Unit 1
Personal Financial Literacy

RyFlip/Shutterstock.com

Technology Applied

Technology is an important part of your world. So, it should be part of your everyday learning experiences. In this text you will find:

- **Pretests** and **posttests** are available for each chapter on the G-W Learning companion website as well as the G-W Learning mobile site. Taking the pretest will help you activate your prior knowledge of the content. Taking the posttest will help you evaluate what you have learned about the chapter content.

- Research skills are critical for college and your career. **Web Connect** at the end of the chapter provides an opportunity to put those skills to work.

G-W Learning Companion Site

The G-W Learning companion website for *Foundations of Personal Finance* is a study reference that contains e-flash cards and vocabulary exercises.

G-W Learning companion website:

www.g-wlearning.com

G-W Learning Mobile Site

The G-W Learning mobile site is a study reference to use when you are on the go. The mobile site is easy to read, easy to use, and fine-tuned for quick access.

For *Foundations of Personal Finance,* the G-W Learning mobile site contains chapter pretests and posttests as well as e-flash cards and vocabulary practice. These features can be accessed by a smartphone or other handheld device with Internet access. These features can also be accessed using an Internet browser to visit the G-W Learning companion website.

G-W Learning mobile site:

www.m.g-wlearning.com

Scan now!

Goodheart-Willcox QR Codes

This Goodheart-Willcox product contains QR codes, or quick response codes. These codes can be scanned with a smartphone bar code reader to access information or online features. For more information on using QR codes and a recommended QR reader, visit the G-W Learning companion website at www.g-wlearning.com.

An Internet connection is required to access the QR code destinations. Data-transfer rates may apply. Check with your Internet service provider for information on your data-transfer rates.

Scan now!

Features Spotlighted

Practical information helps you prepare for your future. Special features add realism and interest to enhance learning.

- **Ethics** offers insight into ethical issues with which you will be confronted as you prepare for your future.
- **Go Green** presents helpful information about how to use natural resources wisely.
- **Event Prep** gives tips to help you prepare for competitive activities in Career and Technical Student Organization (CTSO) competitions.

to sell the merchandise as well as to please the customer. Some do a better job than others.

If you are fair and considerate with salespeople, you are likely to get better service and information that is more reliable. A salesperson who likes you may tell you of an upcoming sale, call you when new merchandise arrives, or give you a straight answer when you need an opinion about a product.

Ethics
Many companies and organizations are well-respected members of the community. When selecting establishments with which to do business, investigate the company and its business practices. Many socially responsible businesses post a code of ethics on their websites. This helps consumers select companies that are respectful and honest in their transactions with customers.

Customer Reviews
Frequently you can learn about products and services from friends, relatives, neighbors, and other consumers. Friends often can give you firsth...
resta...
expe...
or c...
read...

Inte...
...
info...

Go Green
Did you know that the batteries in cell phones and iPods are composed of hazardous materials that will harm the environment if they are disposed of in a landfill? Batteries should always be properly recycled by a reputable organization and never thrown in the regular trash. To be environmentally savvy and save money, consider using rechargeable batteries. Rechargeable batteries, like those in cell phones, can be used many times and will save you trips to the store to purchase disposable batteries.

EVENT PREP
Personal Finance
Personal finance is a competitive event you might enter with your Career and Technical Student Organization (CTSO). The personal finance competitive event may include an objective test that includes banking topics. If you decide to participate in this event, you will need to review basic banking concepts to prepare for the test.

To prepare for a personal finance event, complete the following activities.

1. Read the guidelines provided by your organization. Make certain that you ask any questions about points you do not understand. It is important to follow each specific item that is outlined in the competition rules.
2. Review the vocabulary terms at the beginning of each chapter.
3. Review the Checkpoint activities at the end of each section of the text.
4. Review the end-of-chapter activities for additional practice.
5. Ask your instructor to give you practice tests for each chapter of this text. It is important that you are familiar with answering multiple choice and true/false questions. Have someone time you as you take a practice test.

Economics in Action
Excessive Credit and the Economy
Excessive use of credit can throw the economy off balance and foster inflation. When consumers use credit to buy goods and services, it increases the demand for whatever they are buying. If the demand increases faster than the supply, prices will increase. When governments and businesses join consumers in the excessive use of credit, demand surpasses supply and inflation results. The economy is weakened, and fewer job opportunities exist.

History of Finance
The Silk Road
One of the most famous trade routes was called the Silk Road, created around 100 BC. It was a network of roads that connected Europe, North Africa, and Asia. Caravans of traders exchanged gold, glass, perfumes, and other Western goods for the East's silk, ceramics, spices, and iron. People, plants, animals, ideas, knowledge, and culture also flowed back and forth.

Did you know that the economy plays an important role in becoming a productive citizen? To highlight the importance of the economy in your life, economic concepts are integrated throughout the text. Also, to address specific economic topics, **Economics in Action** and **History of Finance** features highlight insightful information that will be important to you.

Content Connected

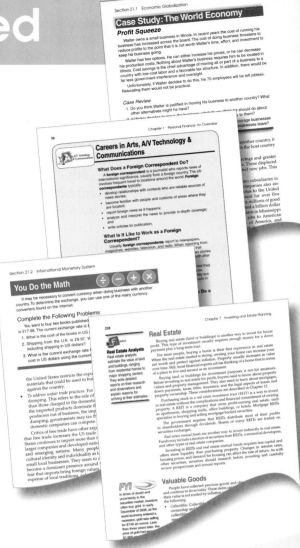

Authoritative content is presented in an easy-to-comprehend and relevant format. The material focuses on the acquisition of research, problem-solving, and academic skills that are required for those taking the next step on the path to college and career readiness.

- **Career** features throughout the text present information about careers in the 16 career clusters. By studying this information, you can learn more about career possibilities for your future.

- **Case Study** features simulate real-world scenarios to give context to issues that arise when learning to be financially responsible.

- **College and Career Readiness Portfolio** activities enable you to create a personal portfolio for use when exploring volunteer, education and training, or career opportunities.

- **You Do the Math** activities focus on math skills that are important to your understanding of personal finance. You are given an opportunity to apply what you learn in context with the material that has been presented in the chapter.

- **Math Skills Handbook** provides you with a quick reference for basic math functions. This helpful information will supplement the content provided in the You Do the Math features throughout the text.

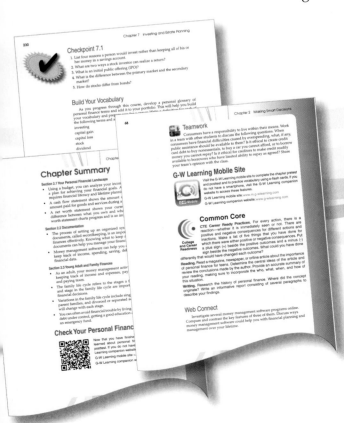

It is important to assess what you learn as you progress through the text. Multiple opportunities are provided to confirm learning as you explore the content. **Formative assessment** includes the following.

- **Checkpoint** activities at the end of each major section of the chapter provide an opportunity to review what you have learned before moving on to the next section in the chapter.

- **Review Your Knowledge** covers basic concepts presented in the chapter so you can evaluate your understanding of the material.

- **Apply Your Knowledge** challenges you to combine what you learned in the chapter with your own experiences and goals.

- **Teamwork** encourages a collaborative experience to help you learn to interact with other students in a productive manner.

- **College and Career Readiness** activities provide ways for you to demonstrate the literacy and career readiness skills you have mastered.

Student Focused

Be prepared for a lifetime of financial decision making. *Foundations of Personal Finance* will help guide you to becoming financially capable as you plan for your future.

Personal Finance—Why It Matters

As a young adult, it is important for you to understand how to earn, spend, and save your money so that you can lead the life you choose. Learning how to set goals and create a plan to meet those goals is a valuable skill that will pay great dividends in your future. To help guide you in creating a personal plan, **Focus on Finance** provides information on topics that gives you a solid foundation of financial information.

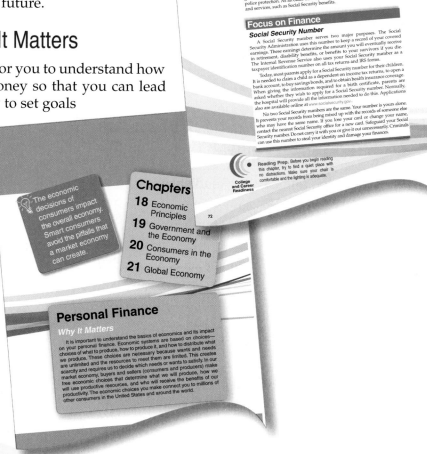

The economic decisions of consumers impact the overall economy. Smart consumers avoid the pitfalls that a market economy can create.

Chapters

18 Economic Principles

19 Government and the Economy

20 Consumers in the Economy

21 Global Economy

Personal Finance

Why It Matters

It is important to understand the basics of economics and its impact on your personal finance. Economic systems are based on choices—choices of what to produce, how to produce it, and how to distribute what we produce. These choices are necessary because wants and needs are unlimited and the resources to meet them are limited. This creates scarcity and requires us to decide which needs or wants to satisfy. In our market economy, buyers and sellers (consumers and producers) make free economic choices that determine what we will produce, how we will use productive resources, and who will receive the benefits of our productivity. The economic choices you make connect you to millions of other consumers in the United States and around the world.

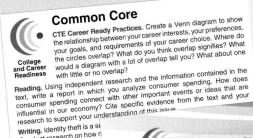

Common Core

CTE Career Ready Practices. Create a Venn diagram to show the relationship between your career interests, your preferences, your goals, and requirements of your career choice. Where do the circles overlap? What do you think overlap signifies? What would a diagram with a lot of overlap tell you? What about one with little or no overlap?

Reading. Using independent research and the information contained in the text, write a report in which you analyze consumer spending. How does consumer spending connect with other important events or ideas that are influential in our economy? Cite specific evidence from the text and your research to support your understanding of this issue.

Writing. Identity theft is a se... Conduct research on how... identity theft. Write an infor... describe your findings of th...

Reading Prep. Review the table of contents for this text. Trace the development of the content that is being presented from simple to complex ideas.

It is all about getting ready for college and career. College and Career Readiness activities address literacy skills to help prepare you for the real world. The Common Core State Standards for English Language Arts for reading, writing, speaking, and listening are incorporated in a **Reading Prep** activity as well as end-of-chapter **Common Core** activities. Common Career Technical Core **Career Ready Practices** are also addressed.

Contents

Unit 4
Planning Your Future...............468

Unit 5
Economic System.....................556

Expanded Table of Contents

Brief Table of Contents

Reviewers

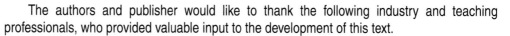

The authors and publisher would like to thank the following industry and teaching professionals, who provided valuable input to the development of this text.

Laura S. Beaton
GED Instructor
Mount Vernon Adult Complex
Henrico, Virginia

David M. Candelaria
Tech Coordinator, Department Chair
Career and Technical Education
Del Norte High School
Albuquerque, New Mexico

Suzanne Dowd, G-W Advisory Council
Team Leader, Family-Consumer Science
Family-Consumer Science Teacher
Plano West Senior High School
Plano, Texas

Lynn Falk, G-W Advisory Council
Business Educator
Bemidji High School
Bemidji, Minnesota

Delia Fernandez, MBA, CFP®
President
Fernandez Financial Advisory, LLC
Los Alamitos, California

Laura Hildebran
Business Teacher
River Bend Middle School
Claremont, North Carolina

Clarissa R. Hobson
CFP® /Senior Financial Planning Advisor
Carnick & Kubik, LLC
Colorado Springs & Denver, Colorado

Michael Koch
Vice President
Insurance Services
Wilder, Kentucky

Christy R. Sellers
Business & IT Teacher
Robert E. Lee High School
Staunton, Virginia

Joy Shannahan
IBCC Coordinator/ BIT-CTE Teacher
J.E.B. Stuart High School
Fairfax County Public Schools, Virginia

Randy R. Sims
Mortgage Loan Officer
Huntington National Bank
Columbus, Ohio

John L. Sorah, EdS
Financial Literacy Instructor
Mill Creek High School
Hochton, Georgia

Cynthia M. Sweeney
Business Teacher
J.M. Alexander Middle School
Charlotte-Mecklenburg Schools
Huntersville, North Carolina

Jenifer C. Richards
Business Education Teacher
Spartanburg High School
Spartanburg, South Carolina

Lois L. Richardson, G-W Advisory Council
Teacher, CTE
Copperas Cove High School
Copperas Cove, Texas

Carin Pankros Roman, CFP®
Financial Planner
CCP, Inc. Financial Planning Services
Palatine, Illinois

Rick V. Wall
Career & Technical Education
Department Chair
Bailey Middle School
Cornelius, North Carolina

Warren Ward
Warren Ward Associates
Columbus, Indiana

Jason Weiss
CTAE Supervisor
Bibb County Board of Education
Macon, Georgia

Barbara Wiegand, G-W Advisory Council
FCS Instructor
Civic Memorial High School
Bethalto, Illinois

Introduction

In today's fast-paced economy, becoming financially capable is more challenging than ever. *Foundations of Personal Finance* helps you meet that challenge. This text provides a comprehensive framework for learning about personal financial literacy. You can discover how to make wise financial decisions that will help you lead a productive life and achieve financial security.

As you progress through this textbook, you will learn how to make financial decisions related to earning money, spending money, and planning for your future. You will learn what you need to know when using credit, buying insurance, purchasing a car, and living on your own. An introduction to economics is also presented to help you connect what you have learned about personal finance to current national economic issues and to the global economy.

A new learning tool has been included to help you study. QR codes are provided to use with your smartphone to go directly to selected text activities. In addition, the G-W Learning mobile site makes it easy for you to study on the go!

Becoming financially capable can begin for you today by studying *Foundations of Personal Finance.*

About the Authors

Sally Campbell is a freelance writer and consultant in consumer economics. She has developed educational materials, including teacher's guides, curriculum guides, textbooks, and student activity materials. She is a former editor and assistant director of the Money Management Institute of Household International, a provider of consumer loans and credit cards. She wrote educational materials related to money management, consumer information, and financial planning. Sally has a master degree in education from St. Louis University and completed the Certified Financial Planning Professional Education Program of the College for Financial Planning. She taught Family & Consumer Sciences and consumer education in the St. Louis public schools. She also served as an educational representative for the McCall Pattern Company.

Robert (Bob) Dansby is an instructor of accounting, business, and personal finance at Chattahoochee Valley Community College in Alabama. He is also an adjunct instructor of accounting at Troy University. In addition to teaching, Bob is also a small business, tax, and personal finance consultant. He is the author of numerous textbooks and workbooks in the area of accounting, cost accounting, business math, and personal finance. He has also written several articles for professional journals, served a five-year term as editor of the Georgia Business Education Association Journal, and has made over 30 presentations at national and regional business education and accounting conferences. Bob holds a PhD in business education from Southern Illinois University at Carbondale.

Library of Congress Cataloging-in-Publication Data

Campbell, Sally R.
  [Confident consumer]
    Foundations of personal finance / Sally R. Campbell, Robert L.
Dansby. --
Ninth edition.
    pages cm
  Revision of the author's The confident consumer.
  Includes index.
  ISBN 978-1-61960-357-8
  1. Finance, Personal. 2. Consumer education. I. Dansby, Robert L.
  II. Title.
HG179.C32 2014
332.024--dc23
                            2012048952

Foundations of Personal Finance

Ninth Edition

Sally R. Campbell
Winnetka, Illinois

Robert L. Dansby
Columbus, Georgia

Publisher
The Goodheart-Willcox Company, Inc.
Tinley Park, Illinois
www.g-w.com

Goodluz/Shutterstock.com

The decisions you make today will affect your finances tomorrow.

from one person to the next. It depends on what the person who makes the decision values.

For example, if spending time with your friends is of primary importance to you, missing time with friends may be the opportunity cost of going to soccer practice or taking an after school job. If getting good grades is a priority, losing time to study may be the opportunity cost of other choices.

Economics in Action

Marginal Analysis

Marginal analysis can help business owners use their resources in the best way possible. For example, suppose five workers in a toy factory produce 100 large, stuffed teddy bears per day. Each worker makes 20 teddy bears. They sew the toy's arms, legs, torso, and head separately. Then they stuff the parts and sew them together. The sewing room has five heavy-duty machines.

The plant manager hires two more workers, but does not buy new machinery. She reasons that time used to stuff the pieces can be done away from the sewing machines. This should leave some machines free for the new workers to sew more teddy bears. The seven workers handle the new work arrangement well and produce 20 teddy bears apiece, or 140 per day.

This success inspires the manager to add one more worker, but she does not get the results she expects. The number of teddy bears produced is only 152, not the 160 she expected. Workers average only 19 teddy bears apiece. They must stand in line to use equipment, which slows them down. The manager realizes that increasing the total production by only 12 teddy bears daily does not cover the cost of the eighth worker.

By using marginal analysis, businesses can determine the right number of workers needed to maximize their profits.

Opportunity cost applies to economic choices of families, businesses, and governments as well as individuals. Weighing opportunity costs is a valuable decision-making tool.

Common Sense Rule

Even before applying laws of economics to help make financial decisions, one rule is obvious. You do not want to spend more than you can afford. The key to financial well-being is spending less than you earn. Living within your means is the only way to have financial peace of mind.

No matter how much money you have, you cannot afford everything you want. Consequently, you need to establish priorities and plan carefully. Make sure to cover your needs before satisfying your wants. If there are family responsibilities, the needs of the family generally come before the wants of individual family members.

Your financial future is in your hands. It pays to develop a clear understanding of your financial situation before making decisions that involve current or future money matters. Today's economic choices determine tomorrow's economic security.

Systematic Decision-Making

When deciding important matters, a systematic or rational decision-making process can help you arrive at the best course of action. **Systematic decision-making** is a process of choosing a course of action after evaluating available information and weighing the costs and benefits of alternative actions and their consequences. It involves five steps, as shown in Figure 1-1 and discussed below.

1. *Define the decision to be made.* You need a clear idea of the challenge to find the best approach. What is at issue? Perhaps you never have time to exercise. Identifying this problem can lead you to set an achievable goal, such as putting aside an hour each day for exercise.

2. *Explore all alternatives.* Analyze possible solutions to your problem. If you need to find an hour to exercise, identify and cut back on time killers. Can you free up an hour by limiting your Internet surfing and TV watching? Can you rearrange your schedule to gain time? Is there an after-school activity you can drop, or can you combine some of your activities?

Steps in the Decision-Making Process		
Step	**Keyword**	**Approach**
1	Problem	Define the problem or challenge.
2	Alternative	Explore alternatives.
3	Choose	Choose the best alternatives.
4	Act	Act on the decision.
5	Evaluate	Evaluate the decision.

Goodheart-Willcox Publisher

Figure 1-1 The five steps of the decision-making process can help you solve problems effectively.

3. *Choose the best alternative.* After considering all alternatives, decide which one best fits your situation. It may be one alternative or some combination.

4. *Act on your decision.* Carry out your plan. For example, if you decide to rearrange your schedule, write a plan for the new routine. Follow it for a few days to see how it works. You may need to make some adjustments. If you decide to limit phone time, it may help to tell friends when you will be taking calls and when you will not be available. Find reminders and aids to help you stick to your new schedule.

5. *Evaluate your solution or decision.* Evaluation is an ongoing process. As you carry out your plan, evaluate your progress toward your intended goal. Is the plan of action working? How can you improve it? The evaluation process can help you stay on track and make better future decisions.

Managing Resources to Reach Goals

Whether you run a big corporation, an average household, or your own personal affairs, you need management skills to get things done. Management skills put you in control. You make the decisions. You carry them out. You benefit from the right choices and occasionally suffer from the mistakes.

Decision-making is an important part of management. However, management involves more than making decisions and solving problems. This three-part process includes planning, action, and evaluation.

Planning

"A job well planned is a job half done." This familiar saying points out the importance of planning. Whether you want to reach a career goal or find a summer job, you need a plan. This applies to almost anything you want to achieve. For example, deciding what to wear to school may involve very little conscious planning. Choosing what to wear to a wedding or a job interview takes more thought. Building an appropriate wardrobe for your lifestyle can be a major planning challenge.

The planning phase of management involves identifying goals, obstacles, and resources. Consider these questions:

- What goals do you want to have or achieve?
- What obstacles stand between you and your goals? What must you overcome?
- What resources can you use to overcome the obstacles and reach your goals?

Two management plans are shown in Figure 1-2. Listed with each goal are the obstacles and resources related to it. Try putting together a similar plan for achieving something you want, such as a summer job, a racing bike, or a part in a school play.

Action

Planning is of little value without action. Action involves putting your resources to work to overcome the obstacles that stand between you and your goals. Success depends on two key characteristics—determination and flexibility.

Determination keeps you focused on the final goal and helps you stick with the project to the end. Determination is especially necessary when things are not

FYI

Systematic decision-making is a skill that can help you solve many challenges that you may encounter.

General Managers

General managers perform a broad range of duties. They coordinate and direct the many support services that allow organizations to operate efficiently. Specific duties vary in degree of responsibility and authority.

Achieving Goals by Overcoming Obstacles		
Goal	**Obstacles**	**Available Resources**
Plan #1 **Complete an English assignment on time**	• Time limitations • Lack of interest in the topic • Difficulty getting started • Tough grading by the English teacher	• Two free hours after school each day • Public library reference room • Knowledge of the topic and where to go for information • Detailed instructions from the English teacher • Writing and computer skills • Computer • Determination to finish on time and get a good grade
Plan #2 **Become president of the student body**	• Popularity of the other candidates • Difficulty in contacting all the voters • Limited time before the election • Lack of organization among supporters	• Knowledge of the job and its demands • Experience in student government • Organizational skills • Public speaking skills • Reputation for leadership • Energy and enthusiasm for planning and running the campaign • Knowledge of what the voters want • Broad support from both the student body and the faculty • Friends who are willing to help run the campaign • Use of school computers and graphics programs • Desire to win

Goodheart-Willcox Publisher

Figure 1-2 Listing your goals, obstacles, and resources will give you perspective on what you can accomplish.

going so well. When working on a tough math assignment, you may feel like giving up. Determination keeps you working until the problem is solved.

Flexibility helps you adjust to new and unexpected situations. It helps you find ways to revise and improve your plans. Imagine that you have two goals for the weekend: earning money for a camping trip and writing a book report. You have a babysitting job on Saturday and plan to spend Sunday afternoon on the book report. When you are called to babysit for much longer than expected, you revise your plans. You write the report while babysitting when the children are asleep. This frees time for something else on Sunday. Flexibility can work to your advantage in all kinds of situations.

Evaluation

Evaluation is a continuous process. When you evaluate a plan of action, you assess your progress as you go through all stages of the management process. What worked? What did not? How could you make it better next time? Evaluation also improves your management skills for future projects. Ongoing evaluation can help you develop better ways of using resources to reach goals. Consider the successes and failures in your planning. How can you do better in the future? Figure 1-3 illustrates the process of evaluation.

Process of Evaluation		
Evaluating Plans	**Evaluating Actions**	**Evaluating Results**
• What are the goals? • What obstacles stand in the way? • What resources are needed? • Are the needed resources available? • Are the goals realistic, given the obstacles and resources? • Are the goals worth the effort and resources required to attain them?	• Is the plan working? • Is there steady progress toward the goals? • Are resources being used to their best advantage? • Are top priority goals getting top priority attention? • Is there room for improvement in the original plans? What adjustments can be made? • Have new or unexpected developments created the need to change the original plans? What changes are needed?	• Were the goals achieved? • Was achieving the goals worth the effort and resources used? • Are the results satisfactory? • What key factors contributed to reaching or failing to reach the goals? • What were the weaknesses in the plans and actions? What were the strengths? • How can future plans be improved?

Goodheart-Willcox Publisher

Figure 1-3 Evaluation is an important part of effective management.

Checkpoint 1.2

1. What are some of the unplanned ways people make decisions?
2. What is an obvious common sense rule?
3. Explain the first step in systematic decision-making.
4. What does the planning phase of management involve?
5. What two characteristics are key in reaching your goals?

Build Your Vocabulary

As you progress through this course, develop a personal glossary of personal finance terms and add it to your portfolio. This will help you build your vocabulary and prepare you for a career. Write a definition for each of the following terms and add it to your personal finance glossary.

cost-benefit analysis   trade-off

marginal benefit   opportunity cost

marginal cost   systematic decision-making

Section 1.3
Financial Influencers

Objectives

After studying this section, you will be able to:

- Identify and explain factors that impact your financial future.
- Describe how the government influences the economy.
- Explain how globalization influences your finances.

Terms

economic conditions

recession

inflation

demographics

culture

technology

globalization

Your Financial Future

There are many important factors and forces that will influence your financial life now and in the future. These include economic, social, cultural, and technological forces. Government actions and advancing globalization affect personal finances as well. Individually and together, these factors will cause you to redefine your financial needs, priorities, and goals over time.

Economic Conditions

Economic conditions are the state of the economy at a given time. When the economy is on the upswing, people are generally optimistic. Businesses make money, grow, and hire more workers. People who want work can find good jobs. Their future income is fairly secure, and they can pay their bills. If they plan carefully, they can save and invest for the future. However, when the economy is plagued by problems, such as recession, inflation, or unemployment, managing personal finances becomes even more important and challenging.

Recession, a period of slow or no economic growth, can have a major impact on personal money management. This is especially true for those who are out of work or whose incomes are stagnant. Recessions spread uncertainty and pessimism over the entire economy. Consumers spend less and save more if possible. Businesses cut back and unemployment rises.

Inflation, or a period of rising prices, also relates to personal money management. As prices go up, the value of a dollar goes down. If income does not rise at the same rate that prices rise, buying power is reduced. Consumers cannot buy or save as much. Sound financial planning and saving can help you cope with challenging economic conditions.

Economics is a science that examines how goods and services are produced, sold, and used. It focuses on how people, governments, and companies make choices about using limited resources to satisfy unlimited wants.

Demographics

To some extent, the way you manage your money and your life in the years ahead will depend on demographics. **Demographics** are the statistical characteristics of a population. Vital statistics include records of births, deaths, and marriages. Social statistics include population breakdowns by age, sex, and race with geographic distributions and growth rates. Other social-economic statistics include education levels, income levels, employment, religion, crime, immigration, and ethnic representation.

The US Census Bureau is a good place to look for the latest demographic statistics. Recent demographic trends have an impact on the overall economy and, in turn, on the financial life of individual consumers. Consider some of the following trends and their economic implications.

- Couples are marrying and having children later in life.
- The percentage of single-parent families is growing.
- The average age of the overall population is increasing.
- Educational requirements for jobs are rising, and job markets are changing.
- Skilled workers are in greater demand.
- More young adults are living at home with their parents.
- The number of unmarried adults is increasing.
- More mothers are working away from home.
- The number of births to single mothers is increasing.

Customer Service Representatives
Customer service representatives interact with customers to provide information. They respond to inquiries about products and services, and handle and resolve complaints.

You Do the Math   ÷ − + ✕

Whole numbers are numbers with no fractional or decimal portion. *Decimals* are numbers with digits to the right of the decimal point. To add a positive number, move to the right on the number line. To subtract a positive number, move to the left on the number line.

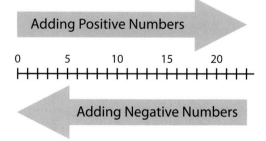

Complete the Following Problems

Find the sum of these equations.

1. $5.87 + 4.956 + 2.011 + 4 =$
2. $34 + 9 + 127 + 783 =$
3. $112.058 + 2.1 + 93.237 =$
4. $987 + 705 + 827 + 4 =$

Government laws and regulations protect you from the cradle to the grave. For a complete listing of government services, regulations, information, and agencies go to www.usa.gov. You will find consumer and citizen services and information on every aspect of personal and financial life.

Monkey Business Images/Shutterstock.com

Culture may influence the way a person makes financial decisions.

Think about these and other demographic factors and how they could affect your financial future. Find examples to show how some of these items relate to personal financial decisions.

Culture

Most urban areas include a variety of racial and ethnic groups. Each group makes an impact on consumer attitudes and buying habits, community services, schools, and many other consumer and family issues. Relationships and marriages between people of different races, cultures, and religions are on the increase. This creates a blending of ethnic traditions, religious beliefs, languages, and concepts of family.

Culture is the beliefs, behaviors, and other characteristics common among members of a group or society. Cultural and ethnic traditions affect many everyday choices and routines. They may dictate the role each person plays in the family, who makes financial and spending decisions, whether both partners work, how the family uses credit, and how the family manages its money.

Technology

New developments and discoveries in communications, medicine, science, and other areas change the way we live in the world. For example, medical advances may result in longer, healthier lives for you and others. New findings on healthful lifestyles include fitness routines, nutritious diets, and stress reduction. You now know how to improve your own health and quality of life. However, living longer makes financial planning even more critical. Your savings must sustain you over a longer life span.

Technology is the application of science and research to human life and environments. Technology brings other changes in the way you live and deal with financial matters. For example, the Internet has altered the way people buy goods and services. You can buy everything from groceries to autos to movie tickets online. Information technology can bring you the latest information from around the world about consumer products, services, and issues. Money management software brings you up-to-the-minute tools for managing money and performing many financial tasks online. You can do your banking, bill paying, investing, and fund transfers online from your home or on the go from your smartphone. The Internet brings an international marketplace to your fingertips.

Advanced technology creates new markets and brings more and cheaper goods and services to consumers. It also creates jobs in many new fields. Unfortunately, it also has fueled *offshore outsourcing* in some fields. This is the business practice of moving factories and jobs overseas and across borders to take advantage of cheap labor and business-friendly government regulations. As a result, many American workers must compete for jobs with lower-paid workers in other countries. This situation has caused layoffs and unemployment, especially among those who work in manufacturing and information technology industries. Today and in the future, the higher-paying jobs will require higher levels of education and training. The right education has never been more important than in today's economy.

Government and the Economy

It would be difficult to overstate the impact of government policies on the economy and, in turn, on consumers. Fiscal and monetary policies affect prices and wages, availability and cost of credit, job opportunities and employment trends, growth and international trade, and a host of other economic conditions.

In the area of consumer information, very few sources can provide more complete information than government. Government publications explain everything from how to raise bees to writing your last will and testament. Much of this information can assist you in financial planning and money management.

Government programs provide direct public assistance largely through Medicaid, Medicare, Social Security, and other less well-known programs. These programs are called *entitlements,* and they account for over 60 percent of the federal budget. Deficit reduction measures are likely to revise and cut expenditures on entitlements in upcoming years. This type of assistance plays an important role in personal financial planning for most citizens. As changes in these programs and in tax laws occur, citizens will need to adjust their financial plans.

History of Finance

Crisis of Ethics

Unethical behavior played a large role in the financial crisis of 2008. Some consumers lied about their income so they could qualify for large mortgage loans. Eager to make money from loans, some financial institutions encouraged consumers to take on too much debt. Other business people sold investments that were riskier and worth less than investors were lead to believe. Many corporate leaders collected large salaries while their companies went bankrupt or received taxpayer money to stay in business. Much of this behavior could be described as unethical. It was driven by the desire for financial gain at the expense of others.

Careers in Arts, A/V Technology & Communications

What Does a Foreign Correspondent Do?

A **foreign correspondent** is a journalist who reports news of international significance, usually from a foreign country. The job involves frequent travel to locations around the world. **Foreign correspondents** typically:

- develop relationships with contacts who are reliable sources of news stories;
- become familiar with people and customs of areas where they are located;
- report foreign news as it happens;
- analyze and interpret the news to provide in-depth coverage; and
- write articles for publication.

What Is It Like to Work as a Foreign Correspondent?

Usually, **foreign correspondents** report to newspapers, magazines, websites, television, and radio. When reporting from a given country, journalists may work in connection with that country's foreign bureau. On-the-scene reporters file news stories live as they occur. Others write their stories in greater depth after events occur, adding human interest and more detail.

Foreign correspondents study the areas and countries they cover and become familiar with the people and their culture. They establish reliable contacts and sources wherever they are covering the news. They also need to know how to stay safe in dangerous and unpredictable locations.

What Education and Skills Are Needed to Be a Foreign Correspondent?

- bachelor degree in journalism or communications
- internships or work experience with local papers or television stations
- fluency in a second or third language
- photography skills
- travel experience
- communication and people skills
- objectivity
- determination and physical stamina

Globalization and Your Finances

Globalization, with all its pros and cons, is today's reality. **Globalization** is the worldwide spread and integration of production, markets, communications, and technology. Your financial and consumer interests are linked to world trade and international economics. On the positive side, globalization gives you access to a vast diversity of goods and services through worldwide markets. News, entertainment, and information travel in seconds to every corner of the globe. Money is equally mobile.

Business competition on a global scale can bring price and quality advantages for consumers. The local and outside world links bring economic and cultural changes. Take a walk through your own home to see how many products, foods, music downloads, and furnishings came from other nations. As products, services, and ideas flow from country to country, you will have opportunities to share common experiences and to understand people from backgrounds and cultures different from your own.

Living in a world economy can bring job opportunities if you prepare to meet the demand in current job markets. It can be devastating for those whose job skills are no longer in demand or whose jobs have moved to other countries. As a young person entering the workforce, you will be competing with workers around the globe. You can benefit by getting the best training and education you can to meet the needs of current and future job markets.

Checkpoint 1.3

1. Name economic conditions that can affect personal financial decisions.
2. List four demographic trends that influence the overall economy and the financial life of individuals.
3. Give three examples of ways technological advances can influence financial decisions and lifestyles.
4. What are some economic conditions that are affected by fiscal and monetary policies of governments?
5. What are some economic advantages of globalization?

Build Your Vocabulary

As you progress through this course, develop a personal glossary of personal finance terms and add it to your portfolio. This will help you build your vocabulary and prepare you for a career. Write a definition for each of the following terms and add it to your personal finance glossary.

economic conditions

recession

inflation

demographics

culture

technology

globalization

Chapter Summary

Section 1.1 Personal Finance Basics

- Financial competence means that you are educated about money matters and can apply your knowledge and skills to making informed and responsible financial choices. You are the manager of your life and will make decisions that matter to you.

- The personal side of consumer choices involves developing a sense of direction and purpose and requires a clear understanding of personal needs, wants, values, goals, and standards. Management involves using resources to reach goals. Goals for spending and well-established priorities can guide you to choices that provide personal satisfaction.

Section 1.2 Managing Your Personal Finances

- Costs, benefits, and trade-offs are factors that influence financial decisions. Economic decision-making tools remind you to live within your means so you can enjoy financial well-being now and in the future.

- Effective management, which includes planning, action, and evaluation, can help you achieve your goals. The process of management also requires making decisions and solving problems.

Section 1.3 Financial Influencers

- The many important factors and forces that influence your financial future are economic, social, cultural, and technological forces. Government actions and advancing globalization affect personal finances as well. Individually and together, these factors will cause you to redefine your financial needs, priorities, and goals over time.

- Fiscal and monetary policies affect prices and wages, availability and cost of credit, job opportunities and employment trends, growth and international trade, and a host of other economic conditions. Public assistance is provided through government programs such as Medicaid, Medicare, Social Security, and other less well-known programs.

- Globalization is the worldwide spread and integration of production, markets, communications, and technology. Globalization gives consumers access to a vast diversity of goods and services through worldwide markets.

Check Your Personal Finance IQ

Now that you have finished the chapter, see what you learned about personal finance by taking the chapter posttest. If you do not have a smartphone, visit the G-W Learning companion website.

G-W Learning mobile site: www.m.g-wlearning.com

G-W Learning companion website: www.g-wlearning.com

Review Your Knowledge

1. Explain what a priority is and how priorities are set.
2. How do standards relate to values and goals?
3. What is a cost-benefit analysis?
4. What are the five steps in systematic decision-making?
5. What steps are in the planning phase of management?
6. What two key characteristics lead to success in the action phase of management?
7. What are the advantages of evaluating a management plan?
8. What is a recession?
9. Explain how cultural and ethnic traditions relate to personal finance.
10. What are three government programs that provide direct public assistance?

Apply Your Knowledge

11. How do priorities guide your consumer and life choices? What are some of your priorities?
12. Why do a person's standards for quality and performance vary from one situation to another?
13. What are your most important and valuable human and nonhuman resources?
14. Apply the decision-making process to an important decision you are facing. Describe the decision, list the alternatives, choose the best alternative, act on the choice, and evaluate the results. Discuss how this process could help you with key decisions and problems in your future.
15. Why are values and goals different for different people? Why and how are values and goals likely to change throughout your life?
16. When you picture yourself as an adult, what standard of living would you like? How much money will you have to earn to achieve this lifestyle?
17. How would you describe the moral principles that define your behavior? What actions do you consider okay and not okay with family, in the school environment, among friends, on a job, in business, and in government?
18. Give three examples of unethical consumer behavior. Discuss the examples.
19. Describe an incident in which people have been a valuable resource to you in reaching an important goal.
20. Describe three financial decisions you have made that reflect your values.

Teamwork

Working with a teammate, discuss how the decision-making process might help in establishing local, state, and federal government policies and budgets. Create a chart and list your ideas. Share your findings with your class. Relate the discussion to actual issues where possible.

G-W Learning Mobile Site

Visit the G-W Learning mobile site to complete the chapter pretest and posttest and to practice vocabulary using e-flash cards. If you do not have a smartphone, visit the G-W Learning companion website to access these features.

G-W Learning mobile site: www.m.g-wlearning.com

G-W Learning companion website: www.g-wlearning.com

Common Core

College and Career Readiness

CTE Career Ready Practices. Create a script for two persons that depicts a positive interaction between two students or coworkers. Be sure to include notes to the actors about body language and facial expressions. Do the same to illustrate a negative interaction on the same topic. What is the essential difference between the two plays/interactions? How does the way you say something influence whether it will be received negatively or positively?

Speaking. Participate in a collaborative classroom discussion about financial competence. Ask questions that connect your ideas to the relevant evidence that has been presented.

Listening. Do an Internet search to find speeches made by wealthy individuals that tell how they became financially independent. Select one speech of your choice and listen to it in its entirety. Describe the line of reasoning, organization, development, and style the speaker used to prepare his or her information. Identify the target audience and the purpose of the speech.

Web Connect

Paying for college can be a huge expense. Many college students receive grants, scholarships, and loans that help with costs. However, for this exercise, assume that you and your parents will be paying the entire cost. A number of websites, such as the College Board, offer online calculators that provide estimates of college costs. Use one of these sites to determine how much money you will need for college. Determine how much money you will need to save per month. Weigh these costs against the benefits of a college education.

College and Career Readiness

College and Career Readiness Portfolio

When you apply for a job, for community service, or to a college, you may need to tell others about how you are qualified for this position. A portfolio is a selection of related materials that you collect and organize. These materials show your qualifications, skills, and talents. For example, a certificate that shows you have completed lifeguard and first aid training could help you get a job at a local pool as a lifeguard. An essay you wrote about protecting native plants could show that you are serious about eco-friendly efforts and help you get a volunteer position at a park. A transcript of your school grades could help show that you are qualified for college.

Two types of portfolios are commonly used: print portfolios and electronic portfolios (e-portfolios). An e-portfolio is also known as a *digital portfolio*.

1. Use the Internet to search for *print portfolio* and *e-portfolio*. Read articles about each type of portfolio. In your own words, write a paragraph and briefly describe each type.

2. You will be creating a portfolio in this class. Which portfolio type would you prefer to create? Write a paragraph describing the type of portfolio you would prefer to create.

Student Organizations

Career and Technical Student Organizations (CTSOs) are a valuable asset to any educational program. These organizations support student learning and the application of the skills learned in real-world situations. There are a variety of organizations from which to select, depending on the goals of your educational programs.

To prepare for any competitive event, complete the following activities.

1. Contact the organization before the next competition. This gives you time to review and decide which competitive events are correct for you or your team.

2. Read all the guidelines closely. These rules and regulations must be strictly adhered to or disqualification can occur.

3. Competitive events may be written, oral, or a combination of both.

4. Communication plays a role in all the competitive events, so read which communication skills are covered for the event you select. Research and preparation are important keys to successful competition.

5. Go to the website of your organization for specific information for the events. Visit the site often as information changes quickly.

6. Select one or two events that are of interest to you. Print the information for the events and discuss your interest with your instructor.

Chapter 2
Making Smart Decisions

Financial security is the ultimate goal of managing your finances. Achieving financial security requires financial literacy and lifelong planning. Different stages in your life cycle will be marked by different financial characteristics. To help create budgets and manage your personal finances, consider using financial planning software or online money management programs. These software packages offer many conveniences to help manage your financial affairs, both daily and over time.

Keep in mind that even with the most competent money management practices, you may face financial difficulties in the future. It pays to know steps you can take to prepare for possible problems and to deal with a financial crisis should the need arise.

Focus on Finance

Reasons to Budget

Where do you want to be financially in 10 years? Can you see yourself owning a car and living in your own house? Will you have a great career and be on your way to financial security? In order to meet goals that you set for yourself, you will need to learn how to manage your personal finances. Budgeting is one way to get started on the path to financial independence. What can budgeting do for you? Budgeting can help you:

- stay out of debt;
- pay your bills on time;
- create a savings account;
- finance your education; and
- buy a car.

Today is the best time to start budgeting your way to the future you hope to achieve tomorrow.

College and Career Readiness

Reading Prep. In preparation for reading the chapter, think about what makes a person successful. How do people measure success? As you read, consider how the information in this chapter supports or contradicts your answers to these questions.

Check Your Personal Finance IQ

Before you begin the chapter, see what you already know about personal finance by taking the chapter pretest. If you do not have a smartphone, visit the G-W Learning companion website.

G-W Learning mobile site: www.m.g-wlearning.com

G-W Learning companion website: www.g-wlearning.com

Sections

Mike Flippo/Shutterstock.com

Section 2.1
Your Personal Financial Landscape

Objectives

After studying this section, you will be able to:

- List and describe the steps in managing your money through the planning and creation of a budget.
- Explain how to create a cash flow statement.
- Explain how to create a net worth statement.

Terms

budget	cash flow statement
income	net worth statement
expense	net worth
fixed expense	asset
variable expense	liability
discretionary expense	wealth
philanthropy	

Budgets

In Chapter 1, you learned about the importance of financial planning. Planning allows you to meet changing needs and goals over your lifetime. It begins with managing daily expenses. A budget can help you make the most of your money and avoid financial problems.

A **budget** is a plan for the use of money over time based on goals, expenses, and expected income. It is the tool that lets you take control of your finances. Planning helps you meet daily needs and achieve your future goals as well.

Start by following the steps in Figure 2-1 to create a budget tailored to your income and needs. These steps can help you create a simple, workable budget.

Creating a Budget	
Step 1	Establish financial goals.
Step 2	Estimate and total your income.
Step 3	Estimate and total your expenses.
Step 4	Analyze current income and spending.
Step 5	Prepare a budget.
Step 6	Evaluate your budget.

Goodheart-Willcox Publisher

Figure 2-1 Following these steps will help you establish a budget tailored to your needs.

Economics in Action

2008 Recession

When the 2008 recession hit the US economy, the impact was felt in millions of homes across the country. Many young adults still struggle to find work. Businesses stopped hiring, and many employees lost their jobs. Demand dropped and growth came to a near standstill. Financial institutions made fewer business and consumer loans. Credit sources dried up.

When people lost their jobs or had their hours reduced, entire families suffered. Long-term goals, such as higher education, starting a business, and buying a home, had to be put on hold. Many unemployed people lost health insurance that was provided by employers. Unemployment led to many families losing their homes.

Loss of income meant lifestyle changes for almost everyone. There was less money and much more anxiety. Retirement savings dropped with the stock market and home values. People who were retired or nearing retirement were forced to work beyond their planned retirement age, if they could find work.

Recovery from the 2008 recession has been slow and is still in progress. Global economic problems contributed to the recession in the United States and continue to impact the economies of most nations.

Establish Financial Goals

Well-thought-out goals can help you direct your dollars to those things you consider most important. Make a list of your important financial goals. Include short-, medium-, and long-term goals, as shown in Figure 2-2. For example, having money for a movie this weekend is a fairly immediate goal. Saving for a 10-day camping trip next year is a medium-term goal. Paying for a new car or future education are long-term goals that require saving over a period of time.

Financial Goals		
	When Wanted	**Estimated Cost**
Short-Term		
Boots	In 2 months	$ 65
Holiday gifts	In 3 months	$ 100
Summer trip	In 9 months	$ 350
Medium-Term		
Laptop computer	In 1 year	$ 500
Used car	In 2 years	$ 6,000
Long-Term		
College expenses	In 5 years	$32,000

Goodheart-Willcox Publisher

Figure 2-2 Organizing your goals on a chart similar to this can help direct your spending and saving to whatever is most important to you at a given time.

Keep in mind that financial goals change over time. Today your goals may include saving money for a smartphone, a car, travel, or college. However, as you move on to college, work, and perhaps marriage and parenthood, your financial goals will evolve and expand.

Estimate and Total Your Income

Determine your budget period—weekly, biweekly, or monthly. This will depend on when you receive most of your income. **Income** is any form of money received, such as an allowance, a paycheck, gifts, and gains from an investment. If you receive money weekly, it makes sense to budget on a weekly basis. If you receive a regular monthly paycheck and pay monthly bills, it may be easier to work with monthly figures.

Estimate your income for each budget period. Using a worksheet, such as the one in Figure 2-3, write your best estimate of how much money you normally receive from each source of income. Total the estimates and enter the amount at the bottom of the sheet.

Estimate and Total Your Expenses

After calculating your income, estimate your typical expenses per budget period. An **expense** is the cost of goods and services you buy. Generally, your expenses will be either fixed or variable.

A **fixed expense** is a set amount that must be paid each budget period. These expenses may include items such as rent or mortgage payments, tuition, insurance premiums, or loan payments. Fixed expenses tend to increase in number and amount as you move into adult life. As a rule, fixed expenses must be paid when due. Therefore, it is important to list them first.

Estimating Income		
Week or Month of _____		
Income Sources	**Estimated**	**Actual**
Jobs		
Babysitting	$ 25	$ _____
Yard work	40	_____
After-school job	200	_____
Allowance	40	_____
Gifts	10	_____
Total Income	**$ 315**	$ _____

Goodheart-Willcox Publisher

Figure 2-3 Use a form similar to this one to estimate expected income. Review your estimates and fill in with actual figures to stay up-to-date on the amount you have to spend and save.

A **variable expense** is a cost that changes both in the amount and time it must be paid. Variable expenses include items such as food, clothing, texting, music downloads, and entertainment. These expenses may be necessary or discretionary. A **discretionary expense** is an amount spent for an item that a person could do without. For example, food is a necessary item. However, the cost of a dinner in an upscale restaurant is a discretionary expense. When you are short of cash, discretionary expenses offer the best opportunities for adjusting your spending.

At this point in your life, you no doubt receive basic necessities from your family or guardians and spend your money mainly on discretionary items, such as music, texting, computer games, and movies. For adults, discretionary expenses often include vacations, gifts, expensive clothing, and other unnecessary goods and services.

Using the worksheet in Figure 2-4 as a guide, list your fixed and variable expenses in the far left column. Then enter the amount you spend on each one. You may want to star discretionary items and start with them if you need to reduce your expenses.

Estimating Expenses		
Week or Month of _____		
Expense Items	**Estimated**	**Actual**
Fixed Expenses		
Bus pass	$ 15	$ _____
Lunches	90	_____
Savings	15	_____
Total Fixed Expenses	**$ 120**	**$ _____**
Variable Expenses		
Snacks	$ 20	$ _____
Movies/concerts/events	40	_____
Clothes	50	_____
CDs/music files	25	_____
Gifts	20	_____
Magazines	15	_____
Grooming aids	25	_____
Total Variable Expenses	**$ 195**	**$ _____**
Total Expenses	**$ 315**	**$ _____**

Goodheart-Willcox Publisher

Figure 2-4 Make adjustments to your variable expenses when you are short on cash.

Savings and Your Budget

You need to include savings in your budget if you want to have cash available for unexpected expenses and emergencies. An emergency fund provides an important financial cushion in case of job loss, disruption to income, or an unforeseen expense. You also will want savings for major purchases and medium- and long-term goals. It is a good idea to include savings as a fixed expense in your budget.

For example, if you wish to take a camping trip in five months, estimate how much money you will need. If the trip will cost $360, figure out how much you will need to save per month or per week to pay for the trip.

- To calculate the monthly savings required, divide $360 by 5. You will need to save $72 each month.
- To calculate the weekly savings required, divide $360 by 20, the number of weeks in five months. You will need to save $18 per week.

You can use this method to plan for any expense if you know the amount you need and when you need it. When you build savings into your budget, you will be better able to deal with unexpected expenses and to reach important goals in your future.

Charitable Giving as an Expense

A *charity* usually refers to an organization that aids those in need, such as the homeless or victims of natural disasters. **Philanthropy** is the act of giving money, goods, or services to meet the needs of others and support organizations and causes that are important to you. You may choose to donate to causes of your choice or to volunteer your time and talents. To determine how much you can give, consider your income, expenses, and outstanding debts.

It pays to investigate before you give. Some charitable organizations are more efficient and effective than others. Some groups may pose as charities but use the funds they collect for personal gain. Be sure to send your money to the group that will make the most effective use of it.

Analyze Current Income and Spending

It is easy to overestimate income and underestimate expenses. A detailed record of spending almost always turns up some surprises and some unnecessary spending. Inspect your record of income and expenses. Are your income figures accurate? Subtract your expenses from your income for each budget period. Are the amounts equal? Do you have money left over? If you have nothing left or if you are "in the hole," you need to find ways to increase income or cut expenses. To increase income, explore the following possibilities.

- Can you earn money by doing some special jobs for your family or neighbors? For example, can you do the grocery shopping, wash windows, reorganize closets and cabinets, or do some yard work?
- Can you get a part-time job? Look for help wanted ads. Have you considered job opportunities in your community? Ask friends, coaches, neighbors, and store managers about job possibilities.
- If you have a job, can you negotiate an increase in wages? Is it possible to work more hours without sacrificing time you need for schoolwork and other important activities?

Business Management & Administration

Bookkeepers

Bookkeepers update and maintain accounting records. They calculate expenditures, receipts, accounts payable and receivable, and profit and loss. They may also handle payroll, make purchases, prepare invoices, and keep track of overdue accounts.

Philanthropy can be a donation of time as well as money.

To reduce spending, study your record of expenses.

- Start with your discretionary expenses. Can you eliminate any items or reduce the cost of items you buy? Perhaps you can make a gift or do something for someone rather than buying a gift. Maybe you can cut back on music downloads and text messaging. Perhaps you can check out books or movies at the library.

- Look at fixed and variable expenses. These expenses may be necessary, but can you reduce their cost by making substitutions? For example, can you pack a lunch instead of buying it? Try a generic shampoo instead of an expensive brand. Drink tap water instead of bottled water.

- Can you cut spending that does not bring you closer to achieving your goals? For example, if good health is a priority, you can stop buying soda and potato chips, or you can walk instead of driving or taking the bus.

After you figure out how to stretch your income to cover your needs, move to next step—preparing a budget.

Prepare a Budget

Now it is time to bring together your goals, income, and expenses into a spending plan. A plan reduces the temptation to spend carelessly. The budget in Figure 2-5 illustrates one way to organize a budget.

First, fill in the planned income amount from the estimated income worksheet. Record the total income on the budget.

Next, record each estimated expense from the estimated expenses worksheet. Total the expenses. Do the expenses equal the planned income?

When a budget period ends, fill in the Actual column in the budget with amounts for actual income and expenses. When a real expense is greater than the amount planned, identify the cause. Did you ignore the plan? Was there an unexpected expense? Was your estimate too low? Adjust your budget to reflect actual income and spending. Try it for a few weeks. You may wish to draft a similar form for your own financial planning.

Put your budget in writing and keep it up-to-date as you go along. The tips in Figure 2-6 can make a budget work better.

Before you give to a charity, research it to understand how your money will be used. There are many resources on the Internet that will help you evaluate an organization and its goals.

Budget		
Week or Month of _____		
Sources	**Estimated**	**Actual**
Income		
Babysitting	$ 25	$ 215
Yard work	40	40
After-school job	200	200
Allowance	40	40
Gifts	10	10
Total Income	$ 315	$ 315
Expenses		
Fixed Expenses		
Bus pass	$ 15	$ 15
Lunches	90	90
Savings	15	15
Total Fixed Expenses	$ 120	$ 120
Variable Expenses		
Snacks	$ 20	$ 20
Movies/concerts/events	40	40
Clothes	50	50
CDs/music files	25	25
Gifts	20	20
Magazines	15	15
Grooming aids	25	25
Total Variable Expenses	$ 195	$ 195
Total Expenses	$ 315	$ 315

Goodheart-Willcox Publisher

Figure 2-5 Use a form similar to this one for your budget. Use your estimates of income and expenses, financial goals, and record of spending to complete your budget.

Quick Tips for Better Budgeting
• Keep it simple.
• Write it down.
• Be specific.
• Be flexible.
• Be disciplined.
• Keep it all together.
• Be prepared for the unexpected.

Goodheart-Willcox Publisher

Figure 2-6 When planning a budget, keep these tips in mind.

Evaluate Your Budget

From time to time, review your overall money management plan to make sure it is working for you. You can expect financial plans to change with significant events in your life. These events include going to college, starting a new job, leaving home, getting married, having children, and changing jobs.

Consider the following questions as you evaluate your budget.

- Is your financial plan working?
- Is your money doing what you want it to do?
- Are you reaching important goals?
- As you achieve goals, do you set new ones?
- Are you controlling your spending?
- Has your income or pattern of spending changed significantly?
- Are there changes in your life that call for adjustments in your financial planning?

When revisions are needed, make the necessary changes to update your budget. Recheck in a week or two to see if the new entries are an improvement. Monitor your finances carefully to make your income work well for you over the years.

Cash Flow Statement

A **cash flow statement** is a summary of the amount of money received and the amount paid for goods and services during a specific period. The cash flow statement shown in Figure 2-7 appears very similar to the budget statement shown earlier. However, there are important differences. In the cash flow statement:

- income is called *Cash Inflow;*
- expenses are called *Cash Outflow;* and
- the term *Actual* heads the column of figures instead of *Planned.*

The cash flow statement goes beyond the budget to reflect actual money inflow and outflow for the month. Prepared at the end of the budget period, it shows real income and spending, not what was planned.

To get accurate figures for the statement, record cash inflows and outflows in an income and expense log, as shown in Figure 2-8. This log is basically

Cash Flow Statement	
Month of October	
Category	**Actual**
Cash Inflow (Income)	
Part-time jobs (babysitting, yard work, after-school job)	$ 265
Allowance	40
Gifts	10
Total Inflow	**$ 315**
Cash Outflow (Expenses)	
Fixed Expenses	
Bus pass, lunches, savings	$ 120
Total Fixed Expenses	**$ 120**
Variable Expenses	
Snacks, clothes, cell phone, grooming aids/makeup, movies/concerts/events	$ 120
Total Variable Expenses	**$ 145**
Total Outflow	**$ 265**
Net Cash Flow	**$ 50**

Goodheart-Willcox Publisher

Figure 2-7 A cash flow statement shows your actual income and expenses.

Income and Expense Log			
Date	**Item**	**Income**	**Expense**
9/10 Fri.	Bus fare—round-trip		$ 4.00
	Lunch		$ 5.00
	Snack		$ 2.00
9/11 Sat.	Babysitting	$ 20.00	
	Snack		$ 3.50
	School supplies		$ 17.00
	Movie ticket		$ 7.00
9/12 Sun.	Gift from uncle	$ 10.00	
	New sneakers		$ 34.00

Goodheart-Willcox Publisher

Figure 2-8 Keeping a detailed log of your income and spending will help you develop a more accurate and realistic budget.

a personal spending diary. Itemize your expenses and record exactly how much money came in. Keep these records until you reach the end of your budget period. You will find that recording cash inflows and outflows leads to more accurate budgeting. Once you finish the cash flow statement, you can prepare the budget for the next month more quickly.

Net Worth Statement

Experts advise evaluating your total financial situation at least annually. A financial or net worth statement can help you do this accurately. A **net worth statement** is a written record of an individual's current financial situation. Your **net worth** is the difference between what you own and what you owe. It measures your financial standing at a particular point in time. A net worth statement is shown in Figure 2-9.

This may not seem necessary now, but as you move into the adult world, your circumstances can change rapidly. Tracking your finances can become more complicated and more important. The net worth statement helps you chart your financial future.

You Do the Math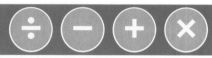

Word problems are exercises in which the problem is set up in text, rather than presented in mathematical notation. Many word problems tell a story. You must identify the elements of the math problem and solve it.

There are many strategies for solving word problems. Some of the common strategies include making a list or table; working backward; guessing, checking, and revising; and substituting simpler numbers to solve the problem.

Complete the Following Problem

Lena Chang, 23, lives alone in a rented apartment. She earns $2,300 a month after taxes and payroll deductions. She has a savings account containing $1,500. She also owns $2,000 in stocks and some jewelry worth about $1,000. Her largest asset is a car that could sell today for $10,000. She still owes $15,000 on a student loan. Her monthly expenses include:

- $200 savings
- $750 rent
- $250 student loan payment
- $250 utilities
- $200 gas, car insurance, and registration
- $230 groceries
- $50 donations to a charity
- $350 extras such as entertainment, eating out, and clothing

Is her net worth statement positive or negative?

Net Worth Statement		
Category	**Amount**	**Totals**
Assets		
Current Assets		
Cash on hand	$_____	
Cash in savings, checking, and money market accounts	$_____	
Cash value of insurance	$_____	
Other	$_____	
Total Current Assets		$_____
Fixed Assets		
Stocks and bonds	$_____	
Mutual funds	$_____	
Individual Retirement Accounts (IRA)	$_____	
Auto	$_____	
Home	$_____	
Furniture and equipment	$_____	
Other	$_____	
Total Fixed Assets		$_____
Total Assets		$_____
Liabilities		
Current Liabilities		
Credit cards and charge account balances due	$_____	
Taxes due	$_____	
Other	$_____	
Total Current Liabilities		$_____
Long-Term Liabilities		
Auto loan	$_____	
Home mortgage	$_____	
Other	$_____	
Total Long-Term Liabilities		$_____
Total Liabilities		$_____
Net Worth (total assets less total liabilities)		$_____

Figure 2-9 A net worth statement helps you determine your net worth at a given point in time.

Assets

An **asset** is an item of value that you own, such as cash, stocks, bonds, real estate, and personal possessions. Assets are divided into two basic categories:

- *Current assets.* These assets, also called *liquid assets,* include cash and savings that can be converted to cash quickly and easily.
- *Fixed assets.* These assets include investments, such as stocks, bonds, and invested funds, that are set aside for long-term goals, such as the education of children or retirement needs. Fixed assets also include a home, auto, personal possessions, and other durable goods that enrich your life through use.

Assets tend to change in value from year to year, so you will want to list them at their current or market value. This amount is an estimated worth at the time you make your net worth statement.

Liabilities

A **liability** is a current or future financial obligation. Liabilities include unpaid bills, credit card charges, mortgages, personal loans, and taxes. Liabilities are divided into two categories:

- *Current liabilities.* These liabilities are items due soon, usually within the year. They include medical bills, taxes, unpaid bills from credit cards and charge accounts, and the amount you borrowed for lunch last week.
- *Long-term liabilities.* These liabilities include obligations to be paid over a long period of time, such as an auto loan or a home mortgage.

Net Worth

Your net worth is the difference between your assets and liabilities. If you own more than you owe, you have a positive net worth. This means that you can meet your financial obligations and possibly reach some of your important financial goals.

Wealthy individuals have assets far in excess of their liabilities. The term **wealth** means an abundance of money and other assets. It includes investments, property, a business, cash, and other items of value that contribute significantly to financial security and a high standard of living and giving.

If your debts exceed your assets, your net worth will be a negative figure. You need to find ways to reduce expenses or increase income. Start with a careful look at expenses. Try to reduce or eliminate all the items that are not essential. Pay credit debts and do not take on more credit obligations. Consider ways to increase income by working more hours or assuming more responsibilities on the job. A job change or additional training may also lead to higher income. Do all you can to create a positive net worth.

Checkpoint 2.1

1. Give three examples of variable expenses.
2. What are some possible ways to increase your income?
3. What are some possible ways to reduce spending?
4. What financial data is shown in a net worth statement?
5. What are three examples of assets?

Build Your Vocabulary

As you progress through this course, develop a personal glossary of personal finance terms and add it to your portfolio. This will help you build your vocabulary and prepare you for a career. Write a definition for each of the following terms and add it to your personal finance glossary.

budget	philanthropy
income	cash flow statement
expense	net worth statement
fixed expense	asset
variable expense	liability
discretionary expense	wealth

Section 2.2
Documentation

Objectives

After studying this section, you will be able to:

- Discuss the importance of good recordkeeping to help you manage your finances.
- Explain how money management software can assist in financial planning.

Terms

recordkeeping

legal document

money management software

Recordkeeping

As you enter the world of work and adult responsibilities, certain documents and papers will become important in managing your affairs. You will need to find a safe place for these documents. Set up a filing system so you can find them as needed. The process of setting up an organized system for financial and legal documents is called **recordkeeping.** A **legal document** is a paper that can be filed with a court officer or used to uphold an agreement in a court of law, such as a marriage certificate, auto loan, mortgage, or credit card agreement. Some records may be printed (hard) copies and others may be digital. The important thing is to know where to find what you need when you need it.

Bills

If you lose track of your bills, you run the risk of paying them late or not at all. If you receive bills by mail, set aside a box or drawer where you place your bills until you are ready to pay them.

Go Green

Did you know that the batteries in cell phones and iPods are composed of hazardous materials that will harm the environment if they are disposed of in a landfill? Batteries should always be properly recycled by a reputable organization and never thrown in the regular trash. To be environmentally savvy and save money, consider using rechargeable batteries. Rechargeable batteries, like those in cell phones, can be used many times and will save you trips to the store to purchase disposable batteries.

Keep track of due dates so you can pay on time and avoid late fees. Many people pay bills on a regular schedule, such as every Sunday night or at the end of the month. The due dates and your paydays will dictate your bill scheduling.

You can pay bills online or by check. You may not have enough money to pay all of your bills at the same time. Pay the bills that are due first. Bill paying is easier if you keep stamps and envelopes on hand. Online payment eliminates the need for these items and makes it even easier to pay your bills.

Financial Documents

Well-ordered records can help you stay within your budget and make adjustments as needed. It is helpful to keep money management records over a period of time so you can review your current financial situation, evaluate your progress, and plan for the future.

File your budget with other money management materials and receipts in one place. Then you will have all the information when you want to evaluate and make necessary revisions in your financial planning. Your files should contain financial records related to your income, spending, and savings. Income records to keep include:

- paycheck stubs;
- statements showing interest earned on savings accounts;
- records of dividends; and
- amounts of cash gifts, tips, and bonuses.

michaeljung/Shutterstock.com

Careful recordkeeping will make financial planning easier to manage.

Case Study

Making Plans

At 28, Myra had no plans to marry or to have children. She is a top-notch photographer and earns $50,000 annually. She also receives outstanding benefits through her job, including health, disability, and life insurance. Myra's parents are in good health, and they both work. Her two brothers have jobs and families of their own. Myra lives in a rented apartment and is thinking about buying a home, something she has always dreamed of doing.

Case Review

1. What changes in Myra's situation could alter her financial needs and plans?
2. Suppose one of Myra's parents becomes ill, resulting in financial problems. How could this affect Myra's financial plans?
3. Suppose Myra's brother and his wife die in an accident and Myra is named guardian of their children. How might this change her financial plans?
4. What are some financial steps Myra should take before purchasing a home? What additional expenses will home ownership bring?
5. What are some key differences in financial planning for those with dependents and those without dependents?
6. How does an individual's age relate to financial planning and decisions?

Spending records to keep include:
- bank statements and checkbook registers;
- receipts from purchases and bills paid;
- statements from credit accounts; and
- cash register receipts for big purchases.

Receipts serve as proof of payments. They are especially important for fixed expenses, such as loan payments, and for major purchases, such as a road bike. They also may be needed for warranty services or settling disputes.

Keeping receipts for minor purchases, such as cosmetics or movie tickets, is a good way to keep track of your spending. If you have trouble staying within your budget, you may want to record all purchases for a time. Then you will have a clear idea of where your money goes. Be sure to keep receipts for any purchases you may need to return, exchange, or have serviced. Proof of purchase is often required for these transactions.

Keeping track of financial records is an important part of money management. In later years, you will need more detailed records for savings, credit transactions, investments, real estate, taxes, and insurance.

Pay yourself first means that you should budget for savings before you budget for spending. If you do not budget for savings, you probably will not save.

Other Documents

Accurate records will be necessary for a variety of transactions and purposes. For example, Figure 2-10 lists items that may be required when you:
- apply for a job, a mortgage, or an apartment;
- make budget and financial planning decisions;

Documents and Records You May Need

Personal

- Birth/marriage/death certificates
- Passports
- Adoption and custody papers
- Military papers
- Separation agreements
- Divorce decree
- Social Security card
- Citizenship papers

Employment

- Résumés
- Copies of completed job applications
- Employment contracts
- Letters of recommendation
- Employment benefit information and documents
- College transcripts and training certificates

Finances

- Budget
- Financial statements
- Bank statements
- Cancelled checks
- Credit card and charge account statements and records of payment
- Loan papers and receipts of payments

Insurance

- Original policies
- List of premium amounts and due date
- Claims information
- List of policies, numbers, company names, and types of coverage
- List of beneficiaries and amounts of expected benefits
- Medical history with names of physicians and record of current prescriptions

Taxes

- Copies of past tax returns
- Record and receipts of deductible expenses
- Record of taxable income
- Paycheck stubs
- W-2 Forms

Property

- Lease/mortgage papers
- Property tax statements and receipts of payments
- Deeds and title papers to property
- Inventory of personal possessions with purchase prices, estimated value, and photos of valuables
- Warranties and instruction manuals
- Service and repair records
- Bills of sale and receipts of payments for valuable purchases
- Receipts for improvements of real estate property
- Appraisals of real estate and valuables

Savings and Investments

- Purchase and sale records for stocks, bonds, and mutual funds
- Investment certificates
- Savings and account records

Estate Planning

- Will (original and copies)
- Individual Retirement Account (IRA) statements
- Pension information
- Social Security records
- Retirement plan documents

Goodheart-Willcox Publisher

Figure 2-10 Keeping these documents organized will help you be a better manager.

- prepare and file income tax returns;
- make loss estimates and insurance claims;
- verify bill payments, tax deductions, insurance claims, and property ownership;
- file for employee or Social Security benefits;

- make savings and investment decisions;
- work on retirement and estate planning;
- draw up a will; or
- settle an estate.

Up-to-Date Information

Along with other important documents, keep financial documents handy for yourself and for anyone you designate to handle your financial and legal affairs if you become unable to do so. Keep the following items in a secure place.

- Savings and checking account numbers, names on each account, and the name of the financial institution where each account is located
- Credit card and charge account numbers, the name of issuer, expiration dates, names of persons authorized to use each account, and numbers to call for lost cards
- PINs (personal identification numbers) for cash or debit cards and passwords for online accounts
- Securities and investment records, including stocks, bonds, and mutual funds with identifying numbers, names of issuers, estimated values, purchase prices and dates, names of brokers, and locations of certificates and accounts
- Other financial and legal documents, such as wills and trusts, adoption papers, insurance policies with claims information, mortgage papers, other loan contracts, tax records, property deeds and titles, pension plans and employee benefit documents, and Social Security and Medicare records
- Names, addresses, and phone numbers for lawyers, investment brokers, physicians, insurance agents, financial advisers, executors, guardians, business partners or co-owners, real estate brokers, and others who should be consulted in the management of your legal and financial affairs; names and contact information for people named in your will
- Inventory of valuable property and possessions with locations, estimated market values, appraisals, and details of purchases
- Household product information with warranties to explain product features, use and care, and servicing options
- Instructions for the management of your affairs, including your will, which outlines provisions for dependents, disposal of property and possessions, other wishes you want carried out if you die, and instructions to be followed if you are incapacitated

Make your recordkeeping system simple and convenient. You can keep many of these records and lists readily available in a secure home file. Use a desk drawer, file cabinet, or sturdy box to keep important papers together in one place. Some people keep their most important financial and legal documents in a safe deposit box at a financial institution with copies in their home files. These procedures will be more significant when you deal with the details of adult life.

Information stored on your computer needs to be organized, secure, and password protected. Data may include bill payment records, contracts, tax

Ethics

As you go to work or school each day, you may encounter others who categorize people using biased words and comments. Using age, gender, race, disability, or ethnicity as a way to describe others is unethical and sometimes even illegal. Use bias-free language in all of your communications, whether verbal or printed, to show respect for others.

forms, and e-mail correspondence related to financial and consumer matters. Set up an online filing system to organize your data. Financial software or web-based money management programs will guide you in setting up your financial affairs so you can locate information as you need it.

To prevent losing important documents should your computer fail, create backup copies on a CD or USB flash drive. Install up-to-date security software to protect against viruses and thieves who target financial information on unprotected websites.

Money Management Software

Just as CAT scans and MRIs provide detailed pictures of what is going on inside your body, money management software can provide a detailed picture of what is going on in your financial life. **Money management software** is a computer program used to organize daily finances and keep track of income, spending, saving, debts, investments, and other financial data.

Money management software allows you to do any or all of the following.

- Create a self-tailored budget and overall money management program.
- Enter income, expenses, and goals.
- Categorize your expenses and evaluate your spending patterns.
- Connect to and interact with your checking, credit, savings, and investment accounts.
- Create budgets, cash flow statements, net worth statements, and other financial documents.
- Track your spending and other financial transactions.
- Access all your financial records at any time.
- Manage and track your investments.
- Prepare and file your income tax returns.

Guided online setup instructions take you through these processes automatically. All you do is fill in your information as directed.

Evaluating Money Management Software

There are many money management software programs from which to choose. Search using the phrase *money management software,* and read the reviews of the most popular programs to help you decide which one would work well for you. These programs generally are very affordable, and some programs may even be free of charge. Many programs are basic and easy to use; others are more advanced and intended for more experienced users. Your choice will depend on the functions you want and your computer skills. It is a good idea to try a demo of a program before you decide whether it will work for you.

Money management software may be available as a web-based service. With a web-based service, your information is stored on a server rather than on your computer. Before enrolling in one of these programs, make sure the company is reputable and is certified as a secured site. If you prefer to store your information on your computer, there are programs you can download from a disc or from a website.

If you take precautions, online money management can be safe and convenient.

Security Online

Whether you are using a web-based program or one on your computer, make sure you have the appropriate virus checkers, malware protections, and backup systems for your data. Should you have a problem with your computer, you want to make sure your information is not destroyed.

Online money management, like many other online activities, requires you to provide confidential information regarding your finances. Take the necessary steps to ensure that your computer and your online connections are secure before providing sensitive personal information. To keep you safe and secure online:

- Protect your computer with up-to-date antivirus and spyware software and a firewall.
- Back up the important data on your computer so you can recover it if the computer is lost or stolen, crashes, or suffers a virus attack.
- Use strong passwords with 14 or more characters, uppercase and lowercase letters, and two or three numbers.
- Do not share personal, financial, or identifying information online unless you know exactly who is to receive it and why.
- Do not enter or access any sensitive information on public computers or Wi-Fi connections.

- Do not open e-mail from people or sources you do not know, particularly if you are asked for sensitive financial or personal information.
- Use secure payment methods, such as credit cards, PayPal, or other online payment processing programs, when purchasing software programs on a website. Avoid using debit cards or money transfers.
- Remove all traces of your personal information before you replace or dispose of your computer.

Checkpoint 2.2

1. What are two ways to pay bills?
2. What are three types of income records you should keep?
3. What does *pay yourself first* mean?
4. What are some tasks you can perform using money management software?
5. Describe three steps you can take to stay safe and secure online.

Build Your Vocabulary

As you progress through this course, develop a personal glossary of personal finance terms and add it to your portfolio. This will help you build your vocabulary and prepare you for a career. Write a definition for each of the following terms and add it to your personal finance glossary.

recordkeeping

legal document

money management software

Section 2.3
Young Adult and Family Finances

Objectives

After you study this section, you will be able to:

- Describe the financial tasks attached to adult life.
- Analyze how the family life cycle influences financial decisions.
- Discuss variations in the family life cycle.
- Outline ways to avoid financial problems.

Terms

written roommate agreement

family life cycle

stages in the life cycle

variations in the life cycle

family financial crisis

On Your Own

As you enter the adult world, your money management activities will expand. You may be eager to leave home and live on your own. Once independent, you may be shocked by the many expenses and responsibilities you must handle that were previously taken care of by your parents or guardians. Managing money well to remain independent becomes the number one financial challenge.

Often, young adults who are newly independent try to hold down costs by sharing living expenses with one or more roommates. Whether you live alone or with friends, you may be surprised at the new financial responsibilities you face. You will need to stay on top of fixed expenses, such as rent, taxes, insurance, car payments, utilities, telephone, and other bills you may be paying for the first time. Planning the use of income to cover expenses will take on new meaning and importance. Following the steps for budgeting that were presented earlier in the chapter can guide you in setting up a budget that will work for you. Some of the financial tasks you will need to assume include:

- keeping track of income and spending;
- planning the use of money to cover expenses;
- learning about household expenses;
- paying bills on time;
- saving and investing for your future;
- protecting against financial losses; and
- computing and paying taxes.

If you choose to live with one or more roommates, you can reduce your overall costs by sharing expenses. Before moving in with roommates, it is a good idea to discuss financial and living arrangements in detail so each of you knows what to expect. Issues to discuss with roommates include the items in the list on the following page.

 man Services

Certified Financial Planners

Certified financial planners have met certification requirements issued by the Certified Financial Planner Board of Standards. They assess the financial needs of clients and use their knowledge of investments, tax law, and insurance to recommend the most beneficial financial options for their clients.

Valeriy Velikov/Shutterstock.com

Whether you move out on your own or with a roommate, you will have many new expenses.

- *Rent.* How much is it? Who pays how much of the total? Is a security deposit required? How will you share it? Who will be responsible for paying the rent on time?
- *Chores.* How will you share cleaning, cooking, shopping, and other tasks?
- *Food.* How will you split the costs and responsibilities related to food?
- *Space.* Who gets each bedroom? How will you share space, time in the bathroom, common rooms, storage areas, and TV time?
- *Cable and utilities.* Will you share these costs? Who will be responsible for paying the bills on time? How will you split any security deposits required for these services?
- *Guests.* What, if any, limitations do you want on overnight guests and parties? Who may have overnight guests and how long may they stay? Do you want advance notice before guests are invited?
- *Privacy.* How will you handle privacy issues with respect to space and possessions?
- *Noise.* What limitations do you wish to put on noise? Do you want designated quiet times?
- *The lease.* What are the terms of the lease? What happens if one tenant moves out before the lease expires? Often when there are co-tenants and one person violates the terms of the lease, the others can be held

responsible for any resulting damages or unpaid rent. Be sure all tenants understand what is expected and decide in advance how you will handle early departures or other violations by one party.

Generally you can avoid future problems by discussing these issues in advance. Once you agree on major issues, it is a good idea to put your "house rules" in writing. A **written roommate agreement** is a document that contains the rules related to the living arrangements and expenses and is signed by all roommates. It lets everyone know what to expect and how problems will be solved.

Family Life Cycle

After a period of living alone or with roommates, many adults marry and start families. Their financial responsibilities increase dramatically again. There are family as well as personal expenses to cover. Perhaps the most important factors affecting family budgeting decisions will be age and stage in the family life cycle.

The **family life cycle** is the stages a family passes through over its lifetime. **Stages in the life cycle** are typical patterns of social and financial behavior families follow at different periods in the life cycle. Your goals and needs, as well as earning and spending patterns, will change with each stage. Becoming familiar with these patterns can provide you with a framework for your own financial planning. See Figure 2-11.

Financial Aspects of the Family Life Cycle		
Stages in the Family Life Cycle	**Career and Income Characteristics**	**Typical Expenses and Obligations**
Beginning Stage		
Marriage Getting started as a couple Establishing a home	Finishing education Making career decisions Entering the workforce Low or no income, with gradual increases	Living expenses Tuition and/or repayment of education loans Auto loan payments and insurance Life, health, and other insurance Home furnishings Savings and retirement contributions Income tax
Expanding Stage		
Infant years Birth/adoption of first child	Increasing income and job responsibilities One or two full-time incomes Decreased income if wife leaves work for childbearing	Child care and baby equipment Education fund Increased insurance coverage Prenatal, birth, and postnatal health care Income taxes Retirement contributions

Goodheart-Willcox Publisher

Figure 2-11 Career and income characteristics, as well as typical expenses and obligations, tend to follow a pattern at different stages of the life cycle.

(Continued)

Financial Aspects of the Family Life Cycle		
Stages in the Family Life Cycle	**Career and Income Characteristics**	**Typical Expenses and Obligations**
Developing Stage		
Toddler, preschool, and elementary school years Children become primary focus	Job advancement likely Increasing income Increasing job responsibilities	Move to larger living space Additional home furnishings Property and income tax increases Increased living expenses Retirement contributions
Adolescent years Involvement in school activities Preparation for launching stage	Continuing job advancement or possible career change Possible return of mother to the workforce Income still increasing	School expenses for extracurricular activities Savings and investments Savings for education Charitable contributions Travel Adolescents' spending Income and property taxes
Launching Stage		
Children leave home Parents adjust to "empty nest"	Heavier job responsibilities Peak performance years Income may peak as well Benefits may increase Retirement planning becomes a priority	Home improvements or new, smaller home Replacement furnishings Education and tuition costs Travel Retirement savings Income and property taxes Weddings of children
Aging Stage		
Parents focus on each other Children marry Grandchildren arrive Elderly parents may require care	Job responsibilities and earnings begin to level off Retirement and estate planning take form	Travel, recreation, and adult education Care for aging parents Increased savings and investments Gifts to help children get established Income and property taxes Long-term care insurance
Retirement years Establishing new routines, interests, and hobbies Grandparenting	Part-time or volunteer work Social Security income Income from retirement savings Wills and estate plans are revised as needed	Health insurance Possible relocation to a retirement area Travel Health care and medications Taxes Long-term care

Goodheart-Willcox Publisher

Figure 2-11 *Continued.*

Beginning Stage

From age 18 to the late 20s, young people are getting established on the job and in life. Those who marry begin the first stage of the family life cycle, called the *beginning stage*. Income for most young adults starts low and gradually increases with time on the job. Two-income couples enjoy the benefits of two incomes. People who marry later may have established careers and higher incomes.

Expenses at this time are likely to include education, college loans, home furnishings, and insurance. The down payment on a home is often the largest single expense for young couples. Other major expenses include an auto, savings, or contributions to a retirement fund. Couples need to tailor savings and investment programs to meet changing needs as they move to later stages in the life cycle.

Expanding Stage

For adults under age 40, life is often characterized by job advancement, rising income, and increasing responsibilities. With the birth or adoption of the first child, couples enter the expanding stage with all its joys and responsibilities. If one spouse leaves the workforce to raise children, income declines. At the same time, expenses increase. Child-related expenses include childcare, children's clothing, baby equipment, toys, and medical expenses.

As the family grows, many couples decide to move to a larger home or to leave city living for a more family-friendly environment in the suburbs. This is a good time to review and expand insurance protection and start an educational fund for children. It also is important to create a will.

Morgan Lane Photography/Shutterstock.com

The different stages of life bring about unique financial challenges as families grow and change.

Developing Stage

School-age children and adolescents bring a new set of circumstances. Family life tends to revolve around the children and their school life. Expenses include a larger clothing budget, sports and hobby equipment, lessons and tutoring, allowances, and savings for future education. Another expenditure for some families is a second car.

During this stage, a spouse who left the workforce may return, either to satisfy career goals or to supplement income. This change may require at least a brief return to school to update education and skills. While income may still climb during parenting years, expenses grow as well. These expenses include housing, insurance, taxes, education, savings, and retirement planning.

Launching Stage

Parents in their 40s and 50s share another set of common experiences. Families enter this stage as the children leave home for college, jobs, or homes of their own. During these years, job advancements often bring higher incomes. Earnings may peak. It is also a time when some people may seek a job or career change. Many families at this stage need extra income to cover college expenses and retirement savings. Retirement planning is critical.

In some families, this is a time when aging parents become a concern. Those in this situation are often called the *sandwich generation*. Parents find themselves *sandwiched* between college-bound teens and their own aging parents. Both financial and emotional demands are great when this happens.

Aging Stage

From the late 50s to retirement, people often need to adjust to new events. Earnings level off. Aging parents may require attention and assistance. Children have left home, creating a situation called the *empty nest*. Many parents become grandparents. Married couples often renew their focus on each other. Many choose to travel or become more active in the community.

Individuals and couples tend to focus on retirement planning during these years. Empty-nest families often move to smaller homes and simplify their lives. Those caring for elderly parents may face heavy health-care costs. Couples need to have reliable health insurance and consider long-term care insurance for themselves. At this stage, estate planning is important. It is also the time to review and revise wills.

For most people, this stage marks formal retirement. Some retirees seek part-time work or volunteer opportunities. For many, free time is a welcome luxury. Those in good health may travel more. Grandchildren are frequently a new focus at this time of life.

Income and most living expenses usually decline during retirement years. Security and comfort depend on the financial planning that occurred in earlier stages. For those who have not planned, the retirement years can bring financial hardship as income drops. Serious spending cutbacks may be required, especially if medical costs rise. Retired adults need to review wills and estate plans and discuss them with their adult children.

Individuals born between 1989 and 2010 are known as *Generation Z* or the *iGeneration.*

Careers in Human Services

What Does a Financial Planner Do?

Financial planners help clients assess their financial affairs and develop a plan to meet their financial goals for the future. They advise clients on investing, insurance, taxes, retirement, and estate planning. **Financial planners** typically:

- advise clients on ways to achieve their financial goals;
- prepare and analyze financial statements;
- provide investment and tax advice;
- advise clients on risk management;
- assist with retirement and estate planning;
- review and revise clients' financial plans as circumstances change; and
- monitor investments, tax strategies, risk management, and the overall financial plan for each client.

What Is It Like to Work as a Financial Planner?

Normally, **financial planners** work with individuals and families. They may do this in a private practice or through an investment firm, bank, or financial service firm. On-the-job training is an advantage of working for a bank or investment firm. Employers often pay fees for the courses required for **financial planners.**

Basically, **financial planners** are salespersons selling financial advice and services. Like most selling jobs, earnings depend on how well they sell. In a bad economy, income may be low. However, a **financial planner** who manages to form long-term relationships with clients can usually establish a reliable income flow.

Financial planners may be paid an hourly fee, a flat fee based on the value of the assets managed, or a commission on securities they sell to clients.

What Education and Skills Are Needed to Be a Financial Planner?

- bachelor degree in finance, economics, or business or law school
- pass the General Securities Representative Qualification Examination Series 7 and any additional exams required by individual states
- registration with state regulators and the Securities and Exchange Commission
- certification from the Certified Financial Planner Board of Standards
- two or more years of work experience in financial planning or a related field
- communication, selling, and computer skills

Variations in the Cycle

Not every family follows the stages of the family life cycle in order as listed in Figure 2-12. **Variations in the life cycle** are patterns that differ from typical families. The number of children and spacing between them can cause the cycle to vary from family to family. Some families skip, overlap, or repeat stages of the family life cycle. For example, couples that do not have children skip the expanding, developing, and launching stages. Parents with children

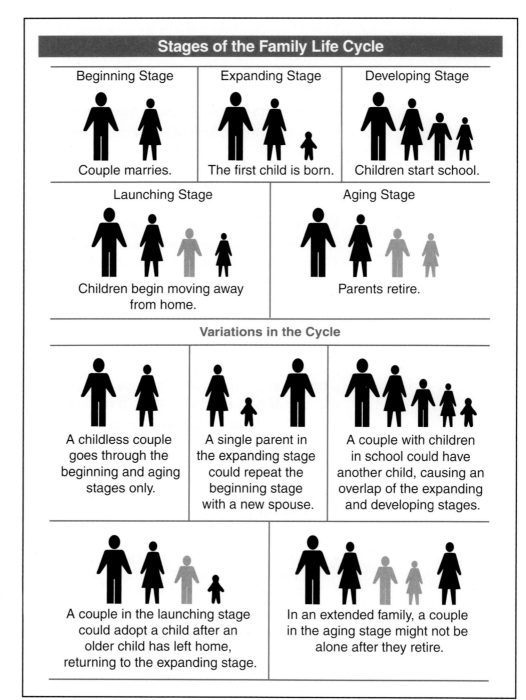

Goodheart-Willcox Publisher

Figure 2-12 Not all families progress through all stages of the family life cycle in the same way.

in school could have more children. This brings an overlap of the developing and expanding stages. Single parents who marry may repeat stages with their new spouses.

As family conditions change, financial planning concerns change, too. For example, single individuals, childless couples, single-parent families, and divorced or separated people have added considerations.

Singles and Childless Couples

Singles and couples with no dependents do not have the expenses related to raising children, such as school and medical expenses. Both groups may spend more throughout the life cycle on travel, leisure, and other extras. Some may choose to give more to charitable causes. Both groups often feel a greater responsibility to help their aging parents.

Single-Parent Families

Females lead most single-parent families. Their income is typically less than that of two-parent families and single-parent families led by males. Saving and planning for future security is sometimes difficult as these families struggle to meet current expenses. Government and community services and assistance can be very helpful for single-parent families.

Separated and Divorced Individuals

Separated and divorced people face a unique set of financial concerns. They may have the following expenses: legal fees, alimony, child support, and property settlement costs. The cost of establishing and maintaining a separate home may be another expense, especially if there are children involved. A divorce or separation may require additional furnishings and moving costs.

No matter what your situation will be, it is wise to begin a savings and investment program early in your adult life to protect against financial risks. These steps are the foundation of financial security in later life. Savings can cover unexpected expenses and emergencies and help you reach goals. Insurance protects against major disasters. By following these three steps, you can feel reasonably comfortable with your financial situation.

Working Through Financial Problems

You can often avoid financial trouble by living within your means and keeping debt under control. This involves taking responsibility for your life, including your financial choices and decisions. Preparation can help you weather a crisis situation if it arises. Getting the best education and job training possible are ways to be prepared. With a good education and job skills, you are better able to find work and advance on the job. Staying current in your field through continuing education and training programs also helps.

Having an emergency fund is another way to prepare for the unexpected. In hard times or during a recession, an emergency fund should equal 8 to 10 months' income. Other preventive measures include:

- sound money management;
- practical credit controls;
- regular savings;
- insurance protection;
- reasonable caution in financial matters; and
- regular family money management discussions.

Preventive measures often help you avoid financial problems altogether. They also can minimize the impact of unavoidable problems, such as the loss of a job in a recession.

There may be times when financial disaster strikes because of circumstances beyond your control. A **family financial crisis** is a major problem that changes the future of the family and its lifestyle. Examples include job loss, divorce, death, disability, serious illness, and natural disasters. When such events occur, you may need to make some serious changes in your financial planning and behavior. If debt problems reach the crisis stage, you need prompt, drastic action to correct the situation.

Start by discussing the problem with adult members of the household, including older children. Make sure that everyone understands the potential impact on their standard of living and what they can do to help. For example, college-bound teens may need to consider work/study programs or a community college near enough to allow living at home while going to school. Knowing they have a stake in resolving the crisis will encourage cooperation of all family members and reduce conflict.

Make a list of financial and nonfinancial resources available to you. In analyzing your situation, consider the following steps you can take to minimize negative financial or other consequences.

- Accept and acknowledge the crisis.
- If debt is a part of the crisis, contact creditors promptly.
- Avoid making any new credit purchases.
- Look for reliable, affordable credit and financial counseling.
- Adjust spending habits and cut expenses.
- Look for every possible source of new income.
- Ask unemployed family members to seek work.
- Look for assistance from extended family, employers, insurance, government programs, and community or charitable organizations.
- Consider selling some assets, such as real estate, investments, autos, and valuable possessions.
- As a last resort, consider bankruptcy.

Some situations may call for the help of professionals. Consider consulting health-care providers, family counselors, financial advisors, and lawyers to determine the full scope of the crisis.

Checkpoint 2.3

1. Name three financial tasks you will need to assume as an adult.
2. What is the purpose of a roommate agreement?
3. What are the typical stages in the family life cycle?
4. What are some common variations in the family life cycle?
5. List three ways to minimize the negative consequences of a financial crisis.

Build Your Vocabulary

As you progress through this course, develop a personal glossary of personal finance terms and add it to your portfolio. This will help you build your vocabulary and prepare you for a career. Write a definition for each of the following terms and add it to your personal finance glossary.

written roommate agreement

family life cycle

stages in the life cycle

variations in the life cycle

family financial crisis

Chapter Summary

Section 2.1 Your Personal Financial Landscape

- Using a budget, you can analyze your income and expenses and create a plan for achieving your financial goals. Achieving financial security requires financial literacy and lifetime planning.
- A cash flow statement shows the amount of money received and the amount paid for goods and services during a specific period.
- A net worth statement shows your current financial situation—the difference between what you own and what you owe. A periodic net worth statement charts progress and is an important tool.

Section 2.2 Documentation

- The process of setting up an organized system for financial and legal documents, called recordkeeping, is an important part of managing your finances effectively. Knowing what to keep and where to file important documents can help you manage your financial affairs.
- Money management software can help you organize daily finances and keep track of income, spending, saving, debts, investments, and other financial data.

Section 2.3 Young Adult and Family Finances

- As an adult, your money management activities will expand to include keeping track of income and expenses, paying bills, saving, investing, and paying taxes.
- The family life cycle refers to the stages a family passes through. Age and stage in the family life cycle are important factors affecting family financial decisions.
- Variations in the family life cycle include singles, childless couples, single parent families, and divorced or separated adults. Your goals and needs will change with each stage.
- You can often avoid financial trouble by living within your means, keeping debt under control, getting a good education and job training, and having an emergency fund.

Check Your Personal Finance IQ

Now that you have finished the chapter, see what you learned about personal finance by taking the chapter posttest. If you do not have a smartphone, visit the G-W Learning companion website.

G-W Learning mobile site: www.m.g-wlearning.com

G-W Learning companion website: www.g-wlearning.com

Review Your Knowledge

1. Give an example of a discretionary expense.
2. What financial data is shown on a net worth statement?
3. What are liquid assets?
4. Current liabilities are usually due within what length of time?
5. What is the purpose of money management software?
6. What strategy do many young, unmarried adults use to help control living expenses?
7. What stage of the family life cycle life is often characterized by job advancement, rising income, increasing responsibilities, and the birth or adoption of a first child?
8. Name three events in life that call for a change in financial plans.
9. What amount of money is recommended for an emergency fund?
10. What are three examples of events that can lead to a family financial crisis?

Apply Your Knowledge

11. Why do you think people often delay serious financial planning?
12. What are the advantages of beginning savings and investment programs at an early age?
13. What are the consequences of putting off saving until age 30? age 40? age 50?
14. What are some financial and other issues roommates need to address before moving in together?
15. How do you think financial security and financial crises affect married couples with children?
16. How do you think financial insecurity affects retired couples?
17. How would a financial crisis in your family affect you personally?
18. Cite an example of ways the economy can influence personal and family money management and lifestyles.
19. How do the demographics of your community affect your family's financial affairs?
20. Has use of technology improved your family's financial affairs? Explain.

Teamwork

Consumers have a responsibility to live within their means. Work in a team with other students to discuss the following questions. When consumers have financial difficulties caused by overspending, what, if any, public assistance should be available to them? Is it ethical to create credit card debt to buy nonessentials, to buy a car you cannot afford, or to borrow money you cannot repay? Is it ethical for creditors to make credit readily available to borrowers who have limited ability to repay as agreed? Share your team's opinion with the class.

G-W Learning Mobile Site

Visit the G-W Learning mobile site to complete the chapter pretest and posttest and to practice vocabulary using e-flash cards. If you do not have a smartphone, visit the G-W Learning companion website to access these features.

G-W Learning mobile site: www.m.g-wlearning.com

G-W Learning companion website: www.g-wlearning.com

Common Core

College and Career Readiness

CTE Career Ready Practices. For every action, there is a reaction—whether it is immediately seen or not. There are positive and negative consequences for different actions and inactions. Make a list of five things that you have done for which there were either positive or negative consequences. Put a plus sign (+) beside the positive outcomes and a minus (-) sign beside the negative outcomes. What could you have done differently that would have changed each outcome?

Reading. Read a magazine, newspaper, or online article about the importance of personal finance for teens. Determine the central ideas of the article and review the conclusions made by the author. Provide an accurate summary of your reading, making sure to incorporate the who, what, when, and how of this situation.

Writing. Research the history of personal finance. Where did the concept originate? Write an informative report consisting of several paragraphs to describe your findings.

Web Connect

Investigate several money management software programs online. Compare and contrast the key features of three of them. Discuss ways money management software could help you with financial planning and management over your lifetime.

College and Career Readiness

College and Career Readiness Portfolio

It is helpful to have a checklist of components that should be included in your portfolio. Your instructor may provide you with a checklist. If not, create your own checklist to use as an ongoing reference as you create your portfolio throughout this class.

1. Decide on the purpose of the portfolio you are creating—temporary or short-term employment, career, or application for college.
2. Research your chosen purpose to find suggested items to include that will help you create a professional portfolio.

Performance

Some competitive events for Career and Technical Student Organizations (CTSOs) have a performance portion. The activity could potentially be a decision-making scenario for which your team will provide a solution and present it to the judges.

To prepare for the performance portion of a presentation, complete the following activities.

1. On your organization's website, locate a rubric or scoring sheet for the event.
2. Confirm the use of visual aids that may be used in the presentation and amount of setup time permitted.
3. Review the rules to confirm if questions will be asked or if the team will need to defend a case or situation.
4. Make notes on index cards about important points to remember. Use these notes to study. You may also be able to use these notes during the event.
5. Practice the presentation. You should introduce yourself, review the topic that is being presented, defend the topic being presented, and conclude with a summary.
6. After the presentation is complete, ask for feedback from your instructor. You may consider also having a student audience listen and give feedback.

Unit 2
Managing Your Finances

Konstantin Chagin/Shutterstock.com

Careful decisions and wise use of resources can help you achieve your financial goals.

Chapters

Personal Finance

Why It Matters

Earning money from a career that is personally satisfying is the first step in gaining financial independence. However, your financial success depends more on how you manage the money you make rather than how much you make. Most people aim toward creating wealth so that they have sufficient money to live their lives comfortably. Wealth does not always come from just a paycheck. It usually comes from the ability to manage your finances and make your money work for you.

Through savings and investing, you can make your money grow. Saving and investing starting at an early age can help you pay for college, buy a car, and retire comfortably. Protecting your health and wealth with insurance can make for a secure future. Estate planning helps you determine your financial needs and ensures your heirs are provided for according to your wishes.

Chapter 3
Income and Taxes

Income gives individuals spending money. Taxes give the various levels of government their spending money, which is called *revenue*. A major way for a government to raise revenue is by taxing each person's income as well as items they buy or own. The government then uses that revenue to provide public goods and services that benefit all. As a teen, you use some of those goods and services now, such as schools, libraries, parks, highways, and police protection. As an older adult, you will use other types of public goods and services, such as Social Security benefits.

Focus on Finance

Social Security Number

A Social Security number serves two major purposes. The Social Security Administration uses this number to keep a record of your covered earnings. These earnings determine the amount you will eventually receive in retirement, disability benefits, or benefits to your survivors if you die. The Internal Revenue Service also uses your Social Security number as a taxpayer identification number on all tax returns and IRS forms.

Today, most parents apply for a Social Security number for their children. It is needed to claim a child as a dependent on income tax returns, to open a bank account, to buy savings bonds, and to obtain health insurance coverage. When giving the information required for a birth certificate, parents are asked whether they wish to apply for a Social Security number. Normally, the hospital will provide all the information needed to do this. Applications also are available online at www.socialsecurity.gov.

No two Social Security numbers are the same. Your number is yours alone. It prevents your records from being mixed up with the records of someone else who may have the same name. If you lose your card or change your name, contact the nearest Social Security office for a new card. Safeguard your Social Security number. Do not carry it with you or give it out unnecessarily. Criminals can use this number to steal your identity and damage your finances.

College and Career Readiness

Reading Prep. Before you begin reading this chapter, try to find a quiet place with no distractions. Make sure your chair is comfortable and the lighting is adequate.

Check Your Personal Finance IQ

Before you begin the chapter, see what you already know about personal finance by taking the chapter pretest. If you do not have a smartphone, visit the G-W Learning companion website.

G-W Learning mobile site: www.m.g-wlearning.com

G-W Learning companion website: www.g-wlearning.com

Sections

Section 3.1 Income

Section 3.2 Tax Returns

Section 3.3 Taxes and
       Government Spending

Blend Images/Shutterstock.com

Section 3.1
Income

Objectives

After studying this section, you will be able to:

* Identify different types of earned income.
* Identify common payroll deductions and determine net pay.
* Describe common types of employee benefits.

Terms

earned income	bonus
wage	gross pay
minimum wage	payroll deduction
overtime wage	net pay
piecework	FICA taxes
salary	compensation
commission	employee benefit
tip	

Earned Income

There are many ways to earn income. Most people work for someone else—an employer. Others choose to work for themselves as self-employed individuals. **Earned income** is the income you receive from employment or from self-employment. For most people, employment is the primary way to earn income.

Wages

A **wage** is payment for work and is usually calculated on an hourly, daily, or piecework basis. A wage is paid on a schedule—often every week or every two weeks. For example, an hourly wage is a fixed amount paid for each hour worked.

Many unskilled and beginning workers are paid the minimum wage. The **minimum wage** is the lowest hourly wage employers can pay most workers by law. Workers who frequently receive minimum wage include food preparers in fast-food restaurants, store salespeople, and workers at a car wash. Contrary to popular belief, most minimum wage workers are adults, not teens.

The US government sets and enforces the minimum wage through the Fair Labor Standards Act (FLSA). Periodically, Congress passes legislation raising the minimum wage so it keeps pace with cost-of-living increases. Some states require a higher minimum wage than the federal wage. If there is both a state and a federal minimum wage, workers get whichever wage is higher.

Yuri Recurs/Shutterstock.com

A minimum-wage job is often a starting point for young workers.

Most wage earners are covered by the overtime provisions of the FLSA. **Overtime wage** is the amount paid for working time in a week that is beyond the standard 40-hour workweek. Eligible workers who put in more than 40 hours per week must receive overtime pay at least 1.5 times their regular hourly rate. For example, Sue Barnwell earns $10 an hour and worked a total of 44 hours last week. Her total earnings for the week are:

regular earnings:	$40 \times \$10$	=	$400
overtime earnings:	$4 \times \$15$ ($\$10 \times 1.5$)	=	60
total earnings:			$460

Some employers pay overtime if an employee works more than eight hours in a day, even if the employee's total hours for the week do not exceed 40. Some employers also pay overtime for weekend and holiday work regardless of the total number of hours worked in the week.

Some employees covered by the FLSA are exempt from receiving the full minimum wage. For example, workers under the age of 20 who are receiving job training can be paid less than the minimum wage. However, this is only during their first 90 consecutive days on the job. High school students enrolled in career education classes can sometimes be paid less than full minimum wage. The Department of Labor in your state can answer questions about wage requirements.

Piecework is a wage based on a rate per unit of work completed. For example, garment workers may be paid by the number of garments completed. The total piecework wages, however, must add up to at least the minimum wage.

On July 24, 2009, the federal minimum wage was set at $7.25 an hour.

Salary

Salary is a fixed payment for work and is expressed as an annual figure. It is paid in periodic equal payments. The payment period is usually weekly, biweekly (every other week), semimonthly (twice a month), or monthly. For example, the salary for a job may be listed as $42,120 a year. However, a worker does not receive a lump sum payment of $42,120. Instead, the salary is divided into equal payments at regular intervals during the year. If the employer pays employees weekly, the worker would receive 52 checks of $810 ($42,120 ÷ 52) throughout the year. Figure 3-1 shows how $42,120 would be broken down and paid in the common pay periods.

Salaried workers are expected to put in as much time as it takes to do the job. Therefore, teachers, managers, supervisors, and professionals are not paid overtime.

Commission

A **commission** is income paid as a percentage of sales made by a salesperson. Some people may work on a commission-only basis. Others may receive a combination of base salary plus commission. Salespeople, who usually work on commission, sell cars, real estate, insurance, and other goods and services.

For a person working on commission, making many sales means income goes up. If customers do not buy, income shrinks. For many salespeople, income varies from month to month and year to year. A good salesperson generally earns more in commissions than in salary.

Tips

A **tip**, or *gratuity*, is money paid for service beyond what is required. A customer leaves a tip as a reward for good service. Tips are also given as incentives for workers to provide good service. This money belongs to workers, not their employers. This form of income is common for food servers, taxi drivers, hairdressers, and other service-industry workers.

Annual Salary of $42,120 in Common Pay Periods				
Pay Period	Salary	Number of Pay Periods in a Year	Calculation	Earnings per Pay Period
Weekly	$42,120	52	$42,120 ÷ 52	$ 810
Biweekly	$42,120	26	$42,120 ÷ 26	$1,620
Semimonthly	$42,120	24	$42,120 ÷ 24	$1,755
Monthly	$42,120	12	$42,120 ÷ 12	$3,510

Goodheart-Willcox Publisher

Figure 3–1 When there are more pay periods per year, the earnings for the pay period are smaller.

According to the US Department of Labor, a tipped employee is one who engages in an occupation in which he or she customarily and regularly receives more than $30 per month in tips. The FLSA requires that tipped employees be paid at least the minimum wage. However, the employer of a tipped employee is only required to pay $2.13 per hour in direct wages. If the $2.13 paid by the employer and the tips received by the employee do not equal the minimum wage, the employer must make up the difference.

Some state laws require an hourly direct wage higher than $2.13 for tipped employees. In those states, employers must pay the higher wage.

Bonus

A **bonus** is money added to an employee's base pay. It is usually a reward for performance or a share of business profits. Bonuses are incentives to encourage workers to perform better. Bonus income is usually based on worker performance, length of time with the company, or company performance.

Self-Employment Income

A growing proportion of the US workforce is self-employed. Unlike employees, who perform services for their employer, self-employed people work for themselves. The form of income earned is called *profit* or *self-employment income.*

This category of workers includes many entrepreneurs in the trades, such as plumbers, carpenters, and painters. Artists and consultants are often self-employed. A teenager who has a part-time job mowing lawns is self-employed.

One of the drawbacks of being self-employed is that you must arrange and pay for your own employment-related benefits. Some of these benefits, especially health care, are costly when purchased by individuals.

Payroll Deductions

The dollar figure on your paycheck is not the same as the dollar figure you are told when hired for a job. **Gross pay,** or *gross income*, is total income before payroll deductions. A **payroll deduction** is a subtraction from your gross pay. Some deductions are mandatory, such as Social Security taxes, Medicare taxes, and income taxes.

The federal income tax system is built on a *pay-as-you-earn* concept. This means a working person pays taxes from each paycheck instead of in one lump sum each year. State and local income taxes usually work this way, too.

When you begin a job, your employer will ask you to complete a Form W-4. *Form W-4* is the Employee's Withholding Allowance Certificate that helps your employer determine how much income tax to withhold from your paychecks as payroll deductions. Money withheld from your check is forwarded by your employer to the IRS or other appropriate government agencies. Figure 3-2 shows a completed Form W-4.

The amount of income tax withheld from your paycheck depends on how much you earn, your marital status, and the number of allowances you claim. An allowance is an amount of earnings not subject to income taxes.

------------------------------- Cut here and give Form W-4 to your employer. Keep the top part for your records. -------------------------------

Form **W-4**	**Employee's Withholding Allowance Certificate**	OMB No. 1545-0074
Department of the Treasury Internal Revenue Service	▶ Whether you are entitled to claim a certain number of allowances or exemption from withholding is subject to review by the IRS. Your employer may be required to send a copy of this form to the IRS.	20--

1 Type or print your first name and middle initial. Kristy A.	Last name James	2 Your social security number 987 65 4321

Home address (number and street or rural route)
1027 Cedar Street

3 ☒ Single ☐ Married ☐ Married, but withhold at higher Single rate.
Note. If married, but legally separated, or spouse is a nonresident alien, check the "Single" box.

City or town, state, and ZIP code
Franklin, IL 65432

4 If your last name differs from that shown on your social security card, check here. You must call 1-800-772-1213 for a replacement card. ▶ ☐

5	Total number of allowances you are claiming (from line **H** above **or** from the applicable worksheet on page 2)	5	2
6	Additional amount, if any, you want withheld from each paycheck	6	$

7 I claim exemption from withholding for 20--, and I certify that I meet **both** of the following conditions for exemption.
  • Last year I had a right to a refund of **all** federal income tax withheld because I had **no** tax liability **and**
  • This year I expect a refund of **all** federal income tax withheld because I expect to have **no** tax liability.
  If you meet both conditions, write "Exempt" here . . . . ▶ | 7 |

Under penalties of perjury, I declare that I have examined this certificate and to the best of my knowledge and belief, it is true, correct, and complete.

Employee's signature
(This form is not valid unless you sign it.) ▶ *Kristy A James*   Date ▶ **01/02/--**

8 Employer's name and address (Employer: Complete lines 8 and 10 only if sending to the IRS.)	9 Office code (optional)	10 Employer identification number (EIN)

For Privacy Act and Paperwork Reduction Act Notice, see page 2.   Cat. No. 10220Q   Form **W-4** (20--)

United States Department of the Treasury, Internal Revenue Service

Figure 3-2 Employees complete the Form W-4. It provides information employers use to determine how much federal tax to withhold from paychecks.

Taxpayers may take an allowance for themselves and for each of their dependents. The more allowances you claim, the smaller the amount of tax that will be withheld from your paycheck by your employer. A worksheet on the Form W-4 will help you calculate your personal withholding allowances. The dollar amount of the allowance is raised each year to keep pace with inflation.

Net pay, or *take-home pay*, is gross pay (plus bonuses, if you get them) minus payroll deductions. For example, see the paycheck stub in Figure 3-3. In a pay period, the worker earned a total of $345.00 in wages and overtime pay. This is gross pay, but the worker's net pay is only $286.75. Gross pay is reduced by payroll deductions. Deductions can lower a paycheck by 20 percent or more.

Based on the information provided on the Form W-4, deductions will be made from your gross earnings. Common payroll deductions are described in the following paragraphs.

People who are self-employed are responsible for the total amount of FICA taxes on their income. They must pay the portion of the tax that the employee would pay plus the portion of the tax that the employer would pay. Self-employed people pay a total of 15.30 percent on net employment earnings.

FICA Tax

Most workers in the United States are covered by the Federal Insurance Contributions Act (FICA). **FICA taxes,** or *Social Security and Medicare taxes*, are taxes paid by the employee and employer that are used to finance the federal Social Security and Medicare programs. The FICA tax is a matching tax. This means that employers must match the amount of FICA taxes that the employees pay. Each pays 7.65 percent—6.2 percent for Social Security and 1.45 percent for Medicare. There is an annual cap on the amount of income that is subject to Social Security taxes. However, there is no cap on income that is taxed for Medicare.

Employers withhold FICA taxes from each employee's paycheck. They add their share of FICA tax and pay the total to the government under the employee's name and Social Security number. The amount of Social Security tax withheld appears on an employee's paycheck.

Town Department Store 111 Broadway Avenue Franklin, IL 65432		Pay Period: 03/08/-- through 03/21/--		Employee: Kristy A. James 1027 Cedar Street Franklin, IL 65432	
Gross Pay	**Federal Income Tax Withheld**	**State Income Tax Withheld**	**FICA Tax Withheld**	**Medicare Tax Withheld**	**Net Pay**
$ 345.00	$ 18.06	$ 13.80	$ 21.39	$ 5.00	$ 286.75
Gross Pay Year-to-Date	**Federal Year-to-Date**	**State Year-to-Date**	**FICA Year-to-Date**	**Medicare Year-to-Date**	**Net Pay Year-to-Date**
$ 8,484.50	$ 444.16	$ 339.38	$ 526.04	$ 123.03	$ 7,051.89

Goodheart-Willcox Publisher

Figure 3-3 This paycheck stub shows some of the common payroll deductions from income.

Federal, State, and Local Withholding Taxes

The amount deducted for taxes is based on your earnings, marital status, and withholding allowances that you claim. Federal income taxes are taxes withheld from the employee's gross pay and forwarded to the federal government. These funds are used for many purposes, such as national security and other government functions.

State income taxes are taxes withheld from the employee's gross pay and are forwarded to the state government. Most states have an income tax. These taxes are used for roads, education, and other purposes.

Local withholding taxes, such as city or county income taxes, are withheld from the employee's gross pay and forwarded to the local government. These taxes are used for police departments, roads, and other services.

Other Deductions

Voluntary deductions may be withheld for health care, dental care, vision care, and other insurance that employees purchase through their employers. These deductions might also include charitable contributions, which are donations that you make to a charitable organization.

Benefits

Compensation is the payment and benefits received for work performed. Some of the most valuable forms of payment to workers are noncash compensation. An **employee benefit,** or *fringe benefit,* is a form of noncash compensation received in addition to a wage or salary. Employee benefits offer important financial advantages.

The availability of employee benefits and other extras depends on the company and type of work. Along with salary or wages, they contribute significantly to the financial well-being of workers and their families. Common types of employee benefits include:

- paid vacation and holiday time;
- paid sick leave;
- life and health insurance; and
- retirement savings plans.

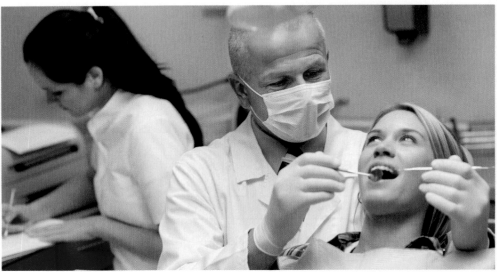

CandyBox Images/Shutterstock.com

Dental insurance is a fringe benefit often provided by employers.

Your employer can help you save money for the future. An employer-sponsored retirement savings plan is an investment program. One example is a 401(k) retirement savings plan. Money is withheld from the employee's gross pay and placed into a savings fund. Employers sometimes match employee contributions. However, with a few exceptions, money must stay in the account until retirement to avoid taxes and penalties. Chapter 7 will present more information about these plans and other valuable financial resources.

Checkpoint 3.1

1. What is earned income?
2. What is the difference between a wage and a salary?
3. For what hours are eligible workers typically paid overtime wages?
4. What are three examples of mandatory deductions from gross pay?
5. Why are FICA taxes referred to as matching taxes?

Build Your Vocabulary

As you progress through this course, develop a personal glossary of personal finance terms and add it to your portfolio. This will help you build your vocabulary and prepare you for a career. Write a definition for each of the following terms and add it to your personal finance glossary.

earned income	bonus
wage	gross pay
minimum wage	payroll deduction
overtime wage	net pay
piecework	FICA taxes
salary	compensation
commission	employee benefit
tip	

Section 3.2
Tax Returns

Objectives

After studying this section, you will be able to:

- List the information needed to file an income tax return.
- Describe basic procedures for filing a 1040EZ tax return.
- Discuss the option of electronic filing of income taxes.
- Give sources of tax information.
- Describe the IRS auditing process.

Terms

Form W-2

unearned income

tax deduction

itemized deduction

standard deduction

exemption

tax credit

Filing an Income Tax Return

The individual income tax is the federal government's largest source of revenue. The Internal Revenue Service, or *IRS*, is the government agency responsible for collecting federal income taxes. Approximately 200 million individuals file a tax return each year. A tax return is a report containing information used to calculate taxes owed by the taxpayer. Tax returns must also be filed with state governments. In many areas, a city tax return may need to be filed. Not filing a tax return is a crime, as is providing false information on a tax form.

Who Must File a Tax Return?

You must file a tax return when your income reaches a level established by the IRS. In a recent year, a single person under age 65 could earn up to $9,500 before being required to file a return. The amount required to file a return is raised each year. To find the current amount, go to www.irs.gov and enter *who must file* in the search box.

If you did not make enough to file a tax return but income taxes were withheld from your paychecks, you should file a return so that you can get a refund. Refunds are never automatic, so you must always file a tax return to receive your refund.

When to File

You must file no later than April 15 of the year after your income was earned. If April 15 falls on a Saturday, a Sunday, or a national holiday, the filing date is extended to the next business day. If you file late, you will be charged a penalty, even if the IRS owes you money.

Yuri Arcurs/Shutterstock.com

A person must file an income tax return in order to receive a refund.

Filing Status

Filing status is a category that determines the tax form you use and your tax liability. It is based on your marital status on the last day of the tax year. When filing your return, you must check one of the following as your filing status.

- *Single.* For individuals who are unmarried at the end of the year.
- *Married filing jointly (even if only one had income).* For couples who are legally married on the last day of the tax year.
- *Married filing separately.* For legally married couples who choose to file separate returns.
- *Head of household (with qualifying person).* For individuals who are unmarried at the end of the year and have at least one dependent child or other dependent relative.
- *Qualifying widow(er) with dependent child.* A special status for an individual with a dependent child whose spouse has died. This status is only available for two years after the death of a spouse and if the taxpayer does not remarry during the two-year period.

It is important to choose the correct filing status. Choosing an incorrect filing status could result in an incorrect tax return.

Documentation

Each year, by the end of January, each of your employers will send you a Form W-2, illustrated in Figure 3-4. **Form W-2** is a Wage and Tax Statement that shows your earnings and the amounts of income, Social Security, and

22222	**a** Employee's social security number 987-65-4321	OMB No. 1545-0008		
b Employer identification number (EIN) XX-XXXXXXX		**1** Wages, tips, other compensation 28956.98		**2** Federal income tax withheld 3020.42
c Employer's name, address, and ZIP code Town Department Store 111 Broadway Avenue Franklin, IL 65432		**3** Social security wages 28956.98		**4** Social security tax withheld 1795.33
		5 Medicare wages and tips		**6** Medicare tax withheld 419.88
		7 Social security tips		**8** Allocated tips
d Control number 123456789		**9** Advance EIC payment		**10** Dependent care benefits
e Employee's first name and initial Last name Suff. Kristy A. James		**11** Nonqualified plans		**12a**
		13 Statutory employee Retirement plan Third-party sick pay		**12b**
1027 Cedar Street Franklin, IL 65432		**14** Other		**12c**
				12d
f Employee's address and ZIP code				

15 State Employer's state ID number IL XX-XXXXXXX	**16** State wages, tips, etc. 28956.98	**17** State income tax 1362.40	**18** Local wages, tips, etc.	**19** Local income tax	**20** Locality name

Form **W-2** Wage and Tax Statement   20--   Department of the Treasury—Internal Revenue Service

Copy 1—For State, City, or Local Tax Department

Goodheart-Willcox Publisher

Figure 3-4 A Form W-2 shows how much an employee was paid during a year and what payroll deductions were taken.

Medicare taxes withheld from your income during the year. This statement will usually be mailed to your home by January 31 of the year after the income was earned.

You will receive a Form 1099-MISC if you earned income from contracted work, royalties, unemployment compensation, and other sources on nonemployee income.

You will need these additional records and forms to prepare your return correctly:

- other records of income, such as from tips
- your Social Security number and numbers for household members
- copies of your tax returns from the previous year you filed
- forms and instructions from the IRS.

Taxpayers who need to itemize may also need these records:

- canceled checks and receipts for deductions or credits entered on your tax return
- itemized bills and receipts for deductible expenses
- bills and receipts for permanent home improvements
- records of interest paid on home mortgages
- real estate closing statements
- investment records, including purchase and sale dates, prices, gains, losses, and commissions

Tax Forms

When filing a tax return, you will use one of three forms: 1040, 1040A, or 1040EZ. These forms and many others are updated each year. Forms and instructions are available for download at the IRS website at www.irs.gov, or printed forms can be picked up at public places, such as libraries and post offices. Selecting the form that is appropriate for you will depend on your tax situation. It is important to use the correct form to ensure that your return is processed quickly. The three forms are described below.

- *Form 1040.* IRS Form 1040 is commonly referred to as the *long form*. It must be used by taxpayers with a taxable income more than $100,000 and by taxpayers who have business or rental income, income or losses from selling assets, or itemized tax deductions. Itemized tax deductions are discussed in the next section of the chapter.

- *Form 1040A.* IRS Form 1040A is commonly referred to as the *short form*. It can be used by taxpayers with a taxable income less than $100,000 who have no business income and who choose not to itemize deductions. Most taxpayers who have dependents, but are not homeowners, use Form 1040A.

- *Form 1040EZ.* IRS Form 1040EZ is the simplest form to use. In order to use it, you must have a taxable income less than $100,000, file as single or married filing jointly, claim no dependents, and have income only from employee compensation, unemployment compensation, and interest. The first tax return you file will likely be a 1040EZ.

You may also need a tax return form to file state taxes. Forty-three states collect personal income tax. Rates vary from state to state and are usually based on adjusted gross income, taxable income, or some other figure taken from your federal return. Filing deadlines for state and local returns usually correspond with filing dates for federal tax forms. The Department of Revenue for your state or municipality can provide the information you need on state and local income, property, and other taxes.

Originally, the 1040A was literally a short form. It was a postcard return that taxpayers filled out and dropped in the mail without the need for an envelope.

Calculating Taxable Income

No matter which form you use, the goal is to calculate how much taxes you owe. First, calculate your gross (total) income for the past year. The less income you earned, the lower your taxes should be.

Income

Earned income is earnings from employment. This includes earned income of wages, salary, commission, tips, and bonuses. The numbers come from Forms W-2 and 1099.

Unearned income is earnings from sources other than work. Unearned income includes the following types of income.

- *Interest received on savings accounts and bonds.* Interest is money paid by financial institutions, governments, and businesses in exchange for the use of the investor's money.

- *Earnings from investments.* Investment earnings are the amount of money received from investments, such as stocks or bonds.

- *Rental income.* Rental income is money received from allowing others to use your property.

- *Social Security and retirement.* Social Security is income received because of retirement or disability. Retirement income comes from sources such as pensions and withdrawals from retirement accounts.

- *Alimony received.* Alimony is money received as a result of a divorce settlement.

- *Unemployment compensation.* Unemployment compensation is money received from a state unemployment fund during periods of temporary unemployment.

Most sources of unearned income are taxable. Some unearned income—such as interest income, rental income, unemployment compensation, and alimony—are taxed at the same rate as earned income. Other unearned income, such as investment income, may be taxed at a lower rate. Social Security is only partially taxable. Depending on its source, retirement income may be fully taxable, partially taxable, or nontaxable.

Adjustments and Adjusted Gross Income (AGI)

Fortunately, your taxes are not calculated based on your gross income. The good news is that your income can be reduced by adjustments. Adjustments are government-approved reductions in gross income. This helps to reduce the amount of tax that must be paid. For example, students or their parents can deduct the interest paid on student loans. You arrive at *adjusted gross income* (AGI) by subtracting your adjustments from your total income.

Tax Deductions

A **tax deduction** is an amount that is subtracted from your adjusted gross income, which further reduces your taxable income. When filing your tax return, you have a choice: itemized deductions or the standard deduction. An **itemized deduction** is an allowed expense that you can deduct from your adjusted gross income. *Itemize* means to list your tax deductions. The specific expenses that can be treated as itemized deductions are determined by Congress. Typical itemized deductions are interest paid on home loans, taxes paid on the value of your home, state income taxes paid, and contributions to recognized charities and churches.

Taxpayers who do not have enough itemized deductions to benefit from them can choose the standard deduction. The **standard deduction** is a fixed amount that may be deducted from adjusted gross income. The standard

imagedb.com/Shutterstock.com

Children who are supported by their parents are claimed as dependents on an income tax form.

deduction amount is set by law and varies according to the taxpayer's filing status (single, married, or head of household). The amount allowed for the standard deduction is adjusted each year to reflect the rate of inflation. According to the IRS, two of three taxpayers take the standard deduction.

Exemptions

In addition to tax adjustments and tax deductions, taxpayers are also allowed tax exemptions. An **exemption** is an amount that a taxpayer can claim for each person who is dependent on that person's income. There are two types of exemptions. Personal exemptions are those you claim for yourself and your spouse if you are married and filing together. Dependent exemptions are those you claim for children or others you support. The amount of money allowed for each exemption follows the rate of inflation. The exemption is phased out when income exceeds a certain amount.

After subtracting the amount of either your itemized tax deductions or the standard deduction and the amount of your exemptions, you arrive at taxable income. Tax rates and allowable tax deductions and exemptions tend to change with each new tax law. In recent years, taxable income in the lowest income bracket was taxed at the rate of 10 percent, while that in the highest income bracket was taxed at the rate of 35 percent.

Tax Credits

You can reduce the amount of taxes you owe with tax credits. A **tax credit** is an amount that is subtracted from the taxes you owe if you are eligible. It is a greater advantage than an exemption or tax deduction because a credit actually reduces your taxes; an exemption or deduction only reduces your taxable income. For example, taxpayers with income under a designated amount can take a $1,000 tax credit for each dependent child under age 17. Tax advisors or the IRS can tell taxpayers which tax credits might be available to them.

Preparing a Form 1040EZ

Form 1040EZ is used by the taxpayer who is single or married filing jointly with taxable income less than $100,000. This is the form that you will use to file your income taxes. Line-by-line directions for completing a Form 1040EZ are found on the back of the form. If you are filing an electronic return, directions are available on the IRS website.

A completed Form 1040EZ for Kristy James is shown in Figure 3-5. Kristy completed her return using the following directions.

Go Green

When filing your tax return, the IRS encourages you to file electronically and allows you to do so free using the e-file software. Filing electronically is faster and more efficient for you, and it saves thousands of trees a year.

Department of the Treasury—Internal Revenue Service

Form 1040EZ

Income Tax Return for Single and Joint Filers With No Dependents (99)   **20– –**

OMB No. 1545-0074

Your first name and initial	Last name	Your social security number
Kristy A.	James	987 : 65 : 4321

If a joint return, spouse's first name and initial	Last name	Spouse's social security number
		: :

Step 1

Home address (number and street). If you have a P.O. box, see instructions.   Apt. no.

1027 Cedar Street

▲ Make sure the SSN(s) above are correct.

City, town or post office, state, and ZIP code. If you have a foreign address, also complete spaces below (see instructions).

Franklin, IL 65432

Foreign country name	Foreign province/county	Foreign postal code

Presidential Election Campaign
Check here if you, or your spouse if filing jointly, want $3 to go to this fund. Checking a box below will not change your tax or refund. ☑ You ☐ Spouse

Step 2

Income

Attach Form(s) W-2 here.

Enclose, but do not attach, any payment.

1	Wages, salaries, and tips. This should be shown in box 1 of your Form(s) W-2. Attach your Form(s) W-2.	**1**	28,956 98
2	Taxable interest. If the total is over $1,500, you cannot use Form 1040EZ.	**2**	200 00
3	Unemployment compensation and Alaska Permanent Fund dividends (see instructions).	**3**	
4	Add lines 1, 2, and 3. This is your **adjusted gross income.**	**4**	29,156 98
5	If someone can claim you (or your spouse if a joint return) as a dependent, check the applicable box(es) below and enter the amount from the worksheet on back. ☐ You ☐ Spouse If no one can claim you (or your spouse if a joint return), enter $9,500 if **single;** $19,000 if **married filing jointly.** See back for explanation.	**5**	9,500 00
6	Subtract line 5 from line 4. If line 5 is larger than line 4, enter -0-. This is your **taxable income.** ▶	**6**	19,656 98

Step 3

Payments, Credits, and Tax

7	Federal income tax withheld from Form(s) W-2 and 1099.	**7**	3,020 42
8a	**Earned income credit (EIC)** (see instructions).	**8a**	
b	Nontaxable combat pay election. 8b		
9	Add lines 7 and 8a. These are your **total payments and credits.** ▶	**9**	3,020 42
10	**Tax.** Use the amount on **line 6 above** to find your tax in the tax table in the instructions. Then, enter the tax from the table on this line.	**10**	2,526 00

Step 4

Refund

Have it directly deposited! See instructions and fill in 11b, 11c, and 11d or Form 8888.

11a	If line 9 is larger than line 10, subtract line 10 from line 9. This is your **refund.** If Form 8888 is attached, check here ▶ ☐	**11a**	494 42
▶ b	Routing number	▶ c Type: ☐ Checking ☐ Savings	
▶ d	Account number		

Amount You Owe

12	If line 10 is larger than line 9, subtract line 9 from line 10. This is the **amount you owe.** For details on how to pay, see instructions. ▶	**12**	

Third Party Designee

Do you want to allow another person to discuss this return with the IRS (see instructions)? ☐ Yes. Complete below. ☑ No

Designee's name ▶   Phone no. ▶   Personal identification number (PIN) ▶

Step 5

Sign Here

Under penalties of perjury, I declare that I have examined this return and, to the best of my knowledge and belief, it is true, correct, and accurately lists all amounts and sources of income I received during the tax year. Declaration of preparer (other than the taxpayer) is based on all information of which the preparer has any knowledge.

Joint return? See instructions.

Keep a copy for your records.

Your signature	Date	Your occupation	Daytime phone number
Kristy A James	3/1/--	Sales Clerk	(123) 456-7890
Spouse's signature. If a joint return, **both** must sign.	Date	Spouse's occupation	If the IRS sent you an Identity Protection PIN, enter it here (see inst.)

Paid Preparer Use Only

Print/Type preparer's name	Preparer's signature	Date	Check ☐ if self-employed	PTIN
Firm's name ▶			Firm's EIN ▶	
Firm's address ▶			Phone no. ▶	

For Disclosure, Privacy Act, and Paperwork Reduction Act Notice, see instructions.   Cat. No. 11329W   Form **1040EZ** (2011)

Figure 3-5 The 1040 EZ is the simplest income tax return form.

Step 1: Enter Name, Address, and Social Security Number

In the spaces provided, write your name, current address, and Social Security number. In the Presidential Election Campaign section, check the box if you wish $3 to go to the Presidential Election Campaign Fund. Checking the box will not reduce your refund or increase the amount you owe. It is a way of designating tax dollars for the public funding of presidential election campaigns. Kristy checked the box to indicate that she does want $3 to go to this fund.

Step 2: Enter Income

- On Line 1, enter the wages, salaries, and tips reported on the Form(s) W-2. Kristy's Form W-2 illustrated in Figure 3-4 shows that she earned $28,956.98 last year. She entered this amount on Line 1.

- On Line 2, enter any interest earned on savings accounts. Interest income is reported on Form 1099INT. Kristy received a 1099INT showing that she earned $200 on her savings account. She entered this amount on Line 2.

- On Line 3, enter any unemployment compensation received. Unemployment compensation is reported on Form 1099MISC. This line is blank on Kristy's return because she did not receive any unemployment benefits during the past year.

- Add the amounts on Lines 1, 2, and 3 and enter the total on Line 4. On Form 1040EZ, the amount on Line 4 is called the *adjusted gross income.* Kristy added the amounts on Lines 1 and 2 to get an adjusted gross income of $29,156.98.

- Check the box on Line 5 if someone else can claim you as a dependent. If not, enter $9,500 if you are single, or $19,000 if married filing jointly. Since she is filing as a single taxpayer, Kristy entered $9,500 on Line 5. The $9,500 is the total of the standard deduction for a single person plus the amount of one personal exemption.

- Subtract the amount on Line 5 from the amount on Line 4 and enter the difference on Line 6. This is the taxable income. Kristy's taxable income is $19,656.98 ($29,156.98 – $9,500.00), which she entered on Line 6.

Step 3: Enter Income Taxes Withheld and Calculate Tax

- On Line 7, enter the amount of federal income taxes withheld from earnings. Kristy's W-2 in Figure 3-4 shows $3,020.42 in federal income taxes withheld. She entered this amount on Line 7.

- On Line 8, enter the amount of the earned income credit (EIC). This is a special credit for taxpayers with earned income below a designated amount. Kristy did not qualify for this credit.

- On Line 9, enter the total of the amounts on Lines 7 and 8. Kristy entered $3,020.42 on Line 9.

- Using the taxable income on Line 6, determine the income tax liability using the tax tables for Form 1040EZ. A partial 1040EZ tax table is illustrated in Figure 3-6. Kristy's taxable income ($19,656.98) falls in the income bracket *At least 19,650 But less than 19,700.* The tax in that bracket for a single person is $2,526. Kristy entered this amount on Line 10.

If Form 1040EZ, line 6, is–		And you are–		If Form 1040EZ, line 6, is–		And you are–		If Form 1040EZ, line 6, is–		And you are–	
At least	But less than	Single	Married filing jointly	At least	But less than	Single	Married filing jointly	At least	But less than	Single	Married filing jointly
		Your tax is–				Your tax is–				Your tax is–	
16,000				**19,000**				**20,000**			
16,000	16,050	1,979	1,603	19,000	19,050	2,429	2,004	20,000	20,050	2,579	2,154
16,050	16,100	1,986	1,608	19,050	19,100	2,436	2,011	20,050	20,100	2,586	2,161
16,100	16,150	1,994	1,613	19,100	19,150	2,444	2,019	20,100	20,150	2,594	2,169
16,150	16,200	2,001	1,618	19,150	19,200	2,451	2,026	20,150	20,200	2,601	2,176
16,200	16,250	2,009	1,623	19,200	19,250	2,459	2,034	20,200	20,250	2,609	2,184
16,250	16,300	2,016	1,628	19,250	19,300	2,466	2,041	20,250	20,300	2,616	2,191
16,300	16,350	2,024	1,633	19,300	19,350	2,474	2,049	20,300	20,350	2,624	2,199
16,350	16,400	2,031	1,638	19,350	19,400	2,481	2,056	20,350	20,400	2,631	2,206
16,400	16,450	2,039	1,643	19,400	19,450	2,489	2,064	20,400	20,450	2,639	2,214
16,450	16,500	2,046	1,648	19,450	19,500	2,496	2,071	20,450	20,500	2,646	2,221
16,500	16,550	2,054	1,653	19,500	19,550	2,504	2,079	20,500	20,550	2,654	2,229
16,550	16,600	2,061	1,658	19,550	19,600	2,511	2,086	20,550	20,600	2,661	2,236
16,600	16,650	2,069	1,663	19,600	19,650	2,519	2,094	20,600	20,650	2,669	2,244
16,650	16,700	2,076	1,668	19,650	19,700	2,526	2,101	20,650	20,700	2,676	2,251
16,700	16,750	2,084	1,673	19,700	19,750	2,534	2,109	20,700	20,750	2,684	2,259
16,750	16,800	2,091	1,678	19,750	19,800	2,541	2,116	20,750	20,800	2,691	2,266
16,800	16,850	2,099	1,683	19,800	19,850	2,549	2,124	20,800	20,850	2,699	2,274
16,850	16,900	2,106	1,688	19,850	19,900	2,556	2,131	20,850	20,900	2,706	2,281
16,900	16,950	2,114	1,693	19,900	19,950	2,564	2,139	20,900	20,950	2,714	2,289
16,950	17,000	2,121	1,698	19,950	20,000	2,571	2,146	20,950	21,000	2,721	2,296

Goodheart-Willcox Publisher

Figure 3-6 Federal tax tables show how much is owed based on taxable income.

Step 4: Determine the Tax Refund or Amount Owed

Compare Line 7 (taxes withheld) with Line 10 (tax liability). If Line 7 is larger than Line 10, a refund is owed. Enter the refund on Line 11a. If Line 7 is less than Line 10, the difference is owed. A balance due is entered on Line 12. Since Kristy's taxes withheld ($3,020.42) exceeded her tax liability ($2,526.00), she is due a refund of $494.42. She entered this amount on Line 11a.

Step 5: Sign the Return

A return must always be signed before it will be processed. An unsigned return will be returned for a signature. If a refund is due, this could delay the return by several weeks. If taxes are owed, it could result in penalties and interest.

Kristy signed her name in the space provided. She also dated the return, entered her occupation, and her phone number.

Electronic Filing

Electronic filing (e-filing) allows you to file your income tax return online. A variety of computer software programs are available today that allow you to file your return using your personal computer. You can purchase a program on CD at major retail stores, online, or download a program from the web page of the company that produces the program.

E-filing programs provide information and advice and walk you step-by-step through the filing process. They can reduce the time required to complete your return and simplify your recordkeeping. Some allow free filing of simple returns.

Ethics

It is unethical to file a fraudulent tax return. In a fraudulent return, a person deliberately reports information that is not correct. A person who intentionally files a tax return that is not accurate may be subject to penalties, interest, and possibly prison time.

The IRS also has a free e-filing service—the IRS e-file. To access details and filing instructions for the IRS e-file, go to www.irs.gov. This site provides all the information you need to file your return online quickly and conveniently. The IRS reports that over 100 million taxpayers e-file each year.

E-filing can be simple and quick. You sign your return with a self-selected personal identification number (PIN) and pay any taxes you owe with either a credit card or a direct debit from your bank. For those who expect a tax refund, online filing usually provides a faster refund than filing a paper return.

Sources of Tax Information and Assistance

Many sources are available for tax planning information and assistance in filing your return. As income increases, finances become more complicated. You may want to find professionals to advise you on tax matters. Several sources of assistance are discussed in the following paragraphs.

Internal Revenue Service (IRS)

Tax rates and laws change from year to year. The IRS publishes free instruction booklets annually, available online or at your nearest IRS office. These materials may also be available at your local library and post office.

Check your local phone directory for the IRS number to call for publications and advice on specific tax questions. The IRS operates a system of recorded phone messages with tax information on a variety of questions. The agency also offers a website and a toll-free hotline for specific questions. Walk-in service is available at some IRS offices across the country.

Volunteer Income Tax Assistance (VITA) Program

The VITA Program is an IRS service that offers free tax help to lower income people who need assistance in preparing their tax returns. IRS-certified volunteers provide free basic income tax return preparation to qualified individuals in local communities. VITA sites are generally located at community and neighborhood centers, libraries, schools, shopping malls, and other convenient locations. Most locations also offer free electronic filing.

Tax Counseling for the Elderly (TCE) Program

The IRS TCE Program provides free tax assistance to individuals who are age 60 and older. Certified by the IRS, TCE volunteers provide fee tax assistance to elderly individuals who qualify for the service. Tax assistance is provided at community locations across the nation. Many of these community locations also offer free electronic filing services.

Tax Preparation Services

If your taxes become complicated by investments, deductions, or other financial circumstances, you may want to call a professional to help prepare your tax return. Services of this type range from one-person offices to nationwide firms specializing in tax preparation.

Business Management & Administration

Payroll Professionals

Payroll professionals collect, calculate, and enter data that are used to create employees' paychecks. They update payroll records when base salary, tax exemptions, and benefit deductions change. They also compile summaries of earnings, taxes, deductions, leave, disability, and nontaxable wages for each employee.

Many tax attorneys and certified public accountants specialize in tax matters. They may prepare your tax return for your signature, based on records and receipts you provide. Some tax preparers guarantee to pay penalties resulting from errors they make. However, the taxpayer has the ultimate legal responsibility for any errors and any penalties for late payment.

Tax Preparation Guides

Each year, tax guides are published by various sources and may be purchased. These guides are also available at many public libraries. Most news and financial periodicals run articles on tax filing, too. These articles appear in the weeks and months before April 15 each year.

You Do the Math

To multiply whole numbers and decimals, place the numbers, called the *factors,* in pairs in a vertical list. When multiplying a percent, move the decimal two places to the left. To find the number of decimal places needed in the final product, add the number of places in each number. Two decimal places plus three decimal places means the product must have five decimal places.

Complete the Following Problems

1. Shelia Stein earns $12 an hour and is covered by the Fair Labor Standards Act. Last week, Shelia worked a total of 42 hours. What is her gross pay?

2. You live in an area that has a general sales tax rate of 8.5 percent on most purchases. How much sales tax would you pay for the following goods and services from area stores?

   A. $150 jacket

   B. $30 haircut

   C. $2 magazine

   The tax rate in a neighboring county is 7 percent. How much can you save on each item by crossing the county line to do your shopping?

3. Using the tax table in Figure 3-6, calculate the amount of John Faye's tax refund or balance due. His information is:

   • Age: 24

   • Filing status: Single

   • Earnings:

     – Form W-2 from his job as assistant manager of a fast-food restaurant showed $30,000

     – Form 1099 from his bank showed $90 in interest income

   • Taxes withheld: Form W-2 showed $2,812 in federal income tax withholding.

IRS Audits

A tax audit is a detailed examination of your tax returns by the IRS. In 2010, the IRS audited approximately 1.1 percent of the more than 141.5 million returns filed. If the IRS audits your return, you have to prove the accuracy of your reported income, tax deductions, adjustments, credits, and other details on your tax return. This situation is when good recordkeeping comes in handy.

It pays to know your rights as a taxpayer if your return is audited. The Internal Revenue Service Reform Act of 1998 guarantees taxpayers due process in their dealings with the IRS. You are expected to answer the IRS agent's questions honestly and completely, providing documentation when necessary. You may take an accountant, attorney, or tax preparer with you to the audit session.

The IRS must provide a detailed statement of your rights and the IRS's obligations during the audit, appeals, refund, and collection process. You have the right to make an audio recording of any audit interview conducted by the IRS. If you disagree with the outcome of a tax audit, you have the right to a conference at the Regional Appeals Office. From there, you can take your case to the US Tax Court, the US Court of Federal Claims, or even the US Supreme court. In the end, you have to pay any additional taxes, interest, and penalties that are assigned.

Checkpoint 3.2

1. What is a tax return?
2. What are three examples of unearned income?
3. What are adjustments to income?
4. Can any taxpayer use the Form 1040EZ when filing a tax return? Explain.
5. What is a tax audit?

Build Your Vocabulary

As you progress through this course, develop a personal glossary of personal finance terms and add it to your portfolio. This will help you build your vocabulary and prepare you for a career. Write a definition for each of the following terms and add it to your personal finance glossary.

Form W-2

unearned income

tax deduction

itemized deduction

standard deduction

exemption

tax credit

Section 3.3
Taxes and Government Spending

Objectives

After studying this section, you will be able to:
- Relate taxation to government spending.
- List three categories of taxable items.
- Discuss tax system reform.
- Describe the social security program.

Terms

entitlement
Social Security
Medicare
disability
Medicaid

Government Spending

The government generates revenue by taxing its citizens and businesses. Tax revenue is used to run the government. However, since its resources are limited, government must make choices. So, like individuals and families, governments create a budget for spending. The budget reflects the priorities and goals of the government and its people.

At present, most taxpayers spend a sizable share of their dollars to pay their income tax, Social Security tax, and other taxes. It is to your advantage to know what your tax dollars buy and how the tax system works.

Paying for government operations, facilities, and services is the primary purpose of taxes. The government provides goods and services that benefit the public. Examples include fire and police protection, schools, highways, airports, parks, and water and sewage treatment.

Besides providing goods and services necessary for society, legislators may raise or lower taxes to achieve one of the following goals.

- *Stabilize the economy.* The government may use taxes to promote economic stability, fight inflation, or slow a recession.

- *Address social challenges.* Some tax dollars are used to provide services and opportunities for the aging and other populations in need. Food stamps, housing subsidies, and veterans' educational benefits are examples of such programs. A less obvious but very important way that government addresses social needs is by supporting an economy that raises the standard of living for people in the country. Less government assistance is needed when people have the ability to improve their financial situations.

- *Influence behavior.* By removing taxes from some items and taxing others, government tries to change peoples' behaviors. For example, the government allows taxpayers to deduct certain charitable donations. This lowers the donor's taxes and encourages giving. The government adds tax on alcohol and tobacco products, which increases their cost and discourages people from using them.

Federal Government Spending

Taxation is the primary source of revenue for both federal and state governments. In those years when the government spends more than it collects, it must borrow money. This is called *deficit spending*, and it increases the national debt. Sources of the federal government's revenue and expenditures are shown in Figure 3-7.

Mandatory Expenses

Each year the federal government spends a large percent of its total budget on mandatory expense items. A mandatory expenditure is a commitment the federal government has made. It must pay these expenses. If enough tax dollars are not available, the government must borrow the money to meet these commitments.

About 60 percent of mandatory expenditures are entitlements. An **entitlement** is a government payment or benefit promised by law to eligible citizens. The largest entitlement program is Social Security, followed by Medicare.

Social Security is a federal program that provides income when earnings are reduced or stopped because of retirement, serious illness or injury, or death. In the case of death, benefits are provided to survivors of the deceased. Benefits are funded by a payroll tax on workers' income and matching contributions from employers.

Medicare is a federal program that pays for certain health-care expenses for older citizens and others with disabilities. A **disability** is a limitation that affects a person's ability to function in major life activities. Medicare is funded by payroll taxes and administered by the US Department of Health and Human Services.

Medicaid is a government program that pays certain health-care costs for eligible, low-income individuals and families. It is administered by state governments. Funding comes from state and federal tax revenues.

Other entitlement programs include federal employee retirement benefits, veterans' pensions and medical care, nutrition assistance, unemployment compensation, and housing assistance. Any reductions or changes in these programs require new legislation.

Interest on the national debt is also a mandatory expense item. This interest must be paid, even if the government must borrow money to pay it. The interest is paid to financial institutions, foreign investors and governments, and individuals who buy government securities. In essence, these institutions and individuals lend money to the federal government, and taxpayers pay the interest.

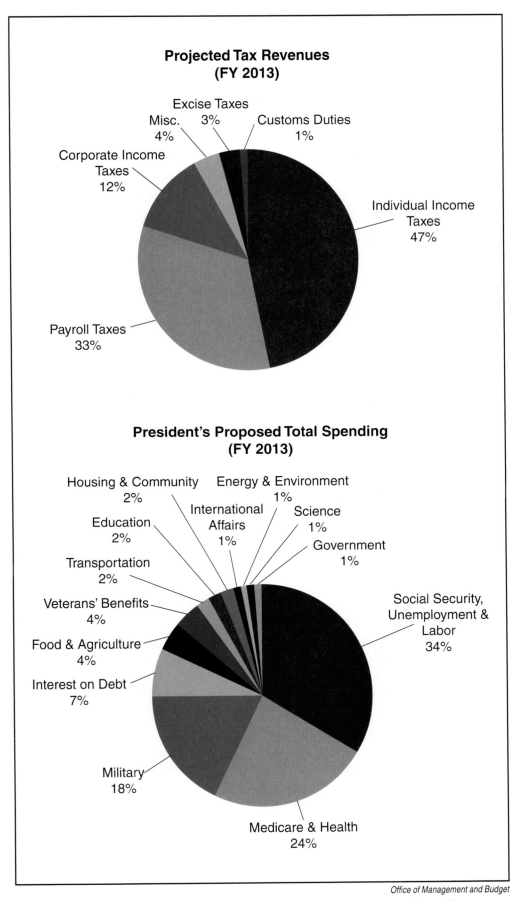

Projected Tax Revenues (FY 2013)

Excise Taxes 3%
Customs Duties 1%
Misc. 4%
Corporate Income Taxes 12%
Individual Income Taxes 47%
Payroll Taxes 33%

President's Proposed Total Spending (FY 2013)

Housing & Community 2%
Energy & Environment 1%
International Affairs 1%
Science 1%
Education 2%
Government 1%
Transportation 2%
Veterans' Benefits 4%
Social Security, Unemployment & Labor 34%
Food & Agriculture 4%
Interest on Debt 7%
Military 18%
Medicare & Health 24%

Office of Management and Budget

Figure 3-7 Where federal government dollars come from, and how they are spent.

Discretionary Expenses

A *discretionary expenditure* is an expense item that can be adjusted according to needs and revenues. National defense and nondefense discretionary spending are the two main categories. Money for national defense is used to equip the armed forces and pay for military personnel, research, and technology. When the nation goes to war or enters a military conflict, defense spending is increased.

Nondefense discretionary spending includes the cost of government operations and a wide array of programs. The federal government also provides funds to state and local governments for certain programs.

State and Local Government Spending

Both taxation and government spending vary widely from state to state and city to city. However, the sources of revenues and categories of expenditures are similar.

Sales, real estate, and personal property taxes make up a large part of state and local revenues. Most states and localities also rely on personal and corporate income tax for a large share of their revenues. These taxes are used mainly to pay for public education, highways, and public assistance programs run by the state. Figure 3-8 shows government taxing and spending at the state and local levels.

Case Study

Tax Reality

Alvira is a high school junior looking for a summer job. She loves animals. This led her to a local veterinarian. Luckily, the vet was looking for an assistant. She needed someone to assist in handling the animals that came in for treatment, grooming, and boarding. Alvira would work 30 hours and earn $240 per week. She would be paid every two weeks.

Alvira's first paycheck was much lower than the $480 she expected. Her paycheck stub showed the following payroll deductions: $29.76 for Social Security, $6.96 for Medicare tax, $62.10 for federal withholding tax, and $28.80 for state income tax. Alvira was shocked and disappointed to receive only $352.38. Still, she had the job she wanted and thought it was pretty good money anyway.

Case Review

1. Do these figures surprise you? What has been your experience with jobs and payroll deductions?
2. Do you think it is fair for Alvira to pay $127.62 in taxes every two weeks? Why or why not?
3. What benefits does Alvira receive from the money she pays in taxes? Does she receive any direct benefits? What services that she enjoys are paid by tax dollars?
4. What information from her paycheck stub will be important when Alvira files her income tax return?

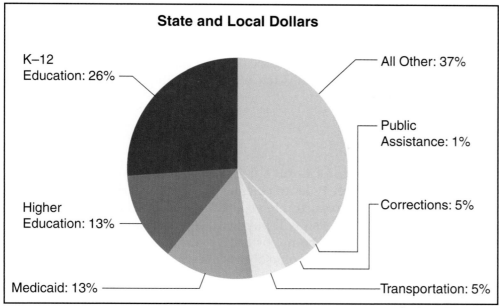

Figure 3-8 How state and local dollars are spent.

Goodheart-Willcox Publisher

Types of Taxes

Different types of taxes apply to different taxable items, including income, purchases, property, and wealth. More than one government body can tax the same item. For example, all levels of government have the power to tax personal income.

Direct and Indirect Taxes

One tax classification has to do with how taxes are paid. *Direct taxes* are those paid directly to the government by the taxpayer. Personal income tax is a direct tax. *Indirect taxes* are taxes levied, or imposed, on one person or entity, but shifted to or paid by another. Sales tax is one example. It is imposed on the seller of goods and services, but paid by the consumer.

Progressive, Regressive, and Proportional Taxes

Another classification of taxes has to do with how the tax rate is applied. A *progressive tax* imposes a higher tax rate on those with higher incomes. Income tax is one type of progressive taxation. As earners' incomes increase, their tax rates increase. In recent years, tax rates ranged from 10 to 35 percent. Progressive tax rates change with new tax laws. However, lower rates always apply to lower incomes, and rates increase as income increases.

A *regressive tax* has the effect of imposing a higher tax rate on those with lower incomes. A *proportional tax* imposes the same tax rate on all individuals or entities regardless of differences in income or ability to pay. Sales tax is one example of proportional tax in that the same rate is applied to purchases of all consumers. However, it also is considered a regressive tax in that it takes a higher percentage of income from consumers with lower incomes.

According to *Forbes Magazine*, the US Treasury may be losing as much as $5 billion a year from fraudulent tax refund claims. Tax fraud shortchanges the government of money that is needed to fund various programs. Tax fraud also hurts honest taxpayers because they must pay higher taxes to make up for the taxes not paid by those who engage in fraud.

For example, two consumers buy a computer for $1,000. Both pay a 7 percent sales tax that comes to $70. The tax is proportional since both pay the same rate. However, if one buyer has an annual income of $30,000 and the other has an annual income of $60,000, the sales tax could be considered regressive because the $70 sales tax represents a higher percentage of the lower income.

What Is Taxed?

The major categories of taxable items are income, purchases, property, and wealth. You pay three types of taxes on money you earn—Social Security, Medicare, and income taxes. You have already learned about Social Security and Medicare taxes. You also will pay a variety of other taxes as you earn, spend, save, invest, buy a home, or start a business. When you die, your estate may have to pay taxes. Some of these taxes are described below.

- *Personal income tax is levied on earnings.* Most earned and unearned income is subject to the federal income tax. Most states also tax the income of its residents.

- *Sales tax is levied by state and local governments on purchases of goods and services.* All but five states have a general sales tax on the goods and services people buy. In many states, food and drugs are exempt from this tax. This eases the burden of sales tax on the poor.

- *Excise tax is levied by federal and state governments on the sale and transfer of certain items.* Examples include cigarettes, alcoholic beverages, air travel, telephone services, gasoline, firearms, and certain luxury items.

- *Property tax is levied on property owned.* It includes real estate property tax and personal property tax. *Real estate tax* is based on the value of land and buildings owned. This is an important source of revenue for local and state governments. Rates vary greatly from area to area and state to state. *Personal property taxes* are assessed in some states on items such as cars, boats, furniture, and other assets.

- *Wealth tax is levied on assets.* There are two main types of wealth taxes. Estates worth over a certain amount are subject to *estate tax*. This is a tax imposed by the federal government on assets left by an individual at the time of his or her death. This tax must be paid out of the estate before assets are distributed. *Gift tax* is levied by the federal government on donors or givers who transfer assets over a given amount to others. The regulations regarding gift tax change from time to time when new tax laws are passed.

Tax System Reform

When the federal income tax system was created in 1914, the tax code was 14 pages long. Today the US tax code contains thousands of pages of complex rules and provisions. The IRS publishes over 450 tax forms and almost 300 forms to explain them. There are also 50 state tax systems and over 80,000 local taxing agencies. Each one has its own set of laws and regulations.

As the cost of providing government services increases, taxes increase. As legislators periodically revise and review the tax code, the tax system becomes more and more complex. In recent years, tax reform legislation has occupied both state and federal lawmakers. Citizens concerned about rising taxes have pushed for measures that limit new taxes.

The federal tax code changes periodically. Congress struggles to meet the need for revenues with a level of taxation voters will accept. Legislators propose new tax laws to increase revenues, to make the tax burden fairer, and to achieve desired economic outcomes.

Since major changes in tax policies can cause major changes in the economy, any new tax legislation needs to be thought out carefully. Here are some issues that are considered when new tax proposals and policies are evaluated.

- *Effectiveness.* Will a new or changed tax law produce adequate revenues? Tax revenues should be great enough to achieve the goals of the tax proposal. Ideally, revenues should be considerably higher than the cost of administering, enforcing, and collecting the taxes. The federal income

History of Finance

Taxes

There were few taxes in the early history of the United States. From 1791 to 1802, the government was supported by what was then called *internal taxes*, or taxes imposed on goods sold inside the country. Items taxed included sugar, carriages, tobacco products, distilled spirits, property sold at auction, corporate bonds, and the slave trade. The costly War of 1812 led to a sales tax on jewelry, gold, and silverware. In 1817, Congress did away with all internal taxes and the government was supported by tariffs (external taxes) on imported goods.

On July 1, 1862, Congress passed The Revenue Act of 1862 to support the Civil War effort. The passage of this act created the nation's first income tax. The Civil War years also saw the creation of additional sales and excise taxes and the first inheritance tax. In 1866, revenue collections reached the highest point in the nation's then 90-year history.

The Revenue Act of 1862 established the office of Commissioner of Internal Revenue. The Commissioner was given the power to assess, levy, and collect taxes. The Commissioner was also given the right to prosecute people who did not pay taxes and seize their property and income. Today, these powers and authority are vested in the Internal Revenue Service and remain very much the same.

In 1868, Congress eliminated the income tax and refocused taxation efforts on tobacco and distilled spirits. The income tax was revived in 1894. In 1895, however, the US Supreme Court declared that the income tax was unconstitutional because it was not apportioned among the states as required by the Constitution.

In 1913, the 16th Amendment to the Constitution made the income tax permanent. The amendment gave Congress legal authority to tax the incomes of both individuals and corporations. The withholding tax on wages was introduced in 1943 to speed up revenue collections needed to support the nation's involvement in World War II.

Employee Benefits Representatives

Employee benefits representatives oversee programs available to employees. Such benefits include health insurance, parental leave, wellness, retirement programs, and others. These specialists help employees take full advantage of the benefits paid completely or partly by their employer.

tax system spends approximately 50 cents for every $100 it collects, which is very cost efficient.

- *Fairness.* Is the tax fair? To be fair, a tax must fit the taxpayer's ability to pay. Tax rates should be no greater than required for essential government services and operations. In addition, the burden should be distributed fairly among taxpayers. Generally, those with similar incomes and resources should be taxed at the same rate. Fairness in taxation is not a new issue. It has been a concern throughout history.

- *Impact.* Is the economic impact of tax legislation minimal or beneficial? Almost all tax legislation shapes the economy to some degree. Tax laws should achieve positive economic goals or at least keep negative results to a minimum. For example, a tax on gasoline can lower demand and slow the depletion of oil reserves. This may discourage unnecessary driving and reduce pollution from automobiles. Since it is spread among many taxpayers, a gasoline tax achieves a reasonable degree of fairness, though it is harder on lower income taxpayers, particularly if they commute to work.

Tax laws should not cause major economic problems or seriously interfere with the forces of supply and demand. For example, an increase in federal income tax during a recession would lower consumer demand at a time when the economy needs the stimulus of greater demand. Eliminating the tax advantages of retirement accounts could reduce savings rates at a time when savings are needed for business growth and expansion.

Social Security

Franklin Roosevelt signed the Social Security Act into law in 1935. Medicare became part of the law in 1965. The Social Security Administration manages the Social Security program. Today, the program covers almost everyone who works. The tax is figured as a percentage of an employee's income and withheld from gross pay. FICA, or Federal Insurance Contributions Act, is the law that requires the collection of Social Security payroll taxes.

Social Security Benefits

When you begin working, your Social Security taxes pay for the benefits others receive. When you retire, or if you become disabled or die, other workers pay Social Security taxes to cover benefits to you and your family. Before a worker or a worker's family can receive benefits, the worker must have paid Social Security taxes for a certain length of time.

As you work, you earn Social Security credits—usually four per year. The amount you must earn to receive a credit has been increased several times. The number of credits required to receive Social Security benefits varies. Most workers need 40 credits or 10 years of work to qualify for benefits. Younger workers who become disabled may require fewer credits to qualify. The benefit amount depends on the worker's age and average earnings over a period of years. The types of benefits the Social Security program provides are discussed in the following paragraphs.

John Wollwerth/Shutterstock.com

Money from Social Security tax is also used to provide disability benefits to people who are physically unable to work.

Retirement Benefits

Workers become eligible for full retirement benefits at age 67. Early retirement can begin as early as age 62, but you only receive about 70 percent of retirement benefit payments. Benefits may also be paid to these members of a retired worker's family:

- unmarried children under 18 (under 19 if full-time high school students) or over 18 with a serious disability beginning before age 22
- spouse who is age 62 or older
- spouse of any age if caring for a retired worker's child under age 16 or disabled

Careers in Finance

What Do Tax Preparers Do?

A **tax preparer** completes a client's tax return, including all supporting schedules, inserts all appropriate information, and calculates the exact amount of money to be paid to or received from the IRS. Preparers may specialize in one area, such as individual returns, business returns, estates and trusts, tax planning, and tax appeals. Some **tax preparers** are self-employed, and others work for tax preparation firms or CPA firms. The Enrolled Agent (EA) designation from the IRS requires either 10 years of working for the IRS or passing an exam. **Tax preparers** typically:

- consult and advise clients on their taxes;
- help clients develop plans to reduce taxes; and
- prepare all tax documentation for clients, such as return forms.

What Is It Like to Work as a Tax Preparer?

A **tax preparer** spends a lot of time working directly with clients. Much time is spent researching tax laws and regulations and inputting data in computer programs. During the tax season, a typical workweek may be in excess of 60 hours and include evenings and weekends.

Tax preparers work in offices, and the working conditions are usually good. Dress is generally business professional attire. In some cases, business casual attire is acceptable.

What Education and Skills Are Needed to Be a Tax Preparer?

- bachelor degree in accounting
- excellent communication skills
- ability to work without direct supervision
- ability to work in a fast-paced environment
- knowledge of tax laws and regulations
- computer skills

Disability Benefits

A worker who becomes disabled before retirement age may receive disability benefits. Getting these benefits often involves an extensive application process. A worker must present concrete evidence that disability prevents him or her from earning a living. The Social Security Administration will review a worker's medical records and other information to determine eligibility. Monthly disability benefits may also be paid to a worker's family members.

Survivors' Benefits

If a worker dies, benefits may be paid to certain members of the worker's family. A single, lump-sum payment may also be made when a worker dies. This payment usually goes to the surviving spouse. Monthly benefits may be paid to these family members of a deceased worker:

- unmarried children under age 18 (19 if full-time high school students) or over 18 if severely disabled, with the disability occurring before age 22
- spouse 60 or older (50 if disabled)
- spouse at any age who is caring for a worker's child under age 16 or disabled
- spouse 50 or older who becomes disabled
- parents who depend on the worker for half or more of their support

Divorced People's Benefits

An ex-spouse can be eligible for benefits on a worker's record under certain circumstances. This eligibility does not affect the amount of benefits the worker and the worker's family are entitled to receive. To qualify for benefits, an ex-spouse must satisfy these requirements:

- married to the worker at least 10 years
- at least 62 years old
- not eligible on his or her own or on someone else's Social Security record

Social Security benefits do not start automatically. When a person becomes eligible, he or she must apply for them at the nearest Social Security office. The Social Security administration calculates benefits and issues monthly payments. The administration also calculates possible future benefits based on current earnings. However, calculations cannot be exact for young workers far from retirement age.

It is a good idea to check your Social Security record every few years to make sure your earnings are being credited to your record. You can get a free postcard form at any Social Security office for this purpose.

Retirees need to contact the Social Security office in their area several months before retirement. This will give the office plenty of time to calculate benefits and begin payments as soon as retiring workers are eligible.

Social Security System Reform

The sound future of Social Security depends on responsible fiscal action today. People are living longer lives. By 2030, there will be almost twice as many Americans of retirement age as there were in 1999. Presently, about three workers pay Social Security taxes for each person who is receiving benefits. By 2030, that number will decrease to two workers to every beneficiary. While the system has some reserves, benefit payments will exceed tax collection around 2013 unless Social Security reforms are enacted soon.

If benefit payments exceed tax collection, the Social Security trust fund will be depleted. There will be no money in the fund to support all the persons who have paid into it. Dealing with this problem will require increasing taxes, decreasing benefits, or both. In the 1980s, Congress called for taxing some retirees' benefits and raising the retirement age. This was done, but it was not enough. Among the other solutions proposed are plans to:

- reduce the automatic cost-of-living allowance (COLAs) increases in benefits;
- raise taxes on benefits to higher-income recipients;
- cut benefits for higher-income recipients;
- raise the retirement age again;
- increase Social Security tax contributions;
- invest Social Security trust fund surpluses in the stock market; and
- permit individuals to invest a portion of their Social Security taxes in personal retirement accounts

As policymakers work toward reform, it will be important to provide dependable benefits regardless of changes in the economy and financial markets. Benefits must continue for the retirees, people with disabilities, and low-income individuals who currently receive payments. One of every three people getting benefits in the current system is not a retiree.

Continued funding of the system will likely require increasing revenues and reducing benefits. It also will require fiscal responsibility, a curb on deficit spending, and a reduction of the national debt. It will be in your best interest to keep up with new developments in Social Security reform as it relates to both taxes and benefits. It is your money at both ends—paying and receiving.

auremar/Shutterstock.com

Consider the posibility that Social Security benefits could change between now and the time you retire.

Checkpoint 3.3

1. What is the primary purpose of taxes?
2. What is deficit spending?
3. What is a progressive tax?
4. What is a sales tax?
5. What are two examples of items on which a state may levy personal property tax?

Build Your Vocabulary

As you progress through this course, develop a personal glossary of personal finance terms and add it to your portfolio. This will help you build your vocabulary and prepare you for a career. Write a definition for each of the following terms and add it to your personal finance glossary.

entitlement

Social Security

Medicare

disability

Medicaid

Chapter Summary

Section 3.1 Income

- There are many ways to earn income. Earned income is the income you receive from employment or from self-employment.

- The federal income tax system is built on a pay-as-you-earn concept. This means a working person pays taxes from each paycheck instead of in one lump sum each year. Net pay is gross pay minus payroll deductions for items such as Social Security taxes, Medicare taxes, and income taxes.

- Employee benefits are a form of noncash compensation received in addition to a wage or salary. Common types of employee benefits include paid vacation, paid sick leave, health insurance plans, and retirement savings plans.

Section 3.2 Tax Returns

- A tax return is a report containing information used to calculate taxes owed by the taxpayer and filed with the government. Not filing a tax return is a crime, as is providing false information on a tax form.

- Form 1040EZ is the simplest federal tax form and can be used if you have a taxable income less than $100,000, file as single or married filing jointly, claim no dependents, and have income only from employee compensation, unemployment compensation, and interest.

- Electronic filing (e-filing) allows you to file your income tax return online.

- Tax information is available from sources such as the Internal Revenue Service, tax preparation services, attorneys, certified public accountants, and tax preparation guides.

- A tax audit is a detailed examination of your tax returns by the IRS, which requires that you show the accuracy of your reported income, tax deductions, adjustments, credits, and other details on your tax return. It pays to know your rights as a taxpayer if your return is audited.

Section 3.3 Taxes and Government Spending

- Paying for government operations, facilities, and services is the primary purpose of taxes. Most taxpayers spend a sizable share of their dollars to pay their income tax, Social Security tax, and other taxes.

- Different types of taxes apply to different taxable items, including income, purchases, property, and wealth. These taxes can be classified based on how the taxes are paid.

- The major categories of taxable items are income, purchases, property, and wealth. Workers pay three types of taxes on money earned—Social Security, Medicare, and income taxes.

- Tax reform legislation has occupied both state and federal lawmakers. Citizens concerned about rising taxes have pushed for measures that limit new taxes.

- Social Security provides income when earnings stop for certain reasons. Retirement, disability, survivors', and divorced people benefits may be provided to those who pay into Social Security during their working years.

Check Your Personal Finance IQ

Now that you have finished the chapter, see what you learned about personal finance by taking the chapter posttest. If you do not have a smartphone, visit the G-W Learning companion website.

G-W Learning mobile site: www.m.g-wlearning.com

G-W Learning companion website: www.g-wlearning.com

Review Your Knowledge

1. What is the difference between earned income and unearned income?
2. What is the difference between gross pay and net pay?
3. What is an employee benefit?
4. What are five types of filing status for a federal tax return?
5. What is a Form W-2?
6. What are the three common forms used for filing federal income taxes?
7. What are some advantages of using e-filing for your federal tax return?
8. Besides providing goods and services necessary for society, what are three other reasons legislators may raise or lower taxes?
9. For the federal government, what are the two largest entitlement programs?
10. Give one example of a direct tax and one example of an indirect tax.

Apply Your Knowledge

11. Give three examples of public goods and services that your taxes buy.
12. Which type of taxes do you consider to be the most fair—progressive taxes or regressive taxes?
13. What government services would you be willing to pay higher taxes to support? Why?
14. If you had the task of reducing federal government spending, what programs or services would you cut or eliminate and why?
15. What do you see as the consequences of continued deficit spending by the government for continuing government services and programs?
16. What do you see as the consequences of continued deficit spending by the government for you and your family?
17. Tax avoidance is a legal strategy for reducing one's income tax. Do you think tax avoidance is an ethical practice? Why or why not?
18. Do you think Social Security reform is necessary? Why or why not?
19. What actions would you recommend for strengthening the Social Security program?
20. Wealthy individuals who paid Social Security taxes during their careers are entitled to Social Security benefits when they retire. Do you agree with this policy? Why or why not?

Teamwork

This chapter discusses taxes and how they impact your paycheck. Working with your team, obtain copies of tax Forms 1040EZ, 1040A, and 1040. These forms can be found on www.irs.gov website. Compare and contrast the three forms. Share your findings with the class.

G-W Learning Mobile Site

Visit the G-W Learning mobile site to complete the chapter pretest and posttest and to practice vocabulary using e-flash cards. If you do not have a smartphone, visit the G-W Learning companion website to access these features.

G-W Learning mobile site: www.m.g-wlearning.com

G-W Learning companion website: www.g-wlearning.com

Common Core

College and Career Readiness

CTE Career Ready Practices. Exceeding expectations is a way to be successful at school and in your career. Make a list of five things that you expect of yourself on a daily basis, such as being on time, completing tasks as assigned, and being courteous. For each of the things you expect from yourself, consider and record what you could do to exceed those expectations. What effect do you think exceeding expectations has on your success?

Speaking. Find out the current amount of the national debt. Using digital media and visual displays of data, prepare a brief report of your findings. Lead a discussion with your class and discuss how the national debt affects the economy and you as a citizen.

Listening. Active listening is fully participating as you process what others are saying. Practice active listening skills while listening to a business report on the radio, the television, or a podcast. Pick a single story about taxes and prepare a report in which you analyze the following aspects of the business story: the speaker's audience, point of view, reasoning, stance, word choice, tone, points of emphasis, and organization.

Web Connect

Visit the IRS website. Make a list of the services the IRS provides for taxpayers. Which one of these services do you think you might need when filing your income tax return?

College and Career Readiness

College and Career Readiness Portfolio

Before you begin collecting information for your portfolio, you should write an objective related to this task. An objective should be a complete sentence or two that states what you want to accomplish. The language should be clear and specific. The objective should contain enough details so that you can easily judge when the objective has been accomplished. Consider this objective: "I will try to get better grades." Such an objective is too general. A better, more detailed objective might read: "I will work with a tutor and spend at least three hours per week on math homework until my math grade has improved to a B." Creating a clear objective is a good starting point for beginning work on your portfolio.

1. Do research on the Internet to find articles about writing objectives. Also, look for articles that contain sample objectives for creating a portfolio.

2. Write an objective for creating a portfolio. Are you creating this for a job interview? a college application? a volunteer position in the community? Include statements for both a print portfolio and an e-portfolio.

Ethics

Many competitive events may include an ethics component that covers multiple topics. The ethics portion of an event may be part of an objective test. However, ethics may also be a part of the competition in which teams participate to defend a given position on an ethical dilemma or topic.

To prepare for an ethics event, complete the following activities.

1. Read the guidelines provided by your organization.

2. Make notes on index cards about important points to remember. Use these notes to study.

3. To get an overview of various ethical situations that individuals encounter, read each of the Ethics features that appear throughout this text.

4. Ask someone to practice role-playing with you by asking questions or taking the other side of an argument.

5. Use the Internet to find more information about ethics and social responsibility. Find and review ethics cases that involve business situations.

Chapter 4
Financial Institutions and Services

Financial institutions make possible most of the economic activity that is conducted on a daily basis in today's modern and increasingly high-tech world. Through their many services, financial institutions enable economic growth in large and small countries all over the world. Without financial institutions, money could not circulate through the world economy. The availability and circulation of money is the basis for all economic growth. Without money, the economy would grind to a halt.

Focus on Finance

Check Cashing

Check-cashing services are not financial institutions, but they are businesses that provide certain financial services for a fee. Even though they are not considered financial institutions, they are still regulated by law. A check-cashing service cannot cash a check, or checks, that total more than $1,000 per day for an individual. Most states regulate check-cashing services to protect consumers against fraud and abuse by these services.

People who turn to check-cashing services generally have no bank account and need cash immediately. Financial experts advise consumers to avoid check-cashing services for two reasons. One, they are not federally insured. Two, they charge high fees, which quickly surpass bank fees. By contrast, many banks offer free checking and low-cost services if the account balance stays above a certain level. Many check-cashing services also make payday loans, which are even more costly. For most consumer needs, bank accounts are less costly and more reliable than check-cashing services.

Reading Prep. Before reading this chapter, review the highlighted terms within the body. Determine the meaning of each term.

College and Career Readiness

Check Your Personal Finance IQ

Before you begin the chapter, see what you already know about personal finance by taking the chapter pretest. If you do not have a smartphone, visit the G-W Learning companion website.

G-W Learning mobile site: www.m.g-wlearning.com

G-W Learning companion website: www.g-wlearning.com

Sections

Section 4.1 Banking Systems

Section 4.2 Checking Accounts

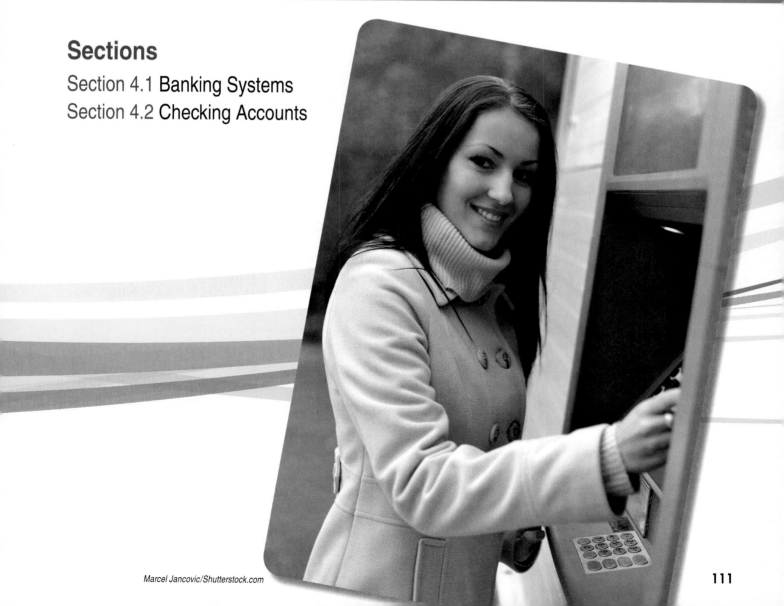

Marcel Jancovic/Shutterstock.com

Section 4.1
Banking Systems

Objectives

After studying this section, you will be able to:

- Identify different types of financial institutions.
- Describe the services of financial institutions.
- Explain special services offered by financial institutions.

Terms

commercial bank
charter
Federal Deposit Insurance Corporation (FDIC)
community bank
savings and loan association (S&L)
credit union
mutual savings bank
electronic funds transfer (EFT)
debit card
ATM card
overdraft
cashier's check
certified check
money order
traveler's check

Types of Financial Institutions

A *financial institution* is an organization that provides services related to money. Our economic system could not function without financial institutions. Examples of financial institutions include commercial banks, savings and loan associations, and credit unions. They keep money flowing throughout the economy among consumers, businesses, and government.

When you deposit money in a bank, the money does not sit in a vault. The bank lends the money to other consumers and to businesses. Consumers borrow money to finance new cars, homes, college tuition, and other needs. Businesses borrow money to pay for new equipment and expansion. State and local governments borrow to build new highways, schools, and hospitals. The interaction that financial institutions create among consumers, businesses, and governments keeps the economy alive, as shown in Figure 4-1.

Without financial institutions, consumers would probably keep their cash under a mattress or locked in a safe. Money could not circulate easily. The nation's money supply would shrink. Funds would not be available for consumer borrowing and spending. Demand for goods and services would fall. Businesses could not get money to modernize plants and develop new products. The economy would slow down. Jobs would become scarce. The economy depends on the flow of money and the services financial institutions provide.

In the past, financial institutions were more specialized. Each type of institution offered a distinct set of services to a specific set of customers. Deregulation, computer technology, and recent economic conditions have made these institutions more alike. Financial institutions and their services are discussed in the following paragraphs.

Commercial Banks

A **commercial bank** is a business owned by investors called *stockholders* or *shareholders*. The primary functions of a commercial bank are to receive, transfer, and lend money to individuals, businesses, and governments. Commercial banks are often called *full-service banks*. They offer a wide range of financial services, including checking, savings, and lending. Many commercial banks, such as Bank of America and Wells Fargo, are very large businesses that operate on a multistate or multinational level.

A **charter** is the license authorizing a bank to operate. Commercial banks may be chartered by the federal government or by a state government. Federally chartered banks are called *national banks* and may use the word *national* in their names. These banks must comply with federal banking regulations. State chartered banks are regulated by state banking commissions.

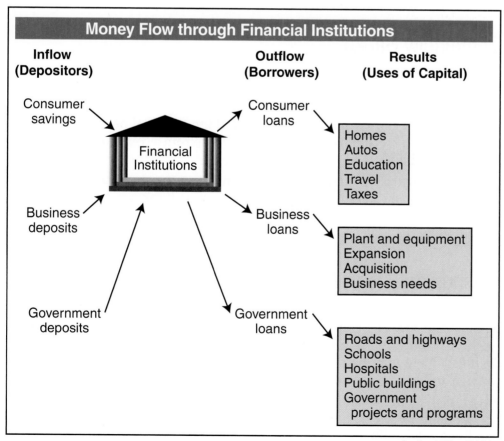

Goodheart-Willcox Publisher

Figure 4-1 Financial institutions keep money flowing through the economy among consumers, businesses, and government.

The **Federal Deposit Insurance Corporation (FDIC)** is an independent agency created by the federal government to protect bank customers by insuring their deposits. The FDIC insures accounts in national banks and other banks that choose to enroll in the program. The FDIC also examines and supervises financial institution policies and operations. Its goal is to help maintain consumer and business confidence in the banking system. When customer deposits are federally insured, it means the bank, savings and loan, or credit union is regularly checked. The institution must pass ongoing examinations of its financial holdings, operations, and management. FDIC insurance guarantees that depositors are protected if the bank fails or cannot repay deposits on demand. Since its creation in 1933, not one person has lost one cent of an insured deposit when a bank failed.

Prior to the global financial crisis that started in 2008, the FDIC insured each customer's deposits in a given bank up to $100,000. To improve confidence in US banks during the crisis, the coverage was raised to $250,000 in 2008. This increase was initially intended to be temporary, but was made permanent in 2010 as part of the *Dodd-Frank Wall Street Reform and Consumer Protection Act*.

For example, Bill Jones has on deposit $240,000 in savings and $10,000 in a checking account at his local bank. If the bank were to fail, the FDIC would return the entire $250,000 to Bill. On the other hand, if Bill has $256,000 in checking and savings deposits, FDIC insurance covers all but $6,000. It is possible for Bill to have multiple types of accounts at the bank. In this case, the total of the Bill's accounts is insured up to $250,000. If Bill opens an account at another bank, the FDIC also insures this account up to $250,000. The law applies to individual owners of the account.

Community Banks

A **community bank** is a type of commercial bank. Unlike multistate and multinational banks, however, community banks are locally owned and operated. All lending decisions are made locally by bank loan officers who live in the local community and understand the financial needs of people in the community. It is often easier to obtain a loan from a community bank than from a larger bank.

Community banks offer all standard banking services, including checking, savings, loans, and safe-deposit boxes. Community banks are governed by the same laws that govern the multistate and multinational banks. Your money is insured by the FDIC just as it would be if you banked with a large bank.

Savings and Loan Associations

A **savings and loan association (S&L)** is a financial institution that offers most of the services commercial banks do. (Savings and loan associations previously only made mortgage loans and paid dividends on depositors' savings.) They may be state or federally chartered. There are two types of savings and loan associations.

- *Mutual savings and loan associations.* These S&Ls are owned by and operated for the benefit of their depositors. These depositors receive dividends on their savings.
- *Stock savings and loan associations.* These S&Ls are owned by stockholders. Like commercial banks, these companies operate for profit.

Deklofenak/Shutterstock.com

Employees at a community bank are often familiar with their clients and the needs of the community.

Prior to 1989, deposits in S&Ls were insured by the *Federal Savings and Loan Insurance Corporation (FSLIC).* However, the FSLIC was abolished in 1989 and responsibility for insuring S&L deposits was transferred to the FDIC. Today S&L deposits, like bank deposits, are insured up to $250,000 per customer by the FDIC.

Credit Unions

A **credit union** is a nonprofit financial cooperative owned by and operated for the benefit of its members. Its services are offered only to members. Traditionally, you gained membership through affiliation with an employer, union, religious organization, community organization, or some other group. In recent years, however, some credit unions have started offering membership on a basis other than job or group affiliation. One criterion may be based on geography, such as a specific community or ZIP code.

Since credit unions are nonprofit organizations, they pay no federal income taxes. Members often run them, and operating costs may be relatively low. For these reasons, successful credit unions can lend funds to members at slightly lower rates than other financial institutions. They may also pay slightly higher interest rates on savings. Today, larger credit unions are run by professional management. They offer most of the services banks and other financial institutions provide.

Credit unions may be either federally or state chartered. The *National Credit Union Administration (NCUA)* grants federal charters and supervises credit unions across the country. NCUA also insures each customer's deposits up to $250,000 in all federally chartered and many state chartered credit unions. "People helping people" is the stated mission of the credit union industry.

The savings and loan crisis during the late 1980s and early 1990s resulted in over 3,000 savings and loan associations closing their doors. Legislation that allowed more freedom for the S&L business was the underlying cause of the closings.

Mutual Savings Banks

A **mutual savings bank** is a financial institution that is owned by its depositors. Earnings are distributed to depositors after operating expenses are deducted and reserve funds are set aside as needed. These earnings are distributed as dividends in proportion to the amount of business a depositor does with the bank. Dividends are a portion of the bank's earnings paid to depositors. Therefore, depositors who have larger deposits receive a greater amount of dividends than those with smaller deposits.

Traditionally, mutual savings banks received and paid dividends on deposits and made home mortgage and improvement loans. Now, they offer a wider variety of financial services.

Mutual savings banks are governed by a board of trustees who perform their duties in accordance with the bank's charter. Only state governments charter mutual savings banks. They exist in only 17 states, mostly in the northeast.

Services of Financial Institutions

When choosing a financial institution, consumers generally look for checking, savings, investment, online, and credit services. These services are also known as *banking products.* Before opening an account, it is wise to do some research. Websites of banks and other institutions offer information about their services and fees. To assess whether an institution has a helpful staff, you may want to visit it in person.

Compare local banks, credit unions, savings and loan associations, and other providers of financial services. Find the place that best serves your current and ongoing financial needs. Once you choose a financial institution, it pays to establish a good working relationship. Make your financial needs known and learn how the institution can help you manage your money.

Before you open an account, find out if the banking institution is insured by the federal government. A sign stating "Insured by FDIC" or "Insured by NCUA" should appear by the front window or near each teller station. You can learn if an institution is insured by the FDIC by checking the Federal Deposit Insurance Corporation's website at www.fdic.gov.

Online Banking

Most large banks now offer easy-to-use, fully secure, and fully functional online banking services. Online banking services allow bank customers to conduct financial transactions on a secure website owned by the bank.

Many regional and smaller banks, as well as some credit unions, also offer at least some online services. Online banking offers many advantages when compared to traditional banking. Unlike conventional banks, online banking sites never close. They are available at all times. In addition, since online banking sites never close, you can keep a close watch on your funds. By keeping a close watch on your funds, you are less likely to bounce a check. You will always be aware of what is happening in your account. An unauthorized transaction can be quickly detected. With online banking, an account holder can:

- pay bills;
- transfer money between accounts;

Online services are increasingly common at all types of financial institutions.

- view account balance and statements;
- view checks and deposits; and
- review the history on an account.

Most online banking sites allow you to download or export your banking activities to popular money management systems, such as Quicken® and Moneydance®. These programs can make managing your finances and keeping important records much easier. The programs allow you to balance your bank statements, pay bills, create budgets, organize expenses, keep detailed records, and transfer money from one account to another.

Safety is a concern with Internet transactions. Even though online banking sites are heavily encrypted, there is always a possibility that hackers will be able to break into the system and divert your funds to their accounts. Accordingly, you should keep your antivirus software and firewalls up to date and never share your personal account information.

While reduced paperwork is an advantage of online banking, there is some risk to having your financial data saved online. Even though banks have backup systems and lost data is rare, problems can still happen. It is in your best interest to print and save statements.

Mobile Banking

In addition to online banking, many banks also offer mobile banking services. By downloading an application from the bank, a customer can use a smartphone for banking transactions. *Applications* (apps) are software programs that let the user perform specific tasks. Typical mobile banking services include the following.

- *Alerts and text banking.* Text banking allows you to request and receive account information quickly via text messages. You can check account balances, view the status of transactions, and receive real-time security alerts.
- *Mobile banking websites.* Mobile banking websites allow you to access account information and make transactions from your phone's web browser or another mobile device.
- *Mobile banking apps.* A mobile app allows you to use a smartphone to do your banking using the phone's built-in functions. Mobile apps are designed specifically for use with a smartphone or tablets, allow quick access to your account, and use 128-bit encryption for safety.

Direct Deposits and Withdrawals

Today many of the services offered by financial institutions are provided through electronic funds transfers. An **electronic funds transfer (EFT)** is the movement of money electronically from one financial institution to another. An EFT is safe, secure, efficient, and faster than paper check payments and collections. Additionally, an EFT is much less expensive than paper check transfers. For example, it costs the US government $1.03 to issue a paper check. However, it costs only about $0.11 to issue an EFT payment. It is also cheaper for businesses and individuals to use EFT.

Customers using EFT service can arrange to have paychecks, Social Security checks, and other payments deposited directly into their accounts. They can also pay bills without writing and mailing checks. Recurring bills, such as car payments, insurance premiums, utility bills, and others, can be automatically paid. Money can be transferred from a checking to a saving account each month, creating an automatic savings program. All these transactions are recorded and included in monthly bank statements. Using ETF in these ways can make managing money more convenient.

Automated Teller Machines

For the convenience of their customers, most banks and credit unions provide *automated teller machines (ATMs).* To use an ATM, you must have an electronically coded card and a *personal identification number (PIN).* Both the card and the PIN are issued by your bank. You can use an ATM to check account balances, make cash withdrawals and deposits, and move money from one account to another. ATMs are located outside bank buildings and other convenient locations, such as shopping malls, airports, grocery stores, college campuses, and sporting arenas. Most ATMs are available 24 hours a day.

Generally, you may use an ATM owned by your bank at no charge. There is usually a charge for any transaction you make at an ATM not owned by or affiliated with your bank. Fees charged for using an ATM card vary; however, they can add up quickly. Make sure you understand these fees and know which ATMs are affiliated with your bank's network.

Since money is withdrawn at ATMs, this makes them a target for crime. Figure 4-2 shows some safety tips for using an ATM. Follow these tips to use ATMs safely.

Safety Tips for Using an ATM

- Memorize your personal identification number (PIN). Do not tell anyone your PIN or carry it with you. If someone stole both your card and PIN, that person would have complete access to your account.
- Protect your privacy. Do not let anyone see you enter your PIN. If a friend is standing too close, politely ask the person to step back. If a stranger is too close, cancel your transaction and use the ATM at another time.
- Watch for suspicious people. Criminals may target ATMs as easy places to steal money. Before approaching, see if anyone is standing around. If so, use another machine or return later.
- Use an ATM in a well-lighted area. Generally, avoid nighttime use, but if necessary, choose a machine in a grocery store or other high-traffic area. If you are at the bank at night, choose a drive-up ATM rather than a walk-up machine.
- Make transactions at walk-up ATMs quickly. Approach the ATM with your card out and ready. Then, leave the area immediately and count your money later.

Goodheart-Willcox Publisher

Figure 4-2 Since money is withdrawn at ATMs, this makes them a target for crime. Follow these tips to use ATMs safely.

Bank Cards

Banks and credit unions issue various types of cards to account holders. When you open an account, most banks will provide you with a debit card as a part of your package of services. A **debit card,** also called a *check card,* allows you to make purchases by swiping your card through a *point-of-sale (POS)* terminal that is usually located at the merchant's checkout counter. Using a debit card has the same effect as writing a check because the amount of the purchase comes directly from your checking account. These transactions are automatic and are deducted almost immediately from your account. It is important to keep track of your balance so that you do not overdraw your account. You can also use a debit card at an ATM to make withdrawals, deposits, and transfer money from one account to another.

Your bank may also provide you with an ATM card. An **ATM card** is a card issued by a bank that allows the holder to check account balances, withdraw and deposit cash, and transfer money from one account to another using an automated teller machine. You cannot make purchases with an ATM card. However, since most debit cards today are dual-purpose cards with ATM access, many banks have stopped issuing separate ATM cards.

Go Green

Many banks today are offering "green" checking accounts to customers. A green checking account is a paperless account in which most, if not all, transactions are completed online. Typical features include electronic statements (e-statements), online banking, and online bill payment.

GeorgeAA/Shutterstock.com

It is important to remember that ATMs can only give you the money that is already in your bank account.

Dual purpose debit cards can also be used for credit purchases. When you make a purchase, the card reader will ask if you want the purchase to be recorded as a debit or as a credit. If you choose debit, you enter your PIN to authorize the transaction and the money comes directly from your checking account. You may also have the option of getting cash back on the transaction. This is like making a purchase and using an ATM at the same time—you simply consolidate your transactions. If you choose credit, you will be asked to sign the sales slip, rather than entering your PIN, and the transaction is treated as a credit purchase. Credit transactions can remain in a pending status for one to three days. The money still comes from your checking account, but it will be several days before the merchant receives the money. Make sure you keep track of the balance in your account so that you do not overdraw.

Most banks and credit unions also offer credit cards. Unlike other cards, however, you usually have to apply for and meet certain conditions to obtain a credit card. If approved, you can use your credit card, such as Visa and MasterCard, to make credit purchases for most consumer items, including food, electronic devices, clothes, movie tickets, motel rooms, jewelry, sporting goods, and many other items. Unlike debit cards, the money does not come directly out of your checking account when you make a purchase or pay a bill with a credit card. Instead, you make monthly payments based on the balance of your account. Some credit cards carry an annual fee and all charge interest on your average unpaid monthly balance. Credit cards are discussed in detail in Chapter 5.

Credit cards, debit cards, and ATM cards offer advantages to the user. They eliminate the need to carry large amounts of cash, allow access to your money at any time, and enable you to purchase goods and services in places where checks are not accepted.

Overdraft Protection

An **overdraft** is a check written for an amount greater than the balance of the account. If you write an overdraft, the bank will charge you an *insufficient funds fee* to cover the transaction. This fee can be costly, and banks normally charge a fee of $30 or higher for each overdraft.

Although overdrafts are not encouraged, some banks offer overdraft protection. With overdraft protection service, a financial institution will honor a check written by you even if it exceeds your account balance. This involves automatically moving money from your savings account to your checking account to cover the amount of the check. However, this service is not free, and a charge will be made against your account.

If you choose to have this service, you will sign up with your bank. The Consumer Overdraft Protection Fair Practices Act of 2009 requires consumers to sign an agreement with their depository institutions to cover and charge for overdrafts. Make sure you read the terms carefully and understand the bank's policies regarding all fees and restrictions that apply to this service.

Overdrafts are also known as *bounced checks.*

Safe-Deposit Boxes

Some financial institutions rent boxes in their vaults to customers for the storage of valuables. Jewelry, birth records, insurance policies, and other important items are often kept in safe-deposit boxes. This is an important service if you need a safe location for valuable or irreplaceable items. Rental charges for these boxes vary.

The contents of a safe-deposit box are *not* insured by the FDIC. However, some banks provide insurance if the contents of a box are lost or destroyed. If you decide to rent a safe-deposit box, be sure to read the contract carefully before you sign it. If items placed in a safe-deposit box are particularly valuable, you should consider buying insurance, such as theft and fire, from a private insurance company.

Financial Counseling and Special Programs

Financial institutions may offer specialized services that include a trust department, tax reporting assistance, brokerage and financial planning, and individual retirement accounts (IRAs). Additional offerings may include money market funds and mortgage loans. A *money market fund* is a specialized type of savings account that has limited check-writing privileges and usually pays a higher interest rate than conventional savings accounts. However, the minimum amount to start one is usually $500. Banks usually charge fees for specialized services.

Loans

Making loans has always been one of the primary services provided by banks and other financial institutions. Individuals can borrow money to finance the purchase of cars, homes, furniture, medical treatment, vacations, home improvements, and other items. Owners of businesses can borrow money to expand operations, purchase inventory, develop new products, buy new equipment, and for many other purposes.

You Do the Math

Using a calculator enables you to apply math concepts as you learn financial responsibility. The calculator on your computer or smartphone will help increase your accuracy.

Complete the Following Problem

Balance a checking account that recorded the following activity since the last statement. How much is in the account?

- Deposits: $25.00 and $120.00
- Checks: $25.00, $8.50, and $98.00
- ATM withdrawals: $20.00
- Bank fee: $3.00 for using an ATM outside the bank's network
- Balance on the last statement: $250.00

Our modern economy could not exist without the ability of individuals and businesses to borrow money. Imagine how many fewer cars and homes would be sold if consumers had to save the entire price before making a purchase. Imagine how many fewer businesses there would be if it were not possible to borrow money for start-up costs. To a very large extent, our entire way of life is directly related to the credit that is available from financial institutions.

Special Services

In addition to the standard services discussed above, many financial institutions offer special services to customers. Some of those services are described in the following paragraphs.

Webmasters

Webmasters develop websites for financial institutions that deliver services of the institution, such as online bill payment and 24-hour banking services. They also make financial sites secure for online banking.

Stop-Payment Order

A *stop-payment order* is a request for a financial institution to refuse to honor a check you wrote, as long as the check has not cleared your account and already been paid. This service is useful if a check is lost or stolen and you want to prevent others from cashing it. A stop-payment order is also useful when you have a grievance concerning goods or services paid for by check. The best way to place a stop-payment order is to go directly to your bank and make the request in person. There are forms the bank will have you complete. The process is much easier if you have all the information regarding the check: the number, the date, the amount of the check, and to whom it was written. You can also issue a stop-payment order by phone. However, you should follow up your verbal request with a written one within 14 days or the original stop-payment order will become invalid. A substantial charge generally applies for this service, but it may be well worth the cost.

Cashier's Check

A **cashier's check** is a special type of check that the bank guarantees to pay. A cashier's check is purchased from a bank and used to make a payment to a person or a business. A cashier's check is paid with cash or from a withdrawal from your checking or savings account. After receiving your payment, the bank teller prepares the check and a bank official signs it. The money is then set aside to pay the check when it is presented for payment. A cashier's check cannot be forged and will not bounce. As a result, some people and businesses prefer to receive a cashier's check because it is more secure. In some situations, such as when making a large down payment to purchase a house or car, the seller may require a cashier's check. Banks usually charge a small fee for this service. However, many banks offer this service free to their established customers.

Certified Check

A **certified check** is a personal check that your bank certifies is genuine and that there is enough money in your account to cover the check. To get a check certified, you write a check in the usual way. You then take the check to your bank where a bank official signs and stamps the word *certified* on it. The money is immediately deducted from your account and becomes unavailable for any other purpose. For example, assume Tracy Taylor has $2,000 in her checking account and is buying a $500 gold necklace from an online seller who only accepts certified checks. Tracy writes the check, takes it to her bank, and goes through the necessary steps to get it certified. Once the check is

Monkey Business Images/Shutterstock.com

A certified check or cashier's check may be required for large payments, such as a security deposit on a rental home.

certified, Tracy's bank immediately limits her available funds to $1,500. The bank is guaranteeing the $500 check will be paid. As with cashier's checks, banks usually charge a small fee for a certified check. A certified check is used to make a payment to a payee who does not accept personal checks that have not been certified.

Money Orders

A **money order** is a payment order for a specific amount of money payable to a specific payee. People who do not have checking accounts may use money orders to send payments safely by mail. Money orders do not contain personal information, and you are not responsible if one is lost or stolen.

Money orders are sold in financial institutions, US Post Offices, and other convenient locations. The charge usually runs between $1 and $5. However, it can be more, depending on the amount of the order and where you buy it.

Traveler's Checks

People who travel and do not want to carry large amounts of cash often use traveler's checks. A **traveler's check** is a special form of check that functions as cash. Traveler's checks can be cashed at many places around the world. If the checks are lost or stolen, they can be replaced at the nearest bank or by the agency selling them. Keep a record of check numbers separate from the checks. You need identifying numbers to replace lost or stolen checks. Sign the checks only at the time you cash them. Unused traveler's checks can be redeemed in cash.

Most banks and credit unions issue traveler's checks. Fees and restrictions on traveler's checks vary. It is a good idea to shop around when buying them. However, many banks offer this service free to their established customers.

Peer-to-Peer (P2P) Payments

A new service that some banks offer is called *peer-to-peer (P2P) payments.* Peer-to-peer payments allow immediate transfer of money from one person to another. Instead of mailing cash or a check to someone, you can log on and send a virtual check. By using an e-mail or cell phone number, a transfer can be made. The receiver will get notification by an e-mail or text message with a code from the P2P system, such as PayPal™, which will allow him or her to transfer the money into an account.

Checkpoint 4.1

1. What are three examples of financial institutions?
2. What are the primary functions of a commercial bank?
3. What are some advantages of using online banking?
4. How does an ATM card differ from a debit card?
5. What are some special services that many financial institutions offer to customers?

Build Your Vocabulary

As you progress through this course, develop a personal glossary of personal finance terms and add it to your portfolio. This will help you build your vocabulary and prepare you for a career. Write a definition for each of the following terms and add it to your personal finance glossary.

commercial bank

charter

Federal Deposit Insurance Corporation (FDIC)

community bank

savings and loan association (S&L)

credit union

mutual savings bank

electronic funds transfer (EFT)

debit card

ATM card

overdraft

cashier's check

certified check

money order

traveler's check

Section 4.2
Checking Accounts

Objectives

After studying this section, you will be able to:
- Describe personal checking accounts.
- Explain how to open and use a checking account.

Terms

checking account
check
check register
endorsement
postdated check
bank statement

Personal Checking Accounts

When earning a regular income, the first financial service many people need is a checking account. A **checking account** is a bank account that allows you to make deposits, write checks, and withdraw money. A **check** is a written order for the bank to pay a specific amount to the person to whom the check is written. Checking accounts are also called *demand deposit accounts* because you can withdraw money or write checks any time you choose—that is, on demand.

A checking account offers a safe place to keep your money. It provides a convenient way to buy goods and services and pay bills. It also provides a record of deposits and receipts of payments. Responsible use of checking accounts aids in money management. It also helps you build a sound credit rating.

Accounts and Services

Look for financial institutions that offer the accounts and services you want in a checking account. Consider the following features.
- *Restrictions and Penalties.* Ask about minimum balance requirements, withdrawal limitations, and penalties for overdrafts or late payments on credit accounts. These items can increase the cost of services and make managing your money more complicated.
- *Fees and Charges.* Ask about all fees and charges associated with the type of account you want. These may include a maintenance fee, charges for ATM use, low-balance penalties, check-writing fees, and check-printing costs. These charges can vary among institutions and different types of accounts. Higher minimum balance accounts usually reduce or eliminate these fees.
- *Interest Rates.* Compare the interest rates on interest-bearing checking accounts. In addition, examine the rates charged to borrow money or use a bank credit card. Look for high interest rates on savings and low interest rates for using credit.

- *Convenience Services.* Look for financial institutions that make banking and other financial transactions easy for you. Services that save you time and effort include convenient hours, ATMs in various locations, online banking, mobile banking, and debit cards.

Checking Account Types

Financial institutions use different names to describe checking account services they offer. There are three common types of checking accounts—basic, interest-bearing, and lifeline. The best account type for you depends largely on the amount you can deposit, the number of checks you expect to write each month, the account features you want, and the fees associated with the account. For interest-bearing accounts, your choice also depends on the interest rate that deposits earn.

When you shop for a checking account, the following questions can help you make the best choice.

- Is there a minimum deposit requirement? If so, what is it?
- What are the charges if the balance drops below the minimum?
- What are the fees per month and per check?
- Does the institution offer an interest-bearing checking account? If so, what is the interest rate and the minimum balance required?
- What other services are offered in connection with different types of accounts?
- What fees are charged for different services and accounts?

AXL/Shutterstock.com

Checking account features vary from bank to bank.

Basic Checking Account

A *basic checking account* permits you to deposit and withdraw your money and write checks. It usually requires a minimum balance to avoid service charges. If the balance falls below this minimum, you are charged a fee. There also may be a monthly service charge and a fee per check. Fees vary from one financial institution to another. A basic account may be a good choice if you write many checks and can keep the minimum balance.

Many banks offer a student checking account that may have minimal fees. This may be a good option to select when opening your first checking account.

Interest-Bearing Checking Account

An *interest-bearing checking account* is a combination savings and checking account. Your money earns interest, and you can write checks on the account. In credit unions, these accounts are called *share drafts*. In banks and savings and loan associations, they are called *negotiable orders of withdrawal* or *NOW accounts*. Financial institutions offer this account with varying interest rates, minimum-balance requirements, and service charges.

Lifeline Checking Accounts

Lifeline checking accounts are relatively new and are intended for low-income customers. In some states, banks are required by law to make these accounts available. They feature low minimum deposit and minimum balance requirements, low monthly fees, and limits on the number of checks that may be written per month. Electronic services may also be limited, unless the account holder pays additional fees.

Opening a Checking Account

Opening a checking account requires only a few simple steps. Certain restrictions may apply if you are under 18 years of age. Some banks require a parent or guardian to be listed on the account with you.

The first thing you will do is provide the bank with personal information, such as a Social Security number, birth date, and address. The bank will also request a personal ID to confirm your identity. You will then be asked to sign a signature card, as shown in Figure 4-3. This is the only signature the financial institution will honor on checks and withdrawal slips. You may also be asked to supply answers to security questions. If you access your account on a mobile device or a computer, you may be asked to answer security questions to verify your identity.

If you want someone else to have check-cashing privileges on your account, he or she also needs to sign a signature card. This may be helpful if you want someone else to be able to access your account in the event that you are unable to do so. If you share an account with a parent or a spouse, it becomes a *joint account*. This requires a clear understanding of who will write checks and how records of transactions will be kept.

When you open a checking account, you receive a book of starter checks. These starter checks are blank but show your account number. You use them until your personalized checks arrive, as shown in Figure 4-4. They will be printed

Bank Checking Draft Signature Card

Submit one card to establish an optional check redemption privilege, which allows you to write checks against your account.

Name of Account			
Account Number		Date	

The registered owner(s) of this account must sign below. By signing this card, the signatory(ies) agree(s) to all the terms and conditions set forth on the reverse side of this card.

Signature	Signature
Signature	Signature

Institutional Accounts:	Joint Tenancy Accounts:
❏ Check here if any two signatures are required on checks	❏ Check here if both signatures are required on checks
❏ Check here if only one signature is required on checks	❏ Check here if only one signature is required on checks

Goodheart-Willcox Publisher

Figure 4-3 When you open a checking account, you will be asked to sign a card with the signature you intend to use for all your financial and legal transactions.

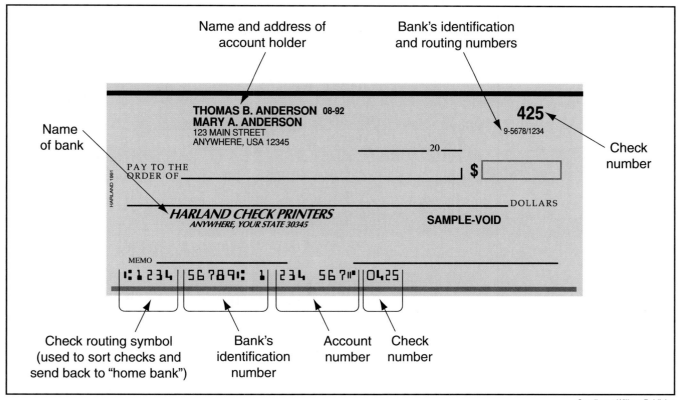

Goodheart-Willcox Publisher

Figure 4-4 Your personalized checks include information financial institutions need to process checks correctly.

with your name, address, and account number. The checkbook includes a register for keeping track of your transactions, as shown in Figure 4-5. A **check register** is a record of account deposits, withdrawals, checks, fees, and interest. It is important to keep track of all of your transactions so you know how much you have in your account.

You may be offered credit, debit, and ATM cards when you open a checking account. Inquire about the service fees associated with using your ATM and debit cards and any limits applying to their use. To avoid errors in your account balance, record all transactions and fees in your check register. Keeping your receipts will also be helpful. If used wisely and responsibly, these cards can provide you with greater financial flexibility.

			RECORD ALL CHARGES OR CREDITS THAT AFFECT YOUR ACCOUNT						
NUMBER	DATE	CODE	DESCRIPTION OF TRANSACTION	PAYMENT/DEBIT (–)	✓ T	FEE (IF ANY) (–)	PAYMENT/ CREDIT (+)	BALANCE $	
	3/1		Opening balance	00			100 00	100	00
								100	00
101	3/2		Lee's Grocery	15 32				15	32
			Groceries					84	68
	3/3		Cash withdrawal	20 00				20	00
								64	68
102	3/4		The Book Shelf	11 75				11	75
			Calendar					52	93
	3/6	DC	No Limits	35 13				35	13
			Jeans					17	80
	3/8	D	Deposit				130 00	130	00
								147	80
103	3/9		Lee's Grocery	18 35				18	35
			Groceries					129	45
	3/11	AP	Unified Utilities	23 07				23	07
			Electric bill					106	38
	3/14	DC	Mary's Dept. Store	34 60				34	60
			Navy shirt					71	78
104	3/16		Richard's Records	21 20				21	20
			CD					50	58
	3/22	D	Deposit				130 00	130	00
								180	58
105	3/26		Lee's Grocery	47 58				47	58
			Groceries					133	00
	3/29		Cash withdrawal	30 00				30	00
								103	00
106	3/30		Dr. Harvey	65 00				65	00
			Dental checkup					38	00
	4/1	D	Deposit				130 00	130	00
								168	00
			Service charge	5 00				5	00
								163	00

Goodheart-Willcox Publisher

Figure 4-5 Make a point of recording all your checks, debits, ATM transactions, and deposits in your checkbook register.

Making Deposits

To deposit money in your account, fill out a deposit slip as a record of the transaction. A *deposit slip* states what is being deposited—currency, coins, or checks—and the amount of each item, as shown in Figure 4-6. Follow these steps when filling out a deposit slip:

1. Write the date.

2. Enter the amount of money being deposited in checks, currency, and coins. If you need more room, you may continue listing checks on the back of the deposit slip.

3. Total the amount of currency, coins, and checks to be deposited. Write this number after the word *Subtotal.*

4. If you want to withdraw cash at the same time you make a deposit, enter the amount after the words *Less cash received.* You must sign the slip if you want cash back from your deposit.

5. Subtract the amount received from the subtotal.

6. Enter the amount deposited after words *Total deposit.*

7. Record the deposited amount in your check register.

Economics in Action

2008 Banking Breakdown

The US economy depends on the flow of money and the services financial institutions provide. When that flow stops, all parts of the economy are negatively affected. Such an event began in the fall of 2008 when global credit markets came to a near standstill as problems surfaced in the financial industry.

Many financial institutions in the United States and around the world lost billions of dollars on risky real estate loans and other investments. Several major financial institutions—such as Lehman Brothers, Fannie Mae, Freddie Mac, and American International Group—failed. Other firms were weakened and taken over by stronger companies. The failure of major financial institutions led to the failure of dozens of banks in the United States.

To address the problem, the Troubled Asset Relief Program (TARP) was signed into law by President George W. Bush on October 3, 2008. The purpose of TARP was to invest money in financial institutions in order to strengthen the financial sector.

Even with billions of dollars pumped into the banking system by TARP, money did not circulate freely. Banks increased qualifications to receive loans and drastically reduced lending, triggering a downward spiral in the economy. Many consumers could not get loans for cars, homes, or other needs. Businesses could not borrow to expand, meet payrolls, or pay for inventories. They grew cautious and cut spending. Firms focused on survival by cutting spending as well as their workforce.

Unemployment grew to new highs. Even consumers who had jobs lost confidence and cut their spending. Demand for goods and services fell. Many businesses posted losses, and eventually some failed. Many businesses that were profitable stopped hiring in fear of the unknown. The economy went into a serious recession that lasted for several years.

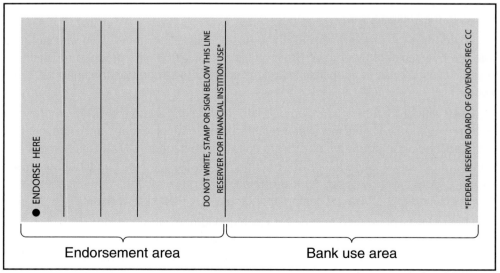

Goodheart-Willcox Publisher

Figure 4-6 A deposit slip is a record of money you put into your account.

When you make a deposit in person, you receive a *receipt*. When you make deposits at an ATM, you also receive a receipt detailing the transaction and showing the current balance in your account. Save your receipts to help balance your check register.

Endorsing Checks

Before a check made out to you can be cashed or deposited, you must endorse it. An **endorsement** is a signature on the back of a check. Its purpose is to transfer ownership of the check from you to the bank. You make the endorsement in the space provided on the left side of the back of the check, as shown in Figure 4-7. When making an endorsement, be sure to sign your name exactly as it appears on the front of the check. There are three ways to endorse a check, as shown in Figure 4-8.

Goodheart-Willcox Publisher

Figure 4-7 On the back of a personal check is an area set aside for endorsements.

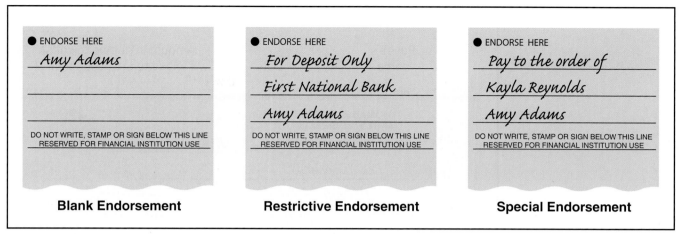

Blank Endorsement   **Restrictive Endorsement**   **Special Endorsement**

Goodheart-Willcox Publisher

Figure 4-8 Three types of endorsements are commonly used.

- *Blank endorsement.* This endorsement requires only the signature of the payee. The payee is the person to whom the check is written. A check endorsed this way may be cashed by anyone. For your protection, you should use this type of endorsement only at the time and place you cash or deposit a check.

- *Restrictive endorsement.* A check with a restrictive endorsement may be used only for the specific purpose stated in the endorsement. For example, if before signing your name, you write "For Deposit Only" and then write the name of your bank, the check cannot be cashed; it can only be deposited in your account. Restrictive endorsements are often used when banking by mail, depositing at an ATM, or when someone else is depositing a check for you.

- *Special endorsement.* A special endorsement is used to transfer a check to another party. Only the person named in the endorsement can cash the check. To use a special endorsement, write "Pay to the order of _____ (the name of the party to receive the check)." Sign your name as it appears on the check.

Ethics

Intentionally writing a check that will bounce is unethical and illegal. Intent to defraud the payee can cause the writer of the check to face criminal penalties.

Writing Checks

A blank check has important information on it. This information helps financial institutions process checks correctly. For checks to be processed, they must also be written correctly. When writing a check, enter the following items in the correct spaces, as shown in Figure 4-9.

1. Date

2. Name of the payee—the person, business, or organization receiving the check

3. Amount of the check in numbers

4. Amount of the check in words

5. Reason for writing the check, after the word *Memo,* if you want a record

6. Your signature, which should look like the one on your bank signature card

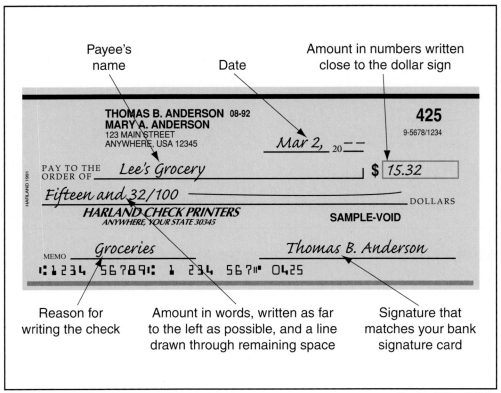

Goodheart-Willcox Publisher

Figure 4-9 Write checks neatly and carefully to avoid mistakes.

Case Study

Online Banking

For her birthday, Alyssa received a new computer that was faster and performed more functions than her old one. She was eager to experiment with all the new things she could do. Alyssa had a checking account at a local bank. She wanted to pay her bills and track her account from home.

Alyssa visited her bank's website to research its online services. Then she signed up for the service. After selecting her user ID and security code, she accessed her account online.

Alyssa directed that her rent and insurance premiums be paid online. She would pay her other bills as she received them. Alyssa also decided to have her paycheck deposited directly to her account. All in all, Alyssa thought she had gained new control over her financial affairs.

Case Review

1. Would you conduct your financial business online?
2. What questions would you ask before signing up for online banking services?
3. What are some of the advantages of online banking? Can you identify any disadvantages?

Careers in Finance

What Does a Bank Teller do?

The first person a bank customer sees is usually a **bank teller.** A **bank teller** communicates with and provides service to the customer. A teller must be educated about bank policies, procedures, and emergency operations, such as what to do if a situation of theft presents itself. **Bank tellers** typically:

- handle all cash transactions, such as cashing a check or depositing money;
- open various accounts for customers; and
- balance the cash drawer.

What Is It Like to Work as a Bank Teller?

The work environment in a bank is generally comfortable, and the surroundings are pleasant. Professional dress and attitude are necessary for the position. Some banks allow tellers to sit, rather than stand, when working at the teller window.

Starting a banking career as a teller is a good first step. Many banking executives learn the business in this entry-level job and work their way up the career ladder.

What Education and Skills Are Needed to Be a Bank Teller?

- high school diploma; college degree preferred
- customer service skills
- excellent math skills
- honest and ethical behavior

For your own protection, write checks in black ink. If you make a mistake, destroy the check and write a new check. Do not make corrections on the check.

When you write a check, record the check number, date, payee, and amount in your check register. Subtract the check amount from your balance. Record a destroyed check by writing its number and the word *void*. When you make a deposit, also record the date and amount of the deposit and add it to your balance. If you follow these guidelines, you will always know how much money is in your account.

Never postdate a check. A **postdated check** is a check written with a future date. Some people postdate a check because they will not have enough money in their account to cover the check until a later date. However, there is no guarantee that the person will hold the check until the date on the check. If the check is cashed early and there is not enough money in the account to cover the payment, you will be overdrawn.

Reconciling a Bank Statement

Once you open a checking account, you will generally receive a bank statement each month. A **bank statement** is a record of checks, ATM transactions, deposits, and charges on your account, as shown in Figure 4-10. Most banks still send statements through the mail. However, many banks will encourage you to access your statement online. When you receive the bank statement, you will *reconcile*, or compare it, with your check register to balance your checking account.

A bank statement usually begins with a summary of your account. It will tell you the beginning balance, the total amount of checks and other payments, the total of deposits and credits, and the ending balance. The summary will be followed by a detailed listing of these items:

- checks paid with the date, number, and amount of each one
- other items paid, such as withdrawals, fees, and bills you authorized the bank to pay for you
- deposits and credits with the dates, descriptions, and amounts

Cancelled checks or photocopies of checks paid from your account may be enclosed with the statement. However, many banks have discontinued this practice, making your cancelled checks and deposit slips available for viewing online.

The first step in reconciling your account is to compare the canceled checks with those recorded in your check register. Compare the deposits in your register with those on the statement and any receipts you may have. Check ATM transactions and fees recorded in your register against those on the statement. If the statement shows any service charges, subtract these from the balance shown in your register. Contact your bank if the statement lists questionable fees or items of which you have no record.

Many banks encourage customers to receive their bank statements online rather than paper. This saves postage, time, and helps protect the environment.

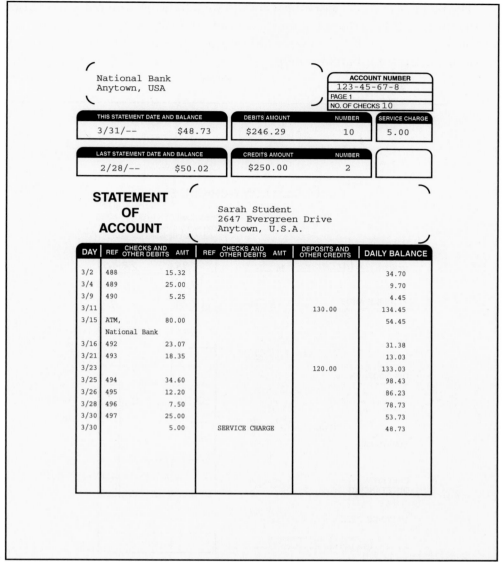

National Bank
Anytown, USA

ACCOUNT NUMBER
123-45-67-8

PAGE 1
NO. OF CHECKS 10

THIS STATEMENT DATE AND BALANCE	DEBITS AMOUNT	NUMBER	SERVICE CHARGE
3/31/-- $48.73	$246.29	10	5.00

LAST STATEMENT DATE AND BALANCE	CREDITS AMOUNT	NUMBER	
2/28/-- $50.02	$250.00	2	

STATEMENT OF ACCOUNT

Sarah Student
2647 Evergreen Drive
Anytown, U.S.A.

DAY	REF	CHECKS AND OTHER DEBITS	AMT	REF	CHECKS AND OTHER DEBITS	AMT	DEPOSITS AND OTHER CREDITS	DAILY BALANCE
3/2	488		15.32					34.70
3/4	489		25.00					9.70
3/9	490		5.25					4.45
3/11							130.00	134.45
3/15	ATM,		80.00					54.45
	National Bank							
3/16	492		23.07					31.38
3/21	493		18.35					13.03
3/23							120.00	133.03
3/25	494		34.60					98.43
3/26	495		12.20					86.23
3/28	496		7.50					78.73
3/30	497		25.00					53.73
3/30			5.00		SERVICE CHARGE			48.73

Figure 4-10 A bank statement is a record of all deposits, checks, charges, and other transactions involving your account during the statement period.

Do not forget about debit card purchases. If you use your debit card to make purchases, these charges were deducted directly from your account.

Next, account for the checks, ATM transactions, and deposits you made that have not yet appeared on your statement. Many bank statements include reconciliation worksheets that can be used for this purpose, as shown in Figure 4-11. Using the worksheet, follow these steps:

1. On the first line, write the closing balance as shown on the bank statement.

2. List all deposits you made that are not on the statement.

3. Add the amounts from steps 1 and 2. Write the total.

4. List by number and amount any checks and ATM withdrawals not included on the statement. Add these amounts together and enter the total for outstanding checks.

5. Subtract the amount in step 4 from the amount in step 3 and enter the balance.

The balance on your worksheet should match the current balance in your check register. If they do not agree, go through the above steps very carefully to check your math. If the figures still do not agree or come close, you may want to contact your bank for help.

RECONCILIATION WORKSHEET

CHECKS AND DEBITS OUTSTANDING
(Written but not shown on statement because not yet received by Bank.)

MONTH __March --__ , 20 __ __

NO. 498	28	40
499	15	00
ATM	25	00

BANK BALANCE shown on this statement $ __48.73__

ADD+ $ __125.00__

DEPOSITS made but not shown on statement because made or received after date of this statement.

TOTAL $ __173.73__

SUBTRACT–

CHECKS OUTSTANDING .... $ __68.40__

BALANCE..............$ __105.33__

The above balance should be same as the up-to-date balance in your checkbook.

TOTAL	68	40

Figure 4-11 This type of worksheet and directions for reconciling an account will appear on the back of most bank statements.

Checkpoint 4.2

1. Why might a person want to have a checking account?
2. What are some fees and charges that may be associated with a checking account?
3. What are three common types of checking accounts?
4. What is the difference between a cashier's check and a certified check?
5. How should a destroyed check be recorded in a check register?

Build Your Vocabulary

As you progress through this course, develop a personal glossary of personal finance terms and add it to your portfolio. This will help you build your vocabulary and prepare you for a career. Write a definition for each of the following terms and add it to your personal finance glossary.

checking account

check

check register

endorsement

postdated check

bank statement

Chapter Summary

Section 4.1 Banking Systems

- Financial institutions, such as commercial banks, savings and loan associations, and credit unions, provide services related to money and help keep the economic system functioning.
- Financial institutions offer consumers banking products, such as checking, savings, investment, online, and credit services.
- Many financial institutions offer special services, such as stop-payment orders, cashier's checks, certified checks, money orders, and traveler's checks.

Section 4.2 Checking Accounts

- The first financial service many people need is a checking account, which is a bank account that allows you to make deposits, write checks, and withdraw money.
- Opening a checking account requires providing your contact information and signing a signature card. You will generally receive a bank statement each month, which you should reconcile with your check register to balance your checking account.

Check Your Personal Finance IQ

Now that you have finished the chapter, see what you learned about personal finance by taking the chapter posttest. If you do not have a smartphone, visit the G-W Learning companion website.

G-W Learning mobile site: www.m.g-wlearning.com

G-W Learning companion website: www.g-wlearning.com

Review Your Knowledge

1. What is the primary function of financial institutions in the economy?
2. Name and briefly describe four common financial institutions serving consumers.
3. Describe electronic funds transfer (EFT) and how it relates to your financial transactions.
4. What is required to use an automatic teller machine (ATM)?
5. What is the purpose of overdraft protection?
6. What are three types of restrictions or penalties that may be associated with a checking account?
7. What is an interest-bearing checking account?
8. What type of information is needed to open a checking account?
9. What is the purpose of endorsing a check?
10. What information is typically included on a bank statement?

Apply Your Knowledge

11. If a person prefers to pay for everything with cash, is a checking account needed?
12. If you had the choice of opening a checking account with a bank or with a credit union, which would you choose? Explain your reasoning.
13. What are some steps you can take to be safe when using an ATM and card?
14. Suppose you need to make a secure payment. Would you use a cashier's check or a certified check? Why?
15. Why would a person choose to bank with a small community bank if there are several large banks in the area?
16. Which type of endorsement for a check would you use most often? Why?
17. Do you think it is important to reconcile your check register and bank statement each month? Why or why not?
18. What payment method would you use if you ordered a class ring through the mail and wanted to use the safest possible method of payment? Explain your answer.
19. Assume you are planning to open a checking account and trying to decide which bank to use. What banking services would you consider most important when making your decision?
20. Banks charge fees for some accounts and services. What are some ways you can reduce your cost of banking?

Teamwork

In this chapter, you learned about checking accounts. Working with a partner, select three banks that offer online banking services. Create a table listing each bank, its features, and its benefits. Present your findings to the class.

G-W Learning Mobile Site

Visit the G-W Learning mobile site to complete the chapter pretest and posttest and to practice vocabulary using e-flash cards. If you do not have a smartphone, visit the G-W Learning companion website to access these features.

G-W Learning mobile site: www.m.g-wlearning.com

G-W Learning companion website: www.g-wlearning.com

College and Career Readiness

Common Core

CTE Career Ready Practices. As a student and worker, financial institutions will play an important part in your life. Describe ways you would use financial institutions in the workplace. Then, describe ways you would use financial institutions in your private life. What do these two uses have in common?

Reading. Read a magazine, newspaper, or online article about the impact of technology on the operations of banking. Determine the central ideas of the article and review the conclusions made by the author. Provide an accurate summary of your reading, making sure to incorporate who, what, when, and how this situation happened.

Writing. Conduct research on EFT systems, how they originated, and how they benefit consumers. Write an informative report based on your findings that consists of several paragraphs describing the implications for the banking industry.

Web Connect

Search the Internet to find three local banks. Access the website for each bank and examine the requirements for opening a basic checking account with no limit on the number of checks written. Create a spreadsheet or table and graphically compare each bank's requirements. (Some banks may offer more than one type of account.) Explain which bank and account you prefer and why.

College and Career Readiness

College and Career Readiness Portfolio

As you collect items for your portfolio, you will need a method to keep the items clean, safe, and organized for assembly at the appropriate time. A large manila envelope works well to keep hard copies of your documents, photos, awards, and other items. Three-ring binders with sleeves are another good way to store your information. If you have a box large enough for full-size documents, it will work also. Plan to keep like items together and label the categories. For example, store sample documents that illustrate your writing or computer skills together. Use notes clipped to the documents to identify each item and state why it is included in the portfolio. For example, a note might say, "Newsletter that illustrates desktop publishing skills."

1. Select a method for storing hard copy items you will be collecting for your portfolio. (You will decide where to keep electronic copies in a later activity.)

2. Write a paragraph that describes your plan for storing and labeling the items. Refer to this plan each time you add items to the portfolio.

Personal Finance

Personal finance is a competitive event you might enter with your Career and Technical Student Organization (CTSO). The personal finance competitive event may include an objective test that includes banking topics. If you decide to participate in this event, you will need to review basic banking concepts to prepare for the test.

To prepare for a personal finance event, complete the following activities.

1. Read the guidelines provided by your organization. Make certain that you ask any questions about points you do not understand. It is important to follow each specific item that is outlined in the competition rules.

2. Review the vocabulary terms at the beginning of each chapter.

3. Review the Checkpoint activities at the end of each section of the text.

4. Review the end-of-chapter activities for additional practice.

5. Ask your instructor to give you practice tests for each chapter of this text. It is important that you are familiar with answering multiple choice and true/false questions. Have someone time you as you take a practice test.

Chapter 5
Savings

Steps to financial security begin with a savings plan. Regular savings builds the foundation for you to acquire most of the things you need and want in life. Establishing a routine for saving can lead to money for college, your first car, your first home, financial assistance to your family, and a comfortable retirement. There are multiple options for savings accounts that are available to you. It is a great advantage to begin your savings program when you are young. The longer your savings accumulate, the more they earn. It is never too early to start saving for your future.

Focus on Finance

Savings Accounts

Many banks offer special checking accounts for students, so be sure to shop around when opening an account. There are four primary factors to consider when opening your first savings account.

- *Convenience.* Unless you bank online, you will probably make frequent trips to your bank. It will be important to select a bank that is convenient to where you live or work.
- *Competitive interest rates.* Shop around and find the highest interest rate available. The higher the interest rate, the more you earn.
- *Low minimum balance.* It usually takes time to build your savings. As a result, you want a bank that does not charge a fee if you have a small balance in your account.
- *No inactivity fees.* Even though you want to save regularly, it is not always possible. You want a bank that is not going to charge you a fee for periods of time when you cannot make a deposit.

Many banks offer special savings plans for young savers. Such plans are designed to attract young savers by offering low fees and low minimum balances. Typical features of plans for young savers include:

- $5 minimum to open an account
- no monthly service charges
- no minimum balance
- no inactivity fees
- unlimited withdrawals

College and Career Readiness

Reading Prep. Before reading this chapter, look at the chapter title. What does this title tell you about what you will be learning? Compare and contrast the information to be presented with information you already know about the subject matter from sources such as videos and online media.

Check Your Personal Finance IQ

Before you begin the chapter, see what you already know about personal finance by taking the chapter pretest. If you do not have a smartphone, visit the G-W Learning companion website.

G-W Learning mobile site: www.m.g-wlearning.com

G-W Learning companion website: www.g-wlearning.com

Sections

Section 5.1 Savings Plans

Section 5.2 Maximizing Savings

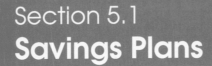

Section 5.1
Savings Plans

Objectives

After studying this section, you will be able to:

- Define personal savings goals.
- List and describe various types of savings instruments that are available from financial institutions.
- Compare and contrast the different types of savings products.

Terms

savings plan	interest-bearing savings account
emergency fund	high-yield savings account
SMART goal	money market account
savings account	certificate of deposit (CD)
annual percentage yield (APY)	

Creating a Savings Plan

A **savings plan** is a strategy for using money to reach important goals and to advance your financial security. Creating a savings plan involves a careful look at your current finances and your important objectives.

Money is a limited resource. Every decision to spend or save has an opportunity cost. The money you spend today cannot meet tomorrow's needs and wants. The opportunity cost of current spending is reduced future spending power. Current spending also costs you the opportunity to earn interest on savings.

Using interest-earning opportunities can help your savings grow. To make the most of your savings dollars, learn how interest is calculated. Compare savings products and services at different financial institutions and choose the type that best meets your needs.

A personal savings plan is a vital part of an overall financial plan. A savings plan consists of budgeting for savings, creating an emergency fund, and setting goals for savings to meet your needs. First, you need to have money that can be set aside for savings.

Budget for Saving

Review the money management section in Chapter 1. Follow the steps outlined to create a simple, workable money management plan. This plan will give you an in-depth look at your current finances. It will also tell you how much money you can use to start a savings program. Once you budget for savings, the following strategies can help you make your savings grow.

- *Pay yourself first.* Rather than waiting until all bills are paid and placing the leftover money into savings, set aside money for your savings first.

Monkey Business Images/Shutterstock.com

Paying yourself first assures that your savings will grow.

- *Budget for savings.* Put savings into your spending plan. Make saving a regular part of your bill-paying routine. When you receive extra money—a gift, a bonus, a tax refund—add it to your savings.

- *Use direct deposit.* Many employers can deposit employees' paychecks directly into their bank accounts. A portion can go into a savings account. This strategy is another way to pay yourself first.

- *Let your savings grow.* Your savings will not build if you are constantly dipping into them. Except for withdrawing money to pay for the savings goals you set, stay out of your savings. If the temptation is too great, perhaps you can choose a savings plan that makes withdrawal difficult.

- *Reduce spending; increase saving.* Keep a spending log as described in Chapter 2. This log will show you where your money goes. Look for places where you can cut spending and add to your savings.

Create an Emergency Fund

The first savings goal is to build an emergency fund. An **emergency fund** is an amount of money you can easily access in case of a job layoff, illness, or unexpected expense. Since most emergencies are unplanned, the money should be kept in an account that allows you to make withdrawals quickly and without a fee. A basic bank savings account, discussed later in the chapter, is a good choice for an emergency fund.

The amount of money in this fund varies depending on your needs. However, a common guideline is that you keep enough money in the emergency fund to cover living expenses for six to eight months. This would include rent or mortgage payments, car and other loan payments, taxes, utilities, food, and all other expenses.

Set Goals for Saving

Once you have an emergency fund, you can save for other things. It is easier to save if you have clearly defined goals. Begin with a list of what you want to achieve with your money. What would persuade you to give up spending now so you can save enough for the future? Next, create SMART goals as shown in Figure 5-1. A **SMART goal** is something you want to achieve stated in terms that are specific, measureable, achievable, realistic, and time related.

Specific

Your savings goals should be straightforward and emphasize what you want to happen. You should outline your goals in exact terms. "Putting together $1,200 for a ski trip next winter" is more specific than "saving money to travel sometime in the future." Likewise, "saving $50 a month to buy a computer next summer" is more specific than "putting money aside in case you need it next year." When you state your goals in specific terms, you can more easily focus your efforts and track your progress.

Measurable

You need to know when you reach your goal. If your goal is to save enough money to buy a laptop computer, you need to be able to determine the point where that goal is reached. Since laptops can range in price from $400 for a basic model to over $4,000 for a powerful gaming model, you will need to decide which type of laptop you can afford and the point in time when you wish to make the purchase. For example, assume you decide that in one year you would like to purchase a particular make of laptop that currently sells for $799. Your research helps determine that, due to improved technology, the computer you want will probably sell for around $600 a year from now. You now have a measured goal. You can now set forth to save $50 a month for the 12-month period you established as your timeframe for the purchase.

Operations Managers

Operations managers at financial institutions are responsible for directing bank operations and overseeing the management of the products and services offered to customers. They may also resolve customer problems, oversee investments, and manage employees and departments.

Figure 5-1 Set SMART financial goals.

Achievable

Goals need to be reasonable and achievable. If you are saving money for the purchase of your first home, for example, consider how much money you will need for the down payment and the amount of your monthly payments. Owning a $1 million home on the beach may be very appealing. However, it is not an achievable goal for most first-time homebuyers. You should set your sights on a home you can afford and create a savings plan that will allow you to achieve that goal. Do not set yourself up for failure by setting goals that are out of reach.

Realistic

Consider your income and expenses, your life situation, and any likely changes. Set up financial goals that you can achieve based on these realities. For example, suppose you can save $300 monthly and you want to buy a car within two years without getting a loan. Buying a used car is a realistic goal while buying a new luxury car is not. What are your goals? Are they objectives you can realistically achieve?

Time Related

Goals should have starting points, ending points, and fixed time periods. You should put your goals and objectives into a timeframe. When will you need your savings? This will vary for different goals.

It is never too soon to start saving for the goods and services you want for your future. Once you know what you want your money to do for you, you can take realistic steps to reach your financial goals.

Savings Products

You can choose from a variety of savings products and plans. A **savings account** is an account designed for accumulating money for future use. Compare the options and decide which one will bring you the highest earnings and most advantageous opportunities for your savings. Important factors to consider are shown in Figure 5-2. You may want to start your search online. Many financial institution websites outline the rates, terms, fees, and services available with different savings products.

Choosing a Savings Product

To decide which form of saving is best for you, consider the following questions.
- How much can you save regularly each week or month?
- When and how often do you expect to deposit money?
- When and how often do you expect to withdraw savings?
- Do you have a specific goal, such as an amount you want to save within a given time?
- Are you saving for a specific purpose or purchase?
- Is it important to be able to convert savings to cash quickly and conveniently?

Goodheart-Willcox Publisher

Figure 5-2 Ask these questions when evaluating a savings product.

The *Truth in Savings Act* requires financial institutions to provide clear information about the costs and terms of interest-earning accounts in uniform terms. The purpose of the Truth in Savings Act is to help consumers compare savings products and make informed decisions. The **annual percentage yield (APY)** is the rate of yearly earnings from an account, including compound interest. This figure is useful in comparing accounts. The act requires advertising and any materials describing savings products to include the following information:

- minimum amount required to open the account

- interest rate

- annual percentage yield (APY) and the period during which that APY is in effect

- minimum deposit, time requirements, and other terms the saver must meet to earn the stated APY

- description of any fees, conditions, and penalties that could lower the yield

As you compare savings products and plans, it is important to make sure your money is safe. As explained in Chapter 4, the Federal Deposit Insurance Corporation (FDIC) insures deposits in many financial institutions up to $250,000. The National Credit Union Administration (NCUA) insures deposits in most credit unions up to $250,000.

Another important consideration is liquidity. *Liquidity* refers to the ease with which an asset can be converted into cash without losing value. You may want part of your savings to be "ready money" for emergencies or other needs. However, you often earn more interest on money you agree to leave on deposit for longer periods of time.

For top earnings on your savings, look for the following.

- *Highest annual interest rate.* Interest is money paid for the use of money. When you deposit money in a savings account, the financial institution will have use of your money. As a result, you will be paid interest. The higher the interest rate, the more interest your money will earn.

- *Highest APY.* The higher the rate, the more your money will earn.

- *Most frequent compounding of interest.* The more frequently interest is compounded, the more interest your savings will earn.

- *Shortest interest periods.* Interest periods may be monthly, quarterly, semiannually, or annually. Generally, shorter interest periods offer more flexibility for depositing and withdrawing money without loss of interest.

Interest rates are expressed as one-year percentages. Convert the rate to a decimal to calculate interest.

Go Green

Using direct deposit for your paycheck is an excellent green practice. No check is generated and no paperwork is created when you make a deposit. To save regularly, you simply specify an amount for your bank to automatically move to your savings account.

- *Fewest restrictions and penalties on the account.* Restrictions and penalties can affect both your earnings and your use of the account. For example, savings accounts may involve a minimum deposit or balance requirements.

- *Lowest fees.* Even small fees can add up over time. A financial institution may charge a fee every time you write a check on an account, for example.

Make sure you find out when interest is credited to your account. If you withdraw savings just before interest is credited, you may not receive the full interest on your savings. To address this problem, some financial institutions offer a *grace period*. During this time, you can receive full earnings on deposits or withdrawals. The grace period often extends from five days before to five days after the crediting date. You may withdraw or deposit money during the grace period and still receive interest for the entire period.

Interest-Bearing Savings Accounts

An **interest-bearing savings account** is a type of demand deposit account that pays interest and allows for regular deposits and withdrawals. Interest-bearing savings accounts have no set maturity date. This means that you do not have to wait until the end of a certain period of time to have access to your money. Instead, you can make withdrawals whenever you choose, and you are also able to close the account when you wish. Common types of interest-bearing accounts are discussed in the following paragraphs.

Regular Savings Accounts

Regular savings accounts, also called *basic savings accounts,* pay interest and allow deposits and withdrawals. These savings accounts generally offer the lowest interest earnings of all savings options. They also have the most liquidity of savings options. Three common types of savings accounts are passbook savings, statement savings, and online savings accounts.

Passbook Savings Accounts

With a *passbook savings account*, a booklet (passbook) is used to record deposits, withdrawals, interest earned, and the current balance. This booklet is presented to a bank teller each time you conduct a bank transaction. Passbook accounts usually allow you to make unlimited withdrawals, have few fees, require a low or no minimum balance, and have a low interest rate. Passbook accounts are most suitable for customers who wish to deal in person with a bank teller. Today, this type of bank account attracts mostly customers who conduct a relatively small number of transactions—such as children opening their first accounts. The passbook savings account is the oldest and simplest type of savings account. However, the popularity of passbook accounts has dropped since the introduction of ATMs and online banking.

Statement Savings Accounts

A *statement savings account* is an account for which the bank sends a statement that summarizes the activity of your account for a specific period of time, usually a month. The statement lists all deposits, withdrawals, and interest earned for the period covered by the statement. As with passbook accounts, statement accounts usually allow unlimited withdrawals, have few fees, require a low or no minimum balance, and have a low interest rate.

Statement savings accounts gained popularity in the 1970s when banks and credit unions started offering to mail automated statements to customers. Most basic savings accounts today are statement accounts.

Online-Only Savings Accounts

Internet banks provide banking services online. Customers access the bank's website to make electronic deposits and withdrawals, transfer funds, or check account balances. Internet banks have minimal operating expenses because they do not maintain or staff physical banks or branch offices. Their lower overhead costs allow them to pay higher interest rates on savings accounts. The higher yield is the primary advantage of online-only savings accounts. It is easy to compare Internet banks and the yields they offer online. See Figure 5-3 for a list of questions to consider when shopping for an online-only savings account.

There can also be some disadvantages to consider if you are interested in online-only savings accounts. For example, you cannot establish a personal banking relationship as you can with people at your local bank or credit union. Every time you e-mail, text, or call with a question or problem, you will likely reach a different person.

There also may be a lag time for both deposits and withdrawals to clear. This can be a problem in an emergency when you need cash immediately. Finally, you may have difficulty accessing your account information and funds if the bank's system goes offline.

High-Yield Savings Accounts

As the name implies, a **high-yield savings account** is an account that pays a higher interest rate than passbook and statement savings accounts. To get the higher rate, however, the bank requires a larger initial deposit and a higher minimum balance. The number of times you can make withdrawals in a year may also be limited. You will usually receive monthly statements of deposits, withdrawals, interest earned, and balances.

Questions to Ask When Shopping for an Online Savings Account

- How do rates and yields compare from bank to bank?
- How easily and quickly can you withdraw your money if you need it?
- How do you make deposits?
- Are accounts covered by the FDIC?
- Does the bank have reliable online security for your personal information?
- How prompt and thorough is the bank in answering your questions and concerns?
- Can you easily link your online account with your local bank to make transfers?
- What other banking services are available in addition to savings accounts?
- Do you feel comfortable and confident dealing with the banking institution?

Goodheart-Willcox Publisher

Figure 5-3 Asking these questions will help you evaluate an online savings account.

Money Market Deposit Accounts

A **money market account** is a type of savings account that typically pays a higher interest rate than regular savings accounts. However, money market accounts (MMAs) have a higher minimum balance—usually $500 but possibly as much as $10,000. Some MMAs pay a flat rate of interest regardless of the balance, while others use a tier structure that pays a higher interest rate on accounts with higher balances.

Most MMAs offer check-writing privileges. When you open an MMA, the bank will issue you a checkbook with which you can write checks against the balance in the account. However, you will be limited to a specified number of checks in a month. Also, there is a minimum amount for each check, which can be as much as $500.

Certificates of Deposit

A **certificate of deposit (CD)** is a savings account that requires a deposit of a fixed amount of money for a fixed period of time or term. When the term is up, you can keep your money in the CD, deposit it in another CD, or take it out. A CD is sometimes called a *time deposit* or *time account.*

Certificates of deposit may offer a fixed annual rate of interest or a variable or floating interest rate. A variable rate moves up and down (floats) with market rates. Usually, it is tied to a specific market rate, such as the rate on US Treasury Bills.

Since CDs require you to commit your money for a period of time, they pay a higher rate of interest than money market and savings accounts. The longer you agree to hold a CD, the higher the rate of interest you can earn. For example, a five-year CD will yield a higher annual rate of interest than a two-year CD.

CDs are not liquid. In order to get the highest interest earnings, you must leave your money in the CD until the term is up. This term may be as little as one month or as much as seven years. If CDs are cashed before the time period is over, a significant amount of interest is lost. Also, there is a penalty for early withdrawal.

History of Finance

Wealth

Early banks only did business with wealthy people. Wealth was held in the form of gold coins, jewels, gold ornaments, fine rugs, silk goods, and other tangible objects of value. By the Middle Ages, global exploration had led to the establishment of trade routes than linked many parts of the world, and traditional objects of wealth could no longer be safely and practically transported for long distances. Shipwrecks and pirates were a constant threat. As a result, early banks developed letters of intent to pay, which were usually printed on durable parchment paper. Along with the letters, a banking network was established that allowed merchants to redeem their letters.

When shopping for a CD, make sure you ask the following questions.

- What is the current APY?
- What is the maturity date?
- What is the dollar amount of earnings if you hold the certificate to maturity?
- What happens to the CD at maturity? Will your money earn interest at the regular savings account rate? Will it be automatically reinvested in another CD? Will the financial institution hold it with no interest until hearing from you? Will you receive notice of the maturity date in advance? This notice gives you time to decide how to put the money to work again.

US Savings Bonds

You have other choices if you are willing to accept less liquidity and commit your funds for a longer period of time. A popular choice is *US savings bonds*. To acquire a savings bond, the common expression is "buy it." However, when you *buy* a savings bond, you are not actually buying anything, but lending money to the federal government.

There are two types of US savings bonds: *EE Bonds* and *I Bonds*. Neither EE Bonds nor I Bonds are insured by the FDIC. However, both are backed by the full faith and credit of the US government. As a result, they are considered exceptionally safe.

EE Bonds

Prior to 2012, EE Bonds could be purchased in paper form from a bank or credit union. When issued in paper form, EE Bonds were always issued at a discount. This means that you would purchase them at half their stated value, called the *face value*. For example, you would pay $25 for a bond with a face value of $50. Likewise, you would pay $50 for a bond with a face value of $100. The bond grows in value as it earns interest. After five years, the bonds could be redeemed (cashed in) without penalty. However, the bond could be held for its stated period and the holder would receive the full face value.

As of January 1, 2012, the US Treasury Department only issues electronic savings bonds, so paper savings bonds can no longer be purchased. Instead, new savings bonds are purchased in electronic form through the TreasuryDirect at www.treasurydirect.gov. *Electronic EE Bonds* are purchased at full face value in amounts of $25 or more, to the penny. *To the penny* means you do not have to invest full dollar amounts. If you so choose, you could invest $25.01. The maximum that can be purchased in one year is $10,000.

EE Bonds earn a fixed interest rate. The rate is based on market yields of *Treasury Notes*, a type of government-backed investment, and other considerations related to savings bonds. New rates are announced every six months.

If you redeem electronic EE Bonds in the first five years, you will forfeit the last three months' interest. If you redeem them after five years, there is no penalty.

Those currently holding paper savings bonds can continue to redeem them at most banks and credit unions. Paper bonds that have not matured but have been lost, stolen, or destroyed can be reissued in paper or electronic form.

I Bonds

I Bonds are sold at face value in denominations ranging from $25 to $10,000. I Bonds pay a fixed interest rate plus a semiannual inflation add-on rate. The Secretary of Treasury determines the fixed interest rate. The interest rate in effect at the time of purchase applies for the life of an I Bond.

The inflation rate is based on the Consumer Price Index, a figure that represents prices consumers pay for goods and services. Every six months, the inflation rate on I Bonds changes. When interest rates are low and inflation is not a threat, the return on I Bonds is relatively low. However, they are good insurance against inflation.

As of January 2012, you can purchase up to $10,000 per year in electronic bonds directly from TreasuryDirect. Also, you can purchase up to $5,000 per year in paper I Bonds as a result of a tax refund. As with EE Bonds, paper I Bonds are no longer sold by financial institutions but can still be issued to replace an existing paper bond that has been lost, stolen, or destroyed.

To buy savings bonds today, you must now create an account with TreasuryDirect. Opening a TreasuryDirect account is free, and there are no paper securities.
To learn more, visit www.treasurydirect.gov.

Summary of Savings Choices

As you have learned, there are a variety of savings options from which to choose. How you save depends on your short- and long-term goals, your income, and the amount you have available to save. Often, savers will have more than one type of savings account. A summary of the savings choices is shown in Figure 5-4.

Summary of Savings Choices		
Type of Account	**Advantages**	**Drawbacks**
Passbook savings account. A printed booklet is used to keep track of each transaction.	• Bookkeeping is automatic. No need to wait for monthly statements. • No or low minimum balance is required. • Money is readily available. • Accounts are FDIC insured.	• Banking may be limited to branch transactions during banking hours. • Passbooks can be lost or stolen. • Interest rates are low compared to other savings options.
Statement savings account. Printed statements are used to summarize account activity.	• No passbook is needed; withdrawals normally only require a driver's license (or other identification) and an account number. • Low or no minimum balance is required. • Accounts often offer ATM cards, making after-hours banking possible. • Accounts are FDIC insured.	• Customer must do some recordkeeping to know the current balance. • Interest rates are only slightly better than passbook accounts.

Goodheart-Willcox Publisher

Figure 5-4 Compare different savings products to determine which one meets your needs.

(Continued)

Summary of Savings Choices

Type of Account	Advantages	Drawbacks
Online Savings account. This type of account is offered by an Internet bank.	• Accounts have higher interest rates than traditional banks. • Convenience is an advantage. • Accounts are FDIC insured. • Accounts have lower fees than traditional banks.	• Accounts have lack of personal contact. • Users are unable to access the account if the bank's computer is offline.
High-yield savings account. This type of account pays a higher interest rate with restrictions.	• Accounts have higher interest rates than passbook or statement accounts. • Accounts are FDIC insured.	• Accounts require a higher initial deposit. • Accounts require a higher minimum balance. • Accounts may limit withdrawals.
Money market account (MMA). This type of account is liquid, offers higher interest, and has restrictions.	• Accounts have higher interest. • Liquidity is good. Most MMAs offer free checking. • Tiered MMAs provide higher interest earnings at higher levels of deposit. • Accounts are FDIC insured.	• Accounts require higher initial deposits and minimum balances to avoid fees. • Accounts restrict withdrawals and transfers. • Accounts limit the number of checks that can be written in a month. • Accounts often require a minimum dollar amount for each check, which can be as high as $500.
Certificate of deposit (CD). This nonliquid savings option provides the highest earnings.	• Accounts have the highest interest rates of FDIC insured products. • Rates increase with longer terms.	• There is no liquidity during the term of the CD. • The interest rate is fixed. • There can be a substantial penalty for early withdrawals.
US savings bonds. EE and I Bonds are issued by the federal government.	• Bonds can be purchased in amounts as low as $25. • Bonds are backed by the full faith and credit of the US government. • It may be possible for deposits to be payroll deducted. • I Bonds can be purchased directly from an income tax refund.	• As of January 1, 2012, savings bonds can only be purchased in electronic form. • Bonds have low interest rates compared to some investments. • A maximum of $10,000 in bonds can be purchased in a calendar year.

Figure 5-4 *Continued.*

Checkpoint 5.1

1. What is a savings plan?
2. What are some reasons you might need to spend money you have saved in an emergency fund?
3. Why is it important for savings goals to be measurable?
4. What are three types of regular savings accounts?
5. What are two types of US savings bonds?

Build Your Vocabulary

As you progress through this course, develop a personal glossary of personal finance terms and add it to your portfolio. This will help you build your vocabulary and prepare you for a career. Write a definition for each of the following terms and add it to your personal finance glossary.

savings plan

emergency fund

SMART goal

savings account

annual percentage yield (APY)

interest-bearing savings account

high-yield savings account

money market account

certificate of deposit (CD)

Section 5.2
Maximizing Savings

Objectives

After studying this section, you will be able to:

- Explain how savings instruments earn interest.
- List and compare alternative places, rather than a bank, to save money.

Terms

simple interest
compound interest
Rule of 72
tax exempt
tax deferred
online-only bank
share account
brokerage firm

Earning More Interest

There are many different places to save your money, and a variety of savings choices. Once you have decided on a safe place (federally insured), your next consideration should be how much interest you will earn. Remember that when you earn interest, you are being paid to save. The more interest you earn, the more you are paid. You can maximize your savings by considering the following.

- *Total amount deposited.* Obviously, the more you deposit the more interest you earn.
- *Interest rate.* The higher the interest rate, the more you stand to gain.
- *Time span of the deposit.* The longer money remains in savings without withdrawals, the more money you accumulate.
- *Interest type.* There are two types of interest. **Simple interest** is interest earned only on the principal, which is the amount of money originally deposited. The principal does not include interest earned. **Compound interest** is an amount calculated using the principal (money deposited) plus the interest it earns. The interest previously earned is included in the total before new interest earnings are computed. Earning interest on the interest makes money grow faster.
- *Frequency of compounding.* The more often interest is compounded, the faster savings grow. Compounding may be done on a daily, quarterly, monthly, or semiannual basis. Over time, compound interest increases the value of your savings, as shown in Figure 5-5. This concept is known as the *time value of money.*

Calculating Compound Interest

Calculating compound interest involves several steps.

1. Multiply the deposit by the annual interest rate.
2. Divide the answer from Step 1 by the rate of compounding. For monthly compounding, divide by 12; for quarterly, divide by 4; for semiannual, divide by 2; for daily, divide by 365.
3. Add the answer from Step 2 to the deposit amount. The result is the new balance with interest.

These steps are shown in Figure 5-6, which illustrates calculating monthly compounding. For example, the savings plan shows a single deposit of $100 and an annual interest rate of 5 percent. Therefore, the deposit amount at the end of Month 2 is $100.84.

Future Value Tables

A future value table provides an easy way to calculate compound interest earnings at different interest rates and times. Future value tables usually

Computer Engineers
Computer engineers design and develop software and systems that make computers work. In the finance industry, these engineers develop and maintain computer programs that manage financial data in a secure, user-friendly environment.

Ethics
Even though banks use computers to process customer transactions, they still make occasional errors. If your bank were to accidently put money into your account that you did not deposit, it would be unethical to withdraw and spend the money.

Watch Your Savings Grow				
Weekly Savings at Different Interest Rates, Compounded Monthly				
Weekly Amount	Interest Rate	Number of Years		
		10	20	30
$10	4.5%	$ 6,550	$ 16,814	$ 32,897
25		16,375	42,035	82,243
50		32,750	84,069	164,486
$10	5.5%	$ 6,910	$ 18,871	$ 39,576
25		17,274	47,176	98,940
50		34,548	94,353	197,880
$10	6.6%	$ 7,294	$ 21,243	$ 47,914
25		18,236	53,107	119,786
50		36,472	106,214	239,572
$10	7.7%	$ 7,707	$ 23,984	$ 58,361
25		19,267	59,959	145,903
50		38,533	119,918	291,807
$10	8.8%	$ 8,148	$ 27,155	$ 71,491
25		20,371	67,888	178,729
50		40,741	135,776	357,459
Original Amounts Saved:				
$10		$ 5,200	$ 10,400	$ 15,600
25		13,000	26,000	39,000
50		26,000	52,000	78,000

Goodheart-Willcox Publisher

Figure 5-5 The dual effects of time and compound interest add value to savings.

show compound interest earnings for either a series of equal annual deposits or a single deposit, as shown in Figure 5-7.

For example, find the future value of a single $100 deposit after 5 years at a 3 percent interest rate. Look across the *5 Years* row to the number in the 3% column. You will find 1.1593. Now, multiply 1.1593 by $100. The $100 deposit would be worth $115.93.

Suppose you made a single deposit of $1,000 instead of $100. To find the future value after 5 years at 3 percent interest, multiply by $1,000. The $1,000 would grow by $159.30.

Rule of 72

If you do not have a future value table, you can use the Rule of 72 to estimate the amount of time or interest it will take for your savings to double in value. The **Rule of 72** is an equation that estimates how long it will take to double an investment with a fixed interest rate.

To calculate the number of years in which your savings will double, divide 72 by the rate of interest. For example, if you deposit $1,000 at a rate of 4 percent, divide 72 by 4. The result is 18. In 18 years, your $1,000 will be worth approximately $2,000.

Calculating Compound Interest			
Month	Step 1 Deposit × Annual Interest Rate	Step 2 Step 1 Answer ÷ Rate of Compounding	Step 3 Deposit + Step 2 Answer = New Balance with Interest
1	$100 × 5% = $5	$5 ÷ 12 = $0.42	$100 + $0.42 = $100.42
2	$100.42 × 5% = $5.02	$5.02 ÷ 12 = $0.42	$100.42 + $0.42 = $100.84
3	$100.84 × 5% = $5.04	$5.04 ÷ 12 = $0.42	$100.84 + $0.42 = $101.26
4	$101.26 × 5% = $5.06	$5.06 ÷ 12 = $0.42	$101.26 + $0.42 = $101.68
5	$101.68 × 5% = $5.08	$5.08 ÷ 12 = $0.42	$101.68 + $0.42 = $102.10
6	$102.10 × 5% = $5.11	$5.11 ÷ 12 = $0.43	$102.10 + $0.43 = $102.53
7	$102.53 × 5% = $5.13	$5.13 ÷ 12 = $0.43	$102.53 + $0.43 = $102.96
8	$102.96 × 5% = $5.15	$5.15 ÷ 12 = $0.43	$102.96 + $0.43 = $103.39
9	$103.39 × 5% = $5.17	$5.17 ÷ 12 = $0.43	$103.39 + $0.43 = $103.82
10	$103.82 × 5% = $5.19	$5.19 ÷ 12 = $0.43	$103.82 + $0.43 = $104.25
11	$104.25 × 5% = $5.21	$5.21 ÷ 12 = $0.43	$104.25 + $0.43 = $104.68
12	$104.68 × 5% = $5.23	$5.23 ÷ 12 = $0.44	$104.68 + $0.44 = $105.12

Figure 5-6 After one year, a single deposit of $100, earning an annual interest rate of 5 percent compounded monthly, will increase to $105.12.

Future Value of $1 (Single Deposit)

Years	Annual Interest Rate							
	1%	2%	3%	4%	5%	6%	7%	8%
1	1.0100	1.0200	1.0300	1.0400	1.0500	1.0600	1.0700	1.0800
2	1.0201	1.0404	1.0609	1.0816	1.1025	1.1236	1.1449	1.1664
3	1.0303	1.0612	1.0927	1.1249	1.1576	1.1910	1.2250	1.2597
4	1.0406	1.0824	1.1255	1.1699	1.2155	1.2625	1.3108	1.3605
5	1.0510	1.1041	1.1593	1.2167	1.2763	1.3382	1.4026	1.4693
6	1.0615	1.1262	1.1941	1.2653	1.3401	1.4185	1.5007	1.5869
7	1.0721	1.1487	1.2299	1.3159	1.4071	1.5036	1.6058	1.7138
8	1.0829	1.1717	1.2668	1.3686	1.4775	1.5938	1.7182	1.8509
9	1.0937	1.1951	1.3048	1.4233	1.5513	1.6895	1.8385	1.9990
10	1.1046	1.2190	1.3439	1.4802	1.6289	1.7908	1.9672	2.1589
11	1.1157	1.2434	1.3842	1.5395	1.7103	1.8983	2.1049	2.3316
12	1.1268	1.2682	1.4258	1.6010	1.7959	2.0122	2.2522	2.5182
13	1.1381	1.2936	1.4685	1.6651	1.8856	2.1329	2.4098	2.7196
14	1.1495	1.3195	1.5126	1.7317	1.9799	2.2609	2.5785	2.9372
15	1.1610	1.3459	1.5580	1.8009	2.0789	2.3966	2.7590	3.1722
16	1.1726	1.3728	1.6047	1.8730	2.1829	2.5404	2.9522	3.4259
17	1.1843	1.4002	1.6528	1.9479	2.2920	2.6928	3.1588	3.7000
18	1.1961	1.4282	1.7024	2.0258	2.4066	2.8543	3.3799	3.9960
19	1.2081	1.4568	1.7535	2.1068	2.5270	3.0256	3.6165	4.3157
20	1.2202	1.4859	1.8061	2.1911	2.6533	3.2071	3.8697	4.6610
25	1.2824	1.6406	2.0938	2.6658	3.3864	4.2919	5.4274	6.8485
30	1.3478	1.8114	2.4273	3.2434	4.3219	5.7435	7.6123	10.0627
35	1.4166	1.9999	2.8139	3.9461	5.5160	7.6861	10.6766	14.7853
40	1.4889	2.2080	3.2620	4.8010	7.0400	10.2857	14.9745	21.7245
50	1.6446	2.6916	4.3839	7.1067	11.4674	18.4202	29.4570	46.9016

Goodheart-Willcox Publisher

Figure 5-7 This table shows the future value (with compounding) of a single deposit of $1.

You Do the Math

Math sometimes requires that you use tables to find specific information. When using a table, use the column on the left to find one of the factors which your problem requires. Use the column at the top to the find the second factor. The point at which the two intersect is the solution.

Complete the Following Problems

1. Use the Future Value Table in Figure 5-7 to find the amount of interest you would earn if you put $4,500 in a savings account for 35 years at an annual interest rate of 3 percent.

2. Calculate the number of years it would take to double a $10,000 deposit in a savings account earning 3 percent interest.

To find the annual interest rate needed to double your savings, divide 72 by the number of years. For example, if your savings were in an account for 20 years, divide 72 by 20. The result is 3.6. Your savings must be in an account paying 3.6 percent for it to double in 20 years.

Inflation and Taxes

Due to inflation, a dollar buys less this year than it did last year. The inflation rate varies from quarter to quarter and year to year. An inflation calculator tells you how much buying power a sum of money will lose between two points in time. One such calculator is available on the Bureau of Labor Statistics website.

When planning for the future, keep in mind that inflation reduces the value of your savings. The goods and services you wish to buy with your savings next year will cost more money than they cost today. Try to find a savings plan that pays higher interest than the rate of inflation.

Taxes also erode savings. Taxes on the money you earn can take 25 percent or more of your income. You minimize taxes by putting money into tax-exempt or tax-deferred savings.

- **Tax exempt** means free of certain taxes. Certain savings accounts for education expenses are tax exempt.

- **Tax deferred** means that taxes on the principal and/or earnings are delayed until the funds are withdrawn. Retirement savings accounts are a common example; taxes are deferred until withdrawals begin at retirement.

When you can reduce or defer taxes on the money you save, you accumulate more money over time. Many employers offer tax-exempt or tax-deferred savings plans. Retirement plans help employees by allowing them to shift some of their tax liability to the future.

You must pay taxes on the interest earned by your savings. After the end of the year, you should receive a Form 1099-INT from each financial institution that holds your savings. It will state the total interest you earned that year. You need to report this amount when filing your taxes.

Inflation is the rate at which prices for goods increase and the value of the dollar decreases.

Case Study

Savings Account

After Morton gets a summer job, his mom convinces him to open a savings account at the bank she uses. The earnings are unimpressive. While surfing the Internet, Morton comes across ads for online high-yield savings accounts.

Morton learns these accounts pay higher interest than his savings are earning. Some accounts also offer auto loans and home mortgages at relatively low rates.

Morton is a little nervous about committing his savings online. However, the Internet banks he investigates are covered by FDIC insurance. After additional checking, he opens an online-only savings account. The procedure is simple because he can transfer funds electronically from one bank to the other.

Case Review

1. What do you think of Morton's decision to move his savings into an online-only account?

2. Go online to investigate online-only savings accounts. Compare two or three accounts at different Internet banks and answer the following questions:

   - What are some of the features of these accounts?

   - How do online-only savings accounts differ from the accounts the local banks offer?

   - What are some of the advantages and disadvantages of online-only savings accounts?

   - How can you open an online-only savings account?

Alternative Places to Save

Most people save their money at banks because accounts are insured by the FDIC. Even when savings rates fell to the lowest levels on record in the years between 2009 through 2012, savers steadfastly maintained the bulk of their savings in US banks. However, there are other places to save that may provide higher returns, and some of them are insured.

Online-Only Banks

Instead of your local brick and mortar bank, you may want to consider the benefits of an online-only bank. An **online-only bank,** also called an *Internet-only bank,* is a financial institution that conducts customer transactions via the Internet. There are three main reasons you might want to consider an online-only bank:

- *Convenience.* Online-only banks usually offer free online bill paying. In addition, you will not have to change banks if you move to another part of the country. Your account is also accessible 24 hours a day, seven days a week.

- *Free or low-cost services.* Often, online-only banks offer 100 percent free checking and low minimum account balances. Online-only banks have lower operating costs, since they only have to support a single online computer network—rather than multiple branch locations, ATMs, and many employees. The lower operating costs are passed on to customers in the form of lower fees.

Careers in Marketing

What Does a Market Research Analyst Do?

Market Research Analysts help companies identify potential customers, determine their needs, and determine what they will pay for goods and services. They study market conditions to estimate the potential sales of products and services. **Market research analysts** typically:

- conduct surveys and research to learn the needs of consumers;
- collect data to forecast sales and consumer demands;
- analyze market conditions;
- collect information on sales, prices, competitors, and market trends;
- report research findings to management; and
- communicate with clients.

What Is It Like to Work as a Market Research Analyst?

Market research analysts work in a variety of industries including finance and insurance, consumer goods and services, and professional and technical services. They may work for a company or for a consulting firm. Normally they work in an office setting with regular hours. However, deadlines may require longer hours and travel may be required. **Market research analysts** spend a lot of time at a computer collecting and interpreting data on consumers and preparing reports on their findings. Companies use these reports to make informed business decisions related to product design, marketing, pricing, and advertising.

What Education and Skills Are Needed to Be a Market Research Analyst?

- bachelor or advanced degree in market research or a related field with coursework in statistics, business, math, and computer science
- written and oral communication skills
- research proficiency
- computer skills
- analytical and creative thinking skills
- at least three years of experience in the market research industry
- Professional Researcher Certification (PRC) from the Marketing Research Association a plus

---

- *Higher interest rates on savings accounts.* Since online-only banks have lower operating costs, they often offer interest rates that are higher than traditional banks.

Most online-only banks are insured up to $250,000 per account by the FDIC. However, always verify FDIC membership before entrusting your money to any bank.

Credit Unions

At credit unions, savings accounts are called **share accounts.** Setting up a share account with a credit union can have several advantages compared to having an account with a bank. Credit unions usually pay a higher rate of interest than banks and allow share accounts to be created with as little as $5. Banks usually require a higher minimum balance—usually between $100 and $500.

If membership in a credit union is based on job affiliation, members can usually have their employers deduct money from their pay and transfer it directly into share accounts. This is a form of paying yourself first. As discussed earlier in the chapter, paying yourself first is an important part of a savings plan. Credit unions are insured up $250,000 by the NCUA.

Brokerage Firms

A **brokerage firm** is a place where you can purchase a variety of investment products as well as open savings accounts. Brokerage firms usually pay higher interest rates than traditional banks and credit unions. However, the accounts may not be insured by the FDIC. The main appeal of a brokerage account is the liquidity and the ability to easily move money from one type of investment to another. Brokerage accounts are covered in greater detail in Chapter 7.

Checkpoint 5.2

1. Why does more frequent compounding of interest result in higher interest earned?
2. Does using the Rule of 72 give an exact amount of time or interest it will take for savings to double in value? Explain.
3. Explain the difference between a tax-exempt account and a tax-deferred account.
4. How does an online-only bank differ from a traditional bank?
5. What information is typically shown on a future value table?

Build Your Vocabulary

As you progress through this course, develop a personal glossary of personal finance terms and add it to your portfolio. This will help you build your vocabulary and prepare you for a career. Write a definition for each of the following terms and add it to your personal finance glossary.

simple interest	tax deferred
compound interest	online–only bank
Rule of 72	share account
tax exempt	brokerage firm

Chapter Summary

Section 5.1 Savings Plans

- Steps to financial security begin with a savings plan. A savings plan is a strategy for using money to reach important goals, and it involves a careful look at your current finances and your important objectives.

- You can choose from a variety of savings products and plans, such as regular, passbook, statement, and online savings accounts. Key features to look for when deciding when and where to save include the annual interest rates, annual percentage yield (APY), lowest fees, and fewest account restrictions.

- High-yield savings accounts, such as money market accounts and certificates of deposit, pay a higher interest rate than passbook and statement savings accounts.

Section 5.2 Maximizing Savings

- The amount of interest earned on savings accounts depends on the amount of money deposited, the interest rate, time the money remains on deposit, and interest type—simple or compound.

- There are places other than traditional banks to save, such as online banks, credit unions, and brokerage firms that may provide higher returns; some of them are insured.

Check Your Personal Finance IQ

Now that you have finished the chapter, see what you learned about personal finance by taking the chapter posttest. If you do not have a smartphone, visit the G-W Learning companion website.

G-W Learning mobile site: www.m.g-wlearning.com

G-W Learning companion website: www.g-wlearning.com

Review Your Knowledge

1. How does creating SMART goals help you reach your savings objectives?

2. What does *pay yourself first* mean?

3. Explain how to use the Rule of 72.

4. What are four primary factors to consider when opening your first savings account?

5. Explain what the APY is and how it is used in reference to savings accounts.

6. What type of account generally offers the lowest interest earnings of all savings options?

7. What is an online-only savings account, and why does it usually pay higher interest than regular savings accounts?

8. What determines the amount of interest you earn on your savings?

9. Why should you keep inflation in mind when planning for your financial future?

10. What might be some advantages of having a share account at a credit union rather than having a savings account at a bank?

Apply Your Knowledge

11. Study the following savings options and list what you consider to be the greatest advantages and disadvantages of each:
    - regular savings accounts
    - high-yield savings accounts
    - money market accounts
    - online-only savings accounts
    - certificates of deposit
    - share accounts at credit unions

12. Assume you are saving for a down payment on your first car, which you plan to buy in one year. What savings instrument would you choose? Explain your choice.

13. Outline your own short-, medium-, and long-term savings goals. Discuss how they are likely to change as you pass through the life cycle stages discussed in Chapter 2.

14. Assume you have $1,000 you can save for one to three years. Compare savings options at three or more financial institutions. Determine which institution will pay the highest rate of interest for your money. Also find out how much you could expect to earn in one, two, and three years. In a short report, explain which savings option you would choose and why.

15. Research and compare different college savings plans. With your family, develop a guide to use for establishing your own savings for college.

16. Go to www.treasurydirect.gov and research how you can buy US savings bonds. Which method do you prefer? Explain why.

17. Give three examples of how regular savings can help you achieve your goals.

18. Accounts insured by the FDIC are the safest places to save money. However, they usually pay the lowest rates of interest. Identify two types of savings instruments that are not insured that you would consider buying in order to earn more interest. Explain reasons for your choices.

19. Much has been written in recent years about cyber thieves and ID theft. Would you trust an online bank to provide the security necessary to protect your funds? Why or why not?

20. In your opinion, what is the safest type of savings instruments? Give reasons for your choice.

Teamwork

A savings plan is crucial for every consumer. Working with a teammate, develop a saver's guide covering local places to save, types of savings accounts, safety and liquidity of saved funds, and questions to ask before committing your money to an account. Create a handout that summarizes the information you discovered.

G-W Learning Mobile Site

Visit the G-W Learning mobile site to complete the chapter pretest and posttest and to practice vocabulary using e-flash cards. If you do not have a smartphone, visit the G-W Learning companion website to access these features.

G-W Learning mobile site: www.m.g-wlearning.com

G-W Learning companion website: www.g-wlearning.com

Common Core

College and Career Readiness

CTE Career Ready Practices. Go online and search using the term *desirable workplace skills.* Then conduct another search using the term *top academic skills.* Create a Venn diagram showing the overlap between the two lists.

Reading. Conduct an online survey of money market deposit accounts. Locate different accounts and read the descriptions to note the similarities. Identify sections of the description that are unique or creative in comparison with other money market accounts about which you have gathered information. After reading, be prepared to present your findings to your class.

Writing. Interview a representative at a financial institution near you to learn the types of savings accounts and services offered at the institution. Pick up literature on different savings programs and determine which one you would find most attractive if you had $200 to $500 to put in savings. Write a two- to three-page report on your choice of a savings program. Explain how you made the decision to select the account that you chose.

Web Connect

Do an Internet search for *FDIC.* Look for information on uninsured investments. Write a paragraph on your findings.

College and Career Readiness Portfolio

College and Career Readiness

You will create both a print portfolio and an e-portfolio in this class. You have already decided how to store hard copy items for your print portfolio. Now you need to create a plan for storing and organizing materials for your e-portfolio. Ask your instructor where to save your documents. This could be on the school's network or a flash drive of your own. Think about how to organize related files into categories. For example, school transcripts and diplomas might be one category. Awards and certificates might be another category, and so on. Next, consider how you will name the files. The names for folders and files should be descriptive but not too long. This naming system will be for your use. You will decide in a later activity how to present your electronic files for viewers.

1. Create a folder on the network drive or flash drive in which you will save your files.

2. Write a few sentences to describe how you will name the subfolders and files for your portfolio.

3. Create the subfolders to organize the files, using the naming system you have created.

Extemporaneous Speaking

Extemporaneous speaking is a competitive event you might enter with your Career and Technical Student Organization (CTSO). This event allows you to display your communication skills of speaking, organizing, and making an oral presentation. At the competition, you will be given several topics from which to choose. You will also be given a time limit to create and deliver the speech. You will be evaluated on your verbal and nonverbal skills as well as the tone and projection of your voice.

To prepare for the extemporaneous speaking event, complete the following activities.

1. Ask your instructor for several practice topics so you can practice making impromptu speeches.

2. Once you have an assigned practice topic from your instructor, jot down your ideas and points you want to cover. An important part about making this type of presentation is that you will have only a few minutes to prepare. Being able to write down your main ideas quickly will enable you to focus on what you will actually say in the presentation.

3. Practice the presentation. You should introduce yourself, review the topic that is being presented, defend the topic being presented, and conclude with a summary.

4. Ask your instructor to play the role of Competition Judge as your team reviews the case. After the presentation is complete, ask for feedback from your instructor . You may consider also having a student audience to listen and give feedback.

5. For the event, bring paper and pencils to record notes. Supplies may or may not be provided.

Chapter 6
Credit

Financially capable people are aware of the importance of obtaining and using credit. Wise use of credit allows for an increased standard of living and the ability to acquire the luxuries and necessities of life. Unwise use of credit can have a negative effect on the quality of life and lead to many financial problems. Good credit management involves financial planning to use credit to meet your needs and weigh your wants to help you enjoy financial security now and in the future.

Focus on Finance

Predatory Lending

Predatory lending is a policy of making loans to high-risk borrowers who are unlikely to be able to repay. Predatory lenders prey on senior citizens, low-income individuals, and others who lack financial knowledge. These loans can be payday loans, mortgages, or other consumer credit. The interest rates are exceedingly high and may increase over the life of the loan, causing the monthly payment to increase substantially each month. When borrowers find they cannot make the larger monthly payments, the lender offers to refinance the loan, lowering monthly payments but increasing the debt. The refinancing terms put the borrower deeper in debt and frequently lead to foreclosure. Always read the fine print on any credit cards, mortgages, or other consumer loans and make sure you understand the terms.

College and Career Readiness

Reading Prep. Before reading this chapter, review the objectives. Based on this information, write down two or three items that you think are important to note while you are reading.

Check Your Personal Finance IQ

Before you begin the chapter, see what you already know about personal finance by taking the chapter pretest. If you do not have a smartphone, visit the G-W Learning companion website.

G-W Learning mobile site: www.m.g-wlearning.com

G-W Learning companion website: www.g-wlearning.com

Sections

Section 6.1 Using Consumer Credit

Section 6.2 Using Credit Cards

Section 6.3 Credit Management

Section 6.4 Consumer Protection

Section 6.1
Using Consumer Credit

Objectives

After studying this section, you will be able to:
- Explain the advantages and disadvantages of using credit.
- Identify the different types of consumer credit.
- Describe secured and unsecured loans.
- Describe how to establish a sound credit rating.
- Describe situations in which it is smart to use credit and others in which it is not.
- Explain what makes up the cost of credit.

Terms

credit
closed-end credit
finance charge
contract
principal
open-end credit
line of credit
secured loan
collateral
unsecured loan
cosigner
creditworthy
credit report
credit score
annual percentage rate (APR)

Consumer Credit

In a cash transaction, you hand over money in exchange for goods or services. Like cash, **credit** is a medium of exchange that allows individuals to buy goods or services now and pay for them later. More specifically, credit is an agreement between two parties in which one party—referred to as the creditor—supplies money, goods, or services to the other party. In return, the receiving party—referred to as the borrower or the debtor—agrees to make future payment by a particular date or according to an agreed-upon schedule.

All credit is based on trust. The creditor believes there is a high likelihood the borrower can and will pay what is owed. For example, suppose you go out to eat with friends. One friend does not have enough money and asks to borrow some of yours. If you trust that friend and can spare the money, you will probably lend it.

StockLite/Shutterstock.com

Learning to manage credit is an important life skill.

Credit also has an element of risk. When you lend a friend money, a DVD, or a shirt, you risk that he or she will not return it. An unpaid debt between friends can harm a friendship. If a friend does not pay you back, you will probably not lend to him or her again.

Consumer credit is the use of credit to purchase goods or services primarily for personal, family, or household use. Using credit to buy goods and services is generally more costly than using cash because fees are usually added to the amount owed. Using credit is costly in another way, too. When you use credit, you spend future income. This means part of your future earnings must be used to pay what you owe. The use of credit reduces future income.

Consumer credit also plays an important role in the economy. It provides the extra buying power needed to support mass production and distribution of goods and services. Therefore, credit helps make more goods and services available to consumers at lower prices.

Governments, businesses, and consumers use credit. Credit plays an important role in personal economics. Used carefully and wisely, it can help people get more of the things they need when they need them. Misused credit can lead to financial disaster. It is important for your own financial well-being to learn how to manage your use of credit.

Types of Credit

There are many types of consumer credit and ways to categorize them. The following paragraphs discuss credit and related terms that you should know.

Closed-End Credit

Closed-end credit is a loan for a specific amount that must be repaid with finance charges by a specified date. A **finance charge** is the total amount paid by a borrower to a lender for the use of credit. In other words, it is the dollar amount paid for credit.

Closed-end credit is given for a specific purpose and is used to acquire more expensive items, such as cars, homes, furniture, major home appliances, and student loans. The creditor takes a risk, but that risk is minimized in several ways. Before the loan is made, the borrower must sign a **contract,** which is a legally binding agreement between the borrower and the creditor. The contract states the terms of the loan. The **principal,** which is the amount of money borrowed, will be stated. Loans are granted by commercial banks, credit unions, finance companies, insurance companies, and credit card agencies. When you take out a loan, you sign a contract stating the amount of the loan, the interest rate, the length of the loan, and other provisions of the agreement.

Open-End Credit

Open-end credit is an agreement that allows the borrower to use a specific amount of money for an indefinite period of time. A **line of credit** is a preapproved amount that an individual can borrow. The maximum is established, and as long as you do not exceed that amount, you can continue charging purchases and repaying on a regular schedule. As long as the borrower makes payments on a schedule, pays any finance charges, and stays within the borrowing limit, he or she can continue to use the credit.

Common examples of open-end credit are:
- credit cards issued by banks;
- credit cards issued by department stores and oil companies;
- overdraft protection on checking accounts; and
- home equity lines of credit.

Types of Loans

When individuals seek credit, they are obtaining a loan. Getting a loan is borrowing money with the intent of repaying in a specified amount of time and within specified conditions. Loans are classified as either secured loans or unsecured loans.

Secured Loans

A **secured loan** is a loan that requires collateral. **Collateral** is property that a borrower promises to give up in case of default. You may pay lower finance charges on a secured loan because the creditor takes less risk when collateral is pledged. The car is collateral in an auto loan. If the borrower were to default, or fail to pay the debt, the creditor may take the property to settle the debt.

Most closed-end credit is offered in the form of installment loans. An *installment loan* is a loan for a specific amount of money that is repaid with interest in regular installments. Finance charges vary with the size of the loan, the interest rate, and the repayment period. Interest rates vary with different lenders and with the collateral pledged.

Unsecured Loans

An **unsecured loan,** also called a *signature loan,* is a loan made on the strength of a signature alone. You sign a contract and promise to repay according to terms of the agreement. An example of an unsecured loan is a credit card.

It is difficult to obtain an unsecured loan unless you have a strong credit rating. However, you still may be able to get an unsecured loan if you have a cosigner. A **cosigner** is a responsible person who signs the loan with the person to whom the loan is granted. By signing the loan, the cosigner promises to repay the loan if the borrower fails to pay. Unsecured loans usually have higher interest rates than secured loans.

The word *credit* is derived from the Latin word *credo,* which means *I trust you.*

Establishing Credit

You may find it difficult to get credit at first. This is because creditors want evidence that you can and will pay your debts. Here are some steps you can take to build a sound financial reputation.

- *Start with a job.* Prove that you can earn money.
- *Open a savings account.* Saving regularly shows a responsible attitude toward financial matters. Your savings also may serve as collateral for a loan.
- *Open a checking account.* A well-managed checking account shows you have experience in handling money. A checking account is often overlooked when people are trying to establish credit.
- *Get a credit card.* Apply to a local department store or an oil company for a credit card. If you are granted credit, make small purchases and pay promptly. This will give you a record of steady payments.

Deklofenak/Shutterstock.com

The first step to establishing credit is proving that you can earn money.

You may also ask a parent or other family member to add you as an authorized user of one of their credit cards. This means their record of the account is copied to your credit report. If your parents or other family members are not comfortable letting you have a credit card with their account, simply have them destroy the card as soon as it arrives. You will still get the favorable credit reporting every month, even though you do not personally use the card.

If you have never used credit, you will need to establish a credit rating. Begin establishing a good credit rating as early as you can. The longer you wait, the more difficult it becomes to find a lender willing to extend credit to you. Without an established credit history, you will also pay a higher rate of interest to lenders willing to give you a loan.

Three Cs of Credit

Creditors want to lend to applicants who are creditworthy. **Creditworthy** means having the assets, income, and tendency to repay debt. Creditors decide whether or not to grant people credit based on their credit ratings. A credit rating is the creditor's evaluation of your willingness and ability to pay debts. It is measured by the *three Cs:*

- *Character.* Character is based on your reputation for honesty and your financial history. The person who has a record of paying bills on time and of assuming financial responsibility will rate high on character.
- *Capacity.* Capacity is your ability to earn money and pay debts. It is measured by your earning power and employment history.
- *Capital.* Capital refers to your financial worth. People with land, homes, cars, savings, or anything of value have capital. Capital gives a person a more favorable credit rating.

Credit Reports

How do lenders get the information to evaluate a consumer's creditworthiness? They look at the application and whether the prospective borrower has a job. They may contact references listed on the application. An important factor is the length of the credit history. If you are unemployed or never have used credit, it may be difficult to get a loan or credit card.

Before making credit available, a creditor reviews the borrower's financial history. Just as you may not lend money to someone who does not repay debts, creditors will not lend to a person with a poor credit reputation. Before making a loan offer, creditors already know the likelihood of the borrower defaulting on the loan. If risk of default is high, most reliable creditors will not lend. Less reputable creditors may lend but with a much higher finance charge and unfavorable terms.

Most lenders consult credit reporting agencies. A *credit reporting agency*, or *credit bureau*, is an organization that collects information about the financial and credit transactions of consumers. Businesses notify the credit reporting agencies when a consumer opens a new account, closes an account, or skips or makes late payments.

There are three major national credit reporting agencies: Equifax, Experian, and TransUnion, LLC. These agencies sell credit reports to creditors.

A **credit report** is a record of a person's credit history and financial behavior. It includes every credit account ever opened and outstanding balances on current credit accounts. It also lists negative information, such as delinquent or late payments and overdue taxes.

The information on credit reports from the different agencies may differ. Carefully review your credit report and check key information in each section. See Figure 6-1 for tips on how to read a credit report. If you find errors, contact the credit reporting agency for instructions on filing a dispute.

Your credit report largely determines whether you can get credit when you need it. With a poor report, you will have trouble getting credit and may have to pay higher finance charges.

Credit Scores

Creditors also evaluate creditworthiness by looking at credit scores. A **credit score** is a numerical measure of a loan applicant's creditworthiness at a particular point in time. It is generated primarily by credit reporting agencies. Your credit score, like your credit report, may differ from one credit reporting agency to another. Each agency has access to different information and uses different mathematical formulas to calculate scores. However, the scores for the same person are usually similar.

How to Read a Credit Report	
Section	**What to Check**
Personal Information	Verify your personal information, such as your name, address, phone number, date of birth, and Social Security number.
Credit Summary	This section summarizes your revolving and installment accounts and any home loans. Check the balances and your total amount of outstanding debt.
Account Information (also called *Credit Items*)	Make sure all accounts listed belong to you. This section may be lengthy, but it is important to check all details for accuracy, including payment history, balance, and account status. Late payments and accounts taken over by collection agencies appear in this section.
Public Records (also called *Negative Information* or *Negative Items*)	Any bankruptcies, garnishments, or liens are shown here. Ideally, this section should be blank.
Inquiries (also called *Credit History Requests*)	Look over the list of creditors that recently viewed your credit report. Applying for a credit card, taking out a loan, submitting an apartment application, or applying for insurance can trigger inquiries.

Goodheart-Willcox Publisher

Figure 6-1 A credit report shows if a person has used credit wisely.

The credit score is also known as the *FICO* score, named for the Fair Isaac Corporation that developed the rating system. FICO scores are calculated based on five categories of information, as shown in Figure 6-2 and listed below.

- *Payment history.* You score high for payment history if you have a record of paying your bills on time.
- *Amounts owed.* This category determines your debt-to-credit-limit ratio. Your debt is the total of all you owe on credit cards, car loans, home loans, and so forth. Your credit limit is the total amount you are allowed under credit card maximums and your original loan amounts. A lower ratio is best.
- *Credit history.* The longer you have used well-managed credit card accounts, the better your credit history will be.
- *New credit.* Several applications for new credit accounts can have a negative effect on your credit score.
- *Types of credit used.* Having a mix of loans and credit cards is slightly favored over using only one type of credit.

The higher a credit score, the greater a person's creditworthiness and the more likely he or she will be able to obtain credit. However, what is considered a good credit score varies. For example, the credit reporting agency Experian uses the VantageScore© system that is based on letters, such as the grades you receive in class. Experian's credit rating system is illustrated in Figure 6-3.

There is no single score standard used by all lenders. What one creditor considers a good score may not be good enough for another. What a creditor considers a good score today may be too low for that same creditor tomorrow.

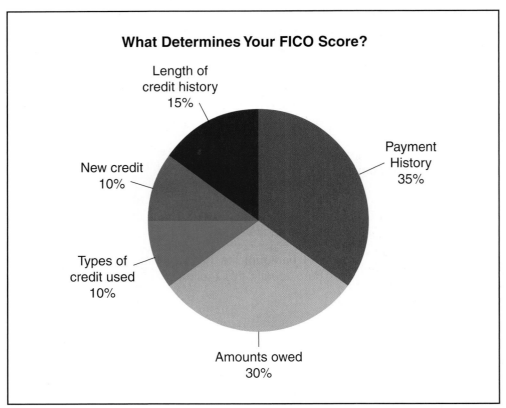

What Determines Your FICO Score?

Length of credit history 15%

New credit 10%

Types of credit used 10%

Payment History 35%

Amounts owed 30%

Figure 6-2 A FICO score is based on five categories of information.

Credit Score Ratings

A   901–990

People who have low risk of defaulting on loans. They often get the best rates and terms from lenders.

B   801–900

People who have managed their credit well and are offered good rates and terms by lenders.

C   701–800

Lenders may consider people in this group for loans, but often require more information.

D   601–700

People in this group have a higher default rate. Lenders may give them credit but at a higher interest rate.

F   501–600

People in this group have a high risk of defaulting on loans. Lenders will often deny them credit. If they get credit, they will pay high interest rates.

Goodheart-Willcox Publisher

Figure 6-3 The VantageScore© credit rating system uses letter grades, just like most schools.

When credit is tight, creditors look for higher credit scores before granting a credit request. A person's credit score changes as his or her financial history and obligations change.

Using Credit

You will find it smart to use credit in some situations but not in others. Several advantages of using credit are as follows.

- *Use of goods and services as you pay for them.* Being able to wear a coat or drive a car while you are paying for it can be a big plus. You have immediate access to an item you need even though you do not have the money to pay cash for it. This is a common reason for using credit.

- *Opportunity to buy costly items.* Many people find it difficult or impossible to save enough to pay for a car or house in one payment. With credit, you can buy goods and services as you need them and pay for them over a period of time. Borrowing is sometimes the only way consumers can pay for major purchases, such as a car.

- *Source of cash for emergency or unexpected expenses.* Even the best money managers encounter unexpected expenses, such as a major car repair. A common way to handle sudden needs for cash is having a line of credit, which is a preapproved amount that an individual can borrow.

- *Convenience and safety.* Credit eliminates the need to carry large amounts of cash. It provides a record of purchases. It usually simplifies telephone, mail, and Internet shopping as well as necessary returns and exchanges.

Since its introduction by the Fair Isaac Corporation in 1970, the FICO Score has become the global standard for measuring credit risk in the banking, mortgage, credit card, auto, and retail industries. Of the top 100 largest financial institutions in the United States, 90 use the FICO Score to make consumer credit decisions.

- *Taking advantage of sales.* Credit allows you to take advantage of sale prices on goods or services you need when you do not have enough cash at the time of the sale.

- *Long-range goals.* Credit can help consumers make purchases that are part of a long-range financial plan, such as paying for education, furniture, or a vacation.

To use credit wisely, you need to be aware of its disadvantages as well as its advantages. Consider the negative aspects when you are deciding how and when to use credit. Here are some disadvantages of using credit.

- *Reduction of future spendable income.* By using credit, you spend future income. You thereby reduce the amount of money you can spend later.

- *Expense.* Using credit usually costs money. The more credit you use and the more time you take to repay, the more you will pay in interest and finance charges. This reduces the amount you will have to spend for other goods and services.

- *Temptation.* Credit makes it easy to spend money you do not have. It can be difficult to resist buying what you cannot afford or can do without when you have ready credit.

- *Risk of serious consequences.* Failure to pay debts on time and in full can cause serious financial problems. You will read about these problems later in this chapter.

Cost of Credit

Using credit is not free, and it can come with hefty charges. When you borrow $10 from a friend, you probably repay the friend an even $10. However, if you borrow money from a financial institution or make credit purchases of goods or services, you usually pay finance charges. You pay finance charges because you have the use of the lender's money. As stated earlier, the finance charge is the total dollar cost of credit. A finance charge has two parts: interest and fees.

The finance charge you pay for the use of credit is expressed as a percentage. An **annual percentage rate (APR)** is the annual cost of credit a lender charges. The higher the APR, the more you pay. The APR factors in all fees and charges that otherwise may be hidden from the borrower. The APR reveals the true rate of interest and helps consumers compare different loans and other sources of credit. Money lenders and credit card companies are required by the federal Truth in Lending Act to state the APR of loans when they advertise a rate.

Go Green

The US Environmental Protection Agency (EPA) rates all vehicles based on greenhouse gas emissions and fuel economy. The most environmentally friendly vehicles receive the SmartWay or SmartWay Elite designation. Some banks and credit unions are offering a lower interest rate to finance the purchase of an EPA designated SmartWay or SmartWay Elite vehicle.

The total amount you pay for the use of credit is based primarily on three factors:

- *Interest rate charged.* As stated previously, the APR is the annual cost of credit a lender charges. The higher the APR, the more you pay. The APR is based on several factors, such as the type of loan, the current market rate of interest, and your credit score.

- *Amount of credit used.* As you learned in Chapter 5, interest is money paid for the use of money. When you borrow money or make credit purchases, you have the use of someone else's money. As a result, the more you borrow or charge, the more interest you pay.

- *Length of the repayment period.* The more time you take to repay the money you borrow or to pay for credit purchases, the longer you have the use of the lender's money. As a result, the longer the period of your loan, the greater the interest you will pay. For example, on July 5, 2012, the interest rate for a 30-year home mortgage was 3.64 percent. However, the rate for a 15-year home mortgage was 3.00 percent.

Checkpoint 6.1

1. What are some items that consumers use credit to buy?
2. What are four common types of open-end credit?
3. List one advantage and one disadvantage of using credit.
4. Identify the five primary factors on which your credit score is based.
5. What three factors determine the amount you pay in finance charges?

Build Your Vocabulary

As you progress through this course, develop a personal glossary of personal finance terms and add it to your portfolio. This will help you build your vocabulary and prepare you for a career. Write a definition for each of the following terms, and add it to your personal finance glossary.

credit
closed-end credit
finance charge
contract
principal
open-end credit
line of credit
secured loan
collateral
unsecured loan
cosigner
creditworthy
credit report
credit score
annual percentage rate (APR)

Section 6.2
Using Credit Cards

Objectives

After studying this section, you will be able to:
- Identify and describe the types of credit cards.
- Identify important factors to consider when shopping for a credit card.
- Describe subprime credit cards.

Terms

credit card
cash advance
store credit card
travel and entertainment card
regular charge account
revolving credit account
acceleration clause
grace period

Credit Cards

A **credit card** is a plastic card that allows the holder to make credit purchases up to an authorized amount. Credit cards are most often used to buy consumer goods and services. You pay for the purchase later, and you may also pay interest.

The most obvious purpose of a credit card is to purchase goods and services. Credit card purchases allow you to track your spending. You have receipts in the event a return is needed or if a replacement of an item needs to be made due to some defect.

Credit cards can also be used to get a cash advance. A **cash advance** is a loan against the available credit on your account. Sometimes the credit card company will mail you checks to use for cash advances. Interest charges on cash advances begin immediately when a check is cashed. Even if you pay by the due date for your credit account, you will still pay interest. There is also a transaction fee on the amount you borrow, and the interest rate may be higher than the rate for regular credit card purchases. A cash advance may not be the best option for borrowing money.

Types of Credit Cards

There are three common types of credit cards: general-purpose cards, store credit cards, and travel and entertainment cards. *General-purpose cards*, such as Visa or MasterCard, are issued by banks, credit unions, and other financial institutions. You can use these cards around the world at the many places where they are accepted. Very often, these cards can also be used like a debit card, allowing you to obtain cash at automated teller machines. They carry a credit limit and require minimum monthly payments. Finance charges and other fees vary. General-purpose credit cards are often referred to as bank cards, even if they are issued by a credit union or other financial institution.

Store credit cards, which are issued primarily by major department store chains, permit you to charge purchases only with the merchant issuing the card. Normally, you have a credit limit and are required to repay a minimum amount each month. Finance charges vary.

Travel and entertainment cards usually require you to pay the entire balance each month. Some cards allow you to pay over a longer period for travel- and vacation-related expenses, such as airfare, tours, cruises, and hotel bills. On these balances, you usually pay a high interest rate and must make minimum monthly payments.

Credit Accounts

Two common types of credit accounts are regular charge accounts and revolving credit accounts. A **regular charge account** lets an individual charge goods and services in exchange for a promise to pay in full within 25 days of the billing date. You receive a bill or statement each month. If you pay on time, there is no finance charge.

A **revolving credit account** is a type of credit agreement that offers a choice of paying in full each month or spreading payments over a period of time. If you choose not to pay in full, there is a finance charge. You must make at least the minimum payment each month. For small balances, the minimum payment is usually a set amount, such as $10. For larger balances, the minimum payment is usually a percentage of the unpaid balance. A typical revolving credit account places a limit on the total amount you may owe at any one time. You may make any number of purchases at any time as long as you do not exceed your credit limit. This type of credit is available through many retailers and through issuers of credit cards, such as Visa, MasterCard, and Discover. The cards can be used to buy goods and services from any seller who honors the card.

micro10x/Shutterstock.com

Be aware of the fees associated with using credit—credit is not free money.

Finance Charges

The finance charge is the total amount paid for the use of credit. There are two parts of a finance charge: interest and fees.

Interest Charges

It is important to understand how interest is calculated. If you pay less than the full amount owed each month, you will pay interest on the unpaid balance. Creditors compute interest charges in different ways, and their methods can result in very different finance charges. You need to read the fine print on credit agreements and monthly statements to learn the methods used to calculate interest. Three methods used for calculating interest are described below.

- *Average Daily Balance.* With this method, the creditor starts with the beginning balance for each day in the billing period and subtracts any payments or credits to your account on that day. Then the balances for each day in the billing cycle are totaled. The total is divided by the number of days in the cycle to arrive at the average daily balance. Interest charges are figured on that amount. New purchases may or may not be added to the daily totals. This is the most common method of computing charges.
- *Adjusted Balance.* With this method, the creditor determines the balance by subtracting payments or credits received during the billing period from the outstanding balance at the end of the previous billing period. Purchases you make during the current billing period are not included. This is the most favorable method for consumers but rarely used by creditors.
- *Unpaid Balance.* With this method, the creditor computes interest charges on the amount you owed at the end of the previous billing period. Payments, credits, and new purchases during the current billing period are not included.

Fees

Find out whether you must pay an annual fee for the privilege of using the card. These fees can be as much as $50 or more. It pays to look for cards with low or no annual fees. Confirm the fees that can be charged to your account and how you can avoid these charges. These charges may include fees for:

- late payments;
- exceeding your credit limit;
- cash advances; and
- balance transfers.

All credit card companies are allowed to advertise interest rates on a monthly basis, for example, 1.5 percent per month. However, they are required to clearly disclose the APR to customers before any agreement is signed.

Shopping for a Credit Card

Shopping for credit is as important as shopping for the goods and services you buy with it. When you want to borrow cash or use credit to finance a purchase, shop around for the best credit terms. The more money you borrow, the more you pay in finance charges. The higher the annual percentage rate, the more you pay in finance charges. The longer you take to repay, the more you pay in finance charges.

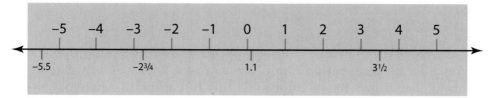

You Do the Math

Integers are positive and negative whole numbers and zero. In other words, they are not decimals or fractions.

Integers

Not Integers

Complete the Following Problems

1. How long will it take to pay off a $1,000 credit card balance that carries an annual 18 percent interest rate if you make no additional purchases and make the minimum monthly payment (typically $10)?

   Go online and find a credit card interest calculator. Use the calculator to illustrate the benefits of paying more than the minimum due on a credit card. Enter the following numbers into the calculator:

   • Amount charged: $1,000

   • Annual interest rate: 18 percent

   • Minimum payment percent: 4 percent

   • Leave minimum payment blank

   Compute the results. How much time and money can you save by paying more than the required 4 percent each month?

2. Fiona's credit card balance is $5,000. The APR is 18 percent and the minimum payment is 5 percent of the balance. What is the minimum payment due? How much of the minimum payment goes to interest? How much of the payment goes to the principal? If Fiona makes the minimum payment this month and does not use her card to make any more purchases, what will her balance be next month? What is next month's minimum payment due?

When applying for a credit card, you will fill out an application with the financial institution. Your application will be verified, and your credit report and credit scores will be reviewed. The credit card company will then decide if you are a good credit risk and if credit will be granted.

The *Equal Credit Opportunity Act (ECOA)* requires that all consumers are treated equally when applying for credit. If your application is denied, contact the financial institution for an explanation. You are entitled to know the specific details pertaining to credit rejection.

Contracts

Using credit involves certain responsibilities for you and the creditor. These responsibilities are spelled out in credit contracts and agreements. The terms outlined in a written agreement are legally binding. They can be enforced in courts of law if you or the creditor fails to carry out the terms of the contract. It is very important to understand exactly what you are agreeing to do before you sign any contract.

Read the contract thoroughly. Be sure all blank spaces have been filled. None should be left open for someone to fill later. Make sure the annual percentage rate and the dollar costs are stated clearly and accurately. Ask questions if there are any terms you do not fully understand.

Study the contract to find out what action the creditor can take if you pay late or fail to make a payment. Also, find out if you can pay in advance. If so, check to see if part of the finance charges will be refunded.

Watch for an acceleration clause. An **acceleration clause** is a statement in a contract that allows the creditor to require full and immediate payment of the entire balance if you miss a payment or fail to abide by the terms of the contract.

Be wary of add-on clauses that allow you to buy additional items before paying in full for goods you have already purchased. The clause may allow the seller to hold a security interest in the items purchased first until you pay for later purchases in full. For example, suppose you buy a washer and dryer; but before paying for them, you buy a refrigerator. The seller can hold title to the washer and dryer until you also pay for the refrigerator.

Read credit contracts thoroughly with particular attention to possible fees, penalties, and consequences of failing to carry out all the terms of the agreement. Do not sign until you fully understand all the terms and the obligations you are assuming.

Disclosures

By law, credit card offers must include certain disclosures or credit terms, as illustrated in Figure 6-4. Before accepting and using any of these cards, you need to read the fine print on any contract you sign and ask questions. Knowing the exact cost of credit can help you compare finance charges and find the best deal. It also helps you decide how much credit you can afford to use.

The APR must be disclosed. As discussed earlier, the APR is the cost of credit expressed on an annual basis. There is usually one rate for purchases and a higher rate for cash advances.

The issuing companies often offer an attractive introductory rate that lasts only three to six months. After this term, you pay the considerably higher regular rate. In this case, it is important to know how long the introductory rate lasts and what the regular rate is. In addition, know the terms of the rate. Can the credit card company raise the rate for any reason, such as missing a payment on this card?

Interest rates can be fixed or variable. A variable interest rate fluctuates with the ups and downs of the economy. It can start out low and reset to a higher rate. A fixed interest rate stays the same, although under certain conditions, such as a late payment, it can change. Most credit cards carry a variable rate, which can be quite high.

Some credit cards have a grace period. A **grace period** is the time between the billing date and the start of interest charges. You have that time to pay the full balance without interest. In a few states, a grace period is mandatory on any new charges made each month. Interest may only be calculated on

Ethics

It is unethical to purposely incur debt with the intention to file bankruptcy to avoid paying what is owed. Businesses extended you credit in good faith. If you do not pay your bills, the creditor suffers the loss of income. By filing bankruptcy, you will jeopardize your financial future and will have difficulty getting credit.

Annual percentage rate (APR) for purchases	2.9% until 11/1/-- after that, 14.9%
Other APRs	Cash-advance APR: 15.9% Balance-transfer APR: 15.9% Penalty rate: 23.9%. See explanation below.*
Variable-rate information	Your APR for purchase transactions may vary. The rate is determined monthly by adding 5.9% to the prime rate.**
Grace period for repayment of balances for purchases	25 days on average
Method of computing the balance for purchases	Average daily balance (excluding new purchases)
Annual fees	None
Minimum finance charge	$0.50

Transaction fee for cash advances: 3% of the amount advanced
Balance-transfer fee: 3% of the amount transferred
Late-payment fee: $25
Over-the-credit-limit fee: $25

* Explanation of penalty. If your payment arrives more than 10 days late two times within a six-month period, the penalty rate will apply.

** The prime rate used to determine your APR is the rate published in *The Wall Street Journal* on the 10th day of the prior month.

Federal Reserve Board
Adapted from Learn More About Your Offer, FederalReserve.gov.

Figure 6-4 On credit card application forms, disclosures are usually shown in a box similar to this one.

outstanding balances from the prior month. There are no interest charges on credit card balances that are paid in full by the due date each month.

Shop around for the best credit card deal. You can compare cards, interest rates, fees, and features online as well as by contacting individual credit card issuers.

Credit Card Statements

You will receive a monthly statement for each credit card account, as illustrated in Figure 6-5. These statements are forms you need to study and understand. Check the statement each month against your own record of charges, payments, and credits. In addition to the date, amount, and business related to each purchase, the statement should tell you the following information:

- date that payments are due
- minimum payment due
- new balance and previous balance

Account Statement

For the period ending Aug 9, 20-- Days in billing cycle: 31

Questions or lost/stolen card? Call Customer Service 1-800-555-1234

Account Number: XXXX-XXXX-XXXX-XXXX

Page: 1 of 4

Summary of Account Activity

Previous Balance	$0.00
Payments	$0.00
Other Credits/Adjustments	$0.00
Purchases	+$152.33
Cash Advances	$0.00
Fees Charged	$0.00
Interest Charged	$0.00
Total New Balance	**$152.33**
Past Due Amount	$0.00
Credit Limit	$3000.00
Credit Available	$2847.00

Payment Information

Total New Balance	**$152.33**
Minimum Payment Due	**$5.00**
Payment Due Date	**Sep 9, 20--**

Late Payment Warning: If we do not receive your minimum payment by the date listed above, you may have to pay a Late Payment Fee of up to $25.00.

Minimum Payment Warning: If you make only the minimum payment each period, you will pay more in interest and it will take you longer to pay off your balance. For example:

If you make no additional charges using this card and each month you pay...	You will pay off the balance shown on this Statement in about...	And you will end up paying an estimated total of...
Only the minimum payment	5 years	$275
$6	3 years	$217 (Savings=$58)

If you are experiencing financial difficulty and would like information about credit counseling or debt management services, you may call 1-800-123-4567.

Goodheart-Willcox Publisher

Figure 6-5 A credit card statement is usually issued monthly.

- total amount of new purchases, fees, and advances
- finance charges as a dollar amount, as well as the periodic and corresponding annual percentage rate
- total amount of payments and credits
- total amount of credit available on the account

Check the statement each month against your own record of charges, payments, and credits.

Lost or Stolen Cards

If a person's credit cards are lost or stolen, the law offers some protection. The cardholder is responsible for only $50 in charges per card if someone else uses the cards. However, if a cardholder notifies the companies that issued the cards before someone else uses them, the cardholder cannot be held responsible for any charges.

Be sure to report credit card thefts or losses as soon as possible by phone. Follow up with a letter or an e-mail. It is a good idea to keep a list of your credit cards on hand. Include the name of the issuer, account numbers, and telephone number for each card.

Subprime Credit Cards

Subprime credit cards are cards offered to people who have a poor credit history. Often they carry very high interest rates, large annual fees, sign-up fees, participation fees, late payment penalties, and other charges. The credit limits are generally low—$250 to $300. Some card issuers limit the credit to an amount equaling the deposit made in a collateral savings account. In other words, if you deposit $300, that is your credit limit; deposit $5,000, and that is your limit.

Subprime cards generally are easy to get, but they are very costly. For example, suppose you are issued a card with a $300 limit. It comes with a sign-up fee of $85, a monthly participation fee of $8, and an annual fee of $50. This leaves $157 of credit. Terms vary with different credit card issuers. Be wary because you almost always lose more than you gain with a subprime credit card. It is better to deal only with reputable creditors.

Checkpoint 6.2

1. What are the three common types of credit cards?
2. What are some items for which you may have to pay credit card fees?
3. What are three methods that may be used for calculating interest for credit cards?
4. What information is typically included on a credit card statement?
5. What are the typical features of a subprime credit card?

Build Your Vocabulary

As you progress through this course, develop a personal glossary of personal finance terms and add it to your portfolio. This will help you build your vocabulary and prepare you for a career. Write a definition for each of the following terms, and add it to your personal finance glossary.

credit card

cash advance

store credit card

travel and entertainment card

regular charge account

revolving credit account

acceleration clause

grace period

Section 6.3
Credit Management

Objectives

After studying this section, you will be able to:
- Outline the steps involved in managing credit.
- Identify steps to take in resolving credit problems.
- Describe types of easy-access credit.

Terms

collection agency

repossession

foreclosure

lien

garnishment

bankruptcy

Chapter 7 bankruptcy

Chapter 13 bankruptcy

credit counseling service

loan shark

easy-access credit

payday loans

pawnshop

rent-to-own

title loan

Managing Your Credit

Credit can make it possible for you to spend more than you earn—temporarily. With careful planning, credit can help you get more of the things you want when you want them. Without planning, credit can create serious, long-lasting financial and legal problems. The information in the following paragraphs will help you handle credit responsibly.

Know Your Financial Personality

A close look at your financial personality can help you decide when and if you can use credit safely. Your financial personality is a combination of your attitudes about money and your spending patterns. You express your financial personality by the way you handle cash and credit.

Financial personalities vary greatly. Some people spend money freely. Others find it hard to part with a dollar. Some people think through each purchase, while others buy on impulse. Answer the following questions to help you consider your money attitudes and habits.
- Do you find it easy to control spending?
- Do you save regularly?
- Do you follow a spending plan?
- Do you consider purchases carefully, particularly major purchases?

- Do you pay bills promptly?
- Do you buy only what you can afford?
- Do you make long-range financial plans?
- Do you handle financial matters with confidence?
- Do you see credit as a tool to use with care and caution?

If you answered "yes" to most of these questions, credit is probably a safe tool for you to use. If you answered "no" to most questions, credit may not be a good option for you.

Keep Track of Spending

Since many credit problems result from poor money management, the development of good management skills outlined in Chapter 2 can help you avoid serious credit problems. These management skills include creating a budget or spending plan. Try not to use more credit than you can pay off each month. You only pay interest charges if you carry a balance to the next month.

Since overspending is easy with a credit card, it is important to keep track of your charges and account balance. Save your receipts. You may want to keep a paper or an electronic log of credit charges so you always know how much you have spent. If you have more than one card, keep track of the total credit spent on all cards.

Look for Alternatives to Using Credit

Usually you have three alternatives to using credit. You may choose from among these options:

- not to buy
- to pay with savings
- to postpone buying now, and buy later with cash

The choice you make will depend on what you want to buy and what you want to achieve with your cash and your credit. Here are some questions to help you evaluate your choices.

How important is making the purchase? If you can do without something, you might be wise not to buy it. Is having the purchase now instead of later worth the extra price you pay for credit?

Are you willing to use all or some of your savings to buy now? Unless you have planned to use money you have saved to make the purchase, reducing or eliminating your savings could be risky. Often it is difficult to replace the savings used for unplanned purchases. You may be left unprepared for unexpected emergencies or financial difficulties.

Can you save your money and buy later? This choice will depend on how long you can wait to make the purchase. It will also depend on your ability to save money. Many people find it easier to make monthly credit payments than to put money in savings.

By waiting and saving, you may miss the satisfaction or pleasure of having what you want now. For example, suppose you want to take a vacation with friends. They are leaving next month for a week at the beach. According to your savings plan, you need three more months to save enough money for the trip. If you wait three months, you will not be able to share the vacation with your friends. In this case, you may decide to use credit to help you finance the vacation.

On the other hand, waiting may help you get more satisfaction from a purchase. Suppose you want to buy a pool table. You want it now, but you do not have enough money. Also, you are not sure what type of pool table you want. You decide to wait and save. As you are saving, you do some comparison shopping. You decide what features you want and where to get the best deal. When you finally buy the pool table, your satisfaction is greater than if you had rushed into a credit purchase. A waiting period can make the purchase more valuable to you.

Check Your Credit Report Regularly

If you make a habit of checking credit reports regularly, you can correct any errors before they cost you a loan, an apartment, or even a job. Checking these reports is the best way to make sure no one has applied for a loan or credit card in your name.

By law, you are entitled to receive one free copy of your credit report from each of the major credit reporting agencies every 12 months. You may receive the report in paper or electronic form.

If you find an error or an incomplete entry in a credit report, make sure you correct it right away. You should immediately report the error to all three credit bureaus, Experian, Equifax, and TransUnion, and request that the incorrect information be removed. Go to the agency website for instructions on how to challenge negative information. You may need to provide copies of any documents that back up your claim.

Credit Problems

Used unwisely, credit can lead to serious financial difficulties. The chart in Figure 6-6 lists some of the danger signals that warn credit users of trouble ahead. The consequences of having a poor credit report are severe and impact more than the ability to get credit. A person with a low credit score may:

- be unable to get loans and credit cards;
- pay higher interest rates for credit;
- have fewer housing choices because property owners check credit reports and reject people with low scores;

Credit Warning Signals
• Stalling one creditor to pay another.
• Receiving past due notices with billing statements.
• Paying only the minimum required each month.
• Charging more than the amount you can pay each month.
• Not paying off credit account balances.
• Routinely running out of money before payday.
• Using credit cards or cash advances for everyday living expenses.

Goodheart-Willcox Publisher

Figure 6-6 Beware of these warning signals when using credit.

- have fewer job prospects because employers avoid job candidates with financial problems; and
- pay higher insurance premiums.

Accurate negative information, such as missed or late payments, may remain on your report for seven years. Bankruptcies may remain for up to 10 years.

When debtors fail to pay, lenders and businesses will try to recover what they are owed. The following paragraphs discuss some of the actions they may take.

Collection Agencies

When debts go unpaid, businesses and creditors often hire collection agencies. A **collection agency** is a business that specializes in debt collection. Often, it is paid with a portion of the money collected. In order to get full payments from you, collection agencies use every lawful means possible. The nonstop pressure they apply causes many debtors to pay in full.

Repossession of Property

Repossession is the taking of collateral when a borrower fails to repay a loan. For example, companies that repossess autos may tow the cars away without notice. The cars are auctioned and the money goes toward paying the debt.

Perhaps the most serious type of repossession is foreclosure. **Foreclosure** is the forced sale of property. The property, usually a home, is taken by the lender because the debtor failed to make loan payments. The residents receive a court order to remove their possessions and leave by a specific date.

The two main types of foreclosure are judicial foreclosure and nonjudicial foreclosure. In *judicial foreclosure*, the lender sells the property under court supervision. In *nonjudicial foreclosure*, the lender is allowed to advertise and sell the property at a public auction without court supervision. Each state specifies the rules and procedures to follow in a nonjudicial foreclosure.

Liens

A **lien** is a legal claim on a borrower's property by a creditor who is owed money. For example, if a person fails to pay state taxes, the state can put a lien on his or her home. To sell or take out a loan on the home, the debtor must pay off the lien first.

Garnishment of Wages

The court may order garnishment of a debtor's earnings. **Garnishment** is a legal procedure requiring a portion of the debtor's pay to be set aside by the person's employer to pay creditors. This reduces the amount of the debtor's paychecks. Some employers fire employees who have repeated garnishments.

Bankruptcy

For those who are overwhelmed by debt, the US Bankruptcy Code allows for a fresh start. **Bankruptcy** is a legal state in which the courts excuse a debtor from repaying some or all debt. In return, the debtor must give up certain assets and possessions. The most common types of bankruptcy are Chapter 7 and Chapter 13.

Chapter 7 bankruptcy is the most common type of bankruptcy filed. A person must pass a *means test* before being approved for Chapter 7 bankruptcy. The means test involves the court looking at the person's income and debt and determining if he or she will be approved to file for Chapter 7. If approved, the court declares the person unable to meet financial obligations. Most debts are discharged or forgiven. This is also referred to as *straight bankruptcy* or *liquidation bankruptcy*. The court then takes and sells the debtor's property and possessions. Proceeds from the sale are divided among the creditors. You may be able to keep you home and your car as these are basic needs for survival.

Chapter 13 bankruptcy permits debtors with regular incomes to pay all or a portion of their debts under the protection and supervision of the court. The court sets up a three- to five-year repayment schedule. It also establishes the monthly amount to be paid toward debts. Once the court accepts the debtor's petition, creditors may not take action against the debtor. This plan has three advantages over straight bankruptcy. The debtor fulfills credit obligations,

Case Study

Using Credit

Chiyo graduated from college recently and has a steady job. She wants the convenience of charging purchases, so she opens a credit card account.

Chiyo's first credit card bill is almost $600. Since she did not keep track of her charges, the bill is a surprise. Her paycheck is only $1,035 a month after deductions. After paying rent and other expenses, she has only $30 left to pay on her credit account each month.

Chiyo did not need most of the credit card purchases. It takes her 24 months to pay off the debt. She pays over $118 in finance charges.

Damian looks at credit as a useful tool. He realizes the importance of establishing credit so he can get loans in the future. Besides, he does not think it is realistic to buy everything with cash.

Although Damian is happy to have his credit card, he is a little afraid of using it. His family had some debt problems when he was younger.

Damian uses his credit card sparingly and keeps track of his charges. He limits his overall debt to an amount he can repay. He uses credit only for things he really needs. His first purchase is a pair of waterproof boots, which he buys on sale. Damian uses his credit card because he does not have enough cash. If he waited until payday, the boots would no longer be on sale. By using credit wisely, Damian saves $20.

Case Review

1. How does offering credit work in the interest of sellers?
2. How can the use of credit work for consumers? How can it create problems?
3. What advice would you give Chiyo for the future use of credit?
4. What did you learn from Damian's example?
5. How can consumers enjoy the benefits and avoid the problems of using credit?

keeps most of his or her own property and possessions, and maintains a reasonably sound credit rating.

Some types of debt cannot be wiped out by declaring bankruptcy. These include most student loans, alimony, child support, and many types of taxes. Also, the *Bankruptcy Abuse Prevention and Consumer Protection Act of 2005* placed restrictions on discharging credit card debt through bankruptcy.

The consequences of filing bankruptcy can haunt a debtor for many years. Once a court declares that a person is bankrupt, a report stays in the credit records for 10 years. The person may be denied loans or credit cards or only be granted credit at inflated interest rates. The person may be denied a job, a business loan, insurance, or housing by anyone who sees the credit report. Bankruptcy should be considered a last resort.

Informing Creditors

If you have trouble paying your bills, notify creditors promptly. Many reputable creditors will work with you. They may help you by renegotiating repayment schedules or setting up a repayment program you can handle. They may be willing to extend your repayment schedules to lower the size of your monthly payments. Of course, this will cost you more in credit charges in the long run, but it may help you get through a difficult period.

The quicker you realize you are having financial problems, the quicker and easier it will be to correct them. It pays to tackle these problems before they get beyond your control. With a sound financial spending and savings plan, some people can correct their own financial problems. However, when financial problems get out of control, it is time to look for outside help. One reliable source of help for people with credit problems is a credit counseling service. A **credit counseling service** is an organization that provides debt and financial management advice and services to people with debt problems at little or no cost.

The National Foundation for Consumer Credit sponsors several hundred credit counseling services throughout the United States and Canada. The service helps a debtor with a stable income work out a practical financial program for repaying debts. The service also helps the debtor plan and control current expenses to avoid further debts.

When debtors are very deep in debt, the counseling service offers another alternative. It tries to arrange new repayment plans with creditors. If creditors agree, the debtor gives the counseling service a set amount from each paycheck, and the service pays the creditors. Credit counseling services of this type help about five of every six applicants.

Unfortunately, some of the businesses that claim to be nonprofit credit counseling services are not. Be cautious of "credit doctors" and for-profit credit repair clinics that promise to fix your credit rating for a fee. These include debt negotiation or debt adjusting businesses that charge high fees. The fees cause their clients to fall deeper into debt. A company that charges high fees or demands that the debtor pay them rather than their creditors should be avoided. Debtors should pay little or nothing for the help they receive. Claims that are too good to be true indicate a problem. The claim might be a guarantee that they can make debt disappear or dramatically reduce total debt. Also be suspicious of those who claim an ability to remove accurate negative information from credit reports.

Repossession Agents

Repossession agents are often contracted by creditors who cannot recover money owed to them. They locate or recover personal property, such as cars, boats, and appliances, sold under a security agreement.

Consumers can contact their local consumer protection agency to get a referral to a reputable consumer credit counseling service. The US Trustee Program of the Department of Justice maintains a list of credit counseling agencies approved for pre-bankruptcy counseling. The list is found on their website. It also is a good idea to check with the local Better Business Bureau or the state attorney general's office for reports of consumer complaints against specific companies.

Easy-Access Credit Trap

You have probably heard the term loan shark. A **loan shark** is someone who lends money at excessive rates of interest. Loan sharks usually use predatory lending tactics and offer easy-access credit. **Easy-access credit** is a short-term loan at a high interest rate that is granted regardless of the borrower's credit history. Even people who are poor credit risks can get these loans if the practice is considered legal in their state. Types of easy-access credit include the following.

- *Payday loans.* A **payday loan** is a short-term, high-interest loan that usually must be repaid on the borrower's next payday. Repayment is guaranteed by the borrower's personal check at the time of the loan or by access to the borrower's bank account. Payday loans carry extremely high finance charges, but some states have laws that limit them.

- *Pawnshops.* A **pawnshop** is a business that gives customers high-interest loans with personal property, such as jewelry, held as collateral. Some pawnshops offer payday loans, too.

- *Rent-to-own agreements.* **Rent-to-own** is an arrangement in which a consumer pays rent for the use of a product and eventually owns it. The advantage is little or no initial payment. The disadvantage to the consumer is paying much more than the product's purchase price by the time the final payment is made.

- *Title loans.* A **title loan** is a short-term loan made using a borrower's car as collateral. The cost of these loans is high, and the borrower risks losing his or her car.

Here is an example of how easy-access credit differs from legitimate sources of credit. Suppose you borrow $1,000 by using a credit card cash advance. The APR is 21.99 percent. That is equivalent to a monthly interest rate of 1.833 percent (APR divided by 12). If you repaid the money in a month, you would pay an $18.33 finance charge. Contrast that to what you would pay if you borrowed from a payday loan company. Finance charges are often $15 or more for every $100 borrowed. At this rate, you would pay $150 to borrow $1,000. You would have to repay $1,150 in two weeks.

If you do not have the money, like many borrowers, you can roll the loan over for another two weeks for an additional finance charge. You owe the lender another $150. After one month, you have paid $300 in fees. What is the annual equivalent of this interest rate? If you continued to roll over the loan for a year, the APR would be 350 percent, or $3,600!

Checkpoint 6.3

1. What are some alternatives to using credit?
2. How can consumers obtain free copies of credit reports? How often are free copies available?
3. What is a collection agency?
4. Why should you notify your creditors promptly if you have trouble paying your bills?
5. Why is Chapter 7 bankruptcy sometimes called liquidation bankruptcy?

Build Your Vocabulary

As you progress through this course, develop a personal glossary of personal finance terms and add it to your portfolio. This will help you build your vocabulary and prepare you for a career. Write a definition for each of the following terms, and add it to your personal finance glossary.

collection agency

repossession

foreclosure

lien

garnishment

bankruptcy

Chapter 7 bankruptcy

Chapter 13 bankruptcy

credit counseling service

loan shark

easy-access credit

payday loan

pawnshop

rent-to-own

title loan

Consumer Protection

Objectives

After studying this section, you will be able to:

- Summarize the laws that govern the use of credit.
- Identify various types of financial fraud and describe ways to protect yourself against these frauds.

Terms

credit fraud
identity theft
phishing

Protecting Your Credit

It is important to carefully review your credit card statements as well as your credit scores on a regular basis. Errors do happen, and if they happen to you, it will be important to take corrective action as soon as possible.

Over the years a number of federal laws have been passed to protect consumers when they use credit. The key points of the most important credit legislation are outlined in this section. Many state governments have also passed laws to protect consumers from illegal or unfair lending practices.

Truth in Lending Act

The *Truth in Lending Act*, passed in 1969, requires creditors to tell consumers what credit will cost them before they use it. Under this law, credit contracts and agreements must include:

- the amount financed or borrowed;
- the total number, amount, and due dates of payments;
- the finance charge in dollar amount and annual percentage rate;
- all charges not included in the finance charge;
- penalties or charges for late payment, default, or prepayment; and
- a description of any security held by the creditor.

For merchandise purchased on credit, creditors must provide additional information. This includes a description of the merchandise, the cash price, the deferred payment price, and the down payment or trade-in. The Truth in Lending Act also prohibits creditors from issuing credit cards you have not requested. The Truth in Lending Act takes precedence over state laws regarding credit and lending.

Equal Credit Opportunity Act

The *Equal Credit Opportunity Act*, passed in 1975, prohibits credit grantors from discriminating against consumers on the basis of sex, marital

Lenders who violate the Truth in Lending Act are responsible for any money damages incurred by consumers. Additionally, attorney's fees and court costs must be paid by the lending institution, not by injured parties.

status, race, national origin, religion, age, or the receipt of public assistance. This means credit can be denied only for financial reasons and not for any of the factors listed above. When applicants are turned down, creditors must provide a written explanation of why credit was denied.

Fair Credit Reporting Act

Passed in 1971 and revised in 1977, the *Fair Credit Reporting Act* requires accuracy and privacy of information contained in credit reports. If you are refused credit because of information supplied by a credit reporting agency, this law gives you the right to:

- receive the name and address of the reporting agency that sent the report;
- find out from the reporting agency what facts are on file, the source of the information, and who has received the information;
- require a recheck of any information you find to be false;
- receive a corrected report if errors are found; and
- require the agency to send the corrected report to all creditors who received false information.

Fair Credit Billing Act

The *Fair Credit Billing Act*, passed in 1975, protects consumers against unfair billing practices. It outlines the procedures to follow in resolving billing errors or disputes. The law requires creditors to send customers a

marco mayer/Shutterstock.com

Under the Fair Credit Billing Act, consumers have a certain amount of time to resolve billing disputes.

written explanation of steps to take when questions arise concerning bills. The customer has 60 days after receiving a bill to notify the creditor of an error. The creditor must answer within 30 days. Within 90 days, the creditor must either correct the bill or explain if it is accurate. Creditors may take no collection action on amounts in question until billing disputes are resolved. However, the customer must pay any amount not in question.

Electronic Funds Transfer Act

Electronic Funds Transfer (EFT) systems use electronic impulses to activate financial transactions instead of cash, checks, or paper records. The *Electronic Funds Transfer Act* protects consumers in these transactions in the following ways.

- Prohibits the distribution of unrequested EFT cards. You receive a card only if you ask for it.
- Requires issuers of EFT cards to provide cardholders with written information outlining their rights and responsibilities for the card and its use.
- Limits to $50 the liability for unauthorized transfers. The cardholder must notify the issuer of card loss or misuse within two business days.
- Requires issuers to provide cardholders with printed receipts of EFT transactions.
- Requires issuers to promptly investigate and correct EFT errors.

Fair Debt Collection Practices Act

Passed in 1978, the *Fair Debt Collection Practices Act* protects consumers against unfair methods of collecting debts. According to this law, debt collectors may not:

- reveal or publicize a debtor's debt to other people;
- contact debtors at inconvenient times (before 8 a.m. or after 9 p.m.) or places (such as work);
- use threats or abusive language;
- make annoying, repeated, or anonymous phone calls;
- make false or misleading statements about the collector's identity or the consequences of nonpayment; or
- collect unauthorized fees or charge debtors for calls and telegrams.

Preservation of Consumers' Claims and Defenses Ruling

The *Preservation of Consumers' Claims and Defenses Ruling* was issued by the Federal Trade Commission. It protects debtors from being forced to pay for goods and services when they have a legitimate dispute with the seller of those goods or services.

This applies when a retailer sells consumer credit obligations or contracts to a third party creditor. The consumer then owes the third party. If the goods or services purchased with credit are unsatisfactory, the debtor still owes the third party rather than the seller. For this reason, the seller does not feel obligated to correct any problems with the goods or services.

This ruling greatly limits the *holder-in-due-course doctrine.* That doctrine says the holder of a consumer contract has a right to collect a debt regardless of any unfair practices on the part of the seller. Here is an example to show how the rule protects you. Suppose you buy a $500 TV from the Viewing Center. You sign an installment contract calling for 18 monthly payments. The Viewing Center offers credit through a sales finance company. Therefore, you owe the finance company rather than the seller.

After the television is delivered, you find that it does not work. You can get sound but no picture. When you complain, the seller refuses to correct the problem. You threaten nonpayment. The seller says that is not the Viewing Center's problem because you owe the finance company.

Economics in Action

Excessive Credit and the Economy

Excessive use of credit can throw the economy off balance and foster inflation. When consumers use credit to buy goods and services, it increases the demand for whatever they are buying. If the demand increases faster than the supply, prices will increase. When governments and businesses join consumers in the excessive use of credit, demand surpasses supply and inflation results. The economy is weakened, and fewer job opportunities exist.

You complain to the finance company, but they tell you the television is the seller's responsibility. Legally, you owe the finance company regardless of the seller's performance.

The Preservation of Consumers' Claims and Defenses Ruling protects you in this type of situation. Under the ruling, you have a right to a legal defense in court if you refuse to pay a creditor because you have a dispute with a seller.

Bankruptcy Abuse Prevention and Consumer Protection Act

The main goal of the Bankruptcy Abuse Prevention and Consumer Protection Act, passed in 2005, was to make the bankruptcy system fairer to both debtors and creditors. However, it has been criticized for disproportionately benefiting the credit card industry.

The law made filing for Chapter 7 bankruptcy more difficult. Those who are allowed to file must pass a means test that takes into account factors such as income and assets. Those who do not pass the means test must file for Chapter 13 bankruptcy, which requires some repayment of debt. Another provision of the law requires debtors to get credit and financial counseling before filing for bankruptcy.

Reorganization, in reference to bankruptcy, is the process of creating a repayment plan to repay debts without liquidating property.

Credit Fraud

Credit fraud is the fraudulent use of someone else's credit information. It usually involves purchasing goods or services and charging them to an innocent person. You can protect yourself through prevention and by quick action if you become a victim.

Identity theft is a form of credit fraud that involves stealing someone's personal information and using the information to commit theft or fraud. Figure 6-7 lists common ways identity thieves can steal your personal information. If someone steals your information, he or she can use it and your name to access funds in your bank or investment accounts. The thief could also write checks on your bank account, make charges on your credit cards, and sign up for cellular phone service.

Identity theft is increasing rapidly. Victims can incur serious financial losses. They also have the inconvenient and time-consuming task of stopping the theft and reestablishing their credit. The costs of just undoing the damage can be substantial.

Identity theft is often committed online using pop-up messages or spam e-mails. Spam e-mails usually come from companies as a form of advertising. Spam e-mails sent by criminals may be phishing schemes.

Phishing is a crime committed online with e-mails that seek your personal information. The phisher claims to be a business where you may

---

Ways Identity Thieves Can Obtain Your Personal Information

- Stealing your wallet or purse.
- Stealing your mail and gaining access to bank statements, credit card statements, and brokerage account statements.
- Going through your trash and dumpster diving.
- Stealing personal information from business databases (for example, businesses such as medical care providers, lenders, and car dealers often have much of your personal information on file).
- Hacking into your personal computer or fraudulent e-mails.
- Bribing people who have access to your personal information.
- Using a cell phone camera to take pictures of your driver's license, credit card, or debit card.
- Diverting your mail to another address by filling a change of address form with the Post Office.
- Stealing your PIN at a gas station or grocery store point-of-sale (POS) system.
- Cloning your credit card number at restaurants and other businesses where sales are rung up out of your sight.
- Using a skimmer, which is a hard-to-detect electronic reader that criminals place on top of card readers that are built into gas pumps. The skimmer is able to copy card and pin numbers, giving criminals free access to victims' accounts without interfering with the legitimate purchase of gas.

Goodheart-Willcox Publisher

Figure 6-7 There are many ways a person's identity can be stolen.

have an account, such as a bank or credit card company. If you open the e-mail, you will be redirected to a website. That website appears to be the financial institution's site, but it is actually a fake site created to collect your information. The message will ask you to confirm, update, or verify the account by giving personal information, such as your name, Social Security number, credit card numbers, passwords, bank account information, or other financial data. Phishing e-mails usually look official. If you provide the information, the phisher uses it to sell your identity or to run up bills and commit other crimes in your name. For your own protection, do not to reply to these e-mails or click on any link they provide. This crime may also be carried out on the phone. Be wary of any call asking for sensitive personal information.

The loss or theft of a wallet can present similar problems if credit cards and identifying information end up in the wrong hands. Ways you can protect yourself against this type of crime are listed below.

- Do not carry your Social Security card or give your Social Security number if other ID will be enough. You may have to disclose your Social Security number when you get a new job, file tax returns, open a credit account, and apply for insurance or financial aid. If your school uses Social Security numbers on student identification cards, ask if something else can be used.

- Do not throw away credit card receipts or monthly statements without shredding them.

- Do not give your Social Security, bank account, or credit card numbers to anyone without knowing that the information will be secure. Also make sure the request for the information is necessary and authentic.

- Periodically, order a copy of your credit report from a credit-reporting agency. Promptly resolve any errors or negative results in the report.

- Carry only the credit cards you really need and use.

- Make photocopies of all the items in your wallet—including the front and back of the cards. This will be very helpful if your wallet is lost or stolen and you need to notify creditors, your bank, or other financial accounts.

- Keep a list of all your credit cards with account numbers, expiration dates, and toll-free customer service phone numbers. You will need this information in case of loss or theft.

If you become a victim of identity theft or lose a wallet, move quickly to minimize the damage. Call credit card companies and other issuers promptly to report missing cards, and follow the call with written confirmation. Contact your bank if you are missing checks, debit cards, or credit cards. File a police report if you are a victim of theft.

If your Social Security card or number has been stolen, contact the Social Security Administration's fraud line at (800) 269-0271 or www.ssa.gov. If your identity is stolen, contact the Federal Trade Commission's Identity Theft Clearinghouse and the Identity Theft Resource Center. These two government websites provide information on financial fraud, on preventing it, and on remedies if you become a victim.

Debt Counselors
Debt counselors help clients resolve financial difficulties. They provide financial counseling about debt, credit, money management, budgeting, and housing issues.

Careers in Finance

What Do Loan Officers Do?

Loan officers evaluate, approve, deny, or recommend approval of loan applications for people and businesses. They assist customers in completing applications and explaining the details of a loan. **Loan officers** typically:

- meet with loan applicants to gather personal information and answer questions;
- explain different types of loans to applicants;
- check the credit scores of applicants;
- verify the earnings of applicants;
- analyze and evaluate the applicant's finances to decide if the applicant should get the loan; and
- approve loan applications or refer them to management for a decision.

What Is It Like to Work as a Loan Officer?

Most **loan officers** are employed by commercial banks, credit unions, mortgage companies, and related financial institutions. Most commercial, mortgage, and consumer loan officers work full time. Some **loan officers** work on a commission basis.

What Education and Skills Are Needed to Be a Loan Officer?

- bachelor degree in business or a related field
- professional license
- excellent communication and listening skills
- customer service skills
- decision-making skills
- attention to detail
- math skills
- computer skills

Checkpoint 6.4

1. What federal law requires lenders to fully disclose to consumers the terms and total cost of credit before a credit agreement is finalized?
2. What federal law was passed to eliminate abusive collection practices by debt collectors?
3. What federal law prohibits credit grantors from discriminating against consumers?
4. Identify four ways identity thieves can steal your personal information.
5. Identify three ways you can protect yourself from identity thieves.

Build Your Vocabulary

As you progress through this course, develop a personal glossary of personal finance terms and add it to your portfolio. This will help you build your vocabulary and prepare you for a career. Write a definition for each of the following terms and add it to your personal finance glossary.

credit fraud

identify theft

phishing

Chapter Summary

Section 6.1 Using Consumer Credit

- Using credit has both advantages and disadvantages. Credit allows individuals to buy goods now and pay for them later, but it may lead to serious debt if misused. Knowing when to use it and understanding the different types of credit can help consumers enjoy the benefits of using credit and avoid problems.

- There are two basic types of consumer credit: closed-end credit and open-end credit. An example of closed-end credit is a car loan and open-end credit is a credit card.

- There are two basic types of loans: secured loans and unsecured loans. A secured loan is a loan that requires collateral. An unsecured loan is made on the strength of a signature alone.

- Creditors want evidence that you can and will pay for your debts. To establish a sound credit rating, a person can get a job, open a savings account and a checking account, and apply for a credit card.

- It is smart to use credit in some situations, such as taking advantage of a sale, but not in others, such as buying items that you do not need or cannot afford.

- The cost for the use of credit is based primarily on the interest rate charged, the amount of credit used, and the length of the repayment period.

Section 6.2 Using Credit Cards

- Credit cards allow the cardholder to buy goods and services on a time-payment plan. There are three common types of credit cards: general-purpose cards, store credit cards, and travel and entertainment cards.

- It is important to shop around for a credit card just as you would shop for goods and services. Factors to consider when shopping for a credit card include the annual interest rate, credit limit, fees, penalties, and other terms of the credit contract.

- Subprime credit cards are offered to people who have a poor credit history. The cards often carry very high interest rates, large annual fees, and other charges.

Section 6.3 Credit Management

- Credit can make it possible for you to spend more than you earn. With careful management, using credit can be beneficial. However, without careful management, credit can create serious, long-lasting financial and legal problems.

- With a sound spending and savings plan, some people can correct their own financial problems. However, others may get help with credit problems from a credit counseling service.

- Easy-access credit consists of short-term loans at high interest rates. Examples are loans such as payday loans, pawnshop loans, title loans, and rent-to-own agreements.

Section 6.4 Consumer Protection

- A number of federal laws have been passed to protect consumers when they use credit. Many state governments also have laws to protect consumers from illegal or unfair lending practices.

- Credit fraud usually involves purchasing goods or services and charging them to another person. Identity theft and phishing are two common types of credit fraud.

Check Your Personal Finance IQ

Now that you have finished the chapter, see what you learned about personal finance by taking the chapter posttest. If you do not have a smartphone, visit the G-W Learning companion website.

G-W Learning mobile site: www.m.g-wlearning.com

G-W Learning companion website: www.g-wlearning.com

Review Your Knowledge

1. How does a credit transaction differ from a cash transaction?
2. Explain the difference between closed-end and open-end credit.
3. What steps can you take to build a sound financial reputation?
4. What is the function of a credit reporting agency?
5. What factors influence a person's credit score?
6. What is wage garnishment?
7. Explain the difference between variable interest rates and fixed interest rates.
8. What are subprime credit cards?
9. What is the main purpose of the Fair Credit Billing Act?
10. What is phishing and how it is typically performed?

Apply Your Knowledge

11. How can the use of credit have a positive influence on the economy?
12. How can the use of too much credit contribute to inflation?
13. Suppose you buy a 10-speed bike using credit. After two weeks, the bike only runs on five speeds. Although the bike has a two-year warranty, the seller refuses to do anything about the problem. Your credit contract has been sold to a finance company, and the seller has been paid. Describe your rights if you refuse to pay the creditor.
14. How can understanding your financial personality help you decide when and if you can use credit safely? How would you describe your financial personality?
15. Why do you think so many students and young people today are incurring so much debt? What are some steps that could be taken to deal with this problem?
16. At what age do you think a person should first receive a credit card? Why?
17. What do you think is the best way for a young person to establish credit?
18. Assume you have a credit card with a balance of $2,000 and an annual interest rate of 21 percent. What would you do to pay the balance off within a two-year period?

19. What are some credit and financial crimes you have read about or have encountered?

20. Assume you have a checking account, a savings account, a credit card, and a debit card. What are some ways you can protect yourself from identify thieves?

 ## Teamwork

In this chapter, you learned about the pros and cons of credit. Working with a teammate, create your own list of pros and cons for the use of credit by teenagers. Make a chart that you can use as a visual aid to discuss with your class.

G-W Learning Mobile Site

Visit the G-W Learning mobile site to complete the chapter pretest and posttest and to practice vocabulary using e-flash cards. If you do not have a smartphone, visit the G-W Learning companion website to access these features.

G-W Learning mobile site: www.m.g-wlearning.com

G-W Learning companion website: www.g-wlearning.com

Common Core

College and Career Readiness

CTE Career Ready Practices. Successful employees also are responsible citizens. Make a list of five things that you can do to show that your are financially responsible when using credit.

Listening. Engage in a conversation with someone you have not spoken with before. Ask the person how he or she manages personal credit. Actively listen to what that person is sharing. Build on his or her ideas by sharing your own. Try this again with other people you have not spoken to before. How clearly were the different people able to articulate themselves? How do you think having a conversation with someone you do not normally speak with is different from a conversation you might have with a friend or family member you speak with every day?

Speaking. Etiquette is the art of using good manners in any situation. Etiquette is especially important when making phone calls since the two parties cannot interact face-to-face. Create a script for a telephone conversation to convince a loan officer that you are a good candidate for an automobile loan. Make a list of the important facts that support why you should be granted a loan. Use please and thank you when appropriate. Ask a classmate to assume the role of the loan officer. Practice your telephone conversation. How would you rate your use of good manners? How does your classmate rate your speech.

Web Connect

How difficult is it for teens to obtain a credit card? Visit the website of a local bank and read the application process for credit cards. Do they offer credit cards to teens? What are the qualifications? Share your findings with the class.

College and Career Readiness

College and Career Readiness Portfolio

Your e-portfolio may contain documents you have created. Scanned images of items, such as awards and certificates, may also be included. You need to decide which file formats you will use for electronic documents. You could use the default format to save the documents. For example, you could use Microsoft Word format for letters and essays. You could use Microsoft Excel format for worksheets. Someone reviewing your e-portfolio would need programs that open these formats to view your files. Another option would be to save or scan documents to PDF (portable document format) files. These files can be viewed with Adobe Reader and some other programs. Having all the files in the same format can make viewing the files easier for someone who wants to review your portfolio.

1. Search the Internet and read articles to learn more about PDF documents. Download a free program, such as Adobe Reader, that opens these files.

2. Practice saving a Microsoft Word document as a PDF file. (Use the **Save As** command. Refer to the program **Help** if needed.)

3. Create a list of the format(s) you will use to store your electronic files.

Case Study

A case study presentation may be part of a Career and Technical Student Organization (CTSO) competitive event. There may be two parts to this event: the objective test and a performance portion of the case.

The activity may be a decision-making scenario for which your team will provide a solution. You will be presented with a case situation in which issues that people face in business must be addressed. The presentation will be interactive with the judges.

To prepare for this event, complete the following activities.

1. Conduct an Internet search for *case studies*. Your team should select a case that seems appropriate to use as a practice activity. Look for a case that is no more than a page long. Read the case and discuss it with your team members. What are the important points of the case?

2. Make notes on index cards about important points to remember. Team members should exchange note cards so that each evaluates the other person's notes. Use these notes to study. You may also be able to use these notes during the event.

3. Assign each team member a role for the presentation. Ask your teacher to play the role of Competition Judge as your team reviews the case.

4. Each team member should introduce him- or herself, review the case, make suggestions for the case, and conclude with a summary.

5. After the presentation is complete, ask for feedback from your instructor. You may also consider having a student audience to listen and give feedback.

Chapter 7
Investing and Estate Planning

Investing is purchasing financial products or valuable items with the goal of increasing wealth over time, in spite of possible loss. You invest in order to create wealth. Investments generally offer greater returns or profit on your money than savings. However, they also present an element of risk. With careful and consistent investing, you can have money for things such as education, travel, retirement, and an overall increase in the standard of living. You can also pass a part of your wealth to the next generation. In this chapter, you will study the reasons for investing, the types of investments, retirement plans, estate planning, and wills.

Focus on Finance

Investments

Making investments is sometimes easier said than done. If you do not have a job, you may think you cannot start a portfolio and make an investment. However, the truth is, even if you have $100 you can make an investment and start a portfolio. How can you do that? There are several investments you can make to get started.

Savings Bonds. Perhaps someone has given you a Series EE US Savings Bond as a gift at some point in your life. The interest rate on these bonds compounds semiannually for 30 years. However, you can cash them before the full 30 years passes.

Treasury Bonds. Treasury bonds are interest-bearing bonds that pay semiannual interest. Maturity and interest rates may fluctuate.

Stocks. Technically, there is no minimum number of shares you must purchase from a publicly traded company.

Mutual Funds. Mutual funds are a great way to create retirement funds or educational funds. Many banks sell mutual funds.

Think big, even if you must start small. Before you know it, you will be on your way to creating an investment portfolio that will get you started on a solid financial path that will help you reach your goals.

College and Career Readiness

Reading Prep. Before reading this chapter, flip through the pages and make notes of the major headings. Analyze the structure of the relationships of the headings with the concepts in the chapter.

Check Your Personal Finance IQ

Before you begin the chapter, see what you already know about personal finance by taking the chapter pretest. If you do not have a smartphone, visit the G-W Learning companion website.

G-W Learning mobile site: www.m.g-wlearning.com

G-W Learning companion website: www.g-wlearning.com

Sections

Section 7.1 Investments

Section 7.2 Investment Strategies and Estate Planning

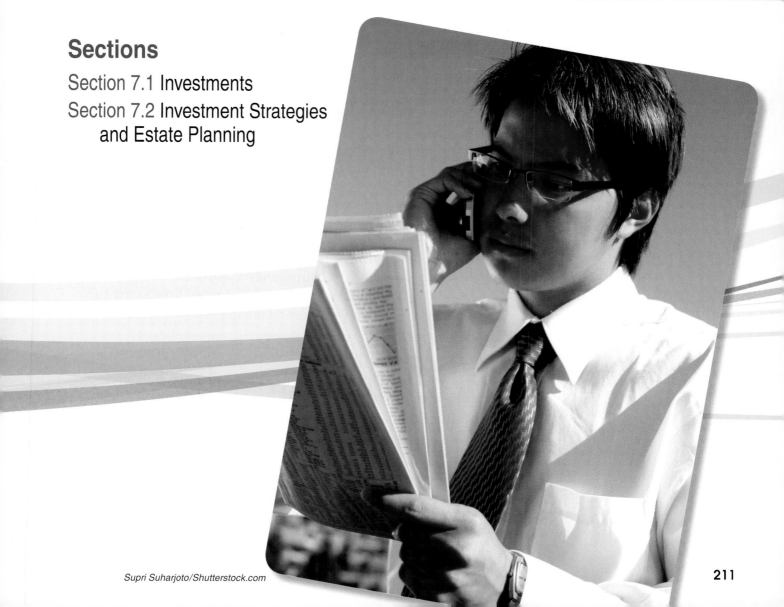

Section 7.1
Investments

Objectives

After studying this section, you will be able to:

- Explain the role of investments in overall financial planning.
- Identify the various types of investment choices.

Terms

investing	securities exchange
capital gain	stockbroker
capital loss	bond
stock	mutual fund
dividend	net asset value (NAV)
common stock	money market fund
proxy	bull market
preferred stock	bear market
stock trade	

Deciding to Invest

Understanding when to put money into savings and when to invest will help you make sound financial decisions. **Investing** is purchasing a financial product or valuable item with the goal of increasing wealth over time in spite of possible loss. Investments generally offer greater returns or profit on your money than savings. However, they also present an element of risk.

As you read in Chapter 5, savings deposited at insured financial institutions are guaranteed against loss up to $250,000 per person for accounts at one financial institution. However, investments are not insured. When you invest, you risk losing some or all of your money. Careful investing for long-term financial goals may reduce risk. Gains usually exceed losses over time.

You are ready to invest when you meet all the following conditions.

- You pay your essential living expenses and have money left over.
- You do not have excessive debt.
- You are not paying finance charges, which may be higher than any earnings on an investment.
- You have adequate insurance protection.
- You have an emergency fund with savings of six to eight months of living expenses.

It is a good idea to set aside a given amount to invest every week or every month. An investment plan is an important step to meeting long-term goals and achieving financial security. People invest for many reasons, as discussed in the following paragraphs.

Stephen Coburn/Shutterstock.com

Investing comes with high risks and the possibility of high reward.

Increase Wealth

Building wealth is a goal that many people aspire to achieve. Having enough money to be financially secure enables a person to buy items that make life comfortable. Building wealth requires a plan, and investments can help you reach that goal. Many people invest with the intention of holding on to the investment and allowing its value to grow over time and increase wealth. Growth, or *appreciation*, refers to an increase in the value of an investment. Various types of investments grow at different rates.

Earn a Steady Income

Some types of investments provide a steady stream of income to the investor, such as interest received from bonds issued by the federal government. Other types of investments can also provide steady income. For example, owners of rental property can earn income from rents collected from tenants.

Beat Inflation

Inflation reduces the value of money and the return on investments. Due to inflation, a dollar will buy less next year than it did this year. To beat inflation, the rate of return earned on an investment needs to be higher than the rate of inflation.

Take Advantage of Tax Benefits

The earnings from some investments are tax exempt, such as interest received from bonds issued by state and local governments. When earnings from an investment are not taxed, the investor has more money available for personal use or to make additional investments.

Some investments are tax deferred, such as most retirement accounts. A *tax-deferred investment* is one where no taxes are paid as the investment earns income and grows in value. Instead, taxes are paid only when withdrawals are made from the account. As a result, the values of tax-deferred investments usually grow more quickly than taxable ones.

Another possible tax benefit of investments is being able to deduct capital losses from income when you file your tax return. A **capital loss** is a loss of money that occurs when the selling price of an investment is less than the purchase price. On the other hand, a **capital gain** is income that results from selling an asset for more than the purchase price. Capital gains are taxable by the federal government and most state governments.

Tax reduction strategies vary greatly from investor to investor and from year to year as tax laws change. Certain investments are especially important for those in high tax brackets. It pays to look for a competent tax accountant, lawyer, or financial planner for advice in this area.

Preserve Wealth in Unstable Economic Times

Both investments and cash can lose value quickly during times of inflation or political and economic instability. Choosing a variety of investments helps protect your investments during periods of economic uncertainty.

Consider your reasons for investing when developing an investment plan. For example, if earning income is important to you, look for investments that pay steady earnings and show high yields. If growth is more important, invest in companies that put earnings back into research, development, and expansion.

Selecting investments to meet your goals and objectives requires careful study. Investments are characterized by these four factors.

- *Degree of volatility. Volatility* refers to quick and unexpected changes in value or price. The change can be either positive or negative. Volatile investments can present greater uncertainty as to risk and to return.

- *Rate of return.* The potential *rate of return* is the expected earnings on an investment for a given period of time. It is often expressed as a percentage. Look for investments that show a history of growth.

- *Risk.* The *level of risk* is the degree to which an investment may deviate from its expected return. Low-risk investments generally offer lower returns, but provide more security. High-risk investments offer the possibility of big gains but also big losses. Most investments fall somewhere between these extremes.

- *Liquidity. Liquidity* is the ease with which an investment can be converted to cash without serious loss. High-liquidity investments are actively traded on security exchanges and are usually sold with nothing more than a phone call or a click of a mouse. Less liquid investments, such as art, antiques, coins, gold, and real estate, are often more difficult to sell.

Your investment goals and objectives will change over time depending on your earning power and your stage in the life cycle. *Risk tolerance* is the amount of uncertainty you can handle. It is connected to your level of comfort with the possibility of loss. Each person needs to determine his or her own emotional and financial risk tolerance and choose investments accordingly.

For short-term goals, use the savings instruments discussed in Chapter 5. The advantage of investing for a long-term goal is having many years before you will need your money. This allows you to keep money invested during the ups and downs of the economy and to achieve gains over time.

Types of Investments

A *security* is a type of investment issued by a corporation, government, or other organization. The most popular investments, stocks, bonds, and mutual funds, are securities. Real estate and valuable goods can also be investments. Valuable goods include rare and usually pricey items, such as gold, gems, antiques, and works of art.

Stocks

A **stock** is a share in the ownership of a corporation. When you purchase stock, you become a stockholder, or shareholder, of the corporation. As a stockholder, you have an ownership interest in the company. The more stock you own, the greater is your ownership interest. Corporations sell stock to

Life cycle, or stages of life, refers to the time between birth and death. You are now a young adult and will later enter into the mature adult and retired adult stages.

Songquan Deng /Shutterstock.com

The New York Stock Exchange (NYSE) in New York City is the oldest continually operating stock exchange in the United States.

raise money for start-up costs, ongoing activities, and expansion. There are two main ways in which investors can realize a return from owning stocks.

A **dividend** is a portion of a company's earnings that is paid to stockholders. Dividends are paid only when declared by the company's board of directors, which is a group of individuals who represent stockholders and oversee the major policy decisions of the company. Dividends are not guaranteed. They are only paid when the board of directors believes it is in the best interest of the company. Instead of paying dividends, some companies put profits back into the company in the hope of increasing its growth and stock value.

If steady income is the reason you are buying stock, you should check the dividend policy of the company before you buy. For example, The Coca-Cola Company has consistently paid a dividend for over 50 years. Likewise, Proctor & Gamble, makers of Pampers diapers and many other consumer products, has paid a dividend every year for almost 60 consecutive years. However, Google has never paid a dividend. Even though Google is an exceptionally profitable company, it is a young company; its cash is being used to fuel the growth of the company. This is typically the case. Young growth-oriented companies usually pay no or little dividends. As a company grows and experiences more consistent profits, however, it usually starts to pay a dividend to its stockholders. For example, Microsoft was founded on April 4, 1975, but it did not pay its first dividend until 2003. Most corporations that pay dividends pay them on a quarterly basis.

If increased wealth and stock value appreciation is the reason you are buying stock, look for opportunity to buy low and sell high. Investors purchase stock when they believe it will appreciate or rise in value. Then they can either sell it at a profit or hold it for further growth.

Stock Classifications

Corporations can issue various types of stock. The most popular types are common stock and preferred stock. When a corporation issues only one type of stock, it is called common stock. **Common stock** is stock that has voting rights and receives dividends declared by the company. Each share of common stock has equal rights with all other shares in the issue. Typical rights of common stockholders are the right to vote in corporate matters and the right to receive dividends when they are declared by the board of directors.

Since common stockholders have voting rights, they elect the company's board of directors. Common stockholders can also vote on other important matters, such as major expansion projects. Typically, common stockholders receive one vote per share, so a stockholder holding 100 common shares would have 100 votes.

Go Green

Investors who are concerned about the environment can choose from a variety of "green" mutual funds and ETFs that are available today. A green mutual fund is one that invests in companies that promote environmental responsibility—such as developing alternative energy, water conservation, waste management, sustainable living, and green transport.

Common stockholders may vote in person at the company's annual stockholders' meeting. Stockholders unable to attend the meeting can vote their shares by proxy. A **proxy** is a stockholder's written authorization to have someone else cast a vote on his or her behalf. The proxy form, called a *proxy statement,* is mailed to the stockholder who completes it and mails it back to the corporation. Proxy votes can also be cast electronically. With an electronic proxy, stockholders vote remotely using their computers, and the votes are received directly by the company. Most common stockholders vote their shares by proxy rather than attending the annual stockholders' meeting.

In addition to common stock, some corporations also issue preferred stock. **Preferred stock** is a type of stock that pays a regular dividend at a fixed rate. All preferred dividends must be paid before common stockholders receive a dividend. In addition, if the company were to fail, the claims of preferred stockholders rank ahead those of common stockholders. However, preferred stockholders usually do not have voting privileges.

The price of common stock usually moves up and down more than preferred stock. However, preferred stock typically does not increase in value as much as common stock.

Being a stockholder does not make you responsible for any of the company's debts if it goes out of business. The company's creditors cannot come after stockholders for payment. However, if a company closes its doors, stockholders may lose their investment in the company along with any unpaid dividends. The first in line for payment from the company's assets are creditors. Next, preferred stockholders' claims are met. Only then are the claims of common stockholders met. Since it is paid first, preferred stock is generally considered a more conservative, safer investment with less risk than common stock.

Stock Categories

When evaluating stock investments, investors often classify stocks into various categories. Besides the common or preferred labels, you may see stock described in one or more of the following ways.

- *Blue-chip stocks.* These are the stocks of large and well-established companies that have proved they can withstand downturns in the economy. They are generally more expensive than other categories of stock. However, they have track records of paying regular dividends and are considered relatively safe and stable investments. The name *blue chip* comes from the blue-colored poker chip, which is typically the most valuable chip in the card game of poker.

- *Income stocks.* These are stocks of companies with a history of paying above-average dividends to investors. These stocks are for investors, such as retirees, who want a consistent source of income.

- *Growth stocks.* These stocks are from companies that put a premium on long-term growth. Most or all profits are put back into the company, and often there are no dividends. Growth stocks are for investors who plan to buy and hold their stocks for long-term gains.

- *Defensive stocks.* These are the stocks of companies whose sales are relatively stable across the ups and downs of the economy. These companies often sell necessities, such as food, health care, and utilities.

Securities/ Investments Analysts
Securities/investments analysts help their clients make investment decisions. They work for investment banks, insurance companies, mutual funds, pension funds, securities firms, and the business media. They examine company financial statements and analyze economic and market factors to determine a company's value and to project its future earnings.

- *Cyclical stocks.* These stocks are from companies whose sales are sensitive to economic ups and downs. The companies provide goods and services that consumers buy when economic conditions are good. Consumers spend less in these areas during economic downturns.

- *Penny stocks.* These stocks are issued by companies with questionable sales forecasts. They are inexpensive, but risky. However, if the company becomes successful, investors can get above-average returns. Penny stocks can cost as little as a few cents or as much as $10 per share.

Additional stock categories exist, each presenting different levels of risk and volatility. Choosing a combination of stocks with varying degrees of risk can reduce overall risk. Additionally, many stocks fall into more than one category. For example, The Coca-Cola Company is a blue-chip stock. However, since the company pays an above-average and consistent dividend, it can also be considered a growth and income stock.

Stock Trading

A **stock trade** is the purchase or sale of shares of a stock. Stock trades occur in two markets: the primary market and the secondary market.

The *primary market*, also called the *new-issues market*, is when a company first sells stock to the public. An *initial public offering (IPO)* is a company's first sale of stock to the public. Companies usually make an IPO to raise capital for expansion or to become publicly traded. The company works with one or more investment banks that help determine the type of stock to issue, the price, and the best time to make the offering. The banks charge a commission to sell the securities to investors. The money raised from the sale of IPO stock, minus the bankers' commission, goes to the company. IPO stocks can be risky investments because the company is often a young business without a long track record of success. Investors who buy shares in an IPO can later sell their stock in the secondary market.

lev radin/Shutterstock.com

Facebook's IPO on May 18, 2012, was a highly anticipated and high-profile event at the NASDAQ stock exchange in New York City.

The majority of stock market activity occurs in the secondary market. Most stock trades in the secondary market are made through organized security exchanges. However, some companies, such as Aflac, Microsoft, and Wal-Mart, have direct stock investment plans that allow investors to buy shares directly from the company.

Securities Exchange

A **securities exchange** is a secondary market where securities are bought and sold through stockbrokers. A **stockbroker** is an agent who executes stock trades for clients. The stockbroker's role is that of a go-between who brings buyers and sellers together. Brokers are licensed by the Financial Industry Regulatory Authority (FINRA) to trade securities. Usually, stockbrokers charge a commission on both buy and sell transactions.

The New York Stock Exchange (NYSE) and the NASDAQ are the major secondary markets in the United States. The NYSE is a traditional brick and mortar exchange located on Wall Street in Manhattan, New York. It is the largest securities exchange in the world; and, unlike newer exchanges, it still uses a large trading floor where brokers conduct transactions.

The NASDAQ (National Association of Securities Dealers Automated Quotations) is an American-based electronic network for trading securities. NASDAQ lists the securities of more than 3,000 companies worldwide. Think of the NASDAQ as a giant electronic flea market where investors all over the world can buy and sell securities. International securities exchanges make it easier and less expensive to invest in foreign companies and for foreign investors to invest in US companies.

A securities exchange does not own stock. Instead, it serves as a market that connects buyers and sellers. The companies that initially issued the stock are not involved in these transactions and receive no additional money from the trades. In other words, in the secondary market, it is astockholders buying and selling among themselves. For example, assume Kelly Larson had the good fortune to buy 100 shares of Google stock for $100 per share when the company held its IPO on August 19, 2004. When the stock soared to $600 per share, Kelly sold her shares.

Kelly bought her shares in the primary market the first time Google sold shares to the public. Later, she sold her shares in the secondary market. In addition, the person who bought Kelly's shares can sell them whenever he or she chooses. This is how the secondary market works. Shares of stock that Google issued in its IPO can be bought and sold over and over again in the secondary market. However, none of the shares Google sold in its IPO can ever again be sold in the primary market.

Over-the-Counter (OTC) Markets

Stocks that are not listed on securities exchanges can be bought and sold at over-the-counter (OTC) markets. OTC markets are virtual markets where dealers and brokers conduct business through an electronic network of computers and telephones. Other types of securities are also traded on OTC markets. OTC markets lack many of the rules and regulations imposed on brokers in securities exchanges. Investors need to be especially alert when trading OTC stock because there can be a high level of risk involved. The largest OTC markets in the United States are NASDAQ's Over the Counter Bulletin Board (OTCBB) and PinkSheets.

The Financial Industry Regulatory Authority (FINRA) was created in July 2007 when the National Association of Securities Dealers (NASD) and the regulatory branch of the NYSE, NYSE Regulation, Inc., consolidated their operations. FINRA is the largest independent securities regulator in the US Its chief role is to protect investors by maintaining the fairness of the US securities markets.

The term *trading stocks* is commonly used in the world of investments. This term may imply that stocks are similar to collectible items, such as baseball cards, which can be physically traded, or swapped, from one collector to another. However, this is not the case. To trade a stock simply means to buy or sell it on any of the financial markets.

Stock Quotes

You can follow the ups and downs of stocks by checking daily stock quotes. To follow a particular stock, you need to know the stock's ticker symbol (trading symbol), which is a series of letters that identify the company. Stocks listed on the NYSE use one, two, or three letters as a symbol. For example, the ticker symbol for Ford Motor Company is F, the ticker symbol for MasterCard Inc. is MA, and the ticker symbol for Wal-Mart Stores Inc. is WMT.

Companies listed on the NASDAQ use four letters as a symbol. For example, the ticker symbol of Google is GOOG, and the ticker symbol for Apple, Inc. is AAPL.

Stock quotes, or listings, appear in the financial section of *The Wall Street Journal* and other major newspapers, similar to Figure 7-1. Listings are also available on the Internet. You can quickly and easily find stock quotes on financial websites. Stock quotes contain valuable financial information. The current yield (Yld%) and the price/earnings ratio (PE) help investors determine the health or weakness of a company and the value of its investments.

Stock Splits

When a corporation is doing well, its stock usually increases in value because investors are willing to pay more for the stock. When a stock's value grows very quickly, the company's board of director's may decide the stock is getting too expensive for employees and average investors to buy on a regular basis. As a result, a corporation may decide to split its stock to create more

Stock Quote										
52 Weeks		Stock	Div	Yld%	PE	Vol 100s	Hi	Lo	Last	Chg
Hi	Lo									
19	13	Corp.X	0.50	3.00	28	19409	17.13	16.00	16.50	−0.25

52-Week Hi/Lo: Highest and lowest prices paid per share over the past year

Stock: Company name or the stock's ticker symbol

Div: Dividend paid per share of stock over the past year

(There will be no number if the stock does not pay dividends.)

Yld%: Yield percentage or rate of return on one share of stock; calculated by dividing the annual dividend (Div) by the current price of the stock

PE: (Price/earnings) A ratio of the price of a share of stock divided by earnings per share for the last 12 months

(Low-risk stocks usually have low PE ratios. Speculative and high-growth stock ratios are often much higher.)

Vol 100s or Sales 100s: Previous day's volume, or total number of shares traded, quoted in hundreds

(For the above listing, sales totaled 1,940,900 shares.)

Hi: Highest price paid per share on the previous day

Lo: Lowest price paid per share on the previous day

Last or Close: Final price paid per share on the previous day

Chg: Compares the final price paid per share today with that paid the previous day

(A positive number indicates a price increase; a negative number indicates a price decrease.)

Figure 7-1 Stock quotes provide essential information for investing in securities and following those you own.

shares, which brings the share price down. For example, assume the stock of Sterling Company has a market value of $100 per share. The board of directors thinks this price is too high and declares a two-for-one stock split. A two-for-one split means that each share of stock now becomes two shares of stock. This doubles the number of the company's shares. The price of the stock would then drop from $100 a share to around $50, making the stock more affordable.

Assume you own 100 shares of Sterling Company stock. Before the split, the total value of the stock was $10,000.

100 shares × $100 = $10,000

After the split, the total value is $10,000.

200 shares × $50 = $10,000

The stock split did not immediately increase the value of your stock, but it increased the number of shares you own. The split makes the share price more affordable, which usually increases the demand for the stock. When demand increases, the share price usually rises. When the share price rises, the total value of your shares rises as well.

Every major corporation in the United States has split its stock at least once. The Coca-Cola company has split its shares 10 times since the company went public in 1919. A split can be in any proportion a company chooses, such as four-for-one, three-for-one, and three-for-two.

Bonds

A **bond** is a certificate of debt issued by a corporation or government. When you buy a bond, you are lending money to the issuer of the bond. Until the bond matures, you, the bondholder, are a creditor. The issuer owes you the amount of the loan plus interest on the bond's face value.

Information stated on a bond includes the following.

- *Maturity date* is the date a bond is due to be repaid to the bondholder. In other words, it is the date bondholders get their money back.

- *Face value*, or principal, is the amount for which a bond is issued and on which interest payments are figured. At maturity, the bondholder receives the face value.

- *Yield* is the percentage of a return on an investment.

  Other important terms relating to bonds include the following.

- *Coupon rate* is the annual interest the issuer promises to pay on the face value.

- *Market value* is the amount for which a bond sells. It may be more, less, or the same as the face value.

- *Current yield* is the annual interest or coupon rate divided by the market price of a bond.

  The three major issuers of bonds are corporations, municipalities, and the federal government.

Corporations

Corporate bonds are issued by businesses that need money to operate and expand. The quality, coupon rates, and yields of these bonds vary with the financial soundness of the issuing corporation. Yields and market prices move up and down as market interest rates change.

Most corporate bonds are bought and sold by brokers. Some bonds are bought and sold on securities exchanges and are listed in newspapers and online. High-grade corporate bonds are considered safer investments than stocks because they are debt instruments. If a company goes bankrupt, it must pay its debts first.

Municipalities

Municipal bonds are issued by state, county, and city governments. Coupon rates and yields depend on market rates and the financial soundness of the issuing municipality. Interest on these bonds is exempt from federal income tax and, in some cases, state and local taxes as well. This makes municipal bonds attractive to upper income investors in high tax brackets.

Most municipal bonds are bought and sold by brokers. Some municipalities may allow investors to purchase bonds directly from the local government. Corporate and municipal bond listings are in the financial sections of major newspapers and online. Look for certain key information when reviewing bond quotes, as illustrated in Figure 7-2.

Corporate and municipal bonds are rated for quality and risk. The most common rating system is by Standard and Poor, illustrated in Figure 7-3. The first four rating categories—AAA, AA, A, and BBB—are recommended for conservative investors. The next four categories—BB, B, CCC, and CC—are considered too risky for average investors. The last two categories—C and D—are for exceptionally risky bonds that are behind on interest payments or in default or both. Only professional investors should consider bonds in these categories.

Bond Quote							
Issuer Name	Symbol	Coupon	Maturity	Rating	Close	Change	Yield %
Bank ABC	B. ABC	2.250%	Mar 20XX	Aaa	100.985	−0.073	1.861
Corp. Y	COR.Y	8.500%	May 20XX	A	106.695	2.375	7.520
Z Corp.	Z.CO	2.250%	Mar 20XX	Aaa	101.042	−0.041	1.839

Symbol: Abbreviated name of the issuing corporation

Coupon: The annual interest paid on the bond
(Coupon rates generally are higher on lower quality bonds to reward buyers for taking greater risks.)

Maturity: The date the principal of the bond is to be repaid to bondholders

Rating: The quality/risk rating of the bond

(As the risk increases, the ratings decline from the highest quality or safest rated, Aaa or AAA, to the lowest quality rated, C or D.)

Close: The closing price of the bond at the end of the day

(Prices are usually shown as a percentage of the face value.)

Change: Compares the closing price with the price paid the previous day

(Some quotes show the change in increments of 1/32.)

Yield: The actual return on investment

(Calculations are based on the coupon rate and the current market value of the bond.)

Figure 7-2 Corporate bond quotes provide the information you need to track bond yields and prices in the marketplace.

Bond Ratings	
Rating	**Bond Credit Quality**
AAA	Highest
AA	Superior
A	Satisfactory
BBB	Adequate
BB	Speculative
B	Highly speculative
CCC	Very highly speculative
CC	Extremely speculative
C	Extremely speculative, behind on interest payments
D	In default

Goodheart-Willcox Publisher

Figure 7-3 Standard & Poor's bond rating categories range from AAA (best) to D (worst).

US Government

US government bonds are issued by the US Treasury and are the safest bonds you can buy. When you buy one, you lend money to the federal government. Treasury bills, notes, and bonds sell in increments of $100.

- *Treasury bills.* Treasury bills (T-bills) are short-term debts with maturities ranging from a few days to 52 weeks. They are the most actively traded

You Do the Math

Many times, you will not need as precise a number as a calculation provides. For example, when working with decimals, especially multiplication and division operations, the final answer may have several more decimal places than you need.

To round a number, locate the value place to which you want to round. Then, look at the digit to the right of this place. If the digit to the right is 5 or greater, add 1 to the value place to which you are rounding. If the digit to the right is less than 5, do nothing to the value place to which you are rounding.

Complete the Following Problem

How many shares of stock would you own at the end of one year if you invested $1,000 each quarter at the following stock prices? Use dollar-cost averaging and round your answer.

- First quarter: $20 per share
- Second quarter: $25 per share
- Third quarter: $30 per share
- Fourth quarter: $35 per share

government debt. Treasury bills sell for less than the face value. They do not pay interest before maturity. You pay less than $100 for a T-bill and receive the full $100 at maturity. The difference between the price you pay and the amount you receive at maturity is the interest.

- *Notes and bonds.* Treasury notes and Treasury bonds are sold at auction and carry a stated interest rate. Buyers receive semiannual interest payments. Treasury notes are short-term securities with maturities of 2, 3, 5, 7, or 10 years. Bonds are long-term investments with maturities of 30 years. Both notes and bonds are sold in increments of $100. The actual price you will pay for these securities depends on the interest coupon and the yield at auction. These may be paper certificates or entered into an electronic account. Today most notes and bonds are sold electronically.

- *US savings bonds.* US savings bonds were discussed in Chapter 5.

Mutual Funds

A **mutual fund** is an investment created by pooling the money of many people and investing it in a collection of securities. Think of a mutual fund as a "basket" of securities. Professional managers at investment firms purchase securities and place them in the basket. Shares of ownership in the basket are then sold to investors. Each investor in the fund owns a tiny part of every security in the basket. Mutual funds may invest in stocks, bonds, commodities, gold, and other securities.

Advantages and Disadvantages of Mutual Funds

There are some key advantages to investing in mutual funds, especially for the beginning investor. These advantages include the following points.

- *Professional management.* Mutual funds are managed by professional investors who follow the markets carefully and are assisted by a team of researchers.

- *Diversification.* Mutual funds offer diversification in a single investment. As mentioned earlier, when you invest in several securities, you spread your risks.

- *Liquidity.* Mutual fund shares are easy to buy and sell. To buy or sell shares in a fund, you simply call the mutual fund company and make the transaction. Most transactions can also be done over the Internet.

Mutual funds also have some disadvantages, including the following.

- *Management fees.* Mutual fund managers charge fees to pay for research, administration, sales, and other operating expenses. Fees are not paid directly by investors, but instead they are deducted directly from the fund's earnings.

- *Sales commissions.* Mutual funds can be load or no load. A *load* is a sales commission paid to the broker or financial advisor who sold you the fund. The load is stated as a percentage. A *front-end load* is deducted when you buy shares in the fund. For example, if you invest $1,000 in a fund with a 5 percent front-end sales load, a $50 ($1,000 × 5%) commission will be deducted from your $1,000 investment. The difference, $950, then goes into your account. A *back-end load* is deducted when you sell the shares. The $50 commission will come out of your

Ethics

It is unethical and illegal for a business to participate in acts of collusion. Collusion occurs when competing businesses work together to eliminate competition by misleading customers, setting prices, or other fraudulent activities. Unethical businesses sometimes collude with other businesses so that they can dominate the marketplace. Collusion is unethical, and it is also illegal.

proceeds when you sell your shares. Some funds are no-load. A *no-load mutual fund* is one sold without a sales commission. Most mutual funds today are sold without a load.

- *Lack of control.* You give up control over the selection and timing of your investments. The fund managers make these decisions.

- *Minimum investment.* Many mutual funds require a minimum investment of $1,000 or more. However, there are some funds with minimum investments as low as $100.

When buying a mutual fund, research the fund's expense ratio. High fees can cut into your earnings significantly and are charged even if the fund is performing poorly.

Types of Mutual Funds

The two basic types of mutual funds are closed-end or open-end. A closed-end fund offers a fixed number of shares. These shares are traded like stocks on securities exchanges and secondary markets. You buy and sell shares in these funds through investment brokers, not through an investment company.

An open-end fund has an unlimited number of shares. It sells and redeems shares at their net asset value. **Net asset value (NAV)** is the total of the fund's assets minus its liabilities divided by the number of the shares the fund has outstanding.

Most mutual funds are open-end funds. Open-end mutual funds may be load or no-load funds. Load funds charge a commission of up to 8 percent of the amount you invest when you buy shares. The average commission is 3 to 5 percent. No-load funds do not charge fees when you buy shares. However, you may be charged fees when you sell or redeem your shares.

Several different types of mutual funds are available, as described in the following list.

- Income funds buy conservative bonds and stocks that pay regular dividends. Their primary goal is to provide current income.

- Balanced funds invest in common stock, preferred stock, and bonds. Their goal is to provide a low-risk investment opportunity with moderate growth and dividend income.

- Growth funds invest in securities that are expected to increase in value. They emphasize growth over income, but involve more risk.

- Specialized funds invest in securities of certain industries or sectors, such as all technology or all health-care companies. They may also invest in certain types of securities, such as all municipal bonds or common stock. Some concentrate on foreign securities.

Mutual funds are often divided into families. Each fund has its own name and investment objectives. Mutual fund quotes display the names of individual funds listed within each family group as shown in Figure 7-4.

A **money market fund** is a type of mutual fund that deals only in interest–paying, short-term investments, such as US Treasury securities, certificates of deposit, and commercial paper. *Commercial paper* is a short-term note issued by a major corporation. The funds are managed and sold by investment companies, brokerage firms, and other financial institutions. The interest earned, minus management fees for operating the fund, is passed along to the depositors. Interest rates on money market funds go up and down with money market rates.

Investing in money market funds has many advantages. These funds provide investors with high yields when interest rates are high. They can be liquidated at any time since they have no term or maturity date. No interest penalties apply for early withdrawals. They can be used as collateral for loans.

Mutual Fund Quote				
Fund	**NAV**	**Chg**	**YTD % return**	**3-yr % chg**
Fund Company 123				
BalFundA	9.89	0.01	28.1	−4.7
SpecFundB	31.72	0.02	28.6	1.2

Fund: Name of the fund company that sells the funds, followed by the names of individual funds offered

NAV: The dollar value of one share of the mutual fund

Chg: The difference between the day's NAV and the previous day's NAV

YTD (Year to Date) %: The percentage gain or loss since the first trading day of the year

3-yr % chg: The fund's total gain or loss over the past three years, indicated as a percentage

Goodheart-Willcox Publisher

Figure 7-4 Mutual funds quotes appear in the financial pages of major newspapers and online.

Money market funds have some disadvantages, too. The rate paid on money market funds changes daily. If money market rates drop, so does the rate of return. A minimum investment of $1,000 or more may be required. Unlike money market deposit accounts, money market funds are not FDIC-insured.

Factors Affecting Returns

In a market economy, the laws of supply and demand determine the price of stocks and many other investments. Supply is the amount of a product or service producers are willing to provide. Demand is the quantity of a product or service consumers are willing to buy. Both supply and demand are closely connected to price.

Certain information can help predict investment returns, including economic indicators, current events and trends, and data about particular economic sectors, industries, and companies.

Business Cycle Fluctuations

When the economy is growing, most businesses and investors do well. However, when economic growth slows, many businesses and investors lose money as sales decline. Cyclical industries are more sensitive to the ups and downs of the business cycle. The performance of these companies is often tied to interest rates, fuel costs, and products that are not immediately essential to the consumer. The stock issued by companies within these industries is categorized as cyclical. Being aware of the ups and downs of the economy can help investors make wise choices.

Interest Rate Fluctuations

Fluctuations in interest rates affect the value of securities and other investments. Bonds and real estate are directly affected by interest rate ups and downs. For example, as interest rates rise, bond prices fall. This is because investors can receive higher returns by investing in bonds with the new higher rates. Conversely, as interest rates fall, bond prices rise. Real estate sales increase as interest rates fall and suffer when they rise. Business growth generally is more robust when interest rates are low and suffers when rates increase.

Stock Market Fluctuations

Bull and *bear* are terms used to describe the strength or weakness of the stock market. **Bull market** is an extended period of consumer confidence and optimism when stock prices rise. The sense of optimism often encourages the exploration of other investment opportunities, including real estate and valuable goods.

Bear market is an extended period of uncertainty and pessimism when stock prices fall. It occurs when investors feel insecure and uncertain about the economy. Fearing further drops in the value of their investments, they often sell them. However, this is often a buying opportunity because prices are low.

Product Innovation

Historically, investors who financed winning products in their infancy, such as the automobile, microwave oven, and cell phone, made handsome profits. Those who invested in products that did not succeed lost their money. The results for most investors fall somewhere between high profits and big losses.

Business failure is caused by many factors, ranging from poor management to new competition to government regulations. Technological advancement can cause new companies and industries to spring up while making outdated companies obsolete.

Government Actions

Actions by governments can impact the value of an investment positively or negatively. Product recalls, new regulations, and increased taxes often have a negative impact on company stock. Trade barriers protecting companies from foreign competition often improve the outlook of stock in protected industries.

Exchange-Rate Risk

For investors who trade securities of companies in other countries, the currency exchange rate needs to be considered. It may be necessary to exchange dollars for another currency. Dividends and gains or losses may be presented in foreign currency. The ups and downs of the exchange rate, whether buying or selling, become a potential risk for the investor.

Real Estate Analysts
Real estate analysts estimate the value of land and buildings, ranging from residential homes to major shopping centers. They write detailed reports on their research and observations and explain reasons for arriving at their estimates.

Real Estate

Buying real estate (land or buildings) is another way to invest for future profit. This type of investment usually requires enough money for a down payment plus a long-term loan.

For most people, buying a home is their first experience in real estate. When the real estate market is strong, owning your home can increase your net worth and protect against inflation. Property usually increases in value over time. Still, most financial experts advise thinking of a home first in terms of a place to live and second as an investment.

Buying land or buildings for investment purposes is not for amateurs. Before investing in real estate for profit, buyers need to know about property values and property management. They also need to learn about mortgages, down payments, taxes, titles, insurance, and the legal aspects of leases and property ownership. These considerations are described in Chapter 12.

Purchasing stock in a *real estate investment trust (REIT)* is a way to invest in real estate without the complications and financial commitment of owning property. A REIT is a company that owns profit-earning real estate, such as apartments, shopping malls, office buildings, or hotels. Mortgage REITs specialize in buying and selling mortgage-backed securities.

The government requires that REITs distribute most of their profits to shareholders through dividends. Shares of many REITs are traded on securities exchanges.

Real estate mutual funds are another way to invest indirectly in real estate. Funds may include a mixture of securities from REITs, commercial developers, and other types of real estate companies.

Investing in REITs and real estate mutual funds requires less capital and offers more liquidity than purchasing property. Changes in interest rates, housing prices, and demand for housing can affect the rate of return. As with other securities, investors should research before investing and carefully review prospectuses and annual reports.

In times of doubt and uncertainty in the securities market, investors often buy gold. In early December of 2008, as the world economy entered a recession, gold was selling for $749 an ounce. Less than three years later, the price of gold had exceeded $1,900 an ounce as investors bought gold as a way of diversifying out of the stock market.

Valuable Goods

People have collected precious goods and objects for thousands of years and continue to do so today. These items can be attractive investments because their value is not eroded by inflation as money can be. Valuable goods include the following.

* *Collectibles.* Collectibles are objects purchased for the pleasure of ownership and because they are expected to increase in value. Common collectibles include rare coins, books, stamps, art, antiques, sports memorabilia, and vintage automobiles.

* *Precious metals.* Precious metals include gold, silver, platinum, and other metals. People buy them in the form of pieces of jewelry, coins, bars, or ingots from banks and dealers. An *ingot* is a bar of metal that is sized and shaped for easy transportation and storage. Why do investors buy gold when gold does not pay interest or dividends? *Gold* is a store of value, and it lasts forever. It does not tarnish, corrode, or degrade. Gold mined thousands of years ago looks the same as gold mined today.

Keith Bell/Shutterstock.com

Investments can take many forms, including this collectible 1931 Ford automobile.

Gold is in demand worldwide and is a way to diversify an investment portfolio.

- *Gemstones.* Precious gemstones include diamonds, emeralds, sapphires, and others. They are collected as stones or as pieces of jewelry.

Consider the risks before you choose these investments. They are less liquid than stocks, bonds, and mutual funds. Like real estate, valuable goods can be difficult to sell quickly. When collectors are ready or forced to sell these assets, they sometimes must accept less than what they originally paid. These valuable goods can also be hard to store and protect from damage and theft.

Judging the worth of valuable items is often difficult unless you have expert knowledge and considerable experience. Only then are you safe in purchasing these items from dealers and online auction sites. Before buying valuable goods for investments, consult a reputable professional with experience in estimating value. Ask for a formal appraisal before making a significant investment in collectibles.

Prices for precious metals, particularly gold, silver, platinum, and copper, are posted on business websites. Prices for these goods are often volatile.

Keep in mind there is no guaranteed return on investments in valuable goods. Putting money into a savings account generates interest. Over time, investing in securities usually pays off. Historically, real estate goes up in value. The rate of return on collectibles, precious metals, and gems is less predictable.

Checkpoint 7.1

1. List four reasons a person would invest rather than keeping all of his or her money in a savings account.
2. What are two ways a stock investor can realize a return?
3. What is an initial public offering (IPO)?
4. What is the difference between the primary market and the secondary market?
5. How do stocks differ from bonds?

Build Your Vocabulary

As you progress through this course, develop a personal glossary of personal finance terms and add it to your portfolio. This will help you build your vocabulary and prepare you for a career. Write a definition for each of the following terms and add it to your personal finance glossary.

investing	securities exchange
capital gain	stockbroker
capital loss	bond
stock	mutual fund
dividend	net asset value (NAV)
common stock	money market fund
proxy	bull market
preferred stock	bear market
stock trade	

Section 7.2
Investment Strategies and Estate Planning

Objectives

After studying this section, you will be able to:

- Describe an investment portfolio.
- Explain investment strategies to consider.
- Describe ways to buy securities.
- Identify retirement investment options.
- Explore the basics of estate planning.

Terms

investment portfolio	estate
diversification	executor
prospectus	will
dollar-cost averaging	trustee
rollover	codicil
traditional IRA	probate
Roth IRA	living will
annuity	trust

Choosing Investments

An **investment portfolio** is a collection of securities and other assets a person owns. Successful investors diversify their portfolios. **Diversification** is spreading risk by putting money in a variety of investments. Building a diversified portfolio involves gathering information, considering strategies, and selecting investment methods.

Consult a professional for advice on complex investments. Financial experts can help in areas where you do not feel confident and competent on your own. A list of financial experts is shown in Figure 7-5.

Online Resources

Today's technology allows you to use the Internet to view important investment information. In the recent past, this type of information was only available to brokerage firms and investment analysts. Investment-related websites provide useful information about individual securities and market movements. On company websites, look at investor information or press releases to evaluate the company's investment potential.

The US Securities and Exchange Commission (SEC) is the government agency that regulates the securities industry. Its mission is to combat fraud as well as to ensure that the securities markets operate efficiently and fairly. All publicly traded companies are required to file financial statements and documents with the SEC. The SEC manages the EDGAR database and keeps it up to date as a guide for investors. Visit www.sec.gov to explore this database.

Financial Experts		
Job Title	**Description**	**Credentials**
Accountant	• Keep, audit, and inspect financial records of individuals and businesses • Prepare financial reports and tax returns	• CPA (Certified Public Accountant) indicates an accountant is certified by the American Institute of Certified Public Accountants.
Financial Planner	• Assist consumers in forming a financial program • Give advice on insurance, savings, investments, taxes, retirement, and estate planning	• CFP (Certified Financial Planner) indicates completion of training and certification administered by the Certified Financial Planner Board of Standards, Inc. • ChFC (Chartered Financial Consultant) may be used by those who have completed additional education and training. • Financial planners are not required by law to be certified or licensed.
Investment Broker-Dealer	• Buy and sell securities and other investment products	• Individuals must be registered with the Securities and Exchange Commission (SEC) and the Financial Industry Regulatory Authority (FINRA).
Registered Representative	• Work for broker-dealers as salespeople, commonly known as brokers	• Individuals must be registered with FINRA and licensed by the appropriate state securities regulator.
Investment Adviser	• Provide information and advice on different types of securities	• Advisors managing over $25 million in client accounts must be registered with the SEC. Advisors managing less must be registered with the state securities regulator.

Goodheart-Willcox Publisher

Figure 7-5 Consulting an experienced professional can help in managing financial and legal matters.

Annual Reports

Most corporate websites offer access to annual and quarterly reports. These sources give a good picture of current and predicted market performance.

One piece of information in annual reports—earnings per share (EPS)—is especially important. When earnings per share increase from year to year, it is an indication the company is doing well. Earnings per share are the total corporate earnings, after taxes, divided by the total number of shares.

Prospectuses

A **prospectus** is a legal document that gives a detailed description of a security. When an investor buys a security, the issuer must provide a prospectus. You may also get a copy mailed to you if you are considering buying a security. A prospectus can usually be found on a company's website or the SEC's EDGAR database.

A prospectus lists company officers, describes business history and operations, and outlines plans for the future. It also includes the following financial information:

- *Risks.* This section spells out the ways an investor can lose money by investing in the security.
- *Performance summary.* This section indicates how the investment has performed and how its performance compares with that of similar investments. Past performance does not necessarily indicate future results.
- *Fees and expenses.* This section outlines any fees or commissions you must pay when buying, selling, or redeeming shares.
- *Management.* This section identifies the qualifications and experience of the directors and officers of the company or fund.

Market Quotes

Stock, bond, and mutual fund quotes, or listings, contain important financial information, including records of past and current performance. Market information on securities appears in the financial section of *The Wall Street Journal* and other major newspapers. For up-to-the-minute information, review listings on the Internet.

Economics in Action

Lost Government Revenue

During an economic recession, the revenues that federal, state, and local governments receive from various forms of taxes are affected. For example, many businesses close or lay off workers. Some workers are forced to take job furloughs or unpaid leave. As the incomes of individuals and businesses fall, so does the share that governments receive in the form of income taxes.

Sales tax revenues also drop. Unemployment or worry about job loss causes consumers to scale back spending. State and local governments that rely heavily on revenue from sales taxes must make do with much less.

Most state and local governments also depend on property tax revenues to fund education, social programs, law enforcement, and much more. During the latest recession, millions of homeowners fell behind in mortgage payments. The banks that provided the mortgage loans took over these homes and sold many of them at less than previous market value.

The market value of a home is, in part, dependent on the sale prices of nearby homes. When a home is sold at a low price, the market value of nearby homes often decreases. When home values drop, so does property tax revenue. With less money coming in, many local governments were forced to cut spending.

At the same time that tax revenues fall during a recession, the need for government services increases. For example, unemployment creates increased demand for social services. In some areas, cities must spend more on law enforcement to enforce evictions caused by foreclosures.

Investment Strategies

Smart investing is a balancing act. It requires balancing risks against returns, as illustrated in Figure 7-6. Younger investors can usually take more risks than older investors. A young investor has many wage-earning years ahead. However, as people get closer to retirement, they need to choose more conservative investments to preserve principal and provide income.

Investing at an early age allows you to benefit from two common investment strategies: buy and hold and dollar-cost averaging.

Buy and Hold

Buy and hold is the strategy of buying securities and holding them for long-term gains as opposed to frequent trading. An investor using this strategy stays invested during market fluctuations. Investors who sell stocks when they drop in value lose money. Investors who hold stocks usually gain in the long run.

If your stock earns dividends, you will earn money over the years you own the stock. Also, if you hold a stock for a period of time, the company may split its stock, increasing your holdings.

Buy and hold does not mean buy and forget. You need to check your investments periodically to know how well they are performing. When an investment is not performing well, it may be time to sell and reinvest in a more promising company. Consult an accountant or tax professional to evaluate the tax implications of selling.

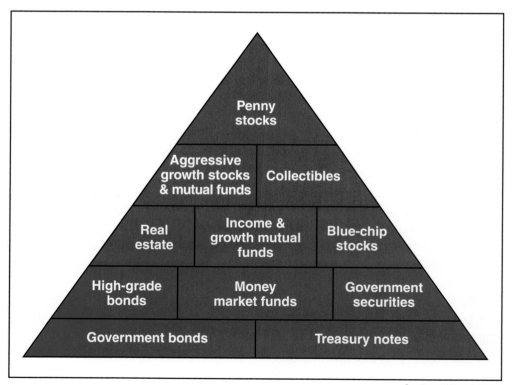

Goodheart-Willcox Publisher

Figure 7-6 High-risk investments, at the top of the pyramid, have a greater chance of earning high returns. Low-risk investments, at the base of the pyramid, usually have low returns.

Dollar-Cost Averaging

Dollar-cost averaging is a strategy of investing a fixed dollar amount at regular intervals, such as monthly, without regard to the price of the investment at the time you buy it. You buy more shares when the price is low and fewer when it is high. This buying strategy reduces the risk of investing a lump sum when it may not be the best time to buy.

Dollar-cost averaging offers the added advantage of convenience. You can set up an automatic payment and make it a part of your overall budget. It helps you make a habit of investing amounts of money you can afford. You can invest as little as $25 monthly. Brokerage firms, mutual funds, and retirement accounts all offer opportunities for dollar-cost averaging.

Buying Securities

Once you have decided on specific securities you wish to buy, there are several ways to acquire them.

Brokerage Firms

To buy stocks, bonds, and other securities, you may open an account with a brokerage or securities firm. The main mission of a brokerage firm is to buy and sell for its customers. The fee you pay for these services is called a *commission.*

The first step to opening an account is to complete an account application with a firm. Once your application is accepted, you call your broker with your orders to buy and sell. Most firms also offer online services.

Full-service brokerage firms maintain research departments to follow market trends and individual securities. In addition, they provide investment advice, portfolio management, and other services. The commission you pay covers the cost of trading and support services provided by the firm. Both experienced and beginning investors can benefit from the expertise of full-service brokerage firms.

Discount brokerage firms execute orders to buy and sell securities, but offer few other services. For instance, a discount brokerage firm does not offer investment advice. The commission is considerably lower than that charged by a full-service broker. However, you will need to do your own research and investment planning when you buy from a discount broker. Some experienced investors may prefer to use discount brokers to save money on commissions.

Online brokerage firms have hundreds of online brokers available to help consumers buy and sell securities. Use the following guidelines when investing through an online brokerage firm.

- *Use reputable brokers.* Check online brokers carefully before becoming involved. Make sure the people you deal with are reputable and legitimate. You can check out brokers and securities firms with your state securities regulator, the nearest SEC office, or at www.sec.gov.

- *Study investment information.* Print information on any investment you are considering. You may also want to obtain other written material, such as a prospectus, an annual report, and recent company news. Study this information carefully. Before placing an order, know exactly what you are buying and what risks are involved.

Brokerage Representatives
Brokerage representatives compute and record data pertaining to securities transactions. They may also take customer calls, create order tickets, record a client's purchases and sales, and inform clients of changes to their accounts.

- *Keep investment documents.* Obtain and keep written confirmations of your buy-and-sell orders and their completion. File all your investment records and information in a safe place where you can locate them easily. You will need these records to file your tax returns.

- *Track performance.* Follow your investments' performance. Prices can rise and fall swiftly in active markets. When you invest directly online, no one will be supervising your account. This makes it essential to follow market trends and prices of securities you own. You want to buy and sell at the most advantageous times.

When you buy and sell securities online or by phone, you will need to use certain types of orders to conduct your trades. These orders are discussed below.

- *Market orders.* A market order instructs your broker to buy or sell a stock at the best price available. The price may be higher or lower than when you placed the order. Stock prices can change between the time you place an order and the time it is executed.

- *Limit orders.* A limit order instructs your broker to buy or sell a certain stock at a set price or better. If the broker cannot buy or sell at the price you request, the order will not be executed.

- *Stop orders.* A stop order instructs your broker to buy or sell a stock when and if it reaches a specific price. It will be carried out only when the stock reaches the target price. This type of order helps you protect your gains and limit losses.

The brokerage firm keeps a record of your transactions. You should receive a statement outlining your account activity periodically, usually every month. You will also receive year-end statements and forms for filing income tax returns.

Monkey Business Images/Shutterstock.com

Young adults have many opportunities to make wise investment decisions.

Investment Clubs

An *investment club* is a group of people who work together to learn about securities and to invest their pooled funds. Most investment clubs become legal partnerships for the purpose of filing income taxes and meeting Internal Revenue Service requirements.

Members attend regular meetings (usually monthly), pay dues, and elect officers. The members decide by vote the amount of the dues each person will pay per month. Members research and follow stocks under consideration or in the club's portfolio. They also buy and sell securities by vote of the majority.

An investment club can be a good way to start investing. It offers the opportunity to invest on a small scale while learning. If you can find a few friends who are interested in learning to invest, you may want to consider forming an investment club.

The National Association of Investors Corporation provides information on starting and running a successful club. You will also find similar information from the Securities and Exchange Commission and Investment Club Central.

DRIPs

A *dividend reinvestment plan (DRIP)* offers a way to bypass brokers and commissions and invest directly in a company. Dividends are automatically reinvested. Many companies offer DRIPs to the public.

To enroll in one of these plans, you need to become a stockholder by purchasing at least one share of stock in your own name. Once enrolled, most companies allow you to invest small amounts routinely. Some even offer a 3 to 5 percent discount from the current market price of the security. Often you can make automatic weekly or monthly stock purchases in amounts as little as $25.

When you wish to sell shares, it may take a few days to complete the transaction. There may also be a fee for selling. You need to keep careful records of dividends, gains, and losses for income tax purposes.

Investing for Retirement

Retirement planning is a key element of financial security. Recent trends indicate more people are retiring earlier and living longer. Early retirees could need income for as long as 20 to 30 years. Providing income for this many years requires early planning, careful investment, periodic review, and proper adjustments to meet changing needs. Starting a retirement investment plan early is the most effective way to provide enough money on which to live after retiring.

You may be able to draw on a variety of income sources for later years. Social Security is a government program financed by joint contributions from workers and employers. While Social Security is not intended to be your sole source of income, it will be an important piece of your retirement picture. For more detailed information on what you can expect from Social Security, see Chapter 3.

The other income sources you may rely on include retirement programs offered by employers, personal retirement plans, and annuities.

Employer-Sponsored Retirement Plans

When job hunting, one important area to explore is the type of retirement plan(s) offered to employees. Having a job you love plus a reliable retirement plan is the ideal combination. Some employers sponsor retirement programs for their employees. These programs vary greatly, but all must meet the standards set forth in the *Employee Retirement Income Security Act (ERISA)*. This 1974 law sets standards for pension and retirement plans to guarantee that workers receive entitled benefits.

Vesting requirements are an important part of this act. *Vesting* means that the employee has completed a fixed number of years of employment and has a legal right to an increasing portion of the money an employer reserves for the employee. Vesting schedules are usually gradual. Typically, after 7 to 10 years, you will be fully vested. Being vested is particularly important if you leave the company for another job or if you are laid off.

401(k) Plans

A *401(k) plan* is a well-known, employer-sponsored retirement plan. The plan is funded with your own before-tax salary contributions and often with matched contributions from your employer. Employer contributions can take different forms, such as employee stock ownership, profit sharing, deferred-compensation plans, or cash. The name *401(k)* comes from the section of the Internal Revenue Code that authorizes this type of retirement plan.

Typical 401(k) plans offer several different investment options, including stock mutual funds, bond mutual funds, and money market funds. Many companies also allow employees to purchase the company stock and hold it inside the 401(k) plan. Diversifying investments helps to minimize risk. Financial experts usually recommend choosing more aggressive investments if you have many years before retirement. In later years, conservative investments should predominate.

Investing in 401(k) plans is one of the better ways to save for retirement, especially when employers match contributions. The great advantage of a 401(k) is the tax-deferred growth of your savings. Plans can vary greatly from employer to employer. They can also be affected by changing tax laws.

Most employer-sponsored retirement plans are portable. That is, you can take your retirement savings with you if you leave your job. A **rollover** is the process of moving retirement savings from one qualified account to another qualified account without incurring penalties and taxes. For example, assume that for the past five years Bill Jenkins had worked for a company that offers a 401(k) plan. Bill found a higher paying job with another company that also offers a 401(k) plan. If the plan of Bill's new employer permits, he can move the balance of his old 401(k) account into the plan of his new employer. However, if Bill's new plan does not permit rollovers, he can roll his old 401(k) account balance into an individual retirement account (discussed in the next section). The rules for a rollover are very specific and strict. For more information, go to www.irs.gov.

403(b) Plans

The *403(b) plan* is a type of retirement plan available to employees of nonprofit organizations—such as public schools, colleges, hospitals, and public libraries. It has many of the same characteristics as the 401(k) plan. Participants in a 403(b) plan are allowed to set aside money for retirement on a pre-tax basis, and the money grows tax-free until withdrawals are made.

Like the 401(k) plan, the 403(b) plan allows workers to choose from a variety of investment options. For instance, a typical 403(b) plan includes several stock mutual funds, bond mutual funds, and stable income funds. Unlike the 401(k) plan, however, the 403(b) plan does not allow participants to invest in individual stocks.

Personal Retirement Plans

You may place part of your earnings in a personal retirement fund. You can start a personal retirement plan at most financial institutions.

When opening a personal retirement account, it is important to choose a sound, reputable financial institution. This institution should provide personal counselors and easy-to-understand guides that inform you of the many issues to consider. Money deposited in a personal retirement plan is usually invested in stocks, bonds, and mutual funds.

IRAs

An *individual retirement arrangement (IRA)* is a personal retirement investment account created by a person. There are many places where you can set up an IRA. For example, you can set up an IRA at a bank, an insurance company, a mutual fund company, and a brokerage firm. An IRA is *not* an investment, but a vehicle that holds the investments you choose. You can hold many types of investments in an IRA, including stocks, bonds, mutual funds, exchange traded funds, REITs, bank CDs (certificates of deposit), and even real estate.

There are two primary types of IRAs: the traditional IRA and the Roth IRA. A **traditional IRA** is an individual retirement account that allows individuals to contribute pre-tax income to investments that grow tax deferred. Contributions to a traditional IRA are tax deductible. This means that amounts you contribute each year can be deducted from your income when you file your tax return. However, when you retire, amounts withdrawn from a traditional IRA are taxable.

A **Roth IRA** is an individual retirement account in which individuals contribute after-tax income and qualified withdrawals are not taxed. Contributions to a Roth IRA are made with after-tax earnings. That is, you cannot deduct your Roth IRA contributions on your tax return. When you retire, however, withdrawals from a Roth IRA are tax free. There are other withdrawals from a Roth IRA that may qualify as tax free, such as withdrawing money for a first-time home purchase.

The process of setting up a traditional IRA and a Roth IRA is identical. When making your application for the IRA, you simply check a box to designate whether you want it to be treated as traditional or Roth. Generally, the Roth IRA is a better choice for most. However, higher income individuals may find it advantageous to open a traditional IRA because the contributions are tax deductible.

Self-Employed Plans

Self-employed individuals can open a simplified employee pension (SEP) plan. Tax-deductible contributions are limited to a percentage of earned income. Earnings grow tax deferred until money is withdrawn at retirement.

A *Keogh plan*, also called an *HR 10,* is another type of personal retirement plan for the self-employed. Tax-deductible contributions are limited to a set

According to the IRS, the organizations that can offer a 403(b) plan are those that are "organized and operated exclusively for religious, charitable, scientific, public-safety testing, literary, or educational purposes." These types of institutions include K–12 public schools, colleges, universities, hospitals, libraries, and churches.

percentage of earned income. The allowable percentage changes periodically. The interest earned on Keogh accounts is not taxed until retirement. Retirement may begin as early as age 59 1/2.

For the latest information and regulations on these personal retirement plans, visit the Internal Revenue Service website at www.irs.gov.

Annuities

An annuity is another form of investment that can be used in personal retirement planning. An **annuity** is a contract with an insurance company that provides regular income for a set period of time, usually for life. Some annuities also provide death benefits. Investors make payments into an annuity over many years or in one large payment. Both the money invested and the interest it earns accumulates in the annuity.

The principal and earnings on an annuity are not taxed until money is either withdrawn or paid out at a future time. Annuities with reputable insurance companies are considered safe, reliable investments. However, investors should shop around and compare costs, fees, and interest rates.

Estate Planning

Estate planning is part of an overall financial plan. An **estate** consists of the assets and liabilities a person leaves when he or she dies. It includes property, savings, investments, and insurance benefits. *Estate planning* is the active management of these assets with directives for managing and distributing them when the owner dies. A **will** is a legal document stating a person's wishes for his or her estate after death. An **executor** is a person appointed to carry out the terms outlined in a will. If a person dies without naming an executor, the court will appoint one.

Ken Hurst/Shutterstock.com

A person creates an estate plan to make arrangements for his or her assets, such as a home, after his or her death.

Case Study

Estate Planning

Kelly and Jerome owned a very successful office supply business. Over the years, they made enough money to buy a house, raise two children, travel, and retire in comfort.

Sadly, Jerome died just a few years after they retired. Not only had Kelly lost her husband, she also faced a sea of financial confusion. Neither Kelly nor Jerome could face the thought that one of them would die, so they had not planned accordingly.

Since there was no will, Jerome's estate was divided according to state law. Half of his property went to their children. The amount Kelly received did not allow her to live comfortably for long. She had no legal right to the money the children inherited. Since Kelly and Jerome also did no tax planning, Kelly had to pay taxes that could have been avoided.

Case Review

1. When does it become important to prepare a will and complete estate planning?
2. Why is a will important even to those who do not have large amounts of money or property?
3. What are some estate planning steps that can ease financial burdens following the death of a loved one?
4. What are some consequences of dying without a will when one leaves young children behind?
5. What advice would you have given to Jerome and Kelly before they reached retirement age?

An estate plan allows people to accomplish these goals:
- decide long before their deaths how they want their assets managed afterward
- provide for their dependents
- minimize tax liabilities
- name an executor
- assign a power of attorney
- prepare a will
- prepare a trust

Power of Attorney

A *power of attorney* is a legal document that gives a person the power to act for another person regarding financial and legal matters. If a person becomes unable to make decisions due to health or other reasons, the person with power of attorney can sign documents and make decisions for that person.

Wills

Anyone who has property to leave or other rights to distribute should prepare a will. In most states, people must be at least 18 to make a will and must be of sound mind. Of sound mind means the person must know what he or she is doing and be mentally competent.

A will guarantees disposal of an estate according to the wishes of the deceased person. This makes settling an estate simpler for beneficiaries, usually family members. Friends may be listed as beneficiaries, as well as a favorite charity, a college, or some other organization.

Generally, it is wise to ask a lawyer for advice on what to include in a will and for help in drawing up the document. A will should do at least three things.

- *Name beneficiaries.* Beneficiaries are the people or groups who will receive assets. Assets include personal property and real estate, money, securities, jewelry, and family heirlooms. A will should clearly outline a person's wishes for the transfer of his or her property.
- *Name an executor.* The executor handles paying funeral expenses, medical bills, taxes, and other liabilities. The executor also performs other duties outlined in the will.
- *Name a guardian.* A guardian is a person responsible for the care of any beneficiaries who are young children. A guardian may also manage an estate on behalf of the dependents, or a trustee may be named to do this. A **trustee** is a person or institution named to manage assets on behalf of the beneficiaries.

A will must be signed in the presence of witnesses. If you change your will after it has been signed, an amendment called a codicil is added. A **codicil** is a document that explains, changes, or deletes provisions in a will. The codicil must also be signed in the presence of witnesses. If you need to make major changes in an existing will, you may wish to write a new will. In this case, it is important to add a clause that cancels all previous wills and codicils.

The cost of preparing a will varies. The more complex the estate, the more expensive the will may be. You can write your own will. A do-it-yourself kit that contains basic information and sample formats may cost less than $20. However, such a kit is unwise for large estates, situations with many tax issues, or when there are complicated instructions for distributing assets.

Since legal requirements for wills vary from state to state and may change with new laws, consulting an attorney is a wise choice. This is especially true for people who own their own businesses or have estates that total more than $1 million. Attorney fees vary, and consumers can usually arrange a free consultation with a lawyer. Your local American Bar Association can refer you to an attorney who can help.

When people die without a will, it is called *dying intestate.* When there is no will, property is divided according to state laws. This is not ideal because it can take a lot of time, and the government decides how to distribute assets.

Probate is a legal process of winding up the affairs of an estate, paying final expenses, and distributing the balance of money and property to beneficiaries. A *probate court* is the government institution that processes a deceased individual's will and estate. The probate procedure requires:

- proof the will is valid;
- an inventory and identification of the deceased person's assets and property;
- property appraisals;
- settlement of debts and taxes; and
- distribution of property according to terms of the will.

Probate can be a costly and time-consuming process that involves paperwork, court appearances, and lawyers. Probate fees are paid out of the

If you die without a will, the state will decide who gets your property and who gets custody of under-aged children.

estate before assets are distributed. The process can take several months, a year, or longer. The executor of the estate must manage the assets during this period. These proceedings are a matter of public record. You can establish a trust to avoid this lengthy and costly process.

Living Wills

A **living will,** or *health-care directive*, is a statement of instructions for specific medical treatment if a person becomes unable to make medical decisions. The primary purpose is to make known the medical treatments you do or do not wish to receive in the case of incapacitating injury or illness. It outlines your desires about medically prolonging your life. Creating a living will is a serious and very personal step to take. It should be discussed with family members, loved ones, and your physician.

Trusts

In addition to a will, you may need one or more trusts, particularly if your estate is complicated or if you wish to make special arrangements for its settlement. A **trust** is an arrangement through which a person transfers assets to a trustee, who then oversees and manages the assets on behalf of beneficiaries.

When you create a trust, you become the *grantor*. As grantor, you decide which assets to transfer to the trust. You name a trustee to manage the assets according to terms outlined in the trust. You also name the beneficiaries who are to receive the assets and when they will receive them.

Unlike a will, a trust account does not have to be probated. This means assets can easily pass to beneficiaries without court involvement. Another advantage of a trust is that it prevents the court from taking control of a person's assets, should the person become incapacitated.

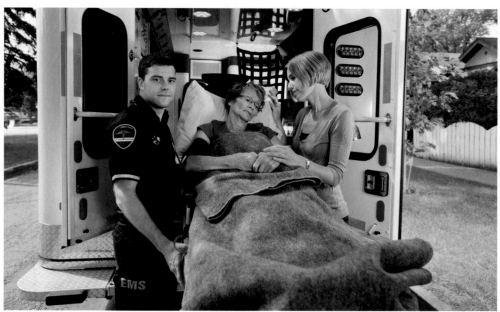

Tyler Olson/Shutterstock.com

A living will makes a person's wishes known in the event he or she is unable to make health-care decisions.

Careers in Finance

What Do Stockbrokers Do?

Stockbrokers are salespeople who buy and sell securities for clients. They advise clients on appropriate investments based on the clients' needs and financial conditions. Clients may be individuals, groups, or businesses. **Stockbrokers** typically:

- contact prospective clients to present information and explain available services;
- counsel clients regarding investment opportunities and market conditions;
- buy and sell securities, such as stocks and bonds;
- buy and sell commodities, such as cotton, corn, oil, and gold;
- monitor financial markets and the performance of individual securities; and
- analyze company finances and make recommendations to clients.

What Is It Like to Work as a Stockbroker?

Stockbrokers usually work in fast-paced office environments. They have access to computer terminals and quote boards that provide continuous current information on availability and prices of securities. Most of a **stockbroker's** day is likely to be spent on the phone pitching stock ideas to clients or prospective clients.

A **stockbroker** may work the standard 40-hour week. Many hours are often spent making client contacts after the trading day and meeting with clients on the clients' schedules. Some **stockbrokers** and financial representatives work exclusively inside banks providing service to walk-in customers.

Stockbrokers are subject to the regulations of the Securities and Exchange Commission (SEC), the stock exchanges, the firms for which they work, and the requirements of the states in which they work. Many belong to the Financial Industry Regulatory Authority (FINRA).

What Education and Skills Are Needed to Be a Stockbroker?

- bachelor degree in business or accounting
- pass the General Securities Representative Qualification Examination Series 7 and any additional exams required by individual states
- sales skills
- ability to analyze large amounts of statistical information
- excellent math skills and an understanding of economics

Trusts are used to achieve different goals. People can use a trust to:

- provide income and asset management for beneficiaries;
- set forth specific provisions for the support and education of minor children or dependents with disabilities;
- have a plan in place for managing financial affairs if they should become incapacitated or unable to manage for themselves;
- minimize estate and gift taxes; and
- protect their privacy and avoid probate court.

You can establish either a living trust or a testamentary trust. A living trust, set up during your lifetime, can provide for the management of your assets before your death and for the distribution of assets as directed after your death. Prior to death, you may serve as grantor, trustee, and beneficiary of the trust. A testamentary trust is set up under the terms of your will and becomes effective when you die.

When setting up a trust account, you will need to decide whether the agreement is irrevocable or revocable. An irrevocable trust is one that you cannot revoke. Stated another way, with an irrevocable trust you cannot change the terms of the trust or end it altogether. A revocable trust, on the other hand, is one which you can revoke; that is, you can change the terms or end it.

Normally, drawing up a trust agreement calls for the services of a competent lawyer who is familiar with estate planning. A representative of a financial firm can also help you set up a trust account.

Checkpoint 7.2

1. What is the purpose of asset diversification?
2. What are typical services offered by full-service brokerage firms?
3. What investment options are typically offered in an employer-sponsored 401(k) plan?
4. What retirement plans are available for a self-employed person?
5. Who should prepare a will?

Build Your Vocabulary

As you progress through this course, develop a personal glossary of personal finance terms and add it to your portfolio. This will help you build your vocabulary and prepare you for a career. Write a definition for each of the following terms and add it to your personal finance glossary.

investment portfolio	estate
diversification	executor
prospectus	will
dollar-cost averaging	trustee
rollover	codicil
traditional IRA	probate
Roth IRA	living will
annuity	trust

Chapter Summary

Section 7.1 Investments

- Investing money offers the opportunity to accumulate more money to meet future needs and goals. An investment plan is an important part of a financial plan designed to meet long-term goals and achieve financial security.

- Investment choices include stocks, bonds, mutual funds, real estate, and valuable goods.

Section 7.2 Investment Strategies and Estate Planning

- An investment portfolio is a collection of securities and other assets a person owns. Successful investors diversify their portfolios. Building a diversified portfolio involves gathering information, considering strategies, and selecting investment methods.

- Factors to consider when choosing investments include the risks, past and expected performance, fees and expenses, and management (the directors and officers of the company or fund). Beginning at an early age allows investors to benefit from two common investment strategies: buy and hold and dollar-cost averaging.

- To buy stocks, bonds, and other securities, you may open an account with a brokerage or securities firm, join an investment club, or take part in a direct reinvestment plan.

- Retirement planning is a key element of financial security and may include retirement programs offered by employers, personal retirement plans, and annuities. Today people are living longer and retiring sooner, which makes early retirement planning even more important.

- Estate planning is the active management of assets with directives for distributing the assets when the owner dies. This includes drawing up a will and possibly a trust to direct the distribution of assets upon one's death.

Check Your Personal Finance IQ

Now that you have finished the chapter, see what you learned about personal finance by taking the chapter posttest. If you do not have a smartphone, visit the G-W Learning companion website.

G-W Learning mobile site: www.m.g-wlearning.com

G-W Learning companion website: www.g-wlearning.com

Review Your Knowledge

1. Define investing.
2. What are the key characteristics of investments?
3. Where are stocks bought and sold?
4. What is the primary market for stocks?
5. Why do mutual funds offer more diversity than buying individual stocks and bonds?
6. What is a prospectus?
7. Describe the dollar-cost average investment strategy.
8. What are some possible sources of retirement income?
9. What goals does an estate plan allow a person to accomplish?
10. What is a trust?

Apply Your Knowledge

11. Name and describe one factor that could affect investment returns.
12. Assume you are ready to make your first investment. Would you choose a mutual fund, individual stock, individual bond, or real estate? Explain your choice.
13. If you were going to invest in stocks, would you buy common or preferred stock? Which is more likely to increase in value? Which do you think is the better investment? What are the advantages and disadvantages of each?
14. Identify and compare the three types of bonds. Which type of bond would you prefer to buy? Why?
15. Mike Burton wants to invest in real estate. However, he does not have enough saved to make a down payment on rental property. Explain how he can indirectly invest in real estate without the complications and financial commitment of owning property outright.
16. Most Americans invest the majority of their retirement savings in mutual funds. Do you agree with this strategy? Include in your answer the advantages and disadvantages of investing in a mutual fund?
17. Go to the website of a publicly traded company with which you are very familiar. Look for a link entitled "Investor Relations" or a similar name. Determine if the company has a direct stock purchase plan and a DRIP. Write a paragraph explaining how direct stock purchase plans and DRIPs are among the most cost effective ways of buying stock.
18. Do you think having a living will is a good idea? Explain your reasoning.
19. Describe the possible consequences of dying without a will. Which ones do you consider the most important?
20. If you were to write a will today, what would it contain? How might it change if you were 30 years old, single, and earning $60,000 annually? How might it change if you were 30 years old, earning the same amount, and married with children?

Teamwork

Form a team of classmates and develop a plan for investing $5,000 over the length of this course. Use the Internet, current financial publications, and books on financial planning for information on developing your plan. Factors to identify and consider include your objectives, types of investments, expected returns, risk tolerance, liquidity, and diversification. Describe your plan in terms of these factors. In the final week of class, compare your team's plans with those of other teams in the class.

G-W Learning Mobile Site

Visit the G-W Learning mobile site to complete the chapter pretest and posttest and to practice vocabulary using e-flash cards. If you do not have a smartphone, visit the G-W Learning companion website to access these features.

G-W Learning mobile site: www.m.g-wlearning.com

G-W Learning companion website: www.g-wlearning.com

Common Core

College and Career Readiness

CTE Career Ready Practices. Each employee has a stake in the profitability of the company for which he or she works. How can an individual employee positively and negatively affect a company's profitability? How do positive and negative customer interactions affect profitability? How does employee productivity and attendance affect profitability?

Reading. Research the laws in your state regarding persons dying without a will. Read closely to determine what the text says. Write several paragraphs, citing the events that affect estate laws. Then, create a visual display that shows the importance of estate planning.

Writing. You are ready to make an investment, and you want to purchase stocks as part of your portfolio. Compose an informative letter or e-mail that you might send to an investment company. Convey the information clearly and accurately through the effective organization of the content. Describe the types of stock you are interested in purchasing and ask for a quote. Be sure to follow the rules of writing a letter or e-mail.

Web Connect

Look up a publicly traded stock on the NASDAQ or New York Stock Exchange. Record the daily closing value each day for two weeks. Compare the value on day 1 with the value on day 14. How did the stock perform?

College and Career Readiness

College and Career Readiness Portfolio

You have identified the types of items you might place in your portfolio. You will begin adding items in this activity and add other items as you continue this class. Locate certificates you have received. For example, a certificate might show that you have completed a training class. Another certificate might show that you can keyboard at a certain speed. You might have a certificate that you received for taking part in a community project. Any certificates you have that show tasks completed or skills or talents that you have should be included. Create a document that lists each certificate and tells when you received it. Briefly describe your activities, skills, or talents related to the certificate.

1. Scan these documents to include in your e-portfolio. Use the file format you selected earlier.

2. Give each document an appropriate name, using the naming system you created earlier. Place each certificate and the list in an appropriate subfolder for your e-portfolio.

3. Place the certificates and list in the container for your print portfolio.

Public Speaking

Public speaking is a competitive event you might enter with your Career and Technical Student Organization (CTSO). This event allows you to showcase your communication skills of speaking, organizing, and making an oral presentation. This is usually a timed event you can prepare for before the competition. You will have time to research, prepare, and practice before going to the competition. Review the specific guidelines and rules for this event for direction as to topics and props you will be allowed to use.

To prepare for the public speaking event, complete the following activities.

1. Read the guidelines provided by your organization. Review the topics from which you may choose to make a speech.

2. Locate a rubric or scoring sheet for the event on your organization's website.

3. Confirm whether visual aids may be used in the presentation and the amount of setup time permitted.

4. Review the rules to confirm if questions will be asked or if you will need to defend a case or situation.

5. Make notes on index cards about important points to remember. Use these notes to study. You may also be able to use these notes during the event.

6. Practice the presentation. You should introduce yourself, review the topic that is being presented, defend the topic being presented, and conclude with a summary.

7. After the presentation is complete, ask for feedback from your instructor. You may consider also having a student audience listen and give feedback.

Insurance plays an important role in our lives. We buy insurance to protect us against financial loss. The types of insurance protection consumers typically buy cover health, disability, life, home, and automobiles. Protection needs in these areas vary with every individual and family. It pays to shop carefully for the best coverage at the best price. A reliable insurance agent can help you select the type and amount of coverage you need. Costs depend on the type and amount of coverage you buy, the deductible amount, the risk factors where you live, and the opportunity for discounts.

Focus on Finance

COBRA

COBRA requires continuation of coverage to covered employees, their spouses, their former spouses, and their dependent children when group health coverage would otherwise be lost due to specific events. Those events include the death of a covered employee, divorce or legal separation from a covered employee, and job termination or reduction in the hours of a covered employee's employment for reasons other than gross misconduct. Coverage periods are:

- Up to 18 months for covered employees, as well as their spouses and their dependents, when workers would otherwise lose their coverage because of job loss or a reduction in hours worked.

- Up to 29 months for employees who are determined to be disabled at any time during the first 60 days of COBRA coverage. The extended coverage period also applies to the disabled employee's qualified beneficiaries.

- Up to 36 months for spouses and dependents facing a loss of employer-provided coverage due to an employee's death, a divorce or legal separation, or certain other qualifying events.

College and Career Readiness

Reading Prep. Before reading this chapter, review the objectives. Based on this information, analyze the author's purpose for this chapter.

Check Your Personal Finance IQ

Before you begin the chapter, see what you already know about personal finance by taking the chapter pretest. If you do not have a smartphone, visit the G-W Learning companion website.

G-W Learning mobile site: www.m.g-wlearning.com

G-W Learning companion website: www.g-wlearning.com

Sections

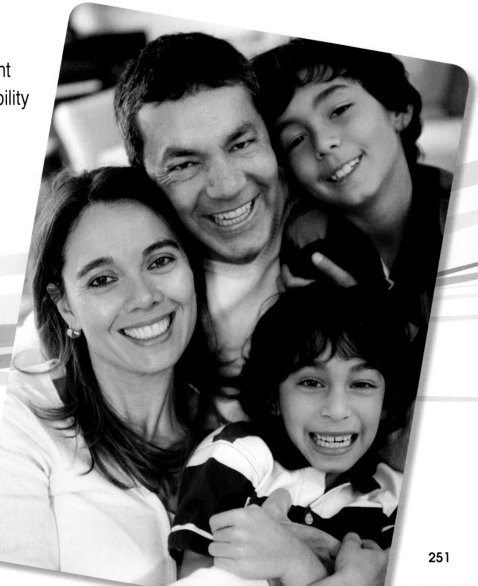

Section 8.1
Risk Management

Objectives

After studying this section, you will be able to:
- Identify and explain two common types of risks.
- Discuss strategies for dealing with risk.
- Explain how insurance protects individuals from financial losses.

Terms

risk	insurance
pure risk	premium
speculative risk	dependent
risk management	policyholder

Risk

Life involves risk. **Risk** is a measure of the likelihood that something will be lost. Some risks are predictable: you will sometimes get sick, and you will grow old. Other risks are unpredictable. These include serious illnesses or injuries, car accidents, house fires, and theft. Some events can limit your ability to earn a living or wipe out your assets. When you earn income, own property, and accumulate savings, these things are too important to lose.

There are various types of risks you will likely face in your lifetime. Some risks have little consequences, such as planning a trip to the beach on a day when there is only a 10 percent chance of rain. Other risks can have much more serious consequences, such as driving a car without insurance. Risks can be classified as pure risks and speculative risks.

Pure Risk

A **pure risk** is a risk with a possibility of loss but no possibility of gain. In such situations, insurance protection is clearly needed. Pure risk can be categorized as personal risk, property risk, and liability risk.
- *Personal risks.* Personal risks are those that affect you directly, such as illness or disability or the illness or disability of an immediate family member.
- *Property risks.* Property risks are those that affect your personal or real property. A car theft and a house fire are examples of property risk. A lightning strike that burns out your electronic equipment is another example of property risk.
- *Liability risks.* Liability risks, also called *legal risks,* result from the possibility of losing money or other property as a result of legal proceedings. For example, suppose Kyle King frequently texts while driving. This practice increases Kyle's liability risk because he would be legally responsible for damages if he accidentally hit another car.

Kinga/Shutterstock.com

You can be liable if a person injures him- or herself on your property, such as by slipping on an icy doorstep.

Likewise, if you invited friends over for a party and the weight of everyone on your deck caused it to collapse, you would be legally liable for any injuries sustained by your friends.

Speculative Risk

Speculative risk differs from pure risk. A **speculative risk** is a risk that may result in either financial gain or financial loss. For example, if you buy gold, silver, land, or the stocks of companies, you could either make or lose money when the property is sold. When the stock of Google was first offered for sale to the public on August 19, 2004, the issue price was $85 per share. The stock soared in value, reaching $714.87 a share on December 3, 2007. Those who bought it when it was first offered speculated that it would go higher and they would make a profit when they sold their shares. Those who bought the stock at higher levels speculated that it would go even higher. However, in late 2008, the world economy fell into a recession, and the market value of Google shares dropped to under $300 a share. Some investors who speculated made money on their Google stock. Other investors who speculated lost money on their Google stock. This is the nature of speculative risk; you may make money, or you could lose money.

Speculative risks generally result in a higher frequency of loss than pure risks. However, most speculative risks are not insurable because they are taken willingly in hopes of making a gain.

Managing Risk

Financial security depends in part on risk management. **Risk management** is the process of measuring risk and finding ways to minimize or manage loss. There are four strategies for dealing with risk. You have probably used several of them.

Ethics

Filing false insurance claims is unethical and illegal. It is important to file accurate information and only request assistance from an insurance company when a claim can be proven. Filing false or misleading claims can result in insurance coverage being cancelled.

Avoidance

One of the best ways to manage risk is to avoid the risk. *Avoidance* is taking steps to eliminate risk. For example, suppose a trail marker warns "Do not go beyond this point!" Hikers may avoid injury by obeying the warning. There may be hazards beyond the sign.

Reduction

Reduction is a strategy of minimizing risks that you cannot always avoid. For example, a reduction strategy for staying healthy is washing your hands often to eliminate disease-causing germs. Wearing a seat belt while driving is a reduction strategy that lowers the chance of injury or death in the event of an accident.

Retention

Retention is assessing risk and making financial preparations for possible future loss. It is also called *self-insurance.* For example, a person may set aside money in a savings account to use in case he or she loses a job. Retention strategies, however, do not work well when potential losses are very high.

Transference

Transference is shifting risk to someone else. The most common way to do this is to buy insurance. By purchasing insurance, you become a member of a large pool of people and transfer your risk to the insurance company. Insurance is a common method of risk management.

Insurance Protection

Insurance is a form of risk management that pools the premiums of a large group of people to cover the expenses of the smaller number within the group who suffer losses. A **premium** is an amount of money regularly paid to an insurance company for a policy. The money collected from the premiums is invested, and the earnings are used to pay claims of insured persons. If you have an accident or another setback, the insurance company pays for your losses. There is little probability that large numbers of people will need payouts at the same time. On average, payouts made by insurance companies will be less than the earnings received from investing the fees paid by the members of the pool.

The main purpose of insurance is to provide protection against specific types of financial losses. Events that could put your finances at risk include

You Do the Math

When adding or subtracting whole numbers and decimals, place each number in a vertical list, aligning the decimal points. Then, complete the operation starting with the column, or place, farthest to the right and work to the left. The result of addition is called the *sum.* In an addition operation, when the sum of a column is greater than nine, the second number is carried to the top of the next column to the left. In a subtraction operation, borrow from the next column to the left when needed. The result of subtraction is called the *difference.*

Complete the Following Problem

Tyrone visits his doctor because he has abdominal pain. The doctor examines Tyrone and sends him to the outpatient testing center at a local hospital for an abdominal scan. Given the following information, how much will Tyrone pay out of his own pocket for the doctor's visit and test? How much would it cost Tyrone if he did not have insurance?

- Doctor's visit: $125

- Abdominal scan: $1,600

- Tyrone's insurance coverage:
    - Deductible: $250 per year (Tyrone has paid $75 toward his deductible.)
    - Copayments: $30 per doctor visit; $10 for generic drugs; $30 for brand-name drugs (Copayments do not count toward the deductible.)

illness or injury, accidents, death, and property losses. The purpose of insurance is to pay for losses that would be difficult or impossible for you to pay for. Taking a careful look at the risks you face and making a plan for managing them with insurance and other resources are basic steps in any financial plan.

Insurance helps mitigate financial losses that are out your control.

Decision-Making Process

Making a decision on purchasing insurance begins by assessing the risks you face, as illustrated in Figure 8-1. The following steps are involved.

Step 1. Identify risks. Determine the possible or probable risks that in some way can affect you. For example, if you live close to a moving stream of water, you probably will need flood insurance on your home.

Step 2. Assess risks. Assess the seriousness of the risks and the likelihood of loss. Focus your attention and resources on the risks that can have serious consequences. Take driving a car, for example. Driving has serious legal and financial risks, so you should never drive without proper insurance.

Step 3. Handle risks. Determine the most effective way to handle the risk. The ways of handling serious risk are avoidance, reduction, and transference. Less serious risks, such as leaving your schoolbooks in an unlocked locker, can be assumed. In other words, you usually do not need insurance for less serious risks because the possibility of loss is too low to justify the cost of insurance.

Step 4. Make a decision. After completing a thorough risk assessment, you can decide the best ways to protect yourself and your property. Consider the losses that could damage or destroy your financial security. Then take steps to protect yourself with appropriate insurance.

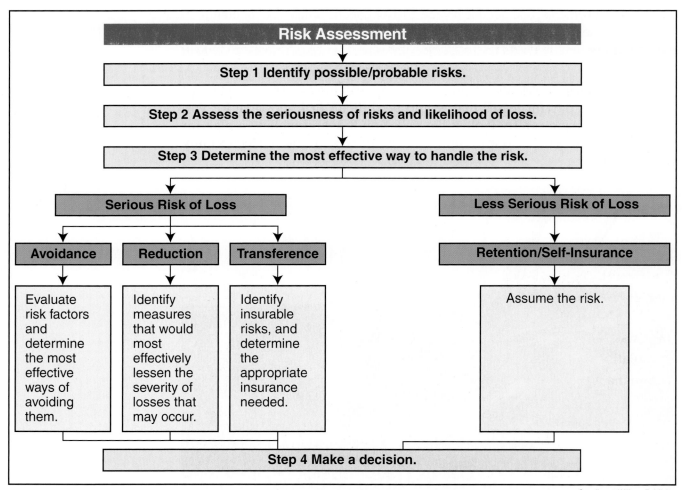

Goodheart-Willcox Publisher

Figure 8-1 Following the decision-making process for assessing risk will help determine your insurance needs.

Buying Insurance

The type and amount of insurance needed varies from person to person. It depends on the risks being covered, the amount available to pay for losses, and the financial obligations of the insured persons. For example, an unmarried person without children generally needs less coverage than a head of a family with several children.

Protection needs increase with each new dependent a person acquires. A **dependent** is an individual who relies on someone else for financial support, such as a child, a spouse, or an elderly parent. Protection needs also increase as additional assets are acquired or there has been an increase in value of assets already owed. For example, if a couple bought a house 20 years ago for $125,000 and the house is now worth $190,000, insurance is needed to cover the current value of the house.

A **policyholder** is a person who has purchased insurance. The premiums you and other policyholders pay are invested by the company to earn money. Both premiums and earnings are used to pay insurance claims. A claim is a bill submitted to the insurance company for payment.

Types of insurance that protect against financial risks include health, disability, life, home, and automobile insurance.

Checkpoint 8.1

1. What are personal risks?
2. Give three examples of property risk.
3. What are liability risks?
4. What are four strategies for dealing with risk?
5. Sue Foster recently bought some gold to hold as an investment. What kind of risk did she incur?

Build Your Vocabulary

As you progress through this course, develop a personal glossary of personal finance terms and add it to your portfolio. This will help you build your vocabulary and prepare you for a career. Write a definition for each of the following terms, and add it to your personal finance glossary.

risk	insurance
pure risk	premium
speculative risk	dependent
risk management	policyholder

Section 8.2
Health and Disability Insurance

Objectives

After studying this section, you will be able to:

- Outline the different types of private health insurance coverage.
- Identify ways to choose an insurance plan.
- Describe types of government-sponsored health insurance programs.
- Explain the purpose of disability insurance.

Terms

deductible

fee-for-service plan

coinsurance

inpatient

managed care plan

copayment

health savings account (HSA)

exclusion

preexisting condition

Private Health Insurance

Health insurance offers protection by covering specific medical expenses created by illness, injury, and disability. Today, approximately 35 percent of health-care costs are paid by private plans offered by insurance companies. Many of these plans are available through employers.

Participants in private insurance plans usually pay a monthly premium. Most plans also carry a deductible. A **deductible** is the amount you must pay toward your medical expenses before your insurance company begins to pay. For example, if your plan has an annual $500 deductible, you must pay the first $500 of medical expenses. Once your deductible is met, your insurance company begins to pay on qualified expenses above the deductible. However, most plans do not pay 100 percent of the expenses above the deductible. Instead, most pay a percentage, usually 80 percent.

Most private insurance programs are group plans sponsored by employers, unions, and other organizations. Individuals may also purchase private health insurance, but it usually costs more and provides less coverage than group plans.

Fee-for-Service Plans

A **fee-for-service plan** is a health-care plan that pays for covered medical services after treatment is provided. An advantage of this plan is that you can usually go to any licensed health-care provider or accredited hospital of your choice.

You are responsible for a deductible and coinsurance. **Coinsurance** is a percentage of the service costs that patients pay. For example, if a medical service costs $100 and the coinsurance is 20 percent, your cost would be $20. In a fee-for-service plan, you pay the $100 at the time of the medical service.

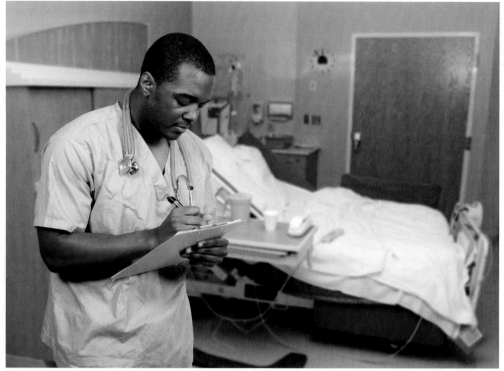

Rob Byron/Shutterstock.com

Health insurance helps offset the high cost of medical care.

Either you or the doctor's office submits a claim to the insurance company. You then receive a reimbursement, or repayment, of $80.

With many fee-for-service plans, your health-care provider will bill your insurance company for you. However, there may be occasions where you have to submit the necessary forms to your insurance company. As a result, you should learn how to file claims and file them promptly. Keep the name and phone number of your plan handy as well as membership numbers and other information you may need to receive services and file claims.

Fee-for-service plans generally offer basic and major medical coverage. Basic coverage includes prescriptions, hospital stays, and inpatient tests. An **inpatient** is a person whose care requires a stay in a hospital. Basic coverage also pays for some doctor's visits, outpatient procedures, and certain other medical services.

Major medical coverage typically covers the costs of serious illnesses and high-cost procedures and injuries. Often fee-for-service plans combine basic and major medical protection in one policy called a *comprehensive plan.*

Managed Care Plans

A **managed care plan** is a type of health-care plan in which the insurance company contracts with specific doctors, hospitals, and other health-care providers to deliver medical services and preventive care to members at reduced cost. Your choice of service providers is limited to those who participate in the plan except for necessary referrals to specialists outside the plan.

You and/or your employer pay a set amount in monthly premiums. You also pay any required deductibles, coinsurance, or copayments. A **copayment** is a flat fee the patient must pay for medical services. Copayments are due at the time of service. For example, when you have a doctor's appointment or a prescription filled, you pay the copayment at that time. Copayment amounts are determined by your health-care plan.

Three forms of managed care are health maintenance organizations (HMOs), preferred provider organizations (PPOs), and point-of-service (POS) plans.

Health Maintenance Organizations (HMOs)

Health Maintenance Organizations (HMOs) provide a list of participating physicians from which you choose a primary care doctor. This doctor coordinates your health care and carries out routine exams and treatments.

Case Study

Life Insurance

Coni is 23 years old and just started her first job after college. She is single with no dependents. Both of Coni's parents are living. A $150 credit card balance and a $1,500 car loan are her only major financial obligations other than her apartment lease.

When Coni is 25, her father dies. His retirement funds leave just enough money for her mother to make ends meet. Coni's mother could become financially dependent on her if she outlives her source of income.

When Coni is 28, she marries Arend. Arend has no dependents. That year, Coni is promoted at work. At age 30, Coni has their first child. Two years later, she has a second child. She works part-time until the children reach school age. This reduces her income temporarily. Coni and Arend start setting aside money for the children's college costs.

When Coni and Arend reach their mid-forties, their children are in high school. They will start college in three and five years. Coni's mother is in a nursing home, and Coni is paying most of the bills. Both Coni and Arend are working and are at the peak of their careers. They expect their salaries to remain fairly stable during the remaining 20 years of work.

Now Coni and Arend are in their mid-fifties. Both children graduated from college. Coni's mother passed away. Coni and Arend begin to consider travel and retirement.

Case Review

1. When Coni was single and both her parents were alive, do you think she needed life insurance? Explain.
2. When Coni's father died, what changes should she have made in her insurance program? Why?
3. What type of insurance program would you recommend for Coni and Arend when they first married? Why?
4. What insurance and other financial planning would be suitable for a couple with young children?
5. How would Coni and Arend's financial planning change when they reached their forties?
6. What changes do you think they should make in their insurance program now? Why?

The plan normally covers only treatments provided by doctors who participate in the plan. If you go outside the plan for care, you pay part or all of the bill.

Normally, you must go through your primary care doctor for a referral to a specialist if you require specialized treatments, consultations, or procedures. Your primary care doctor and a referral specialist from the HMO will determine which treatments and procedures are covered.

Preferred Provider Organizations (PPOs)

Preferred provider organizations (PPOs) arrange with specific doctors, hospitals, and other caregivers to provide services at reduced costs to plan members. You receive services at lower costs by going to participating caregivers, but you may go outside the plan if you are willing to pay the extra cost. For example, the plan may pay 80 percent of the cost of care within the plan and only 60 percent outside the plan. This offers you more choices than an HMO offers.

Point-of-Service (POS) Plans

Point-of-service plans connect you with a primary care doctor who participates in the plan and who is your "point of service" provider. That doctor supervises your care and makes referrals as necessary to participating or nonparticipating specialists.

POS plans combine features of both HMOs and PPOs, providing the freedom of a PPO with the lower cost of an HMO. There usually is no deductible, and copayments are limited if you see doctors within the plan. You may also choose health-care providers outside the plan; but a deductible may apply, and copayments are higher.

Health Savings Accounts

A **health savings account (HSA)** is a tax-advantaged savings account available to people enrolled in qualified high deductible health plans (HDHPs). In an HDHP, the patient pays a high deductible before the insurance begins to pay. However, the monthly premiums are usually lower than for other types of plans.

If you have an HSA, you may contribute pre-tax dollars into the account. The maximum annual amount you can contribute is adjusted each year based on the rise of the consumer price index (CPI) in the previous year. Current HDHP deductible amounts and HSA contribution levels are available on the US Treasury Department website.

You may use savings in the account to pay for health-care costs. Unused funds in the account may accumulate tax-free. However, if you use funds for purposes other than health-care costs, you will incur tax penalties.

An HSA can save you money three ways. The high deductible feature in your health-care coverage makes monthly premiums less expensive. When filing your tax return, you can deduct the amount you contribute to your HSA, thus reducing your taxes. The unspent savings in your account are allowed to accumulate tax-free until you need them to pay health-care expenses.

You may be able to set up an HSA through your employer. Employer-sponsored plans result in pre-tax deductions. This means that your employer deducts your plan contributions from your pay before taxes are determined, reducing the amount of your income subject to taxes. For example, Claudia Cole earns $2,000 a month and contributes $200 monthly to her HSA. Each month, Claudia's employer deducts her $200 contribution from her pay. Her income taxes are calculated on the difference, $1,800 ($2,000 − $200).

If your employer does not offer these accounts, you may be able to establish one on your own. You can do an Internet search for a list of companies that offer HSA-eligible plans in your state.

COBRA

If you are covered by an employer-sponsored group plan and lose your job, you are likely to lose your health-care coverage as well. In this case, you may be entitled to continue your health benefits under the *Consolidated Omnibus Budget Reconciliation Act (COBRA)*.

This law gives covered workers the right to continue their group health-care coverage for up to 18 months after job loss. (In some cases, the coverage can be extended up to 36 months.) However, the covered worker must pay the premiums for continuing coverage. A covered worker is anyone who is (or was) provided coverage under an employer's group plan.

COBRA generally applies to all group health plans maintained by private companies with at least 20 employees and by state and local governments. Employers may require individuals who elect continuation coverage to pay the full cost of the coverage plus a 2 percent administrative fee. The required payment for continuation coverage is often more expensive than the amount that active employees pay for group health coverage since the employer usually pays part of the cost of employees' coverage. However, the COBRA payment is usually less expensive than individual health coverage. For information on COBRA and its possible benefits, contact the nearest US Department of Labor office.

Individual Plans

People who are not eligible for group insurance may purchase health insurance on their own. However, individual policies are more expensive and may offer fewer benefits than group plans. Premiums for an individual can be as much as $800 a month. Families often pay more than $1,000 a month.

Many families and individuals cannot afford high premiums, so they go without health insurance. However, it is risky to be uninsured. A serious illness or injury can easily wipe out a person's life savings, assets, or business.

Many health insurance companies sell individual plans. An application process includes filling out a medical history questionnaire and sometimes submitting to medical tests or a complete physical exam. Healthy young applicants are usually accepted. However, people suffering from serious injuries, illnesses, or chronic physical or mental health problems may be denied coverage. If they are accepted, they pay high premiums.

Some insurance plans may contain many exclusions. An **exclusion** is a medical service that is not covered in an insurance plan. Examples include dental care or treatment of preexisting conditions. A **preexisting condition** is an illness or an injury a person has before signing up for health-care insurance. Generally, these conditions are not covered by a new plan for a stated period of time, if at all.

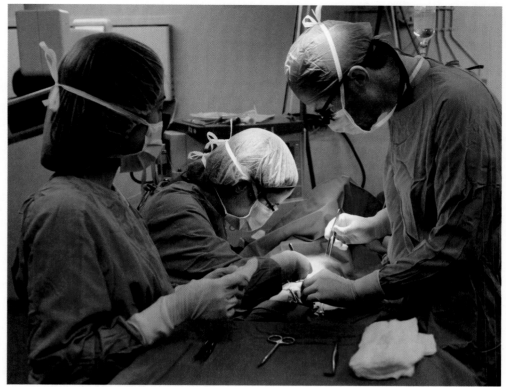

An unexpected illness or injury can mean financial hardship for an uninsured person.

Coverage for Young Adults

Many health insurance plans cover the policyholder's children until they reach a certain age. The recent *Affordable Care Act* includes limited provisions for young adults to remain on family policies until age 26. Full-time college students can usually remain on their parents' plan. However, once they leave college, change their student status to part-time, or get married, they may no longer be eligible. Eligibility requirements vary from state to state.

Many colleges offer student medical insurance for major medical expenses. For routine health problems, students can visit free or low-cost campus health and mental health clinics. Young people who do not go to college often get health coverage through an employer. However, health coverage is usually not available to part-time, temporary, and contract employees.

Many young people do not have health coverage because of high monthly premiums and deductibles. Healthy young people may not want to pay for health insurance, but serious illness is always a possibility. Also, accidents are a leading cause of injury and death among young adults. Experts recommend carrying major medical insurance to pay for hospitalization, tests, and surgery in case of serious illness and injury.

Long-Term Care

Long-term care insurance covers certain costs of care in a nursing home, an assisted living facility, or at home. The plan pays for the assistance needed by a person with a chronic illness or disability who cannot safely live alone.

Older consumers are the primary purchasers of long-term care insurance. Plans vary in cost and the services provided. Premiums for this coverage increase with the age of the purchaser.

Choosing a Plan

Many different types of private insurance programs are available. If you are looking for an individual plan, it pays to shop around. The website for the Department of Insurance for your state may offer consumer information and assistance.

If you have access to a group plan through your employer or some other affiliation, you can usually sign up during an enrollment period. At this time, policyholders can also change plans or renew coverage. Carefully review the insurance materials provided and choose the plan that meets your needs.

In evaluating health insurance plans, consider the services covered, the choice of health-care providers, and the costs.

Services

No plan will pay for all your medical expenses or cover all the services you may need. *Maximum benefits* refer to the maximum paid for specific types of treatment or the maximum number of days care is covered. For example, payment for mental health care may be limited to $1,000 annually; the number of days in a hospital may be limited as well.

Plans also may require preauthorization and utilization reviews for certain services. A *preauthorization* is an approval from the plan before receiving certain procedures and treatments. A *utilization review* is an insurance company's examination of requests for medical treatments and procedures to make sure they are covered and the patient truly needs them.

Be sure to find out if preauthorizations and utilization reviews are required. Look for coverage of the services that are most important to you. Important services may include:

- inpatient hospital services
- outpatient surgery
- office visits
- preventive care and screenings
- maternity care and well-baby care
- medical tests
- emergency room care
- physical therapy
- X-rays
- mental health services
- drug and alcohol abuse treatment
- prescription drugs
- home health care
- dental care
- eye care

Business Management & Administration

Risk Managers

Risk managers identify potential problems and predict their probability of occurring. They suggest ways of appraising and controlling risk and minimizing its effects. Their input helps to determine the amount people pay for insurance.

Choice

Some plans allow you to choose your doctors regardless of where they practice or their hospital affiliation. Other plans limit you to participating health-care providers. Consider the following questions.

- How important is it to choose your own doctor and hospital or continue with the providers you already use?
- What health-care providers, including doctors, hospitals, and labs, participate in the plan? Where are they located?
- What are the provisions for seeing a specialist if you believe you need one?
- Can you change doctors without prior approval if you are dissatisfied with your primary care physician?

Cost

Make sure you know the answers to the following questions before choosing a plan.

- What premiums must you pay?
- Is there a deductible? If so, how much is it? Which services are subject to the deductible?
- What are the costs of using nonparticipating providers and facilities?
- What health costs should you be prepared to pay? Check any exclusions, service limitations, or restrictions on preexisting conditions that may apply to you.
- What portion of the charges requires a copayment? Do copayments apply to every medical service you receive or only to specific items, such as office visits and prescription drugs?
- In a managed care program, find out whether copayments are higher if you go outside your health-care plan for treatment.

Figure the total cost of the premiums you would pay together with the deductible. Certain plans have lower premiums, but higher copayments or deductibles. Other plans may have the reverse. Very often, you can reduce monthly premiums by choosing a plan with a higher deductible. This can save you money if you typically require only routine health-care services.

You can control your health-care costs by developing habits that make the most of your health-care dollars. See Figure 8-2 for ways to lower health-care costs.

Go Green

Some insurance companies encourage consumers to be eco-friendly by offering special rates for fuel-efficient cars or environmentally-friendly housing. By offering these special rates, insurers can help customers reduce their carbon footprint.

Ways to Lower Health-Care Costs

- Make good health a priority. Follow a balanced approach to diet, exercise, sleep, stress control, and accident prevention.

- Find out what free or low-cost health services and programs are available through your school, employer, community, and government.

- Know exactly what expenses your health insurance covers, keep accurate records, and file claims promptly for covered expenses.

- Discuss fees and prices with health-care providers. Cost-conscious patients can often avoid unnecessary expenses.

- Lower hospital costs by asking for outpatient care, if possible, and minimum hospital stays.

- Get a second opinion before agreeing to nonemergency surgery or costly procedures.

- Obtain necessary authorizations before receiving treatments to be sure they are covered by your insurance.

- Keep track of out-of-pocket spending on health-care expenses. If these are more than a certain percentage of your income, they may be tax deductible.

Goodheart-Willcox Publisher

Figure 8-2 Individuals can lower the cost of health care by following these recommendations.

Government-Sponsored Health Insurance

The government offers health insurance to certain eligible people, including older adults, people with disabilities, low-income families, and children. What each person pays, if anything, depends on various factors.

Medicare

Medicare covers specific health-care expenses for eligible citizens age 65 and older. It also covers those under age 65 with certain diseases or disabilities. The government funding for Medicare comes from payroll taxes. Four different parts of Medicare provide coverage for specific services.

Part A Hospital Insurance

Part A helps pay for inpatient care in hospitals and skilled nursing facilities up to a specified number of days. It does not cover long-term care, but it covers some home health care and hospice care. Hospice care is for people with a terminal illness.

Most recipients do not pay a monthly premium for Part A coverage if they paid Medicare taxes while working. The current Medicare tax rate is 1.45 percent of earnings. Employers withhold the Medicare tax from the pay of employees and match it dollar for dollar for a total tax of 2.9 percent (1.45×2). Self-employed people pay the full 2.9 percent.

A deductible must be met before Medicare will pay for hospital stays. If a patient needs care beyond the specified number of days allowed for home health, hospice, and skilled nursing care, the patient is responsible for paying certain costs. Current deductible rates and patient costs are available online at www.medicare.gov.

Part B Medical Insurance

Part B is a voluntary program that helps pay for a variety of health-care costs. These include doctors' fees, outpatient hospital services, home health services, certain tests, and other health-care costs. To obtain Part B coverage, enrollees must pay a monthly premium.

Patients also pay an annual deductible each year before Part B will pay for services. In addition, patients pay coinsurance for certain services. For example, patients pay 20 percent of the cost for a physical therapy session. Premiums, deductibles, and coinsurance rates change periodically.

Part C Medicare Advantage Plan

Private health insurance companies contract with Medicare to provide this type of plan. Medicare Advantage Plans combine Part A and Part B benefits under one plan. Some people prefer this type of plan because it simplifies enrollment and payment procedures. In most cases, prescription drug coverage is also included. Plans vary in coverage and costs.

Part D Prescription Drug Coverage

Part D helps to lower prescription drug prices and protect against higher future drug prices. Those who enroll in this program pay a monthly premium. Private insurance companies provide the coverage. There are a variety of plans offered, and subscribers choose the one that best suits their medical needs.

Medigap Insurance

Medigap insurance helps pay for health-care costs not covered by Medicare, such as copayments and deductibles. Private insurance companies sell this type of protection—not the government. Usually, this insurance is only available for patients who have both Medicare Parts A and B.

The insurance is available in up to 12 standard benefit packages that provide varying degrees of coverage. The broader the coverage, the higher the premium will be. It pays to shop carefully for a reputable, reliable insurance company with a good record of customer service.

Medicaid

Medicaid is a health insurance program for eligible low-income persons and those with certain disabilities. It is a state-administered program financed by federal and state tax revenues.

Patients apply for Medicaid at public aid offices within their state. The services provided vary from state to state. Most Medicaid programs pay for inpatient and outpatient hospital services, clinic care, X-rays, and laboratory services. Some states also pay for family planning, home health-care services, dental care, eye care, and other medical needs.

Children's Health Insurance Program (CHIP)

Many American families earn too much to qualify for Medicaid but not enough to afford private health insurance premiums. The Children's Health Insurance Program (CHIP) gives federal funds to states to provide health insurance coverage for children ages 18 and younger. The program rules vary slightly among states. Taxes on the sales of cigarettes and other tobacco products are used to fund the program. For more information, go to www.healthcare.gov.

Disability Insurance

Disability insurance pays a portion of income lost to a worker who is unable to work for a prolonged period because of illness or injury. Many people do not think they need disability insurance. However, the loss of income because of an inability to work can be financially devastating.

Disability insurance may replace as much as 60 to 70 percent of the income normally earned. The two types of disability insurance are short-term plans and long-term plans. Short-term coverage normally requires a waiting period of up to 14 days and provides coverage for up to two years. Long-term coverage may have a waiting period of several weeks or months, and it pays for a number of years or for life.

Many employers provide limited disability insurance to their workers as a benefit. The employer pays the premium for these group plans. If an employee wants a higher level of insurance through the group plan, he or she may be able to pay for it. Consumers may buy this type of coverage independently if they are not part of employer health-care plans or other insurance programs.

Shop carefully if you are buying disability insurance because plans vary greatly from company to company. Important questions to ask when buying disability insurance include the following.

- What benefits are promised? How much money will you receive?
- What is the waiting period if benefits do not start immediately? Is there is a waiting period of weeks or months? If you opt for a longer waiting period, your insurance premium will often be lower.

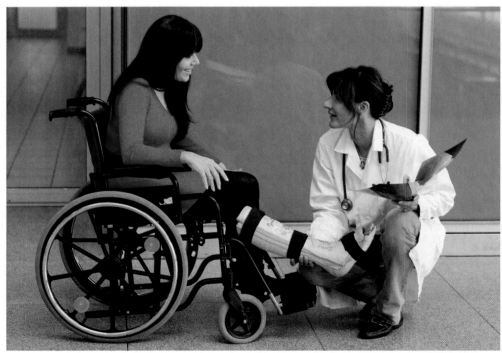

An injury or illness may leave you unable to work.

- How long are benefits available? The length of time a person can receive benefits varies. This can be a few years, until retirement, or for a lifetime.
- Can the policy be canceled by the insurer? A noncancelable clause means that the insurance company cannot cancel your coverage so long as you pay the premiums. A guaranteed renewable clause means that you can renew the coverage with the same benefits but usually at a higher cost.

You may have to give up some of the features you want to get an affordable premium. For example, lowering the amount of the benefit or lengthening the waiting period will reduce the premium you must pay.

Workers' compensation insurance is another type of disability insurance. It provides a safety net for workers with work-related illnesses or injuries. It covers medical care and pays for a portion of lost wages. Workers' compensation insurance also pays for medical treatment and rehabilitation that injured workers may require. The entire cost of workers' compensation insurance is usually paid by the employer. The cost depends on several factors, including the number of employees, risk factors associated with the job, and the company's past history of accidents.

When workers are permanently disabled, they may receive benefits for life. If injuries and illnesses are fatal, workers' compensation provides death benefits to survivors.

Employers in every state are required to provide some form of workers' compensation insurance. Employees must file claims through their employers to apply for workers' compensation. Each state has its own laws and time limits for filing claims. Applicants must prove they are disabled and usually must submit to examinations by insurance company doctors. To find out more about your state's workers' compensation laws, check with the state Workers' Compensation Board.

Checkpoint 8.2

1. What is an advantage of fee-for-service health insurance plans?
2. What coverage does the typical health insurance policy provide?
3. Why is a health savings account (HSA) referred to as a tax-advantaged account?
4. What is the purpose of COBRA insurance?
5. What is the purpose of disability insurance?

Build Your Vocabulary

As you progress through this course, develop a personal glossary of personal finance terms and add it to your portfolio. This will help you build your vocabulary and prepare you for a career. Write out a definition for each of the following terms, and add it to your personal finance glossary.

deductible

fee-for-service plan

coinsurance

inpatient

managed care plan

copayment

health savings account (HSA)

exclusion

preexisting condition

Section 8.3
Life Insurance

Objectives

After studying this section, you will be able to:

- Describe types of life insurance and endowment policies.
- Explain how to select appropriate life insurance coverage.

Terms

beneficiary

term life insurance

whole life insurance

endowment insurance

Life Insurance

The right life insurance choices can help provide financial security for you and your family. Life insurance protects dependents from loss of income and helps pay expenses after the death of the insured person. The larger your financial responsibilities, the more important it is to have adequate coverage. Life insurance is especially important if you have a spouse, children, or elderly parents who depend on your income.

When an insured person dies, the face value of his or her policy is paid to the beneficiary. The face value is the amount for which the policy is written. A **beneficiary** is a person or organization named by a policyholder to receive the death benefit of an insurance policy after the policyholder's death.

The three traditional types of life insurance are term, whole life, and endowment. Each type is available in slightly different forms and with different features.

Term Life

Term life insurance is a type of insurance that provides protection only for a specific period of time. This time period may be 1, 5, 10, or 20 years or until a specified age. When the term ends, so does the protection. Term policies often include a renewable option that allows you to renew the coverage at the end of the term, usually at higher rates.

The advantage of term insurance is that it offers the most protection for your insurance dollar. Policies offering only protection cost less than policies with savings features. For those people who really need insurance and cannot afford high premiums, term coverage may be the best choice.

Whole Life

Whole life insurance is a type of insurance that provides basic lifetime protection so long as premiums are paid. Whole life insurance is also called *straight life insurance*. The face amount is paid to the beneficiaries upon death of the insured. The coverage builds cash value over the years. *Cash value* is the

szefei/Shutterstock.com

Life insurance protects those who are financially dependent on you.

amount of money a policyholder would receive if the policy were surrendered before death or maturity.

You may be able to borrow against the cash value of whole life insurance at a relatively low interest rate. However, until repaid, benefits are reduced by the amount of the loan. You can also surrender the policy for its cash value if you want to change or eliminate coverage. New types of whole life insurance were developed in recent years to meet today's needs and demands. The new types include limited payment policies, variable life, adjustable life, and universal life.

Limited Payment Policies

Limited payment policies offer lifetime protection. They require premium payments over a stated period of time, such as 20 years, or until you reach a certain age. During the payment period, premiums are higher and cash value builds faster than for standard whole life coverage.

Variable Life

Variable life insurance premiums are fixed. The insurance protection is combined with an investment feature. The face value varies with the performance of the fund in which the premiums are invested. However, the face amount may not fall below the original amount of the insurance. These policies guarantee a minimum death benefit. The benefit may be higher than the guarantee, depending on the earnings of the premium dollars invested.

The advantage of this type of life insurance is the potential of earnings when the value of the fund rises. The main disadvantage is it may not offer the best of either insurance or investment opportunities.

Adjustable Life

You can revise an adjustable life insurance policy as your needs change. Within limits, you may raise or lower the premiums, face value, and premium payment period. Coverage may start with term insurance for a given amount, premium, and term. All these factors may change as needed. Flexibility is the key advantage of adjustable life coverage. The need to constantly monitor coverage may be a disadvantage.

Universal Life

Universal life insurance permits the adjustment of premiums, face value, and level of protection. In addition, it offers an investment feature. The cash value is invested to earn interest at current market rates. An annual statement shows the current level of protection, cash value, and interest earned. The statement also includes a breakdown of how premiums are allocated to protection, investment, and expenses.

An advantage of universal life is flexibility, both in the amount of the premiums and in the level of protection. Earnings also keep pace with current market rates. If interest rates go down, however, your earnings decrease. You pay no taxes on the accumulated interest until you cash in your policy. This can be an advantage for persons in high income tax brackets.

Endowment Insurance

Endowment insurance is a type of insurance that pays the face value of the policy to beneficiaries if the insured dies before the endowment period ends. It pays the face amount to the insured if he or she lives beyond the endowment period.

The advantage of endowment insurance is the combination of protection and savings. It is a type of investment. Disadvantages are the high premiums and possible tax consequences.

Choosing a Plan

Each person's needs are unique. The life insurance coverage that is right for one person or family may be wrong for another. Finding the type and amount of protection that works best for you requires careful planning.

The amount and type of life insurance protection you need depends on two key factors: your present and future earning power and your financial responsibilities and obligations.

Amount of Protection

Protection is often based on the amount of earnings that would be lost if the insured died prematurely. It is also matched to the needs of survivors for whom the insured is financially responsible. These needs depend on the number of survivors, their marital status, their earning power, and their lifestyles.

Other factors to consider include the share of family income provided by the insured and income available from other sources. Careful analysis is

Goodluz/Shutterstock.com

A knowledgeable insurance agent can help you determine which plan suits your needs.

needed to determine the amount of protection to buy. Consider the following questions to decide how much coverage you need.

- What are the ages and financial needs of those depending on your income? Dependents may include aging parents or relatives as well as a spouse and young children.

- What amount of money would your dependents need to maintain their standard of living without your income? Ideally, money would be left to cover a home mortgage and everyday living expenses. It might also cover major future expenses, such as college educations for children.

- What other sources of income that would be available for dependents? Would dependents be able to draw on Social Security benefits, savings, employee benefits, or their own earnings? You want enough coverage to fill the gap between what is available from other sources and what your dependents would need.

- What amount of cash would be needed to pay burial costs and unpaid debts? Even if you are single with no dependents, you need enough life insurance to take care of these costs. Then your financial obligations will not burden your parents or other relatives.

Types of Protection

You can buy life insurance in a variety of forms and with many special benefits. The decision depends on how much coverage you need, what you can afford to spend, and the special features you want.

Group life insurance is a form of term insurance that covers a large number of people under a single policy. Group insurance may be available through your employer, union, or another group to which you belong. As a rule, group coverage costs less than an individual policy for the same amount of coverage. Very often, group coverage is provided as a fringe benefit where you work. The

Claims Representatives, Examiners, and Investigators
Claims investigators handle insurance claims when a company suspects fraudulent or criminal activity, such as arson, falsified claims, staged accidents, or unnecessary medical treatments. They often perform surveillance work.

employer may pay all or part of the premium. If you rely on group protection, look for a conversion clause. This permits you to convert to an individual policy without proof of insurability if you should leave the group.

Individual policies, though more expensive, generally can be tailored to the policyholder's needs. Features to consider when choosing life insurance protection include the following.

- *Guaranteed renewability* allows you to keep coverage in force at the end of a term without new evidence of insurability. Premium rates increase with each new term.
- *Double indemnity* provides for double benefits if death is the result of an accident. This may also be called an *accidental death benefit.*
- A *disability benefit* provides for a waiver of premiums if the insured becomes permanently and totally disabled. While this provision often is available as a feature on a life insurance policy, more comprehensive, separate disability coverage is usually desirable.
- A *convertible provision* permits you to convert or exchange a term policy for another form of protection without new evidence of insurability.

Finally, consider how life insurance fits into your overall plan for future security and eventual retirement. Future financial security depends on the right mix of savings, insurance, and investments. Some people plan to use insurance as a form of savings. In this case, be sure the earnings on your insurance match or exceed those on other forms of savings and investments.

Choosing a Company, Agent, and Policy

When purchasing life insurance, always select a company that is respected within the insurance industry, by its policyholders, and by people in the financial field. Check whether the company has a reputation for settling claims fairly and promptly. Also be sure the company is licensed to operate in your state.

You can research and compare life insurance companies by reviewing *Best's Insurance Reports.* These reports can be found in most public libraries or on Best's Insurance Reports website. You can also research an insurance company through the Department of Insurance for your state.

Look closely at policies that offer the benefits and options important to you. Be sure to compare the premiums charged by different companies for the same types and amounts of coverage. If you are considering whole life insurance, compare the cash value accumulation rates. Additional information on buying life insurance is available from a number of financial publications and online.

The life insurance agent you choose is also important. Very often, the agent is the key to the quality of service you receive. All states require a special license to sell life insurance. Initials following an agent's name indicate completion of specific studies in the insurance field. *CLU* indicates a Chartered Life Underwriter. *ChFC* indicates a Chartered Financial Consultant. *LUTCF* indicates a Life Underwriters' Training Council Fellow. Members of the National Association of Life Underwriters subscribe to the ethical standards of that group.

Choose an agent who can clearly explain the different types of coverage and benefits available. A good agent advises you honestly about the type and amount of coverage you need. He or she also helps you evaluate your coverage as your needs and finances change. Finally, a responsible agent handles policy revisions and claims promptly.

Once you choose a company and an agent, select a policy. Talk honestly with your agent as you discuss your needs.

After you buy a policy and it is delivered to you, review it carefully. Be sure the policy you are given is the one you chose. If the policy does not meet your expectations, most companies allow you to return it within ten days without obligation. As you review the policy, check to see that it states the following information.

- name of the company
- name of the insured and the beneficiaries
- type of coverage
- amount of coverage and benefits
- amount and due dates of premiums
- terms for borrowing money against accumulated cash value, if applicable
- schedule of cash value accumulation, if applicable
- benefits and options of the policy

Be sure to ask questions about any terms, provisions, or sections you do not understand. Once you are insured, inform your family and beneficiaries of the coverage and the location of the policy.

Checkpoint 8.3

1. What is the primary purpose of life insurance?
2. What is group life insurance?
3. What is the main difference between term life insurance and whole life insurance?
4. Name four types of limited payment policies.
5. The amount and type of life insurance protection you need depends on what two key factors?

Build Your Vocabulary

As you progress through this course, develop a personal glossary of personal finance terms and add it to your portfolio. This will help you build your vocabulary and prepare you for a career. Write out a definition for each of the following terms, and add it to your personal finance glossary.

beneficiary

term life insurance

whole life insurance

endowment insurance

Section 8.4
Home and Auto Insurance

Objectives

After studying this section, you will be able to:

- Outline the key factors to consider when buying home insurance.
- Outline the key factors to consider when buying auto insurance.

Terms

umbrella policy

depreciation

endorsement

bodily injury liability

property damage liability

no-fault auto insurance

Home Insurance

Once you invest in a home of your own, you want to protect it with insurance. Homeowners insurance provides coverage for liability and damage to property under certain conditions. It provides two basic types of coverage: property protection and liability protection.

Property coverage insures the policyholder against financial loss due to damage to or loss of a dwelling and personal property and possessions, such as clothes and furnishings. It may also pay for additional living expenses if you should need to move out of your home because of damage to the property. The specific losses covered depend on the type of policy you buy. Floods and earthquakes are not covered by property and casualty insurance. These types of insurance are purchased separately.

Homeowners liability coverage protects a homeowner if others are injured on the policyholder's property. For example, if someone falls and is hurt in your home, liability coverage pays for any loss incurred.

This coverage also protects you if you, your family, your pets, or your property accidentally damages the property of others. It pays for the legal costs of defending yourself if you are sued because of injuries or damages.

Additional coverage can be purchased through an umbrella policy or extended liability policy. An **umbrella policy** is an insurance policy that covers loss amounts that are higher than those covered by primary policies.

Amount of Coverage

The first step in buying the right homeowners coverage is to find out how much it would cost to rebuild your home. This may be more or less than the price you paid for the home or the amount it would bring if you sold it today. The cost of rebuilding your home depends on local building costs and the type of home you own. Today, most insurance companies recommend enough insurance coverage to rebuild your home if it should be completely destroyed.

To keep insurance coverage up to date, inform your insurance agent of any major home improvements you make. You may also want to add an inflation-guard clause to your policy. This automatically adjusts policy renewal coverage to reflect current rebuilding costs.

Read the policy to learn about the coverage provided for personal possessions. Compare the contents limit with the total value of your possessions. If coverage is not adequate, you should talk to your insurance agent about increasing protection.

Knowing whether your personal property is insured for replacement cost or actual cash value is also important.

- *Actual cash value* is the replacement cost minus depreciation. **Depreciation** is a decrease in the value of property as a result of age or wear and tear.
- *Replacement value* covers the cost of replacing what you lose without deducting depreciation.

For example, a five-year-old TV set, even in good condition, is no longer worth what you paid for it or what a new similar set would cost. If the set were stolen, actual cash value recovery would not pay for a new one. If it were insured for replacement value, you could recover the full cost of a new TV set of comparable quality. Obviously, it pays to insure possessions for replacement rather than actual cash value.

When insuring a home and possessions, make a complete inventory of your belongings. Include the purchase date and price for costly items. It is a good idea to take photos or videos of each room. This helps you remember the contents and establish your claims in case of major losses. See Figure 8-3.

viki2win/Shutterstock.com

Home improvements can increase the value of your house, which affects the amount of insurance coverage needed.

Filing a Home Insurance Claim

Follow these steps to file a claim on your home insurance.

1. Report any burglary or theft to the police immediately.

2. Notify your insurance agent or company promptly by phone or e-mail with a written follow-up report. Determine the exact coverage your policy provides and find out whether the loss exceeds the deductible. Ask about details of filing a claim and about records and estimates you may need to file a claim for repairs or replacements.

3. Make temporary repairs and take necessary steps to prevent further damage. Keep receipts and records of expenses involved for reimbursement.

4. Make a list of lost or damaged articles with estimated replacement costs and confirming records of purchase and replacement prices.

5. Keep records and receipts for living expenses if damage to your property requires you to find a place to live while repairs are being made.

6. Provide your insurance agent or company with the necessary receipts, records, and information required to handle and settle your claim.

7. Check your policy to find out what steps are involved in settling a claim. If you are dissatisfied or have questions concerning the final settlement, discuss matters with your agent or the claims adjuster.

8. If you find a settlement unsatisfactory or are not satisfied with your insurance company's handling of your complaint, you can contact the department of insurance for your state or call the National Insurance Consumer Helpline for assistance.

Goodheart-Willcox Publisher

Figure 8-3 These guidelines can help you file a home insurance claim.

Insurance Representatives

Insurance representatives interact with agents, insurance companies, and policyholders. They handle much of the paperwork related to insurance policies, such as sales, policy applications, and changes and renewals to existing policies.

Cost of Home Insurance

Be sure to call or visit with an independent agent or representatives from several companies and comparison shop before you buy insurance. Compare company reputations for honoring and prompt processing of claims. The cost of protecting your home and personal possessions depends primarily on the following factors.

- *Type and amount of coverage.* The higher the amount of protection purchased and the more perils covered, the higher the premium will be. A policy with replacement value coverage is more expensive than one with cash or market value protection.

- *Size of the deductible.* The higher the deductible is, the lower the insurance premium will be.

- *Risk factors where you live.* The type of home you own and its location influence premium rates. For example, you pay more for fire protection on a frame house than on a brick house. You pay more for protection against theft and vandalism in high-crime areas than in low-crime areas.

- *The insurance company.* The cost of insurance premiums varies from company to company.

- *Opportunity for discounts.* Check with your insurance agent to see if you qualify for premium reductions for having more than one policy with the company, such as home and auto coverage. Also, check to see if discounts are available for devices such as a smoke detector or burglar alarm, for nonsmoker policyholders, or for long-term policyholders. These discounts can reduce your homeowner premiums considerably.

When you are ready to buy home insurance, take time to study the types and amounts of coverage available. Then find an informed, reputable insurance agent or broker who can advise you on the type and amount of coverage you need. Ask friends and business associates about their experiences with insurance agents and companies.

A.M. Best Company rates insurers for financial stability. The ratings are published in *Best's Insurance Reports: Property-Casualty*. This publication is available in the reference section of most public libraries and at the company's website. The Department of Insurance for your state may also help you evaluate a company's service and complaint record. In addition, you can find information online about home insurance coverage, companies, and rates.

Renters Insurance

Many renters mistakenly believe they do not need insurance because their property owner's policy will cover any loss they may suffer. However, the property owner's policy does not cover the personal items of a renter. As a result, it is a good idea for renters to purchase a renters insurance policy. Renters insurance covers losses due to damage or loss of personal property and possessions. These include electronics, furniture, bedding, and so forth. The property owner carries coverage on the dwelling itself.

Renters should look for a policy with liability insurance. If guests were harmed in a rented home or apartment, liability insurance would cover any expenses incurred by the resident.

College students living in a dorm or renting an apartment may need renters insurance to protect their possessions. However, an endorsement to their parents' homeowners insurance may be necessary to cover a child's personal possessions while living in a dorm. An **endorsement** is an attachment to existing insurance coverage, such as a family policy, to protect a computer, a television, and other expensive items taken to college.

Auto Insurance

Auto insurance gives policyholders coverage for liability and property damage under specified conditions. When you own or lease a car, you take certain personal and financial risks. If you are involved in a car accident, you may be required to pay thousands of dollars for injuries and property damage. If you are in an accident where you are at fault or claims are filed against you, it can cost thousands of dollars in legal fees as well as damages. Practically no one can afford the financial risks of extensive property damage, serious injury, or death without insurance coverage.

All 50 states have *financial responsibility laws* that require drivers to show proof of their ability to pay stated minimum amounts in damages after an accident. Most states also have compulsory auto insurance laws that require car owners to buy a minimum amount of bodily injury and property damage liability insurance in order to legally drive their cars.

When you are ready to buy auto insurance, shop carefully to get the coverage you need at the best price. An auto insurance policy may include several types of coverage for the insured individual or family.

Types of Auto Insurance

Of the six basic types of auto insurance coverage, two are liability coverage. They pay other parties for losses you cause. The other auto policies pay you, the insured, for losses outlined in the policy.

Bodily injury liability is insurance coverage that protects you when you are responsible for an auto accident that results in the injury or death of other parties. **Property damage liability** is insurance coverage that protects you when you are responsible for an auto accident in which the property of others is damaged.

These policies cover the policyholder, family members, and any person driving the car with the owner's permission. They pay damages to the other parties involved in an accident you cause. Both types of liability coverage pay the legal fees for settling claims. They also pay for damages assessed against you, up to limits stated in the policy. These damages include injuries to other parties or damage to the property of others.

Types of auto insurance coverage that pay the insured are discussed in the following list.

- *Medical payments* or *personal injury protection (PIP)* pays you, the insured, for medical expenses resulting from an accident in your car, regardless of who is at fault. It covers you and any person injured in or by your car.

- *Collision insurance* pays you for damage to your car due to an auto accident or collision with another car or object.

- *Comprehensive physical damage insurance* pays you for loss or damage to your car resulting from fire, theft, falling objects, explosions, earthquakes, floods, riots, civil commotions, and collisions with a bird or animal.

pedalist/Shutterstock.com

Your driving record partially determines the cost of your insurance premiums

- *Uninsured* and *underinsured motorist insurance* pays you for injuries caused by an uninsured or hit-and-run driver. It covers insured persons driving, riding, or walking. It covers you if you are injured as a pedestrian. It also covers passengers in the insured person's car.

There are additional types of insurance that you may purchase, such as roadside assistance and rental reimbursement insurance.

Cost of Auto Insurance

Auto insurance is a costly service. Coverage for young drivers is particularly high because they have more accidents. Premium rates and service for the same coverage may vary greatly from company to company. It pays to shop carefully.

To compare insurance costs, check the cost of coverage you need with several reliable insurance companies. Once you buy auto insurance, read your policy carefully, and know what coverage you carry. It is also a good idea to keep the policy and records of premium payments and claims together in one place so you can find them as needed. You must also carry proof of your insurance coverage in your vehicle in most states. The guidelines in Figure 8-4 can help you select the automobile insurance you need. The cost of auto insurance depends on the factors discussed in the following paragraphs.

Driver Classification

Driver classification is determined by the age, sex, and marital status of the driver. Driving record and habits are also considered. It can be difficult for individuals with poor driving records to buy insurance. Insurers consider these drivers too great a risk. In such cases, it may be possible to obtain coverage through an assigned risk plan. This is a state-supervised program in which high-risk drivers are assigned to insurance companies. The companies are required to provide coverage, but premiums are considerably higher than for drivers with better driving records.

Suggestions for Buying Automobile Insurance

- Decide the types and amounts of coverage you need. If you now have a policy, review your coverage and its cost before renewal time.

- Check with several reputable insurers. Keep in mind that the least expensive coverage is not necessarily the best for you. Consider such things as the company's reliability and its reputation for service, including claims handling. If you are in doubt about a company, check with the Department of Insurance for your state.

- Consider the amount you would save by paying a higher deductible. You may find it pays in the end to take care of small losses yourself.

- Check with your agent regarding your eligibility for premium discounts.

- Consider special coverages or higher policy limits if you frequently drive other commuters to work or groups of children to school or other events.

- Consider reducing or dropping collision coverage as cars get older.

Goodheart-Willcox Publisher

Figure 8-4 These guidelines can help you select auto insurance.

Young, single males are involved in more serious accidents than other classes of drivers. Therefore, they tend to pay the highest insurance premiums. If a young man marries, his insurance costs may decrease because married men have fewer serious accidents than single men. Rates for women, single and married, are lower than for males.

A poor driving record tends to increase premiums as does a record of previous claims and costly settlements. When your driver classification changes, so might your insurance rates.

Rating Territory

The number and amount of claims an insurance company processes in your area determines rates for auto insurance. Premiums are higher in frequent claim areas, such as big cities and high traffic districts.

Premium Discount Eligibility

Some companies offer discounts to drivers with the following characteristics:

- have a safe driving record
- get good grades (if still in school)
- have installed antitheft devices
- are over a certain age
- have two or more cars on a policy
- have a good credit score

Check with your insurance company about possible discounts.

History of Finance

First Life Insurance

Ancient Rome is credited with being the birthplace of life insurance. The first policies were granted by burial clubs. These clubs, called *Fratres*, covered the cost of funeral expenses for members and provided financial assistance to surviving family members. Money left over after the cost of the funeral was typically given to the surviving family members to help them with financial problems that often accompanied the loss of a family member. Members who were more than six months behind with their club dues did not qualify for help with the funeral costs of a family member.

The first insurance company in the United States was formed in Charleston, South Carolina, in 1732. However, life insurance was not added to its product line until around 1760. In the beginning, many opposed the concept of life insurance because it was viewed as benefiting from death.

Careers in Finance

What Does an Insurance Sales Agent Do?

An **insurance sales agent** is a client's first contact person when buying insurance. For that reason, an **insurance sales agent** must be customer-service oriented. **Insurance sales agents** may sell insurance to individual consumers as well as businesses. **Insurance sales agents** typically:

- help determine customer needs, types of insurance, and levels of insurance that fit the customer's requirements;
- facilitate the application process and submits the information to an underwriter;
- prepare reports and maintains records; and
- find potential customers.

An **insurance sales agent** may sell only one company's insurance. However, there are also independent agents, also known as *insurance brokers,* who may sell products for multiple insurance carriers.

What Is It Like to Work as an Insurance Sales Agent?

An **insurance sales agent** spends most of his or her time working with clients. The insurance environment is professional, and agents will generally dress in business attire. Clients may come to the insurance business office, or agents may travel to the client's home or place of business. Hours may be flexible and include evenings and weekends.

An **insurance sales agent** must communicate with customers of many different social and ethnic backgrounds. Because insurance is serious in nature, an agent must follow accepted guidelines for use of e-mail, social networking, blogs, and texting.

What Education and Skills Are Needed to Be an Insurance Sales Agent?

- college degree preferred
- professional license
- excellent communication skills
- expertise in financial products
- ability to work without direct supervision
- computer skills

Over 90 percent of US insurance companies use credit scores as a factor in establishing insurance rates. If you have a high credit score, you will usually get better auto insurance rates than someone with a low credit score.

Insured Car

Cars that are costly to repair or that are favorite targets of thieves cost more to insure. Premiums are higher for luxury, sports, and new cars than for standard models and older cars. For older cars, collision insurance may not be cost effective. Very popular models cost more to insure than more ordinary cars. Check the insurance costs for different models before buying a car.

Deductible Amount

Increasing the deductible amount can reduce premiums for collision and comprehensive damage coverage. The higher the deductible is, the lower the premium will be.

Coverage Amount

The more protection you buy, the higher the premium will be. However, the cost per dollar of coverage is usually less for more coverage. For example, a $100,000 policy costs less per dollar of coverage than a $50,000 policy. Just remember to buy the amount of coverage you need. A reliable agent can help you decide.

No-Fault Auto Insurance

No-fault auto insurance is a type of insurance plan that eliminates the faultfinding process in settling claims. When an accident occurs, each policyholder makes a claim to his or her own insurance company. Each company pays its own policyholder regardless of who is at fault. No-fault insurance is designed to simplify and speed up payments to accident victims. It also acts to lower insurance rates by reducing costly court trials to determine fault.

State legislators decide whether their state adopts a no-fault insurance plan and what form it takes. Most states with a no-fault plan have a combination no-fault and liability insurance. The no-fault pays for claims up to a set amount, called a *threshold*. However, in most states individuals can sue for additional damages when an accident involves severe injuries, death, or major medical bills. Liability insurance pays for damages over and above the threshold amount.

Auto accidents are an unfortunate reality of life. According to the National Highway Traffic Administration, an auto accident happens every 60 seconds, resulting in upwards of 40,000 highway deaths annually in the United States. Further, car accidents are a leading cause of permanent disability in the United States and the world.

You can reduce your chances of an auto accident by keeping your car in good running condition, driving within the speed limit, and minimizing distractions while driving, such as eating, drinking, texting, and talking on a cell phone. However, if you are involved in an accident, there are certain procedures you should follow at the scene of the accident and when filing an insurance claim. Those procedures are summarized in Figure 8-5.

Auto Accidents and Insurance Claims	
At the Scene of an Accident	**Filing an Insurance Claim**

At the Scene of an Accident

- Stop your car safely beyond the accident and out of traffic. Turn on a flasher or warning light.
- Assist the injured, but do not move anyone unless absolutely necessary.
- Administer any first aid you are qualified and trained to provide.
- Stay calm and help others to do the same.
- Get help as quickly as possible. Call or have someone call the police and an ambulance if needed.
- Provide police with information they request.
- Ask for a copy of the police report.
- Write down names, addresses, and phone numbers of those involved in the accident and of any witnesses; license number, make, and model of cars involved; driver's license numbers of drivers involved; insurance company and identification number of each driver involved; and names and badge numbers of police officers and other emergency assistants.
- For a collision with an unattended or parked auto, try to find the owner. If unsuccessful, leave a note with your name, number, and address. Damages over a certain amount must be reported to the police in most states.

Filing an Insurance Claim

If your car is involved in an auto accident; damaged by fire, flood, or vandalism; or stolen, follow these steps in filing a claim for your losses:

- Phone your insurance agent or a local company representative as soon as possible to report the incident.
- Ask the agent how to proceed and what forms or documents are needed to support your claim. These may include medical and auto repair bills and a copy of the police report.
- Obtain and provide the information the insurer requires. Cooperate fully with your insurance company in the investigation and settlement of claims.
- Turn over copies of any legal papers you receive in connection with the accident and losses you are claiming. If you are sued or claims are brought against you, the insurance company will provide legal representation for you.
- Keep copies of any paperwork and documents you submit with your insurance claim.
- Keep records of any expenses you incur as a result of an automobile accident. They may be reimbursed under the terms of your policy.

Note: If involved in an accident, it is unlawful to leave the scene without proper notification if there is injury, death, or property damage over a certain amount. Check the laws on reporting accidents in your state.

Goodheart-Willcox Publisher

Figure 8-5 Follow these steps if you are involved in an auto accident and must file an insurance claim.

Checkpoint 8.4

1. What two basic types of coverage does homeowners insurance provide?
2. What is the first step to consider when buying homeowners insurance?
3. What does renters insurance cover?
4. What is auto liability coverage?
5. The cost of auto insurance depends on what factors?

Build Your Vocabulary

As you progress through this course, develop a personal glossary of personal finance terms and add it to your portfolio. This will help you build your vocabulary and prepare you for a career. Write a definition for each of the following terms, and add it to your personal finance glossary.

umbrella policy	bodily injury liability
depreciation	property damage liability
endorsement	no-fault auto insurance

Chapter Summary

Section 8.1 Risk Management

- Risk is a measure of the likelihood that something will be lost, and risks can be classified as pure risks and speculative risks.
- Financial security depends in part on risk management. Four strategies for dealing with risk are avoidance, reduction, retention, and transference.
- Insurance is a form of risk management that pools the premiums of a large group of people to cover the expenses of the smaller number within the group who suffer losses.

Section 8.2 Health and Disability Insurance

- The high cost of medical care makes it important to investigate all options for obtaining health insurance. Private health insurance includes fee-for-service plans, managed care plans, group plans, individual plans, and long-term care plans.
- When choosing a health insurance plan, consider the services covered, the choice of health-care providers, and the costs.
- Older citizens and certain groups may be eligible for government insurance programs. The government offers health insurance, such as Medicare and Medicaid, to certain eligible people, including older adults, people with disabilities, low-income families, and children.
- Disability insurance pays a portion of income lost to a worker who is unable to work for a prolonged period because of illness or injury.

Section 8.3 Life Insurance

- Adequate life insurance coverage guarantees income for the policyholder's survivors. The three types of life insurance, term, whole life, and endowment, are available in different forms and with different features.
- The amount and type of life insurance protection you need depends on two key factors: your present and future earning power and your financial responsibilities and obligations. Life insurance may also offer investment features.

Section 8.4 Home and Auto Insurance

- Once your own a home, you need insurance to protect it. When buying home insurance, factors to consider include the type and amount of coverage, deductible amounts, risk factors, premiums, and discounts.
- Carrying adequate auto insurance is a major responsibility for car owners. When buying auto insurance, factors to consider include the types and amounts of coverage, deductible amounts, policy limits, premiums, discounts, and the company's reputation for service.

Check Your Personal Finance IQ

Now that you have finished the chapter, see what you learned about personal finance by taking the chapter posttest. If you do not have a smartphone, visit the G-W Learning companion website.

G-W Learning mobile site: www.m.g-wlearning.com

G-W Learning companion website: www.g-wlearning.com

Review Your Knowledge

1. What are two types of risk?
2. What is the most common way to transfer risk?
3. How does insurance protect individuals from financial losses?
4. What factors should be considered when evaluating health insurance plans?
5. What are the differences between Medicare and Medicaid?
6. What does the term deductible mean as it relates to insurance?
7. What are the differences between whole life and endowment insurance?
8. What four major factors determine the cost of home insurance?
9. What is no-fault auto insurance?
10. What determines driver classification for auto insurance?

Apply Your Knowledge

11. Develop a risk management plan that best suits your tolerance for risk.
12. Identify one or more speculative risks you would consider taking. Give reasons for your choices.
13. Make a list of possible losses for which you would be willing to assume the risk of loss.
14. What type of insurance is most important to you? Why?
15. Prepare a list of factors that would be important to you when selecting a health insurance policy.
16. Using various research methods—the Internet, newspapers, the library—find possible hazards (storms, tornados, and hurricanes) that pose the greatest threat to loss of property in the area where you live. How would you protect yourself from these hazards?
17. Visit the Department of Motor Vehicles website in your state. List the laws regarding uninsured motorist insurance.
18. What type of health insurance plan would you recommend for an elderly person? Why?
19. List the factors you would consider to be the most important to you when selecting a life insurance company.
20. Explain the basic types of coverage home insurance policies provide. Check with insurance providers in your area and compare the coverage offered by similar policies.

 ## Teamwork

In this chapter, you learned about various types of risk and how insurance helps an individual manage personal risk. Working with a teammate, research disability and long-term care insurance offered by three major insurance companies. Find out about coverage, costs, and factors to consider in deciding whether and how much of this type of coverage someone might wish to consider at different stages of life. Create a chart to show your findings and share it with the class.

G-W Learning Mobile Site

Visit the G-W Learning mobile site to complete the chapter pretest and posttest and to practice vocabulary using e-flash cards. If you do not have a smartphone, visit the G-W Learning companion website to access these features.

G-W Learning mobile site: www.m.g-wlearning.com

G-W Learning companion website: www.g-wlearning.com

Common Core

College and Career Readiness

CTE Career Ready Practices. Read the Ethics feature presented throughout this book. What role do you think that ethics and integrity have in risk management? Think of a time when you used your ideals and principles to make a decision that involved some type of risk. What process did you use to make the decision? In retrospect, do you think you made the correct decision? Did your decision have any consequences?

Listening. Perform an Internet search on the average age of persons covered by automobile insurance. Look for opinions regarding how claims impact the historical model of pricing automobile insurance. After reading a few expert opinions on this topic, use this information to form your own opinion. Discuss your findings and reasoning with the class. Respond to any questions you are asked. As you listen to your classmates' opinion on this topic, take notes and ask questions about positions or terms you do not understand. Evaluate your own position. How does their reasoning contribute to your understanding of the cost of automobile insurance? Does your opinion change or is it strengthened?

Speaking. The way you communicate with others will have a lot to do with the success of the relationships you build with them. There are formal and informal ways of communicating your message. Create a speech that will introduce you to a new insurance agent. The agent should be a person you have never met. Deliver each speech to your class. How did the words, phrases, and tone you used influence the way the audience responded to the speech?

Web Connect

The law requires that drivers carry certain types and amounts of auto insurance. These requirements vary among states. Using the Internet, find the legal requirements of your state. Do you believe the requirements are sufficient? What changes would you make? Why?

College and Career Readiness Portfolio

Community service is an important activity that interviewers expect candidates to have performed. Serving the community shows that the candidate is well rounded and socially aware. In this activity, you will create a list of your contributions to community organizations.

Many opportunities are available for young people to serve the community. You might volunteer for a community clean-up project. Perhaps you might enjoy reading to residents in a nursing facility. Maybe raising money for a shelter for homeless pets appeals to you. Whatever your interests, there is sure to be a related service project in which you can take part.

Interviewers for jobs or colleges look for your service activities on applications. Volunteering helps show social awareness and commitment to others or to a cause. In this activity, you will create a list of your service activities. Remember that this is an ongoing project. You will update this list when you have activities to add.

1. List the service projects or volunteer activities in which you have taken part. Give the organization or person's name, the dates, and the activities that you performed. If you received a certificate or award related to this service, mention it here.

2. Give the document an appropriate name, using the naming system you created earlier. Place the file in your e-portfolio.

3. Place a copy of the list in the container for your print portfolio.

Business Law

Business law is a competitive event you might enter with your career and technical student organization (CTSO). Business law is an individual event in which participants take an objective test that covers multiple legal topics. Participants are usually allowed one hour to complete the event. One of the topics that may be included on the test is *insurance as a means of risk management.*

To prepare for a business law event, complete the following activities.

1. Well in advance of the date of the event, visit the organization's website.

2. Download any posted practice tests.

3. Conduct research on the Internet regarding the legal topics that will be covered on the test. Print out the information you find to use as study material.

4. Visit the organization's website often to make sure information regarding the event has not changed.

Unit 3
Managing Your Spending

mangostock/Shutterstock.com

To save money and build wealth, you must spend less than you earn. Being a smart shopper helps you accomplish this.

Chapters

Personal Finance

Why It Matters

As a consumer, you make decisions every day related to routine spending for food, clothing, health care, and personal needs. Most consumers also face some big spending decisions involving the choices of transportation and housing.

In the world of so many choices, you want to get the most for your dollars. How do you do that? You accomplish this goal by prioritizing your needs and wants and spending within your means. Acquiring smart shopping skills and knowing where to shop and how to find information will help you make wise decisions.

When you are making buying decisions, be a smart consumer. Know your rights, responsibilities, and where to go for help if you believe your consumer rights have been violated.

Chapter 9
Smart Shopping Basics

Smart shopping can make $50 seem like $100. If you develop sound, basic shopping skills, you can buy far more than an unskilled buyer who spends the same amount of money. As a smart shopper, you will get greater satisfaction for your dollars. Your shopping experiences will be rewarding rather than frustrating.

Shopping smart is largely a matter of understanding the marketplace, knowing what you want, using reliable information, and making sound decisions. There are countless places to shop and items to buy. However, choosing from so many alternatives can be a challenge. Knowing what you want and seeking out reliable consumer information can help you make the right spending choices.

Focus on Finance

Impulse Buying

When you shop, do you find yourself buying things you do not need? Before the next shopping trip, take some time to evaluate your buying habits. Make a list of what you really need and what you want. Identify why you need the product and what would be the consequences if you did not buy the item. You may decide an item is not a need but a want. Once you finalize your shopping list, stay focused and avoid impulse buying. Impulse buying refers to unplanned buying or purchases made on the spur of the moment. If possible, pay cash for your purchases. Using a charge card can influence you to overspend. Using cash instead of plastic will help you control spending on things that you really do not need. Life is not all about saving; it is also about enjoying things that make you happy. By making good buying decisions, you can enjoy all those things that make your life fun.

College and Career Readiness

Reading Prep. Think of some of your life goals. How are these goals affected by your personal finances? As you read the chapter, focus on how goals affect the spending habits of consumers.

Check Your Personal Finance IQ

 Before you begin the chapter, see what you already know about personal finance by taking the chapter pretest. If you do not have a smartphone, visit the G-W Learning companion website.

G-W Learning mobile site: www.m.g-wlearning.com

G-W Learning companion website: www.g-wlearning.com

Sections

Section 9.1 Shopping Basics

Section 9.2 Before You Shop

Diego Cervo/Shutterstock.com

Section 9.1
Shopping Basics

Objectives

After studying this section, you will be able to:

- Compare and contrast brick and mortar stores with nontraditional sellers.
- Describe selling techniques used by sellers to get consumers' attention.

Terms

marketplace	infomercial
brick and mortar businesses	buying incentive
telemarketing	coupon
t-commerce	rebate
e-commerce	loss leader
consumer cooperative	game of chance
advertising	focus group
product placement	

Marketplace

The **marketplace** is the place buyers and sellers meet to exchange goods, services, and money. Our free enterprise economy is characterized by free economic choice, the profit motive, and competition. Within the framework of these three characteristics, the forces of supply and demand create a vast arena of sellers and buyers. Business can operate out of traditional brick and mortar stores or from nontraditional, virtual, or online enterprises.

Brick and Mortar Stores

Retail stores sell directly from their place of business. These are usually called **brick and mortar businesses** because they operate out of a physical location. Retailers include department stores and specialty shops, superstores and warehouse clubs, discount stores and factory outlets, and resale shops. Stores may be independently owned and centered in one region, or they may be chain stores located across the country. Many retailers also operate active catalog and Internet businesses.

Department Stores and Specialty Shops

Department stores sell a wide variety of goods and services in a single store. Merchandise is divided into departments. Sections include clothing, cosmetics, linens, shoes, jewelry, and more. These stores offer one-stop shopping plus a variety of customer services.

Specialty shops sell a specific type of merchandise or service, such as shoes, toys, or gifts. Barbershops and beauty salons also are examples. Generally, these stores offer a broad selection of their specialty, and the salespersons are well informed about products and services they sell.

Superstores and Warehouse Clubs

Some *superstores* specialize in specific products, such as electronics, sporting goods, foods, or office supplies. Others sell a wide variety of merchandise similar to the department stores. *Warehouse clubs* sell memberships to customers who want buying privileges. They usually offer a wide variety of merchandise at relatively low prices. These "big box" stores offer price advantages to consumers but they also threaten local stores that cannot compete with their pricing.

Discount Stores and Factory Outlets

Discount stores sell certain lines of merchandise at relatively low prices. Services such as deliveries, credit, and returns may be limited. Most discount stores are self-serve operations.

Factory outlets sell brand name merchandise directly to consumers. Frequently, a variety of factory outlets will be located in an outlet mall. Outlet prices are usually lower than prices for the same merchandise in other stores.

Resale Shops

Resale shops sell used merchandise. Extras, such as warranties, guarantees, exchanges, and credit privileges, are rare; but prices may be exceptionally low. It is important to inspect merchandise carefully to be sure items are in good condition. *Thrift shops* sell donated merchandise. Churches, hospitals, or charitable organizations usually run these shops, and proceeds benefit the organization. *Consignment shops* accept merchandise to sell and pay the owners a percentage when items are sold.

Nontraditional Sellers

Nontraditional sellers provide products and services without a brick and mortar location. You can shop at home from catalogs or television or by using the telephone or Internet. Shopping at home is a convenient way to buy what you need. Internet and television bring worldwide markets into your living room. These technologies let you shop and compare products at any time. Shopping at home saves time, energy, and fuel. However, you cannot see the seller in person or inspect the merchandise prior to purchase. When you buy from a distance, it is important to check out carefully both the seller and products. Remember that shipping costs may be added to the price of the item.

Catalogs

Customers can use *catalogs* to order goods and services featured on their pages. It is important to check the reliability of the seller and to understand the policies on returns or exchanges.

Telemarketing

Telemarketing is the sale of merchandise by phone. Telemarketers sell everything from toys to insurance to burial plots. Unfortunately, they may call at inconvenient times with offers that do not interest you. Consumer protection laws require telemarketers to state clearly the company and caller name, the purpose of the call, and the type of goods or services being offered. They may not call before 8 a.m. or after 9 p.m. or misrepresent the goods and services they are selling.

If you do not wish to receive telemarketing calls, you can place your phone number on the *National Do Not Call Registry* by going online to a website. Telemarketers are not allowed to call registered numbers.

T-Commerce and E-Commerce

T-commerce is the sale of merchandise on television through shopping networks or TV commercials. The networks display and sell their goods and services on TV broadcasts around the clock. Most networks also offer featured items online along with a full Internet catalog of other items they sell.

TV commercials for products include a number to call for purchase or for more information. T-commerce lets you see the products on TV, order by phone, pay by credit card, and have the item delivered to your home.

Interactive television (ITV) lets you use your remote control to make purchases. If you see a TV commercial for a pizza or a piece of fitness equipment, you can buy it instantly by using your remote control to place your order.

E-commerce is buying and selling goods and services online. You can access thousands of retail sites online and buy almost everything you can buy in stores. Offerings include books, clothing, food, furniture, vacation and business travel, automobiles, investments, cosmetics, and prescription drugs.

szefei/Shutterstock.com

The sale of an item goes to the highest bidder at the close of an Internet auction.

Online brokers offer shopping search engines called *bots* that search the web for the best values for different products. You select a category and then type in the name of the product to find comparative prices, features, and other information.

Internet Auctions

Internet auctions offer items for sale to the highest bidder. In some cases, the seller sets a reserve price, which is the lowest acceptable price for an item. Auctions are announced, and bidding closes at a preset time. The highest bidder wins (purchases the item). Items with reserve prices are sold only if the highest bid exceeds the reserve price.

In person-to-person Internet auctions, buyers and sellers connect at the close by e-mail or telephone to arrange payment and delivery. In business-to-person auctions, the auction site controls payment and delivery arrangements.

Before you buy or sell at an Internet auction site, download a copy of the Federal Trade Commission publication *Internet Auctions, A Guide for Buyers and Sellers.* You also will want a copy of the auction rules and policies.

Craigslist and similar sites are other online sources of goods and services. They offer free classified listings for almost any product or service you could possibly want. Community-based listings are currently available in over 450 cities. However, there is very little oversight, and users need to be cautious when exchanging personal information and arranging for pick up or delivery of items purchased or sold.

Consumer Cooperatives

Consumer cooperatives are nonretail associations owned and operated by a group of members for their own benefit rather than for profit. Members contribute services and pay dues to participate in the cooperative. Prices usually are lower than in retail stores. However, merchandise and customer services are limited to what the membership can provide.

Selling Methods

When you enter the marketplace to buy goods and services, remember that businesses are there to sell and make a profit. You enter to buy at the best price. The purpose of the market is to arrive at a transaction and price that is acceptable to both seller and buyer.

Businesses use a number of selling methods to increase sales and profits. As a consumer, you can make these selling methods work for you as long as you remember that their main purpose is to sell goods and services.

Advertising

Advertising is any paid public announcement promoting the sale of a product or service. The goal of the advertiser is to send a message to the consumer in the hopes of making a sale. Businesses spend billions of dollars annually to put their messages before you in newspapers and magazines, on television and the radio, on websites and blogs, in direct mail, and on billboards.

Ethics

If you purchase a piece of clothing, wear it, and then decide you no longer want it, it is unethical to return the merchandise to the store. Do not repackage the item and pretend that you have not used it. Unless the merchant states that used products are permissible to be returned, accept your loss and keep the item you purchased.

E-Merchandising Managers

E-merchandising managers are responsible for meeting sales goals for their area of merchandise sold online. They work to optimize online navigation and review site traffic. They also review competitive websites to evaluate merchandise, promotion strategies, customer experiences, and product presentations.

Keep in mind that only positive information about a product or service is likely to appear in an ad. Although law prohibits false and misleading advertising, you still should expect some exaggerated claims. It pays to develop a healthy skepticism toward advertising claims. Try not to let ads convince you to buy what you do not need or cannot afford. Some techniques sellers use to convince consumers to buy their products are listed as follows.

- *Green ads* associate the use of a product or service with saving the planet, conserving resources, or some other environmental benefit. Key words may include *natural, organic, pure, green,* and *healthful.*
- *Humor* uses a funny character, picture, or situation to get attention.
- *Insecurity* appeals to the consumer desire to be popular, attractive, and appealing to the opposite sex.
- *Testimonials* show real people using a product or service.
- *Celebrity endorsements* use famous personalities to promote products.
- *Bandwagon* commercials try to show that a product is fashionable or trendy; everyone is buying it.
- *Puffery* uses exaggerated claims about a product or service.
- *Nostalgia* is associating a product or service with the "good old days," childhood memories, or a time when life was simpler and more satisfying.
- *Statistics* that are shocking or provocative may be used in advertisements.

Finding new ways to reach potential customers challenges advertisers. Bombarded by so many commercial messages, consumers have become cynical about advertising. It is harder for advertisers to get consumers' attention. **Product placement** is a means of showing a brand name product or its trademark in movies and television programs. This happens when you see an actor or actress driving a particular car or drinking a specific soft drink onscreen. Very often, advertisers pay movie and TV studios to put products in a scene.

Many of the advertisers' techniques are not really harmful, but it pays to look more closely at the product than at the advertising appeals. There is an art to reading an ad or hearing a commercial. Look for information you can use, such as:

- factual descriptions of products or services offered for sale;
- listings and demonstrations of special product features and qualities;
- descriptions of the differences between advertised items and similar goods and services on the market; and
- details on prices, availability, places to buy, special offers, and terms of sale.

Go Green

Buying from retailers who respect the environment is a good practice to adopt. When possible, look for stores that offer products made from recycled or sustainable materials. Always take your shopping bags with you to avoid wasting paper or plastic bags.

Words or terms that should alert you to possible deception are *free, one-time offer,* and *valued at.* When an offer sounds too good to be true, you can be almost sure that it is false.

The Better Business Bureau (BBB) publishes a *Code of Advertising* booklet that sets advertising standards. Businesses that belong to the Better Business Bureau should follow this code. A copy of the booklet is available from your local bureau or on the BBB website.

Infomercials

An **infomercial** is a paid television program designed to sell a service, product, or idea. It is sometimes called a *direct response television advertisement (DRTV)* because the aim is to sell directly to the viewer via interactive television or by telephone.

Infomercials are usually program-length advertisements. The format often resembles actual television programming, and the products or services being promoted are demonstrated. Products you may see in an infomercial include cosmetics, exercise equipment, kitchenware, and health-care devices.

Advertisements may offer easy payments and risk-free trials. They also may claim limited availability to encourage viewers to buy immediately. While infomercials can offer valuable product information and demonstrations, consumer advocates recommend a thorough investigation of the sponsor, product or service, and advertising claims.

Direct Mail Advertising

Direct mail advertising includes advertising circulars, catalogs, coupons, and other unsolicited offers that arrive through mail or another delivery service. Fundraisers also use direct mail. Direct advertising comes via telephone and e-mail as well. Some consumers find this direct approach helpful, while many consider it a nuisance.

Direct mail is also known as *junk mail.*

Special Sales and Promotions

Businesses hold special sales and promotions to attract customers and increase sales. When price reductions and promotions increase sales and profits, they benefit the seller. When you buy what you need on sale, you benefit as well. However, if special sales persuade you to buy what you do not need, you lose. To take advantage of sales and promotions, follow these suggestions.

- Know what you need and want with or without sales.
- Stay within your preset price limits for given items, buying only what you can afford.
- Stick to an overall spending plan and do not be sidetracked by sales, especially for major purchases.
- Anticipate reduced prices, such as preseason specials and end-of-season sales.
- Control the urge to buy what you do not need or want just because it is on sale.

Businesses offer special sales and promotions to encourage shoppers to purchase specific items.

It is in your best interest to know the meaning of the following terms frequently used to sell merchandise:

- *Clearance sale* indicates a reduction from previous prices on merchandise.
- *Closeout sale* refers to products that are no longer being produced and have been discontinued.
- *Going-out-of-business sale* refers to sellers who are closing their business and are selling goods at reduced prices to hasten the closing. Note that sellers cannot legally use this phrase if they are not closing.
- *Introductory offer* indicates new merchandise selling at a price that will increase after the initial offer.
- *Liquidation* refers to the sale of merchandise at reduced prices in order to aid in converting inventory to cash.

Buying Incentives

A **buying incentive** is a special offer by sellers designed to help sell goods and services. They include loyalty cards, coupons, contests, games, rebates, premiums, and prizes. Incentives are often found in magazines or newspapers. Sometimes they come with the purchase of goods and services. You benefit from this form of selling as long as you limit purchases to the goods and services you would ordinarily buy or try. You lose if you buy something you do not really want just to get loyalty points, use a coupon, or win a prize.

A **coupon** is a printed or electronic offer giving a discount for products or services bought before a certain date. Coupons are given as incentives to purchase a new product or increase sales of established products.

Rebates also are a type of buying incentive. A **rebate** is a cash back offer. For example, a seller advertises a $75 rebate on the purchase of a $600 TV. Ideally, the buyer sends the proof-of-purchase to the manufacturer and receives the $75 rebate. However, rebates usually come with rules and deadlines and sometimes have complicated instructions. Before you buy on the strength of a rebate, study the offer carefully.

Two-for-one offers, bargain buys, and other forms of special pricing are also buying incentives. Some sellers offer loss leaders to bring customers into the store. A **loss leader** is an item priced at or below cost to attract buyers in the expectation that they will purchase other merchandise as well.

Contests and sweepstakes are games of chance sponsored by a business to engage prospective customers. **Games of chance** mean that the participant must wager something to win. The wager could be buying a chance to win or submitting personal information to enter. Contests require customer participation so the business can capture data for future campaigns or customer research.

Customer loyalty programs are popular incentives to shop. These programs usually issue a frequent buyer card to the customer. The customer can then build points with each purchase for future gifts or discounts at the store.

Packaging and Display Tools

Experts carefully plan and study every aspect of a product's presentation, from its color and size to its name and labels. **Focus groups** are groups of consumers that evaluate products before they go on the market.

Once a product is ready for sale, sellers calculate which locations and stores will bring the most sales. Take a walk through a large supermarket or drugstore. Study the packages and product displays. Note how many items seem intentionally placed to attract your attention. Can you identify some of the eye-catching techniques used? Studies indicate that items placed at floor level attract the least notice. When the same products are raised to waist level, sales increase by almost 60 percent. At eye level, they jump almost 80 percent.

Products you are likely to buy on impulse are often placed near the checkout counter. These products may also be in display racks in the aisles where you can pick them up with ease.

Staples in the supermarket, such as dairy products, breads, meat, poultry, and produce, will be located well into the store. Nonessentials will be near the front. This way, you are drawn into and through the store. Then you are apt to see and buy more products than you intended.

Packaging can be a powerful selling tool. Notice the color, shape, size, and labels on the packages that attract you most in your walk through the store. You will feel the urge to reach for some products more than others. See if you can figure out what draws you to different packages.

In addition to appearance, packages may sell for their convenience features or their ecological claims. Ecological selling terms include *recyclable* and *earth friendly*. Convenience innovations include boil-in-the-bag foods, juice boxes, squeezable bottles and tubes, pull-tab cans, and spray containers.

Checkpoint 9.1

1. What is the difference between brick and mortar stores and nontraditional sellers?
2. What are some different types of brick and mortar stores?
3. What are some advantages to using nontraditional online businesses?
4. What is the goal of advertisers?
5. What information should you look for when reading an ad or hearing a commercial?

Build Your Vocabulary

As you progress through this course, develop a personal glossary of personal finance terms and add it to your portfolio. This will help you build your vocabulary and prepare you for a career. Write a definition for each of the following terms and add it to your personal finance glossary.

marketplace

brick and mortar businesses

telemarketing

t-commerce

e-commerce

consumer cooperative

advertising

product placement

infomercial

buying incentive

coupon

rebate

loss leader

game of chance

focus group

Section 9.2
Before You Shop

Objectives

After studying this section, you will be able to:

- Recognize and develop the shopping skills you need for different types of shopping.
- Make suggestions on how to shop for various types of personal goods.
- Evaluate warranty promises and coverage for products you buy.

Terms

comparison shopping	work order
nutrients	warranty
equilibrium	limited warranty
organic food	implied merchantability
unit price	implied fitness
EnergyGuide label	extended warranty
ENERGY STAR program	obsolete

Shopping Tips

Every shopping decision has an opportunity cost. Since money is a limited resource, spending it now means giving up the opportunity to spend it later. Consumers who realize this and look at the costs and benefits of different spending alternatives come out ahead. Smart shopping depends on making rational decisions. To be a smart shopper, you need well-defined goals and a clear view of your resources.

A spending plan based on sound decisions works to your advantage both for routine shopping and big purchases. Spending plans need to fit into an overall budget tailored to your specific income and needs. This type of planning gives you a framework for making decisions and can help you avoid impulse buying. A clear picture of your needs can also help you choose the best quality level for different purchases, as shown in Figure 9-1. Planning can help you stay within price ranges you can afford.

You need a variety of shopping skills to help you get value for your dollars. Handle money with care whether you shop with cash or credit. Keep receipts and sales slips for possible returns or exchanges. When using credit, be sure to keep track of purchases and limit total charges to an amount you can pay on time. When paying by mail, send a check or money order; never send cash. This is safer, and it gives you a record of the payment. Take care to keep track of purchases for both cash and credit cards as you shop.

Deal only with reliable sellers. Countless consumer problems arise each year as a result of trading with dishonest sellers and being taken in by shady selling schemes.

Levels of Quality		
Best Quality	**Medium Quality**	**Lower Quality**
Upper Price Range • top of the line • most and best features	**Medium Price Range** • standard features • customary materials, design, and performance	**Lowest Price Range** • few features • adequate materials, design, and performance
Buy when: • you can afford the best and owning it is worth the cost. • top quality and performance are needed for frequent or extended use.	**Buy when:** • medium quality suits your purpose and is affordable. • the best is not necessary for the amount of use it will get. • durability, practicality, and reasonable price are important. • extra features are not required.	**Buy when:** • the item is necessary, and it is all you can afford. • lower quality suits your purpose. • the item will be used only occasionally or temporarily. • the item will be outdated or outgrown soon.

Goodheart-Willcox Publisher

Figure 9-1 The way you will use a product and your budget will determine the quality level you select.

Copywriters

Copywriters work with artists to conceive, develop, and produce effective advertisements. They create the written message in print ads, posters, brochures, and web pages as well as the scripts of radio and television ads.

Compare products, services, and places to shop. Check prices, quality, performance, and anything else that is important to you for a specific purchase. Find out about policies concerning returns, exchanges, credit, and customer satisfaction. Check service and repair policies for products that may require servicing.

Consider the value of time and energy as well as money. The price of a product may be lower in a shopping center than in a neighborhood store. Getting to the shopping center takes time, energy, and fuel. When you weigh these disadvantages against the potential savings, is it worth going to the shopping center?

Do your homework before buying expensive goods and services. If you are unfamiliar with a product or service, take time to learn more about it before you shop. Basic knowledge of prices, ratings, and recommended features can help you make informed decisions.

Report unfair or dishonest business practices to appropriate authorities and organizations. Places to look for action or assistance are listed in Figure 9-2. Consumer protection departments of local and state governments and the state attorney general's office can also help resolve conflicts between a customer and a seller. Often law enforcement agencies depend on the help of consumers to track down wrongdoers in the marketplace. By contacting the proper authorities, you can help put dishonest sellers out of business.

Deal fairly and honestly with others in the marketplace. Follow the guidelines in Figure 9-2 as you deal with businesses, salespeople, professionals, and other shoppers. You will get more respect and better service by being honest, courteous, and fair.

Fairness Guide	
With Salespeople	**With Professionals**
• Show courtesy to salespeople and others who serve you in the marketplace. • Wait your turn when stores are crowded and salespeople are busy. • Avoid shopping just before closing time. • Ask for salespeople who have been helpful in the past, and thank them for their help. • Handle merchandise with care to avoid soiling or damaging it. • Return merchandise to its proper place after you handle it. • Inform salespeople if you come across damaged or broken products. • Be as free with compliments for good service as you are with complaints for poor service.	• Respect the expertise, training, and education a professional person offers. Understand that professionals are selling their time; do not waste it. • Be on time for appointments or give plenty of notice if you must be late or cancel. • Pay promptly unless you have made credit arrangements. • Call during office hours except when emergencies require calling at other times. • Remember, in most cases, you are in partnership with the professionals who serve you. Working together is the best way to achieve mutual goals.
With Other Shoppers	**With Businesses**
• Wait your turn when several shoppers want help at the same time. • Avoid pushing, shoving, raising your voice, and blocking aisles or doorways. • Control children, pets, and shopping carts. • Respect the needs and belongings of other shoppers.	• Let merchants and manufacturers know what you like or dislike about their products, services, and policies. • Make necessary returns and exchanges promptly, particularly when merchandise is seasonal. • Be businesslike about handling problems and registering complaints. • Avoid damaging merchandise or making unfair returns, exchanges, or demands.

Goodheart-Willcox Publisher

Figure 9-2 Fairness in the marketplace is a two-way street that both businesses and consumers travel.

Shopping for Goods

When you buy merchandise, inspect it first. Look products over carefully. Read labels, hangtags, seals, and manuals. Look for information about the price, quality, and performance features. Also, consider any extra costs for delivery, installation, upkeep, and servicing. Be sure to know exactly what you are buying, the quality you are getting, and the terms of the sale.

For certain goods, it may pay to buy in quantity. For example, soap at three bars for $2.75 is a better buy than $1.00 per bar. When buying in large quantities, make sure the merchandise will keep. Only buy what you can conveniently use and store.

Monkey Business Images/Shutterstock.com

When shopping for food, consider nutritional options such as fruits and vegetables.

Always compare stores as well as products to find the best values. You may be able to save a lot of money by comparison shopping. **Comparison shopping** is the process of gathering information about products, services, and prices to find the best buy among similar products and services. Knowing what features, performance requirements, quality, and price range you want gives direction to your shopping. It will also help you evaluate quality and performance.

If you are buying goods at a sale, do not let price reductions tempt you to buy what you do not really want. A $90 white jacket on sale for $35 is no bargain if it does not fit. Figure the cleaning or repair costs if items are soiled or damaged. If the $90 jacket is marked down to $35 but is soiled, add the cost of dry cleaning to the sale price when figuring the total price of your bargain. Also, look for possible flaws to see if they would affect your use of the product. Usually, you cannot return or exchange sale items. Find out policies on sale items before you buy. Are returns or exchanges allowed? If a product is marked "second," "irregular," or "as is," it may be flawed in some way.

Try to plan your purchases to match the timing of sales. Seasonal sales usually offer the best buys. Knowing when to expect price cuts on certain products and services can help you plan your purchases to get the best values for your dollars. Check ads and store mailings to know what is on sale in your area.

Food

When you know the foods and nutrients your body requires, you can select safe, nutritious foods that have a positive effect on your health. The food you eat affects the way you look, feel, and function. Learning to shop for the best food values can have a positive effect on your budget.

Nutrients are chemical substances found in foods. They furnish energy, build and maintain body tissues, and regulate body processes. You need six types of nutrients: proteins, fats, carbohydrates, vitamins, minerals, and water. *Fiber* is also essential for good health. It is the indigestible or partially digestible part of plants. It helps move food and digestive by-products through the large intestine and promotes good digestion. Whole grains, fruits, and vegetables are good sources of fiber.

In 2010, the US Department of Agriculture developed new dietary guidelines for Americans. *MyPlate* is a part of a communications initiative based on *2010 Dietary Guidelines for Americans* to help consumers make better food choices. When Americans eat healthy, they can get the nutrients they need and make good spending decisions. MyPlate illustrates the recommended choices and amounts of different foods from the basic food groups: grains, vegetables, fruits, protein, and dairy, as shown in Figure 9-3. The US Department of Agriculture provides detailed and interactive information on healthy eating and diets tailored to individual needs.

To access up-to-date information on MyPlate, go to www.myplate.gov.

Eating Out

When you eat out, you pay for more than just the food. You pay for someone to buy, prepare, and serve the food. Usually, meals in restaurants cost more than similar meals you prepare at home. You also will need to leave a tip of 15 to 20 percent when meals are served to you. In expensive restaurants where service is very good, a 20 percent or slightly higher tip is appropriate. Consider how much and how often you want to pay someone else to shop and cook for you.

Before choosing a restaurant, it pays to find out about the type of food served and the prices. An advance call or a visit to a restaurant's website will let you know if reservations are required or accepted, whether there is a dress code, and if credit cards are accepted. Websites often provide menus as well. Restaurant reviews in newspapers, magazines, and online will give you detailed information on food, service, and customer experiences and recommendations.

United States Department of Agriculture

Figure 9-3 MyPlate is a nutrition guide that helps consumers make better food choices.

When eating out with friends, decide in advance how you will pay. Separate checks save figuring and hassling when the bill comes if each person wishes to pay his or her own way. If food portions are large, you can often save money by splitting an order.

Before You Shop

There are many factors that affect the price of food. When the supply of a specific food is greater than demand, prices fall. When demand is greater than supply, prices rise. Rising prices tend to encourage more production and increase supply, thus lowering demand. Falling prices tend to discourage production and decrease supply, thus increasing demand. Prices tend to go up and down until price equilibrium is reached. **Equilibrium** is the point at which the demand and supply curves intersect. That occurs when supply and demand for a given product at a given price are in balance, as shown in Figure 9-4.

The demand curve shows how much people will buy at different prices. The supply curve shows how much product will be produced at different prices.

Manufacturers market *brand name products* that are sold in most grocery stores. These products generally carry a name you recognize and are of consistent quality and taste wherever you buy them. Chain stores and other

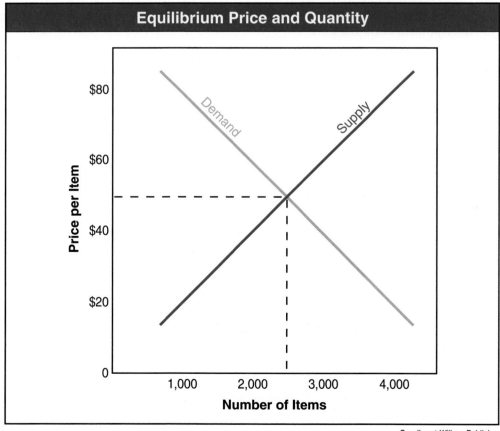

Goodheart-Willcox Publisher

Figure 9-4 The demand curve shows how much people will buy (*x*-axis) at different prices (*y*-axis). The supply curve shows how much product will be produced (*x*-axis) at different prices (*y*-axis). Equilibrium, $50, is the point at which the demand and supply curves intersect.

Case Study

Winners and Losers

Morris is a high school senior. He and a friend are planning a cross-country camping trip right after graduation. Morris needs a sleeping bag. While searching for a bargain online, he finds a website advertising a good selection of sleeping bags at reduced prices. The website belongs to a store that has a location in town that carries the same merchandise. At the store, Morris buys a $150 down sleeping bag that is marked down to $100. Morris saves $50.

Susan sees the same website with marked down sleeping bags. She has never been camping, but she figures she will go someday and will need a sleeping bag. She heard that down sleeping bags are the best. Susan picks up her paycheck and heads for the sports shop. She buys a $120 bag reduced to $80. Susan does not see how she can go wrong with a bargain like this, although it eats up most of her paycheck. Susan never does go camping. The sleeping bag sits in her closet in its original wrapping. She loses her $80.

Case Review

1. What advantages do sales and promotions offer shoppers?
2. What experiences have you had buying goods and services during special promotions and sales?
3. Why was the purchase of a sleeping bag that was on sale a bargain for Morris and a costly mistake for Susan?
4. Why are people so often tempted to buy at a sale even if the goods and services do not meet real needs?

large retailers often sell store brand or generic products that compete with brand names on the grocery shelves. Generally, brand name items are more expensive than generics. By comparing the two products, you may find that many store brands satisfy your needs very well and often provide considerable cost savings. It pays to make the comparisons. It is estimated that consumers can save as much as 30 percent by shopping for generic products.

Organic food is a food produced without synthetic fertilizers, pesticides, growth stimulants, or genetic engineering. Regulations for organic foods also severely restrict the use of additives, such as preservatives, monosodium glutamate (MSG), or artificial sweeteners, colorings, and flavorings. Organic meats and poultry must come from animals raised without the use of growth hormones, antibiotics, or feed made from animal parts. Organic foods are costly to produce and market. They tend to be more expensive than their nonorganic counterparts. The USDA Organic stamp may be used only on foods that are certified at least 95 percent organic, as shown in Figure 9-5.

Create a Budget

A food budget can be an important shopping tool. It focuses attention on what you need to buy and prevents impulse buying and overspending. The amount you spend for food will depend on your income, living expenses, food needs, and personal preferences. Since food is a flexible expense, you can often adjust your food budget to the amount of money available. You can eat steak, go to your favorite restaurant, or throw a party when your pockets

United States Department of Agriculture

Figure 9-5 Foods that are certified as organic by the USDA may carry this stamp.

are full. You can stay home and eat canned tuna when you need money for car repairs, medical bills, or other pressing expenses.

Before you go to the store, plan your purchases. Shop with a grocery list and a spending limit in mind. Try to keep track of the amount you actually spend each week. If spending exceeds the amount planned without a good reason, you may need to adjust your food choices and control impulse buying.

Compare pricing of similar items. The **unit price** of a product is the cost per unit, weight, or measure. The unit price is usually listed on the shelf label where products are displayed. You can use unit pricing to find the best values by comparing the price per unit of various items. For example, you can compare:

- different brands and sizes of the same product;
- different forms of a product, such as canned versus frozen versus fresh; and
- one product to a similar product, such as canned peas versus canned green beans.

Clothing

Most people want clothes that look good and feel comfortable. Having the right clothes for the way you live takes careful planning and shopping. When you enter the workforce, your clothing choices and needs may change. The way you dress can be a factor in taking you from an interview to a job, and it can contribute to your advancement in the workplace. For an interview, let the type of job be your guide on what to wear. Once on the job, a careful look at what most other employees wear can be a good guide to what is appropriate. Some employers issue guidelines or have employees follow a dress code that makes your choices easier. When you are unsure of the proper attire on a new job, ask your employer. Workplace dress codes often are classified as *business* or *business casual*. Your employer will define what is expected for business or business casual dress.

A careful look at your wardrobe needs will help you achieve the look you want at a price you can afford. Before shopping for clothing and shoes, look seriously at your budget and your clothing needs.

What you buy will depend largely on how much money you can spend. As you plan, consider the:

- total amount you have to spend;
- total amount of your essential expenses other than for clothing;
- importance of clothing and personal appearance to you; and
- amount you can allow for clothes after meeting other essential needs.

When you are ready to start shopping, it is a good idea to prioritize your needs and focus on the most important items first. You need to know how to judge quality and what quality level will best serve different purposes. It also is important to keep your spending limits in mind. Catalog and online outlets often have values and variety that may be hard to find in local stores.

Clothing labels and tags provide important information. Most labels will identify the manufacturer, designer, or seller; the country where the garment was made; and the fiber content. If a special finish has been applied to the fabric, it is usually listed. Labels also give care instructions and size information.

Much of the information on labels of clothing and other textile products is required by law. Four of the most important laws and regulations that govern the labeling, marketing, and safety of clothing and textile products are described in Figure 9-6.

Regulations Governing Clothing and Textile Products	
Wool Products Labeling Act	Requires products containing wool to be labeled with the percentage and type of fibers used—new or virgin wool, reprocessed or reused wool. This act is enforced by the Federal Trade Commission.
Textiles Fiber Products Identification Act	Requires textile products to be labeled with the generic name, fibers used, and the percentage of each fiber present by weight. The name or identification of the manufacturer and the country of origin, if the item is imported, must also be listed. This is required for wearing apparel, accessories, and textile products used in the home such as draperies, upholstered furniture, linens, and bedding. This act is enforced by the Federal Trade Commission.
Permanent Care Labeling Rule	Requires manufacturers to attach permanent care labels to apparel explaining the best way to clean a garment including methods and temperatures for laundering, drying, ironing, and dry cleaning. Fabrics, draperies, curtains, slipcovers, upholstered furniture, carpets, and rugs must also be labeled with care instructions. This rule is enforced by the Federal Trade Commission.
Flammable Fabrics Act	Sets flammability standards for children's sleepwear, general wearing apparel, carpets, rugs, and mattresses to protect consumers from unreasonable fire risks. This act is enforced by the Consumer Product Safety Commission.

Goodheart-Willcox Publisher

Figure 9-6 These laws regulate the labeling, marketing, and safety of clothing and textile products.

Yuri Arcurs/Shutterstock.com

Before purchasing an electronic device, learn about special performance features, ease of use, and servicing.

Electronics and Appliances

Technological advances have created a steady stream of new consumer electronics and appliances. These goods and services can improve the ways people communicate, learn, spend their leisure, and do business. However, consumers need to examine their needs and budgets before they spend their money. Shop around before you buy. Identical products vary in price from store to store.

Before You Shop

As you shop, consider safety, ease of use, performance features, energy efficiency, warranties, and servicing. Be sure to check and recheck the size and dimensions of a new purchase against the size and shape of the space where you will put it. Read the labels, seals, and instruction booklets that come with products. They provide facts and information on use and care, performance, safety, energy efficiency, and proper disposal or recycling.

The more *durable* a product is, the longer it will last. Begin with a careful check of construction features. Appliances should be sturdy, well built, and evenly balanced. Look for hard, durable finishes that do not scratch or dent easily.

Before buying an appliance or electronic device, determine your needs. The following questions can help.

- What jobs do you need the product to perform for you?
- What size (physical dimensions, power level) do you need?
- What special features are important to you?

- Do you have the space required to use all the product's features?
- What special safety features do you want?
- Is the appropriate power source available and convenient to the product's location?

After determining your needs, figure out how much money you can spend. Look at your savings to see how much cash you have on hand. Study your budget to determine how much money you have to spend for monthly operating costs, service charges, or loan payments.

If you need more than one product, set priorities. For example, having a working refrigerator is a need. Without one, you must eat most of your meals out, which is expensive and inconvenient. However, a new smartphone is a want. For most consumers, purchasing a refrigerator will take priority over buying a smartphone. Based on your savings and budget, decide how much you can spend for the appliance or electronic device you want to purchase. Consider the following questions.

- Will you buy on credit or can you pay cash?
- How much more is the credit price than the cash price? Is it worth the difference?
- If you choose to use credit, how much can you afford to pay in monthly installments? What are the total finance charges?
- How much money will you need for installation, servicing, and operating costs?

The time to obtain information on appliances and electronic devices is before you buy. It pays to find out what is new before you shop. This is particularly true when you buy costly products you expect to enjoy for a long time.

Most manufacturers' websites provide information about their products related to functions, features, power, and dimensions. You may need to dig deeper to learn about installation requirements, warranties, use, and care. Collecting and comparing this information on different brands can help you make a wise choice.

Sources of information also include consumer publications and materials from retailers, governments, trade associations, utility companies, and consumer groups. Look especially for articles that compare similar products or different brands. The Internet is an excellent, comprehensive source of information on products, features, energy efficiency, and prices. Almost every type of product offers a variety of performance features. Generally, more features mean higher prices and possibly higher operating costs. Features that extend a product's life or make it safer, more efficient, and easier to use may be worth the extra cost.

The easier it is for you to keep a product well maintained, the more you will use and enjoy it. Be sure you understand what you need to know about its installation, use, and care. Choose products with controls that are easy to read, understand, and operate.

Ask salespersons for demonstrations before you buy. When installing major appliances, insist on qualified service persons to make the required gas, electrical, and plumbing connections. For some products, installation may be included in the purchase price. Do-it-yourself installations and servicing are risky unless you are trained to do these jobs. Employing service people who are not authorized to do the work may also jeopardize warranty coverage.

Marketing

Sales Promotion Managers
Sales promotion managers direct programs that combine advertising with purchase incentives to increase sales. They use direct mail, telemarketing, media advertising, catalogs, exhibits, websites, store displays, and special events to establish closer contact with consumers.

You Do the Math

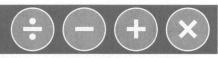

The number that is going to be multiplied by another number is called the *multiplicand*. The number by which the multiplicand is multiplied is called the *multiplier*. Many times, you will not need as precise of a number as the calculation provides. To round a number, locate the value place to which you want to round. Then, look at the digit to the right of this place. If the digit to the right is less than 5, do nothing to the value place to which you are rounding.

Complete the Following Problems

1. A bike shop has a bicycle on clearance sale for $265. That same bike is available from a web-based business for $220. The sales tax rate for both is 6 percent. The Internet business charges $25 for shipping and handling. The bike shop bicycles are assembled free of charge. The bike available online is shipped unassembled. It costs $35 to have someone put it together. Which offer is a better deal?

2. Store A has flip-flops on sale at two pairs for $5.50. Store B has them on sale for 25 percent off their normal price of $3.50 a pair. Store C gives you one free pair of flip-flops if you buy a pair at the regular price of $5.

   A. How much do the flip-flops cost per pair at each store?

   B. Which store has flip-flops at the lowest price per pair?

   C. Which store charges the highest price?

3. The cereal you want to buy comes in two different sizes. What is the unit price of each one? Which one is the better deal?

   •   Box A 10-ounce box for $5.00

   •   Box B 6-ounce box for $3.50

Energy Efficiency

When you buy appliances and electronic products, it pays to consider energy efficiency and operating costs. This is especially true for major home appliances and products you expect to use for a number of years.

Energy efficient equipment and appliances cost less to own and operate. Over time, even if the purchase price of an energy efficient product is high, it may still be a bargain. Energy efficiency saves you money in lower utility bills. It reduces air pollution and helps conserve natural resources at the same time.

You can also save energy by unplugging electronic devices when they are not in use. Even though they are turned off, televisions, computers, and even device chargers draw electricity.

As you shop, look for the EnergyGuide labels that appear on refrigerators, freezers, dishwashers, clothes washers, water heaters, air conditioners, and furnaces. An **EnergyGuide label** is a label that shows the estimated annual cost of operating an appliance and other information. By comparing the average cost estimates for similar appliances, you can determine which would be the most energy efficient and least costly to own and operate.

These labels tell you the estimated yearly energy used in operating an appliance based on national average utility rates. The lower part of the label gives an estimate of the electricity or gas the appliance uses in one year based on typical use. You can multiply this figure by your local electric or gas rate to estimate costs for your area.

Energy efficiency rating labels appear on climate-control equipment, such as air conditioning and furnaces. These labels show the range of efficiency ratings for competing equipment of the same cooling or heating capacity.

The **ENERGY STAR program** is a voluntary partnership of the US Department of Energy and the Environmental Protection Agency, product manufacturers, local utilities, and retailers. Its purpose is to encourage the purchase of the most energy-efficient consumer electronics and appliances. The ENERGY STAR label, as shown in Figure 9-7, appears on appliances and home electronics that meet strict energy- and water-saving criteria. The label on a clothes washer, for example, means the model uses one-third less energy and one-half the water of those without the label.

By choosing products labeled with the ENERGY STAR, you can conserve energy and water and keep your utility bills down. You will also help to protect the environment.

Services

Buying services is different from buying goods. When you buy a product, you can see it, inspect it, try it on, or handle it. After using a product once, you can usually expect it to be the same when you buy it again.

When buying a service, you do not really know what you are getting until after you receive it. For the most part, you buy on faith. Most services require special knowledge or skills. Examples are dental and medical care, auto and household repairs, and legal and financial advice. When buying such services, investigate the service provider's qualifications and reputation. Check education, training, experience, and membership in business or professional

United States Environmental Protection Agency

Figure 9-7 ENERGY STAR label identifies products that are energy efficient.

organizations. Choose only qualified professionals whom you can trust to do a good job.

Know or find out who performs the service. Ask how long the service takes, how much it costs, and what the price includes. For expensive services, such as auto repairs and home improvements, get several written estimates. Compare estimates carefully, reading all the details. Look for reasonable price estimates along with assurance the job will be done right, on time, and with appropriate guarantees.

You also want to give a clear and complete description of what you want. For example, when you get a haircut, describe the type of cut you want or bring a picture of the style. If you do not know what you want, ask for advice. Professional service providers who know their fields can give you valuable guidance.

Work orders and contracts are common when buying services on your car or home or other costly work that is performed over a period of time. A **work order** is a document that describes the work that will be performed. For expensive or lengthy service jobs, you will want a written contract that includes this information:

- name, address, phone number, and license number of the service provider
- description of the work to be done and materials to be used
- starting date and estimated completion date
- total cost and a schedule of payments
- description of the grounds for terminating the contract by either party along with the consequences of termination

Ask to see a copy of the service provider's liability insurance certificate if it is applicable. If a *building permit* is required, ask the service provider to apply for it in his or her name. Be sure to thoroughly inspect the work before paying in full or signing a completion certificate.

After the Purchase

Buying goods and services can be a large part of your budget. When you spend your dollars, check to make sure that the vendor who is selling you the product stands behind the purchase.

Warranties

When you shop, compare warranty coverage just as you compare other features. A **warranty** is a guarantee that a product will meet certain performance and quality standards. The warranty provides for specific remedies if the product does not live up to stated promises. Warranties are included in the purchase price. Warranties can guide you both in the purchase of products and in later needs for service and satisfaction. By law, you have the right to read product warranty promises before you buy.

Written warranties may be full or limited. A *full warranty* must provide the following:

- free repair or replacement of defective products or parts
- repair or replacement within a reasonable time

- no unreasonable demands on you as a condition of receiving repairs or replacement
- replacement if a number of attempts at repair fails
- transfer of coverage to a new owner if the product changes hands during the warranty period

A **limited warranty** is a guarantee for service, repairs, and replacements only under certain conditions. You may be required to pay labor costs or handling charges. It may cover repairs only and not replacement. It may also require return of the product to the seller or an authorized service center for warranty servicing.

Most warranties cover products for a stated period of time, such as 90 days or one year. Warranties do not protect against failure caused by misuse of a product.

In addition to the written warranty, most products carry unwritten implied warranties of merchantability and fitness. **Implied merchantability** is an unwritten guarantee that a product is what it is called and does what its name implies. A computer printer must print documents; a heater must produce heat. The product must be in working order.

Implied fitness is an unwritten promise that a product must be fit for any performance or purpose promised by the seller. If a salesperson or hangtag suggests roller skates for outdoor use, they must be fit for outdoor skating. Implied warranties apply to the condition of a product at the point-of-sale. They cover defects that are present but may not be obvious at the time of purchase.

You usually need proof of purchase to receive warranty service, so be sure to keep the sales receipts, warranties, and model numbers of the products you buy. To make the best use of a product warranty, read it carefully to learn:

- how long coverage lasts;
- whether it covers the entire product or only parts;
- performance and characteristics that are guaranteed;
- whether labor costs are included;
- party responsible for carrying out warranty promises;
- what you must do to receive warranty benefits.

Service contracts are often available for both electronic products and home appliances. If you use appliances correctly, care for products as directed, and buy from reputable manufacturers and dealers, warranty servicing usually is adequate. A *service contract* may be worth considering if you move frequently and need installations and follow-up services with each move. Someone who expects to give an appliance maximum use may also consider purchasing a service contract. For example, a clothes washer in a household of five or more members may need more servicing than a similar machine in a couple's home.

When you buy major appliances, autos, or electronic products, the seller often offers a service contract or extended warranty for an additional cost. An **extended warranty** covers servicing and repairs that may be required after the initial warranty expires. Before you buy this type of protection, consider the following questions.

- What is the cost of an extended warranty or service contract? Must you pay a deductible?

Marketing

Product Planners
Product planners are responsible for the entire life cycle of a product. They are involved in the acquisition, distribution, internal allocation, delivery, and final sale of a product.

- What is covered by the agreement and what must you do to obtain the services promised? Must you provide proof of periodic maintenance?

- Does the extended warranty cover services already guaranteed in the original warranty?

- What would repair services cost without an extended warranty? What would it cost to simply replace the product if it fails? It may be cheaper to replace some products than to buy the extended warranty.

- Who and where do you call for service? Check out service providers with a consumer protection group, such as the Better Business Bureau.

- Can you buy the service contract at a later date or after the warranty expires?

Extended warranties often are expensive. If you want to buy this type of protection, you may want to buy it directly from the manufacturer rather than the retailer or other third party. Compare the available sources of protection.

Product Service

Most appliances and electronic products require service or repair at some point. You can reduce the need for repairs by buying well-built products and carefully following directions for use and care. If the product is under warranty or you purchased a service contract, take advantage of the services to which you are entitled.

If the product is not under warranty, service or repairs can be expensive. The first question you need to ask is whether repair costs are as much or more than the price of a new model. If the answer is yes, buying the new product is the better choice.

History of Finance

Shopping and the Economy

Except for a few brief periods, the late twentieth and early twenty-first centuries were prosperous times for most Americans. Unemployment and inflation were low. Climbing stock market levels created wealth for most investors. Homeowners benefited from rising property values. Taxes were low.

During the prosperous times, Americans spent more than they saved. Consumer spending was high, and people used credit to buy more goods and services. In 2008, the US economy went into recession. Businesses suffered and laid off workers. Unemployment climbed.

Consumers stopped spending and focused on paying off debt and saving money. People delayed major purchases with hopes of better times ahead. Although saving is a good financial strategy for individuals, strong consumer spending is crucial to the health of the US economy in a recession.

American consumers contributed to a global economic boom. During the recession, imports slowed. Other countries cut production and their workforces. Hotels and restaurants around the world struggled without American tourists. When Americans stopped shopping, the impact was felt thousands of miles away.

For electronics and appliance purchases, keep copies of warranties and records of servicing with dates and charges.

Keep important paperwork filed and ready for reference as you need it. Paperwork includes receipts of appliance purchases, copies of warranties, and records of servicing with dates and charges. Have your file in hand when you call for service. Service providers will want to know the make, model, and serial number of the product. They will also need the date of purchase and details of the problem you are experiencing.

Finding a reliable service facility is the key to getting the most for your service dollars. It is a good idea to do this before you have problems. This way, you know where to call for prompt, reliable service when you need it.

Check your warranty for a list of service centers. You can also ask friends, neighbors, and appliance dealers for recommendations. Once you have the names of several service centers, check with your local Better Business Bureau or consumer protection agency. If complaints have been filed against a facility and not resolved to the customer's satisfaction, it may be best to look for servicing elsewhere. Finding the answers to the following questions can help you choose a service center.

- Is the center authorized to work on the specific products you own?
- What are the qualifications of service technicians? Ask about years of experience, special training, certification, or licensing.
- How much does the center charge for basic repair services, house calls, pickups, and deliveries? Compare fees of several service centers.

- Does the center provide emergency service?
- Do the technicians guarantee their work?
- How long will it take to have your appliance or electronic product serviced?

One sure way to trim costs for appliance repairs is to avoid unnecessary service calls. In most cases, when a service person comes to your home, you pay even if there is nothing wrong with the product. An estimated 30 percent of all calls for service are unnecessary. Often the product is unplugged, not set properly for operation, or not running because of a blown fuse.

Look to the owner's manual for items to check before calling for service. Most manuals provide a troubleshooting section that can help you identify problems and fix those you can take care of yourself. When servicing is necessary, make sure you understand what caused the problem and what was done to correct it.

Product Safety

When purchasing electronics and home appliances, check for seals and labels showing that products meet safety standards. For example, the UL seal of Underwriters Laboratories, Inc. indicates that products have been tested for electrical, thermal, and fire hazards.

You can prevent many home accidents by following these simple precautions.

- Before using an electric appliance, make sure the appliance and the cord are in good condition.
- Avoid the use of extension cords. If needed, use them only for low-wattage appliances. Extension cords are not safe for high-wattage products, such as irons, toasters, and coffeemakers.
- Turn off equipment before connecting or disconnecting at outlets.
- Be sure to avoid using several electric appliances on a single circuit. Overloading circuits can blow a fuse and create a fire hazard.
- If you have gas appliances, promptly call the gas company if you ever smell gas or suspect a leak. Since gas leaks are very dangerous, most gas utility companies will check your home for suspected gas leaks for little or no charge.

Obsolescence

Most products eventually break or outlive their usefulness which mean they become obsolete. **Obsolete** means something is no longer useful because a newer version exists. *Obsolescence* gives manufacturers the opportunity to introduce new products and increase sales. Consumers benefit when obsolete products are replaced by something better. Better can mean something cheaper, more powerful, more efficient, or with more features.

Obsolescence also benefits producers because it stimulates demand. The more often consumers replace an outdated product with a new one, the more they buy overall. Consumer electronics products are especially susceptible to obsolescence because of the constant new developments in technology. Companies also strive to outdo each other in competitive markets. Every company wants to introduce something new.

Careers in Education & Training

What Does a Consumer Education Teacher Do?

A **consumer education teacher** teaches consumer education concepts and skills. The teacher is part of the faculty and may have responsibilities outside, as well as inside, the classroom. **Consumer education teachers** typically:

- teach important consumer skills and concepts;
- grade assignments and monitor progress;
- manage the classroom and supervise student activities outside the classroom;
- communicate with parents regarding student performance; and
- participate as a faculty member in school administration and activities.

What Is It Like to Work as a Consumer Education Teacher?

Consumer education teachers normally work in high schools or post-secondary institutions. They may teach several classes a day as well as supervise student activities in the school.

Consumer education teachers usually work closely with other staff members and school administrators to enhance the overall school environment and learning experience. Most states have tenure laws that provide a measure of job security. A large number of teachers belong to a teachers' union that represents their interests.

In most schools, teachers work school hours, but they often need to take work home. The school year is typically 10 months with several vacation breaks throughout the year. Salaries may depend on the qualifications and educational levels of individual teachers.

What Education and Skills Are Needed to Be a Consumer Education Teacher?

- bachelor degree with major or additional training in content area
- completion of a teacher education training program
- state license or certification; requirements vary by state
- continuing education for advancement
- communication and computer skills
- teaching skills
- patience

Mediators

Mediators listen to two parties involved in a dispute, sort through differences between them, and find a compromise. Mediators must be neutral and have excellent listening and communication skills.

Planned obsolescence, or built-in obsolescence, occurs when products are designed to become obsolete or to break down after a certain amount of time or after a certain amount of use. Obsolescence is created in the following ways.

- *Discontinued parts or service.* If consumers cannot have a product fixed, they are forced to buy a new one.

- *Discontinued upgrades.* Consumers must buy a new product when the older one cannot use the latest upgrades and applications. For example, newer computer software programs often require more memory than older computers possess.

- *Unavailable parts or refills.* In the past, for example, when printer ink cartridges ran out of ink, the entire cartridge had to be replaced at a high cost. Today, most cartridges are refillable.

- *Use of parts that wear out or break.* Use of cheap, breakable parts during manufacturing can cause a product to wear out sooner.

- *Superficial design changes.* Consumers may be convinced they need to buy new products because they are better looking, more fashionable, or trendy. In the clothing and footwear market, for example, new trends quickly make current fashions obsolete.

As a consumer, you can protect your wallet by continuing to use products you own as long as they meet your needs. Buy new products only when improvements offer significant advantages.

Because there are new product developments each year, you will want to find out what is new on the market before buying. Over time, electronic products and appliances will become obsolete. Carefully consider the benefits versus the costs before upgrading to a new model or product.

Blend Images/Shutterstock.com

Old products become obsolete when new products become available to replace them.

Checkpoint 9.2

1. How can a spending plan help you make smart shopping decisions?
2. Name five tips for getting value for your dollars.
3. Describe the major difference between buying products and buying services.
4. What information should you keep with product warranties?
5. List five questions to ask before buying an extended warranty.

Build Your Vocabulary

As you progress through this course, develop a personal glossary of personal finance terms and add it to your portfolio. This will help you build your vocabulary and prepare you for a career. Write a definition for each of the following terms and add it to your personal finance glossary.

comparison shopping	work order
nutrients	warranty
equilibrium	limited warranty
organic food	implied merchantability
unit price	implied fitness
EnergyGuide label	extended warranty
ENERGY STAR program	obsolete

Chapter Summary

Section 9.1 Shopping Basics

- Traditional brick and mortar stores, such as department stores, operate out of a physical location. With nontraditional sellers, consumers shop at home from catalogs or television or by using the telephone or Internet.

- To get consumers' attention, businesses use advertisements, product placements, infomercials, direct mail advertising, special sales, promotions, and buying incentives.

Section 9.2 Before You Shop

- You need a variety of shopping skills to help you get value for your dollars. Smart shopping depends on making rational decisions. To be a smart shopper, you need well-defined goals and a clear view of your resources.

- When buying personal goods, look products over carefully. Read labels and consider information about the price, quality, and performance features. Be sure to know exactly what you are buying, the quality you are getting, and the terms of the sale.

- When you shop, compare warranty coverage just as you compare other features. A product may carry a full or a limited warranty. An extended warranty or service contract may be worth considering.

Check Your Personal Finance IQ

Now that you have finished the chapter, see what you learned about personal finance by taking the chapter posttest. If you do not have a smartphone, visit the G-W Learning companion website.

G-W Learning mobile site: www.m.g-wlearning.com

G-W Learning companion website: www.g-wlearning.com

Review Your Knowledge

1. How do warehouse clubs operate?
2. What is an advantage of buying at a resale shop? What are some disadvantages?
3. What can you do if you do not wish to receive telemarketing calls?
4. What are three techniques sellers use in advertisements to convince consumers to buy products?
5. What is a loss leader and how can using a loss leader increase sales?
6. What information should you consider with comparing products, services, and places to shop?
7. What are four guidelines you can follow when dealing with other shoppers?
8. What does comparison shopping involve?
9. What does the term *implied merchantability* mean?
10. How can consumers benefit from product obsolescence?

Apply Your Knowledge

11. In what ways have technological advancements changed the marketplace over the past 20 years?
12. What sources of information do you find most helpful when buying goods and services?
13. How do needs, wants, trends, prices, and quality affect your shopping decisions?
14. Describe a time when specific needs and goals helped you make a sound buying decision.
15. Describe your most successful and least successful shopping experiences. Why do you think one was successful and the other disappointing?
16. What do you see as the pros and cons of buying from online sellers?
17. What are some items you would consider buying at a resale shop? What are some items you would not consider buying at a resale shop? Give reasons why you would not want to buy these items at this type of store.
18. What products have you used in the past that are now obsolete? Why are the products obsolete?
19. Do you prefer to shop at traditional brick and mortar stores or at online stores? Gives reasons for your preference.
20. Have you purchased an item through an Internet auction? When you received the item, was it as you expected it to be? Describe the experience.

 ## Teamwork

Working with your team, investigate service contracts and extended warranties on the Internet to answer the following questions.

- When, if ever, does buying a service contract make sense?
- What are the advantages and disadvantages of an extended warranty?
- What do sellers and manufacturers have to gain from selling service contracts?
- What should consumers know before buying a service contract or extended warranty?

G-W Learning Mobile Site

Visit the G-W Learning mobile site to complete the chapter pretest and posttest and to practice vocabulary using e-flash cards. If you do not have a smartphone, visit the G-W Learning companion website to access these features.

G-W Learning mobile site: www.m.g-wlearning.com

G-W Learning companion website: www.g-wlearning.com

Common Core

College and Career Readiness

CTE Career Ready Practices. Create a Venn diagram to show the relationship between your career interests, your preferences, your goals, and requirements of your career choice. Where do the circles overlap? What do you think overlap signifies? What would a diagram with a lot of overlap tell you? What about one with little or no overlap?

Reading. Using independent research and the information contained in the text, write a report in which you analyze consumer spending. How does consumer spending connect with other important events or ideas that are influential in our economy? Cite specific evidence from the text and your research to support your understanding of this issue.

Writing. Identity theft is a serious problem for business as well as consumers. Conduct research on how much money businesses lost in the last year due to identity theft. Write an informative report consisting of several paragraphs to describe your findings of the implications for consumers.

Web Connect

Use the Internet to comparison shop to find the best deal. Search for several sellers of three products or services you want to buy. Record the name of each seller, the price charged, and any additional charges, such as shipping and taxes. Identify the best deal for each product.

College and Career Readiness Portfolio

College and Career Readiness

Your portfolio should contain items related to your schoolwork. These items might include report cards, transcripts, or honor roll reports. Diplomas or certificates that show courses or programs you completed should also be included.

At some point, you will likely apply for a particular job or volunteer position. At that time, list the classes you took that helped prepare you for the job or volunteer position. Describe the activities you completed or topics you studied in these classes that relate to the job or volunteer duties. This information will be helpful when you apply for the position by letter or talk with an interviewer.

1. Identify a job or volunteer position for which you could apply. Write a paragraph that gives the classes you took and activities completed that relate to the position. You can use this document as a model when you are actually ready to apply for a position.

2. Scan other documents related to your schoolwork (grade reports, transcripts, and diplomas). Place the model paragraph and other documents in your e-portfolio.

3. Place hard copies in the container for your print portfolio.

Objective Test

Some competitive events for Career and Technical Student Organization (CTSOs) require that entrants complete an objective part of the event. This event will typically be an objective test that includes terminology and concepts related to a selected subject area. Participants are usually allowed one hour to complete the objective part of the event.

To prepare for an objective test, complete the following activities.

1. Read the guidelines provided by your organization.

2. Visit the organization's website and look for objective tests that were used in previous years. Many organizations post these tests for students to use as practice for future competitions.

3. Look for the evaluation criteria or rubric for the event. This will help you determine what the judge will be looking for in your presentation.

4. Review the Checkpoint questions at the end of each section of this text.

5. Review the end-of-chapter activities in this text for additional practice.

6. Create flash cards for each vocabulary term with its definition on the other side. Ask a friend to use these cards to review with you.

7. Ask your instructor to give you practice tests for each chapter of this book. It is important that you are familiar with answering multiple choice and true/false questions. Have someone time you as you take a practice test.

Chapter 10
Consumer Power

Some consumers seem to know what they want. Others tend to make the wrong choices. They sometimes take on too much debt. They never seem to be in control of their finances. Most people probably fall somewhere in between the consumer who is confident and the uncertain, inexperienced consumer.

There is a basic set of skills you need to make the most of your consumer dollars. You need to learn where to find reliable information about products and services, consumer legislation, and economic conditions. As a consumer, you enjoy certain rights and carry certain responsibilities. For example, you are entitled to safety in the marketplace—safe products and services. However, you are responsible for using products as directed and for heeding safety precautions and warnings. You have the right to be heard and the responsibility to speak out when you have a problem with products, services, or sellers. Consumers are guaranteed certain rights in the marketplace, but they also have responsibilities to know and exercise these rights.

Focus on Finance

Trial Offers

Beware of companies that offer free trial offers or other free products. These offers may be made on the phone by a telemarketer, in a store at which you are shopping, or in a television advertisement. If a company offers you a trial offer, pay close attention to the terms and conditions. Understand who you are dealing with and what you are agreeing to. By accepting the offer, you may be required to give a credit card number to receive the product or service. If you do not cancel during the trial period, your credit card may be charged for the product or service offered for the trial period. By accepting the trial offer, you may have agreed to pay if you do not cancel before the trial period ends. The Federal Trade Commission (FTC) recommends that before you give the okay to a free trial offer, ask the seller questions about how to cancel, who to call to cancel, and whether you will be billed automatically. Visit the FTC website for more information before you accept such a transaction.

College and Career Readiness

Reading Prep. Scan this chapter and look for information presented as fact. As you read this chapter, try to determine which topics are fact and which ones are the author's opinion. After reading the chapter, research the topics and verify which are facts and which are opinions.

Check Your Personal Finance IQ

Before you begin the chapter, see what you already know about personal finance by taking the chapter pretest. If you do not have a smartphone, visit the G-W Learning companion website.

G-W Learning mobile site: www.m.g-wlearning.com

G-W Learning companion website: www.g-wlearning.com

Sections

Section 10.1 **Be an Informed Consumer**

Section 10.2 **Protecting Your Rights**

Blend Images/Shutterstock.com

Section 10.1
Be an Informed Consumer

Objectives

After studying this section, you will be able to:

- Identify and use reliable sources of consumer information.
- Describe the process of evaluating consumer information.

Terms

labeling law
testing and rating service
review

Sources of Information

The information you need to be an informed consumer includes constantly changing facts and figures. Products, services, laws, and economic conditions can change substantially from year to year. There is no substitute for reliable information when you go shopping. As goods, services, and markets become more varied and complex, knowledge is ever more important.

Knowing how to find, evaluate, and use available information can help you become a smarter shopper. It pays to stay up to date. Information you need to make the best buying decisions comes from a variety of sources including labels and hangtags, testing and rating services, salespersons, other consumers, and the Internet.

Christophe Testi/Shutterstock.com

Food labels provide shoppers with information about ingredients and nutritional value.

Labels and Hangtags

Information on labels and hangtags tells you about the content, quality, performance, care, and maintenance of various products. This information helps you select, use, and care for items you buy. A **labeling law** is a government regulation that requires certain information be placed on labels for certain products. Clothing and textile products must be labeled with clear and complete care information, fiber content, the name of the distributor or manufacturer, and the country of origin.

Food packages must carry a list of ingredients, the name and address of the manufacturer, the quantity by weight and number of servings, and specific nutritional information. Look also for the nutritive values, grade and quality levels, expiration dates, preparation, and storage instructions.

Drugs and cosmetics must be labeled with ingredients, directions for use, and cautions against misuse. Laundry supplies, household cleaning agents, pesticides, and herbicides must be labeled with directions for safe use and disposal. They also should contain warnings against hazards of misuse.

Look for age-of-user advice on toy labels, such as "suitable for ages four to six" or "not recommended for children under three years old." Many manufacturers voluntarily provide additional useful information on labels, such as recipes and serving suggestions on food packages. Regardless of the product you are buying, its label can be an important source of practical, reliable information.

Testing and Rating Services

A **testing and rating service** is a group or organization that tests products and rates them according to certain criteria. The testing and rating of consumer goods helps you evaluate features and compare different models and brands of similar products and services. Two common forms of testing and rating results are seals of approval or certification and ratings in consumer publications.

Seals usually rate products as *certified, approved, tested,* or *commended.* Organizations that test products issue seals for the products that meet their standards. A common seal is shown and explained in Figure 10-1.

Consumers Union publishes *Consumer Reports,* which carries ratings of tested products and services. These ratings can help you compare similar goods and services.

FYI

For detailed information on labeling required by law on various products, go to www.ftc.gov and search using the term *labeling laws.*

The Seal	Where It Is Found	What It Means
UL ® **Underwriters Laboratories, Inc.**	On appliances, computer equipment, furnaces, heaters, fuses, smoke detectors, fire extinguishers, and thousands of other products.	Products passed initial tests and periodic factory evaluations, indicating they continue to meet UL standards for safety.

Goodheart-Willcox Publisher

Figure 10-1 This seal indicates that an appliance meets specific performance and safety standards.

Before relying on testing and rating information, you need to know answers to the following questions.

- Who sponsored or conducted the testing? Are the ratings objective or designed to promote the product? Consider the qualifications, interests, and intentions of the testing organization.
- Were product performance and features that are most important to you tested?
- What test methods were used and under what conditions? Were products tested for the type of use you will give them? If TV reception was tested under ideal conditions, it may not be meaningful to you if you live where there is a lot of interference.
- What do the test results mean? Read explanations of seals and ratings carefully to find out exactly what they mean.
- When were products tested, and which models were included? Products tested one year could be better or not as good the next year, particularly in product lines where research brings frequent innovations. If you use test results and ratings as a guide, be sure they include the models you are considering.
- What important factors are not included in testing? Consider price, availability, credit terms, delivery, installation, and reputation of the seller. Most of these items are not covered by product testing and rating services.

Salespersons

Knowledgeable salespeople can be one of your best sources of information. They should know how different brands and models compare and what features are most important. They should also know when new merchandise is expected, when sales are scheduled, and a host of other facts that can help you make sound buying decisions.

Of course, not all salespeople are well-informed and helpful. Their job is to sell the merchandise as well as to please the customer. Some do a better job than others.

If you are fair and considerate with salespeople, you are likely to get better service and information that is more reliable. A salesperson who likes you may tell you of an upcoming sale, call you when new merchandise arrives, or give you a straight answer when you need an opinion about a product.

Customer Reviews

Frequently you can learn about products and services from friends, relatives, neighbors, and other consumers. Friends often can give you firsthand information about everything from new fashions and movies to restaurants and electronic products. They can tell you about their personal experiences with products, services, and sellers. A **review** is a critical report or comments about an item. Many websites have a section where you can read reviews of products that have been posted by other customers.

Internet

The Internet is one of the most complete, up-to-date sources of consumer information available. The Internet allows you to:

Ethics

Many companies and organizations are well-respected members of the community. When selecting establishments with which to do business, investigate the company and its business practices. Many socially responsible businesses post a code of ethics on their websites. This helps consumers select companies that are respectful and honest in their transactions with customers.

Rob Marmion/Shutterstock.com

Carefully evaluate the source and content of consumer information and reviews.

- find out the latest on consumer laws and protection;
- compare product prices, features, and availability;
- check the reliability of sellers, order merchandise, and file complaints;
- access both private and government agencies that protect your interests; and
- research and buy almost anything you want.

Customer reviews of products and services have become a prominent feature on the Internet. Many consumers rely on these reviews to guide their buying decisions. Products and services frequently reviewed include hotels, restaurants, and autos. Bookseller sites often allow readers to post book reviews. Consumer reviews have expanded to include all types of services, including those of doctors and other professionals.

Reviews are available on company websites, independent rating websites, government websites, and consumer advocacy websites. Many of these sites are free. Others charge a fee or require membership to access evaluations. An increasing number of websites review local goods, services, and businesses ranging from restaurants and movies to physicians and therapists to contractors and repair services. The next time you are looking for a restaurant, an auto repair shop, or a fitness instructor, do research on one of the customer review websites covering your area.

Video Graphics Designers

Video graphics designers plan, create, and analyze video communications. They also develop material for websites, interactive media, and multimedia projects. They must be able to use color, illustrations, photography, and animation techniques to enhance communications.

Evaluating Information

After identifying sources of information, you may want to begin a consumer information file. This will put the latest facts and figures at your fingertips when you, the intelligent consumer, are making decisions. The following guidelines will help you evaluate materials in your file.

Is the Source Reliable?

A reliable source on one subject may not be the best place for facts on other topics. For example, a banker may give sound financial advice, but he or she may know nothing about buying furniture. A medical association can tell you how to find a doctor but not how to buy a car. The Food and Drug Administration can tell you how to read a nutrition label, but you would not expect them to be a good source of information on how to judge auto repair services.

What Is the Purpose of the Information?

Is the information intended to inform the buyer or to sell a product, service, or idea? Both news articles and advertisements can offer useful information, but ads generally present only positive, sometimes exaggerated facts.

How Useful Is the Information?

Look for material that is up to date and easy to understand. Read to see if recent developments on the product or subject are discussed. Consider whether the data is complete. Does it tell what you need to know?

Once you begin collecting consumer materials, you will need to organize the information for easy use. Find a drawer or box large enough to hold all the materials you collect. Then sort according to subject matter. As you gather new materials, add them to your file. Periodically review what you have filed and discard information that is no longer current or useful. If you keep information electronically, organize it by folders.

Go Green

Be a smart consumer and turn off the lights. It is a common practice in Europe to unplug equipment that is not in use, including lights and computers. A business can *save some green*, as in dollars, by going green. Up to 25 percent can be saved on energy costs by just turning off and unplugging equipment at the end of the day. Less energy usage also reduces negative effects on the environment.

Checkpoint 10.1

1. Name five sources of consumer information.
2. What information are you likely to find on clothing labels?
3. How can product rating information guide consumer purchases?
4. What are some types of websites that may have product reviews?
5. What three questions can help you evaluate consumer information?

Build Your Vocabulary

As you progress through this course, develop a personal glossary of personal finance terms and add it to your portfolio. This will help you build your vocabulary and prepare you for a career. Write a definition for each of the following terms and add it to your personal finance glossary.

labeling law

testing and rating service

review

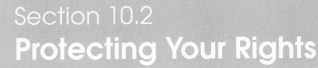

Section 10.2
Protecting Your Rights

Objectives

After studying this section, you will be able to:

- Describe the rights and responsibilities of consumers.
- Discuss the importance of consumer laws.
- Identify reliable consumer advocates.
- Recognize and guard against various forms of deceptive practices in the marketplace.
- Outline steps for consumer self-defense.

Terms

bait and switch
pyramid scheme
Ponzi scheme
chain letter
sweepstakes
lottery
skill contest

caveat emptor
consumer advocate
binding arbitration
small claims court
class action lawsuit
lawsuit

Consumer Rights and Responsibilities

In a free market economy, you enjoy certain rights and responsibilities when you enter the marketplace. Some of your important rights are discussed in the following paragraphs.

Consumer Bill of Rights

In a message to Congress in 1962, President John F. Kennedy outlined four basic consumer rights. In 1985, the United Nations General Assembly added four more rights. These eight rights listed below are now called the *Consumer Bill of Rights*. The original four basic consumer rights are:

- the right to safety;
- the right to be informed;
- the right to choose; and
- the right to be heard.

Four additional rights that were added in 1985 are:

- the right to satisfaction of basic needs;
- the right to redress;
- the right to consumer education; and
- the right to a healthful environment.

Today, these eight consumer rights have been endorsed by the United Nations and affirmed by Consumers International, a worldwide consumer organization. Each of these rights carries responsibilities. Together they form the basis for fairness in the marketplace.

Safety: Rights and Responsibilities

Consumers have the right to protection against products, production processes, and services that could be hazardous to their life, health, and personal finances. The government plays an important role in establishing and enforcing safety standards in the marketplace. The Consumer Products Safety Commission handles problems involving hazardous products. The Food and Drug Administration deals with health and safety issues related to food, drug, and cosmetic products. Several federal agencies oversee consumer financial services including credit, investments, savings, and insurance.

It is the consumer's responsibility to read and follow directions for the safe use, care, storage, and disposal of products, as shown in Figure 10-2. Consumers are also responsible for reporting product-related health and safety problems promptly to sellers and manufacturers. Serious safety hazards should be referred to the government agency that can take prompt action to prevent injury or accident.

Truthful Information: Rights and Responsibilities

Consumers are entitled to accurate information on which to base their buying decisions. The government protects this right through various agencies

Product Design Engineers
Product design engineers develop new electronics, appliances, and accessories to meet consumer needs. They evaluate the design's overall effectiveness, cost, reliability, and safety. The engineers also design the equipment and processes needed to make the new products.

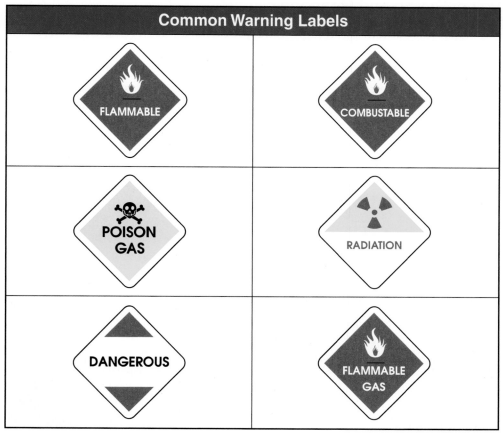

Goodheart-Willcox Publisher

Figure 10-2 These labels are required on products containing hazardous substances.

and regulations. The law requires labels with specific consumer information on certain products. It also mandates specific facts to be clearly stated on any contracts you may be required to sign. In addition, the government prohibits false and misleading advertising.

With the right to truthful information comes the responsibility to seek, evaluate, and use available consumer information. Before you buy, investigate. Check a store's reputation for honesty and fair play and carefully evaluate advertising claims and product performance. Finally, shop and compare quality, features, and prices of goods and services before you buy.

Choice: Rights and Responsibilities

Consumers have the right to choose from a variety of quality goods and services at competitive prices and are free to decide where to shop. Laws protect free choice in the marketplace by prohibiting practices such as monopolies and price fixing.

Consumers are responsible for choosing products and services that will best meet their needs at prices they can pay. Choosing is not always an easy matter and calls for informed and careful decisions.

The responsibilities of choice go beyond personal buying decisions. Consumers have an obligation to deal with reliable, reputable businesses for their own protection and for the overall good of the marketplace. Every buying choice expresses approval of the purchase and the seller. It pays to be aware of the messages you send with the dollars you spend.

Voice: Rights and Responsibilities

When consumers have legitimate problems or concerns, they have the right to speak up, to be heard, and to receive a reasonable response to their concerns. Both businesses and governments have a responsibility to respond.

Consumers are responsible for speaking out and expressing concerns to appropriate business and government representatives. This means learning

Alexey Stiop/Shutterstock.com

According to the Consumer Bill of Rights, consumers have the right to safety and the right to a healthful environment.

and using appropriate and effective means of communication. Let businesses and government representatives know what you like and want as well as what you dislike.

Satisfaction of Basic Needs: Rights and Responsibilities

Consumers have the right to access goods and services required to meet basic needs. These include adequate food, shelter, clothing, health care, education, and sanitation. These basics should be available to all consumers. To satisfy basic needs, you need both enough income to purchase essentials and a marketplace that provides them.

Governments play a role both in defining basic needs and helping citizens satisfy them through various programs, such as public housing, Medicare, Medicaid, Social Security, tax-supported schools and hospitals, sewer and sanitation systems, and fire and police protection.

Responsibility for satisfying basic needs includes putting essential needs ahead of wants when spending, learning about and taking advantage of services available in the marketplace or provided by governments, and getting the training and education needed to earn a living wage.

Redress: Rights and Responsibilities

Consumers have the right to a fair settlement of legitimate disputes. This includes some form of compensation for misrepresentation, shoddy goods, or unsatisfactory services.

Here again, consumers share some of the responsibility to present disputes clearly to the appropriate authorities and make demands reasonable.

Consumer Education: Rights and Responsibilities

Consumers have a right to consumer education. This involves training in the knowledge and skills needed to make informed, confident choices in the marketplace. Consumers can fulfill their responsibilities related to this right by taking consumer education or personal finance courses and by keeping up to date on consumer issues.

Healthful Environment: Rights and Responsibilities

Consumers have a right to live and work in an environment that is nonthreatening to the well-being of present and future generations. This means having pure water and air, safe and responsible waste disposal, preservation of natural resources, and respect for the earth and overall environment. Chapter 17 outlines environmental concerns, government action, and consumer rights and responsibilities related to environmental issues.

Additions to Consumer Rights

Over time, new consumer rights have been declared as the need becomes apparent. These recent protections are discussed in the following paragraphs.

Consumer Privacy Bill of Rights

In 2012, the Obama administration proposed a *Consumer Privacy Bill of Rights* to protect the personal data of consumers. It gives individuals more control over personal information that businesses and organizations collect

Arts, A/V Technology & Communications

Commercial Food Photographers
Commercial food photographers take photos that show food looking its best. They spend hours planning each photo's lighting, props, and setting. When the food is in place, photographers shoot quickly to avoid melting, drying, and shriveling of the food due to hot lights.

You Do the Math

Number sense is an ability to use and understand numbers to make judgments and solve problems. For example, suppose you want to add three basketball scores: 35, 21, and 18.

First, add 30 + 20 + 10 = 60.

Then, add 5 + 1 + 8 = 14.

Finally, combine these two sums to find the answer: 60 + 14 = 74.

Complete the Following Problem

Molly wants to purchase several items of clothing. She is not sure she has enough money to buy the items she wants. Her budget is $95 before tax. The prices of each of three items are $16, $42, and $35. How can she figure the total cost of the three items without using a calculator?

---

from them. The Consumer Privacy Bill of Rights gives consumers the right to information about privacy and security practices of any organization collecting personal data. They have a right to expect secure and responsible handling of personal data. Consumers should be able to access personal data that has been collected and to correct any erroneous information on record. Consumers have the right to expect organizations that collect personal data to use and disclose that information in ways that are consistent with the reason for collecting the information. The bill allows consumers to prevent personal information from being shared with individuals or companies without their permission

Airline Passenger Bill of Rights

Over the years, airline passengers have complained frequently about airline services. A consumer advocacy group, Flyers Rights, has worked for legislation to provide passenger rights. Current provisions in the *Airline Passenger Bill of Rights* include:

- restrictions on the number and length of tarmac delays;
- prominent listing of all ticket costs and fees, eliminating the hidden costs of flying;
- compensation to passengers who are bumped;
- refunds of baggage fees for lost luggage; and
- changes in reservations within 24 hours of booking without penalties.

Airlines are fighting some of these provisions, and final rulings are being negotiated. If you plan to fly, it may pay you to check for the latest information on passenger rights.

Credit Cardholders Bill of Rights

A law known as the *Credit Card Accountability, Responsibility, and Disclosure (CARD) Act of 2009* applies to existing credit card accounts as well as new accounts. The legislation requires credit providers to mail bills at least 21 days before the due dates. They also must give at least 45 days' advance notice of rate hikes or any other important changes to the credit card agreement and at least 30 days' notice prior to an account closure. The law includes special provisions regarding credit cards issued to minors. Credit providers may not offer credit card accounts to minors who have no proof of financial means to pay debts incurred unless there is a cosigner over age 21 who has the ability to pay. The law also requires any advertisements for free credit reports to make clear that free credit reports are available under federal law.

Consumer Laws

In the United States, there are many laws at both the federal and state levels that protect the consumer. These laws protect against fraudulent advertising, unfair trade practices, and a variety of other issues. The Federal Trade Commission Bureau of Consumer Protection provides extensive consumer protection information.

Some examples of federal consumer laws are as follows.

- *Consumer Product Safety Act*—develops safety rules and recalls for products
- *Federal Trade Commission Act*—regulates trade and prevents unfair competition
- *United Stated Do Not Call Registry*—stops telemarketers from calling consumers
- *Fair Credit Reporting Act (FRCA)* —regulates sharing of consumer data
- *Health Insurance Portability and Accountability Act (HIPPA)*—regulates availability of health plans

Consumers should check with their state of residence for specific state protection legislation.

Visual Merchandise Managers

Visual merchandise managers are responsible for designing and implementing window and store displays for retail stores. Visual merchandisers create displays that maximize the space of the store while appealing to the senses of their target customers.

History of Finance

Denim Jeans

In the United States, cotton denim jeans were first made by entrepreneurs Levi Strauss and Jacob Davis. They received a patent for their pants in 1873. The first jeans were created for miners working in California's gold rush. The popularity of denim jeans spread to others who sought durable and comfortable work pants.

Perhaps more than any other garment, jeans are associated with an attitude and a lifestyle. In the 1940s, they became synonymous with freedom and the Wild West because of their popularity among cowboys. During the 1950s, some parents and educators prohibited teenagers from wearing jeans because of their association with rebellion and delinquency.

During the 1970s, jeans became canvases of the wearer. Young people painted, embroidered, and beaded their jeans. Cutoff jeans were also popular. During the 1980s, designer jeans and stonewashed denim were popular. Jean styles became baggy and were worn below the hip. Ribbed, faded, decorated, and designer labeled, denim jeans have been a favorite wardrobe item for generations of Americans.

Health and Sanitary Inspectors

Health and sanitary inspectors examine establishments where foods are manufactured, handled, stored, or sold. They enforce legal standards of sanitation, purity, and grading.

Consumer Advocates

While consumer rights have been declared and defined in local, federal, and international forums, you still may find your rights denied or diminished in some situations. When this happens and you cannot settle differences directly with sellers, it often helps to contact outside agencies. Both government agencies and private organizations offer consumers assistance with problems in the marketplace. A **consumer advocate** is a group or an individual who promotes consumer rights. Advocates address consumer interests in various areas, such as health and safety, education, redress, truthful advertising, fairness in the marketplace, and environmental protection.

Government Agencies

When dealing with dishonest and fraudulent business practices, contact the appropriate government regulatory agency. Most federal agencies will have local or regional offices. In addition, local and state governments provide regulatory and law enforcement functions to deal with fraud in the marketplace. Figure 10-3 lists some of the federal government agencies that provide services and protection for consumers.

Other Organizations

Consumer advocacy comes from a variety of other sources and offers a range of services to consumers. The advocacy groups fall primarily into the following categories.

- *Better Business Bureaus (BBBs).* These are nonprofit organizations supported largely by local businesses. They promote ethical business practices and, in some cases, offer dispute resolution programs.

- *Consumer organizations.* Consumer interest groups advocate for consumer causes and provide educational materials and information on

Government Agencies
• United States Department of Agriculture
• Consumer Product Safety Commission
• Environmental Protection Agency
• Federal Trade Commission
• Food and Drug Administration
• Health and Human Services
• Housing and Urban Development
• National Institutes of Health
• United States Postal Service
• United States Department of Justice
• United States Department of Transportation
• Securities and Exchange Commission
• Social Security Administration

Goodheart-Willcox Publisher

Figure 10-3 There are many government agencies that provide services and protect consumers.

Orhan Cam/Shutterstock.com

Government regulatory agencies enforce laws to protect the rights of consumers.

products and services. Many of these groups are nonprofit organizations that work actively on behalf of consumers. One example is the Consumers Union, which publishes *Consumer Reports.*

- *Trade associations and dispute resolution programs.* Many companies that produce or sell the same types of goods and services often belong to an industry association. These associations often act as go-betweens for the companies they represent and consumers. They provide consumer information on products and services and may offer dispute settlement programs. One example is the Major Appliance Consumer Action Board. This board is a group of representatives from the home appliances industry that helps resolve consumer complaints.

- *Corporate consumer departments.* Many companies operate consumer affairs departments that deal with consumer concerns and resolve disputes. When you cannot get satisfaction at point of sale, try contacting the consumer affairs or customer relations department at the company headquarters.

Consumer Deception

Certain deceptive practices, though illegal, still exist in the marketplace. For example, it is against the law for sellers to make false or misleading statements about products, services, prices, or guarantees. It also is illegal to advertise sale items that are not actually available for sale or to use false statements such as *special price* or *clearance price* when items are not selling at reduced prices. As a consumer, it pays you to be alert and a bit skeptical when interpreting advertising and sellers' claims. There are many deceptive techniques, some of which are described in the following paragraphs.

Bait and Switch

Bait and switch is a strategy that involves advertising one item and then substituting another item. An item is advertised at a very attractive price to attract customers. When customers come to buy, the seller claims to be out of that item and attempts to sell a substitute. The substitute may be a more expensive item, or it may be an inferior product offered at the same price. This technique is against the law. If you come across bait and switch selling, report it to the Federal Trade Commission or your state consumer fraud agency.

Pyramid and Ponzi Schemes

Pyramid and Ponzi schemes are similarly deceptive. Both promise investors big returns with low risk. A **pyramid scheme** is a fraudulent investment plan. The pyramid scheme calls for each participant to invest a given amount of money and sign up a certain number of additional participants to do the same. The only way to produce the promised profits is to recruit new participants who will recruit others. The many at the bottom of the pyramid end up paying money to the few at the top. Eventually, the pyramid collapses because there are not enough new investors to pay all the earlier investors.

A **Ponzi scheme** is an investment operation in which money from new investors is used to pay earlier investors. The operation works as long as new investors contribute money. Ponzi scheme organizers promise to invest in high-return, low-risk opportunities. In fact, however, they focus on attracting new investors to pay earlier investors and to cover their own personal expenses. These schemes are illegal, fraudulent operations. One of the most famous Ponzi schemes was run by Bernie Madoff who pled guilty in March 2009 on 11 federal felonies.

Pyramid and Ponzi schemes are illegal and should be reported to the Federal Trade Commission and the Securities Exchange Commission. Warning signs of pyramid schemes include:

- The promise of quick, easy money and high returns on your investment
- A large initial investment required to participate
- No available money-back or exit plan
- An unknown promoter or company making the offer with no detailed information available
- Profits dependent on recruiting new members into the plan
- A sense that the program is not legitimate

Chain Letters

Chain letters are US letters or e-mails that promise a big return for a small investment. They may promise anything from recipes, to socks, to huge financial rewards. To get the rewards, you must send as little as a recipe, a pair of socks, or $5 to someone at the top of a list, removing that person's name from the list and adding your own to the bottom. Then you send copies of the letter to a certain number of people with instructions that they do the same. The theory is that by the time your name reaches the top of the list, you will receive oodles of whatever is being sent, such as recipes, socks, or money. Remember the following information about chain letters.

- If you start or send one of these letters that involves money or valuable items, you are breaking the law.
- You are not likely to receive what is promised in the quantity promised. Most certainly, it will not make you rich.
- If you receive a chain letter scam via e-mail, you should contact your service provider and forward the letter to the Federal Trade Commission.

Sweepstakes, Lotteries, and Skill Contests

Sweepstakes, lotteries, and many games of skill are forms of gambling. The odds of winning depend on how many entries you submit, how many prizes are offered, and the total number of entrants. Odds are almost always against the players. People who regularly buy lottery tickets or chances to win big prizes can spend a sizable amount of money over time. This sort of gambling can become addictive and have a negative effect on a person's employment or a family's well-being.

A **sweepstakes** is a promotional offer that gives participants the chance to win items of value or prizes. Some sweepstakes require with no purchase or entry fee to participate. The offers come via direct mail, the Internet, or television. Prizes range from relatively small items, such as personal media players, digital cameras, and smartphones, to large items, such as vacations, cars, cash, and dream homes.

Lotteries are similar to sweepstakes except prizes are awarded to participants by chance in exchange for some form of payment. Most states run lotteries to help fund government operations. Critics of public lotteries claim that they prey on the poor. On the other hand, state lotteries often benefit public schools and other necessary public services.

Skill contests offer the opportunity to win prizes by skill instead of chance. There may be an entry fee or purchase required to enter the contest.

The law regulates these types of promotions, but you also need to be alert on your own behalf. Before you enter a sweepstakes, lottery, or game of skill for a chance to win prizes, follow these guidelines.

Case Study

Consumer Electronics

Laticia saved $250 she received for her birthday to buy a smartphone. At a local phone store, a salesperson demonstrated several phones. There are many different features and options for each phone.

Laticia wants a camera and text messaging, e-mail, and Internet access. The only phone offering all the features she wants costs more than $300.

The service plan is $99 per month, plus a $35 sign-up fee. If she signs a two-year contract, the cost of the phone is reduced by 50 percent. There is a $175 release fee for breaking a contract.

Laticia cannot afford $99 per month. Feeling discouraged, she leaves the store to think it over. The salesperson cautions that the prices will not last forever and urges her to make a decision soon.

Case Review

1. How might Laticia have prepared for her trip to the cell phone store?
2. What are some ways Laticia can lower the costs of buying a phone and the monthly service charges?
3. What experience have you had with cell phones and service plans?
4. What do you think are the basic phone features needed?
5. What advice would you give Laticia?
6. What should you find out before signing a phone contract?

- Look for a full description and an estimate of the value of any prize or winning.
- Find out exactly who sponsors the offer and what the sponsor stands to gain.
- Read and be sure you understand all the rules, including small print.
- Know exactly what is required to participate.
- Know all the fees, charges, or expenses involved in participating.
- Find out the tax consequences attached to big winnings.

Food and Beverage Managers

Food and beverage managers oversee food and beverage inventory and budget control. They assist with menu planning and make sure prepared dishes meet quality and safety standards.

Consumer Self-Defense

Looking after your own interests is an essential consumer skill. Most sellers are honest and reputable, and most products are what they claim to be. However, there are times when you need to apply the principle of caveat emptor. **Caveat emptor** means *let the buyer beware.* The risk in the transaction is on the buyer's side. If you have any question about a seller's reliability or the quality of a product, proceed with caution. This is particularly true when a sizable amount of money is involved or when you are signing a contract.

Self-defense also involves following up when products and services do not meet your expectations or the seller's claims. It calls for settling differences with sellers and seeking the help of third-party consumer advocates when necessary. Consumer advocates promote consumer interests in many areas. Consumer self-defense may require legal action when all else fails.

Successful Complaining

What do you do when a product fails or you are overcharged because of a billing error? What if repairs do not fix your car or a salesperson is rude? To address any of these problems, you need to complain to the right person in the right way. The art of complaining is an essential self-defense tool.

You can often handle simple exchanges and returns of unsatisfactory merchandise by taking purchases back to the seller and explaining your dissatisfaction. Most reliable merchants take care of simple matters on the spot.

Here are a few guidelines to follow when problems are more involved or complicated.

- Put your complaint in writing. Explain the problem clearly, rationally, and briefly. Include important facts, figures, and dates along with copies of receipts.
- Be prompt. Do not wait weeks to act. Put your case in writing right away, and send it by registered mail. The receiver must sign for a registered letter, and you receive a record of its delivery.
- Direct your complaint to the right person and place. If an adjustment requires approval from higher up, the department or store manager is the person to see. Contact the credit department for billing errors and other credit problems. Complain to top management if a problem is serious or is not solved at lower levels.
- Be specific and factual. Clearly identify the product or service in question and describe the problem. Include the date and place of purchase, the product name and model number, and the purchase price.

Careers in Business Management & Administration

What Does a Business Ethics Consultant Do?

A **business ethics consultant** assesses the culture and value system of a company or organization to determine whether its practices and policies meet ethical standards. **Business ethics consultants** assist businesses in developing an ethical culture and value system. **Business ethics consultants** typically:

- ensure that practices and policies of an organization conform to laws and regulations;
- help solve problems that occur within their organization;
- advise on crisis control when problems occur with customers and government agencies;
- implement training programs for employees in corporate culture and core values; and
- educate employees in the legal, ethical, and reputational interests of the organization.

What Is It Like to Work as a Business Ethics Consultant?

Business ethics consultants may work in corporations or nonprofit organizations or as independent agents. A **business ethics consultant** serves as an internal police force to help businesses understand and follow the various laws and regulations governing their operations. With today's emphasis on corporate social responsibility, career opportunities for **business ethics consultant**s are expanding. They work in a variety of fields, including environmental sustainability, banking and finance, health care, communications, public relations, and human resources.

What Education and Skills Are Needed to Be a Business Ethics Consultant?

- bachelor or master degree in business administration
- courses in business ethics, economics, and finance
- oral and written communication skills
- work experience
- knowledge of regulations and compliance procedures for the field in which one works

Include your account number or the last four digits of your credit card number if the purchase was charged.

- Be reasonable. You are more likely to get a satisfactory response if you state your problem reasonably and sympathize with the reader. For example, you might write, "I realize it takes time to correct a computer error, but…." Or you might say, "I know it must be difficult to give one-day service on appliances, but...." Threatening or sarcastic letters rarely lead to satisfactory solutions.

- Suggest a solution. You may not always get your way, but it helps to outline the solution you are seeking. Do you expect a repair, a replacement, a refund, or an apology?

- Be businesslike. Put your grievances in writing. Keep a written record of phone conversations with the date, the name of the other party, and promises made or action to be taken. Keep important receipts and records together. You may need to furnish papers or documents, such as sales slips, bills, receipts, warranties, and previous correspondence. Send copies of these papers and keep the originals.

- Be persistent. Most problems can be solved with one letter directed to the right person. However, if you do not get the desired results, write a follow-up letter. Enclose a copy of earlier correspondence and indicate a date by which you expect some action. If a third letter is necessary, include copies of the previous letters and outline the action you will take if the matter is not settled by a certain date. You may want to copy a consumer protection agency or organization with your third letter.

Seeking Resolution

Difficult problems may require some form of legal action. However, legal action is costly and time consuming, and a favorable outcome is not guaranteed. For these reasons, most consumers consider it only as a last resort. Other options depend on the nature of the problem and the amount of money involved. These options include the following.

- *Binding arbitration.* **Binding arbitration** is a method of settling disagreements through an objective third party. Once both parties agree to arbitrate, each presents his or her case to the arbitrator. The arbitrator's decision is final and legally binding. Arbitrators are chosen from a pool of volunteers or professionals, depending on the program. Binding arbitration is quick, low cost, relatively simple, and informal.

- *Small claims court.* A **small claims court** is a part of the court system that offers a simple, prompt, and inexpensive way to settle minor differences involving small amounts of money. Procedures are relaxed with consumers normally representing themselves without a lawyer. They collect and bring documentation and evidence to support their cases. Claim amounts are limited to a maximum of $1,200 in some states and up to $5,000 in others. Since procedures vary from state to state, contact your local courthouse for more information.

- *Class action lawsuits.* A **class action lawsuit** is a legal court action brought by a group of individuals who have been similarly wronged. The court permits members of a common class to pool their grievance and sue for damages on behalf of the entire class or group. Laws governing this type of lawsuit vary from state to state.

- *Individual lawsuits.* A **lawsuit** is a civil action brought by a person (a *plaintiff*) against another party (the *defendant*). The plaintiff claims to be damaged or negatively impacted by actions of the defendant. He or she seeks a legal remedy to be determined by the court. If the plaintiff is successful, a judgment will be entered in his or her favor. The judgment may involve court orders to enforce the plaintiff's rights or to award

Mediation is a way to attempt to settle a dispute using a neutral party.

damages to the plaintiff. The court may also issue an order to prevent or compel specific action by the defendant.

Right of Refusal

It pays to exercise the right of refusal when sellers promote items you do not need, do not want, or cannot afford. As long as the economic system guarantees free economic choice, no one can make you buy what you do not need or want. You always have the ultimate right of refusal. Use this right to protect your financial interests.

On a larger scale, you can use the right of refusal to influence demand in the marketplace. Collectively, consumers have the power to strengthen the demand for what they buy and to weaken the demand for what they refuse. Thus, the economic system, as well as your own financial welfare, depends on the intelligent use of the power of refusal.

Smart shopping is a skill almost anyone can develop. It involves knowing about different places to shop and different types of sellers. The marketplace offers you many comparison-shopping opportunities to find the goods and services you want at the best prices.

Collecting, evaluating, and using information as it applies to different purchases is part of smart shopping. Smart shopping also calls for rational decision making and a personal spending plan. Specific suggestions apply to buying products and others apply to buying services. Shopping at sales calls for another set of techniques to get the best bargains. You want to develop a set of personal skills and tools to defend and promote your interests in the marketplace.

Checkpoint 10.2

1. What eight consumer rights are listed in the Consumer Bill of Rights?
2. What are three examples of federal consumer laws?
3. List three deceptive practices consumers may encounter in the marketplace.
4. List three guidelines to follow when making a consumer complaint.
5. Name four methods consumers can use to resolve disputes.

Build Your Vocabulary

As you progress through this course, develop a personal glossary of personal finance terms and add it to your portfolio. This will help you build your vocabulary and prepare you for a career. Write a definition for each of the following terms and add it to your personal finance glossary.

bait and switch	caveat emptor
pyramid scheme	consumer advocate
Ponzi scheme	binding arbitration
chain letter	small claims court
sweepstakes	class action lawsuit
lottery	lawsuit
skill contest	

Chapter Summary

Section 10.1 Be an Informed Consumer

- Knowing how to find, evaluate, and use available information can help you become a smarter shopper. Information comes from a variety of sources, including other consumers, advertising, labels and hangtags, testing and rating services, salespersons, and the Internet.

- When evaluating consumer information, consider whether the source is reliable, what the purpose of the information is, and how current and complete the information is.

Section 10.2 Protecting Your Rights

- In a free market economy, consumers enjoy certain rights and responsibilities in the marketplace. Many of these rights are listed in the Consumer Bill of Rights.

- In the United States, there are many laws at both the federal and state levels that protect the consumer. These laws protect against fraudulent advertising, unfair trade practices, and a variety of other issues.

- A consumer advocate is a group or an individual who promotes consumer rights. Both government agencies and private organizations offer consumers assistance with problems in the marketplace.

- Certain deceptive practices, though illegal, still exist in the marketplace. Some of these practices include bait and switch selling, pyramid schemes, and chain letters.

- Consumer self-defense involves looking after your own interests and being skeptical when interpreting advertising and sellers' claims. It also involves following up when products and services do not meet your expectations or the seller's claims.

Check Your Personal Finance IQ

Now that you have finished the chapter, see what you learned about personal finance by taking the chapter posttest. If you do not have a smartphone, visit the G-W Learning companion website.

G-W Learning mobile site: www.m.g-wlearning.com

G-W Learning companion website: www.g-wlearning.com

Review Your Knowledge

1. What are two ways you can learn about products from other consumers?
2. What information is typically included in labeling for food items?
3. What are two common forms of testing and rating results for products?
4. How can you use the Internet to help you be a smart shopper?
5. Why is it important to know whether product information is intended to inform the buyer or to sell a product or service?
6. What government agency handles problems involving hazardous products?
7. What are some issues that may be addressed in an Airline Passenger Bill of Rights?
8. What is the main focus of the Fair Credit Reporting Act?
9. What are three federal government agencies that provide services and protection for consumers?
10. What course of action can you take if you cannot get a serious consumer problem solved by contacting the seller or manufacturer?

Apply Your Knowledge

11. Do you think reading customer reviews is a good way to learn about products? Why or why not?
12. Do you usually read the labels and hangtags when shopping for clothes? What information found on the labels and tags is most important to you?
13. Think of two stores where you shop regularly. Are the salespersons knowledgeable and helpful to you? Describe your experiences.
14. Knowing the source of the information and knowing how current the information is can be helpful when reviewing information about products. Which of these two factors do you think is the most important? Why?
15. Have you ever been offered a free product or a free trial offer? Did you accept the product or offer? If not, why not? If yes, describe the experience.
16. What do you see as the pros and cons of state lotteries?
17. Describe a situation in which a specific consumer protection law worked for you. What was the law and how were you protected?
18. Select a specific consumer protection law and apply a cost/benefit analysis to it. Consider costs and benefits for the consumer, for businesses involved, and for government enforcement agencies.
19. Describe a situation in which you complained or wanted to complain about a product or service. How did you go about complaining, or if you did not complain, explain why.
20. Have you used the Internet to find or research a product or service? Describe the outcome.

Teamwork

Working with your team, make a list of the qualities and features you would want in a smartphone or other electronic product. Determine a price range. Investigate the product and develop a buying guide that includes a product description, features, warranty terms, energy efficiency data, and price.

G-W Learning Mobile Site

Visit the G-W Learning mobile site to complete the chapter pretest and posttest and to practice vocabulary using e-flash cards. If you do not have a smartphone, visit the G-W Learning companion website to access these features.

G-W Learning mobile site: www.m.g-wlearning.com

G-W Learning companion website: www.g-wlearning.com

Common Core

College and Career Readiness

CTE Career Ready Practices. The ability to read and interpret information is an important workplace skill. As a consumer, it is important that you understand your consumer rights. Research the Consumer Bill of Rights. Read and interpret the information you locate. How do these rights influence consumer behavior? Then write a report summarizing your findings in an organized manner.

Speaking. Select a member of your class to whom you will present the information you learned from the last activity about the Consumer Bill of Rights. Make use of any displays or demonstrations to enhance the presentation.

Listening. Practice active-listening skills while listening to your teacher present a lesson. Were there any barriers to effective listening? Evaluate your teacher's point of view and use of material in the presentation.

Web Connect

Visit the Better Business Bureau (BBB) website. How does the BBB help consumers? Describe three ways in which consumers can get assistance from the BBB.

College and Career Readiness

College and Career Readiness Portfolio

Your portfolio should contain samples of your work that show your skills or talents. Now is the time to start collecting items. You can decide which documents to include later when you prepare your final portfolio. Look at past school or work assignments you have completed. Select a book report, essay, poem, or other work that demonstrates your writing talents. Include a research paper, letter, electronic slide show, or other items that illustrate your business communication skills. Look for projects that show your skills related to critical thinking and problem solving. Have you completed a long or complicated project? Write a description of the project and tell how you managed various parts of the assignment to complete it on time. Include samples from the completed project. What career area interests you most? Select completed work from classes that will help prepare you for jobs or internships in that area.

1. Save the documents that show your skills and talents in your e-portfolio. Remember to place the documents in an appropriate subfolder.

2. Place hard copies in the container for your print portfolio.

Communications Skills

Competitive events may also judge communications skills. Presenters must be able to exchange information with the judges in a clear, concise manner. This requirement is in keeping with the mission of CTSOs: to prepare students for professional careers in business. Communication skills will be judged for both the written and oral presentation. The evaluation will include all aspects of effective writing, speaking, and listening skills.

To prepare for the business communications portion of an event, complete the following activities.

1. Visit the organization's website and look for specific communication skills that will be judged as a part of a competitive event.

2. Spend time to review the essential principles of business communication, such as grammar, spelling, proofreading, capitalization, and punctuation.

3. If you are making a written presentation, ask an instructor to evaluate your writing. Review and apply the feedback so that your writing sample appears professional and correct.

4. If you are making an oral presentation, ask an instructor to review and listen for errors in grammar or sentence structure. After you have received comments, adjust and make the presentation several times until you are comfortable with your presentation.

5. Review the Common Core activities that appear at the end of each chapter of this text as a way to practice your reading, writing, listening, and speaking skills.

6. To practice listening skills, ask your instructor to give you a set of directions. Then, without assistance, repeat those directions to your instructor. Did you listen closely enough to be able to do what was instructed?

Chapter 11
Health and Wellness

Staying healthy starts with taking care of yourself. Routine checkups, appropriate health care, and learning to read and follow the directions for medications are important to your well-being. A fitness and weight-loss program is also an important part of a good health routine, so you will want to follow your own path to fitness and weight management. Staying healthy includes having fun. Having fun begins with knowing what you enjoy and then planning the use of time and money you spend on fun and recreation. Travel and vacation planning skills will also lead to good times and productive use of your time and money.

Focus on Finance

Health-Care Costs

Health-care costs in the United States are our fastest growing government expenditure. Avoiding emergency room (ER) visits for all but real emergencies offers the possibility of huge cost savings for an individual and the government. The costs of ER visits, even for relatively simple procedures, can run between $600 and $800. The average cost of common treatments at walk-in clinics runs an estimated $60 to $75. In addition, a visit to a walk-in clinic rarely takes more than 20 to 30 minutes while a trip to the ER often runs to 2 to 3 hours or more. Investigate the availability and quality of walk-in clinics in your area before you need emergency services.

College and Career Readiness

Reading Prep. Before reading the chapter, skim the photos and their captions. As you read, determine how these concepts contribute to the ideas presented in the text.

Check Your Personal Finance IQ

Before you begin the chapter, see what you already know about personal finance by taking the chapter pretest. If you do not have a smartphone, visit the G-W learning companion website.

G-W Learning mobile site: www.m.g-wlearning.com

G-W Learning companion website: www.g-wlearning.com

Sections

Section 11.1 Staying Healthy

Section 11.2 Fitness and Leisure

Darren Baker/Shutterstock.com

Section 11.1
Staying Healthy

Objectives

After studying this section, you will be able to:

- Describe ways to always be at your best.
- State your consumer rights as a patient.
- Select qualified health-care professionals and evaluate the quality of care provided in health-care facilities.
- Explain correct ways to purchase drugs and medicines that you need for your health.

Terms

primary care physician

specialist

walk-in clinic

prescription drug

over-the-counter drug

generic drug

dietary supplement

At Your Best

When you look and feel your best, you get more out of life. Developing health, fitness, and grooming routines are the first steps in improving the way you look and feel. Pursuing leisure activities can improve your mental and emotional health.

Keys to looking and feeling your best at every stage of your life are listed in Figure 11-1. It is nearly impossible to look and feel your best without a

Keys to Looking and Feeling Your Best at Every Stage of Life
• Adequate sleep, rest, and relaxation
• Regular exercise and physical activity
• A well-balanced, nutritious diet
• Maintaining a healthy weight
• Competent medical and dental care
• Attention to known safety precautions
• Attention to posture and grooming
• Challenge, achievement, involvement
• Positive mental attitude
• Family, friendship, and support
• Effective control of stress
• Avoidance of tobacco and drugs

Goodheart-Willcox Publisher

Figure 11-1 This chart outlines the keys to good health and good looks.

bikeriderlondon/Shutterstock.com

Adequate sleep is needed to look and feel your best.

balanced approach in these areas. Still, thousands of people routinely ignore one or more of these basics. At the same time, people spend billions of dollars on products that promise effortless beauty and fitness.

Your lifestyle and the choices you make are the keys to staying healthy and preventing life-threatening diseases. Quality self-care involves developing healthful eating habits. It also involves avoiding illegal drugs and tobacco products and limiting alcohol consumption. Getting adequate rest and physical activity and finding ways to deal with life's stressful situations are critical.

Medical attention when you need it is also important. Regular physical and dental checkups may help you avoid serious illnesses or at least identify them in their early stages. Knowing how to evaluate health-care professionals and medical facilities can help you get adequate health care when you need it.

Your Rights as a Consumer

As a consumer, it is important for you to understand your rights as a patient. On March 23, 2010, President Obama signed the *Affordable Care Act* into law. The Affordable Care Act put new consumer protections in place, giving you tools to make informed medical decisions.

As a part of this new act, a *Patient's Bill of Rights* took effect on September 23, 2010. The Patient's Bill of Rights put an end to some of the worst insurance abuses and put consumers, not insurance companies, in control of their health care. The list of rights that follows can be found at www.healthcare.gov.

- *Provides coverage to Americans with pre-existing conditions.* You may be eligible for health coverage under the Pre-Existing Condition Insurance Plan.

- *Protects your choice of doctors.* Choose the primary care doctor you want from your plan's network.

- *Keeps young adults covered.* If you are under 26, you may be eligible to be covered under your parent's health plan.

- *Ends lifetime limits on coverage.* Lifetime limits on most benefits are banned for all new health insurance plans.
- *Ends pre-existing condition exclusions for children.* Health plans can no longer limit or deny benefits to children under 19 due to a pre-existing condition.
- *Ends arbitrary withdrawals of insurance coverage.* Insurers can no longer cancel your coverage just because you made an honest mistake.
- *Reviews premium increases.* Insurance companies must now publicly justify any unreasonable rate hikes.
- *Helps you get the most from your premium dollars.* Your premium dollars must be spent primarily on health care—not administrative costs.
- *Restricts annual dollar limits on coverage.* Annual limits on your health benefits will be phased out by 2014.
- *Removes insurance company barriers to emergency services.* You can seek emergency care at a hospital outside of your health plan's network.

Health-Care Providers

The best time to choose a physician, dentist, or specialist is when you are healthy. Most people go to a primary care physician for routine health-care needs. A **primary care physician** is a physician trained to diagnose and treat a variety of illnesses in all phases of medicine. This doctor oversees general treatment for most patients. When a specific health problem arises, your primary care physician may refer you to a specialist.

A **specialist** is a physician who has had further education and training in a specific branch of medicine. Figure 11-2 describes some of the many medical and dental specialists. These specialists are qualified and licensed to practice general medicine or dentistry, but they focus on care within their specialties.

A physician or specialist is a doctor of medicine, or MD. In your search for a physician, you may also come across a doctor of osteopathy, or DO. Both MDs and DOs are qualified to provide complete medical care. Both may decide to go beyond basic medical education into a chosen specialty. Both must pass comparable state licensing exams. Both practice in accredited, licensed hospitals and other care facilities.

Look for primary care physicians who are:
- graduates of approved medical or dental schools;
- licensed to practice in your state;
- board certified in their area of practice;
- members in one or more local, state, and national professional societies and associations; and
- well established in their practice with a good reputation among both patients and fellow professionals.

Friends, relatives, employers, and coworkers may be able to recommend qualified health-care providers.

The following are also sources of information on medical professionals.
- If you move to a new area, your former doctor may be able to refer you to a new physician.
- Medical or dental schools in the area often can provide a list of faculty doctors and graduates who practice in the area.

Health-Care Specialties

Medical	Area of Treatment
Cardiology	Diseases of the heart
Dermatology	Diseases of the skin, hair, and nails
Gynecology	Women's reproductive system
Internal medicine	Wide range of physical illnesses and health issues
Neurology	Disorders of the brain, spinal cord, and nervous system
Obstetrics	Medical care of pregnant women
Oncology	Diagnosis and treatment of tumors and cancer
Ophthalmology	Care of the eyes
Orthopedics	Fractures, deformities, and diseases of the skeletal system
Otolaryngology	Diseases and disorders of the ear, nose, and throat
Pediatrics	Development and care of children
Psychiatry	Mental and emotional issues and disorders
Surgery	Operations to diagnose or treat a variety of diseases or physical conditions
Urology	Urinary tract and male reproductive system
Dental	**Area of Treatment**
Oral surgery	Operations to extract teeth or to treat injuries and defects of the jaw and mouth
Orthodontics	Irregularities and deformities of the teeth, often with braces

Goodheart-Willcox Publisher

Figure 11-2 There are many medical specialties in the health-care field.

- National and state medical associations operate referral services.
- Local hospitals often can recommend qualified licensed providers.

If you receive care through a managed care program, you may be required to choose a physician, hospital, or other care provider that participates in the plan. Before you make a final decision about a doctor, find out what services are performed in the office. Some doctors' offices are equipped to take X-rays and perform other tests that require special equipment. Tests performed in the office can save you a trip to the lab, hospital, or clinic. Ask in advance about charges and fees for routine office visits, a complete physical, and other services you may need.

You may also want to consider the location of the office, the office hours, and the backup staff available in the doctor's absence. If you have any special medical needs, make sure the doctor or group practice you choose can meet them.

In addition to physicians, you may wish to turn to chiropractors, optometrists, podiatrists, or psychologists for the medical services they can provide. A *chiropractor* treats problems of the musculoskeletal system and their impact on the nervous system. Treatments may include manipulating parts of the body, particularly the spinal column. An *optometrist* tests eyes for vision defects and prescribes corrective glasses and contact lenses. A *podiatrist* diagnoses and treats minor foot ailments. A *psychologist* diagnoses and treats mental and emotional problems and learning difficulties.

Licensing requirements for these fields vary from state to state. Do not rely on these health-care providers for medical advice beyond their limited fields. Coverage of these services varies with insurance and managed care plans.

Hospitals and Medical Facilities

Doctors normally arrange for the hospitalization of their patients who need hospital care. The hospital or clinic where patients go for treatment may be determined by their choice of a primary care physician or their health-care plan. Managed care plans often require that members use specific doctors or medical facilities.

Nevertheless, patients are wise to evaluate the facilities that provide care as well as the health-care professionals who supervise their hospital stays. If a patient is unable to do this, a family member or a friend acting as an advocate can often help. The following questions are useful in assessing health-care facilities.

- Is the hospital accredited? A hospital should be accredited by the Joint Commission on Accreditation of Health Care Organizations or by the American Osteopathic Association. An accredited hospital must meet certain quality standards in providing health care.

- Who owns or finances the hospital? A nonprofit hospital is supported by patient fees, contributions, and endowments. A proprietary hospital is owned by individuals or stockholders and operated for profit. A government-supported hospital is operated with local, state, or federal funds. Ownership can make a difference in the eligibility for treatment, the services offered, and the charges.

- Is it a teaching hospital? Hospitals and clinics affiliated with a medical or nursing school generally provide a high level of training for students. As a result, they are likely to provide high-quality medical services.

- Who staffs the hospital? Does the hospital employ an adequate, qualified staff of physicians, specialists, nurses, therapists, and technicians? If a hospital is understaffed or if the staff is underqualified, patients may not receive the quality of medical care they need.

- What types of facilities are located at the hospital or clinic? Is there an intensive care unit? Is the emergency room well equipped and staffed? Look for the up-to-date equipment and facilities required to provide quality care.

- What type of care and services are provided? An acute care facility diagnoses and treats a broad range of illnesses and emergencies. A special disease facility diagnoses and treats a specific illness or group of diseases. A chronic disease facility provides continuing care for ongoing illnesses.

- Does the hospital enjoy a good reputation in the area? Look for medical facilities that are highly regarded by both medical professionals and patients.

- Is the staff sensitive to patient needs for privacy and honest information on diagnosis and treatment? Do nurses and others who deal directly with patients look after the patients' comfort and special needs.

It pays to check out emergency room and ambulance services in the area before you are in an emergency situation. Knowing you are being treated in a facility that provides quality medical care can have a positive effect on your mental and physical health.

Walk-in Clinics

A **walk-in clinic** is a health-care facility that provides certain routine medical attention. Usually it will be staffed by health-care providers who are trained to work in clinics. These providers can write prescriptions and give

History of Finance

Changes in Health-Care Costs

Today you hear a lot about health-care costs and quality of care. Since 1960, annual health-care expenditures in the United States climbed from approximately $3,000 (in today's dollars) to over $14,000 per household. During the same time period, group insurance rates also advanced from $740 (today's dollars) to over $14,000. Currently, total health-care expenditures in this country come to more than $8,000 per capita annually. This is twice as much as medical spending in Australia, Canada, United Kingdom, Germany, or Japan, without better health outcomes.

High health-care expenditures put pressure on employers who are required to provide worker health insurance coverage or pay penalties, with exceptions for small businesses. Health-care costs also create hardships for individuals and families without employer-sponsored coverage as they try to find affordable care and protection on their own. According to credit counseling agencies, medical debt is a frequent factor in personal bankruptcy filings. Finally, health-care costs drain government budgets at the federal, state, and local levels. Government covers close to 50 percent of total health-care expenditures.

In 2010 Congress passed health-care reform legislation called the Affordable Care Act (ACA). This new law is designed to expand access to health insurance to over 30 million uninsured Americans, to set forth a Patients' Bill of Rights, and ultimately to curb rising costs. In addition, the law outlines ways to improve the health-care delivery system, and it emphasizes disease prevention and healthful lifestyles. Its most controversial provision was the individual mandate that requires everyone to have health insurance. The constitutionality of this provision was debated, and finally the Supreme Court settled the matter by upholding the major provisions of health-care law. However, the debate continues as some people vow to continue their opposition to the ACA.

Health-care reform will continue to command the attention of legislators and the public as costs continue to rise and take a sizable share of government and private spending. Watch for upcoming developments.

vaccinations as needed. The clinics also have a doctor on call if consultation is necessary.

These clinics generally offer quick, economical service with short waiting times. They may be located in pharmacies, workplaces, stores, or shopping malls. Often, they are open on evenings and weekends.

Walk-in clinics typically treat sinus and upper respiratory infections, bladder infections, strep throat, minor injuries, and other relatively minor illnesses. They may provide routine physicals and tests along with vaccinations.

The costs of services at a walk-in clinic will normally be less than services of hospital emergency rooms. Generally, you pay by cash, check, or credit card. Some clinics take insurance, but not all insurance companies pay for treatments at a walk-in clinic.

Ideally, these clinics cut down on emergency room visits and unnecessary trips to the doctor. However, under some conditions, you need to go directly to an urgent care clinic or emergency room. A partial list of these conditions includes:

- a fever over 103 degrees in connection with strep throat or other infections
- deep tissue damage or blistered burns
- stiff neck or severe pain along with ear or respiratory infections or strep throat
- life-threatening illness, such as a severe asthma attack, or injury
- heart attack symptoms, including chest discomfort, shortness of breath, and/or nausea, lightheadedness, and cold sweats
- complicated health problems

Emergency Health Care

Emergency rooms or emergency care centers should be used only when there is an emergency. Using these facilities for common ailments may prevent someone else from getting the care they need.

You need to go to a hospital emergency room or an emergency care center if you have an injury or sudden illness that requires immediate attention. When you go for emergency care, be ready to give this information:

- your name, address, and phone number
- information on your injury or illness
- your managed care or insurance card and identifying data
- information on your current medications and any allergies you have

In an emergency situation, it is preferable to call 911 rather than driving yourself to the hospital. If you call an ambulance, *emergency medical technicians* (EMTs) can make an immediate, accurate diagnosis and give temporary treatment on the way to the hospital.

Alternative Medicine

Alternative medicine includes a group of health-care practices and products that are not presently a part of conventional medicine. Alternative health-care treatments include:

- mind-body interventions, such as patient education, cognitive-behavioral counseling, hypnosis, meditation, and music and art therapy
- biological-based approaches, such as herbal products, diet supplements, and natural therapies

- manipulative and body-based methods, such as manipulation and/or movement of the body as done by chiropractors, some osteopaths, and massage therapists

- energy therapies, such as acupuncture, therapeutic touch, and magnetic field therapies

Some conventional health-care providers combine alternative treatments with conventional methods. It is advisable to check with your health-care provider before relying on alternative treatments.

Drugs and Medicines

Drugs and medicines eat up a sizable portion of the health-care dollar. Drugs fall into two major groups—prescription drugs and over-the-counter drugs. A **prescription drug** is a medication that can only be obtained with a physician's orders. Insurance normally covers part of the cost of prescription drugs and medicines. Consumers pay a percentage or a set fee per prescription.

An **over-the-counter drug** is a nonprescription medication available on supermarket and drugstore shelves. They are considered safe to use when you follow label directions and warnings. These drugs include more than 300,000 different drugs. Painkillers, antacids, cough medicine, antihistamines, and vitamins are examples.

Brand-Name and Generic Drugs

Most drugs are available either by generic names or by trade and brand names. A **generic drug** is a drug that is sold by its common name, chemical composition, or class. Usually it costs considerably less than a similar

Physical Therapy Assistants

Physical therapy assistants work on health teams with doctors, nurses, and physical therapists. They help physical therapists provide treatment that improves patient mobility, relieves pain, and prevents or lessens patients' physical disabilities. They work in hospitals, rehabilitation centers, and schools.

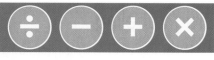

You Do the Math

To multiply numbers that are stated as a percentage, first change the percentages to a number with decimals. This is done by dropping the percent sign and moving the decimal two places to the left. Next, multiply the numbers to get the answer. Count the total decimal places to the right in both numbers. Then move the decimal point in the answer to the left the total number of places.

Complete the Following Problems

Suppose the average consumer coinsurance is 23 percent for generic drugs and 36 percent for brand-name drugs.

- Drug A (generic): $49
- Drug B (generic): $75
- Drug C (brand name): $125

1. What is the total amount a consumer owes when filling prescriptions for drugs A, B, and C?

2. The generic version of drug C costs 40 percent less than the brand name. What is the total amount a consumer owes after switching to the generic drug C?

Certain medications can only be obtained with a prescription from a doctor.

brand-name drug. All prescription and over-the-counter drugs must meet the same federal standards. Generic drugs are required to have the same active ingredients and effects as their brand-name equivalents.

When a physician prescribes a medication by brand name, a patient can ask if the generic equivalent may be substituted. If so, the doctor needs to write this on the prescription. Many health management and insurance plans require the use of generic equivalents, but patients can get brand-name medications with an increased copayment.

Drug Labeling

With the ever-rising costs of drugs, consumers are asking more questions about what their doctors prescribe. They should also become better informed about the many over-the-counter drugs available without prescription. Labels on over-the-counter drugs serve as keys to choosing products and comparing generics with brand names. Information on these labels must include:

- name and address of the manufacturer, packer, or distributor
- quantity of contents in weight, measure, or count
- purpose of the medication
- directions for use and storage
- recommended dosages for different purposes, ages, and conditions
- number of times and length of time the medication may be used
- conditions under which the drug should not be used
- warnings and precautions related to use, possible side effects, and interactions with other drugs
- list of active ingredients and the quantity of each per dosage
- list of all other ingredients with the name and quantity of any habit-forming drug in the product
- the expiration date after which the product should not be used

Prescription drug labels dispensed by doctors or pharmacists are exempt from certain labeling requirements. These labels state:

- pharmacist's name and address
- prescription number
- date of the prescription
- name of the prescribing physician
- patient's name
- directions for use
- any cautionary statements contained in the prescription
- number of refills, if any
- expiration date of the medication

Many pharmacies also provide leaflets with more complete information on prescription drugs.

Questions to Ask About Medicines

To be an informed partner in your own health care, ask the following questions when your doctor prescribes medicine for you.

- What are the brand and the generic names of the drug? Is there a lower-cost generic equivalent?
- What is the drug intended to do? Is it really necessary?
- How much of this drug should you take, at what time of day, and for how long?
- Is the medication habit-forming?
- What, if any, side effects should you expect?
- What activities, other drugs, foods, or beverages should you avoid while taking the drug?

Be cautious with both over-the-counter and prescription drugs to prevent interactions with other drugs, alcohol, herbal supplements, and various foods.

Dietary Supplements

A **dietary supplement** is a product that is intended to enhance your diet. It contains various ingredients, such as vitamins, minerals, herbs, amino acids, and other substances. Normally, supplements come in pill, capsule, tablet, or liquid form. They must be labeled "dietary supplement" and carry a supplement facts label on the product.

Supplements can be helpful, harmless, risky, or dangerous. This depends on what substances they contain and the quantity you take. It also depends on the potential interaction with prescription medications or other supplements you may use and the body's reaction to the product.

People take supplements for a variety of reasons. Some look to vitamin and mineral supplements to provide nutrients they think are not present in adequate quantities in their regular diet. Others look to supplements for weight loss, bodybuilding, a boost in energy and performance, extra brainpower, or other promised effects.

Weight-loss products are among the more common dietary supplements. You can find a number of weight-loss pills and supplements at your drugstore

Ethics

Ethical communication is very important in both business and personal life. Distorting information for your own gain is an unethical practice. An ethical communicator depends on honesty, accuracy, and truthfulness to guide all communication. Communication must be presented in an unbiased manner. Facts should be given without distortion. If the information is an opinion, label it as such. Do not take credit for ideas that belong to someone else; always credit your sources.

or food store and online. Most of these products have not been proven safe or effective. Some are dangerous and can produce unwanted side effects. To date, there is no known way to lose weight without eating less and getting more physical activity.

Dietary supplements are not tested or approved by the Food and Drug Administration (FDA) or any other government agency. Proof of safety and effectiveness is up to the manufacturer/distributor of the products.

The FDA *Dietary Supplements Final Rule* requires that products be produced under controlled conditions, free of contaminants or impurities, and accurately labeled. The rule also explains the requirements for testing ingredients and final products and for recordkeeping and handling of consumer product complaints.

The FDA can take action to ban or restrict the sale of any product that is shown to present risk of illness or injury. For your own protection, thoroughly check any supplements you may be considering. Before using a dietary supplement, follow these guidelines.

- Discuss the product with your health-care provider or pharmacist. Be sure to let this person know what medications and other supplements you take.
- Read the label carefully, particularly the supplement facts panel.
- Take a hard look at the advertising claims for the product. Are they believable?
- Determine whether you really need the supplement.
- Decide whether the product is worth its cost.

You can find more detailed information on dietary supplements by visiting the websites of the organizations shown in Figure 11-3.

Buying Drugs, Medicines, and Supplements Online

Many consumers buy both prescription and over-the-counter drugs and supplements online. Drugs and other health products are available through thousands of websites on the Internet. These include sites for familiar drugstore chains as well as legitimate independent pharmacies.

Online sites offer various advantages, such as shipping and delivery, easy comparison of products and prices, easy access to product information, and links to additional sources of information. Reliable sites also offer consultation

Go Green

When you go to the store to buy office supplies or other items, be sure to bring your own reusable bag. By using reusable bags to carry products home from the store, thousands of pounds of landfill waste can be saved every year. While there are different schools of thought on this topic, it is generally accepted that plastic bags take almost 1,000 years to degrade. Additionally, discarded plastic bags can pose threats to wildlife and the soil. Did you know that store owners have to purchase the plastic or paper bags and that they pass on the cost to the consumer through higher product prices?

Sources of Information on Supplements
• Food and Drug Administration
• National Institutes of Health
• Federal Trade Commission
• American Dietetic Association
• American Pharmacists Association
• National Council on Patient Information and Education

Goodheart-Willcox Publisher

Figure 11-3 Before using a dietary supplement, research it thoroughly and discuss the product with your health-care provider.

with a pharmacist who is qualified to answer consumer questions concerning medications. In some cases, Internet drug shopping saves consumers money.

To use an Internet pharmacy, you usually open an account and submit your credit card and insurance information. Once your account is established, you submit a valid prescription that may be called or faxed in by your doctor. Medications are usually delivered within a few days; or for an extra fee, they may be shipped overnight.

Although online shopping is convenient, there are many websites that sell unapproved products and do not follow the established procedures for filling prescriptions. For example, some of these sites distribute prescription drugs without requiring a lawful prescription, direct medical supervision, or a physical examination performed by a licensed health professional.

Consumers buying from such sites risk harmful drug interactions, and they may risk buying outdated, counterfeit, or contaminated medications. You can protect yourself if you buy medicines online. Refuse to buy from sites that follow these practices:

- sell prescription drugs without a lawful prescription
- do not identify themselves or provide a US address and phone number
- do not provide access to a registered pharmacist who is qualified to answer questions
- advertise new cures and quick cures for all types of illnesses and ailments
- make unsubstantiated and unbelievable claims

Tobacco Products

Smoking tobacco is linked to many diseases, including heart disease, cancer, lung diseases, digestive problems, and infertility. It is also a cause of premature aging, yellow teeth, and bad breath. Chewing tobacco products can lead to cancers of the throat, lips, and gums. Just being around people who smoke and breathing in secondhand smoke can raise your risk of becoming ill.

Aside from the serious health risks, tobacco products cost a lot of money over time. A pack of cigarettes may cost as much as $7. At that price, a pack a day would cost $2,555 per year and $12,775 over five years. Smokers also pay more for insurance than nonsmokers. Health and life insurers charge smokers higher premiums because they are more likely to get seriously ill than nonsmokers.

Obviously, smoking carries a large price tag and many risks. If you smoke, quitting now can lower your risk of disease. In addition, you will save thousands of dollars each year. If you do not smoke, do not start and avoid secondhand smoke.

Health and Medical Records

Up-to-date health and medical records are valuable for many reasons. If you switch doctors or health-care plans, you will need to give your new care providers a thorough knowledge of your medical background.

Some medical history also will be required if you are admitted to a hospital. Health and medical records can help doctors with the diagnosis and treatment of illnesses as well as with the prevention of certain diseases. Having health facts readily available is very important for anyone with health conditions that would require special treatment in an emergency.

Data from health histories is also helpful when filling out school records and insurance forms. Organized receipts for paid medical bills and the purchase of medications are needed for filing insurance claims and tax forms.

Figure 11-4 lists types of information to keep in personal and family medical records. You may want to write some of this information on a card to carry with you. You need to carry a medical identification card as well. This

---

Personal Medical Records

- Name, address, date and place of birth, height, weight, occupation, and blood type
- Persons to notify in an emergency with addresses, phone numbers, and relationship
- Personal physicians and health-care providers with names, addresses, and phone numbers
- Allergies
- Medications with dosages, prescription numbers, prescribing physician, and pharmacies
- Chronic illnesses with important details on history, medication, and treatment
- Visual or hearing defects and other disabilities
- Immunizations, screening tests and results, and dates for follow-up
- Infections and childhood diseases with important details
- Hospitalizations, injuries, and surgeries with dates and details
- Physical checkups and laboratory tests with dates and details
- Social Security, Medicare, and Medicaid numbers
- Details of employer-sponsored or individual health insurance or managed care plans including names, addresses, and phone numbers of plan managers or claims officers, medical services covered, policy and membership numbers, premium amounts and due dates, claims records, agent or contact person, and related membership data
- Dental treatment records
- A copy of advance directives, if any

  (An advance directive is a legal document describing what kind of care you want if unable to make medical decisions, such as when you are in a coma.)

Goodheart-Willcox Publisher

Figure 11-4 Record this type of medical information for each family member.

card identifies your insurance company or managed care plan and gives the necessary information to confirm your coverage.

Checkpoint 11.1

1. What are four keys to looking and feeling your best at every stage of your life?
2. What are three rights included in the Patient's Bill of Rights?
3. What are some things you should look for when choosing a primary care physician?
4. What types of medical problems are treated at a walk-in clinic?
5. What are some advantages of buying drugs online?

Build Your Vocabulary

As you progress through this course, develop a personal glossary of personal finance terms and add it to your portfolio. This will help you build your vocabulary and prepare you for a career. Write a definition for each of the following terms and add it to your personal finance glossary.

primary care physician

specialist

walk-in clinic

prescription drug

over-the-counter drug

generic drug

dietary supplement

Objectives

After studying this section, you will be able to:

- List factors to consider when evaluating a fitness and weight-loss program.
- Compare and evaluate personal grooming products and services.
- Manage the money and time you spend pursuing fun and leisure activities.

Terms

physical fitness
body composition

hypoallergenic

Fitness and Weight-Loss Programs

Physical fitness is a state in which all body systems function efficiently. It includes heart health, muscle strength, power, endurance, flexibility, and body composition. **Body composition** is the proportions of muscle, bone, fat, and other tissues that make up body weight.

Inactivity puts you at unnecessary risk for developing serious life-threatening chronic diseases, such as cancer, heart disease, diabetes, high blood pressure, and others.

You can improve your fitness through diet and exercise. There are many benefits to following a sound fitness program tailored to your needs and abilities, as shown in Figure 11-5.

Rewards of a Sound Physical Fitness Routine		
Health	**Performance**	**Appearance and Well-Being**
• Improved heart and lung efficiency • Lowered cholesterol levels • Improved muscle strength • Lower blood pressure • Weight management • Stronger immune system • Stronger bones and bone density • Fewer injuries • Better resistance to minor and serious illnesses	• Mental alertness and agility • Stress management • Higher productivity • Better balance • More energy • Better sleep • Improved memory • Better focus and concentration • Quicker thinking and reactions	• Weight control • Improved muscle tone • Better posture • Improved self-image • Lower anxiety levels • Improved emotional stability • An alert, healthy look • Opportunity to meet new people and share activities • Positive mental outlook

Goodheart-Willcox Publisher

Figure 11-5 These are some of the rewards for following a sound fitness program.

To begin your own fitness program, start with a close look at your present fitness level. Decide where you want to improve and what physical activities you would enjoy. Once you decide on the sports and exercises you want to pursue, plan your approach. It often is helpful to put your plan on paper and make adjustments as your needs and interests change. It will also be important to build fitness activities into your daily routine.

Organized Fitness Programs

Today, many schools emphasize fitness and offer programs as part of the curriculum or as extracurricular activity. If your school has such offerings, it would be a good place to start your own routine. As another option, you may want to go to a fitness center, a health club, or scheduled workout sessions. The following guidelines can help you find the best fit for your needs and wallet.

- Look for a convenient location and hours that work for you. Find out whether classes and equipment you want will be available at times you want them.

- Ask about the classes and training, and check out the equipment.

- Find out whether personal trainers and instructors are certified. The American Council on Exercise (ACE) operates a certification program you can check out on their website.

- Consider the overall atmosphere. Is the facility clean, well equipped, and well staffed? Is the environment friendly and inviting? Is equipment in working order? Will you feel comfortable working out there?

- Review the costs and payment arrangements. Is there a membership fee? What fees will you pay for extras, such as personal training sessions or fitness classes? What are the payment options? Must you sign a contract? Are there refunds if you opt out? Is there a sign up special offered? Will payments fit into your budget? Carefully study any contract you are asked to sign.

- Investigate the reputation of the facilities you are considering. Talk with current members about their satisfaction. Check with the local Better Business Bureau as to whether there have been complaints registered against the facility. Find out whether the facility is a member of the International Health, Racquet, and Sportsclub Association. Members follow a code of ethics that protects the health and safety of club members.

- Finally, find out whether you can sign up for a single session or a short trial membership before joining or signing on for a longer time period.

Activity Coordinators

Activity coordinators develop and coordinate activity programs to meet the needs, interests, and capabilities of clients. They also develop and implement special events. They often work at schools, assisted living facilities, health and sports clubs, or theme parks and other tourist attractions.

Weight-Loss Programs

Selecting a weight-loss program requires careful investigation. If you wish to lose weight, talk with your doctor first to determine your ideal weight and to learn how much you need to lose. Most health-care providers can help you find a weight-loss plan that will work for you. They also can advise you on the safety of any dietary supplements or special diets you may be considering.

If you do sign on for a weight-loss program, be sure that it encourages healthy behaviors. These involve healthful eating and more physical activity to achieve gradual weight loss—usually at a rate of one-half to two pounds per week. The plan also should include access to medical care if you are following a program that requires monitoring by a physician. A few specifics to look for in a weight-loss program include:

- counseling or group classes on diet and lifestyle changes
- diet recommendations and/or meal plans
- physical activity or exercise monitoring
- an ongoing plan for maintaining a desirable weight

Look into the qualifications of the staff and supervisors of the program. Find out whether there are any health risks connected with the program. It also is a good idea to inquire about the typical results of participating in the program and to discuss it with pervious participants.

Finally, take a close look at the costs. Are there sign-up fees, attendance fees, special foods or supplements to purchase, or printed material you must buy? Is there a contract or agreement you are expected to sign? Be sure you fully understand all the details of any weight-loss program you are considering before signing on.

Guarding Against False Claims

In the fitness and weight-loss field, you may come across exaggerated and false claims and promises made by the sellers and promoters of a variety of remedies and procedures. Be wary of these claims:

- quick and easy weight loss
- quirky diets and nutrition supplements that supposedly cure serious diseases
- effective secret cures your doctor does not know
- cure-alls to treat a wide range of unrelated diseases
- untried or unproven remedies

Personal Care Products

Using personal care products can help you look and feel your best. Cosmetics or grooming aids can cleanse, beautify, or alter the appearance of the body. They do not alter body structure or functions. They include lipstick, nail polish, hair gel, hair straighteners, moisturizers, teeth whiteners, and other products.

However, certain cosmetics also fit the definition of a drug. That is, they are intended to treat or prevent disease or to affect the functions of the body. These include fluoride in toothpaste, hormone creams, acne treatments, sunscreens, and antiperspirants.

Cosmetics and drug products must be labeled with their active ingredients and must meet Food and Drug Administration (FDA) standards for safety and effectiveness. The FDA is the government agency that regulates the safety and labeling of cosmetics.

When you buy a cosmetic or grooming aid, keep in mind these four questions.

- Is it safe to use?
- Will it work?

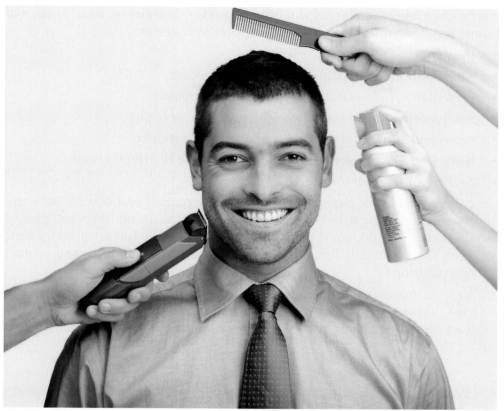

Yuri Arcurs/Shutterstock.com

Personal care products should be used to maintain a clean and well-kept appearance.

- Is it a good buy?
- Do I need it?

As you shop, read labels to compare the contents and prices of different products and brands. Often, salespersons can help you make the best choices. Read directions on how to use products before you buy and again before you use them.

Look for special prices and sales on products you have tried and want to use again. For products you have never used before, it is a good idea to buy a small size to see if you like it. If you are dissatisfied with a product or it does not meet specific advertising claims, return it. Some products have a money-back guarantee, and most retailers will allow reasonable returns.

Cosmetics, Safety, and the Law

Though law does not require it, reputable cosmetic manufacturers test products thoroughly before marketing. They test for safety, effectiveness, and customer appeal. Many manufacturers also voluntarily register their formulas with the FDA. They may make safety data available before marketing a product.

The FDA requires manufacturers who do not test a product for safety to place a warning on the label. The warning reads, "The safety of this product has not been determined." The FDA can also ban unsafe or misbranded cosmetics. However, the agency must first prove that the product is unsafe or misbranded.

Product labels can be helpful buying guides. The *Federal Food, Drug, and Cosmetic Act* requires labels on cosmetic products to state:

- the name of the product;
- a description of the nature or use of the product;
- ingredients in descending order of predominance;
- net quantity of contents by weight, measure, or count;
- name and address of the firm marketing the product;
- name of the manufacturer if different from the distributor; and
- country of origin if imported.

Labels must also carry warnings and adequate directions for safe use of any products that may be hazardous if misused. In addition to labeling requirements, tamper-resistant packaging is required for certain cosmetic products. These include liquid oral hygiene products, eyedrops, and contact lens preparations.

Keep in mind that cosmetics labeled hypoallergenic are not necessarily safe for persons with allergies. **Hypoallergenic** means that a substance or product does not contain ingredients likely to cause allergic reactions. There

Case Study

Your Health

Greg is feeling stressed out. He recently started high school and is finding the schoolwork a little tough. He is on the football and debate teams and plays in the band. He also likes to jog, read, and watch TV. Whether he is working or playing, he worries about everything else he should be doing. He is falling behind in his classes, and nothing is fun anymore.

Sixteen-year-old Eleni has lots of interests, but she never seems to have time for any of them. She tends to sleep late in the morning and barely arrives at school on time. Eleni eats with friends and relaxes for 45 minutes during her lunch break. In study hall, she surfs the Internet or looks at fashion magazines. Eleni often stops for something to eat with friends on the way home from school.

Once at home, she usually watches TV even though the late afternoon programs are boring. Soon it is time for dinner. After dinner, she likes to watch her favorite TV shows and talk to friends on the phone or online. However, her parents will not let her do these things until her homework is done. Eleni thinks she does not have time in the evening to do the things she really likes.

Case Review

1. Have you ever signed up to do more than you could handle?
2. How might Greg deal with his problem? How might he have avoided it?
3. Do you know someone with a problem like Eleni's?
4. What time-wasters do you see in Eleni's day?
5. How do you think Eleni might solve her problem?
6. What time-wasters rob you of hours for fun?
7. Do you often think you have too much to do and not enough time? If so, what can you do about it?

is no way to produce a cosmetic that is totally nonallergenic for all users. Learn what you can about the manufacturer as well as the product before you buy.

For your own safety, keep a record of any harmful reactions you experience from cosmetic products. Avoid buying anything that irritates your skin. If you have a serious reaction to a specific product, contact both the manufacturer and the FDA. Manufacturers need to know of any adverse reactions caused by their products so they can address the problem. The FDA investigates products that cause unusual reactions and will take corrective action if necessary.

Selecting Grooming Appliances

Personal care appliances include blow dryers, curling irons, electric shavers, electric toothbrushes, and a host of other products. There are many brand names, models, features, and prices for each appliance. The money you spend on these products will bring you greater satisfaction if you make the best choices for your wants and needs. When buying an appliance, consider these guidelines.

- Make sure you really need it and will use it.
- Look closely at the product features. Do not pay extra for features you will not use.
- Make sure the appliance is made by a reputable company and sold by a reliable retailer.
- Look for the Underwriters Laboratories symbol to be sure products meet industry safety standards.

Compare prices of similar appliances that have the same features. It also pays to compare prices at several stores. The cost of the same product can vary greatly from one retailer to another. Once you buy a grooming appliance, read and carefully follow directions for its use, care, and storage, as shown in Figure 11-6.

Use Appliances Safely

- Read the manufacturer's use and care instructions before using an appliance. Follow the directions carefully.
- Use and store electrical appliances away from water.
- Turn off appliances before connecting or disconnecting them. Disconnect by pulling the plug—not the cord.
- Disconnect any appliance that gives a shock. Have it checked and repaired before using it again.
- Keep electrical cords and plugs in good repair.
- Avoid coiling cords tightly.
- Check the wattage rating stamped on appliances. Avoid connecting more than 1600 watts on any single electrical circuit.

Goodheart-Willcox Publisher

Figure 11-6 Follow these guidelines for safe use of grooming appliances.

Buying Grooming Services

Beauty and grooming services include haircuts, hair coloring, hair removal, facials, massages, manicures, pedicures, and other procedures. Buying a service is different from buying a cosmetic product or grooming appliance. You cannot see the results of the service until after it is performed.

When deciding where to get a haircut or any type of service, consider the location of the shop, its business hours, cleanliness, and any other factors important to you. Be sure to find out what the prices include ahead of time. For example, does the cost of a haircut include a shampoo and styling? If you are unsure how much to leave for a tip, ask what is appropriate. Find out all the details to avoid any surprises.

Planning for Leisure

Planning leisure activities, such as hobbies, sports, or travel, contributes to your overall health and wellness. Recreation can help reduce stress and tension and improve the way you feel. Pursuing the activities you like most will take time and probably money. Getting more out of your limited recreation hours and dollars calls for careful planning and decision-making.

Selecting Sports and Hobby Equipment

The money you spend for pleasure will include equipment, supplies, and special clothes. It may also include lessons or coaching. Costs will depend on the activities you choose. The following paragraphs discuss guidelines to follow as you shop for leisure products.

Anticipate Costs

Unless you already have the equipment, some sports and hobbies may be expensive. Golf, skiing, sailing, and photography require expensive equipment. Before becoming involved in a sport or hobby, find out how much it will cost. When money is limited, you may want to choose less costly activities, such as hiking, chess, or dancing.

Do Your Homework

Personal Trainers
Personal trainers work one-on-one with clients either in a gym or in the client's home. They help clients assess their level of physical fitness and set and reach fitness goals. Trainers also demonstrate various exercises and help clients improve their exercise techniques.

Before making any major purchases, check *Consumer Bulletin* and *Consumer Reports* product ratings. Also look for information in specialized sports and hobby magazines and from manufacturers and retailers. Talk with people who have experience in the sport or hobby that interests you. Coaches, pros, instructors, and experienced salespersons can offer good advice on the purchase or rental of hobby and sports equipment. You can also find information on individual sports and hobbies online. Find out what kinds of equipment are recommended and how much you are likely to pay.

Learn to Judge Quality and Performance

Find out the important quality and performance features of a piece of equipment before you spend your money. For example, suppose you want to buy a tennis racquet. You will need to decide on the head size and length, weight and balance, frame stiffness and string pattern, and the best grip and

Samot/Shutterstock.com

Consider the costs of a new hobby. Golf, skiing, and photography require expensive equipment and additional costs.

handle. Do you want a top-of-the-line or beginner's racquet? A little online research can guide your choice. Buy the equipment that best suits your ability, interests, and budget.

Rent Equipment

If you are not sure what equipment to buy or if you are not sure of your interest in a new sport or hobby, try renting equipment first. Sometimes rental fees can be applied toward the purchase of equipment if you later decide to buy. People often rent ski equipment and musical instruments first and buy later.

Look for Money Savers

When you need costly equipment, you may want to consider buying used equipment. Other ways to save are to check discount stores for good buys or to wait for end-of-season sales. Snow skis, for example, will sell for less in April than in November. Look for equipment exchanges in your area, and check the classified ads in local papers. Online sites also may offer bargains.

Travel and Vacation Planning

Each year, consumers spend billions of dollars on travel within the United States and abroad. For most people, however, time and money for travel and vacation are limited. It takes careful planning to get the most fun and satisfaction out of these limited resources.

Smart travelers begin their vacation planning at the library or online. They check out articles, books, and websites on areas they want to visit and the special activities they like, such as biking, rafting, climbing, or skiing. Most airlines, hotels, resorts, restaurants, and cities operate their own websites you can use to plan your travel.

Careers in Health Science

What Does a Dietitian/Nutritionist Do?

Dietitians and nutritionists advise people on foods to eat that promote good health and achieve specific dietary goals. They often supervise food-service programs for schools, hospitals, nursing homes, airlines and other organizations that serve food in large quantities to people with different dietary needs and preferences. **Dietitians and nutritionists** typically:

- assess nutritional and dietary needs;
- educate people on nutrition, meal planning, and the connection between diet and the prevention and management of specific diseases;
- develop meal plans based on nutritional needs, costs, and food preferences;
- stay up-to-date on research related to nutrition and health; and
- supervise meal plans in hospitals and places where there are different dietary needs and restrictions.

What Is It Like to Work as a Dietitian/Nutritionist?

Dietitians and nutritionists plan nutrition programs that promote good health and disease control. Most work full time in institutions. However, some work as self-employed consultants with individual clients or organizations. They may also counsel individuals and families about specific nutritional needs, dietary plans, and food preparation. **Dietitians and nutritionists** may consult with physicians and health-care personnel to determine nutritional needs and diet restrictions of patients or clients.

What Education and Skills Are Needed to Be a Dietitian/Nutritionist?

- bachelor degree with concentration in dietetics, food and nutrition, or related area
- supervised postgraduate training
- state licensing and/or certification; requirements vary by state
- registered dietitian (RD) credential
- organizational, communication, and people skills

Questions for Travelers

Before you make travel or vacation plans, ask yourself the following questions.

- How will you get there? The transportation you choose will depend on where you are traveling and how much time and money you have to spend. Before buying airline or train tickets, check for any travel restrictions and penalties for changes or cancellations. Some tickets are nonrefundable.

- Where will you stay? Investigate hotels, motels, resorts, youth hostels, and campgrounds. Find out about reservations and rates. Rooms are easier to get and rates are lower during off-season months.

- What are the special things to see and do? Are there seasonal festivals, sightseeing tours, athletic events, or historical sites? Check to see if you need tickets in advance for any special events.

- How much will it all cost? Make a list of estimated expenses for transportation, lodging, and meals. Also estimate costs for equipment rental, sports activities, or sightseeing. Check your estimates against your budget to be sure you have enough money to cover your costs.

Package Tours and Trips

Throughout the year, travel agencies, airlines, and resorts offer many vacation packages and group tours at special rates. Before you sign up for a package trip, find out exactly what is included. For example, consider the following factors:

- length of the trip and dates of departure and return
- type and quality of accommodations
- meals and other items included and not included in the price
- total costs itemized
- available options
- penalties for cancellations
- size and makeup of the tour group

Deal only with a reliable travel agency or tour company. If possible, talk with other travelers who have dealt with the agency or company and find out if they were satisfied with their travel arrangements.

Checkpoint 11.2

1. What are some areas in which you may see improvements when following a sound fitness program?
2. What are some things to look for in a weight-loss program?
3. What four questions should you keep in mind when buying a cosmetic or grooming aid?
4. What are some sources of information for travel and vacation planning?
5. What are the advantages of renting rather than buying expensive hobby or sports equipment when you are unsure of your ongoing interest?

Build Your Vocabulary

As you progress through this course, develop a personal glossary of personal finance terms and add it to your portfolio. This will help you build your vocabulary and prepare you for a career. Write a definition for each of the following terms and add it to your personal finance glossary.

physical fitness   hypoallergenic

body composition

Chapter Summary

Section 11.1 Staying Healthy

- When you look and feel your best, you get more out of life. Developing health, fitness, and grooming routines are the first steps in improving the way you look and feel.

- As a consumer, it is important for you to understand your rights as a patient. The Affordable Care Act put new consumer protections in place, giving you tools to make informed medical decisions.

- A primary care physician oversees general treatment for most patients. When a specific health problem arises, you may be referred to a specialist. You may receive health-care services at a doctor's office, hospital, walk-in clinic, emergency room, or other treatment facility.

- Drugs fall into two major groups—prescription drugs and over-the-counter drugs. A generic drug usually costs less than a similar brand-name drug. Labels on drugs provide valuable information about the drug's use and possible side effects.

Section 11.2 Fitness and Leisure

- To begin a fitness program, start with a close look at your present fitness level. Decide where you want to improve and what physical activities you would enjoy. Choose a weight-loss plan that encourages healthy behaviors, such as healthful eating and physical activity to achieve gradual weight loss.

- As you shop for personal grooming products and services, read labels to compare the contents and prices of different products and brands. Check the qualifications and experience of persons performing personal care services before you purchase the services.

- Getting good value for your limited recreation hours and dollars calls for careful planning and decision-making. Before making any major purchases for sports or hobby equipment, check the product ratings. When planning travel, do research on destinations, travel costs, places to stay, and activities to find the best values.

Check Your Personal Finance IQ

Now that you have finished the chapter, see what you learned about personal finance by taking the chapter posttest. If you do not have a smartphone, visit the G-W Learning companion website.

G-W Learning mobile site: www.m.g-wlearning.com

G-W Learning companion website: www.g-wlearning.com

Review Your Knowledge

1. What factors are involved for quality self-care and physical fitness?
2. What law includes a Patient's Bill of Rights that gives certain protections related to health care to consumers?
3. What is the difference between a primary care physician and a doctor who is a specialist?
4. What are four questions that are useful in assessing health-care facilities?
5. When should you go to a hospital emergency room or an emergency care center for treatment?
6. What are three treatments that would be considered part of alternative health care?
7. What are some claims you should be wary of when choosing a fitness or weight-loss program?
8. What information is required on labels on cosmetic products?
9. What are some guidelines to follow as you shop for leisure products?
10. What factors should you consider before you sign up for a package trip?

Apply Your Knowledge

11. Have you or any of your family members ever received treatment or diagnosis for a health issue at a walk-in clinic? What do you see as the advantages of walk-in clinics?
12. What, if any, dietary supplements have you used? Did you find them effective? Why is it important to check with a health-care professional or pharmacist before taking dietary supplements?
13. Bring a dietary supplement container to class and discuss the information on the label.
14. What grooming aids do you use routinely? How do you decide which aids to buy and use?
15. How many grooming appliances do you and your family own? Do you use every appliance on a regular basis? What appliances could you do without? What more do you need?
16. What would you recommend to get inactive teens involved in a sports or fitness program?
17. What has been your experience with grooming services? How do you choose a barber or hair stylist or manicurist?
18. What are your favorite active sports and hobbies? What ways have you found to save money on sports and hobby equipment?
19. Have you or your friends ever rented sports equipment? What are some advantages of renting equipment rather than buying it?
20. What has been your favorite vacation or travel experience? Describe what made it a special experience and how you might plan future travel and vacations. What are some cost-saving travel tips?

Teamwork

Working with your team, make a list of the cosmetics and grooming aids you own. Estimate the total amount you spend on these items monthly. How much do you spend each month?

G-W Learning Mobile Site

Visit the G-W Learning mobile site to complete the chapter pretest and posttest and to practice vocabulary using e-flash cards. If you do not have a smartphone, visit the G-W Learning companion website to access these features.

G-W Learning mobile site: www.m.g-wlearning.com

G-W Learning companion website: www.g-wlearning.com

Common Core

College and Career Readiness

CTE Career Ready Practices. Maintaining a healthy lifestyle has an impact on how you function physically and mentally in your personal life and in the workplace. What unhealthy behaviors could have an effect on how well you do your job? How do you think employers should deal with behaviors that affect the personal health of their employees? Write several paragraphs to support your opinions.

Reading. In order to retain information that you read, it is necessary to focus and read with a purpose. The Food and Drug Administration regularly recalls products that may cause harm to consumers. Do an Internet search for Food and Drug Administration recalls. Select one product and list the brand name, the product description, the reason the product was recalled, and the company that produced the product. Share your findings with the class.

Writing. Select a generic drug with which you are familiar. Conduct a short research project to answer questions about the history of the drug's creation. Use multiple authoritative print and digital sources. Write several paragraphs about your findings to demonstrate your understanding of the process that led to the development of the product.

Web Connect

Visit the websites of two fitness centers and health clubs in your area to learn what facilities and programs they offer, the cost of joining, the qualifications of staff members, and the benefits of membership. Which one would you join if you were looking for a place to work out? What impressed you both positively and negatively about the different centers?

College and Career Readiness

College and Career Readiness Portfolio

You have collected documents that show your skills and talents. However, some skills and talents are not shown effectively using only documents. Do you have a special talent in an area such as art, music, or design? Have you taken part in volunteer activities? Create a video to showcase your talents and activities. For example, if you are an artist, create a video that shows your completed works. If you are a musician, create a video with segments from your performances. If you have taken part in a volunteer or service activity, create a video that tells viewers about it. Suppose you volunteer with a group that helps repair homes for elderly homeowners. The video could show scenes from the work sites and comments from the residents. (Be sure you have permission to include other people in your video.)

1. Place the video file in an appropriate subfolder for your e-portfolio.

2. Print a few screen shots from the video. Create a document that describes the video. State that the video will be made available upon request or tell where it can be viewed online. Place the information in the container for your print portfolio.

Financial Math

Financial math is a competitive event you might enter with your career and technical student organization (CTSO). The financial math event may include an objective test that includes financial literacy topics. If you decide to participate in this event, you will need to review basic banking concepts to prepare for the test.

To prepare for a financial math event, complete the following activities.

1. Read the guidelines provided by your organization. Make certain that you ask any questions about points you do not understand. It is important you follow each specific item that is outlined in the competition rules.

2. Review the vocabulary terms at the beginning of each chapter.

3. Review the Checkpoint activities at the end of each section of the text.

4. Review the You Do the Math features for additional practice.

5. Ask your instructor to give you practice tests for each chapter of this text. It is important that you are familiar with answering multiple choice and true/false questions. Have someone time you as you take a practice test.

Over the years, you will probably spend a large portion of your income on a place to live. Consider the choices very carefully. The home you choose will influence the way you live, the people you meet, and your overall sense of well-being. The word *home* has different meanings for different people. To some people, a home is a base of operations—a headquarters. To others, a home is a secure shelter from an unfriendly world. It may be a place to relax and entertain, or simply a wise investment. A home may mean all of this and more. It is whatever people make it. In this chapter, you will study the types of housing and the advantages and disadvantages of renting and buying.

Focus on Finance

Renters Insurance

Many renters do not worry about insurance because it is widely assumed that all property owners protect their property by carrying insurance. While it is true that the overwhelming majority of property owners do carry insurance, the property owner's policy does not cover your personal possessions or damage that you may cause to the property. As a result, it is important to take out renters insurance to protect you. Renters insurance typically provides coverage for:

- damage to your personal property from fire or wind;
- theft of your property;
- personal liability in the event you are sued over accidental injury to others who are in your apartment;
- accidental damage to the property of others in your care; and
- living expenses if you are forced to live elsewhere while your apartment is being repaired.

There are many other reasons you may need renters insurance, such as electrical surges that damage computers, televisions, and other electronic equipment. The amount of insurance you need depends on the value of the items you own. You will also need coverage to protect yourself in case your actions cause damage to another person or to another person's property.

Reading Prep. Before reading, preview the illustrations. As you read the chapter, cite specific textual evidence to support the information in the illustrations.

College and Career Readiness

Check Your Personal Finance IQ

Before you begin the chapter, see what you already know about personal finance by taking the chapter pretest. If you do not have a smartphone, visit the G-W Learning companion website.

G-W Learning mobile site: www.m.g-wlearning.com

G-W Learning companion website: www.g-wlearning.com

Sections

Section 12.1 Housing Decisions

Section 12.2 Rent or Buy

Objectives

After studying this section, you will be able to:

- List key factors to consider when choosing a housing location.
- Compare and contrast renting a residence to buying a residence.
- Discuss the moving process.
- Make suggestions for obtaining furnishings.
- Describe the importance of home maintenance.

Terms

apartment

cooperative

single-family house

townhouse

condominium

manufactured home

landominium

Housing Location

When making housing decisions, location is one of your most important considerations. You also need to decide what type of housing you want and how much you can spend. Finally, you want to weigh the pros and cons of buying versus renting a home at different stages in your life. Once you have a home, you will need to furnish, decorate, and maintain your living space.

The location of your first home away from your childhood home may be determined largely by what you are doing. Will you be working, going to school, or getting married? Very often, a job or school will dictate in part where you live. Even so, you will be able to make some choices within existing limitations.

Consider how you like to live. Would you prefer living in the country, a small town, a city, or a suburb? Some people like the pace and excitement of city living. Others like rural areas with lots of open space. Still others try to have both by living in the suburbs. There is more to choosing a location than deciding between city and country though. Some other factors to consider are discussed in the following paragraphs.

Employment Opportunities

What types of jobs are available in the areas that appeal to you? Will you be able to find the type of work you want? How much money can you expect to earn if you work in the area? Local or state employment offices and chambers of commerce are places to check out employment opportunities in different areas. You can also find job listings and career opportunities for different areas and in different fields online.

Cost of Living

What is the average cost of housing in different areas? The Bureau of Labor Statistics publishes cost of living figures for different cities and parts of the country. Business and world almanacs also give cost of living and other economic information on different places. Cost of living comparisons are available from a number of sites online.

It pays to find out the costs of food, housing, health care, transportation, and utilities for places where you would like to live. What are the rates for home and car insurance? What are the sales, income, and real estate tax rates? The cost of maintaining similar lifestyles in different areas can vary greatly.

Climate

What type of weather do you like—warm, dry, wet, cold, or mild? Is a change of seasons important to you? Would you rather live near the desert, the mountains, or the ocean? A world almanac or the National Climatic Center of the US Department of Commerce can provide weather statistics for different cities. These statistics include average high and low temperatures, rainfall and snowfall, humidity, and wind speed.

Lifestyle

Will you be living alone or with a roommate or spouse? Do you expect to have children? Young, single persons or childless couples may prefer living in the heart of a city. Families with young children may want to live in a suburb or small town where there is more space and a stronger sense of community.

Try to decide what is most important to you. Do you want to live close to your family or friends? Do you want to live near a college or university to further your education? Do you want to be close to the mountains so you can ski in the winter? Would you rather be near water so you can enjoy water sports? Your answers to these and similar questions will help guide your choice of location.

Neighborhood

Once you have narrowed your choices to a specific region or city, you can begin evaluating different neighborhoods. Appearance is one of the most obvious factors to consider in a neighborhood. Are the buildings attractive? Do the architectural styles offer both variety and harmony? Are both private and public areas well kept? Are the yards attractively landscaped with trees, bushes, and flowers? Is the street layout attractive and functional?

What is the overall character of the neighborhood? Does it appear residential, commercial, industrial, or mixed? What zoning laws and building codes apply to the neighborhood? Is the area relatively free of heavy traffic, noise, and air pollution? How would you assess property values now and in the future? Does the neighborhood seem safe and crime-free? Local newspapers and law enforcement agencies may have information about crime rates.

You may want to consider the ages, interests, occupations, and educational backgrounds of the people in the area. Is the overall income level similar to your own? Are most people living in the area single or married? Are there children in the neighborhood? Are there enough similarities to make life comfortable and enough differences to make it interesting?

Ethics

When submitting an application for rental property or to buy property, it is important to be truthful in your application. Making up information is unethical and could cost you a future opportunity to find housing. This means always telling the truth about your job, savings, and other financial information that is requested. Intentionally giving incorrect information is not only unethical but also illegal in some states.

Community Facilities

Check out the community services and facilities. Are services convenient to use and reasonable in cost? Is fire and police protection adequate? What is the cost of utilities? Does the community provide trash pickup, recycling, and snow removal? Are streets and other public areas well maintained? Learn what you can about health care in the area. Is public transportation convenient and reliable?

Look for services and activities that are important to you. For example, does the community sponsor athletic programs and cultural events? Are citizens actively involved in local government? Will you have access to a public library, churches, parks, and athletic facilities? Are there a variety of shops and stores?

Schools

The education system is important because its quality affects local property values. It is also important if you have children. Find out whether the schools in the area are noted for quality education. What are teacher qualifications and pay scales? What is the average class size? Are textbooks and lab equipment up to date? Are special education programs offered? What extracurricular activities are offered?

Sources of Information

Be sure to check out a location carefully before you settle. Moving into a place that does not suit you can be costly in terms of happiness, time, and money. The following sources can provide helpful information about specific regions and communities:

- chambers of commerce
- local newspapers and magazines
- classified ad pages and local government listings in phone books
- long-time and new residents of an area
- travel books and almanacs
- community organizations in the area
- real estate brokers
- the Internet

Your First Residence

At different times in your life, you will most likely choose different types and styles of housing. Your choices will be based on what you need and want, what you can afford, what is available, and whether you want to be a renter or a homeowner.

No matter what decision you make, you will need professionals to help you through the renting or purchasing process. Figure 12-1 lists some professionals who can help.

Rent

When you move out on your own, you will more than likely rent a place to live. An **apartment** is a living unit that is often among similar units. An

Surveyors

Surveyors measure and identify water, land, and airspace boundary lines. They record their results for legal documents, such as deeds and leases. They also prepare maps and reports. Surveyors work outdoors and often use technology, such as global positioning devices, to gather preliminary data.

Experts		
Job Title	**Description of Services**	**When To Use an Expert**
Real Estate Agent	• Brings buyer/tenant and seller/landlord together; negotiates a deal acceptable to both • Provides helpful information on community tax rates, schools, services, shopping, property values, etc. • Recommends lenders; helps arrange financing for home purchase • Represents the seller in a sale; is paid a commission for services—usually a percentage of the price	• You need help finding the housing you want in an area you like at a price you can pay • You are unfamiliar with an area and need facts to decide exactly where and what to buy or rent • You need help finding professional services and home financing • You want to sell a home at a fair price in a reasonable length of time
Property Manager	• Meets with and shows properties to prospective renters • Explains and discusses the lease and explains the terms of occupancy	• You are looking for a place to rent • You are unfamiliar with an area and need to see different properties
Lawyer	• Represents either buyer or seller in transferring real estate • Protects client's interests when selling, buying, building, or leasing a home • Draws up agreements for the client; checks agreements drawn by others before the client signs • Represents the client at the closing of a real estate transaction	• You buy or sell a residence • You have questions about a housing contract or lease • You become involved in a dispute with a property owner, seller, builder, or buyer in a real estate transaction • Before you sign any contract or agreement involving more money or time than you can afford to sacrifice
Architect	• Draws up plans for building or remodeling • Chooses suitable building materials • Helps find a lot suited to the house design or design a house suited to the lot • Hires and works with the contractor and supervise building	• You want to build a residence or do extensive remodeling • You want a custom-designed residence
Contractor	• Accepts responsibility for building or remodeling a home • Orders building materials • Hires and supervises workers • Sees that work is done according to specifications and terms in the contract	• You want to build a residence or make improvements

Goodheart-Willcox Publisher

Figure 12-1 Experts can help you with renting or buying.

apartment complex is a large group of multi-family dwellings where residents share common areas, such as lobby, grounds, laundry facilities, and other building facilities.

A studio apartment is an apartment that has a bathroom and one large room that serves as the living room, bedroom, and kitchen. Studio apartments are smaller than traditional apartments, but they generally cost less.

Apartment buildings vary in the types of services and facilities they offer. They may or may not have laundry equipment, parking space, recreational facilities, and other extras.

You may also have an opportunity to rent a house or another piece of property that belongs to another person. When renting a residence, the checklist in Figure 12-2 will help you evaluate the rental property.

Regardless of the property you rent, you will more than likely sign a lease from the owner. Some owners will allow you to pay on a month-to-month basis without a long-term contract. However, most owners will require at least a six-month lease agreement. The amount of monthly rent is usually lower if you sign a lease for a year or longer.

Own

At some point in your life, you may have an opportunity to own your own place. If you are planning to buy a residence, there are a number of factors to consider.

A **single-family house** is a detached house, usually with a front and back yard, a driveway, and often an attached carport or garage. The single-family house is still the most popular type of housing.

Rental Property Checklist		
Building and Grounds	**Services and Facilities**	**Inside Living Space**
• Attractive, well-constructed building • Good maintenance and upkeep • Clean, well-lighted halls, entrances, stairs • Reliable building management • Locked entrances, protected from outsiders	• Laundry equipment • Parking space (indoor or outdoor) • Swimming pool or tennis courts • Convenient trash disposal • Adequate fire escapes • Storage lockers • Locked mailboxes • Elevators • Engineer on call for emergency repairs	• Adequate room sizes • Windows located to provide enough air, light, and ventilation • Windows have screens and storm windows • Attractive, easy-to-clean floors • Furnished appliances in good condition • Clean, effective heating, thermostatically controlled • Up-to-date wiring • Conveniently placed electric outlets • Well-fitted doors, casings, cabinets, and built-ins • Extras (air conditioning, dishwasher, fireplace, patio)

Goodheart-Willcox Publisher

Figure 12-2 Using a checklist will help you evaluate rental property.

A **condominium,** commonly referred to as a *condo,* is a form of multi-family housing in which a person typically owns the unit he or she occupies. The common grounds and building structure are jointly owned by the owners of the individual units. Owners pay a monthly assessment or maintenance fee to cover the costs of operating, maintaining, and repairing the shared property. The owners generally elect a board of managers to make policy and management decisions for the shared property.

A **landominium,** also called a *planned unit development,* is a type of residential property in which the homeowner owns both the home and the land on which the home is built. Landominium communities often include features such as golf courses, tennis courts, clubhouses, walking trails, and parks. A landominium owner typically has greater maintenance responsibilities than a condo owner. For example, a landominium owner may be responsible for windows, patio doors, decks, skylights, and walkways on the property. Like a condo, a landominium is part of a community where the landscaping, maintenance, and other services are provided by a homeowners' association. Unlike a condo, however, common areas, such as clubhouses and golf courses, are owned by the homeowners' association, not jointly by the residents.

A housing **cooperative,** commonly called a *co-op,* is a form of home ownership in which a person buys shares in a corporation that owns the apartment building. The size and type of apartment the buyer lives in is based on the number of shares purchased. As with a condo, owners of a co-op pay a monthly fee that covers their share of maintenance and service costs. The fee also covers the building mortgage and taxes. Usually, it is necessary to obtain approval from an elected board of directors before selling or remodeling a unit.

Similar to condos and co-ops, a **townhouse** is a home that is attached to adjacent houses. Unlike a condo or co-op, however, the owner of a townhouse typically also owns the land on which the unit is built. Townhouses can be grouped together as a small number of units, such as a row of five to ten homes. They are usually two-story buildings with the bedrooms on the second floor. Townhouses can also be part of a huge townhouse complex. Owners of townhouses often do not pay a monthly maintenance fee and are responsible for all inside and outside maintenance costs. Older townhouses in large cities can have as many as six floors and an elevator.

A **manufactured home** is a single-family house built in a factory and shipped to the home site where it is erected. These homes are constructed in compliance with the Department of Housing and Urban Development (HUD) Code. The HUD Code was originally called the *Manufactured Homes Construction and Safety Standards Code.* Manufactured homes generally cost considerably less than other types of housing with comparable living space

Cooperatives are more common in the Northeast than other parts of the country. They are a dominant form of home ownership in New York City.

Go Green

Homeowners and renters are going green with programmable thermostats. Using a programmable thermostat, you can preset the times your heating or air-conditioning systems are turned on. As a result, you do not use as much energy when you are asleep or away from your residence, and you save money.

Although some people hire the service of professional movers, others may choose to move their own possessions with the help of friends or family.

and equipment. Maintenance costs are usually low, too. However, over time they may decrease rather than increase in value. They often are located in manufactured home communities, but they may be built on private lots. The homeowner may purchase the lot that the manufactured home rests on. The lot may also be owned by a business that charges the homeowner a monthly rent.

Moving Your Possessions

For some people, finding a place to live is easy compared with moving their belongings. People who do not own much furniture often move themselves. A borrowed or rented truck and a few friends can accomplish a move in an afternoon. You can check advertisements for free boxes given away by people who have recently moved. As you accumulate furniture and possessions, moving becomes more complicated and expensive. Moving a short distance away can also be handled by local movers. Moving to another state requires a national carrier. Consider and compare all the possibilities.

You will need to notify utilities, the cable company, newspaper, and other services of your move. Either terminate existing services or have them transferred to the new address. The businesses need to know where to send a final bill. The utilities and businesses that service your new home will need to know when you will move in. They may also require that you fill out contracts and pay a refundable deposit.

If you hire a mover, it pays to check out a moving company thoroughly. Many consumer complaints involve moves and moving companies. Contact the Better Business Bureau to check for complaints against the company. Talk to friends and acquaintances to get the names of movers they used with good results.

If you use a mover, follow these guidelines to make a move go smoothly.

- Get rid of excess baggage. The more items you move, the more you pay. Get rid of items you do not need or want before moving.

- Get cost estimates from several movers. Be sure estimates include everything that is to be moved. Find out what services are included in the estimates. Rates for interstate moves are regulated by laws and are based on weight and distance. Packing and other services add to the cost.

- Time the move. If you have a choice, move between mid-October and mid-April. You often get better service and lower rates than in the peak moving months of summer. The middle of a month is better than the first or last days of a month.

- Collect information to help you move. Most major carriers offer helpful publications for planning a move and settling in a new area. Interstate movers are required to give you a copy of the pamphlet, *When You Move: Your Rights and Responsibilities*. Carriers should also give you information about filing claims in case of loss or damage to your possessions.

- Check insurance coverage. A mover's liability for your possessions is limited to an amount per unit of weight. This often is less than replacement value for most items. Find out what additional protection is available if you need it. Make sure your possessions are adequately insured before you move.

Before your move, take an inventory of your possessions. As you pack, label moving cartons with a list of contents and their intended location in your new home. Supervise both pickup and delivery to be sure everything is moved and delivered to your new address.

Read the shipping order and bill of lading carefully. A *bill of lading* is a receipt listing the goods shipped. Make sure these forms accurately state pickup and delivery dates, estimated charges, and services to be performed. They should also state any special agreements or arrangements between you and the mover.

You should be prepared to pay for your move on delivery with a certified check. Ask for an itemized receipt. In the event of loss or damage to your possessions, file reimbursement claims promptly.

Furnishing Your Residence

When furnishing a residence, consider the items you will need to buy. At first, you may want to consider buying furniture for only certain rooms in your home. Start with essential items, such as a bed, a comfortable chair, a light for reading, a clock, and other necessary items. Add other furnishings as you can afford them.

As you add furniture, consider items that are multiuse. For example, a sofa bed can serve as a couch and also as a bed if you have overnight company. Likewise, lightweight chairs can be carried from room to room, allowing them to be used for different purposes.

Plan the best ways to use your money, time, and talents. Can you paint, wallpaper, sew, or upholster? Using color is a great way to decorate without spending a lot of money. A simple coat of paint can transform a dark, dreary room into a cheerful space. Put your talents to work.

There are many places where you can find items needed to furnish your place to live. If you are budget conscious, bargain hunting and do-it-yourself jobs may become important. Great places to look for bargains include:

- garage and yard sales;

Residential Moving Coordinator

Residential moving coordinators help plan individual and family moves within the same city or to points throughout the world. They coordinate all aspects of relocating, such as completing an inventory of items, packing, delivery, and unpacking of items.

- flea markets and secondhand stores;
- classified sections of newspapers;
- furniture warehouses;
- online discounters; and
- estate sales.

In most major cities and suburbs, you can rent furniture. If you move frequently or do not have enough money to furnish a first home, renting may be a reasonable option. Often, it is possible to rent with an option to buy. This lets you apply the rent to the purchase price. Furniture rental companies may also be a source of used furniture at attractive prices.

Furniture rentals usually involve applying for credit, signing a lease agreement, and paying a security deposit and delivery charges. Read the contract carefully and be sure you understand all the terms of the agreement before signing.

Do not confuse furniture rental agreements with aggressive *rent-to-own* (RTO) plans. RTO plans are not regulated under the Truth in Lending Act or state credit laws. Fees typically add up to much more than rented items are worth and more than the cost of buying on credit. For example, a $500 television might be offered at $60 per month for 18 months. That comes to a total cost of $1,080.

Case Study

Furnishing Your Home

Carmen is moving to Kansas City to begin her first full-time job. It will be necessary for her to arrive a week early to find an apartment. Since she is new to the city, she needs to use the Internet to find an apartment to lease. A list of her requirements includes:

- Close to work
- One bedroom
- Utilities included
- Must fit within the $600 per month rental expense budgeted

Carmen found several potential apartments on apartment location websites. She called the rental office for two different apartment complexes. However, in order to meet her requirements, she discovered that she must increase her budget amount for rent expense to $650. She also found out that she must make a security deposit equal to one month's rent. She had not budgeted for this amount of money. The rental agent also told her she must sign a one-year lease.

Case Review

1. Carmen had an unexpected expense of a security deposit for which she had not budgeted. How could she have avoided this surprise? How would you feel about making a security deposit?
2. If you were Carmen, how would you go about finding an apartment in a new city where you were moving?
3. What criteria would you require for a first apartment to lease?
4. How important would it be to you to meet all your requirements for an apartment?
5. How would you feel about signing a lease?

Protect yourself if you consider renting furniture or appliances. Determine the total cost by multiplying the amount of each rental payment by the number of payments required in the contract. Compare this total with the cash price and the credit price of similar merchandise at reputable stores. Find out what will happen if you miss a payment. Check out provisions for servicing or repairs on rented appliances, insurance requirements and fees, and penalties for late payment or default. Read the fine print carefully.

Home Maintenance

When you move into your first home, whether it is a one-room apartment or a house, you will face home care and maintenance responsibilities. In a rental apartment, this is largely a matter of keeping the space clean and caring for the appliances. If problems arise with the heating, air conditioning, plumbing, or major appliances, the property owner is usually responsible. When you buy a home, you become your own property owner and your responsibilities increase dramatically.

Maintaining a home is both costly and time consuming. When you buy a home, housing experts recommend setting aside 1 to 3 percent of the purchase price each year to cover maintenance and repairs.

Maintenance involves routine chores you can often perform yourself. These include keeping drains running freely, faucets drip free, toilets flushing, and floors and carpets clean and in good condition. You also need to periodically clean gutters, windows, the garage, and the basement.

Yards and plantings need seasonal attention, too. To maintain home appliances and equipment, follow instruction manuals and owners guides. Many manufactures operate interactive websites to address your questions and problems with their products.

Home repairs can become more involved. They include attention to roof leaks, broken windows, fallen trees, plumbing problems, and foundation

AVAVA/Shutterstock.com

Routine cleaning is needed to maintain the care of a home or apartment.

damage. The electric and the heating and cooling systems also need routine maintenance as well as occasional repairs and replacement. Regular inspection and maintenance is the best way to keep a home in good condition. It also helps you catch small problems before they become major and costly repair jobs.

Use care when selecting people to repair or work on your home. The bigger the job the more thoroughly you need to investigate them. Some tips include the following.

- Contact your local government. Find out if permits must be obtained before the work is started. Ask about any guidelines you should follow in hiring people to work on your property.

- Find reputable workers by asking acquaintances for the names of people they have used with satisfaction. Check for memberships in trade or professional organizations and the local Better Business Bureau. These memberships offer some assurance of a worker's qualifications and reliability. Investigate carefully before hiring someone who comes to your door unsolicited.

- Interview the worker before you hire him or her. Ask for work experience and references from other customers. Follow up and check references. Ask workers about licensing and insurance. They should be insured and bonded. Ask to see the insurance certificate. Look for coverage that protects you from property damage workers may cause and any other financial risks associated with the work being done.

- Interview several candidates and get several written estimates for the work to be done. After you select someone, you will probably be asked to sign a contract. Read it carefully and ask any questions you might have before you sign. If a job is lengthy and expensive, you should refuse to pay the entire cost before work is begun. You will probably be asked to pay for a portion up front and the rest upon completion of the job.

Checkpoint 12.1

1. What are some factors to consider when choosing a housing location?
2. What factors will influence your choice of a home?
3. What are some guidelines you can follow to make a move go smoothly if you use a mover?
4. What are some places to look for bargains when furnishing a home?
5. What does home maintenance involve? Give some examples.

Build Your Vocabulary

As you progress through this course, develop a personal glossary of personal finance terms and add it to your portfolio. This will help you build your vocabulary and prepare you for a career. Write a definition for each of the following terms and add it to your personal finance glossary.

apartment	cooperative
single-family house	townhouse
condominium	manufactured home
landominium	

Objectives

After studying this section, you will be able to:

- Compare the advantages and disadvantages of renting a place to live and buying a home.
- Discuss the process of renting a residence.

Terms

equity

security deposit

lease

lessee

lessor

rental agreement

rental inventory checklist

eviction

Monthly Housing Costs

Most financial advisors suggest that total monthly housing costs come to no more than one-third of monthly take-home pay. Take-home pay is the amount of money you receive after taxes and other deductions are subtracted from your paycheck.

Housing costs include rent or mortgage payments, utilities, maintenance, property taxes, and homeowners or renters insurance. You can use the budgeting information in Chapter 2 to determine your monthly housing allowance. In summary, a budget takes you through the following steps.

1. Total the amount you have to spend each month. Include all income and earnings.
2. Total monthly expenses other than housing. Include food, clothing, transportation, recreation, loans, insurance, taxes, and any other ongoing obligations.
3. Subtract the expenses from total monthly income to arrive at the amount you can afford for housing each month.
4. Adjust earnings, spending, and housing costs as needed.

If you do not have enough money for the home you want, you have three choices. You can try to increase your income, spend less on other expenses, or choose a less expensive home. Before choosing a place to live, determine how much money you can spend on housing. The amount you can afford will depend on several factors. These include your income, other expenses and obligations, housing needs, and your expected future income.

Since housing is generally a monthly expenditure, begin by figuring a reasonable monthly housing allowance. If you plan to buy a home, you will need to determine a purchase price, a down payment, closing costs, and a mortgage you can handle over a long period of time. The cost of moving and furnishing your home should also be considered. Home buying expenses are covered later in this chapter.

Renting

The primary financial responsibility of renting a place to live is to pay the rent each month. The renter is also responsible for taking reasonable care of the rental unit and paying any utility bills that are not included in the rent. In turn, the property owner is responsible for making the property habitable and providing the tenant quiet and peaceful possession of the property.

Renting a home offers certain advantages. They include the following.

- *Fewer financial responsibilities.* You do not need a large sum of money for a down payment. Rent is generally lower than a mortgage payment. You do not have to pay property taxes. Renters do not pay for major repairs and maintenance, such as a new roof or purchase of major appliances.

- *More free time.* Since renters are often not responsible for home maintenance, such as landscaping, and home repairs and improvements, they have more free time.

- *Less financial risk.* Renters do not need to worry about property values or the inability to pay a mortgage.

- *Greater mobility.* Renters can usually move at the end of their lease if they give a month's notice.

The disadvantages of renting include the following.

- *No investment.* Buying a home is an investment and renting is not. Over time, homes generally increase in value. The mortgage payments that homeowners make are payments on an asset that they eventually own. Rent payments do not benefit renters beyond providing a place to live; they go into the pockets of property owners.

- *Little control.* Renters have less control over their living space. At the end of a lease period, property owners can raise the rent or ask them to move out. They may not be allowed to own pets, hang pictures on the walls, or paint and decorate. Some renters have irresponsible property owners

You Do the Math

It is easy to convert between percentages, fractions, and decimals. A percentage is simply the numerator of a fraction with a denominator of 100. The word *percent* means for every one hundred, or per one cent. To change a fraction to a percentage, first convert it to a decimal by dividing the numerator by the denominator. The numerator is the top number and the denominator is the bottom number of the fraction. For example, 1/3 would be 1 divided by 3 = 0.33.

Complete the Following Problem

What is the maximum amount each of the following people should spend on housing given their monthly take-home pay? Experts say that monthly housing costs should be no more than one-third of take-home pay.

- Consumer 1 earns $1,000 a month.

- Consumer 2 earns $4,000 a month.

- Consumer 3 earns $400 a month.

- Consumer 4 earns $2,250 a month.

bikeriderlondon/Shutterstock.com
There are a number of advantages to owning as well as renting.

who do not maintain properties or make needed repairs. Inadequate heat, hot water, and pest control are just a few of the problems these renters endure.

- *No tax benefits.* Because rent payments are not tax deductible, there are no tax benefits from renting.

Buying

For many people, owning a home gives a sense of permanence and financial security. It is a source of pride and satisfaction. Buying a home can be a smart move for the following reasons.

- *Increased wealth.* **Equity** is the difference between the market value of property and the amount owed on the property. As a homeowner, you build equity as your home increases in value and your home loan is paid down. You are buying something you often can resell, perhaps for a profit.
- *Tax benefits.* Home mortgage interest and property taxes paid on a home are deductible expenses when figuring federal and state income taxes. Rent payments are not tax deductible. As a result, renters do not receive the tax advantages enjoyed by homeowners.
- *Greater control.* When you buy a home, you generally have the freedom to make most of the decisions concerning your property, such as what color to paint it, where to hang pictures, whether or not to put in a swimming pool, etc. Condominiums and some housing subdivisions have rules that limit homeowners' freedoms.

The disadvantages of buying a home include the following.

- *Greater costs and financial responsibilities.* When they purchase a home, most homeowners make a down payment. This is often a large sum of money. Monthly costs include mortgage payments, homeowners insurance, and property taxes. Owners are also responsible for repair and maintenance costs.

- *Less mobility.* Moving usually involves selling a home, which is often complicated and time consuming. In a slow real estate market, it can take many months to sell a house or condominium.
- *Complicated relationships.* When friends or roommates buy a home together, they usually plan to live together for some time. However, if they decide to go their separate ways, it can be difficult to agree on what to do with the home.
- *Greater financial risk.* Although property values generally rise over time, homeowners risk losing money if property values drop or if they cannot keep up with mortgage payments. People who do not pay their mortgage can lose their homes.

Another factor to consider when making the decision to rent or buy is how long you will live in the property. Most financial experts agree that if you are going to live in the property for at least five years, buying makes more financial sense. However, if you plan to live in the property for less than five years, renting makes more financial sense.

Renting a Living Space

If you live with your parents or guardians, you may look forward to moving out on your own in the future. Like any other goal, this one requires planning and saving. Putting away a portion of your income in a savings account that earns interest can help you accumulate what you need to make this goal a reality.

Many young people, especially during difficult financial times, do not have the funds to move out on their own. They find that continuing to live with their families allows them to save money on rent, utilities, food, and other expenses. Parents may require working young adults to contribute to

Gunnar Pippel/Shutterstock.com

A lease or rental agreement should be signed prior to renting an apartment.

household expenses. However, these contributions are usually less than the cost of renting their own place.

Roommates

Many college students and young adults make living expenses more affordable by sharing housing with roommates. However, prospective roommates should have a clear understanding about financial obligations and house rules before moving in together. The following questions should be discussed before signing the lease.

- When is rent due, and what is each person's share of the rent?
- Is there a security deposit? How will that be divided if there are charges for damage to the residence?
- How long will each person live in the apartment? Who will pay the rent for the rest of the lease term if someone moves out early?
- How are utility bills to be divided?
- Will furniture, televisions, and appliances be shared? If they are damaged, who will pay for repair or replacement?
- Will food and meals be shared? How will food costs be divided?

Other issues that need to be negotiated concern privacy. For example, which part of the apartment is public and which parts are private or off limits? Will guests be allowed? If so, how often? How will housework be divided? Discuss these issues honestly before moving in with someone or having someone move in with you.

Finding a Rental

Once you have narrowed your search to particular communities or areas, you can tour the area looking for "For Rent" or "Apartment Available" signs. A phone number for the management company, realtor, or owner will probably be written on the sign. Many apartment buildings have on-site managers who are usually available to show apartments and take applications. The manager's apartment may be flagged on the buzzer panel or mailboxes.

Other sources of information about available rentals include:

- classified ads in newspapers and online;
- real estate agencies;
- college housing offices;
- bulletin boards at local grocery stores, coffee shops, community centers, etc.; and
- friends, acquaintances, and people who live in the area.

Make a good impression on the property owner or manager by showing up looking clean and neat and by being polite. You should be given a tour of the rental unit. Make sure you ask questions about parking, laundry, pets, and other concerns.

If possible, find an opportunity to talk with several tenants. There are some questions that only those who live in a building can answer accurately. For example, are apartments warm enough in winter and cool enough in summer? Are other tenants agreeable? Is the noise level acceptable, and is privacy adequate? Find out if current tenants are satisfied with maintenance and repairs, building services, security, and the overall atmosphere.

Application for Renting

You will probably have to fill out an application if you find a place you want to rent. Besides your name and contact information, you may be asked for the name, address, and phone number of your employer; financial information; names and contact information of references; and a list of previous addresses and landlords. Make sure you have this information with you.

You may also have to give your Social Security number, pay a fee, and give permission for your credit report or credit score to be checked. Property owners are allowed to request a credit report on prospective tenants. Credit reporting agencies require them to provide your name, address, and Social Security number to get a report. Property owners usually will not rent to people with low credit scores. There may be other fees as well.

If you rent an apartment or house, you are expected to pay the first month's rent and sign a lease. Normally, renters must also pay a security deposit. A **security deposit** is an amount a renter pays to help protect the property owner against financial losses in case the renter damages the property or fails to pay rent. It usually must be paid before moving into a rental unit. The amount of the security deposit generally comes to one or two month's rent. The deposit should be returned, usually with interest, when the lease expires provided there is no damage to the property.

Leases and Rental Agreements

Most renters are asked to sign a lease when they begin renting. A **lease** is a contract that specifies the conditions, terms, and rent for the use of an asset, as illustrated in Figure 12-3. The term of a lease varies, but the term is typically 6 months or 12 months.

The lease must be signed by the **lessee,** the person who rents the property, and the **lessor,** the person who owns and rents the property. An apartment lease explains the legal rights and responsibilities of both a tenant and a property owner.

Before signing a lease, read it carefully and know the answers to the following questions.

- *Rent.* How much is the rent and when must it be paid? What are the penalties for late payment?
- *Security deposit.* Is a security deposit required? If so, how much is it? Will it draw interest? How do you get the deposit back? Under what circumstances may the property owner keep part or all of it?
- *Utilities.* What utilities are included in the rent? How much should you expect to pay for utilities that are not included? (Ask to see a record of previous billings.)
- *Furnishings, appliances, services.* What furnishings and appliances are included? What building services and facilities are available? What is included in the rent and what costs extra?
- *Lease period.* What term or period of time does the lease cover? What are the beginning and ending dates of the lease? When do payments begin? When can you move in? When must you renew the lease or give notice that you will not renew? What happens if you leave before the lease expires? Can you sublet or assign the lease to someone else? What are the conditions for doing so? What are your responsibilities if the person taking over does not pay the rent?

A lease clearly states the rights and responsibilities of both the property owner and tenant.

- *Upkeep, maintenance, repairs.* Who is responsible for upkeep, maintenance, and repairs? What does the property owner maintain, and what must you maintain? What can either of you do if the other fails to carry out upkeep and maintenance responsibilities? Where and how do you contact the property owner or rental agent with questions, problems, or complaints?

- *Legal remedies.* What legal remedies are available? What can you do if the property owner breaks the lease in some way, such as failing to make necessary repairs or to provide adequate heat? What can the property owner do if you break the lease by not paying the rent or failing to obey building rules? Does the lease outline ways, such as arbitration or legal action, to handle disagreements with the property owner? Who pays the legal costs of settling differences?

- *Other conditions of use.* Can you paint, hang wallpaper, and decorate? If you install shelving, carpet, or equipment, can you remove it later? Can you keep pets? Can you have a roommate?

Before signing, make sure all spaces in the lease are filled in accurately, including dates, dollar amounts, addresses, and names. All verbal agreements

History of Finance

Home Ownership

Home ownership has long been regarded as the American dream. Until the second half of the 20th century, however, the idea was more of a dream than a reality. In the first four decades of the 20th century, less than half of all Americans owned their own homes. The rate of home ownership declined in three of the decades. The Great Depression that started in 1929 had a profound effect on the housing market. Between 1929 and 1933, new housing starts fell by 95 percent and over half of all home mortgages were in default. In an effort to stabilize the market, President Herbert Hoover signed the *Federal Home Loan Bank Act* in 1932. This law laid the foundation for government support of the housing market.

In 1933, President Franklin Roosevelt created the Home Owners' Loan Corporation (HOLC) to provide low interest loans to help out homeowners who were in foreclosure. In 1934, the federal government created the Federal Housing Administration (FHA), which set standards for home construction, created 25- and 30-year mortgages, and lowered interest rates. In 1938, the Federal National Mortgage Association (Fannie Mae) was created to provide a secondary market in mortgages. In 1944, mortgage assistance programs were created to help veterans returning from World War II to obtain home mortgages.

These programs, along with available credit, boosted the rates of home ownership quickly. By 1950, the percent of Americans who owned their own home had risen to 55 percent. By 1970, the figure had risen to over 60 percent. With the exception of the 1980s—when mortgage interest rates hit record highs—the rate of home ownership steadily increased until the financial crisis that started in late 2008. Today, more than two-thirds of Americans own their own homes.

WB-20 APARTMENT LEASE
Approved by Wisconsin Real Estate Examining Board

Nelco Forms
P.O. Box 10208
Green Bay, WI 54307-0208

APARTMENT LEASE

	1 2	This lease of the apartment identified below is entered into by and between the Landlord and Tenant (referred to in the singular whether one or more) on the following terms and conditions:
PARTIES	3	Tenant: *Raoul Doe* Landlord: *Sawdusky Realty*
		Ilse Doe
		Agent for maintenance, management: name *Mike Manning* address *1210 Fixit St.* *Anytown, USA*
APARTMENT ADDRESS	10	Building address: street *1000 Collect St.*
		Agent for collection of rents: name *Lisa Brown* address *1000 Collect St.* *Anytown, USA*
		city, village/town *Anytown,*
		county *Anycounty* State *St*
		Agent for service of process: name *Myra Lee* address *508 Process St.* *Anytown USA.*
	24	Apartment number: *208*
TERM	25	Lease term: *8/1/-- to 8/1/--* ~~Month to Month~~ (strike if not applicable)
	26	First day of lease term: *8/1/--* Last day of lease term: *8/1/-- One Year Later*
RENTALS	27	Apartment: $ *950.00* per *MO.* Other: *Garage Sp.* $ *30* per *Mo*
	28	Payable at *Apt. 101, 1000 Collect St.* on or
	29 30	before the *First* day of each *Month* during the term of this lease.
UTILITIES	31 32	Utility charges, other than telephone, are included in the rent, except: *Heat And Electricty*
	33 34	which Tenant shall pay promptly when due. If charges not included in the rent are not separately metered, they shall be allo-
	35 36	cated on the basis of: *Separate meters are installed*
SPECIAL CONDITIONS	37 38 39 40	Special conditions: *No Pets*
RENEWAL OF LEASE TERM	41 42 43 44 45 46	(Strike clause 1 or 2; if neither is striken clause 2 controls.) 1. This lease shall be automatically renewed, without notice from either party, on identical terms for a like suc- cessive lease term unless either party shall, at least 45 days before the expiration of the lease, notify the other in writing of the termination of the lease. However, Landlord must, at least 15 days but not more than 30 days prior to the time specified for giving the notice as herein set forth notify Tenant in writing of the above provision for automatic renewal or extension.
	47 48	~~2. This lease shall be automatically renewed, without notice from either party, on identical terms, except that it shall be a month-to-month tenancy.~~
ASSIGNMENT SUBLETTING	49 50 51	Tenant shall not assign this lease nor sublet the premises or any part thereof without the prior written consent of Landlord. If Landlord permits an assignment or a sublease, such permission shall in no way relieve Tenant of Tenant's liability under this lease.
SECURITY DEPOSIT	52 53	Upon execution of this lease Tenant paid a security deposit in the amount of $ *950.00* to be held by *Sawdusky Realty*
ASSIGNMENT SUBLETTING	54 55 56 57 58 59 60 61 62 63	If the person holding the security deposit is a licensed real estate broker, acting as agent, it shall be held in the broker's trust account. The deposit, less any amounts withheld, will be returned in person or mailed to Tenant's last known address within 21 days after Tenant vacates the premises. If any portion of the deposit is withheld, Landlord will provide an accompanying itemized statement specifically describing any damages and accounting for any amount withheld. Failure to return the deposit or provide a written accounting within 21 days will result in the waiver of any claim against the deposit. The reasonable cost of repairing any damages caused by Tenant, normal wear and tear excepted, will be deducted from the security deposit. Tenant has 7 days after the beginning of the lease term to notify Landlord in writing of damages or defects in the premises; no deduction from Tenant's security deposit shall be made for any damages or defects of which notification is given. Landlord will give Tenant a written description of any physical damages charged to the previous tenant's security deposit as soon as such description is
LANDLORD'S RIGHT TO ENTER		
VACATION OF PREMISES	64 65 66	available. (If none, so specify_____.) (Strike paragraph if no security deposit is paid.) Tenant agrees to vacate the premises at the end of the lease term or the extended lease term, and promptly deliver the keys to Landlord.
LANDLORD'S RIGHT TO ENTER	67 68 69 70 71	Landlord may enter the premises at reasonable times and with 12 hours advance notice, with or without Tenant's permission to inspect the premises, make repairs, show the premises to prospective tenants or purchasers, or to com- ply with any applicable law or regulation. Landlord may enter with less than 12 hours advance notice upon specific consent of Tenant. No advance notice is required for entry in a health or safety emergency or where entry is neces- sary to preserve and protect the premises from damage in Tenant's absence.
ABANDONMENT BY TENANT	72 73 74 75 76	If Tenant shall abandon the premises before the expiration of the lease term, Landlord shall make reasonable efforts to re-lease premises and shall apply any rent received, less costs of re-leasing, to the rent due or to become due on this lease, and Tenant shall remain liable for any deficiency. If Tenant is absent from the premises for three successive weeks without notifying Landlord in writing of such absence, Landlord, at Landlord's sole option, may deem the premises abandoned.
DISPOSAL OF TENANT'S PROPERTY	77 78 79	If Tenant shall leave any property on the premises after vacation or abandonment of the premises, Tenant shall be deemed to have abandoned the property, and Landlord shall have the right to dispose of the property as provided by law.
TENANT OBLIGATIONS	80 81	During the lease term, as a condition to Tenant's continuing right to use and occupy the premises, Tenant agrees and promises:
USE	82	1. To use the premises for residential purposes only by Tenant and Tenant's immediate family.
	83 84	2. Not to make or permit use of the premises for any unlawful purpose or any purpose that will injure the reputa- tion of the premises or the building of which they are a part.
	85 86	3. Not to use or keep in or about the premises anything which would adversely affect coverage of the premises or the building of which they are a part under a standard fire and extended insurance policy.
	87 88	4. Not to make excessive noise or engage in activities which unduly disturb neighbors or other tenants in the build- ing which the premises are located.
PETS	89	5. Not to keep in or about the premises any pet unless specifically authorized as a special condition in this lease.
GOVT. REG.	90	6. To obey all lawful orders, rules and regulations of all governmental authorities.
MAINTENANCE	91 92	7. To keep the premises in clean and tenantable condition and in as good repair as at the beginning of the lease term, normal wear and tear excepted.
IMPROVEMENTS	93 94 95	8. If obligated to pay for heat for the premises, to maintain a reasonable amount of heat in cold weather to prevent damage to the premises, and if damage results from Tenant's failure to maintain a reasonable amount of heat Tenant shall be liable for this damage.

WB20   NTF 0074

Goodheart-Willcox Publisher

Figure 12-3 The lease clearly states the rights and responsibilities of both landlord and tenant.

should be written into the lease. You should understand all clauses, obligations, and consequences. If you have serious questions or doubts about signing the lease, you may want to get a lawyer's advice. Make sure you receive a copy of the signed document and keep it in a safe place.

As mentioned earlier in the chapter, the longer the term of your lease, the lower your rent typically is. For example, the rent under a 12-month lease is usually lower than a 6-month lease. However, you may not want to be under a lease contract for that long. An option is to find a property that allows you to have a rental agreement rather than a lease. A **rental agreement** is a written agreement that permits the tenant to move out at any time as long as the required notice is given. Rental agreements usually run month-to-month. This means you can continue renting as long as you pay your monthly rent, but you can move out any time after giving a one-month notice. The downside of a month-to-month rental agreement is the cost. Since month-to-month rentals are more likely to experience more frequent periods of vacancy than a leased property, the property owner usually wants a higher amount of rent.

Renter Protection

There are a variety of federal, state, and local laws and regulations that protect renters. For example, the Title VIII of the *Civil Rights Act of 1968*, also called the *Fair Housing Act*, prohibits discrimination against consumers who are looking to buy, rent, or get financing for a dwelling. Consumers cannot be discriminated against because of race, color, national origin, religion, sex, familial status, or disability.

Other laws state that property owners cannot enter a renter's dwelling except in the case of an emergency. If property owners need to access homes to do maintenance, they are required to give tenants a certain amount of notice.

The lease protects renters as well as property owners. The rent that is stated in the current lease cannot be raised until the lease period is over. Some cities have laws that limit how much property owners can raise the rent on their tenants. If heat is included in the rent, it must be provided when temperatures are low. Property owners are required to install fire alarms.

When you gain access to your new residence, the first thing you should do is conduct an inspection and complete a rental inventory checklist. The **rental inventory checklist,** which may be supplied by the property owner, is a detailed list of property items and their condition. Make a note of problems on the inventory checklist or the lease, such as a scratched floor, a dirty oven, and a dripping faucet. The property owner should fix some of these right away. Other problems should be documented so you are not charged for them when you move out. Take the time to fill out the form carefully and thoroughly and make a copy for yourself.

Renters should purchase renters insurance to protect against losses due to theft, fire, or other damages.

Being a Good Tenant

Tenants also have responsibilities to their neighbors and property owners. The main responsibility is to pay the rent on time. Failure to pay rent can result in late fees, termination of the contract, or eviction. **Eviction** is the legal process of removing a tenant who is not paying rent from a rental property

Building Code Officials

Building code officials examine buildings, highways, and streets; sewer and water systems; bridges; and other structures. They ensure that their construction, alteration, or repair complies with building codes and ordinances, zoning regulations, and contract specifications

Careers in Transportation, Distribution & Logistics

What Do Property Managers Do?

When owners of homes, apartments, office buildings, and other rental properties lack the time or expertise needed for the daily management of properties, they often hire a **property manager. Property managers** make sure the property looks presentable, assume responsibility for repairs, and work to keep properties rented. **Property managers** typically:

- meet with and show properties to prospective renters;
- explain the lease and terms of occupancy;
- collect monthly rental fees from tenants;
- arrange for repairs and equipment as needed;
- clean and prepare a property for a new renter;
- contract for trash removal, landscaping, security, and other services;
- investigate and settle complaints, disturbances, and violations; and
- stay current on housing laws.

What Is It Like to Work as a Property Manager?

Property managers normally work out of an office. However, many **property managers** spend much of their time away from their desks overseeing the property. Some **property managers** work for realty companies. Others work for a property owner and may be required to live in the apartment complex where they work. Most **property managers** work full time. On-site managers often live in an apartment rent-free as part of their compensation.

What Education and Skills Are Needed to Be a Property Manager?

- high school diploma
- knowledge of property management
- ability to work independently
- strong interpersonal and communication skills
- reliability and able to put client needs first
- problem-solving skills
- negotiation skills

if the tenant does not leave voluntarily. Evictions are often reported to credit bureaus, which could lower the tenant's credit score and could make it hard to obtain another lease. Tenants are also expected to:

- meet the terms of the lease;

- keep the dwellings clean and free of pests;
- prevent damage to the property;
- report problems, such as leaks or broken windows, right away;
- avoid noise and behaviors that could disturb neighbors;
- give notice before they move out as required in the lease; and
- clean up before moving out.

Checkpoint 12.2

1. What do housing costs include?
2. What are four advantages of renting a home?
3. What are three advantages of buying a home?
4. What are some sources of information for finding a place to rent?
5. How does a lease differ from a rental agreement?

Build Your Vocabulary

As you progress through this course, develop a personal glossary of personal finance terms and add it to your portfolio. This will help you build your vocabulary and prepare you for a career. Write a definition for each of the following terms and add it to your personal finance glossary.

equity	lessor
security deposit	rental agreement
lease	rental inventory checklist
lessee	eviction

Chapter Summary

Section 12.1 Housing Decisions

- When making housing decisions, location is one of your most important considerations. Some factors to consider when choosing a housing location include employment opportunities, cost of living in the area, the climate, your lifestyle, the neighborhood, community facilities, and schools.

- At different times in your life, you will most likely choose different types and styles of housing. Renting a home and buying a home both have advantages and disadvantages.

- Moving a short distance away can be handled alone, with the help of friends, or by local movers. Moving to another state requires a national carrier. You will need to notify utility companies and others who provide services of your move.

- When furnishing a residence, you may want to start with essential items and add other furnishings as you can afford them. Renting furnishings is another option to consider.

- When you move into your first home, you will face home care and maintenance responsibilities. In a rental apartment, this is largely a matter of keeping the space clean. Maintaining a home involves many tasks and is both costly and time consuming.

Section 12.2 Rent or Buy

- Some advantages of renting a home include fewer financial responsibilities, less financial risk, and greater mobility. Disadvantages of renting include no buildup of equity, little control of the home, and no tax benefits. Some advantages of buying a home include increased wealth and tax benefits. Disadvantage of owning a home include greater costs and financial responsibilities, less mobility, and greater financial risk.

- The process of renting a residence involves finding a suitable place that is affordable and coming to an agreement with the owner. A lease or rental agreement should state the terms of the agreement. A variety of federal, state, and local laws and regulations that deal with discrimination and other issues protect renters.

Check Your Personal Finance IQ

Now that you have finished the chapter, see what you learned about personal finance by taking the chapter posttest. If you do not have a smartphone, visit the G-W Learning companion website.

G-W Learning mobile site: www.m.g-wlearning.com

G-W Learning companion website: www.g-wlearning.com

Review Your Knowledge

1. When choosing a housing location, what questions related to employment opportunities should you consider?
2. Where can you find information about the cost of living in different areas?
3. Who are some business professionals you may need to consult to help you through the renting or purchasing process?
4. Why is it important to take an inventory of your possessions before you move?
5. What items should you acquire first when furnishing a first home?
6. When you buy a home, housing experts recommend setting aside how much of the purchase price each year to cover maintenance and repairs?
7. How can you use budget amounts to determine the amount you can afford to spend for housing each month?
8. What are the responsibilities of a renter?
9. What is the main advantage of signing a lease as opposed to renting month to month with a rental agreement?
10. What are some things that good tenants are expected to do?

Apply Your Knowledge

11. What are the factors that are most important to you when deciding where to live?
12. Assume you have taken a job in a large city and are making plans to move. You plan to live alone and are looking for an inexpensive apartment in a safe area. What type of apartment would you choose? Why?
13. How does a person's lifestyle tend to influence housing location? Give examples.
14. What sources of information do you find to be the most helpful when looking for a place to live?
15. Assume you have a job that requires you to move frequently. Is home ownership a good option for you? Why or why not?
16. Assume you are renting your first apartment. You found a desirable property and the owner makes available two options: a 12-month lease for $575 per month and a month-to-month agreement for $600. Which would you choose? Why?
17. What do you consider to be the most important renter protection law? Why?
18. Would you consider renting furniture a good alternative to buying? Why or why not?
19. What are some things you would do to save money if you were decorating and furnishing a home?
20. If you were on a budget and furnishing your first place, which pieces of furniture would you start with and which would you add as your budget allowed?

Teamwork

In this chapter, you learned about finding a place to live after you leave your current dwelling. Working with a teammate, research the cost of an apartment. Create a budget based on the two of you sharing an apartment. Include rent, utilities, food, insurance, and any other costs that you might have. How much will it cost per month for the apartment?

G-W Learning Mobile Site

Visit the G-W Learning mobile site to complete the chapter pretest and posttest and to practice vocabulary using e-flash cards. If you do not have a smartphone, visit the G-W Learning companion website to access these features.

G-W Learning mobile site: www.m.g-wlearning.com

G-W Learning companion website: www.g-wlearning.com

Common Core

College and Career Readiness

CTE Career Ready Practices. Career-ready individuals learn how to solve problems by using a decision-making process. Imagine yourself renting an apartment that you will share with a roommate. What decision-making processes would you use to find an appropriate apartment? Create a flowchart to show the steps you would take.

Listening. Passive listening is casually listening to someone speak. Passive listening is appropriate when you do not have to interact with the speaker. Listen to a classmate as he or she is having a conversation with you. After the person has finished talking, write down what you remember.

Speaking. There will be many instances when you will be required to persuade the listener. When you persuade, you convince a person to take a course of action which you propose. Prepare for a conversation with a real estate agent to persuade the person to find you an apartment to rent.

Web Connect

Do an Internet search for tips for renting an apartment. What kinds of information did you find? Were there any surprises?

College and Career Readiness

College and Career Readiness Portfolio

As part of a job interview, you may be asked about your travel or other experiences with people from other cultures. Companies are interested in this information for good reasons. Many companies serve customers from a variety of geographic locations and cultures. Some companies have offices or factories in more than one area or country. As an employee, you may need to work with people from other cultures. Your job may involve travel to company locations in other areas or countries. Employees that speak more than one language and have traveled, studied, or worked in other areas can be valuable assets. These employees can help the company understand the needs and wants of its customers. They may also be better able to communicate and get along with coworkers.

1. Identify travel or other experiences you have had that helped you learn about another culture.

2. Write a paragraph that describes the experience. Tell how the information you learned might help you better understand customers or coworkers from this culture.

3. Save the document file in your e-portfolio. Place a printed copy in the container for your print portfolio.

Teamwork

Some competitive events for Career and Technical Student Organization (CTSOs) have a performance portion. If it is a team event, it is important that the team making the presentation prepare to operate as a cohesive unit.

To prepare for team activities, complete the following activities.

1. Read the guidelines provided by your organization.

2. Practice performing as a team by completing the team activities at the end of each chapter in this text. This will help members learn how to interact with each other and participate effectively.

3. Locate on your organization's website a rubric or scoring sheet for the event to see how the team will be judged.

4. Confirm the use of visual aids that may be used in the presentation and amount of setup time permitted.

5. Review the rules to confirm if questions will be asked or if the team will need to defend a case or situation.

6. Make notes on index cards about important points to remember. Team members should exchange note cards so that each evaluates the other person's notes. Use these notes to study. You may also be able to use these notes during the event.

7. Assign each team member a role for the presentation. Practice performing as a team. Each team member should introduce himself or herself, review the case, make suggestions for the case, and conclude with a summary.

8. Ask your instructor to play the role of competition judge as your team reviews the case. After the presentation is complete, ask for feedback from your instructor. You may consider also having a student audience to listen and give feedback.

Owning a home has long been called the American dream. Buying a home, however, is a huge financial commitment and can be a complicated event for the buyer and the seller. Consumers should shop for the best mortgage that fits their financial situations. They should study the multitude of legal documents that must be signed and seek professional help when needed.

Focus on Finance

Mortgage Calculators

Buying a residence is a big step in your life. Before you start the process of buying, you should do your homework and make sure the property is financially affordable. There are many mortgage calculators on the Internet that will help you figure the cost of a loan. These calculators will help you estimate how much you can afford now as well as how much you will pay over the life of the mortgage. The first piece of information you will need to use the calculator is the amount of the loan for which you are applying. This will typically be 80 percent of the purchase price of the house. This is called the *principal amount*. Next, decide for how many years you want the loan; a period of 15, 20, or 30 years is the common time span. You will then enter the interest rate of the loan. The mortgage calculator will then do the work for you.

By estimating the monthly payment, the mortgage calculator will help you decide if you should move forward with applying for a loan. Of course, there are many other factors to consider, such as your credit rating, your salary, and other financial details. However, this is the first step in deciding if this is the right decision for you.

Reading Prep. Before you begin reading this chapter, Iconsider how the author developed and presented information. How does the information provide the foundation for the next?

College and Career Readiness

Check Your Personal Finance IQ

Before you begin the chapter, see what you already know about personal finance by taking the chapter pretest. If you do not have a smartphone, visit the G-W Learning companion website.

G-W Learning mobile site: www.m.g-wlearning.com

G-W Learning companion website: www.g-wlearning.com

Sections

Section 13.1 Buying a Home

Section 13.2 Financing a Home

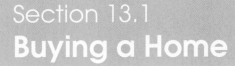

Section 13.1
Buying a Home

Objective

After studying this section, you will be able to:

- Discuss important points to consider when buying a residence.
- Identify the steps in buying a home.

Terms

real estate broker

exclusive buyer agent

purchase agreement

earnest money

contingency clause

Selecting a Home

Selecting your first home is an important decision. Choose a residence that is conveniently designed for your lifestyle and housing needs. Looking at different types of options can help you decide what you like best.

If you are buying a single residence, solid construction is of great importance. Be sure to check both outside and inside construction features. It pays to carefully evaluate the outside of the house, the yard, and the neighborhood, as well as the inside living space. Single-family residences are built in a variety of ways.

- *Custom-built.* Homes are usually designed by architects to meet the specific needs and wishes of their clients. A contractor is hired to build the house according to an architect's plan. This can be a costly and lengthy project.

- *Tract.* Neighborhoods of new homes are built by developers who erect many houses at once within a given area. These houses are built from similar plans in order to keep costs down. Most tract houses look alike and lack the individuality of custom-built houses. They are less expensive; however, and builders often make minor alterations to meet individual buyers' needs.

- *Modular and kit.* These homes are partially built in factories. They are then moved in sections to the home site for completion. These houses are relatively inexpensive. Quality depends on the manufacturer as well as the builder who puts the house together.

When buying a condominium, landominium, cooperative, or townhouse, it is important to do some thorough homework. The soundness of this type of investment depends greatly on the management, restrictions, operating policies, and types of people involved in both ownership and management. A few questions to answer before buying are listed as follows.

- How is the property managed and by whom? What voice do owners have in management decisions?

- Are current residents generally satisfied with the management and the building?

- What is the financial status of the building? Is there a mortgage on the property? Are any major repairs or renovations anticipated? If so, are funds available to cover the costs? Does the appraised value compare favorably with the selling price?

- How much is the monthly maintenance fee or assessment? What does it cover? When and how can it be increased?

- What control do occupants have over their units? Are there restrictions on selling, remodeling, refinancing, or renting? Are pets permitted?

- How does the unit compare with similar units in other buildings and with other forms of available housing in the area?

When buying a residence, a checklist like the one in Figure 13-1 can help you with an initial evaluation.

Checklist for Single-Family Houses

Outside House and Yard

- Attractive, well-designed house
- Lot of the right size and shape for house and garage
- Good drainage of rain and moisture
- Mature, healthy trees, placed to give shade in summer
- Well-kept driveway, walks, patio, and porch
- Parking convenience (garage, carport, or street)
- Well-lighted and sheltered entry

Outside Construction

- Durable siding materials, in good condition
- Solid brick and masonry, free of cracks
- Solid foundation walls
- Weather-stripped windows and doors
- Noncorrosive gutters and downspouts, connected to storm sewer or splash block to carry water away from house
- Copper or aluminum flashing used over doors, windows, and joints on the roof
- Screens and storm windows

Inside Construction

- Sound, smooth walls with invisible nails and taping on dry wall surfaces
- Well-done carpentry work with properly fitted joints and moldings
- Properly fitted, easy-to-operate windows

- Level wood floors with smooth finish and no high edges, wide gaps, or squeaks
- Well-fitted tile floors (no cracked or damaged tiles, no visible adhesive)
- Good possibilities for improvements, remodeling, expanding
- Dry basement floor with hard, smooth surface
- Adequate basement drain
- Sturdy stairways with railings, adequate head room, not too steep
- Leakproof roof in good condition
- Adequate insulation for warmth and soundproofing

Living Space

- Convenient work areas (kitchen, laundry, workshop) with adequate drawers, cabinets, lighting, workspace, electric power
- Bedrooms located far enough from other parts of the house for privacy and quiet
- Social areas (living and dining room, play space, yard, porch, or patio) convenient, comfortable, large enough for family and guests
- Adequate storage—closets, cabinets, shelves, attic, basement, garage
- Windows located to provide enough air, light, and ventilation
- Usable attic and/or basement space
- Extras (fireplace, air conditioning, porches, new kitchen and baths)

Goodheart-Willcox Publisher

Figure 13-1 A checklist can help you with an initial evaluation of a residence that you are considering for purchase.

In some ways, owning a condo, landominum, or co-op is like owning a traditional house. Most people obtain a mortgage when buying their home and make monthly mortgage payments. They also pay property taxes and have the same tax and equity benefits as the traditional house owner.

Home Buying Process

Buying a home involves many considerations and decisions. Chapter 12 discussed the importance of selecting a location. Once you have decided on an appropriate location, there are other important questions to ask. For example, do you want a house or a condominium? Do you want a house in a newly constructed subdivision or an older established neighborhood? Do you have a preference for a ranch-style home or a two-story house?

Begin by making a list of the home features you want and decide which ones are most important. This will help you narrow your options and stay within a budget. Factors to consider include the number of bedrooms and bathrooms you prefer, the size of the yard, and if you must have a garage. Evaluate whether you want a place in move-in condition or whether you are willing to do some home renovation. Once you have an idea of what you are looking for, you can begin your search.

Real Estate Agents

Many consumers looking for a home work with real estate brokers. A **real estate broker** is a person licensed to arrange for the purchase and sale of real estate for a fee or commission. Some brokers specialize in commercial

History of Finance

Subprime Mortgage Crisis

From 1998 to 2006, the United States experienced a housing boom. Many consumers purchased homes because interest rates were low. The increase in demand caused housing prices to rise. Some homes doubled in value in just a few years.

Eager to reap the benefits of a good housing market, many lenders loosened mortgage requirements. They gave high-risk loans to borrowers with poor or no credit history. The lenders bundled the subprime mortgage loans together and sold them to investors and other financial institutions.

Many of the loans given during the housing boom were adjustable rate mortgages. When interest rates eventually rose, home owners faced higher monthly payments. Many consumers could no longer afford to pay and defaulted on their loans. Thousands of people had their homes repossessed.

Lenders and investors who purchased the bundled subprime mortgages experienced serious losses. Afraid of more losses, lenders stopped making loans to consumers, businesses, and other financial institutions. The freeze in the credit market affected the global financial system. Some banks failed, and huge financial institutions went bankrupt. In 2008 the government had to step in to help ease the recession triggered largely by failures in the subprime mortgage market. The crisis raised awareness to the risks associated with subprime lending and the need for mortgage reform.

auremar/Shutterstock.com

A knowledgeable real estate agent can assist buyers with selecting and purchasing a home.

properties. Others work with residential properties. Many brokers can also assist in arranging rental housing.

Real estate brokers usually employ sales agents to work for them. When a homeowner lists a home with a broker, the broker or a sales agent provides a variety of services. This person helps the homeowner price the home, advertise it, show it, and negotiate the sale with a prospective buyer. Brokers and agents post their listings online on sites such as the Multiple Listing Service (MLS). Good brokers or agents know the territory in which they work. They have multiple contacts with people in the community and with other professionals in the business.

For their services, brokers and agents receive a commission, usually between 3 and 6 percent of the home's final sale price. The seller usually pays the commission.

People searching for a home may also work with exclusive buyer agents. An **exclusive buyer agent** is a real estate agent who works for the buyer and not the seller. Meet with the agent and ask questions about his or her experience. You should feel comfortable with the person and satisfied with the responses to your questions. An experienced broker or agent can provide valuable information about the real estate market, including home prices, zoning laws, and property taxes. He or she can help buyers find neighborhoods that best meet their search criteria. Your agent will interview you about the type of home you are looking for and ask how much you can spend. Then he or she will alert you to homes that meet your criteria and arrange showings.

Since many people look at as many as 50 homes before they buy, brokers help them make the best use of their time. They set up appointments to tour houses, help find financing, and negotiate the sale.

Case Study

Choosing Where to Live

Milt just finished an automotive technology training program and accepted a job in another city. He needs to move closer to his work. Milt wants a two-bedroom house rather than an apartment. He needs a place for his car and a yard for his dog.

Online listings are not very helpful because Milt does not know the city. Here are some of his other options:

- Contact the chamber of commerce for a map of the city and information on apartments.
- Make appointments to see some rental property listed online.
- Take a day or two to drive around the city and see the neighborhoods.
- Ask his employer about places to live.
- Use a real estate or apartment finder agency to help find a potential rental property.
- Check into a hotel for a few weeks until he is more familiar with the city.

Case Review

1. If you were Milt, how would you search for a place to live?
2. Which ideas from Milt's list might you use in searching for a place to live?
3. What should Milt consider before he chooses a house to rent?
4. If Milt wanted to share an apartment with a roommate, how could he go about finding someone

The National Association of Exclusive Buyer Agents can help you find an exclusive buyer agent in your area.

Your Offer

Buying a home is not like going to a department store to buy a jacket. Homebuyers usually do not pay the initial asking price. There is usually some *negotiation*, or back-and-forth haggling, between the buyer and the seller. For example, assume a home you like is listed for sale at $200,000. You may offer less, perhaps 5 percent or $10,000 less. The seller can accept or reject your offer of $190,000. The seller may also reject your offer but counter with another price, such as $195,000. Now you must decide whether or not to accept the new reduced price or make another offer.

Before making an offer, a buyer needs to research the sale price of comparable homes in the area. For example, if the home you are interested in is a three-bedroom, two-bath home with a two-car garage, look for other homes of that description that have sold in the previous months in that neighborhood. What were the asking prices and the prices paid? A real estate broker can do this research for you. Use the prices paid as a guide to formulate your bid.

If the property is an exceptional value and others are also submitting offers, you will want to submit the asking price or near the asking price. However, there are many reasons to offer less than the asking price. A buyer may offer less in these situations:

- the property needs repairs.
- the home has not sold despite being on the market a long time.
- other comparable homes nearby sold for much less.

- the seller is desperate to sell.
- the buyer is flexible about the move-in date.
- the market for selling homes is bad, and there are many homes on the market.
- there are a number of foreclosures in the neighborhood and in the area.

The financial crisis that started in late 2008 had a profound effect on the housing market. Many people lost their jobs and could no longer afford to make monthly mortgage payments. Some people walked away from their homes and let the lenders foreclose. The result was a flooding of the market with homes and a reduction in home values. A neighborhood with many foreclosures means that home values have dropped. In this situation, you always offer the lowest reasonable price. In a housing crash, you never know when home prices have hit their bottom. Considering this, do not pay the potential value of a home; pay the current value or less.

Purchase Agreements

When you have an offer price, then an agent or real estate attorney can draw up a purchase agreement. When the buyer agrees to buy and the seller agrees to sell, they both sign a purchase agreement. A **purchase agreement** is a contract between a homebuyer and a seller that includes a description of the real estate, its location, the purchase price, the possession date, and any other conditions and terms of the sale. Sometimes this contract is called a *sales agreement*.

The agreement should state all of the conditions and terms of the sale. For example, if the seller agrees to make any home repairs, these should be stated in the agreement. If the owner promises to leave the draperies, dishwasher, range, and refrigerator, these should also be listed and described.

When you sign a purchase agreement, you must also give the seller an earnest money check. **Earnest money** is a deposit you make when you sign a purchase agreement to show that your offer is serious. This prohibits the seller from selling the home to someone else. This is usually a percentage of the home price. It is applied toward the down payment at the closing of the sale. Buyers can lose the earnest money if they fail to go through with the agreement. A home purchase agreement may contain a contingency clause. A **contingency clause** is part of a contract that calls for certain requirements to be met before the contract is binding. For example, the validity of the agreement may depend upon obtaining a mortgage within a certain period of time or at a certain rate. It may be made contingent upon the sale of the buyer's current home.

Home Inspection

A common contingency is that the home must pass an inspection by a home inspector hired by the buyer. For a fee, home inspectors examine the home for problems that may affect the value of the home or require costly repair. These problems include cracks in the foundation, a leaky roof, and plumbing and electrical problems. Inspectors also check to make sure appliances work.

Buyers who live in areas where termites thrive or where mold is common may also have the home inspected for these problems by specialists. Specialized

StockCube/Shutterstock.com

A home inspection will often identify the need for minor and major repairs.

inspectors can be hired to find problems related to lead or asbestos exposure. If problems are found, buyers can ask sellers to fix them before they purchase the home. Buyers can also use the inspection findings to negotiate a reduction in the sale price.

Checkpoint 13.1

1. How does a real estate broker differ from an exclusive buyer agent?
2. What information should be included on a real estate purchase agreement?
3. What are some reasons a potential buyer might offer less than the asking price for a home?
4. What is the purpose of an earnest money payment?
5. What is the purpose of a home inspection in the home purchase process?

Build Your Vocabulary

As you progress through this course, develop a personal glossary of personal finance terms and add it to your portfolio. This will help you build your vocabulary and prepare you for a career. Write a definition for each of the following terms and add it to your personal finance glossary.

real estate broker   earnest money

exclusive buyer agent   contingency clause

purchase agreement

Financing a Home

Objectives

After studying this section, you will be able to:

- Explain how a mortgage amount is calculated.
- Describe different types of home mortgages.
- Identify various government-sponsored financing programs.
- Describe how to shop for a mortgage.
- Explain the closing process.
- Identify ways to save money on a mortgage.

Terms

mortgage	home equity loan
amortization	closing cost
private mortgage insurance (PMI)	point
escrow account	property survey
fixed rate mortgage	appraisal
adjustable rate mortgage (ARM)	title
graduated payment mortgage	title insurance
subprime mortgage	

Home Mortgage

Most homebuyers get loans to finance home purchases. A **mortgage** is a type of secured loan used for buying property. The lender is usually a bank or a mortgage company. The borrower promises to repay the lender the loan amount plus interest. The mortgage is paid in monthly installments over a set number of years. The home is the collateral for the loan. If the borrower fails to pay according to the terms of the mortgage contract, the lender can foreclose on the property. As you learned in Chapter 6, foreclosure is the

Go Green

A green house is one that is energy efficient and friendly to the planet. A green home will contain some or all of the following earth friendly features: an alternative power system, such as solar or wind power, recycled building materials, a solar powered water heating system, and no-VOC (nontoxic) paints and stains. Green home communities are being built throughout the United States in an effort to lessen the carbon footprint humans leave behind

process in which the lender takes possession of the property if the borrower fails to make the mortgage payments.

Amortization is the process of paying back a loan in equal monthly installments. Each installment decreases the outstanding loan amount, or principal, each month. Most home mortgages are amortized. In the beginning, payments are applied largely to interest. As the loan is repaid, an increasing amount of each payment is applied to the principal. This means the borrower builds up equity, or ownership, in the property as the loan is repaid.

The amount of your monthly mortgage payment depends on four factors: the size of your mortgage, your down payment, the interest rate, and the term of the loan.

Size of Mortgage

First, consider how much you need to borrow. What is the maximum size mortgage your income and resources will support? Many homebuyers, especially first-time homebuyers, overestimate what they can afford and take out a mortgage that results in payments that are difficult to make. Most mortgage lenders require that the buyer spend no more than 28 percent of gross monthly income on mortgage, property tax, and home insurance payments. For example, if Mac McKenzie has total monthly earnings of $3,000, his monthly mortgage payment should not exceed $840 ($3,000 × .28).

Down Payment

Real Estate Appraisers
Real estate appraisers estimate the value of land and buildings, ranging from residential homes to major shopping centers. They write detailed reports on their research observations and explain reasons for arriving at their estimates.

How much money can you afford as a down payment for a loan? The more you pay down, the less your monthly payments and total interest charges will be. If your down payment is less than 20 percent of the purchase price, most lenders will require you to obtain private mortgage insurance. **Private mortgage insurance (PMI)** is an insurance policy that protects the lender from loss if the borrower defaults on the loan and the home goes into foreclosure. The reason for PMI is that if borrower is unable to make a down payment of 20 percent or more, lenders will typically look at the loan as a riskier investment. By requiring PMI, the bank is guaranteed an added layer of protection. The PMI payment is usually paid monthly as part of the overall mortgage payment.

After the borrower has paid between 20 and 25 percent of the home's purchase price, PMI is not required. The *Homeowners Protection Act of 1998* requires the automatic termination of PMI when the equity in the home reaches 22 percent of the property's value at the time the mortgage was taken. Homeowners can request early termination of PMI if they can provide proof that the equity in their home has risen to 22 percent of the property's current market value. Many borrowers either forget or do not know that PMI can be dropped once a home's value reaches the accepted level.

Interest Rate

The interest rate you pay can have a significant impact on the amount of your monthly mortgage. For example, monthly principal and interest payments (rounded to an even dollar amount) on a $150,000, 30-year mortgage at various interest rates are listed as follows.

Interest Rate	Monthly Payment
4%	$716
5%	$805
6%	$899
7%	$998
8%	$1,101

A higher interest rate not only increases the amount of your monthly mortgage, but also adds thousands of dollars to the total interest paid over the life of a loan. Interest rates can vary greatly from year to year. If you buy when interest rates are high, you may have to look at lower-priced homes. If you buy when interest rates are low, you may be able to afford a more expensive home.

When inflation is higher or expected to rise in the near future, mortgage rates will increase because the value of the dollar is decreasing at a higher rate. On the other hand, when the economy is in recession and homes sales are sluggish, interest rates fall. The financial crisis that started in late 2008 lead to a collapse in the housing market. Home prices dramatically fell, and interest rates fell to the lowest on record. The graph in Figure 13-2 shows the drop in interest rates as home sales remained sluggish for years after the start of the financial crisis.

The interest rate on a 30-year fixed rate mortgage dropped to a then record low of 3.53 percent on July 19, 2012. Unfortunately, not all potential homebuyers can qualify for the best rates. Your credit score is one of the most significant factors in determining the interest rate you get.

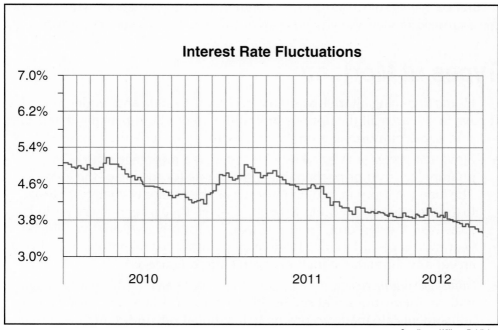

Goodheart-Willcox Publisher

Figure 13-2 Interest rate pattern on 30-year fixed rate mortgages can fluctuate regularly.

Ethics

In an effort to make a sale, some homeowners may be tempted not to mention defects in the home. If you bought a home and discovered that the seller did not disclose all defects, you will probably have grounds for a lawsuit against the seller. It is unethical to sell a home and not disclose material defects to the buyer. All material defects should be noted in the seller's property disclosure and posted on the MLS (multiple listing service) listing of the house.

Term of the Loan

Interest is a factor of time. The longer you finance your home, the more interest you will pay over the term of the loan. Historically, the 30-year mortgage has been the most popular. However, taking out a mortgage for a shorter period means that you do not have the use of the lender's money as long; therefore, you get a better interest rate.

For example, assume Becky and James Quinn are borrowing $150,000 to purchase their first home. They have been quoted a rate of 4.00 percent on a 30-year mortgage and 3.25 percent on a 15-year mortgage. Figure 13-3 compares the monthly payment and total interest paid on the two loans.

As you can see, a 30-year mortgage results in monthly principal and interest payments of $716. Over the life of the loan, however, a total of $107,805 in interest will be paid. The $1,054 monthly payment with the 15-year mortgage is substantially higher. However, over the life of the loan, only $39,721 in interest will be paid. As a result, the 15-year mortgage will save Becky and James $68,084 ($107,805 − $39,721) in interest.

Most lenders offer a variety of terms you can choose for your mortgage. In addition to the two most popular terms, 30-year and 15-year, other common terms offered are 10-year, 20-year, and 25-year. Each borrower must decide which type of mortgage works best for him or her.

Property Taxes and Insurance

When you buy a home, you will have to pay real estate taxes and property insurance premiums. Rather than paying these expenses separately, you can choose to have an escrow account set up and pay them as a part of your monthly mortgage payment. An **escrow account** is an account for holding money in trust for others. With a mortgage, the lender sets up an escrow account for you. You pay part of your insurance and taxes each month along with your mortgage payment. That way, you save gradually for the cost of taxes and insurance instead of making a lump sum payment. The lender will then take the escrowed money and pay your taxes and insurance when they are due.

Types of Mortgages

Home financing alternatives vary from state to state and lender to lender. It pays to research all the options to find the method of financing that is best for you. Types of mortgages on the market today include the following.

- *Fixed rate mortgage.* A **fixed rate mortgage** is a mortgage with a guaranteed fixed or unchanging interest rate for the life of the loan. The loan rate does not go up or down as the economy changes. These loans are normally written with 20-, 25-, or 30-year repayment periods. However, shorter term, fixed rate loans are another alternative. Fifteen-year mortgages dramatically increase monthly payments, but they bring an equally dramatic reduction in total interest charges.

- *Adjustable rate mortgage.* An **adjustable rate mortgage (ARM)** is a mortgage with an interest rate that can be adjusted up or down periodically. The adjustments are made according to a national rate index and other predetermined factors. These loans are often offered at lower interest rates than fixed rate mortgages. However, borrowers take the risk that interest rates and loan payments will increase when adjustments are made.

Mortgage Rates					
Term of Loan	Amount of Loan	Rate	Monthly Payment	Total Payments	Total Interest
30-Year	$150,000	4.00%	$716	$257,805	$107,805
15-Year	$150,000	3.25%	$1,054	$189,721	$39,721

Goodheart-Willcox Publisher

Figure 13-3 A 15-year mortgage can save money over a 30-year mortgage.

- *Graduated payment mortgage.* A **graduated payment mortgage** is a mortgage that allows the buyer to pay low monthly payments at first and higher payments in the future. It has the advantage of low monthly payments in the early years of the loan. Those who take this type of mortgage generally expect their earnings to increase.

- *Subprime mortgage.* A **subprime mortgage** is a mortgage made by lenders who charge higher than prime rates to borrowers who have poor or no credit ratings. Often, these borrowers do not qualify for mortgages from other lenders. Subprime lenders often bundle these mortgages together and sell them to financial institutions that are willing to absorb the risks.

- *Home equity loan.* A **home equity loan**, also called a *second mortgage*, is a type of loan in which the borrower uses the equity in his or her home as collateral for the loan. As you learned earlier, equity is the difference between a home's market value and the amount the homeowner still owes on the loan. These loans can be used by homeowners to pay for home improvements, vacations, college costs, and other debts, such as medical bills and credit cards. In a home equity loan, the home serves as collateral. If the homeowner cannot repay the debt, the lender can repossess the home. Therefore, homeowners should use care in taking out these loans.

Andy Dean Photography/Shutterstock.com

First-time buyer programs provide assistance, reduced down payments, and tax benefits to eligible buyers purchasing a first home.

Government-Sponsored Financing Programs

Several government programs encourage home ownership. Some of these programs are described as follows.

- *First-time homebuyer programs.* First-time homebuyer programs provide buyers with assistance, including financial incentives, to buy a home. These incentives include reduced down payments, tax breaks, and lowered requirements for obtaining credit.

- *FHA-insured loans.* An FHA-insured loan is guaranteed by the Federal Housing Administration (FHA) and helps people with low and moderate incomes purchase homes. The FHA makes no loans, but it insures lenders against borrowers' defaults. The maximum loan amounts are determined by a formula based on average cost of homes in the area. Down payment for FHA-insured loans can be as low as 3 percent. Borrowers can take up to 30 years to repay. Interest rates may be lower than for conventional loans because the government insures the lender. The home being bought and certain loan terms must meet FHA standards.

- *VA-guaranteed loans.* A VA-guaranteed loan is insured by the Veterans Administration. Only veterans of the US Armed Forces are eligible for these loans. They are long-term, fixed rate mortgages. The Veterans Administration sets rates. There are no down payment requirements. Interest rates usually are lower than the current market rate. Borrowers can take up to 30 years to repay.

Consult a lawyer before signing any home financing agreement. Small mistakes can have big consequences.

Shopping for a Mortgage

Consumers can take steps to ensure that they are eligible for the best loan terms, including the lowest interest rates, when they are ready to buy. The key is maintaining the highest credit score possible. As discussed in Chapter 6, lenders look at credit reports and credit scores to evaluate the creditworthiness of loan applicants. Consumers with higher scores are offered the most favorable financing terms, including lower interest rates.

In the years leading up to buying a home, consumers can take steps to boost their credit scores. These steps include the following.

- Maintain steady employment.
- Establish a credit history by using credit wisely.
- Pay bills and taxes on time.
- Repay car loans, student loans, and other debts on schedule.
- Guard your financial information to avoid identity theft.
- Check your credit reports regularly.

As discussed earlier in the text, you are entitled to one free copy of your credit report from each of the three major credit reporting agencies each year. If you find inaccuracies, have them corrected. Fixing problems on your credit report can be time consuming, but it can raise your credit score.

Loan Officers

Loan officers work for financial institutions. They assist in gathering documentation that is needed for loan approval. They analyze and assess the creditworthiness of potential borrowers to determine if they qualify for a loan.

You Do the Math

It is important to understand the terms of a mortgage and how much it will cost. One way to calculate the total interest charged over the lifetime of a loan is to follow these steps:

1. Multiply the amount of monthly payment times 12 months in a year times the number of years of the loan.

2. Subtract the answer from the original amount of the loan. The difference will be the total amount of interest paid.

Complete the Following Problem

Perry and Susan obtained a mortgage for $250,000. Their monthly payment will be $998 for 30 years. How much interest will they pay over the life of the

When you are ready to shop for a mortgage, shop carefully and ask questions. Sources of home loans include commercial banks, savings banks, mortgage companies, and credit unions. It pays to be thorough. Shop at least three sources to compare rates and terms.

Nationwide mortgage search services report on mortgage terms and availability in different localities. Quotes are also available online. These services or a licensed mortgage broker might help you. Using a computerized program, they can help find the best mortgage package for your situation.

When you apply for a mortgage, the lender will ask detailed questions related to your financial circumstances. You should be prepared with facts and figures, as shown in Figure 13-4.

When you shop for home financing, the terms you are quoted often apply only at the time you apply for the mortgage. These terms may change by the time your mortgage is approved. You may want to ask for a mortgage lock-in, sometimes called a *rate lock* or *rate commitment*. This is a promise from the lender to honor the quoted rates and terms while your application is being processed.

FYI

According to Bankrate, Inc., borrowers with credit scores above 760 get the best rates. However, those with credit scores under 500 may not be able to qualify for a mortgage.

Items Lenders Require with an Application for a Mortgage Loan
• Income tax returns
• Paycheck stubs
• Employment information
• Property listing with a legal description
• Savings account records
• Real estate sales contract
• Debt history
• Application fee

Goodheart-Willcox Publisher

Figure 13-4 This chart lists some of the information lenders will require to process a loan application.

Closing

After the seller accepts a buyer's offer, both parties set a deadline to finalize the sale of the home. This is called the *closing date*. On this day, the buyer, seller, lender's representative, real estate agents, and sometimes attorneys for the buyer or seller meet to sign documents and to settle all outstanding matters. The buyer gives the seller a certified check for the down payment. Other fees must be paid.

Before the closing date, the buyer must obtain a mortgage, a process that can take weeks or sometimes months. The lender investigates the buyer's credit history and the property itself.

A **closing cost** is a fee or settlement charge that must be paid before the sale of a home is final. As of January 1, 2010, the US Department of Housing and Urban Development (HUD) requires lenders and brokers to give homebuyers a standard *good faith estimate (GFE)* when they apply for a mortgage. This form clearly states important loan terms and closing costs. It makes it easy to compare from lender to lender the actual and estimated costs of obtaining a mortgage and closing on the purchase of a home. The good faith estimate will include fees for many of the following services.

- *Points.* A **point** is an amount that is charged by lenders at closing and equals one percent of the mortgage. Most lenders charge one to four points. Four points on a $100,000 mortgage comes to $4,000. It may be possible to negotiate for a lower rate of interest if you are willing to pay more points at the time of purchase. Find out how many points different lenders charge.

AVAVA/Shutterstock.com

Making an additional mortgage payment each year allows homeowners to save money in interest payments.

Careers in Marketing

What Do Real Estate Agents Do?

Real estate agents help clients buy, sell, and rent properties. **Real estate agents** work through real estate brokers who are licensed to manage their own real estate businesses. Most **real estate agents** sell residential property. However, some sell commercial, industrial, agricultural, or other types of property. **Real estate agents** typically:

- solicit clients to buy, sell, and rent properties;
- help sellers set the price of a property;
- advise clients on mortgages and market conditions;
- take prospective buyers or renters to see properties;
- promote properties through open houses, advertising, and listing services;
- prepare documents, such as purchase offers; and
- attend closings with clients.

What Is It Like to Work as a Real Estate Agent?

Real estate agents often work more than 40 hours a week. They often have irregular schedules that include evenings and weekends. However, most are able to set their own schedules. The majority, if not all, of their earnings comes from commissions. As a result, earnings can fluctuate widely each year.

According to the Bureau of Labor Statistics, the majority of **real estate agents** are self-employed. This means they get no expense reimbursements and are fully responsible for their own income taxes and payroll taxes.

What Education and Skills Are Needed to Be a Real Estate Agent?

- high school diploma or equivalent
- real estate license
- must be 18 years old
- must be able to work independently
- strong interpersonal and communication skills
- selling skills
- problem-solving skills
- negotiation skills

- *Property survey.* A **property survey** is a map of the property drawn by a surveyor to show size, boundaries, and characteristics of a property. Lenders usually require a survey to make sure the building is on the land according to its legal description. It is normally the seller's responsibility to hire a surveyor and pay for a survey.

- *Appraisal.* An **appraisal** is a written estimate of the value of the real estate. The buyer usually pays the appraisal fee. Before approving a mortgage loan, the lender will usually require an appraisal. It helps the lender decide if the home is worth its price and if the mortgage is a good investment.

- *Title search and title insurance.* A **title** is a legal document that proves ownership of property. An *abstract of title* is a summary of the public records regarding the ownership of a property. The buyer should have an attorney or title insurance company review the abstract of title to be sure that the seller is the legal owner and that the property is free of debts or title problems. The title company also offers **title insurance,** which is a type of insurance that protects the buyer if problems with the title arise after the purchase. The buyer usually pays the title search fee and the one-time fee for title insurance.

- *Recording the deed.* Recording fees must be paid to record the deed. This document transfers the ownership of the property from the seller to the buyer.

- *Credit report.* Credit report fees are charged to the borrower. When someone applies for a mortgage, the lender orders the borrower's credit report and/or credit score.

- *Loan application.* Loan application fees are charged by most lenders to process new loan applications.

Other expenses due at or after closing are commissions paid to real estate brokers and fees for attorneys' services. Some lenders require buyers to set up escrow accounts to cover real estate taxes and property insurance.

Saving Money on Your Mortgage

You have already heard that you can save money you pay on a mortgage by making a bigger down payment or by locking in a low interest rate. Other strategies include the following.

- *Avoid paying private mortgage insurance (PMI).* As discussed earlier in the chapter, most lenders require PMI if the borrower is unable to make a 20 percent down payment. PMI can add as much as $50 a month to the mortgage payment. One strategy to avoid PMI is a piggyback loan. With a piggyback loan, the borrower takes out two loans simultaneously. One loan is for 80 percent of a home's value, and the other loan is to make up for whatever cash is lacking for a 20 percent down payment.

- *Make an additional mortgage payment each year.* This can result in thousands of dollars of interest savings because the loan will be paid off early. (The shorter the term of a loan, the lower the amount of interest paid.)

- *Pay additional amounts against the principal.* This will reduce the cost of the loan. Many loans are structured so that the bulk of the early loan payments go toward the finance charges. When you pay an additional amount on the principal, you reduce the amount on which the interest

The US Department of Housing and Urban Development (HUD) has free state-by-state information on buying a home. HUD also sponsors housing counseling agencies throughout the country to provide free or low-cost advice.

charge is based. This practice will not reduce the amount of your monthly payment, but you can pay the loan off years early.

- *Consider an adjustable rate mortgage.* If you will move within a few years, it may be wise to look to the adjustable rate mortgage. This mortgage usually is available at lower rates than long-term, fixed rate mortgages. If you plan to live in a home for many years, the long-term, fixed rate mortgage may be a better choice if rates are low at the time of purchase.

- *Refinance your mortgage.* If interest rates drop below the rate you obtained for your mortgage, you may want to refinance your mortgage. Refinancing at a lower rate can save you money on monthly payments. However, refinancing costs extra money for closing costs, points, and so forth. You only want to refinance if the savings are more than the costs.

Checkpoint 13.2

1. What four factors determine the amount of a monthly home mortgage payment?
2. Why is the interest rate on a 15-year mortgage lower than the rate on a 30-year mortgage?
3. What risk does a buyer take with an adjustable rate mortgage?
4. What buyers are eligible for a VA-guaranteed loan?
5. What are four sources of a home mortgage?

Build Your Vocabulary

As you progress through this course, develop a personal glossary of personal finance terms and add it to your portfolio. This will help you build your vocabulary and prepare you for a career. Write a definition for each of the following terms and add it to your personal finance glossary.

mortgage	home equity loan
amortization	closing cost
private mortgage insurance (PMI)	point
escrow account	property survey
fixed rate mortgage	appraisal
adjustable rate mortgage (ARM)	title
graduated payment mortgage	title insurance
subprime mortgage	

Chapter Summary

Section 13.1 Buying a Home

- Selecting your first home is an important decision. Single-family residences are built in a variety of ways, so consider all of your options.
- Buying a home involves many considerations and decisions. You must find a home you want, perhaps with the help of a real estate agent, and make an offer. You may sign a purchase agreement, pay earnest money to the seller, and arrange for an inspection of the home.

Section 13.2 Financing a Home

- A mortgage is a type of secured loan used for buying property. The borrower promises to repay the lender the loan amount plus interest. The mortgage is paid in monthly installments over a set number of years with the home serving as collateral for the loan.
- Home financing alternatives vary from state to state and lender to lender. Types of mortgages include a fixed rate mortgage, an adjustable rate mortgage, a graduated payment mortgage, and a subprime mortgage. A home equity loan, also called a *second mortgage*, is another type of loan.
- Several government programs encourage home ownership. Some of these programs are first-time homebuyer programs, FHA-insured loans, and VA-guaranteed loans.
- When you are ready to shop for a mortgage, carefully compare rates and terms for at least three sources. Sources of home loans include commercial banks, savings banks, mortgage companies, and credit unions.
- After the seller accepts a buyer's offer, the parties set a closing date. On this day, the buyer, seller, lender, and real estate agents meet to sign documents and to settle all outstanding matters. This process is called *closing*.
- You can save money you pay on a mortgage by making a bigger down payment or by locking in a low interest rate. There are also other ways to save, such as avoiding paying private mortgage insurance, making an additional mortgage payment each year, and refinancing when terms are favorable.

Check Your Personal Finance IQ

Now that you have finished the chapter, see what you learned about personal finance by taking the chapter posttest. If you do not have a smartphone, visit the G-W Learning companion website.

G-W Learning mobile site: www.m.g-wlearning.com

G-W Learning companion website: www.g-wlearning.com

Review Your Knowledge

1. How much commission do brokers and agents usually receive for their services? Who pays the commission?

2. What is the purpose of a contingency clause in a contract? Give one example of a contingency clause.

3. If problems are found during a home inspection, what remedies might the buyer request?

4. Suppose you make an offer to buy a house and give the seller earnest money. What happens to the earnest money if you later decide not to buy the house? What happens to the earnest money if you do buy the house?

5. What percent of gross monthly income do most lenders allow for mortgage, property tax, and home insurance payments?

6. What federal law requires the automatic termination of PMI when the equity in the home reaches 22 percent of the property's value at the time the mortgage was taken?

7. What is a mortgage lock-in?

8. Why do lenders require a survey of property?

9. What is the purpose of a property appraisal?

10. What is an abstract of title and why should the buyer view the abstract of title before purchasing a property?

Apply Your Knowledge

11. How would you prefer to finance a home if you were buying today? Why?

12. What type of mortgage do you consider to be the most advantageous? Why?

13. Why do you think most mortgage lenders require a significant down payment?

14. Suppose you are applying for a home loan for $125,000. The lending agent you are working with stated that an adjustable rate mortgage (ARM) would give you the lowest possible monthly payment during the first three years for the mortgage. Would you consider an ARM? Why or why not?

15. Assume you are taking out a mortgage and you are given the option of escrowing your insurance and property taxes or paying them separately. Which method would you choose? Why?

16. Assume you are into your fifth year of a 30-year mortgage and you decide you want to pay off the loan early. What steps would you take?

17. What could you do to avoid paying for private mortgage insurance if you do not have the required 20 percent down payment on a property you are buying?

18. Assume you are buying a house. You have been quoted a $674 monthly payment on 30-year mortgage and a $986 monthly payment on a 15-year mortgage. Assuming you can afford the higher payment, which option would you choose? Why?

19. Would you use the equity in your home to finance a new car? Why or why not?

20. What do you think is the best way to save money when shopping for a mortgage?

Teamwork

Working with your team, survey several realtors and home mortgage lenders. Find out the range of current interest rates, what is required to qualify for a mortgage, and what forms of financing most buyers are using to purchase homes. Create a chart to compare and contrast your findings and share with your class.

G-W Learning Mobile Site

Visit the G-W Learning mobile site to complete the chapter pretest and posttest and to practice vocabulary using e-flash cards. If you do not have a smartphone, visit the G-W Learning companion website to access these features.

G-W Learning mobile site: www.m.g-wlearning.com

G-W Learning companion website: www.g-wlearning.com

College and Career Readiness

Common Core

CTE Career Ready Practices. Making small improvements in the way things are done can bring about great benefits in your personal life and in your career. Do an Internet search for the phrase *buying your first house.* Review the information that is provided. How do you think you could improve the suggested process of buying your first house?

Reading. Go to a real estate site that sells homes in your neighborhood. Choose three house listings and read each posting carefully. Create a Venn diagram that shows the characteristics of each property, the cost, and any other information that is important to making a decision. If you were in a position to buy a house, which one of the three would you choose?

Writing. Interview a real estate agent in your area. Ask that person what he or she likes best and least about the job as well as several other questions of your own. Write a one-page paper describing what you learned from the interview.

Web Connect

Use the Internet to investigate housing issues in your area to learn what is being done about housing for low- and middle-income families, problems of the homeless, and zoning for different types of housing.

College and Career Readiness

College and Career Readiness Portfolio

Your portfolio should not only showcase your academic accomplishments but also the technical skills and talents you have. Are you exceptionally good at working with computers? Do you have a talent for playing a musical instrument? Technical skills and talents are very important. Interviewers will want to know what talents and skills you have.

1. Write a paper that describes the technical skills or talents you have acquired. Describe the skill or talent, your level of competence, and any other information that will showcase your skill level.
2. Save the document file in your e-portfolio folder using an appropriate filename.
3. Place a printed copy in your container for your print portfolio.

Role-Play and Interview

Some competitive events for Career and Technical Student Organization (CTSOs) require that entrants complete a role-play or interview. Those who participate will be provided information about a situation and given time to practice. A judge or panel of judges will review the presentations or conduct the interview.

To prepare for the role-play or interview event, complete the following activities.

1. Read the guidelines provided by your organization.
2. Visit the organization's website and look for role-play and interview events that were used in previous years. Many organizations post these events for students to use as practice for future competitions. Also, look for the evaluation criteria or rubric for the event. This will help you determine what the judge will be looking for in your presentation.
3. Practice in front of a mirror. Are you comfortable speaking without reading directly from your notes?
4. Ask a friend or an instructor to listen to your presentation or conduct an interview. Give special attention to your posture and how you present yourself. Concentrate on the tone of voice. Be pleasant and loud enough to hear, but do not shout. Make eye contact with the listener. Do not stare, but engage the person's attention.
5. After you have made your presentation, ask for constructive feedback.

Chapter 14

Transportation

Whether you drive the family car, buy or lease your own car, or ride a bus, you will do a lot of traveling over the years. Americans spend billions of dollars each year on transportation. You personally will spend thousands of dollars transporting yourself in your lifetime.

In the United States, the car is the most widely used form of transportation. If you plan to own a car, you will face many decisions. This chapter presents information on choosing, paying for, insuring, and maintaining a car. Since cars are not the answer to everyone's transportation needs, public transit, bicycles, mopeds, and motorcycles will also be covered.

Focus on Finance

Fuel Efficiency

Fuel economy is a topic on everyone's mind. Gasoline prices continue to rise while resources decrease. Auto manufacturers continue to experiment with other sources of power to reduce dependence on fuel and to reduce carbon dioxide emissions.

Hybrid vehicles are autos that use two or more sources of power. Hybrids frequently combine a gasoline or diesel engine with an electric motor. The cars have a gas tank and small gasoline or diesel engine along with an electric motor powered by a battery. An onboard computer balances power between the gasoline engine and the electric motor, using both for high speeds and for heavy acceleration.

Neighborhood electric vehicles (NEVs) are powered by electricity and used for short distances at speeds not exceeding 25 to 30 miles per hour. These vehicles are particularly useful in small communities.

The US government is also helping to promote fuel efficiency. For vehicles manufactured in the 2011 model year, fuel efficiency standards were raised for the first time in over 20 years. In the past, passenger cars were required to meet a standard of 24.1 mpg (miles per gallon). Vehicles in the 2011 model year had to meet 30.2 mpg. By 2020, passenger cars will be required to meet at least 35 mpg.

Reading Prep. Before reading this chapter, review the objectives. Based on this information, write down two or three items that you think are important to note while you are reading.

College and Career Readiness

Check Your Personal Finance IQ

 Before you begin the chapter, see what you already know about personal finance by taking the chapter pretest. If you do not have a smartphone, visit the G-W Learning companion website.

G-W Learning mobile site: www.m.g-wlearning.com

G-W Learning companion website: www.g-wlearning.com

Sections

Section 14.1 Transportation Choices

Section 14.2 Finding and Financing an Automobile

Section 14.3 Consumer Protection and Responsibility

Objectives

After studying this section, you will be able to:

- Identify various types of transportation.
- Explain how to evaluate transportation choices.

Terms

mass transit

commuter service

moped

motor scooter

Forms of Transportation

Transportation is a necessity of life. Individuals must have transportation to get to and from work, to shop, to receive health-care services, for leisure, and for education. The transportation choices open to you depend partly on where you live. In most urban and suburban communities, you will be able to choose from several forms of public and private transportation. *Public transportation* is any form of transportation that charges set fares, runs a fixed schedule, and is available to the general public. *Private transportation* is any form of transportation that you control and is not available to the general public. You may have access to buses, trains, subways, and taxis. In rural areas, riding a bike or taking the school bus may be the only alternatives to driving a car. Whatever way you choose to get from here to there, it pays to look carefully at the advantages and disadvantages of each option.

Mass Transit

In urban areas, large cities and their suburbs, residents often rely on mass transit for their major transportation needs. **Mass transit** is public transportation where a large number of people can travel at the same time. Examples include airplanes, buses, trains, subways, and trolleys. Using mass transit usually costs less than owning a car, and for many it is the only choice. People who use public transit frequently can save money by purchasing transit fare cards if they are available. City governments favor mass transit over cars because a large number of people moving together reduces congestion, pollution, and accidents.

Some mass transit systems cater mainly to *commuters,* or people who must travel some distance between home and work. A **commuter service** is a type of mass transit that runs mainly during business hours. Most commuter services rely on trains. Commuter trains include those that run on traditional above ground tracks and those that use underground subway lines. Some waterside areas, such as New York, San Francisco, and Puget Sound in Washington state, also have ferryboat services for passengers, cars, and some types of freight.

bikeriderlondon/Shutterstock.com

Using a taxi can be a convenient option for transportation, especially in areas where parking is limited.

The quality, cost, safety, and reliability of mass transit systems vary from city to city. One of the major advantages of using public transportation is freedom from car ownership responsibilities. In the city, a car can be a nuisance as well as an expense because of heavy traffic and limited parking areas.

On the downside, it may be difficult to match your travel schedule with the transit schedule. Unless you plan carefully, you may waste a lot of time waiting for the bus or train. If public transit is not within walking distance, you may have to drive or be driven to the station. You may also have to pay to park at the stop or station. If you use mass transit during rush hours, it can be difficult to find a seat. If you travel during off hours or late into the night, there may be safety concerns connected with using public transit.

According to the International Association of Public Transport, public transportation offers many advantages over other forms of transportation. Those advantages are listed in Figure 14-1.

Public Transportation
• Costs less to the community
• Needs less urban space
• Is less energy-intensive
• Pollutes less
• Is the safest mode
• Improves accessibility to jobs
• Offers mobility for all

Source: International Association of Public Transport
Goodheart-Willcox Publisher

Figure 14-1 Public transportation has many advantages for the consumer.

Taxicabs

Taxicabs offer door-to-door service with no parking problems and no car ownership responsibilities. However, using taxis on a regular basis is very costly. It can also be difficult to find a taxi during rush hours or in bad weather. For most consumers, taxis are not a reliable, affordable form of transportation.

Cars and Other Passenger Vehicles

Cars and similar vehicles, such as trucks, vans, and sport-utility vehicles (SUVs), are the preferred answer to the transportation needs for most Americans. Many people take pride and pleasure in owning a car. When you drive your own car, you can come and go as you please. If your work involves time on the road, having your own car may be a necessity.

Although a car is a convenient and comfortable form of transportation, it is also a major responsibility and expense. The purchase price of a car is only the beginning. Other expenses include insurance, licensing, maintenance, fuel, and parking. In some urban areas, parking and traffic problems are serious enough to make owning a car more trouble than it is worth.

A carpool is economical for people who come from and go to the same places at the same times. Carpooling can save energy, minimize parking problems, and reduce traffic congestion. During times of particularly high gas prices, such as in 2008 and 2012 when the cost of regular gas exceeded $4.00 a gallon, carpooling can save a significant amount of money. Carpooling can also reduce repairs because of the reduced use of your car. You can also take advantage of the high occupancy vehicle (HOV) lane offered in many large cities. HOV lanes typically have fewer cars, so the traffic moves more quickly than it does in the other lanes.

Carpooling can have drawbacks. Some may find carpooling inconvenient. Since the needs of other riders must always be considered, carpooling offers only limited flexibility. Also, it does not provide an answer to transportation needs outside the pooling situation.

Two-Wheelers

Two-wheelers may offer adequate transportation in some situations. Riding a bicycle, moped, or motorcycle can be a convenient and economical way to get around. Two-wheelers conserve energy, require little parking space, and are easy to maneuver in traffic. Bicycles are pollution-free, and

According to the Surface Transportation Policy Partnership, most American families spend more on driving than on health care, education, or food. The average American spends 18 cents out of every dollar on transportation, making it second only to housing as the largest household expense. The vast majority of that spending, 98 percent, is for the purchase, operation, and maintenance of automobiles.

Go Green

Today's meaning of a *green car* is not a car that is painted green. A green car is a car with fewer emissions and greater fuel efficiency, and it is friendlier to the environment than other cars. Hybrid vehicles are the most popular form of green vehicles. A greater number of totally electric vehicles are being produced; however, their popularity substantially trails hybrids.

powered cycles use less fuel and pollute less than cars and other passenger vehicles.

A major disadvantage of two-wheelers is the high accident rate, particularly on highways and in heavy traffic. Riding a bike, moped, or motorcycle safely requires special skill, constant attention, and appropriate safety equipment. This type of transportation is also uncomfortable in bad weather and inconvenient if you need to carry passengers, baggage, or supplies.

If you can satisfy part or all your transportation needs with a two-wheeler, there are many choices to consider. Bicycles, scooters, mopeds, and motorcycles come in many styles and sizes. Choose your two-wheeler according to how you will use it, what size and style you prefer, and how much money you have to spend.

Bicycles

Bicycles are the most energy efficient means of transportation and cost less than most motorized two-wheeler vehicles. People who bike rather than drive, just for trips of three miles or less, save sizable amounts each year in fuel costs and reduce pollution. With worldwide environmental concerns, many countries and some major cities in the United States are working to make cycling a convenient and safe alternative to driving an automobile. Cycling also offers pleasure and fitness advantages.

If you can use a bicycle for some or most of your transportation needs, finding the right bike is the first step. The many types and styles from which to choose can be overwhelming unless you know exactly what you want. If you plan to invest a sizable amount in a bicycle you hope to ride often and for many years, buy from a reliable bike or sports shop. If you are already knowledgeable about bikes, you may want to shop for one at a superstore, a discount store, or online. You can find used bikes for sale in classified listings, auctions, house sales, and bike shops.

Bike prices range from under $200 to $5,000, depending on a bike's type, style, and performance. Special features can be expensive, so weigh the benefits against their costs. Expect to pay a considerable amount for a top-of-the-line bike in any category. You might find a good used bike for much less if you shop carefully. Remember to include the cost of accessories in your budget. These extras can add up, and prices vary from dealer to dealer.

Mopeds and Motor Scooters

Mopeds and motor scooters may be either gas powered or electric. These low-powered vehicles can be an efficient, economical means of transportation and are suited to local riding for short distances.

If buying a moped or motor scooter, check state and local laws on insurance, permits, licensing, and rules of the road. The technical definition of low-powered cycles varies from state to state. Generally, a **moped** is a motorized two-wheeler with an engine capacity less than 50cc. The vehicle may or may not have pedals in addition to the motor. Top speed is about 25 miles per hour, and the vehicle is suitable only for off-highway riding. A **motor scooter** is a two-wheeled motor vehicle with an engine capacity of 50cc to 250cc. It is larger than a moped. It typically reaches speeds of 30 to 40 miles per hour and is designed primarily for off-highway riding.

Ethics

To make a sale, some car sellers—both dealers and private sellers—fail to disclose to potential buyers all known defects in a vehicle. It is unethical for a seller to sell any vehicle without disclosing to the buyer all known defects. In most states, car sellers are legally liable to the buyer if it can be established that known defects were either covered up or undisclosed.

Motorcycles

Over six million Americans choose a motorcycle for transportation and riding pleasure. There are several basic models; each model is designed for a different type of cycling. Visit a dealership or go online to compare models. A motorcycle averages 35 to 60 highway miles per gallon and costs relatively little to drive. However, insurance is essential and will be expensive. Since motorcycles are considered a greater risk than cars, insurance companies charge higher premiums. The types of insurance coverage offered is similar to that provided by auto insurance. Motorcycle licensing, registration, and traffic laws vary from state to state. For example, some states require cycle drivers to wear helmets and other states do not. A good helmet is a safety necessity whether required by law or not.

When shopping for a motorcycle, check out the dealers as you would car dealers. The cost of a motorcycle can be substantial, ranging from $5,000 to $25,000. Visit several dealers and test drive different makes and models. You should feel comfortable and confident riding the bike you buy.

Evaluating the Choices

One person's ideal means of transportation may not work for the next person. As you consider your transportation alternatives, follow these guidelines.

- *Determine transportation needs.* Where do you live? Where must you go? When and how often do you need to travel?

- *Identify available choices.* Do you have access to mass transit? Could you join or form a carpool? Do you own a bicycle, moped, or motorcycle you

TonyV3112/Shutterstock.com

A scooter or motorcycle is an economical choice of transportation which requires less fuel than a car.

can use to get around? Can you walk to most of the places you need to go? Is a family car available to you? Would buying or leasing a car be a practical and affordable alternative?

- *Compare costs.* What are the daily, weekly, and monthly fares for public transportation? Can you afford to own and maintain a car? How much would it cost to carpool?

- *Consider comfort and convenience.* Is public transportation close to your home? Will it take you where you want to go? Is it reliable and safe? Does it run at convenient times? If you drive your own car, would there be a problem with traffic and parking? Would the weather permit you to ride a bicycle, moped, or motorcycle?

- *Consider safety.* What is the safety record of the mass transit system? Would you feel safe getting on and off or waiting at the transit stop during the hours you travel? If driving, would you have to travel on congested highways during rush hours? Is your car, bicycle, moped, or motorcycle equipped with important safety features?

- *Consider personal preferences.* Do you want a car of your own? Would you rather not have the responsibilities and expenses of car ownership? Do you prefer public transportation to driving your own car?

Checkpoint 14.1

1. List three forms of mass transit systems.
2. What is a major advantage of using public transportation?
3. Are taxicabs a form of mass transit? Explain.
4. What is the preferred means of transportation for most Americans?
5. What is an advantage of using two-wheel vehicles? What is a disadvantage of using two-wheel vehicles?

Build Your Vocabulary

As you progress through this course, develop a personal glossary of personal finance terms and add it to your portfolio. This will help you build your vocabulary and prepare you for a career. Write a definition for each of the following terms and add it to your personal finance glossary.

mass transit   moped

commuter service   motor scooter

Objectives

After studying this section, you will be able to:

- Evaluate types of car sellers.
- Evaluate car makes and models.
- Identify sources of information you can use when shopping for a pre-owned car.
- Identify common costs associated with buying and maintaining a car.
- Describe the final four-point check.
- Identify sources for financing a car.

Terms

certified used car	vehicle identification number (VIN)
bill of sale	down payment
option	depreciation

Automobile Marketplace

The way people acquire autos has changed dramatically in the past few years. Traditional auto dealerships have become more user friendly as a result of competition from auto superstores and the Internet. The result is a competitive market and a confusing array of ways and places to look for the car of your choice. All of this can work to your advantage.

Traditional Dealerships

Traditional dealerships usually represent one or two manufacturers and sell new and used cars. Many dealerships, as well as auto manufacturers and superstores, sell certified used cars with full warranties. Certified used cars provide some buyer protection. A **certified used car** is a previously owned vehicle that has received a thorough mechanical and appearance inspection along with necessary repairs and replacements.

Most certified vehicles meet age and mileage restrictions. They pass inspections that include checks for damage, top-off of fluids, and repair or replacement of damaged parts. Once a vehicle passes this process, the dealer or manufacturer often extends the existing warranty or issues a new 12-month or 12,000-mile warranty.

Dealerships will offer financing and take your car as a trade-in if you have one. As you shop, check out the service department. Is it well-equipped and staffed with skilled, certified automotive technicians?

You can usually earn top dollar for a used car by selling it to another individual. However, if you plan to trade in a car, take time to research its resale value beforehand. Sources of information on used cars are given later in this chapter. Also, dealers will usually offer trade-in customers one price that includes the new car with the trade-in value subtracted. You will usually get a better deal if you negotiate separately on the price of your car and the price of the car you wish to buy.

On the Internet, you can find up-to-the-minute information on new and used vehicles, financing, and insurance, and compare different makes and models. Most manufacturers and many dealerships have online services. If you do not want to do your own shopping and bargaining, car-buying services, such as Autobytel and Autoweb, will find and price the car you want and put you in touch with a dealer near you.

Auto Superstores

Auto superstores sell both new and used vehicles that are inspected, serviced, and warranted. They typically carry huge used car inventories. Most superstores are computerized. You can enter into the system the type of vehicle you want, the price you are willing to pay, and other details, and the computer will locate cars in stock that meet your requirements. Prices are normally fixed. Financing, insurance, and auto servicing can be arranged as well as trade-ins if you own a car to trade.

Private Sellers or Auctions

Private sellers or auctions are other options if you are buying a used car. Normally, you receive no warranty coverage from private sellers unless the original warranty is still in force. Cars sold at auction are usually sold as is, which offers no protection if you later have problems with the vehicle. In these cases, you want to make very careful inspections and have the vehicle checked by an

Flashon Studio/Shutterstock.com

To select a car that is best for you, consider the size, safety features, fuel efficiency, and appearance when making comparisons.

independent, certified automotive technician. When buying a used car, always obtain a **bill of sale,** which is a legal document that spells out important features of the sale and transfers rights from the seller to the buyer.

Assessing Car Needs

It helps to enter the marketplace knowing what you want and how much you can afford. You will need to shop carefully to determine your preferences and match your car choice to your transportation needs and budget. Think about why you want a car and how you will use it. Is a car primarily a necessity, a convenience, or a pleasure? Will you drive mostly on city streets, in heavy traffic, on highways, or on rugged country roads? Will you travel short or long distances? Will you drive frequently or only occasionally?

Case Study

Choosing a Vehicle

David needs a car to carry supplies and equipment for his job as a painter. He has $2,000 cash to make a down payment. David makes the following list of his car needs:

- used, but in good condition
- large enough to carry paint, supplies, and equipment
- useful for personal driving
- fuel efficient
- sold by a reliable dealer or private seller
- equipped with good tires, air conditioning, a radio, and a luggage rack

David reads the classified ads in the local paper and online. He also visits several used car dealers. After test-driving several vehicles, he narrows his choices. One choice is a five-year-old van in good condition, but it is missing some of the features he wants. It would be perfect for his job needs but awkward for personal use. It comes with a warranty.

Another choice is a four-year-old station wagon. It is not in the best condition, but it costs only $1,500. This would leave him $500 to make improvements. It is adequate for both job and personal use, and it includes all the features he wants. However, an individual is selling it, so it has no warranty.

The third choice is a small wagon priced at $1,400. A reliable dealer is selling the car with a used-car warranty. The car has the features he wants and gets good gas mileage. The only drawback is its size. It is fine for personal driving, but it is a little small for his business needs. However, David can carry his extension ladder on the car's luggage rack, and he can squeeze everything else inside.

After much debating, David decides to buy the small wagon. It comes closest to meeting all his work and personal transportation needs.

Case Review

1. How do you think systematic decision-making helped David make a good choice?
2. How did David's list of goals help him make a decision?
3. What goals would you have if you were in the market for a car?
4. How can a list of goals help someone shop for cars and talk with car dealers?

You may want to rank certain car characteristics from most to least important in meeting your needs. For example, consider the importance of these items in evaluating a car for your use:

- size
- appearance and styling
- performance and handling
- safety record and features
- model or body type
- features and options
- fuel efficiency
- hybrid or standard
- domestic or imported
- warranty coverage

Plan to research online and make several shopping trips before you buy. This will let you become familiar with different makes and models, compare prices, and check out options without falling prey to high-pressure salespersons. Keep in mind that most new and used car prices are negotiable. As you research different cars, you may want to consult the following resources online and at local bookstores or libraries.

- *Kelley Blue Book* and *Edmunds* list the estimated resale value of new and used cars.
- *Official Used Car Guide* from the National Automobile Dealers Association lists general information on cars by the make, model, and year.
- Auto Safety Hot Line, a toll-free number, gives safety data on various car models from the National Highway Traffic Safety Administration. It should be listed in your local phone directory.
- Websites, such as Autobytel, Autotrader.com, Edmunds, Intellichoice, SmartMoney Auto Guide, and individual car manufacturers, provide new and used car information, such as pricing, safety, and more.
- Magazines, such as *Automobile Magazine, Car and Driver, Motor Trend,* and the auto issues of *Consumer Reports, Consumer Research,* and *Kiplinger's Magazine,* provide useful information on car buying and ownership.

Dispatchers
Dispatchers schedule and dispatch workers, equipment, or service vehicles to carry materials or passengers. Some dispatchers take calls for taxi companies, for example, or for police or ambulance assistance. They keep records, logs, and schedules of the calls that they receive and of the transportation vehicles that they monitor and control.

Size, Style, and Make

Cars come in a variety of standard sizes and styles. You can find compact, small, mid-size, and large cars in almost all styles and makes. Common styles or body types include two- and four-door sedans, station wagons, hatchbacks, convertibles, sport cars, pickups or light trucks, sport-utility vehicles (SUVs), mini-vans, and full-size vans. Consider how much space you will need for carrying passengers or cargo.

Options

An **option** is a feature available for a particular car. Some options contribute to safety, performance, and economy. Others are primarily for appearance and convenience. The chart in Figure 14-2 outlines common options and categorizes them according to purpose.

Common Options				
Safety options or features	• Air bags • Antilock brakes • Child restraint seats • Automatic restraint system • Alarm system • Rear wiper and defrost • Fog lights • Daytime running lights	**Convenience and preference options or features**	• Air conditioning • Sound system • Sunroof • Electronic instrument panel • Power seats • Intermittent windshield wipers • Rear wiper and defroster • Leather seats • Plush interior • Power mirror adjustment • Trip computer • Adjustable steering column • Adjustable ride control • Electronic vehicle monitor • GPS (global positioning system)	
Performance options or features	• Automatic transmission • Power steering • Front-wheel or four-wheel drive • Large engine • Cruise control			
Security options or features	• Antitheft alarm system • Single switch lock • Wireless cell phone connectivity • Remote keyless entry			

Goodheart-Willcox Publisher

Figure 14-2 These options or features are usually available at additional costs, although a few of these may be standard equipment for certain cars.

Standard options come at no additional cost. Different makes and models come with different sets of standard options or features. *Extra options* can add significantly to the price of a car.

Every year, manufacturers add to the available options or features on new cars. Very often, you will find option packages offered at special prices. Try not to pay for any options you do not really want and be sure you know the cost of each extra option.

Warranty

A car warranty is a written promise to the customer that should something break, malfunction, or otherwise go wrong with a vehicle within a stated period of time, the manufacturer will make necessary repairs at no cost. Normally, new cars carry full warranty protection on some parts and limited protection on others. Items such as the air conditioner, radio, and tires carry separate warranties. When shopping for a car, study the warranties to learn just what they cover and what you must do to receive warranty coverage.

Auto warranties usually run for three years or for the first 36,000 miles; however, some manufacturers offer much longer warranties. Most warranties set forth specific maintenance requirements the owner must meet during the warranty period. If the car needs any repairs during that time, they must be made by a factory-authorized service department to keep the warranty valid. However, routine maintenance may be done by an independent service center as long as the work and the parts meet specifications in the owner's manual.

If you want protection beyond the warranty period, you can buy an extended warranty from the manufacturer. You can also purchase a private used-car warranty. However, such warranties are often costly, and you should always totally understand the terms and limitations of one before you purchase.

Shopping for a Pre-Owned Car

If you buy a new car, your car loses 15 to 20 percent of its value when you drive it off the lot. This is not so with used or pre-owned cars. Used cars can be great bargains. However, buyers who do not do some research first can end up with a *lemon,* a car with serious problems that are costly to repair. Unscrupulous dealers and private sellers may hide problems so they can charge more money for a car. The tips in this section can help you get a good deal.

Buyers Guide Sticker

One source of information is the *Buyers Guide sticker*. The *Federal Trade Commission's Used Car Rule* requires a Buyers Guide sticker on the window of any used car sold by a dealer. This guide describes warranty coverage or lack of it. It directs the buyer to ask that all promises from the dealer be in writing.

The sticker suggests the buyer ask to have the vehicle inspected by an independent automotive technician. It also lists some major defects that may occur in used cars. Look up performance, safety, and service records for the make and model you are considering. The Federal Trade Commission's Used Car Rule is discussed in greater detail later in the chapter.

VIN Check

You can check the history of a used car online using its vehicle identification number (VIN). A **vehicle identification number (VIN)** is a unique number assigned by the automobile industry and used to identify an individual auto. An auto VIN will be found on the car dashboard, on a sticker on the driver's side doorjamb, and in the title documents of the car. The history report will include information on accidents, flood damage, theft, recalls, liens on the vehicle, odometer records, and manufacturing details.

To access the VIN history online, enter *VIN* in the search engine of your choice. You will find a number of websites that perform VIN searches. Fees range from about $15 to $30 for one report to $40 or more to check several cars. Generally, this is a good investment if you are buying a car.

Previous Owner

If you buy the car from the owner, ask a lot of questions. Normally you receive no warranty coverage, so it is important to learn all you can about the reliability of the car. Is the seller the original owner? Try to find out how the car was driven and maintained. Ask for service and other records on the car. If you buy from a car dealer, you can also ask for these records.

Estimating Car Costs

Before you make any commitments, it is important to be sure you can pay all the expenses associated with owning a car. The chart in Figure 14-3 outlines some of those expenses. The figures will vary from car to car, owner to owner, and area to area. You will need to estimate how the figures are likely to apply to you and how much money you can spend on car ownership expenses.

When buying a car, you need to consider both the purchase price and the ongoing costs of car ownership. This initial cost of a car is only the beginning. Most car buyers do not pay the full purchase price at once. They pay a portion of the purchase price, called a **down payment,** and take out a loan to pay for the balance. These buyers will make monthly payments on the auto loan that include interest charges until the loan is paid off. Taxes and fees are also paid when a car is purchased. These taxes and fees will be discussed later in the chapter.

Auto costs will also include many of these expenses:

- insurance premiums, usually paid monthly or semi-annually
- licensing and registration, usually paid annually
- operating costs, such as gasoline
- maintenance, such as oil changes, new batteries, new tires and tire rotations, car washes, and interior cleanings
- car repair costs, such as repairs to brakes, transmissions, etc.
- possibly parking

The worksheet shown in Figure 14-3 can help you figure annual costs of owning and operating a car. You may want to check *Consumer Reports* ownership costs ratings for different makes and models of cars.

Calculating the cost of gasoline can help you estimate the expenses associated with owning a car. Figure 14-4 illustrates how to calculate the cost of gas.

Car Ownership Costs		
Ownership costs		
Depreciation	$ _____	
Insurance	$ _____	
Sales tax	$ _____	
License and registration	$ _____	
Finance charges	$ _____	
Total ownership costs		$ _____
Operating costs		
Fuel and oil	$ _____	
Maintenance and repairs	$ _____	
Tires	$ _____	
Parking	$ _____	
City permits	$ _____	
Total operating costs		$ _____
Total annual car costs		
Costs per mile (Divide total annual costs by number of miles driven.)		$ _____

Goodheart-Willcox Publisher

Figure 14-3 This worksheet can help you calculate the annual costs of owning a car.

Calculating Gas Costs		
Starting with a full tank of fuel, record the mileage on the odometer. From that point on, record how many gallons of gasoline you buy, the price, and the odometer reading. Example:		
Full tank	Cost	Odometer 8,500
10 gallons	$35.00	Odometer 8,725
13 gallons	$46.15	Odometer 8,970
9 gallons	$31.32	Odometer 9,243
Total gallons = 32	Total cost = $112.47	Total miles = 743 (9,243 ÷ 8,500)
Miles per gallon: 743 miles ÷ 32 gallons = 23.22		
Cost of gas per mile: $112.47 ÷ 743 miles = 15 cents		

Goodheart-Willcox Publisher

Figure 14-4 Calculating the cost of gasoline can help you estimate the expenses associated with owning a car.

Depreciation

Depreciation is a major cost of car ownership. **Depreciation** is a decrease in the value of property as a result of use and age. It represents the difference between the amount you pay for the car and the amount you get for it when you sell it or trade it in for another car.

Although it is not an expense you actually pay, depreciation can represent a sizable amount of money, particularly if you buy a new car. For example, you buy a new car this year and plan to sell or trade it in three years. Its value is likely to drop by close to 50 percent. You lose less to depreciation if you buy a used car.

For first-time buyers, the used car market can be the best place to satisfy both budget and transportation needs. Used cars cost less to buy and to insure. They also depreciate more slowly. You can choose from a wide selection of makes, models, and sizes. Generally, it is a good idea to look for a two- to three-year-old car that has low mileage and is in good condition. It is a plus if the manufacturer's warranty is still in force.

What You Can Afford

Buying a car typically is not a spontaneous purchase. Many people save money for months and even years before they accumulate enough to buy a car.

To determine how much you can afford to spend on a car, start with the amount of cash you have on hand for a down payment and initial costs. If you own a car you can sell or trade, add its value to the amount you can spend. You will also need cash up front for licensing, registration, taxes, and insurance.

Next, determine how much you can spend each month to cover ongoing costs of car ownership. These costs will include fuel, maintenance, loan payments, insurance, parking, and an allowance for miscellaneous expenses.

A hybrid vehicle uses two types of energy—a conventional gasoline engine and a battery pack—that share the demand for power between these two sources. This sharing results in much better gas mileage than traditional gasoline powered vehicles. J.D. Power and Associates, an automotive research company, expects the amount of hybrid cars on the road to triple between 2012 and 2015.

Take a look at your overall income and expenses. Total your monthly income after deductions and subtract your total monthly expenses. You will need to pay monthly car costs out of the amount left. To buy the car you want, it may be necessary to increase your income or cut your spending in other areas. Figure 14-5 shows the 2012 average cost of driving common passenger vehicles.

Final Four-Point Check

After answering the many questions about car buying, you may be ready to zero in on the car of your choice. However, before you part with your money, take time to check the car over carefully—in the driver's seat, on the road, under the hood, and on paper.

In the Driver's Seat

Sit in the driver's seat and see if you are within comfortable reach of the steering wheel, foot pedals, and controls. Also check for good visibility. Make sure you can see well out the front, side, and rear windows. Check seat position and adjustments for comfort.

On the Road

Test-drive the car to see how well it handles in traffic, on the open road, and when starting, stopping, turning, and parking. Is it comfortable and easy to drive? Also test all the equipment and controls, such as the emergency brake, turn signals, horn, radio, windshield wipers, and headlights.

Under the Hood

A careful check of the engine and working parts of a car is particularly important when buying a used car. Unless you know all about cars, ask an independent, certified automotive technician to look under the hood with you.

Take an overall look at the engine. Check the levels of all the fluids—oil, water, brake, transmission, and power steering. If fluid levels are low, it could be a sign of leakage or of poor maintenance.

Environmental Engineers

Environmental engineers use the principles of science and chemistry to solve environmental problems. In the automotive industry, environmental engineers work to minimize the effects of automobile emissions on the environment by developing hybrid or alternative fuel vehicles.

Average Driving Costs						
Based on Driving 15,000 Miles Annually	Small Sedan	Medium Sedan	Large Sedan	Average Sedan	Four-Wheel Drive SUV	Minivan
Cost Per Mile	44.9 cents	58.5 cents	75.5 cents	59.6 cents	75.7 cents	63.4 cents
Cost Per Year	$6,735	$8,775	$11,325	$8,940	$11,355	$9,510

Goodheart-Willcox Publisher
Source: American Automobile Association

Figure 14-5 Average Driving Costs in 2012

Also check the condition of the tires. Then start the engine. If you hear any strange noises, find out the cause. The car should idle smoothly and should not emit any burning odors.

On Paper

When the car you are considering passes the four-point check, you are ready to buy with confidence.

Wherever you shop, whether you buy or lease, start the process with a low offer. Negotiate the cash price of the car first, and then negotiate the trade-in allowance, if any. Do not be afraid to walk away if you are not getting what you want. You always can come back.

If you are looking at a used vehicle, ask to see the service record, which will tell you how the vehicle has been maintained. Check out the VIN history as well.

Be sure the title is in order, and get all the figures and quotes in writing when you are shopping. Take a day or two to think over the deal you are offered before committing.

Financing

Most purchases of new and used cars are financed. This means the buyer takes out a loan and pays for the car with monthly payments. Financing a car costs more than paying cash because you pay interest on the amount borrowed. By understanding the ins and outs of financing a car, you will be able to shop more intelligently for auto loans.

Transportation, Distribution & Logistics

Automotive Technicians

Automotive technicians inspect, maintain, and repair automobiles and light trucks. They perform simple mechanical repairs as well as high-level, technology-related work. They use computerized shop equipment and work with electronic components while also using their skills with traditional hand tools.

History of Finance

History of the Car Loan

In the early days of the automobile industry, dealers had to pay cash for all cars they purchased from manufacturers. This meant that most dealers could only buy a few cars at a time. However, with the development of the assembly line manufacturing process, manufacturers wanted dealers to buy vehicles in large quantities so they could keep the factories running regularly.

Automobile dealers today do not buy the cars they keep on their lots and in the showrooms. Instead, they acquire vehicles on a credit plan from the manufacturer, which is a process called *floor planning*. Dealers take possession of vehicles and pay the manufacturer interest until the inventory can be sold. This practice allows dealers to have a large inventory and, hopefully, generate more sales.

Since many people cannot afford to pay cash for cars, consumers can also buy cars using credit. The ability to finance cars brought the automobile into reach for many people who otherwise would have been shut out of the market. Founded in 1919, General Motors Acceptance Corporation (GMAC) was the first large nonbank financing source for automobile loans. However, the practice of financing automobiles was not warmly received by all, including Henry Ford. He believed the practice would be the financial ruin of the country. The critics were terribly wrong. Many similar companies followed, and today automobile financing is a multibillion-dollar business.

Sources of Financing

Common sources of car loans include auto dealers, banks, credit unions, and finance companies. It is a good idea to shop around for loans before you go to the car dealer.

In general, the minimum age for obtaining a car loan is 18. When you apply for a car loan, the lender will want proof that you have a job and earn income. The lender will also look at your credit report and/or credit score to determine whether or not you are creditworthy.

Dealer financing is a convenient, on-the-spot source of financing. Rates may also be attractive when dealers are overstocked and need to sell cars to reduce their inventories. When asking a dealer about auto financing, be sure to insist on separate quotes for the car and the financing. This is the only way you can accurately compare finance charges and terms with other loan sources. Be wary of a dealer who tries to package the car and the financing together. This can be a costly package.

After looking at the dealer's credit terms, check financing terms from other sources. You can always come back to the dealer. Credit unions generally offer the lowest rates for auto loans. You can also investigate financing sources online and compare rates and terms.

To obtain an auto loan, the borrower pledges the car as security or collateral. This means the creditor will hold the title to the car until the loan is paid in full. If the borrower fails to repay the loan, the lender may legally take back or *repossess* the car and sell it.

The installment loan is the most common form of auto financing. It is repaid in monthly payments over a period of time. The size of the monthly payments and the length of the repayment period for installment loans vary greatly. Loan periods are usually between three and seven years for new cars

You Do the Math

When multiplying numbers, the answer you get is called the *product*. Before multiplying percentages, you must change the percentage to a decimal. To change a percentage to a decimal, move the decimal point two places to the left. For example, 25.7 percent is equal to the decimal 0.257.

Complete the Following Problems

1. You find the car of your dreams at a used car lot. You negotiate the price down to $5,000. You make a down payment of $2,000 and borrow the rest. The dealer offers you a car loan with an APR of 8 percent for 36 months. How much interest will you pay for the loan?

2. A hybrid car costs $30,000 and gets 55 miles per gallon. A comparable car that is not a hybrid costs $22,000 and gets 25 miles per gallon. Consumer A drives 125 miles a week. Consumer B drives 500 miles a week. Assuming each customer pays cash for the sticker price of the cars and fuel stays at $3 a gallon, how many years would each consumer need to drive the car before fuel savings justify the higher price?

and two to five years for used cars. This makes it relatively easy for car buyers to obtain loans they can afford to repay comfortably.

Cost of Financing

The overall cost of auto financing varies with the principal, which is the original amount borrowed, the annual percentage rate (APR), and the length of the repayment period. Consider them carefully if you shop for a loan.

The more money you borrow, the more interest you pay, as illustrated in Figure 14-6. You want to make the biggest down payment you can and pay for taxes, title, and other fees up-front to lower the amount you need to borrow.

The higher the APR, the more money you will pay in interest. The longer the repayment period, the more interest is paid. A low monthly payment with a long repayment period is often no bargain.

You can use the principal, the APR, and the repayment period length to compare the cost of credit between different loans, as illustrated in Figure 14-7. Using the figures in Figure 14-7 as a starting point, you can calculate the finance charges on different amounts of principal. For example, if you borrow $4,000, multiply the finance charge in the chart by four.

In summary, you can save money on car loans by taking these actions:

- shopping for the lowest rates available
- increasing the down payment and decreasing the size of the loan
- increasing the size of monthly payments
- shortening the repayment period

Interest	
Finance Charges	**Loan Amount (Principal)**
$ 99.28	$1,500
$132.37	$2,000
$198.56	$3,000

Goodheart-Willcox Publisher

Figure 14-6 This chart shows how much interest is paid on loans from $1,500 to $3,000. Each loan has an APR of 12 percent and is repaid in 12 monthly payments.

Interest			
Repayment Period	**Annual Percentage Rate**		
	6%	**8%**	**10%**
12 Months	$32	$ 43	$ 54
24 Months	$63	$ 85	$107
36 Months	$95	$128	$161

Goodheart-Willcox Publisher

Figure 14-7 This chart depicts the estimated finance charges for a $1,000 loan given different rates and repayment periods.

Leasing

Today, over 50 percent of consumers lease their cars. An auto lease is similar to an auto loan in that the lessee makes an initial payment and makes monthly payments for a set period of time. Generally, the lessee's initial costs and monthly payments are less than those of a buyer. However, the lessee does not own the car at the end of the lease term. Like buyers, lessees must also pay fees for registration, licensing, and other charges.

If you lease a car, your initial payment usually includes the first monthly payment, a security deposit, and a *capitalized cost reduction.* Familiarize yourself with the following terms before negotiating a car lease.

- *Capitalized cost* of a leased car is the price or value of the vehicle on which the lease is based. The lower the figure, the lower monthly payments will be.

- *Capitalized cost reduction* may include a cash down payment, trade-in allowance on a car you are trading, rebates, and other buying incentives. These things reduce the capitalized cost which will lower your monthly payments.

- *Residual value* is the worth of a car at the end of the lease. The higher the residual value, the lower monthly payments will be. The residual value is based on depreciation estimates. Consult the *Automotive Lease Guide* at your local library or bookstore for a list of the residual values of leased cars.

- *Lease term* is the length of the lease—usually 24, 36, or 48 months. Try to limit the lease term to the length of the car warranty.

- *Mileage limitations* are stated in the lease. You will usually be limited to 12,000 or 15,000 miles annually. Check out extra charges for excess mileage and wear and tear.

- *Money factor* is the interest you pay, usually stated as a small decimal such as .00265. To convert this to an annual interest rate, multiply by 24 (for example, $.00265 \times 24 = 6$ percent). The money factor should be similar to or lower than new car loan rates. Compare lesser offers with your own sources.

Negotiate all the terms of the lease, including the capitalized cost of the car. Be prepared to negotiate the trade-in allowance or capitalized cost reduction if you are trading a car or making a down payment. It also is important to be aware of the penalties if you terminate the lease early. Try not to do this. It can be very costly.

Check the lease for turn-back condition requirements and car care packages you may be required to purchase. Review the warranty and be sure it is good for the entire term of the lease. Consider buying gap insurance, which covers you if the car should be stolen or totaled in an accident. It pays the difference between what you owe on the lease and what the car is worth. Finally, look for a fixed residual price option to buy at the end of the lease if you think you may want to own the vehicle rather than lease a new car.

Get answers to any questions you have and be sure you understand all the terms of the agreement before you sign a lease contract. Review all the charges you must pay up front and at the termination of the lease. Get all the figures and promises in writing.

Checkpoint 14.2

1. How does buying a certified used car help protect you?
2. What is an auto superstore?
3. What are two sources where you can find the estimated resale value of cars?
4. Identify four common sources for car loans.
5. What is normally included in the initial payment of a leased car?

Build Your Vocabulary

As you progress through this course, develop a personal glossary of personal finance terms and add it to your portfolio. This will help you build your vocabulary and prepare you for a career. Write a definition for each of the following terms and add it to your personal finance glossary.

certified used car

bill of sale

option

vehicle identification number (VIN)

down payment

depreciation

Objective

After studying this section, you will be able to:

- List major consumer protections for car buyers.
- Describe the responsibilities of car ownership.

Terms

lemon

lemon law

FTC Used-Car Rule

Consumer Protection for Car Buyers

Most states have consumer protection laws that prohibit car dealers from using deceptive and misleading practices to sell vehicles. A dealer must honestly answer all a consumer's questions. In addition, some states require that car dealers reveal any information they have concerning used vehicles, such as whether the vehicle was leased, was a fleet vehicle, or was a demonstrator. The dealer must reveal such information whether or not the buyer asks.

Truth in Lending Act

The *Truth in Lending Act* requires creditors to provide borrowers with a complete written account of credit terms and costs. According to this law, a loan contract must state this information:

- amount borrowed or financed
- total amount to be repaid
- dollar cost of finance charges, which is the total amount paid for the use of credit, including interest charges and any other fees
- annual percentage rate or APR
- date charges begin to apply
- number, amount, and due dates of installment payments
- list and explanation of any penalties for late payment, default, or prepayment
- description of the security pledged, which is usually the car

A loan with a prepayment penalty does not allow the borrower to pay off the loan early and save on interest charges. Avoid these types of loans. If the agreement is with the dealer, the contract must also state this information:

- full description of the car
- retail or cash price of the car
- deferred payment price (price with credit charges)
- amount of the down payment

Before signing any loan agreement, be sure to read it carefully. Ask questions if any part of the contract is unclear. Make sure there are no blank spaces or lines to be filled in later. Also, pay special attention to the creditor's legal rights in case of late payment, default, or prepayment. You should be aware of any possible consequences. More information on buying a new or used car is available on the Federal Trade Commission (FTC) website at www.ftc.gov.

Finally, review your financial situation one more time. Be sure you can carry out your responsibilities and make payments according to the terms set forth in the contract.

Lemon Laws

A **lemon** is a vehicle that has serious mechanical problems that the manufacturer has been unable to fix after a reasonable number of attempts. To protect consumers against such vehicles, federal and state lemon laws have been passed in recent years. A **lemon law** is a law that requires a seller or manufacturer of a defective vehicle either to replace or repair it or to refund the buyer's money. The defect must be extensive and must occur within a certain time or mileage period, usually 12 to 24 months or 12,000 miles. You can check the lemon laws by searching for *lemon laws* and the name of your state.

Unfortunately, receiving help under a lemon law is not an automatic and straightforward process. You need to document the problem and attempts to fix it clearly. Your state may require arbitration, where a third party is involved in working out a solution. Some consumer experts recommend that you seek the help of a lemon law attorney at the start of the process. Figure 14-8 lists what you should do in case you have a lemon.

Magnuson-Moss Warranty Act

Lemon laws do not provide protection to buyers of used vehicles. However, there is a federal law that may. The *Magnuson-Moss Warranty Act* provides protection for purchasers of any product that costs over $25 and has a manufacturer's warranty. The act states that when a motor vehicle needs repairs three times or more for the same problem, the repairs provide proof

What to Do If You Buy a Lemon

- Get copies of all repair orders. Prepare a list identifying the problems, the repairs performed, and the dates that the car was in the dealer's repair shop.
- Provide the dealer with a list of problems.
- Contact the manufacturer to report the problem. Some state laws require that you do so to give the manufacturer an opportunity to fix the problem(s).
- Contact your state or local consumer protection office for information on the laws in your state and the steps you must take to resolve your situation.
- If the defect is serious and the car is a danger to drive, file for arbitration immediately.
- If your car qualifies as a lemon, draft a letter to the dealer and the manufacturer demanding that you receive a refund or replacement. Send a copy of the letter to your state or local consumer protection agency.
- Contact an attorney if the dealer and manufacturer have not addressed your concerns to your satisfaction.

Goodheart-Willcox Publisher

Figure 14-8 If you by a car that turns out to be a lemon, follow these steps to resolve the situation.

of the ineffectiveness of the manufacturer's warranty. Under the act, buyers may have a right to receive damages for the reduced value of the vehicle. Unlike lemon laws, buyers may not only receive money but can also keep the vehicle. Additionally, if a buyer incurs legal expenses related to the problem, the manufacturer must pay the legal expenses.

FTC Used-Car Rule

Buyers of used vehicles are often concerned if the vehicle has hidden problems or defects that could result in costly repairs. The Federal Trade Commission's Used-Car Rule, commonly called the **FTC Used-Car Rule,** requires dealers to fully disclose to buyers what is and is not covered under a used vehicle's warranty. The rule covers cars, light trucks, vans, and certain demonstrators and program cars. Any dealer that sells five or more vehicles over a 12-month period is covered by the FTC Used-Car Rule.

The rule requires dealers to post a *Buyers Guide* sticker on all used vehicles before offering them for sale or permitting potential buyers to examine them. On a Buyers Guide, if the *AS IS–NO WARRANTY* box is checked, the buyer is responsible for all flaws and repairs after the sale. If the *WARRANTY* box is checked, the dealer pays for repairs as outlined in the warranty. The FTC Used-Car Rule does not apply to banks or financial institutions selling used vehicles, nor does it apply to private sellers.

Buying a car from a private seller often costs less than buying from a dealer. Additionally, in many states you will not pay the retail sales tax that must be paid if a vehicle is purchased from a dealer. However, a vehicle purchased from a private seller usually does not have a warranty unless there is some time left on the manufacturer's warranty. When shopping for a used car, it is wise to consider a certified used car.

Car Owner Responsibilities

Once you become a car owner, you assume two major responsibilities. You are expected to carry adequate auto insurance and to operate and maintain your car properly and safely. Failing to carry out these responsibilities can endanger lives and financial resources of the car owner as well as passengers, other drivers, and pedestrians. Auto insurance is covered in Chapter 8.

You have much to gain by operating and maintaining your car properly. Rewards include better car performance, driving safety, and car reliability. You will have fewer breakdowns and repairs, better fuel economy, and greater trade-in value. You will also create less pollution.

Maintaining Your Car

Keeping your car in good driving condition is necessary for safety, economy, and performance. Study and follow the owner's manual for routine maintenance and service schedules. Manufacturer's instructions offer guidelines for lubrications, tune-ups, and other routine servicing. However, if you drive a car under severe conditions, your car may need more frequent attention than indicated in the owner's manual.

One key to long car life is anticipating and avoiding potential problems. Listen to your car and investigate strange noises and sluggish performance. Pay

kurhan/Shutterstock.com

Before servicing your automobile, shop around and investigate to learn more about the reputation and competence of your chosen mechanic or repair center.

attention to warning lights, gauge readings, and any leaks, drips, or unusual odors. Check out irregularities promptly. If you ignore little sounds and changes in performance, a small problem may become major and costly. Your car may have to be towed, or you may have to take the car to the nearest service station or repair shop. Then you may not get the best service at the best price.

For safer driving and better fuel economy, keep the tire pressure at the recommended level. Replace worn tires with the proper size as recommended in the owner's manual. Tires also need to be rotated periodically.

Service Shops and Mechanics

It pays to investigate service centers before you need one. Look for a service shop or mechanic you can trust and go to the same place whenever your car needs service or repairs. Basically, you have three choices: a dealer, a chain auto service center, or an independent, certified automotive technician. For warranty servicing, it may be necessary to go to the dealership. For routine repairs and maintenance, it pays to shop around. Evaluate service and repair centers according to the following guidelines.

Reputation

Look for membership in such organizations such as the local Chamber of Commerce or Better Business Bureau. Also ask several customers of the shop about their satisfaction with services and prices.

Competence

Look for experienced, well-trained automotive technicians. Certification is one indication of competence. ASE certified technicians have completed the training and passed the tests of the *National Institute for Automotive Service Excellence.*

Careers in Transportation, Distribution & Logistics

What Does an Auto Finance Manager Do?

The **auto finance manager** is typically the final person you talk with before completing the purchase of an automobile. The **auto finance manager** helps customers complete necessary paperwork and sells additional insurance, services, and warranties. **Auto finance managers** typically:

- prepare all documents necessary to complete a sale or lease;
- assist in preparing auto loan paperwork;
- sell and explain additional services offered by the dealer, such as credit life insurance and extended warranties;
- check the customer's credit history and determine if the customer can get credit and with which lender;
- check if there are any outstanding liens on the vehicle;
- summarize daily transactions so the front office has all the paperwork it needs for bookkeeping.

What Is It Like to Work as an Auto Finance Manager?

Auto finance managers work for auto dealerships. Working conditions are usually good and in an office environment. Most **auto finance managers** work full time and may meet with clients in the evenings or on weekends.

What Education and Skills Are Needed to Be an Auto Finance Manager?

- high school diploma
- good customer relations skills and sales skills
- willingness to remain current on insurance products, consumer credit, and industry-related legislation
- excellent communication and listening skills
- decision-making skills
- attention to detail
- initiative
- math skills
- computer skills

Certified technicians receive credentials listing their areas of competence. They usually wear the blue and white ASE insignia. Where these technicians are employed, an ASE sign usually appears on the premises. The sign may also appear in Yellow Pages listings of auto repair shops.

An endorsement by the *American Automobile Association* is another indicator of reliable servicing. Endorsed repair centers must meet the high standards of the association.

Facilities, Equipment, and Parts Inventory

Look for auto service shops and centers that are adequately equipped to care for your car and to perform the specific services required. Also ask about the availability of necessary parts.

Convenience

It pays to find servicing in convenient locations when you need to leave your car for service. Business hours that work well for you may also be important when dropping off or picking up your car. Before taking your car in for service, it is a good idea to call for an appointment and to ask how long you can expect to be without your car.

Charges

Compare fees and charges for routine maintenance jobs, such as a lubrication, a wheel alignment, and an oil change. You can often make these comparisons on the telephone. Though it is not certain, it is likely that shops with reasonable charges for routine maintenance will be reasonable on bigger jobs as well.

Paperwork

It pays to get certain things in writing when you buy costly services. Be sure you receive written estimates, itemized bills, and written guarantees on the work performed. When you leave your car to be serviced, make it clear you want to be contacted before any unexpected major repairs or services are performed. Keep your own file of auto records for purchases, maintenance, repairs, and insurance claims.

Checkpoint 14.3

1. What federal law requires creditors to provide borrowers with a complete written account of credit terms and costs?
2. Do lemon laws provide another form of vehicle warranty? Explain.
3. What protection for consumers is provided by the Magnuson-Moss Warranty Act?
4. What federal law requires dealers to fully disclose to buyers what is and is not covered under a used vehicle's warranty?
5. What is an advantage to buying a used car from a private seller? What is a disadvantage to buying a used car from a private seller?

Build Your Vocabulary

As you progress through this course, develop a personal glossary of personal finance terms and add it to your portfolio. This will help you build your vocabulary and prepare you for a career. Write a definition for each of the following terms and add it to your personal finance glossary.

lemon

lemon law   FTC Used-Car Rule

Chapter Summary

Section 14.1 Transportation Choices

- The transportation choices open to you depend partly on where you live. You may be able to choose from several forms of public transportation, such as buses, trains, subways, and taxis. Private transportation in the form of cars or similar vehicles is the preferred answer to the transportation needs for many Americans.

- To evaluate transportation choices, first determine your transportation needs and identify available choices. Then compare the cost, convenience, and safety of the choices.

Section 14.2 Finding and Financing an Automobile

- The way people acquire autos has changed dramatically in the past few years. Traditional dealerships and auto superstores usually sell both new and used cars. Private sellers or auctions are other options if you are buying a used car.

- You will need to shop carefully to determine your preferences for the make and model of a car and to determine which cars you can afford. You will also need to consider options and warranties when evaluating car choices.

- Used cars can be great bargains; however, you should do some research before buying. One source of information for used cars is the Buyers Guide sticker. You can check the history of a used car online using its vehicle identification number (VIN). If you buy the car from a private owner, ask for service and other records on the car.

- When buying a car, you need to consider both the purchase price and the ongoing costs of car ownership. These costs include insurance premiums, yearly licensing and registration fees, operating costs, maintenance costs, and repair costs.

- Once you feel that you have found the right car to meet your needs and budget, employ the final four-point check. Be sure to sit in the driver's seat, test drive the car on the road, check under the hood, and go over all of the paperwork.

- Many purchases of new and used cars are financed. Common sources of car loans include auto dealers, banks, credit unions, and finance companies. It is a good idea to shop around for loans before you go to the car dealer.

Section 14.3 Consumer Protection and Responsibility

- Most states have consumer protection laws that prohibit car dealers from using deceptive and misleading practices to sell vehicles. Federal laws, such as the Truth in Lending Act and the Federal Trade Commission's Used-Car Rule, also protect consumers. A dealer must honestly answer all a consumer's questions, including questions related to credit terms and warranties.

- Once you become a car owner, you assume two major responsibilities. You are expected to carry adequate auto insurance and to operate and maintain your car properly and safely.

Check Your Personal Finance IQ

Now that you have finished the chapter, see what you learned about personal finance by taking the chapter posttest. If you do not have a smartphone, visit the G-W Learning companion website.

G-W Learning mobile site: www.m.g-wlearning.com

G-W Learning companion website: www.g-wlearning.com

Review Your Knowledge

1. Name two advantages and two disadvantages of mass transit.
2. How does a commuter service differ from other forms of mass transit?
3. In addition to the purchase price of a car, what other expenses are involved with having a car?
4. What are some websites that provide information about new and used cars?
5. What are some security options that may be offered on a car?
6. What does the Buyers Guide sticker for a used car sold by a dealer describe or include?
7. What is depreciation as it applies to a car?
8. What two major responsibilities do you assume once you become a car owner?
9. How can early attention to car problems save hundreds of dollars?
10. Is declaring a car a lemon a straightforward process? Explain.

Apply Your Knowledge

11. If you were to organize a carpool of four to six people to go to and from work or school, what rules or policies would you want to make clear to each rider?
12. Assume you are thinking about buying a late-model used car. What would you do in order to find the best possible car at the best possible price?
13. How can you decide if you have enough money to buy, operate, and maintain a car?
14. When shopping for a car loan, you think that the rate quoted by your bank is a little high. What would you do to secure a better rate?
15. What steps would you take to operate a car safely and smoothly?
16. What are some things you would do to get reliable auto servicing?
17. Assume you bought a car that you think may be a lemon. What steps would you take to establish your claim?
18. If you were buying a used car, what is the first step you would take? Why?
19. Would you consider riding a bicycle to work or school? Why or why not?
20. What are some factors you would consider if you were buying a motorcycle?

Teamwork

Working with a teammate, research four sources of auto financing in your area and compare credit costs and terms for a two-year, $5,000 loan for a used car and a two-year, $15,000 loan for a new car. Create a chart to compare how the annual percentage rate, the amount of the loan, and the repayment period affect credit costs. Also, explain why credit costs differ for used and new cars. Share your findings with the class.

G-W Learning Mobile Site

Visit the G-W Learning mobile site to complete the chapter pretest and posttest and to practice vocabulary using e-flash cards. If you do not have a smartphone, visit the G-W Learning companion website to access these features.

G-W Learning mobile site: www.m.g-wlearning.com

G-W Learning companion website: www.g-wlearning.com

College and Career Readiness

Common Core

CTE Career Ready Practices. Employ valid and reliable research strategies as they apply to ways to save energy through wise transportation choices. Select two modes of transportation and list the pros and cons of each. Which would result in greater savings of energy?

Listening. Research the positives and negatives of buying a previously used car. Using the Internet, find video footage of at least three speeches or news broadcasts that discuss the opportunities for finding a vehicle with a previous owner. Compare and contrast the speakers' information, points of view, and opinions. How are they similar and different? Using the information presented, create a list of positives and negatives that you might encounter when buying a previously used car.

Speaking. Working in small groups, develop a list of regulations that you would like to see developed for buying a new automobile. Develop a presentation in which you attempt to persuade your classmates to adopt your regulations. Then, develop a separate presentation in which you attempt to persuade your teacher, acting as a member of an automobile dealership, to adopt your regulations. How will you alter your presentations for these two different audiences?

Web Connect

Select three new cars you would consider buying. Specify make, size, style, and features. Shop for these cars online and locate the best buys in your area. Create a chart that shows your findings and share with the class.

College and Career Readiness

College and Career Readiness Portfolio

Employers and colleges review candidates for various positions. The ability to communicate effectively, get along with customers or coworkers, and solve problems are important skills for many jobs. These types of skills are often called *soft skills*. You should make an effort to learn about and develop soft skills you will need for your chosen career area.

1. Do research on the Internet to find articles about soft skills and their value in helping employees succeed.

2. Make a list of the soft skills that you possess that you think would be important for a job or career area. Select three of these soft skills. Write a paragraph about each one that describes your abilities in this area. Give examples that illustrate your skills.

3. Save the document file in your e-portfolio. Place a printed copy in the container for your print portfolio.

Business Calculations

The business calculations event is an objective test that covers multiple problems related to various business applications. Participants are usually allowed one hour to complete the event.

To prepare for a business calculations test, complete the following activities.

1. Well in advance of the date of the event, visit the organization's website.

2. Download any posted practice tests.

3. Time yourself taking the tests with the aid of a non-graphing calculator. Check the answers and correct any mistakes you may have made.

4. Review the Math Skills Handbook in this text.

5. Visit the organization's website often to make sure information regarding the event has not changed.

Unit 4
Planning Your Future

bikeriderlondon/Shutterstock.com

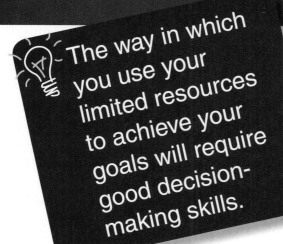

The way in which you use your limited resources to achieve your goals will require good decision-making skills.

Chapters

Personal Finance

Why It Matters

As a young adult, one of the keys to your personal financial success will be your ability to transition from school to a career. Now is the time to begin creating a financial plan to fund the training and education that you will need to open doors to future opportunities. Adequate planning for funding will affect the quality of your choices of careers. The career you choose will determine the people you meet, the places you travel, and the amount of money that you make. It is one of the most important decisions you will make in your lifetime. Waiting until you graduate from high school to create a plan to pay for tuition might be too late to enable you to make the choices that you prefer. By investigating funding options, scholarships, and other resources now, you can help ensure that the future choices you make are the ones that will make you happy. Life is not all about making money. However, selecting the career that is a good fit for you will lead to personal and financial success.

Chapter 15
Planning for Your Career

Most Americans enter the workforce at some point in their lives. People work primarily to earn money for life's necessities and a few extras. Most people begin working during their teens or early 20s and continue to retirement age. Because you will likely be working for many years, it pays to get the training and education that will lead to good jobs and good pay.

If you are like most young people, entering the world of work will be a major step. It calls for thoughtful choices. You will spend about one-third of your waking hours at the occupation you choose. Therefore, you will want to find work you can do well and enjoy. This can be a challenge.

Some people seem to know from an early age what they want to do with their lives. Most people have to search out the jobs that will bring adequate income and job satisfaction. For high school students who plan to go on to college or enter a training program after graduation, the world of work may seem far away. However, it is not too early to begin thinking about your future and the career choices that will bring you satisfaction.

Focus on Finance

529 College Savings Plan

A 529 College Savings Plan is a state-sponsored, tax-advantaged investment vehicle that allows parents, grandparents, other relatives, and even friends to plan and invest for a child's college education. Plans are usually sponsored by a state; however, participation in the plan is not restricted to residents of that state. For example, if a 529 investor does not like the plan of the state in which he or she lives, a plan of another state can be chosen.

All money invested under the plan grows tax-free. Your investment can grow at a faster pace than it would in a taxable account. Withdrawals from the plan are also tax-free, as long as they are used to pay for the qualified higher education expenses for the specified beneficiary. Qualified expenses include tuition, fees, supplies, tutoring, rooming, and transportation.

Most states allow in excess of $200,000 in contributions into a 529 College Savings Plan. Unused funds of a beneficiary can be transferred to a sibling.

College and Career Readiness

Reading Prep. As you read this chapter, determine the point of view or purpose of the author. What aspects of the text help to establish this purpose or point of view?

Check Your Personal Finance IQ

Before you begin the chapter, see what you already know about personal finance by taking the chapter pretest. If you do not have a smartphone, visit the G-W Learning companion website.

G-W Learning mobile site: www.m.g-wlearning.com

G-W Learning companion website: www.g-wlearning.com

Sections

Section 15.1 Career Plan

Section 15.2 Preparing for a Career

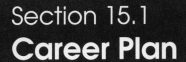

Section 15.1
Career Plan

Objectives

After studying this section, you will be able to:

- Identify the personal interests, aptitudes, abilities, and personality traits that influence career decisions and prepare a career plan.
- Identify the career clusters.
- List sources of job and career information.
- Identify employment trends.

Terms

career plan	ability
interest	career cluster
aptitude	career ladder

Making a Career Plan

Even if college and training stand between you and the work world, you can begin a career plan once you decide which career fields interest you the most. A **career plan** is an outline of steps or actions you can take to reach a career goal. It will include required courses and training, job-related experiences, and extracurricular activities and projects that will help prepare you for the career of your choice. Very often, career plans are set up over a number of years from junior high school through college and beyond.

It may be too soon to choose a lifetime career path, but it is not too early to begin thinking about what you would like to do in the world of work. Career planning begins with a careful look at yourself—at what is important to you, what you like to do, what you do well, and how you see yourself both now and as an adult. Your interests, aptitudes, skills, and abilities will determine to a large degree what type of career will be right for you. Your values and goals will also be important indicators of the type of work that will bring you satisfaction.

Identify Your Interests

An **interest** is an activity you enjoy, a subject you like, an idea that fascinates you, a sport you play, or a hobby you enjoy. Some of your interests may be key factors in choosing work you will enjoy. Very often, identifying your interests can start with a look at your life. What are your favorite hobbies, subjects, and extracurricular activities?

Projecting yourself into the work world can include a look at you in the present school setting. Consider subjects you have taken. List those you like most. List also the hobbies, activities, and part-time jobs you have pursued outside of school. Which of these interested you the most?

Consider the ways school and nonschool interests could carry over into a job or career. For example, if you are a member of a school athletic team, what skills and learning might you develop that would make you a better employee? Maybe you write for the school newspaper, are great with numbers, or are really at home in the science lab. How might these experiences and talents help you find a job? You may be president of the student council, act in the school play, or play in the band. What might you learn that will help you in the work world? What part-time jobs have you held? Has part-time work given you any insight into what you do or do not want to do with your future?

Identify Your Aptitudes and Abilities

A look at your strengths, weaknesses, talents, and skills can lead to deeper self-knowledge. An **aptitude** is a natural physical or mental talent. For example, if you score high in verbal aptitude, you may find it relatively easy to learn language arts. You may be well suited for work in written or oral communications. If you do well in math, you may find work with numbers satisfying. It may be possible to take aptitude tests through your school guidance department.

An **ability** is a physical or mental skill developed through learning, training, and practice. You are born with certain aptitudes, but your abilities are learned.

When aptitude and ability go together, you are likely to learn quickly and well. For example, if you are highly coordinated and athletic, you could learn a sport quickly and play relatively well. If you are interested in playing tennis but do not have athletic aptitude, you might overcome a lack of coordination with hard work and practice. When you can put interests, aptitudes, and abilities together into a job choice, you are likely to be successful on the job.

Try to picture yourself at work. If you have a burning desire to paint, act, dance, protect the environment, teach, or practice medicine or law, find out what jobs will let you follow your dream. Take the path that leads to your ultimate goal.

Ethics

When applying for a job, submitting an application for acceptance into a university, or even applying for a position as a volunteer with an organization, it is important to be truthful in your application and résumé. Making up experience or education to gain a position is unethical and could cost you a future opportunity to be a part of that organization. Always tell the truth about your skills, experience, and education. Play up your strengths without attempting to create the illusion of being someone you are not. Present your information in a positive light, but keep it honest. Potential employers will usually discover untruths, and this discovery will cause you to miss the opportunity you are seeking.

Eric Fahrner/Shutterstock.com

As you begin to plan for your future career, consider your interests, aptitudes, and abilities.

If you enjoy a number of activities but are not clear on a career path, you will need to keep your options open. It might help to consider job categories in terms of what you do well and what you like doing. For example, try completing this sentence: "I like working with _____." Possible answers might be *words, numbers, people, animals, plants, machinery, computers, books, ideas, cars,* or whatever else you really enjoy. List your options and try to rank them in order of importance. Start with what you like the most and work down to what you like least.

Assess your strengths by completing another sentence: "I am particularly good at _____." Possible answers might include *communication, selling, research, acting, design, sports, problem solving, science, helping people,* or *teamwork.* Again, list your strengths; then rank them starting with your greatest strength.

Look at Your Personality

Personality traits also provide a clue to the type of work you can do well and enjoy doing. Seeing yourself as others see you is not always easy, but it is a useful exercise when trying to match yourself to a job. Think about the type of person you are. For example, would others describe you as quiet or talkative, shy or outgoing, tense or easygoing? Are you an energetic self-starter or do you often need a push to get going? Are you quick to try new things, or are you more comfortable with familiar things? Are you cautious, or are you willing to take risks?

Try to write a paragraph describing your personality. Pretend you are writing to a prospective employer for a job you really want. Which of the adjectives in Figure 15-1 would you use?

You Do the Math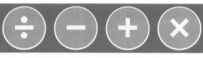

Whole numbers are numbers with no fraction or decimal. When adding whole numbers, place each number in a vertical list. The result of addition is the *sum*. In subtraction, the result is the *difference*.

Complete the Following Problems

You are considering going to college to get a teaching degree. If you attend the local university, you could live at home and save money. However, you are really interested in going to a school two hours from home and living on your own. Make a comparison of the costs for the first year of school. These are the largest expenses. Remember, however, there will be expenses for other things, such as insurance, transportation, and entertainment.

- Tuition $20,000
- Apartment $12,000
- Books $2,400
- Food $2,600

1. What is the cost for going away to school?
2. What is the cost for attending a local university?
3. How much more money would you need if you go away?

Which of the following adjectives would you apply to yourself?		
• Organized	• Cautious	• Imaginative
• Responsible	• Intellectual	• Willing
• Persistent	• Helpful	• Determined
• Enthusiastic	• Friendly	• Loyal
• Honest	• Trustworthy	• Sensitive
• Thorough	• Creative	• Hardworking

Goodheart-Willcox Publisher

Figure 15-1 These are just a few of the many terms you might use to describe your personality.

Assess Your Values and Goals

Consider what you want to do with your life. This will be closely connected with your personal values and goals. *Personal values* are the ideals and principles that are important to you. Goals are the specific achievements or objectives you want to reach. The two are usually related. For example, you may place importance on a clean and safe environment. A related work goal may be a job that involves environmental research and protection, waste management, or conservation.

Analyzing personal values and goals can help you make the most appropriate career and job choices. What is really important to you? What contribution do you want to make? Most people need to feel that the work they do has importance and meaning. What job or career will make you feel you are making a difference?

Many people find satisfaction in jobs that serve others. It is possible to serve others in almost any career. However, there are more opportunities in fields such as social work, health care, education, the ministry, and other services to the public.

Career Clusters

A **career cluster** is a grouping of general occupational and career areas. Figure 15-2 shows 16 career clusters. The clusters were developed by a partnership among the states, educators, and employers. The object of the career clusters concept is to link material learned in school to a career path and identify the knowledge and skills learners need as they move toward their career goals. Within each cluster are subgroups called *career pathways,* which are areas of concentration. Each pathway contains a group of careers requiring similar academic and technical skills as well as similar industry requirements and education. The pathways help guide students to the course of study they will need to achieve their career goals.

You may be drawn to one or two of the clusters based on interests, aptitudes, and abilities. If you focus on one career cluster and pathway, you will learn knowledge and skills related to different occupations in that pathway. This will allow you to be somewhat flexible in choosing an occupation. You can more easily explore different occupations within your areas of interest.

The career pathways include jobs from entry-level to management positions. With this information, you can establish a career ladder in a chosen pathway. A **career ladder**, as illustrated in Figure 15-3, is an outline of jobs in

According to the US Department of Labor, the average US worker changes careers three to five times during his or her lifetime.

The 16 Career Clusters

Careers involving the production, processing, marketing, distribution, financing, and development of agricultural commodities and resources. 	Careers involving management, marketing, and operations of foodservice, lodging, and recreational businesses. 
Careers involving the design, planning, managing, building, and maintaining of buildings and structures. 	Careers involving family and human needs. 
Careers involving the design, production, exhibition, performance, writing, and publishing of visual and performing arts. 	Careers involving the design, development, support, and management of software, hardware, and other technology-related materials. 
Careers involving the planning, organizing, directing, and evaluation of functions essential to business operations. 	Careers involving the planning, management, and providing of legal services, public safety, protective services, and homeland security. 
Careers involving the planning, management, and providing of training services. 	Careers involving the planning, management, and processing of materials to create completed products. 
Careers involving the planning and providing of banking, insurance, and other financial-business services. 	Careers involving the planning, management, and performance of marketing and sales activities. 
Careers involving governance, national security, foreign service, revenue and taxation, regulation, and management and administration. 	Careers involving the planning, management, and providing of scientific research and technical services. 
Careers involving planning, managing, and providing health services, health information, and research and development. 	Careers involving the planning, management, and movement of people, materials, and goods. 

States' Career Clusters Initiative 2008

Figure 15-2 There are 16 career clusters. Each cluster contains several career pathways.

a given career field that are available at different levels of education, training, and experience. This gives you some idea of work opportunities in your chosen field as you progress from one level of learning to the next. The career plan in Figure 15-4 shows how one person planned ahead for a career in the consumer and resource management field.

Job and Career Information

Knowing a few basic facts about different jobs and careers can help you make the right choices in the work world. Study the job market as you make

Career Ladder for Work in Consumer and Resource Management	
Advanced Degree	• Family counselor • Family and consumer sciences educator or extension agent • Consumer advocate • Consumer affairs director for a corporation or financial institution • Executive director of a consumer interest organization
College Degree	• Financial planner • Consumer journalist • Product researcher • Consumer information specialist • Consumer advocate • Consumer education director
Advanced Technical Training	• Consumer product tester • Consumer product representative • Credit counselor • Family debt counselor • Financial services salesperson • Consumer consultant • Consumer representative for a utility company • Public relations officer for a business
High School Diploma	• Consumer hotline operator for the state consumer services office • Personal shopper • Customer service representative for department store • Consumer complaint handler • Product demonstrator • Research assistant
Pre-High School Graduation	• Food planner and shopper for the family • Part-time checkout clerk at a supermarket • Reporter on consumer issues for the school paper

Goodheart-Willcox Publisher

Figure 15-3 This career ladder outlines some of the job opportunities in the consumer and resource management field at different levels of education and training.

Career Plan for College Professor in Consumer and Resource Management			
	Education and Training	**Work Experience**	**Personal Projects and Activities**
Junior High School	• Family and consumer sciences courses • Extra credit projects related to consumer issues	• Operate an errand service for neighborhood families	• Family meal planner and food shopper • Comparison shopper for family purchases
Senior High School	• Take college prep courses with emphasis on consumer economics	• Part-time checkout clerk at the supermarket	• Start a consumer study group at school • Research consumer product purchases
College	• Take bachelor degree program in family and consumer sciences	• Part-time consumer product tester	• Volunteer in student financial aid department • Consumer issues editor for student newspaper
After College	• Enroll in graduate consumer sciences program • Complete graduate degree	• Part-time consumer research assistant • Assistant professorship in family and consumer sciences • Full professor and department head	• Continue involvement in consumer issues

Goodheart-Willcox Publisher

Figure 15-4 This career plan shows the planned steps toward a career goal beginning in junior high school and going through college.

career decisions. What careers and occupations do you think will be in the greatest demand over the next 10 to 20 years? Take a look at the help-wanted sections in the newspapers and online to learn which fields offer the most job opportunities in the present.

It is important to learn what you can about the occupations and careers that interest you. You will want to look for job areas that offer the most and best opportunities for the future. Early planning can help you find the courses and experiences that will open career doors for you later. Some of the many sources of career and job information that are readily available are discussed in the following paragraphs.

Career Guides

The US Department of Labor sponsors a variety of career information resources including the following:

- O*NET (www.onetonline.org) is the principal source of information about occupations in the United States. You can use the site to search for specific occupations or search for jobs that are currently in high demand.
- The *Occupational Outlook Handbook* (www.bls.gov/oco) updated every two years, profiles over 250 jobs. For each job, it describes work activities, earnings, education and training requirements, personal qualifications, and outlook for employment.

- *CareerOneStop* (www.careeronestop.org) provides information about education and training, salary and benefits, and résumés and interviews.
- *Occupational Outlook Quarterly* (www.bls.gov/opub/ooq) includes practical, up-to-date information about job choices and preparation for the careers of your choice in the job markets of today and tomorrow.

Internet

The Internet can be used for researching colleges, jobs, career information, and employment opportunities. Most colleges and universities have websites that provide information on the school, courses of study, tuition, financial aid, scholarships, and other details. You may even be able to take certain courses online.

The Internet also allows you to post your résumé, locate job listings and related information, research individual companies, and explore career opportunities and employment trends. You can also apply for some jobs online.

History of Finance

Practical Education

The original purpose of college was not practical education designed to prepare students for a career. Originally, college was for the enlightenment of the mind. Students, primarily male, went to college to study the arts, literature, philosophy, history, and law. The growth and expansion of the nation following the end of the Civil War led to the need for practical education. The apprentice system was no longer able to provide all the skilled workers the nation needed. As a result, private business colleges were founded to fill the void. One of the original such schools was Folsom's Merchantile College, which opened in 1848 in Cleveland, Ohio. Among the courses offered by the school were penmanship, bookkeeping, and drawing. Schooling lasted only two to three months, and night classes were offered for those who worked during the day. John D. Rockefeller, founder of Standard Oil, graduated from Folsom in 1855.

Folsom became the model for the national chain of Bryant & Stratton Business Schools. Many other proprietary business schools sprang up, and the for-profit education industry played a significant role in preparing Americans for the workforce well into the twentieth century.

In the early part of the twentieth century, practical education started to make its way into colleges and public high schools. By the mid-twentieth century, most colleges offered degrees in business and other practical fields. Most high schools were also offering practical education. Around 1960, public vocational/trade schools were starting to open in many states. These schools offered courses of study ranging from accounting to welding, and they were designed to put students in the workforce within a year.

By 1975, junior colleges had become community colleges, offering practical as well as academic courses of study. Four-year and two-year schools continue to expand offerings in practical education. With the advent of online education, the trend is likely to continue.

Social media networking sites can be very effective in finding job information. Twitter, Facebook, and YouTube are several examples of free social media tools businesses use for research purposes.

School Guidance Counselors

In many schools, guidance counselors offer a wealth of job information. They can help you determine the areas best suited to your aptitudes and abilities. The Guidance Department at your school may provide files of information on education, training, and careers. Counselors may also help you evaluate your options, direct you to more information, and guide you in the choice of a college or training program. Check out the Guidance Department in your school to find out what services it offers.

Libraries

School and community libraries also offer a host of information. Some libraries may have an education and employment section containing a variety of books and publications. When searching online or in card catalogs, look under headings such as *careers, colleges and universities, jobs*, and *occupations*. In addition, check headings related to specific career fields that interest you.

Career Events

Special career days at school and career fairs in the community can provide up-to-date information on jobs, education, and training. In addition, college or business representatives often visit high schools to speak with interested students. It is a good idea to take advantage of both. You can learn firsthand

Golden Pixels LLC/Shutterstock.com

School guidance counselors can provide information related to college and career decisions.

about opportunities in the work world. It is also helpful to talk to people who work in fields that interest you.

Job fairs are a great way to meet potential employers. Various organizations sell booth space for employers to present information about their businesses. Attendees can visit the booths to discuss job opportunities, submit résumés, and complete applications.

Employment Trends

In job markets, it is very possible that today's opportunity will become tomorrow's dead end. It is important to stay abreast of new technology and to follow the trends in industry. Consider where the best jobs are likely to surface given current trends and developments. The *Occupational Outlook Handbook* can help you keep up with these changes. Following the news and relating it to the work world will also give you timely clues to upcoming opportunities.

New technology requires highly trained and skilled workers in a variety of fields. Untrained workers will either be unemployed or remain at bottom-level, low-paying jobs. Not only is initial training important, the willingness to retrain over the years is equally important. Technology makes dramatic and sometimes sudden changes. These changes often lead to a demand for workers with different types of skills and training. You need to learn and relearn work skills over a lifetime.

Economic factors, both at home and around the world, can seriously affect employment in different fields. Recession, inflation, tax policies, and international trade all have an impact on what and how many jobs are available. These factors also affect the qualifications workers will need to find employment. For example, when unemployment is high and jobs are hard to find, training, education, and competence become even more important in finding and keeping a job. When taxes and interest rates are high, there may be fewer jobs because businesses are less likely to expand and are more likely to cut back on hiring.

Economic conditions can vary around the world and from one part of the country to another. It pays to look at opportunities in different areas when you are searching for employment. Supply and demand in the job market varies greatly from one field of employment to another and from one area to another.

Think long and hard about your career goals. The work you choose will affect the way you live, the people you meet, the money you earn, and the satisfaction you get out of work and life. Try to decide what will be the best preparation for the work you want. Will you need a college degree or occupational training? Will the job require an internship, an apprenticeship, or previous work experience? Will you need a combination of these to achieve your career goals? This is a good time to start planning for your future.

Checkpoint 15.1

1. What does a career plan include?
2. What is the difference between an aptitude and an ability?
3. What is the object of the career clusters concept?
4. What are some sources of career and job information?
5. What are some economic factors that can affect employment in different fields?

Build Your Vocabulary

As you progress through this course, develop a personal glossary of personal finance terms and add it to your portfolio. This will help you build your vocabulary and prepare you for a career. Write a definition for each of the following terms and add it to your personal finance glossary.

career plan   ability
interest   career cluster
aptitude   career ladder

Objectives

After studying this section, you will be able to:

- Describe the education and training you will need.
- Discuss the importance of college access.
- Outline the steps you can take to pay for the education and training you will need.

Terms

education

community college

training

occupational training

continuing education

internship

apprenticeship

Reserve Officers' Training Corps (ROTC)

college access

529 plan

Education and Training

In the years ahead, a college education or training will be required for many jobs. It will be an advantage in almost all occupations. Preparation for the work you want will typically pay off in the form of higher earning power, better job opportunities, greater job satisfaction, and security. It can enrich your life in other ways as well.

Following high school, you will find many opportunities for further education and training. Your choices will depend largely on the career path you want to pursue.

Education

Education is the general process of acquiring knowledge and skills. You will obtain education throughout your lifetime. Some education is formal and some is informal. *Formal education* is the education you get from a school, college, or university. When you attend one of these institutions, you will usually receive a diploma, degree, or other document that confirms you successfully completed a course of study. Informal education is learning in an unstructured setting. You might get informal education from reading articles on the Internet or learning a skill from a coworker.

High School

A high school diploma is the minimum educational requirement for most jobs. A high school diploma indicates that you have basic skills in reading, writing, and math.

Some high school students complete a cooperative education program. A cooperative education program, or co-op program, prepares students for an

Andresr/Shutterstock.com

You can begin planning for your future career before graduating from high school.

occupation through a paid job and classes at school. Students take classes for half a day, and they work the other half of the day. These programs are a good way to get hands-on experience in a job.

Many high schools offer career and technical student organizations. A career and technical student organization (CTSO) is an organization for high school students interested in a career area, such as business or family and consumer education. Examples are DECA—an Association of Marketing Students, Future Business Leaders of America (FBLA), Business Professionals of America (BPA), and SkillsUSA.

CTSOs provide a variety of activities that enable students to learn more about the career; meet professionals in the field; and develop interpersonal, leadership, career, and technical skills. In addition, many career and technical student organizations offer scholarships.

A CTSO will usually have a chapter in a school. Through the school chapter, students participate in chapter meetings and civic, service, social, and fundraising activities. In addition, many CTSOs have competitive events. These competitive events provide the opportunity for students to develop career and technical skills. Students can compete at the school, state, national, and international levels. Participating in competitive events can be a motivating experience.

Postsecondary School

Postsecondary education is available at professional career schools, vocational-technical schools, and community colleges. A **community college** is a two-year postsecondary school offering both academic and occupational courses. These educational institutions offer education for specific careers. The programs can last from six months to two years, depending on the program. They usually include a combination of classroom learning and hands-on experience. These schools offer certificates, diplomas, and associate degrees in a variety of careers.

College or University

Higher education will be the first choice for many high school students. It can be the single most costly investment of a lifetime. It can also bring the best returns in higher earnings, better job opportunities, and a fuller life. If college is in your plans for the future, start planning now. There are many factors to consider in choosing a school and field of study.

Take a look at your reasons for going to college. Are you interested in a specific field of study? Do you want to learn more in broad areas to help you decide what you want to pursue in greater depth? Is your primary goal to learn and broaden your horizons or to qualify for a particular career? Answers to these questions can help you choose the path to your future education and career choices.

Consider whether a small or large school appeals more to you. Do you want to be near home or far away? What part of the country attracts you most? Weigh the pros and cons of an urban versus a rural setting and private versus state schools.

Colleges look at grades, test scores, class ranks, activities, special talents, and other achievements of prospective students. Some schools are more competitive than others. However, if you have a reasonably good record and really want to go to college, there will be a school for you. Prepare a résumé and outline your strongest points to present to the admissions office of the schools that interest you.

Schools differ greatly. No doubt several will meet your needs and accept you as a student. When looking at colleges, check out and compare the following factors.

- *Programs of study.* Look at the courses offered in different fields, foreign study opportunities, work-study, student-designed majors, and exchange programs with other schools.

- *Faculty.* Consider the number of doctorates, the faculty/student ratio, and the academic reputation of the school—particularly in the field you want to pursue.

Case Study

Career Choices

Lee loves computers. He works part time at Compumart doing sales and service. Compumart offered him a full-time position when he graduates from high school. The money will be good, and Lee already knows a lot about the business. The best part is the opportunity to develop new programs and work with the latest equipment.

Eventually, Lee might become a computer programmer or a systems analyst. Both careers require more schooling; so for the moment, he just plans to enjoy his job.

Case Review

1. What are the advantages of being able to move right into the job you want from high school? Do you see any disadvantages for Lee?
2. Under what circumstances would Lee be smart to delay his computer job and go to college or enroll in an advanced training program?
3. What are some of the occupations that are open to high school graduates?
4. What other hobbies or activities can you think of that could lead to satisfying full-time employment?

- *Facilities.* Check out the library, science labs, computer labs, athletic facilities, fitness programs, and other items of special interest to you.
- *Environment.* Find out about dormitories and living quarters, the makeup of the student body, extracurricular activities, campus size and setting, existence and importance of fraternities and sororities, safety on campus, and other factors that are important to you.
- *Geographic location and campus setting.* Think about whether you wish or need to be close to home. Do you wish to go to school in a different part of the country? What advantages do you see in one part of the country versus another? Do you prefer an urban or more rural setting?
- *Cost.* Determine the total amount of tuition, room and board, fees, books, and overall cost of living.
- *Financial aid.* Investigate loans, scholarships, grants, part-time job opportunities, and work-study programs.

You also may want to compare private versus public schools, coed versus gender, religious versus nondenominational, and small versus large schools. Visit the colleges you are considering if possible to get a sense of life on campus and the academic focus.

Training

Training is typically instruction on a specific skill or task needed for a job. Training may happen on the job or by taking a training program at a college, university, professional association, or private company. Training offerings include college and university courses, training for specific occupations, certification programs, and company-sponsored employee training. You may be able to earn a college degree online or complete certification requirements in a variety of fields. This also is an excellent way to continue your education, enhance career advancement, and enjoy lifetime learning.

On-the-Job Training

Most jobs typically provide some training on the job. If a company gets new equipment or develops new procedures, it will usually provide on-the-job training for all employees using the new equipment or procedures.

Occupational Training

Preparing for employment in a specific field may be a smart move for many students. This type of education generally costs less and takes less time than a college degree. **Occupational training** is education that prepares you for a specific type of work. It is available through a variety of schools and programs in addition to online offerings.

Occupational schools are usually privately owned and depend on satisfying students for their continued success. Training, equipment, facilities, and qualifications of instructors vary greatly. Check thoroughly before enrolling.

Adult education programs include academic and occupational courses offered in a night school setting. They may be an extension of a nearby college or university or offered through the local board of education. Course offerings vary in different areas. These programs are perfect for the worker who needs advanced training but has little time to spend going to school.

Since the quality and content of occupational education varies greatly, investigate carefully before enrolling. Be sure you understand all the terms of any agreement or enrollment contract before you sign it. In making your choices, look for these factors:

- Qualified, experienced instructors
- Adequate, up-to-date equipment and facilities
- State licensing or accreditation from industry or educational agencies
- Recommendations from prospective employers and former students
- Reasonable costs for tuition, equipment, supplies, and fees
- Fair policies on transferring credits and refunds for non-completed courses
- Degrees or certifications you need for the employment you seek

Continuing Professional Education

Continuing education is learning you pursue after you complete your formal education and training. It can take many forms, from individual courses to complete programs. You may choose to continue your education in order to advance on a current job, to qualify for employment in a new field, or simply for personal satisfaction. Many of the education and training opportunities already discussed offer continuing education possibilities. Some careers require a specific program of continuing education. Keeping up to date in your field is an advantage in almost all occupations.

Internships

An **internship** is a short-term position with a sponsoring organization that gives the intern an opportunity to gain on-the-job experience in a certain field of study or occupation. Internships are available in a variety of career areas.

Apprenticeships

An **apprenticeship** is a combination of on-the-job training, work experience, and classroom instruction. About 350 apprenticeships are registered with the Bureau of Apprenticeship and Training, a division of the US Department of Labor. Over 800 occupations fall into the apprentice category. The jobs involve manual, mechanical, or technical skills. An apprenticeship requires on-the-job work experience along with classroom or

According to the US Department of Labor, 62 percent of all US jobs now require two-year or four-year degrees and higher or postsecondary occupation certificates or apprenticeships.

Go Green

The USB flash drive is becoming a popular alternative to rewritable CDs (CD-RWs). Even though CD-RWs are reusable, they can be easily damaged and may end up in a landfill after just a few uses. USB drives, on the other hand, are more durable, reusable, and easy to carry and store. Have you seen the new ecofriendly bamboo USB drives? Bamboo is one of the fastest growing woody plants on the planet, so this renewable resource is a good choice for the case of a USB drive.

Dragon Images/Shutterstock.com

An apprenticeship offers on-the-job training and work experience.

other types of learning. These programs offer pay and job benefits, training by experienced trades people, certification, and improved employment opportunities. The regulations governing apprenticeships were updated in 2008. For more information, contact the nearest regional or state office of the Bureau of Apprenticeships and Training.

Armed Forces

The military offers a wide range of education and training programs at little or no cost both through recruitment services and the Reserve Officers' Training Corps (ROTC). **Reserve Officers' Training Corps (ROTC)** is a college program for training commissioned officers for the United States armed forces. Some high schools offer Junior Reserve Officers' Training Corps (JROTC) to prepare high school students for leadership roles. If your school has this program, you may want to investigate its benefits. Each branch of the service also offers a service academy where students can earn tuition-free college degrees.

In colleges, ROTC involves taking ROTC courses and training along with college courses. Participants enter the service as officers upon graduation. ROTC graduates make up approximately 39 percent of all active duty officers in the Department of Defense. The service commitment varies, but it usually calls for several years of active duty followed by a period of time in the reserves. The ROTC program is slightly different in each branch of the service.

In addition to education and training opportunities, those who enter the military through the ROTC program generally receive good salaries and generous benefits, such as health care, housing, travel opportunities, and use of social and athletic facilities. However, once in the service, there is always the possibility of being called to active duty during times of war. Participants are also required to serve out the entire term of their contracts—two, four, or six years. In most cases, it is not possible to resign or quit early.

Business Management & Administration

Human Resources Specialists

Human resources specialists focus on the recruitment and management of the people who work for an organization. They deal with hiring, firing, performance management, structuring of employee positions, safety, wellness, benefits, employee motivation, communication, and training.

College Access

Have you heard the term *college access*? **College access** refers to building awareness about college opportunities, providing guidance regarding college admissions, and identifying ways to pay for college. College access includes access to all kinds of postsecondary institutions, including colleges, universities, and trade schools.

Gaining access to a postsecondary institution to further your education is a critical step in your career plan and your financial future. However, preparing to go to college presents many challenges to students and families both academically and financially. The sooner you begin planning, the better. It is never too early to begin.

As you plan for your education, you will want to learn as much as possible about what it takes to gain admission to the college of your choice and how to create a financial plan to pay for your education. Academic preparation includes taking the right courses and doing your best. Make the most of your remaining high school years. If you have always been a good student, do not slack off. If you have not been performing to your potential, you can demonstrate your abilities and commitment by showing improvement. Doing the very best you can and becoming involved in organizations at your high school or in your community will provide greater access to college. Most schools are looking for well-rounded individuals who participate in a variety of activities.

There are many websites that provide information to help you gain access to college. Many sites offer guidance for every stage of the planning process, starting with exploring careers in grade school through applying for college. Because there are so many websites, you will need to determine which sites offer the best information for your particular situation.

You can start by searching the Internet for resources offered in your state. Search using the term *college access* plus the name of your state to get started. If you have already been thinking about a specific college, make sure you check the school's official website to learn about admission requirements and to find out what financial help might be available to you. The US Department of Education has a website that provides information about the benefits of more education, steps to continuing your education, and ways to manage the cost of your education. Visit www.college.gov to learn more about going to college—reasons to go, what to do, and how to pay.

The College Board website offers an assortment of college planning tools, including information about finding a college, applying to college, and paying for college. One of the tools you will find on the website is a financial calculator to help project the cost of an education.

The National College Access Program Directory provides information about college access programs across the country. Visit its website and search for programs that might meet your individual needs.

If you have not already done so, talk to your family, friends, and guidance counselor today for information to begin planning for college.

According to *The Huffington Post*, people with a bachelor degree make 84 percent more over a lifetime than high school graduates.

Funding Your Education

When you invest, you are using money to make money. Education is an investment in you. Higher education and job training programs can cost thousands of dollars. Deciding how much you can afford to invest and how

Vocational Rehabilitation Counselors

Vocational rehabilitation counselors counsel people coping with personal, social, and vocational difficulties that result from birth defects, illness, disease, accidents, or the stress of daily life. They help to maximize each client's independence and employability, assess client needs, and design and implement rehabilitation programs that may include personal and vocational counseling, training, and job placement.

you will pay for it requires careful thought. The following are a few steps to guide you in financing your education.

- Estimate the cost of attending the colleges or occupational schools you are seriously considering.
- Estimate the resources available to you, including savings, investments, student earnings, and family income.
- Measure estimated costs against estimated resources to determine how much additional money you need.
- Consider ways to cut costs without sacrificing important goals and objectives for your future.
- Search for additional resources—scholarships, grants, loans, and earnings—to help pay for your education.

As you are making decisions on your schooling, you will need to create a financial plan for paying for your education. Whether you attend a trade school, community college, or university, someone has to pay the cost of the education. Funds to pay for college come from a variety of sources. Each student's financial situation is different. You will need to figure out which sources are available to you and which ones fit your needs.

Some families can afford to pay for college with current income or savings. If your parents or other family members are able and willing to pay for a college education for you, by all means take advantage of their generosity. You can thank them by studying hard and earning your degree. You may be fortunate enough to have a family who established a 529 plan for you to fund your college education. A **529 plan** is a savings plan for education operated by a state or educational institution. These plans are tax-advantage savings plans and encourage families to set aside college funds for their children. These funds may be used for qualified colleges across the nation. Each state now has at least one 529 plan available. Plans vary from state to state because every state sets up its own plan. There are restrictions on how this money

Jason Stitt/Shutterstock.com

Online cost calculators can help you plan a budget for financing your college education.

can be used, so make sure you understand how the plan works. You will be penalized if you use money invested in a 529 plan for anything other than college expenses.

Even if your family has a 529 plan, the amount saved might not be enough to pay for all your college expenses. Many families pay for college

Careers in Education & Training

What Does a Career Counselor Do?

Career counselors help people with career decisions. They explore and evaluate the client's education, training, work history, interests, skills, and personality traits. Aptitude and achievement tests can be arranged through a counselor to help individuals make career decisions. **Career counselors** work with clients to develop their job search skills and assist in locating and applying for jobs. **Career counselors** typically:

- use assessment measures to help clients evaluate their interests, skills, and abilities
- evaluate clients' background, education, and training to help them develop realistic goals
- guide clients through making decisions about their careers
- help clients learn job search skills, such as interviewing, networking, and preparing effective résumés
- assist clients in locating or applying for jobs
- help clients select and apply for educational programs to obtain the necessary degrees, credentials, or skills

What Is It Like to Work as a Career Counselor?

Some **career counselors** work in high schools and colleges. Some work in outplacement firms and assist laid-off workers to transition into a new job or career. Others work in corporate career centers to assist employees in making decisions about their career path within the company. Still others work in private practice.

Most **career counselors** work full time. Work is usually performed in an office environment or professional setting. Hours worked may be irregular, depending on the schedules of individual clients.

What Education and Skills Are Needed to Be a Career Counselor?

- bachelor degree (master degree in counseling with a focus on career development preferred)
- people skills
- listening skills
- written and oral communication skills
- compassion

using savings, current income, and loans. Parents, other family members, and students often work together to cover the cost of college. You might contribute money you have saved, money you earn if you work while attending school, and money for loans you will have to repay.

There are many online college cost calculators that can help you estimate how much money you will need to fund your education. Once you have an idea of how much it will cost to go to college, you need to figure out how you will pay for it. More than half the students attending college get some form of financial aid. Figure 15-5 shows potential sources of funding for your education.

Financial aid is available from the federal government as well as nonfederal agencies. There is more than $100 billion in grants, scholarships, work-study, need-based awards, and loans available each year. Some states also offer college money to attend a state school if you have good grades

Potential Sources of Funding a College Education		
Source	**Brief Description**	**Repayment**
529 Plans	Tax-advantage savings plan designed to encourage saving for future college costs. Plans are sponsored by states, state agencies, and educational institutions.	No repayment.
Grants	Money to pay for college provided by government agencies, corporations, states, and other organizations. Most grants are based on need and some have other requirements.	No repayment.
Scholarships	Money to pay for college based on specific qualifications including academics, sports, music, leadership, and service. Criteria for scholarships vary widely.	No repayment.
Work-study	Paid part-time jobs for students with financial need. Work-study programs are typically backed by government agencies.	No repayment.
Need-based awards	Aid for students who demonstrate financial need.	No repayment.
Government education loans	Loans made to students to help pay for college. Interest rates are lower than bank loans.	Repayment is required. Repayment may be postponed until you begin your career.
Private education loans	Loans made to students to help pay for college. Interest rates are higher than government education loans.	Repayment is required.
Internships	Career-based work experience. Some internships are paid and some are not. In addition to experience, you will likely earn college credit.	No repayment.
Military benefitss	The US Military offers several ways to help pay for education. It provides education and training opportunities while serving and also provides access to funding for veterans. The US Reserve Officers' Training Corps (ROTC) programs and the military service academies are other options to consider.	No repayment, however a service commitment is required.

Goodheart-Willcox Publisher

Figure 15-5 There are multiple alternatives for funding a college education.

in high school. Grants, scholarships, work-study programs, and need-based awards are some examples of financial aid.

- A *grant* is typically provided by a nonprofit organization, such as a government or other organization. Grants are generally need based, do not have to be repaid, and are usually tax exempt. A Federal Pell Grant is an example of a government grant.

- A *scholarship* may be based on financial need or some type of merit or accomplishment. There are scholarships based on ACT or SAT scores, grades, extracurricular activities, athletics, and music. There are also scholarships available for leadership, service, and other interests, abilities and talents. It is surprising how many scholarships and grants go unused because no one has applied for them. Do not fail to apply for help just because you do not want to write the essay or fill out the application. Talk to your school counselor and be persistent if you think you might qualify for college money.

- *Work-study programs* are usually part-time jobs on campus that are subsidized by the government.

- *Need-based awards* are available for students and families who meet certain economic requirements. Income and other demographics determine if a student qualifies for this assistance.

The *Free Application for Federal Student Aid (FAFSA)* is the application form used to determine your eligibility for federal financial aid. Many institutions require the FAFSA form if you are applying for any type of financial aid. You can file your application online at www.fafsa.ed.gov. In addition to the financial aid application, the FAFSA website has resources to help you plan for college. Visit the website and click on the links under the heading Thinking About College?

Checkpoint 15.2

1. How will preparation for the work you want typically pay off in the future?
2. What is a cooperative education program?
3. What are some factors you should compare when selecting a college?
4. What does the term *college access* describe?
5. What is a 529 plan?

Build Your Vocabulary

As you progress through this course, develop a personal glossary of personal finance terms and add it to your portfolio. This will help you build your vocabulary and prepare you for a career. Write a definition for each of the following terms and add it to your personal finance glossary.

education

community college

training

occupational training

continuing education

internship

apprenticeship

Reserve Officers' Training Corps (ROTC)

college access

529 plan

Chapter Summary

Section 15.1 Career Plan

- Your interests, aptitudes, skills, and abilities will help determine what type of career will be right for you. A career plan is an outline of steps or actions you can take to reach a career goal. It will include required courses and training, job-related experiences, and extracurricular activities and projects that will help prepare you for a career.

- A career cluster is a grouping of general occupational and career areas. Sixteen career clusters have been developed by a partnership among the states, educators, and employers. The object of the career clusters concept is to link material learned in school to a career path.

- Knowing a few basic facts about different jobs and careers can help you make the right choices in the work world. Some sources of career and job information include career guides, the Internet, school guidance counselors, libraries, and career events, such as job fairs.

- It is important to stay abreast of new technology and to follow the trends in industry. Consider where the best jobs are likely to surface given current trends and developments. The Occupational Outlook Handbook and news about current events can help you keep up with these changes.

Section 15.2 Preparing for a Career

- Your choices for further education and training will depend largely on the career path you want to pursue. You may get formal education or training from a school, college, or university. You might get informal education in an unstructured setting, such as from reading articles on the Internet or learning a skill from a coworker.

- College access refers to building awareness about college opportunities, providing guidance regarding college admissions, and identifying ways to pay for college. College access includes access to all kinds of postsecondary institutions, including colleges, universities, and trade schools.

- Higher education and job training programs can cost thousands of dollars. Deciding how you will pay for it requires careful thought. Financial aid is available from the federal government as well as nonfederal agencies. Grants, scholarships, work-study programs, and need-based awards are some examples of financial aid.

Check Your Personal Finance IQ

Now that you have finished the chapter, see what you learned about personal finance by taking the chapter posttest. If you do not have a smartphone, visit the G-W Learning companion website.

G-W Learning mobile site: www.m.g-wlearning.com

G-W Learning companion website: www.g-wlearning.com

Review Your Knowledge

1. How do interests, aptitudes, and abilities apply to education and career choices?
2. What are career pathways in the career clusters?
3. How can you use the Internet to find information about jobs and careers?
4. What is a job fair?
5. How does new technology affect the job market?
6. How does informal education differ from formal education?
7. Where can you find information about internships and apprenticeships?
8. How can you find resources related to college access in your state?
9. What steps can you follow to guide you in financing your education?
10. What are some examples of financial aid you may be able to get to help pay for college?

Apply Your Knowledge

11. Choose a career that you may be interested in pursuing. Use the Internet or other sources to find out the employment outlook, education required, and other important information needed about your choice. Write a one-page report summarizing your findings.
12. Discuss the key advantages and disadvantages of going from high school to each of the following: college, occupational training, an internship, an apprenticeship, the armed forces.
13. Research three colleges or trade schools that you would consider attending. Create a chart that shows tuition, room and board, books, and other costs that you may incur. How did the three compare? Share your findings with the class.
14. What types of experiences and activities in high school do you think would be helpful in getting full-time employment? Explain.
15. Ask your guidance counselor for information about grants and scholarships for which you may be eligible. What is required to apply for these opportunities? Make a list of requirements and information needed to complete the application.
16. Completing application forms takes a lot of information. Ask your counselor for an application for financial aid or download one from the Internet. Using a good quality pen, complete the form as accurately as possible. Submit to your instructor for feedback.
17. What types of training and education do you think would be required to obtain the type of employment and position you want to achieve?
18. What does lifelong learning mean to you?
19. Do you believe a four-year college degree is worth the time and expense? Why or why not?
20. What career field do you think will be in most demand in the next 10 years? Give reasons for your answer.

Teamwork

Working with your team, take turns describing skills that you have acquired from doing activities, such as volunteer work, babysitting, or hobbies. On a flip chart or whiteboard, list one or two skills for each team member. Work together to create a list of skills that you could use when you begin looking for a job or applying to college.

G-W Learning Mobile Site

Visit the G-W Learning mobile site to complete the chapter pretest and posttest and to practice vocabulary using e-flash cards. If you do not have a smartphone, visit the G-W Learning companion website to access these features.

G-W Learning mobile site: www.m.g-wlearning.com

G-W Learning companion website: www.g-wlearning.com

Common Core

College and Career Readiness

CTE Career Ready Practices. You may have been taught to treat others how you would like to be treated. This is often referred to as the golden rule. Productively working with others who have a background different from yours may require that you learn to treat others as they wish to be treated. Conduct research on the Internet about cultural differences related to personal space, time, gestures/body language, and relationship toward authority figures. List four differences and how you would approach each.

Reading. Read a magazine, newspaper, or online article about the cost of a college education. Determine the central ideas of the article and review the conclusions made by the author. Provide an accurate summary of your reading, making sure to incorporate the who, what, when, and how of this situation.

Writing. Research the topic of college access. Where did the concept originate? Write an informative report, consisting of several paragraphs to describe your findings.

Web Connect

Research salaries of college graduates. How much can a college graduate expect to earn over a lifetime? How does that amount compare to someone with a high school diploma?

College and Career Readiness

College and Career Readiness Portfolio

Employers and colleges review candidates for various positions. For example, the abilities to communicate effectively, get along with customers or coworkers, and solve problems are important skills for many jobs. These types of skills are often called soft skills. You should make an effort to learn about and develop soft skills you will need for your chosen career area.

1. Do research on the Internet to find articles about soft skills and their value in helping employees succeed.

2. Make a list of the soft skills that you possess that you think would be important for a job or career area. Select three of these soft skills. Write a paragraph about each one that describes your abilities in this area. Give examples that illustrate your skills.

3. Save the document file in your e-portfolio. Place a printed copy in the container for your print portfolio.

Proper Attire

Some Career and Technical Student Organization (CTSOs) require appropriate business attire from all entrants and those attending the competition. This requirement is in keeping with the mission of CTSOs: to prepare students for professional careers.

To be sure that the attire you have chosen to wear at the competition is in accordance with event requirements, complete the following activities.

1. Visit the organization's website and look for the most current dress code.

2. The dress code requirements are very detailed and gender specific. Some CTSOs may require a chapter blazer to be worn during the competition.

3. Do a dress rehearsal when practicing for your event. Are you comfortable in the clothes you have chosen? Do you present a professional appearance?

4. In addition to the kinds of clothes you can wear, be sure the clothes are clean and pressed. You do not want to undermine your appearance or event performance with wrinkled clothes that may distract judges.

5. Make sure your hair is neat and worn in a conservative style. If you are a male, you should be clean-shaven. Again, you do not want anything about your appearance detracting from your performance.

6. As far in advance of the event as is possible, share your clothing choice with your organization's advisor to make sure you are dressed appropriately.

Chapter 16
Entering the Work World

Entering the world of work is a major step for most people. Being employed not only provides you with the means to obtain what you need and want in life, it also gives you a sense of identity and security. For many people, what they do defines who they are.

Finding a job is often a lengthy process. The job seeker can enhance his or her chances of success by becoming aware of standard job seeking practices, such as the proper way to apply for a job and good interviewing skills.

For some people, entry into the world of work does not mean finding a job. Many people prefer to become self-employed and work for themselves. Being self-employed offers many advantages, but it comes with much responsibility and some drawbacks. As with all else in the work world, becoming self-employed should be a decision that has been well-researched and thought about carefully.

Focus on Finance

Citizenship

Life is not all about making money. Being a good citizen is important to your personal and financial success. Good citizens are ethical. You probably hear the term *ethics* almost every day. Personal ethics serve as a moral compass that helps you decide what is right and wrong in different situations. Ethical behavior centers on honesty, fairness, integrity, and well-defined values. Ethical behavior is expected when representing yourself and the business for which you work. Avoid the temptation to "twist the truth" and always keep your communications honest.

Good citizens are socially responsible. *Social responsibility* involves concern for the welfare of those around you in the community and in the world. You show your concern for others through participation in community life, shared problem solving, and good citizenship. Examples include keeping up to date on local issues, voting in every election, and contributing your time and talents to meet needs in your school, job, and community.

Personal ethics and social responsibility are keys to a well-lived life and to success in financial and business matters, as well as personal relationships.

Reading Prep. Before reading this chapter, flip through the pages and make notes of the major headings. Compare these headings to the objectives. What did you discover? How will this help you prepare to read new material?

College and Career Readiness

Check Your Personal Finance IQ

Before you begin the chapter, see what you already know about personal finance by taking the chapter pretest. If you do not have a smartphone, visit the G-W Learning companion website.

G-W Learning mobile site: www.m.g-wlearning.com

G-W Learning companion website: www.g-wlearning.com

Sections

Section 16.1 **Career Application Process**

Section 16.2 **Success in the Workplace**

Section 16.3 **Entrepreneurship**

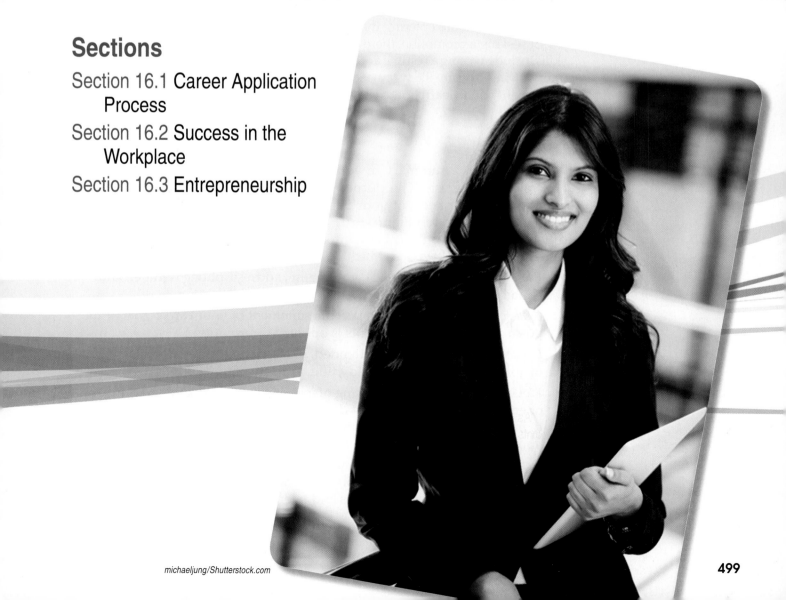

Section 16.1
Career Application Process

Objectives

After studying this section, you will be able to:

- Demonstrate skills needed for success in the job application process.
- Describe the responsibilities of a first job.
- Explain why a Form I-9 is required for new employees.

Terms

résumé	interview
reference	Form I-9
cover message	social responsibility

Job Application Process

Whether you are entering the workforce for the first time, looking for a new job, or seeking a promotion, there are several skills you will want to master. These skills include writing a résumé and cover letter, filling out an application form, and interviewing. You are likely to need these skills more than once in your lifetime. It will benefit you to learn how to be successful in each situation.

Résumé

A **résumé** is a summary of your educational background, work history, and relevant interests. The purpose of a résumé is to draw an employer's attention to key aspects of your background. As an example, Kim Garcia's résumé is illustrated in Figure 16-1. You may need to tailor your résumé for different purposes, but the basic information and general format will be the same. It should be keyed and include the following information.

- *Personal information.* Include your name, address, phone number, and e-mail address.
- *Goals or objectives.* Include a specific statement of your career goal or the position you are seeking. (This is optional information.)
- *Education.* Include schools attended, dates, degrees earned, class rank, major and minor areas of study, and courses completed.
- *Work experience.* Include a listing of jobs held with names and addresses of employers, dates, and brief descriptions of responsibilities. Be sure to include both paid and volunteer positions that give a true picture of your previous experience.
- *Activities and honors.* Include names of school or community activities and organizations in which you have participated, offices held, honors received, and any specific skills and talents you possess if they would be assets on the job.

Kim R. Garcia
1036 Spring Street
Vallejo, California 94590
(707) 555-3214
kgarcia@provider.com

Objective

Mature and responsible high school senior seeks an entry-level job as an office assistant.

Work Experience

Watkins Sportswear, Vallejo, CA

- 9/20-- to present
- Retail Salesperson
- Assisted customers with clothing and athletic shoe selections; scanned purchases and collected payment from customers; inventoried stock monthly; returned merchandise to racks and shelves.

Ojay's Restaurant, Vallejo, CA

- 6/20-- to 9/20--
- Grill Crewperson
- Prepared and cooked food; cleaned work area.

Volunteer Experience

Solano County Food Bank

- 12/20-- to present
- Solicited food donations from grocery store and restaurant managers; prepared bags of food for clients; designed and distributed informational flyers to community groups.

Vallejo Recreation Department

- 6/20-- to 9/20--
- Coached elementary school students in playing soccer.

Education

- Vallejo High School, Vallejo, CA
- 20-- to present; Graduation date: 6/12/20--
- Emphasis on business education and accounting.

Honors and Activities

- National Honor Society, 20-- to 20--
- Business Professionals of America, member, 20-- to 20--.
- Treasurer during junior year.
- Vallejo High School Student Council during sophomore year.
- 4-H member for eight years.

Skills

- Proficient with Microsoft Word, Excel, PowerPoint, and Internet. Fluent in Spanish.

Figure 16-1 Your résumé is one of the first things that introduces you to your potential employer. It pays to give it careful, detailed attention.

A list of references might include previous managers, teachers, or volunteer leaders.

A **reference** is a person who is qualified and willing to speak on your behalf. References may include former teachers, employers, counselors, or others with knowledge of your character and qualifications. Always ask permission from anyone you wish to use as a reference. Provide the name, title, address, and phone number of each reference.

Use good quality paper when you print your résumé and never use colored paper. Some potential employers may ask for an *electronic résumé*. In these cases, save your prepared résumé in a separate file without formatting, such as in text only format. Then you can attach this file to an e-mail to the employer contact. Be sure not to save over your original résumé, with its spacing, special font use, and other formatting.

Your résumé is one of the first things that introduces you to a prospective employer. It pays to give it careful, detailed attention. You can find free résumé templates on the Internet. Microsoft Word has templates that will help you prepare a job-winning résumé. Remember that your résumé is your introduction to a new company; it is usually the first impression of you that a potential employer gets. As a result, it needs to be prepared very carefully and be exceptionally readable.

The origin of the résumé can be traced back to feudal England (in the Middle Ages) when men traveling to different parts of the kingdom were given a letter of introduction by a lord or a head of a local guild.

Cover Message

A **cover message** is a letter or e-mail that you send with your résumé. It also gives you an opportunity to expand on material in the résumé. For example, Kim Garcia's cover letter is illustrated in Figure 16-2. If you are mailing your letter and résumé, use good-quality paper. Most career counselors agree that your cover letter should be printed on paper that matches your résumé. Always take care to use correct spelling and punctuation. Include:

- the purpose of the message, which is to ask for an interview or information about a position;
- a brief statement of your interest in the school, job, or program for which you are applying;

Kim R. Garcia
1036 Spring Street
Vallejo, California 94590
(707) 555-3214
kgarcia@provider.com

April 25, 20--

Mr. Robert Drake
Personnel Manager
Whitaker Publishing Company
1822 W. Meridian St.
Vallejo, CA 94590

Dear Mr. Drake:

Introduction — Through Mr. James Mitchell, vocational counselor at Vallejo High School, I learned your company plans to hire a full-time office assistant in June. I know your company is a worldwide leader in outdoor publications and I would like to apply for this position.

Body — To prepare for office work, I have taken a number of business courses in high school. As mentioned in my résumé, I am skilled in Microsoft Word, Excel, PowerPoint, and navigating the Internet. I am also fluent in Spanish. I am presently gaining on-the-job experience as a retail salesperson with Watkins Sportswear. With my education and work experience, I feel confident I can perform well as an office assistant for your company.

Conclusion — May I have an interview to discuss the job and my qualifications in greater detail? I can be reached at 707-555-3214 or at kgarcia@provider.com. I will appreciate the opportunity to talk with you. Thank you for taking time to consider my application.

Sincerely,

Kim R. Garcia

Kim R. Garcia

Goodheart-Willcox Publisher

Figure 16-2 A cover message gives you an opportunity to make a positive impression on a potential employer.

- highlights from your résumé along with other pertinent information on your experience or qualifications;
- a mention of follow-up steps you plan to take, such as calling to arrange an interview;
- how and where you can be reached for an interview or more information; and
- a thank you.

Application Form

It pays to master application forms because you will complete applications in one situation or another throughout your life. You complete application forms for jobs, schools, credit, apartments, mortgages, and insurance. Kim Garcia's job application is illustrated in Figure 16-3. Some pointers to help you complete a typical application form are listed as follows.

- Copy the form so you can work on it before completing the final form to submit.
- Read the entire form before filling in any spaces. Be sure you understand each question before trying to answer it.
- Follow directions with care, making sure to write clearly and spell correctly.
- Complete all the questions that apply to you on the front and back of the form. For those that do not apply, write "Not applicable" or "NA."
- Give factual, accurate, and positive answers to questions about your education, work history, and past experience.
- Include names, titles, addresses, and phone numbers of former employers and references.

Economics in Action

Financing Education

In an extended economic downturn, many families find it difficult to save money for college or job training. Normal sources of cash for college become scarce. Grants and loans become harder to get. Investments in savings programs lose value. Colleges and universities experience declining values in their endowments and dwindling contributions. State governments are often forced to cut funding for state schools, which means increases in tuitions and fees.

Demand for financial aid becomes stronger, which makes it difficult to qualify for available assistance. While financial aid becomes more limited, college costs are rising. In 2012 the average annual tuition cost for a full credit load for in-state students at four-year universities came close to $8,700. At some private schools, the cost was over $29,000. At the same time, education has never been more important for individual students and for the country.

In order to finance an education, families need to start planning and saving as early as possible. As a student, you should work toward a high school record of achievement that will appeal to college admissions boards. Explore every possible source of money for college—scholarships, grants, loans, savings, work/study programs, and part-time work. Also remember to complete and submit a Free Application for Federal Student Aid through www.fafsa.gov.

APPLICATION FOR EMPLOYMENT

PERSONAL INFORMATION

Date _April 25, 20– –_   Social Security Number _Will provide if hired_

Name _Garcia_ (Last)   _Kim_ (First)   _R._ (Middle)

Present Address _1036 Spring Street_ (Street)   _Vallejo_ (City)   _CA_ (State)   _94590_ (Zip)

Permanent Address _1036 Spring Street_ (Street)   _Vallejo_ (City)   _CA_ (State)   _94590_ (Zip)

Phone No. _(707) 555-3214_   E-mail _kgarcia@provider.com_

If related to anyone in our employ, state name and department _N/A_   Referred by _Mr. James Mitchell Vocational Counselor_

EMPLOYMENT DESIRED

Position _Office Assistant_   Date you can start _June 10, 20– –_   Salary desired _Open_

Are you employed now? _yes_   If so may we inquire of your present employer? _yes_

Ever applied to this company before? _no_   Where _N/A_   When _N/A_

EDUCATION

Name and Location of School

Grammar School _Spring Grove School_
Vallejo, CA

Middle School _Vallejo Middle School_
Vallejo, CA

High School _Vallejo High School_
Vallejo, CA

College _N/A_

Technical, Business or other School _N/A_

Subject of special study or research work

What foreign languages do you fluently speak? _Spanish_   Read? _Spanish_   Write? _Spanish_

U.S. Military or Naval service _N/A_   Rank _N/A_   Present membership in National Guard or Reserves _N/A_

Activities other than religious (civic, athletic, fraternal, etc.) _National Honors Society, Business Professionals of America, Vallejo High School Student Council, 4-H_

Exclude organizations the name or character of which indicates the race, creed, color or national origin of its members

FORMER EMPLOYERS List employers starting with last one first

Date Month and Year	Name and Address of Employer	Salary	Position	Reason for Leaving
From _9/20--_ To _Present_	Watkins Sports Wear 1122 Market Street Vallejo, CA, 94590	$8.50/Hour	Salesperson	Seeking full-time job after graduation
From _7/20--_ To _9/20--_	Ojays Restaurant 1301 Main Street Vallejo, CA, 94590	$8.00/Hour	Grill Crewperson	Summer job
From To				
From To				

REFERENCES List below at least two persons not related to you whom you have known at least one year

Name	Address	Job Title	Years Acquainted
1 Mr. James Mitchell	Vallejo High School 3300 W. Glendale Ave. Vallejo, CA 94590	Vocational Counselor	3
2 Ms. Angelica Ortiz	Watkins Sportswear 1122 Market Street Vallejo, CA 94590	Store Manager	1
3			

I authorize investigation of all statements contained in this application. I understand that misrepresentation or omission of facts called for is cause for dismissal.

Date _April 25, 20– –_   Signature _Kim R Garcia_

Goodheart-Willcox Publisher

Figure 16-3 Most job application forms call for similar information to that on this example.

Interview

An **interview** is the employer's opportunity to meet with you and discuss the job and your qualifications for the job. This is an important meeting and calls for careful preparation. Pluses here include appropriate clothing, prompt arrival, and a firm handshake. Also, keep the following in mind: eye contact, direct answers to questions, intelligent questions of your own, and a confident manner.

Be Prepared

Materials to bring include copies of your résumé, application form, correspondence, references, and transcripts. Be ready to discuss your class rank or grade point average and other facts that may be requested. Bring a pen and paper to take notes.

Find out as much as you can about the company for which you are applying. Be informed about your field of interest, if it is established at this point.

Anticipate Questions

Think about questions you may be asked and about how you will answer those questions. You may be asked questions such as the following.

- Why do you want to work for this company or apply for this position?
- What can you contribute to this organization?
- What are your strengths and weaknesses?
- What are your educational and professional goals?
- What type of work do you most enjoy? least enjoy?

Ask Questions

Ask specific questions about job responsibilities, opportunities for advancement, and other items that fit the situation. When the interview is complete, be prepared to ask closing questions. For example, will you be contacted, or should you call to learn the results of the interview? Should you send additional information or materials? Let the interviewer know where and when you can be contacted.

Follow Up

Be sure you note the interviewer's name and title so you can use it in a follow-up letter. The purpose of the letter is to thank the interviewer and indicate that you are (or are not) still interested in the job. Also include your name, address, and phone number; the date of the interview; and the job you applied for. If you do not receive a response from your interview within two or three weeks, call to inquire about the results.

Your First Job

Landing the job you want is just a beginning. You want to do all you can to succeed and advance in your chosen field. Some work habits and traits will be important for success in almost any job, from stock clerk to top

Tyler Olson/Shutterstock.com

To be successful in the workplace, an employee must be able to work with others as a cooperative member of the team.

executive. These habits and traits include promptness, reliable attendance, dependability, a positive attitude, and eagerness to do the work as best you can. Meeting the dress standards of your work environment will help you fit in and move ahead. If there is no dress code to guide you, take your cue from reliable coworkers or ask superiors what is appropriate. This applies to "casual Fridays," too.

You will need to master basic communication skills, such as meeting and greeting clients and customers, interacting with other employees and your superiors, and handling business telephone calls and e-mails. Most jobs call for written communication skills. Face-to-face communications call for eye contact, a firm handshake, and an easy conversational manner. Listening to what other people say is important as well. Concentrate on names, dates, information, and instructions you will need to remember. Take notes when you are receiving detailed instructions or information you will need later.

A businesslike approach to your job will take you a long way. This means taking job responsibilities seriously. Stick to the work you have to do and try not to be idle during working hours. If you find yourself with time on your hands, ask for more work to do. If you end up with more than you can complete, discuss the situation with your superior before falling hopelessly behind. There are some behaviors you should avoid on the job. Do not send and receive personal e-mail and phone calls on company time. Do not let friends drop by to see you at your workplace.

In many workplaces, it is important that you be able to work as a team member. You will be working with others toward common goals. To do this successfully you will need to cooperate with coworkers, give others credit for their ideas and contributions, do your fair share of the work, and be a reliable part of the group. Very often, experience on an athletic team or group project in school provides a helpful background in cooperating with others to achieve a common goal.

Business Management & Administration

Employment Interviewers

Employment interviewers help job seekers find suitable job openings and employers find qualified staff. They may work for private employment agencies, state government employment services, or private companies. They interview applicants to explore their interests and abilities. They then attempt to match the applicants with jobs that are on file.

As you learn to work with a team, you may discover that you have leadership qualities. Being a leader means more than giving directions to others. Leaders have the ability to motivate others to participate in tasks. Encouraging open communication among team members is another important aspect of this role. Effective leaders make sure that each team member feels valued and that each voice is heard. They identify the individual strengths of each team member and make sure team members are recognized for accomplishments. They encourage team diversity and value all cultures.

In addition to the role of employee, you also fill the role of citizen. Good citizens participate, volunteer, and accept responsibility for themselves. They respect the environment, behave ethically, and often accept responsibility for helping others as well. A part of good citizenship is **social responsibility**, which is a general sense of concern for the needs of others in the community, country, and world. Social responsibility is about an individual's duty to take care of others and the world they share. It also involves finding constructive approaches to current social issues and needs. Many workplaces encourage their employees to be socially responsible by participating in community and charitable activities. Social responsibility can include providing relief for disaster victims, working at shelters, and raising money for charity. Protecting the environment and conserving natural resources are other aspects of social responsibility.

Employment Eligibility

Following acceptance of a position, you will be required to complete an Employment Eligibility Verification Form, or a Form I-9. A **Form I-9** is used to verify an employee's identity and that he or she is authorized to work in the United States. Figure 16-4 illustrates the portion of this form that declares

Department of Homeland Security
U.S. Citizenship and Immigration Services

Form I-9, Employment Eligibility Verification

Read instructions carefully before completing this form. The instructions must be available during completion of this form.

ANTI-DISCRIMINATION NOTICE: It is illegal to discriminate against work-authorized individuals. Employers CANNOT specify which document(s) they will accept from an employee. The refusal to hire an individual because the documents have a future expiration date may also constitute illegal discrimination.

Section 1. Employee Information and Verification *(To be completed and signed by employee at the time employment begins.)*

| Print Name: Last | First | Middle Initial | Maiden Name |

| Address *(Street Name and Number)* | | Apt. # | Date of Birth *(month/day/year)* |

| City | State | Zip Code | Social Security # |

I am aware that federal law provides for imprisonment and/or fines for false statements or use of false documents in connection with the completion of this form.

I attest, under penalty of perjury, that I am (check one of the following):
- [ ] A citizen of the United States
- [ ] A noncitizen national of the United States (see instructions)
- [ ] A lawful permanent resident (Alien #) _____
- [ ] An alien authorized to work (Alien # or Admission #) _____
  until (expiration date, if applicable - *month/day/year*)

Employee's Signature   Date *(month/day/year)*

Department of Homeland Security

Figure 16-4 A portion of the Employment Eligibility Verification Form I-9.

citizenship status. Both citizens and noncitizens must complete this form. You will be required to present one of many documents the government will accept as proof of employability. The employer may not specify which document you must present. Common documents would be a valid driver's license, photo ID, or passport. It must include a photo or information such as name, date of birth, gender, height, eye color, and address.

The employer must keep this form on file for three years or one year after the employee is terminated. It must be made available for inspection by authorized US government officials, such as representatives of the Department of Homeland Security, Department of Labor, or Department of Justice.

Checkpoint 16.1

1. What categories of information should be included on a résumé?
2. What is the purpose of a cover message?
3. Why should you read the entire application form before you begin to answer questions on the form?
4. What can you do to be prepared for an interview?
5. What are some basic communication skills you will need to master for work?

Build Your Vocabulary

As you progress through this course, develop a personal glossary of personal finance terms and add it to your portfolio. This will help you build your vocabulary and prepare you for a career. Write a definition for each of the following terms and add it to your personal finance glossary.

résumé	interview
reference	Form I-9
cover message	social responsibility

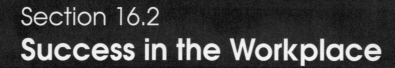

Section 16.2
Success in the Workplace

Objectives

After studying this section, you will be able to:

- Describe the importance of workplace law.
- Discuss safety practices on the job.
- Define workplace ethics.
- Make recommendations on the proper way to leave a job.

Terms

Occupational Safety and Health
   Administration (OSHA)

falling hazards

lifting hazards

material-storage hazards

ergonomics

copyright

license

software piracy

freeware

shareware

netiquette

phishing

cyberbullying

software viruses

Workplace Laws

The US Department of Labor enforces laws that protect workers. There are over 180 federal laws that apply to the workplace. Figure 16-5 shows a brief summary of laws that protect the rights of workers.

In 1970, the *Occupational Safety and Health Act* was passed. The Occupational Safety and Health Administration was established a year later. The **Occupational Safety and Health Administration (OSHA)** is a federal agency that enforces safety and health regulations in the workplace. OSHA's efforts have led to a significant decline in workplace injuries and deaths since the 1970s.

Workplace Accidents

Falling hazards, lifting hazards, and material-storage hazards account for most of the workplace accidents that occur in offices. **Falling hazards** are sources of potential injuries from slipping or falling. Falls are the most common workplace accident in an office setting. Falls can result in broken bones, head injuries, and muscle strains. To avoid workplace falls:

- close drawers completely;
- do not stand on a chair or box to reach; and
- secure cords, rugs, and mats.

Lifting hazards are sources of potential injury from improperly lifting or carrying items. Most back injuries are caused by improper lifting. To avoid injuries resulting from lifting:

Worker Protection Laws	
Law	**Key Provisions**
Fair Labor Standards Act (FLSA)	Establishes the minimum wage, overtime pay, child labor standards, and other workplace conditions that affect covered workers
Family and Medical Leave Act (FMLA)	Requires employers to allow eligible employees up to 12 weeks of unpaid job-protected leave annually for birth or adoption and care of a child, care of a seriously ill family member, or a serious personal health condition
Consolidated Omnibus Budget Reconciliation Act (COBRA)	Gives eligible workers who leave their place of employment the right to continue their employer-sponsored group health insurance, including coverage for preexisting conditions, for up to 18 months at their own expense
Occupational Safety and Health Act (OSHA)	Promotes and enforces safety and health standards in the workplace
Equal Employment Opportunity Comminisson (EEOC)	Protects employees against discrimination based on race, color, disability, religion, sex, age, and national origin in hiring, promoting, firing, wages, testing, training, and all other terms and conditions of employment
Employee Retirement Income Security Act (ERISA)	Outlines employees' rights as participants in an employer's pension and/or profit-sharing plans

Figure 16-5 These federal laws protect the rights of workers.

- make several small trips with items rather than one trip with an overly heavy load;
- use dollies or handcarts whenever possible;
- lift with the legs, not the back; and
- never carry an item that blocks vision.

Material-storage hazards are sources of potential injury that come from the improper storage of files, books, or office equipment. A cluttered workplace is an unsafe workplace. Material stacked too high can fall on employees. Paper and files that are stored on the floor or hall are a fire risk. To prevent injuries:

- do not stack boxes or papers on top of tall cabinets;
- store heavier objects on lower shelves; and
- keep aisles and hallways clear.

Maintaining a safe workplace is the joint responsibility of the employer and employee. The employer should make sure the facility and working conditions are such that accidents are unlikely to occur. The employee should use common sense and care while at the office.

Workplace safety in the United States has continuously improved since the beginning of the 20th century. Gradually, workplace injury, death, and illness have declined. This is due to a change in the type of work done today and in the safety precautions that have been put in place. Many workers now spend extended periods of time in front of computers. This work can also result in injury. **Ergonomics** is the science of adapting the workstation to fit the needs of the worker and lessen the chance of injury. Figure 16-6 depicts the best way for a worker to sit at a computer workstation.

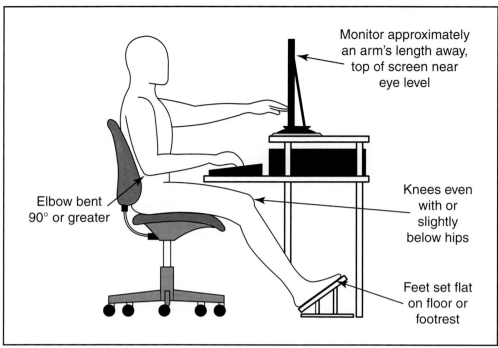

Monitor approximately an arm's length away, top of screen near eye level

Elbow bent 90° or greater

Knees even with or slightly below hips

Feet set flat on floor or footrest

Goodheart-Willcox Publisher

Figure 16-6 An ergonomic workstation is safe and comfortable.

Workplace Ethics

Ethics in the workplace is a significant issue in the business world. *Ethics* are a set of moral values that guide a person's behavior. They help a person determine what is right and wrong in given situations. Ethics are based on traits, such as trustworthiness, honesty, loyalty, respect, responsibility, and fairness. Over 90 percent of business schools now require ethics courses as part of their curriculum.

An employee with strong ethics will always try to do the right thing. Employees demonstrate their ethics through honesty, integrity, and loyalty. *Honesty* is the quality of being truthful and sincere. *Integrity* is strong moral character. Employees with integrity will consistently refuse to compromise their ethical principles, regardless of any outside influence, punishment, or reward. *Loyalty* is faithfulness to a commitment. In the business world, it is faithfulness to an employer or a supplier.

Companies differ in their approach to workplace behavior. Some companies simply assume that employees bring their own standards to the job, and management offers very little guidance. Some companies rely on an informal corporate culture that guides job-related decisions and actions. Other businesses follow a carefully developed program. This program may include a statement of corporate values and a code of ethics to guide employees.

Today, more and more businesses are adopting clearly formulated ethics programs to guide behavior and decisions in the workplace. In companies that take ethics seriously, top management will project the value system that drives behavior. A company may convey its expectations for ethics on the job in different ways. These ways include employee handbooks, training sessions or seminars, or printed formal statements of company values and ethics.

The standards only have meaning when the message comes from management and is enforced by example. Stated codes of ethics generally

Business Management & Administration

Human Resources Recruiters

Human resources recruiters recruit and place workers. They maintain contacts within the community and may travel considerably, often to college campuses, to search for promising job applicants. They screen, interview, and occasionally test applicants. They may also check references and extend job offers.

You Do the Math   ÷ − + ×

Subtraction is the process of taking away from a larger whole. The large number is the *minuend*, the number that is being subtracted is the *subtrahend*. The difference is the *remainder*.

Complete the Following Problems

According to the US Census Bureau, individuals with college degrees have higher earning power than those without a degree. Assume that someone with a high school diploma will have lifetime earnings of $1.2 million; someone with a bachelor degree, $2.1 million; and someone with a master degree, $2.5 million.

1. What are the increased earnings from a high school diploma to a bachelor degree?

2. What are the increased earnings from a high school diploma to a master degree?

3. What are the increased earnings from a bachelor degree to a master degree?

address relationships of the business with employees, customers, suppliers, investors, creditors, competitors, and the community. Business codes of ethics frequently relate to issues such as fair treatment of employees, teamwork, competition, and conflicts of interest. Other issues include use of business resources and assets, confidentiality, and environmental concerns.

When you apply for jobs, inquire about an employer's policies regarding employee decisions and behavior on the job. If ever in doubt about what is and is not acceptable, ask before you act.

Software

It is unethical, and illegal, for an employee to download software that has not been purchased and registered by the employer. All software is protected by a copyright; however, some software may be released by its owner for free use. A **copyright** is the exclusive right to copy, license, sell, or distribute material. In the United States, an original work is copyrighted as soon as it is in tangible form. When you buy software, you are buying a license. A **license** is the legal permission to use a software program. All software has terms of use that outline what the license allows and how the software may be used.

If you buy software, you have the license, and you can use the software on your computer. If a business buys software, the business has the license for the software. A software license allows you to use the software, just like a driver's license allows you to drive a car. **Software piracy** is the illegal copying or downloading of software. This includes scanning or downloading images or music. Never engage in software piracy.

Some software may only be lawfully used if it is purchased. These programs are known as *for-purchase software*. Demo software may be used without buying it, but demos are either limited in functionality or time. Other software, known as **freeware,** is fully functional and can be used forever without purchasing it. To be considered freeware, the software cannot be

Almost everything found on the Internet is copyrighted, including images, music, videos, and textual information. A copyright statement is *not* required, and lack of a copyright statement does not mean the work has no copyright.

a demo or restricted version of software meant for purchase. **Shareware** is software that can be installed and used without cost. You purchase the software if you decide to keep using it. Shareware usually has a notice screen, time-delayed startup, or reduced features. Purchasing the software removes these restrictions. Figure 16-7 identifies the differences between software types.

The difference between a demo of for-purchase software and shareware is subtle. Typically, shareware software is not limited. This means that the software remains functional forever with restrictions. Shareware is based on the honor system. Those who continue to use the software are expected to purchase it. A demo of for-purchase software, however, typically stops working after a period of time. In the case of a limited-feature demo, the best features are either not functional or are functional only for a limited time.

Public-domain software is similar to freeware in that it is free. However, freeware is copyrighted, while public-domain software either has no copyright or the copyright has expired. Some photographs, music, videos, and textual information are in the public domain.

Business Devices

Company equipment is to be used for business-related functions, not personal use. Office equipment includes everything from the computer on your desk to the photocopy machine and the company phone. All employees must be aware of appropriate use of office equipment.

Hardware, such as computers and photocopiers, are provided to employees to improve efficiency. In many cases, it would be impossible for an employee to even do the basics of his or her job without this equipment. Always be aware of what you are doing when using company hardware. For example, computers are company property and, as such, the company

Ethics

While you are at work or school, it is important to be respectful in your use of computer equipment. The computer is available for your use as a tool for research or to accomplish a task. It is unethical to use the computer, without permission, for personal means, such as playing games, shopping, or other activities that are outside of your assignments. It is also unethical to access confidential information, download copyrighted material, or harass others. Many organizations monitor users to make certain that the computer activity is ethical and legal. Users may also be required to sign an agreement that the computer will only be used for specific purposes.

michaeljung/Shutterstock.com

Company equipment, such as tablets, computers, and cell phones, should be used for work-related purposes only and not for personal or leisure use.

Characteristics	Software Type		
	For-Purchase	Freeware	Shareware
Cost	• Must be purchased to use • Demo may be available	Never have to pay for it	• Free to try • Pay to upgrade to full functionality
Features	Full functionality	Full functionality	Limited functionality without upgrade

Goodheart-Willcox Publisher

Figure 16-7 Ethical software use depends on whether the software is for-purchase, freeware, or shareware.

can look at information stored on them at any time. Do not store personal or inappropriate information on company computers.

Mobile devices, such as smartphones or tablets, provided by the company for employee use are company property. Always be aware that you represent the company when you use one of these devices. They should not be used for personal reasons without company approval. Additionally, be aware of any communication you send with these devices. Be sure it follows company policies for acceptable communication and behavior.

Internet Access

Internet access provided by the company should be used only for business purposes. Checking personal e-mail or shopping online is not acceptable. When communicating using the Internet, you are a representative of the company. Proper netiquette should be followed.

Netiquette is the accepted social and professional guidelines for communicating using the Internet. Never use texting language in a business environment. It is unprofessional to do so. Also, always proofread and spell-check e-mails before sending them. If you are sending e-mail to a customer in response to a question, texting a coworker, blogging about a company product, or any other communication, it is important to follow the same common courtesy you would follow for a face-to-face discussion.

If you create publications or blogs for the company, perhaps as a marketing function, you might think of using images, video, text, or sounds you find on the Internet. Remember, almost everything on the Internet is protected by copyright. This material is the result of someone's work and creativity. Without appropriate permission, you cannot use this material.

Phishing, which is pronounced *fishing*, is a fun-sounding name for an activity that is not fun at all. **Phishing** is the use of fraudulent e-mails and copies of legitimate websites to trick people into providing personal, financial, and other data. The most common form of phishing is done by sending an e-mail to the intended victim. The e-mail message pretends to be from a legitimate source, such as the victim's bank. The e-mail asks the victim to send certain information, such as an account number and password, or it provides a link to a web page. If the victim goes to the web page, the site looks

Business Management & Administration

Equal Employment Opportunity Specialists

Equal employment opportunity specialists provide advice to management concerning how to prevent discriminatory practices in recruiting, hiring, promotions, pay, and benefits. They analyze workforce characteristics and organizational structure and make recommendations to ensure compliance with laws and requirements.

legitimate, but it collects the information the victim enters. The information can then be used to commit fraud.

Businesses can protect customers from phishing e-mails by keeping their customers' information secure. They can also warn customers if information has been stolen or if the company knows that phishing e-mails pretending to be from the company are circulating. Customers can protect themselves by using software that filters their e-mail. Legitimate businesses do not request confidential information via e-mail.

Cyberbullying is using the Internet to harass or threaten an individual. Cyberbullying includes sending threatening messages or something as simple as intentionally flooding someone's e-mail. Do not participate in any activity that could be considered bullying another individual.

Software Viruses

Viruses can be introduced by downloading infected programs from the Internet. Using the Internet at school or work without following guidelines can put the computer and the network at risk. **Software viruses** are computer programs that cause harm to computer systems. A virus may destroy customer data on the computer or collect information from the company's network

Case Study

Starting a Business

Martin got his first computer at age three. His computer knowledge and expertise grew with each passing year. After high school graduation, Martin took computer technician and business courses at the Institute of Electronics. With certification in the field in which he excelled, Martin decided to open his own business.

Martin contacted the local office of the US Small Business Administration for information and guidance. He got a $10,000 loan and rented a small storefront. He also used the money to purchase parts, tools, and software.

Martin then created a website advertising computer repairs, installations, consultations, and tech support by a certified computer technician. He distributed fliers to small businesses and homes in the area.

Most customers want on-site service, so Martin only opens the store for three hours a day. Since most business is from repeat customers, Martin now offers services on a contract basis. This provides a more predictable monthly income.

Case Review

1. What do you think of Martin's dream of having his own business?
2. What do you see as the advantages and disadvantages of going into computer technology as your own boss versus working for an established computer tech company?
3. Under what circumstances would you be willing to take the risks and devote the time and effort required to start and run a business?
4. How would you evaluate Martin's approach to reaching his goal?
5. What factors do you think will contribute to the success or failure of Martin's business over time?

and transmit it to some other location. They can also be contained in e-mail attachments or transmitted by visiting websites. In general, viruses can be file infections, boot-sector infections, worms, and Trojan horses.

Never open an e-mail attachment that you are not expecting. It is better to send an e-mail asking about the attachment before opening it than to deal with a virus infection. Avoid visiting questionable websites or downloading files from unknown sources to the computer.

Leaving a Job

Leaving a job, whether by resignation or job termination, is something most workers experience at some time. Knowing how to leave can help you make a positive transition into a new job. If you leave by choice, it is a good idea to have a new job before you leave your present position. Keep in mind that it is almost always easier to find a job when you have one. It is important to give appropriate notice, usually two weeks, before leaving a job. Put your resignation in writing to document the communication and help avoid misunderstandings. The letter, addressed to the appropriate person in the human resources department, should be a simple statement of your intent to leave and the date on which you will be leaving. Include the date on your letter and your signature, address, and phone number. It pays to leave with as much goodwill as possible. You may need references or cooperation of coworkers and superiors in future positions.

If you are fired or your job is terminated, you need to know your rights and benefits under the law. In most states, you can be fired for incompetence, breaking company rules, excessive absence or tardiness, and many other reasons. You also may be laid off because business is not good and your employer is downsizing or merging with another company. However, you cannot legally be fired for any form of discrimination, such as age, race, religion, sex, marital status, sexual orientation, or disability.

If you think your rights have been violated, it is important to contact the appropriate government office. This will usually be the nearest Equal Employment Opportunity Commission (EEOC) office or your state's Department of Human Rights office. Find out whether you are eligible for unemployment benefits and employer-sponsored health insurance.

Checkpoint 16.2

1. What federal law promotes and enforces safety and health standards in the workplace?
2. What types of hazards account for most of the workplace accidents that occur in offices?
3. What are ethics?
4. Explain the difference between freeware and public-domain software.
5. Why is netiquette important in the business world?

Build Your Vocabulary

As you progress through this course, develop a personal glossary of personal finance terms and add it to your portfolio. This will help you build your vocabulary and prepare you for a career. Write a definition for each of the following terms and add it to your personal finance glossary.

Occupational Safety and Health Administration (OSHA)

falling hazards

lifting hazards

material-storage hazards

ergonomics

copyright

license

software piracy

freeware

shareware

netiquette

phishing

cyberbullying

software viruses

Objectives

After studying this section, you will be able to:

- List advantages and disadvantages of becoming an entrepreneur.
- Identify major parts of a business plan.

Terms

entrepreneur

sole proprietorship

partnership

limited liability company (LLC)

corporation

franchise

business plan

Becoming an Entrepreneur

Becoming an **entrepreneur**, a person who owns and operates a business, is another way to enter the world of work. It involves investing your money and talents to earn a profit (income).

Entrepreneurs have always played a key role in the growth and success of the American economy. A few of the most successful entrepreneurs have names you will recognize. Bill Gates, Walt Disney, and Oprah Winfrey are all well-known entrepreneurs. Most major corporations were started by one person who had an idea and a plan. These individuals started with a dream and a willingness to work hard and take risks.

You may think big businesses dominate the marketplace, but small businesses are the backbone of the US economy. Since the mid-1970s, more than two-thirds of the new jobs in the nation were created by small businesses. Small firms employ approximately 60 percent of the nongovernment workforce. Approximately 21 million small businesses exist in America today. Most of these employ fewer than 20 workers. For those who like to be their own boss, becoming an entrepreneur may be the answer.

Starting a business can be risky. Thousands of small businesses fail each year. To succeed in a business of your own, it is a good idea to have previous work experience with the service or product you plan to sell or produce. You need to know how to manage a business, sell your goods and services, and deal with customers and suppliers. You need to keep accurate financial records and know the legalities involved in running a business. You will require enough money to get started and operate until the business begins to pay for itself.

There are some disadvantages to being an entrepreneur. To establish your own business, you will need to work long and hard. Unfortunately, there is no sure income and no guarantee of success. There is very little financial security when you begin. However, for those who do succeed, the advantages and rewards can be great. They include not only income and profits, but also independence and personal satisfaction.

Odua Images/Shutterstock.com

Entrepreneurs play an important role in the growth of the US economy.

The word entrepreneur is of French origin and means to undertake or to make an undertaking.

Figure 16-8 shows a summary of the forms of ownership. A business of your own can take four basic forms:

- a **sole proprietorship** is a business that has a single owner;
- a **partnership** is a business that has two or more owners;
- **limited liability company (LLC)** is a business that is organized as a proprietorship, but the liabilities (debts) are limited to the assets of the business; and
- a **corporation** is a business that is a separate legal entity that is owned by investors called *stockholders* or *shareholders*.

Rather than starting a business completely on their own, many entrepreneurs prefer franchising. A **franchise** is an agreement that permits

Go Green

At school and in the office, paper helps people communicate. Paper is used to take notes, write reports, and countless other tasks. Although business articles have long discussed a "paperless office," workers still find many reasons to print rather than to save information digitally. According to the EPA, the average office worker in the United States will use approximately 10,000 sheets of paper in a year. Considering how much paper is used each year and how much ink or toner is needed to print those pages, planning printing needs can help conserve resources.

Forms of Business Ownership				
Form of Business	**Is formal application to the state required?**	**Ease of Formation**	**Cost of Formation**	**Are owner(s) personally responsible for debt if the business fails?**
Sole Proprietorship	No	Easy	Low	Yes
Partnership	No	Easy	Low	Yes
Limited Liability Company (LLC)	Yes	Moderate	Moderate	No
Corporation	Yes	Involved	High	No

Goodheart-Willcox Publisher

Figure 16-8 Each type of business ownership has unique advantages.

the franchisee to market and sell goods and services in a given area that are provided by the franchiser. Fast-food restaurants, car rental companies, and cleaning services are among the many franchise businesses.

Writing a Business Plan

If you decide to start your own business, you will need to write a business plan. A **business plan** is a formal document that states the goals of your business and includes a detailed strategy of how you will achieve your goals and grow your business. A business plan will be necessary if you need to obtain a loan or other funding to start the business.

The US Small Business Administration (SBA) provides a wealth of information and resources for businesspeople and entrepreneurs. These resources include an online training course in business planning and business plan samples. These samples can be very helpful when writing a business plan.

Purpose of a Business Plan

A business plan serves several purposes. It helps an entrepreneur think through his or her ideas and set goals and objectives. An effectively written business plan can help convince investors and bank loan officers to put money into a new or already existing company. A business plan should be updated as a business grows. Goals and objectives, as well as strategies for achieving them, may change over time.

Parts of a Business Plan

Writing a business plan should be the first step in creating a business. According to the SBA, a business plan consists of several parts, which are discussed in the following paragraphs.

Careers help students set realistic academic and career goals and develop a plan to achieve them;

evaluate students' abilities and interests through aptitude assessments and interviews; and

develop strategies with teachers, administrators, and parents to help students succeed.

What Is It Like to Work as a High School Guidance Counselor?

Most **high school guidance counselors** work full time. They work in private and public schools. They often have private offices so that they can meet with students and have confidential conversations. In some schools, they also teach classes. Some have summers off when school is not in session.

What Education and Skills Are Needed to be a High School Guidance Counselor?

- master degree in school counseling or a related field, such as school psychology
- people skills
- listening skills
- written and oral communication skills
- compassion
- patience
- attention to detail
- ability to work with parents, teachers, and other school staff members

docent/Shutterstock.com

A business plan should be updated regularly as the company grows and changes its goals and objectives.

1. Executive Summary

The executive summary is a succinct one- to two-page description of the business. It should grab the reader's attention and make him or her want to learn more. Although it comes first in the plan, it is written last.

2. Company Description

The company description section gives details about the business and who will run it. It should include the following information.

- Mission and vision statements, or brief descriptions of the business's purpose and its plan for future growth
- Company goals and objectives
- Company history
- List of company principals, or key employees

3. Market Definition

An overview of the industry and market are given in the market definition section. This includes the current and projected size of the entire market and who the competitors are. The plan provides an estimate of how much of that market the entrepreneur hopes to capture. Characteristics of target customers are given, as well as the customer needs the business will satisfy.

4. Products and Services

The goods and/or services the business creates, as well as prices charged, are described in the products and services section. Business plan writers must address the issue of competitiveness, explaining why the products and services they produce will be successful despite competition from other companies.

5. Organization and Management

The organization and management section details how the company is organized, including its legal structure (proprietorship, partnership, or corporation). It may include an organizational chart that shows the relationships among various departments and employees. Biographies of company leaders and any special licenses and permits held by the business are given.

6. Marketing and Sales Strategy

The target market was defined in the market definition section. How the business will reach this market is outlined in this section. It includes the following information.

- The positioning information describes the niche this product or service will fill relative to products and services already available.
- The pricing information describes what competitors charge and what customers are willing to pay. It gives a rationale for pricing.
- The promotion information outlines advertising, sales events, and other strategies to get product or service information out to consumers.
- The place information discusses how the product will be distributed or put into the hands of consumers.

7. Financials

This section gives financial statements for the business. The statements that should be included are described below.

- A balance sheet measures the net worth or value of a business at a particular time.
- An income statement reports the revenue and expenses of a business and shows a net income or net loss.
- A cash flow statement reports how cash moves in and out of a business.

Financial statements for a proposed business should contain estimates of these costs over one year, as well as a summary of start-up costs and budgets.

8. Appendices

Appendices may include information such as company brochures, résumés of those in leadership roles, copies of published articles about the business, photographs of products, and contracts.

Checkpoint 16.3

1. Which type of business is owned by investors called stockholders or shareholders?
2. Small firms employ what percentage of the nongovernment workforce?
3. What are some disadvantages to being an entrepreneur?
4. What is the purpose of a business plan?
5. What financial statements should be included in a business plan?

Build Your Vocabulary

As you progress through this course, develop a personal glossary of personal finance terms and add it to your portfolio. This will help you build your vocabulary and prepare you for a career. Write a definition for each of the following terms and add it to your personal finance glossary.

entrepreneur

sole proprietorship

partnership

limited liability company (LLC)

corporation

franchise

business plan

Chapter Summary

Section 16.1 Career Application Process

- Whether you are entering the workforce for the first time, looking for a new job, or seeking a promotion, there are several skills you will want to master. These skills include writing a résumé and cover letter, filling out an application form, and interviewing.

- Some work habits and traits will be important for success in almost any job. These habits and traits include promptness, reliable attendance, dependability, and a positive attitude. You will need to master basic communication skills, take job responsibilities seriously, and be able to work as a team member.

- An Employment Eligibility Verification Form, or Form I-9, is a record of your identity and your eligibility to work in the United States. When filling out this form, you must present a document that proves employability, such as a driver's license or passport.

Section 16.2 Success in the Workplace

- The US Department of Labor enforces laws that protect workers. These laws relate to worker safety, employment eligibility, medical leave, health insurance, minimum wage, overtime pay, child labor standards, and other issues that affect workers.

- Ethics in the workplace is a significant issue in the business world. Some companies rely on an informal corporate culture to guide job-related decisions and actions. Other businesses follow a carefully developed ethics program.

- Social responsibility is a general sense of concern for the needs of others in the community, country, and world. Social responsibility is about an individual's duty to take care of others and the world they share. It also involves finding constructive approaches to current social issues and needs.

- Knowing how to leave a job can help you make a positive transition into a new job. If you leave by choice, it is important to give appropriate notice. If you are fired or your job is terminated, you need to know your rights and benefits under the law.

Section 16.3 Entrepreneurship

- An entrepreneur is a person who owns and operates a business. The business may be formed as a sole proprietorship, a partnership, a limited liability company, or a corporation.

- For entrepreneurs who succeed, the advantages and rewards can be great. They include not only income and profits, but also independence and personal satisfaction. There are some disadvantages to being an entrepreneur. To establish your own business, you will need to work long and hard. There is no sure income and no guarantee of success.

- A business plan helps an entrepreneur think through his or her ideas and set goals and objectives. These parts are typically included in a business plan: executive summary, company description, market definition, products and services, organization and management, marketing and sales strategy, financials, and appendices.

Check Your Personal Finance IQ

Now that you have finished the chapter, see what you learned about personal finance by taking the chapter posttest. If you do not have a smartphone, visit the G-W Learning companion website.

G-W Learning mobile site: www.m.g-wlearning.com

G-W Learning companion website: www.g-wlearning.com

Review Your Knowledge

1. What is the purpose of a résumé?
2. What information should be included with a cover message that you send with your résumé?
3. What is the purpose of a follow-up letter sent after an interview?
4. What should you do if you find yourself with time on your hands at work? What should you do if you have more work to do than you can complete?
5. What type of accident is the most common in an office setting? What steps can you take to prevent this type of accident?
6. What is the fair use doctrine for copyrighted material?
7. When you resign from a job, why should you put your resignation in writing? What are the main points the letter should include?
8. When is it appropriate to use texting language in a business message?
9. What are three types of businesses that are often operated as franchises?
10. What are some things you need to succeed in a business of your own?

Apply Your Knowledge

11. Discuss pointers for using a résumé, an interview, and an application form to present yourself as a suitable job candidate.
12. Completing applications correctly takes time and practice. Do an Internet search for a job application and print one of your choice. Practice completing the form several times until you are comfortable using a pen and printing the information.
13. Review the sample resume in this chapter. Using it as an example, create your own personal resume that you may use for a job application.
14. Review the cover message in this chapter. Using it as an example, create a cover message to request an interview.
15. Assume you just completed a successful interview for a position. Write a thank you letter to the person with whom you interviewed.
16. If you were starting a business, what form of ownership would you choose? Why?
17. Do you consider franchising a good option for starting a business? Why or why not?

18. Do you think taking the time to write a business plan is worthwhile when starting a new business? Why or why not?

19. What do you think is the most important part of the business plan?

20. Do an Internet search for sample business plans. Which one(s) do you find most interesting? Why?

Teamwork

In this chapter, you read about the importance of workplace safety. Working with a teammate, brainstorm safety ideas for your school. Make a list of steps that can help make your school a safer place. Create a poster that outlines these steps and present to your class.

G-W Learning Mobile Site

Visit the G-W Learning mobile site to complete the chapter pretest and posttest and to practice vocabulary using e-flash cards. If you do not have a smartphone, visit the G-W Learning companion website to access these features.

G-W Learning mobile site: www.m.g-wlearning.com

G-W Learning companion website: www.g-wlearning.com

Common Core

College and Career Readiness

CTE Career Ready Practices. When planning a career, it is necessary to use career planning tools and strategies. Make a list of strategies you would recommend that a person use to enter a career for which they are qualified.

Speaking. Participate in a collaborative classroom discussion about college and career readiness. Ask questions to participants that connect your ideas to the relevant evidence that has been presented.

Listening. Do an Internet search on speeches about college education. Select one speech of your choice and listen to it in its entirety. Present your findings and supporting evidence of the line of reasoning, organization, development, and style the speaker used to prepare his or her information. Identify the audience and the purpose of the speech.

Web Connect

Do a search for financial aid applications or ask your school counselor for forms. Completing applications requires a lot of personal information and time. Practice completing a form using a good quality pen.

College and Career Readiness

College and Career Readiness Portfolio

Employers and colleges review candidates for various positions. For example, you may discuss software programs you can use or machines you know how to operate. These abilities are often called hard skills. You should make an effort to learn about and develop the hard skills you will need for your chosen career area.

1. Do research on the Internet to find articles about hard skills and their value in helping employees succeed.

2. Make a list of the hard skills that you possess that you think would be important for a job or career area. Select three of these hard skills. Write a paragraph about each one that describes your abilities in this area. Give examples that illustrate your skills.

3. Save the document file in your e-portfolio. Place a printed copy in the container for your print portfolio.

Job Interview

Job interviewing is an event you might enter with your organization. By participating in the job interview, you will be able to showcase your presentation skills, communication talents, and ability to actively listen to the questions asked by the interviewers. For this event, you will be expected to write a letter of application, create a résumé, and complete a job application. You will also be interviewed by an individual or panel.

To prepare for a job interview event, complete the following activities.

1. Use the Internet or textbooks to research the job application process and interviewing techniques.

2. Write your letter of application, résumé, and complete the application (if provided for this event). You may be required to submit this before the event or present the information at the event.

3. Make certain that each piece of communication is complete and free of errors.

4. Solicit feedback from your peers, instructor, and parents.

Chapter 17
Your Role in the Environment

Protecting the world around you is one of your most critical roles as a consumer, citizen, and taxpayer. Individuals, governments, and businesses share responsibility for preserving the environment and being good *stewards*, or managers, of the earth's natural resources. Protecting the environment is one of the most pressing challenges today. It calls for the attention, participation, and best efforts of all of everyone—individuals, local communities, governments, and businesses. Climate change, waste disposal, dwindling resources, and urban sprawl are some of the environmental challenges that need attention and action.

You can take an active role in protecting the earth. Stay informed about current environmental issues. Learn to conserve resources in your own life and participate in community environmental protection programs.

Focus on Finance

Fuel Economy

In the United States, the *Drive 55* campaign is an effort to educate drivers about how much less fuel efficient a vehicle becomes once it exceeds a speed of 55 miles per hour (mph). All vehicles lose fuel economy at speeds over 55 mph. For example, driving 55 mph instead of 75 mph can reduce your fuel cost by as much as 25 percent. Driving 65 mph instead of 75 mph can save you up to 13 percent. In addition to reducing speed, if you turn your engine off if you are stopped for more than three to four minutes you can save money. You can save up to 19 percent of fuel costs by not letting your engine idle too long while stationary. Avoid jack rabbit starts and stops. Mild accelerations and moderate slowing can increase fuel efficiency by more than 30 percent. Rotate tires every 5,000 to 8,000 miles, and check the tire alignment at least once a year. Tires that are not properly aligned can cause the car to scrub, which lowers mileage and causes unnecessary tire wear. Look for other ways you can save money on your automobile.

College and Career Readiness

Reading Prep. As you read this chapter, stop at the Checkpoints and take time to answer the questions. Were you able to answer these questions without referring to the chapter content?

Check Your Personal Finance IQ

Before you begin the chapter, see what you already know about personal finance by taking the chapter pretest. If you do not have a smartphone, visit the G-W Learning companion website.

G-W Learning mobile site: www.m.g-wlearning.com

G-W Learning companion website: www.g-wlearning.com

Sections

auremar/Shutterstock.com

Section 17.1
Environment

Objectives

After studying this section, you will be able to:

- Discuss the importance of natural resources in modern society.
- Outline today's major environmental challenges.

Terms

sustainable	landfill
conservation	hazardous waste
ecology	fossil fuel
environmentalist	renewable energy
climate change	biofuel
global warming	nonrenewable energy

Limited Natural Resources

Natural resources are naturally occurring elements that people use to produce the necessities and luxuries of life. For example, crude oil is needed to produce gasoline that the world society depends on for commerce and transportation. Iron is needed in the production of many modern products, including automobiles, household appliances, buildings, surgical instruments, and industrial equipment. Coal is needed to generate electricity and other fuels. There are many other natural resources that modern society relies on to produce the products and services needed to maintain good health and a high standard of living.

As essential as they are, most natural resources are of limited supply. For some, the existing reserve is down to a few years. For example, cadmium is a metal used to make batteries. Because of heavy demand and extensive mining, scientists predict it will only be available for another 35 to 70 years. The reserve of antimony, used in the production of credit cards and car parts, is projected to last only 16 to 35 years. The reserve of silver, used not only to make jewelry but also used for film, batteries, and X-ray imaging, is limited to 14 to 28 years.

Scientists predict a future in which shortages of basic natural resources—water, food, and fuel—will affect a growing number of people. By 2040, the world's population is expected to reach over 9 billion people. Sustainable practices and conservation preserves natural resources. **Sustainable** means able to be kept in existence. As this term relates to the environment, it refers to using resources responsibly to prevent depletion or permanent damage. **Conservation** is the protection and management of the environment and valuable natural resources.

You will pay the costs of protecting the planet and solving environmental problems far into the future. Your tax dollars pay for research to find earth-friendly ways to meet basic human needs. Your votes for policymakers will decide how the country manages natural resources. Learning how your money is spent and what environmental choices you have is in your own best interest.

Environmental Challenges

Ecology is the study of the relationship between living things and their environment. Scientists who study ecology have found that life on earth exists in a delicate balance. When that balance is disrupted, the consequences can be serious, unpredictable, and irreversible.

An **environmentalist** is a person who is concerned with the quality of the environment and how to maintain it. Current environmental issues include climate change, water and air pollution, depletion of natural resources, and land use. All of these issues can disrupt the balance needed to preserve the environment.

Climate Change

Climate change is the shifts in measurements of climate—such as temperature, precipitation, or wind—that last decades or longer. It is linked to **global warming,** the steady rise in average temperatures near the earth's surface. Warming temperatures are causing climate changes throughout the world.

Both natural processes and human activity contribute to climate change. In recent decades, however, human activity has been an increasingly dominant cause of global warming. Activities such as driving cars and generating

It took from the beginning of humankind to 1950 for the world population to grow to approximately 2.5 billion people. In the next fifty years, from 1950 to 2000, the world population more than doubled to over 6 billion people. By 2012, it had grown to 7 billion.

spirit of america/Shutterstock.com

The job of an environmentalist involves working to improve environmental issues such as water and air pollution, natural resources, climate change, and land use.

Modern society has become a disposable one. Each year, millions of tons of disposable products, such as baby diapers, plastic drinking cups, plastic garbage bags, plastic water bottles, and plastic milk cartons, are dumped in landfills. Plastic can take hundreds of years to decompose.

electricity by burning coal release carbon dioxide, one of the greenhouse gases (GHG). Like a greenhouse roof, these gases form a layer in the atmosphere that prevents heat from escaping.

Adding to global warming is the problem of *deforestation,* which is the clearing of forests. Large tracts of trees are cut down by loggers and removed by farmers. The trees are sold as timber, and the land is used for grazing animals, growing crops, and building towns. Trees and other plants filter carbon dioxide from the air, using it and sunlight to grow. With fewer plants to absorb carbon dioxide, more remains in the atmosphere. If carbon dioxide and other greenhouse gases continue to collect in the atmosphere, experts predict serious consequences, as shown in Figure 17-1.

Waste Disposal

In 1960, the average US citizen generated about 2.5 pounds of garbage a day. Today, the average US citizen generates about 4.3 pounds of garbage each day. All that waste must be disposed somehow. Some solid waste is disposed through burning, but most household waste is buried in a landfill. A **landfill** is a permanent waste disposal site for most solid, non-hazardous waste.

Special sites are devoted to the disposal of hazardous waste. **Hazardous waste** is a substance—liquid, solid, or gas—that is dangerous or potentially harmful to health or the environment. Hazardous wastes are discarded by-products of agricultural, manufacturing, medical, national defense, and other sources. Households discard hazardous waste, too. Some examples are paint, cleaners, auto products, pesticides, and flame-retardants. Also hazardous are fluorescent lamps, batteries, consumer electronics, and anything with mercury, such as fever thermometers.

Existing landfills are filling up, and building new landfills is costly. Few communities are willing to permit landfills in their area, so new sites are

---

Possible Results of Climate Change

- *Rising sea levels and flooding.* Ice in arctic regions and high altitudes would melt faster if temperatures rise. This would release large volumes of water, possibly flooding many coastal areas.
- *Weather pattern changes.* Some regions would suffer water shortages and drought. Warmer oceans would trigger more hurricanes, which could cause flooding.
- *Famine.* Extreme weather changes would threaten crop production in many regions, causing food shortages.
- *Animal and plant extinction.* Weather would probably change faster than many plants and animals could adjust. In the short term, animals would probably try to migrate to more comfortable climates that supported familiar food supplies. Plants, however, would likely die off.
- *Human migrations.* Flooded coastal areas plus shortages of food and safe water could force millions of people from their homes. This might lead to regional conflicts.

Goodheart-Willcox Publisher

Figure 17-1 Climate change could permanently alter weather and other conditions.

located further from the areas they serve. This requires transporting waste for long distances at considerable cost.

Improper disposal of waste poses serious threats to human health and the environment. If hazardous waste is placed in landfills, it can contaminate groundwater and cropland. Without proper controls, burning waste can release greenhouse gases that contribute to climate change.

Dwindling Resources

Natural resources, such as land, water, forests, fuel, and wildlife, are valuable economic assets. As stated earlier, most natural resources are of limited supply. Everyone shares the challenge of making sure these resources continue to be available to future generations.

Fossil Fuels

A **fossil fuel** is an organic substance, such as coal, petroleum, and natural gas, derived from the decomposed remains of animals and plants that lived in prehistoric times. Burning fossil fuels is the major source of greenhouse gases. Fossil fuels provide more than 85 percent of all energy consumed in the United States. This includes gas that powers cars and heats homes and coal that produces electricity.

Energy sources can be classified as renewable or nonrenewable. **Renewable energy** is a power source that is continually available or can be replenished. Examples include wind, water, solar (sun), and biofuels. A **biofuel** is a fuel composed of or produced from biological raw material. An example is ethanol made from corn or sugar beets.

Nonrenewable energy is a power source that can be used up or cannot be used again, as shown in Figure 17-2. Once nonrenewable energy is gone, it cannot be replaced. Fossil fuels are nonrenewable energy sources. Nuclear energy is also a nonrenewable resource because it is created from uranium, a substance available in limited amounts.

At present, the United States depends on foreign sources for over 50 percent of its petroleum. This dependence is a big concern because the United States

Go Green

Recycling is important so that landfills do not become overloaded. Paper and cans are often recycled; communication tools should also be recycled. Cell phones, printers, monitors, computers, and other office equipment are considered electronic waste. Electronic waste should be properly disposed of and not just placed in the trash. Some components may be toxic, such as the materials in a battery. Electronic equipment can be donated to charities to be refurbished for use in locations that are in need of electronic equipment. However, if the equipment is beyond repair, locate a reputable electronic manufacturer, reseller, or community service center that will make sure the equipment is properly recycled.

Energy Sources			
		Description	**Disadvantages**
Renewable Energy Source	**Solar**	• Sun's radiation that reaches the earth • Can be converted to electricity and heat • Produces almost no undesirable side effects • Used most often and most effectively in warm climates • In cloudy areas, solar energy systems usually need to be used with other forms of power	• Cannot be concentrated into high-grade, usable fuel in large enough quantities • Limited use at night and on cloudy days unless new storage systems are installed to absorb, store, and release energy as needed
	Wind	• Large windmill-like turbines turn wind energy into electricity • A wind farm is a business that generates power from multiple turbines at one location	• Many areas lack sufficient wind or space to set up wind turbines • Not a constant or dependable source of energy • Getting wind energy to places that need it requires creating a system of power lines across many miles • Equipment to harness wind energy requires an investment • People who live near wind farms complain about disturbances, such as light deflection off turbine blades
	Hydro	Captures the power of ocean waves or water flowing over a dam to create electricity	Depends on the presence of enough water
	Geothermal	Uses hot water and steam produced deep inside the earth to create energy	Sources of geothermal energy are very limited
	Biofuels	• Made of biological matter from plants and animals that can be converted to energy • Ethanol is made from grains—corn, sorghum, wheat, sugar cane, etc. • Ethanol is usually mixed with gasoline • Biodiesel is made from plant and animal oils and fats	• Not yet possible to produce adequate quantities of usable energy from any of these sources • Depends on availability of farmland and forests • When land is used to grow sources of biofuels it cannot be used to grow food

Goodheart-Willcox Publisher

Figure 17-2 Dependence on nonrenewable energy sources will eventually use up remaining supplies.

Continued.

Energy Sources			
		Description	**Disadvantages**
Nonrenewable Energy Source	**Petroleum and natural gas**	• Fossil fuels • Main forms of energy used in the United States today	• Use contributes to air pollution and climate change • Oil spills foul water and kill wildlife • United States is dependent on imports to meet demand • Supplies and prices are controlled by other governments, including some hostile to the United States
	Coal	• Also a fossil fuel • Plentiful US source of energy and a major export • Likely to be a major source of energy well into the future	• Difficult to transport • Burning coal contributes to air pollution and climate change • Strip-mining causes long-lasting damage to the land • Converting coal to a gaseous or liquid form is a costly process
	Nuclear	• Energy is produced from nuclear fission, (splitting apart) of uranium in nuclear power plants • Produces 20 percent of the electric power in the United States, which is 8 percent of the nation's total energy production • Releases few greenhouse gases • Used as the main source of energy in some countries, including France and Japan	• Questions persist about plant safety and safe waste disposal • Nonrenewable because uranium is scarce • Nuclear waste, improperly handled, could cause catastrophic environmental damage

Goodheart-Willcox Publisher

Figure 17-2 (Continued)

has little or no control over the supply or price of fuel imports. Achieving energy independence will require greater fuel efficiency and conservation. It will also require development of new energy sources that are renewable, affordable, and environmentally safe.

Clean Water

Most people in the United States take fresh, pure water for granted. In many parts of the country, water is plentiful and relatively cheap. This natural resource, which is vital to all forms of life, is becoming more precious. Many of the common items you buy require huge amounts of water to manufacture. For example, hundreds of gallons of water are used in the production of one pair of denim jeans.

Crude oil is traded on the world market. This means that when demand increases in other heavily populated countries—such as China and India, each with a population over a billion people—residents of the United States pay a higher price even if demand here is declining.

You Do the Math

Word problems are exercises in which the problem is set up in text rather than presented in mathematical notation. Many word problems tell a story. You must identify the elements of the math problem and solve it.

Complete the Following Problem

Assume a car gets 20 miles per gallon (mpg) going 70 miles per hour (mph). If the car gets 20 percent better fuel economy going 55 mph, how much farther does it travel per gallon of fuel at the lower speed?

Both the availability and quality of water are important environmental issues. Water scarcity creates severe problems. Demands for fresh water increase dramatically with population growth. In the years ahead, conserving water and keeping the water supply clean will become vitally important.

Urban Sprawl

Before the invention of cars, most people worked and went to school within walking distance of their homes. Everything a person needed was concentrated in a compact town center. If public transportation was available, most people used it.

Cars gave people more mobility. Homes and businesses were built along highways that led to and from city centers. Open land was converted into housing developments, roads, malls, and business parks. This dispersed development is described as urban sprawl. Many environmental groups oppose urban sprawl, especially when it replaces forests or prime farmland.

Transportation, Distribution & Logistics

Environmental Compliance Inspectors

Environmental compliance inspectors examine, evaluate, and investigate eligibility for or conformity with laws and regulations governing contract compliance of licenses and permits. They also perform other compliance and enforcement inspection activities. They work to control and reduce the pollution of water, air, and land.

silver-john/Shutterstock.com

Water is a natural resource that is a necessity for all life forms.

They argue that sprawling areas require more roads, more driving, and more services than well-planned, concentrated business and residential developments.

While some areas of the country allow unchecked growth, other areas carefully plan new developments. Many towns and communities focus on smart growth policies that protect ecologically sensitive regions yet address future population needs.

Checkpoint 17.1

1. What are natural resources? Give two examples.
2. What is the expected size of the world population by 2040?
3. What are some issues with which environmentalists are concerned?
4. What are some possible results of climate change?
5. Why do some environmental groups oppose urban sprawl?

Build Your Vocabulary

As you progress through this course, develop a personal glossary of personal finance terms and add it to your portfolio. This will help you build your vocabulary and prepare you for a career. Write a definition for each of the following terms and add it to your personal finance glossary.

sustainable	landfill
conservation	hazardous waste
ecology	fossil fuel
environmentalist	renewable energy
climate change	biofuel
global warming	nonrenewable energy

Section 17.2
Addressing Environmental Challenges

Objectives

After studying this section, you will be able to:

- Explain steps individuals can take to conserve natural resources and protect the environment.
- Explain steps citizen groups can take to conserve natural resources and protect the environment.
- Identify the role of government in protecting the environment.
- Explain steps businesses can take to reduce their impact on the environment.

Terms

biodegradable

home energy audit

recycle

composting

What You Can Do

"Think globally; act locally" is a guideline often used to address environmental challenges. There are many steps you can take in your home and community to improve and protect your world. Making a few small changes in your shopping habits, reducing your water and energy use at home, reducing waste, and conserving fuel all make an impact on sustaining the environment.

Shop Wisely

Green has become the symbolic color of earth-friendly products, policies, and lifestyles. Many products now carry "green" labels identifying them as *earth-friendly*, *eco-friendly*, or *environmentally-friendly*. These terms have no official definition. A careful examination of the manufacturer's goals and accomplishments can help you judge if the company's practices benefit the environment.

The following tips can help you address environmental issues when shopping for goods and services.

- Look for energy-saving features when buying products, such as autos, appliances, furnaces, air conditioners, and electronic equipment. Look for water-saving features when buying dishwashers, clothes washers, toilets, and bathroom showerheads.
- Buy pre-owned consumer goods when they address your needs. You can buy used items at resale shops, garage sales, and online auction and sales sites.

- Buy products with packaging that is biodegradable. **Biodegradable** means able to be broken down naturally by microorganisms into harmless elements. Cardboard is an example of a biodegradable material. Also, bring your own reusable bags when you shop.

- Support businesses and manufacturers that operate recycling and take-back programs, such as permitting consumers to return old electronics for disposal when they purchase a new model.

- Shop locally. Transporting food and other products uses fuel. Look for locally grown foods at farmer's markets and grocery stores.

Conserve Energy

Most people can conserve a considerable amount of energy without major inconvenience. Often it simply involves a new mindset to get into the habit of using less, economizing, and saving. Some ways to reduce personal and family energy use are discussed in the following paragraphs.

Conduct a Home Energy Audit

A **home energy audit** is an assessment of how much energy your home uses. It also identifies ways to reduce consumption.

Your electric and gas meters measure the amounts of electricity and gas you use each month. Look at your bills or visit utility company websites to

Economics in Action

Can Pollution Credits Work?

The US government uses market incentives to tackle environmental problems. New programs create markets where "pollution credits" are bought and sold like stocks and bonds. The laws of supply and demand set credit prices.

For example, conservation banking programs reward landowners and local governments for preserving open space, endangered species, and habitats. They earn credits that can be sold. Other people or businesses must buy credits to offset environmental damage they cause. Having to buy credits is costly and discourages practices that are harmful to the environment.

Another example is a cap-and-trade program for greenhouse gas (GHG) emissions. The government sets a cap, or maximum allowable amount, for GHG emissions. Businesses get an initial allowance of credits from the government. They are awarded additional credits for good environmental stewardship, such as planting trees.

If a business exceeds the emission cap, it must pay the government with credits. If a business doesn't have enough credits, it can buy them from lower-polluting businesses. Having to purchase credits is like paying a fine.

These programs, especially the cap-and-trade program, are controversial. Program promoters say they minimize the cost of government regulation. Business owners, not government regulators, decide how to keep their emissions under the cap. However, some environmentalists say the programs do not do enough to curtail fossil fuel burning and other environmental damage. Other critics say they create undue hardship for businesses and will boost energy prices for consumers.

learn how to read your electric and gas meters. Your utility company may provide free or low-cost energy auditing services. You can also hire a company that provides this service.

The government's Home Energy Saver™ calculator, available at http:// hes.lbl.gov, is an easy way to get a quick assessment of the energy used at a residential address. The calculator also computes greenhouse gas emissions.

You can visit the government's Energy Star website at www.energystar.gov. The Home Energy Yardstick can help you see how your home's energy use compares with similar homes across the country.

Monitor Heating and Cooling

Home heating and cooling consumes the greatest share of energy in the home. You can use the thermostat in your home to conserve energy. Consider saving energy by setting the thermostat no higher than 68° F in winter and no lower than 78° F in summer.

You also conserve energy by keeping equipment clean and in good working order. Be sure to change or clean filters regularly.

When heating or cooling equipment is in use, you can save energy by closing off unused rooms and keeping all outside doors and windows tightly closed. Also, keep heating and cooling vents clear of furniture, rugs, and other obstacles.

Insulate Your Home

Well-fitted storm doors and windows prevent winter heat loss and the escape of cool air in the summer. You can buy inexpensive weather-stripping kits and materials that can be used to stop drafts through loose-fitting windows and doors.

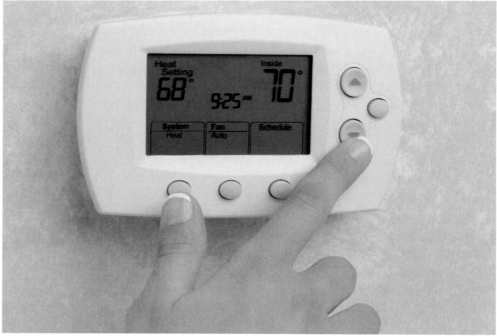

Steve Cukrov/Shutterstock.com

Monitor the temperature in your home throughout the day to conserve energy.

Case Study

Environmental Issues

Maxine recently attended a community presentation titled "Survival on Planet Earth." The speaker outlined five critical environmental issues:

- Solid waste disposal
- Energy conservation
- Climate change
- Water purity and conservation
- Hazardous waste disposal

The speaker also shared powerful *what you can do* directives. After the presentation, Maxine started forming a Mother Earth action group at her high school. Within a week's time, Maxine had 25 enthusiastic members. The group wants to take steps in each of the five areas. They hope to gain both individual and community participation.

Case Review

1. Choose two environmental issues and outline at least three actions the Mother Earth group could take in each area. Include individual and community projects.
2. Discuss environmental protection and conservation projects that might work in your home, school, and community.

Insulation is necessary in all homes, especially older homes. Insulation is a material used to slow the movement of hot or cool air. It is installed in ceilings, walls, and floors to help maintain the desired indoor air temperature. Although insulating a home can be costly, it more than pays for itself in lower fuel costs over time.

Conserve Hot Water

The gas or electric water heater is a major energy user in the home, but insulating the hot water tank cuts energy use. Less energy will be needed to keep the water hot. If you buy a new water heater, look for one with high energy-efficiency ratings.

Water heaters have an adjustable thermostat. Set the temperature no higher than 140°F to avoid scalding.

Use Appliances and Electrical Devices Wisely

Electrical appliances and equipment account for about 23 percent of energy used at home. Some energy-use strategy tips are as follows.

- Replace incandescent bulbs with compact fluorescent lightbulbs (CFLs). They use about 75 percent less electricity and last up to 10 times longer. Look for dimmable bulbs if you have dimmer controls.
- Turn off the television, computer, lights, and other electrical equipment when not in use.
- Keep appliances and equipment in good working condition. Periodically check and clean refrigerator and freezer door seals to make sure they fit tightly. Open doors for only as long as necessary.

- Use the appliance that takes the least amount of energy for the job. For example, use your microwave if you have one. It uses approximately one-third of the energy of a conventional oven.
- Use dishwashers, clothes washers, and clothes dryers in the early morning or late evening to ease energy demand during peak usage times. Use dishwashers only for full loads and select the shortest cycle able to do the job well. For greater energy efficiency from clothes dryers, clean the filters after each use.

Buy Green Energy

Many homes are heated by *conventional power,* such as coal, natural gas, oil, and power created by nuclear power plants. In some parts of the country, homes and businesses can choose to purchase electricity from companies that supply green power. *Green power* includes forms of renewable energy, such as wind and solar power.

Some major energy suppliers also offer green energy sources as an alternative or as a supplement to conventional energy. You may be charged more for green power than for conventional power. However, as green power becomes more widely available, the costs should come down.

For information about green power sources in your area, go to the website of the Office of Energy Efficiency and Renewable Energy of the US Department of Energy. Look under *Green Power Network.*

Conserve Water

There are many ways you can cut down on water usage. The following tips will help you save on your water bill as well as conserve a valuable resource.

- *In the bathroom.* Take shorter showers and install a low-flow showerhead. Turn off water while brushing your teeth or shaving. When installing a new toilet, buy a water-saving model. For new installations, this is required by law in most communities.
- *In the kitchen.* Do not let water run while washing or rinsing dishes or cleaning vegetables and fruits. Repair leaky faucets promptly. When using the dishwasher and clothes washer, wash only full loads.
- *Outdoors.* Water gardens and lawns in the early evening to prevent evaporation by the sunlight. Use a soaker hose, which waters more efficiently than sprinklers. During dry spells, water trees and plantings rather than the grass. Lawns will normally recover after a drought, while big trees and delicate plantings can suffer permanent damage.

Reduce Waste

Reducing trash involves an overall sense of economizing—buying less, using less, reusing, and recycling. **Recycle** means to reprocess resources so they can be used again. Recycling reduces waste in landfills, conserves resources, and saves energy. Almost every community provides some type of recycling and waste disposal programs. Many areas offer pick-up services for recyclables and others have drop-off centers.

Reducing paper trash is a good place to start. You can reduce the junk mail you receive by contacting the Direct Marketing Association. By signing

iculture, Food & Natural Resources

Recyclers
Recyclers turn old products, used appliances, and automobiles into useful, environmentally safe raw materials. They may analyze waste reduction and recycling opportunities and design and implement programs to reduce, reuse, and recycle materials. They may operate machines that compress materials into easy-to-transport bundles.

auremar/Shutterstock.com

Reduce waste by recycling used plastic, glass, and paper.

up with their Mail Preference Service, you will stop getting unsolicited mail from direct-mail marketers. You can have your bills and bank statements sent to you electronically instead of on paper. Many utilities and financial institutions provide this service.

Some communities encourage composting as a method of reducing and recycling yard and other organic waste. **Composting** is a natural process that transforms materials, such as food waste, leaves, and grass clippings, into useful soil-like particles. Find out whether your local government sponsors a composting project or offers information on home compost measures.

Most areas also provide specified pick-up days or drop-off sites for disposal of hazardous waste and electronic products. Find out how your community handles household waste and direct your waste to the appropriate place. You can also locate sites for various types of waste disposal and treatment online at www.epa.gov.

The mercury in compact fluorescent lightbulbs (CFLs) makes them more efficient. They release no mercury when in use. However, because of the mercury content, you must use extra care when disposing of used or broken bulbs. Many retailers who sell CFLs will accept used bulbs for recycling. You can also check in your community for recycling programs. Go to the EPA site for information on recycling CFLs and on the procedures to follow if a bulb breaks.

In caring for your yard and garden, limit or eliminate the use of pesticides. In household cleaning, look for biodegradable, nontoxic products with low or no phosphate and chlorine content.

Websites provide helpful information on recycling and responsible disposal of home appliances and electronic products. Check the government listings in your phone book or look for the Environmental Protection Agency's E-Cycling page online.

Ethics

As an employee of a company, you may hear confidential information about employees or the company business. It is unethical to share any confidential information you learn, and doing so may cost you your job. Repeating information is sometimes known as gossiping, and some people find it harmless. Television shows present taking part in "water cooler" talk and listening to the "grapevine" as fun office activities. However, depending on the confidentiality of the topic, sharing information may be considered as slander. Always protect any confidential information you learn and respect the situation in which you learned it. This will not only promote ethical behavior in the organization, it may build your reputation as a trusted person.

Make Each Mile Count

Transportation accounts for almost two-thirds of the petroleum used in the United States. There are many opportunities for energy conservation and pollution control in this area. The greatest difference you can make is switching from driving to biking, walking, or taking public transportation. Limiting airplane travel can also help reduce petroleum use.

Drivers can conserve fuel and cut down costs by following these tips:

- Consider buying a small car to reduce fuel needs.
- Plan trips carefully, combining errands when possible.
- Carpool when possible.
- Lower your driving speed. Most cars get about 20 percent better fuel economy on the highway at 55 miles per hour than they do at 70 miles per hour.
- Maintain your car to improve engine life and performance.

What Citizen Groups Can Do

At the local level, citizen action is often the driving force that protects a community's environment. The grassroots efforts of citizens working together have led to investigations of polluting industries and the establishment of local air and water quality standards. Citizen groups also help launch recycling and composting centers. In some communities, they promote programs for recycling electronic products and safe disposal of hazardous waste. These groups frequently organize clean-up days for local public areas, such as beaches, parks, and playgrounds.

Some communities have managed to turn solid waste into an asset by producing energy from gas built up in landfills. Other landfills are turned into golf courses and recreational areas.

Many communities sponsor a variety of programs to protect and enhance the environment. These include restrictions on land use, emissions controls, and environmental education and awareness programs. To reduce air pollution from cars, some communities restrict downtown parking, ban auto traffic in certain parts of the city, and improve public transportation. Other areas encourage carpooling by establishing express highway lanes for cars with two or more passengers.

Local action is the speediest, most direct way to deal with problems in and near your community. Watch for activities in your community. Take whatever steps you can to protect the air you breathe, water you drink, and parks and open spaces you enjoy. The organizations listed in Figure 17-3 are good sources for information.

What Government Can Do

An important function of government is to ensure a safe and healthy environment for its citizens. Because both the environment and the economy are critical issues, the methods used to protect and conserve the environment and its resources need to be cost effective.

Many environmental problems, such as climate change, deforestation, and water pollution, among others, are global. The government frequently pursues environmental interests at the international level.

Regulation and Legislation

In 1970, the federal government passed legislation creating the Environmental Protection Agency (EPA). The agency serves as the national watchdog and coordinating bureau for matters affecting the environment. The EPA focuses on air and water quality, noise, solid waste, hazardous waste, toxic substances, and other ecological issues.

Under a 1975 law, the Department of Energy (DOE) was required to set efficiency standards for major home appliances and several commercial products. The goal of the standards was to reduce the nation's energy use. Since then, the list of products under the DOE's review has grown. Besides

Sources of Environmental Protection Information
Government
• National Aeronautics and Space Administration (NASA) on Global Climate Change
• US Department of Energy and US Environmental Protection Agency ENERGY STAR Program
• US Department of Energy Office of Energy Efficiency and Renewable Energy
• US Environmental Protection Agency
• US Fish & Wildlife Service Endangered Species Program
• United Nations Environment Programme
Consumer Groups and Nonprofits
• Basel Action Network
• Center for Resource Solutions
• Consumers Union
• National Resources Defense Council
• The Nature Conservancy
• Ocean Conservancy
• World Wildlife Federation
Business/Industry Groups
• American Council for an Energy-Efficient Economy
• Association of Home Appliance Manufacturers
• Consumer Electronics Association
• E-Cycling Central, Telecommunications Industry Association
• US Chamber of Commerce Institute for 21st Century Energy

Goodheart-Willcox Publisher

Figure 17-3 You can find information about the environment on the websites of these organizations.

setting minimum efficiency standards, it also sets maximum water-use standards for certain products. The DOE is charged with periodically reviewing opportunities for more energy- and water-savings from the items under its authority. These reviews involve input from manufacturers and consumers.

In addition, many state and local regulations govern environmental activities. To find out how your state is involved, go to your state website and look for the department or agency that deals with environmental issues.

Taxation

The use of taxes as a tool in fighting pollution is a recent concept. The so-called green tax offers a way to charge the cost of pollution to the polluter, whether producer or consumer. Examples of possible items subject to a green tax include excess household waste and auto emissions.

Green taxes could take the form of direct tax, fines, or user fees. They would provide greater incentive and pressure to find cost-effective ways of reducing and controlling pollution. Green taxes would also produce revenues that could be used to help clean up waste and pay for government pollution control services.

In some cases, government can use tax incentives to reward and encourage good environmental stewardship by both consumers and business. Examples include tax benefits for insulating homes, using solar energy, or purchasing fuel-efficient cars and appliances.

Clean Energy Development

Energy policies and choices affect jobs, prices, industries, the environment, and lifestyles here and around the world. It is clear that dependence on nonrenewable and polluting sources of energy must be severely curtailed. Harnessing the energy of the sun, wind, and water may provide a large share of the energy used in the future. Scientists and entrepreneurs are also developing other sources of energy. Government is heavily involved in these efforts both through its own laboratories and through funding of research in leading universities.

Other actions government could take on energy issues include the following.

- Tax fossil fuels to encourage greater efficiency and discourage excessive energy consumption.
- Provide incentives for industries to conduct comprehensive clean energy research.
- Work out a cooperative policy with other nations for the development, allocation, and efficient safe use of world energy resources.

Water Conservation

Areas experiencing water shortages can lower the system-wide operating pressure to reduce the flow of water. Government can also enact bans, restrictions, and rationing for different types of water usage. These normally are temporary measures taken during periods of severe shortages. More permanent conservation measures include:

Hazardous Waste Technicians

Hazardous waste technicians identify, remove, package, transport, and dispose of various hazardous materials, including asbestos, radioactive and nuclear materials, arsenic, lead, and mercury. They often respond to emergencies where harmful substances are present. They transport and prepare materials for treatment or disposal.

- local building codes that require water-efficient faucets, toilets, showerheads, and appliances in new construction
- utility billing that imposes higher rates for excess water usage
- increased recycling of industrial water
- public education programs to encourage voluntary reductions in water usage
- water meter accuracy and leak detection

What Businesses Can Do

Manufacturers and retailers share responsibility for the environmental impact of the production, use, and disposal of their products. Product stewardship is an environmental concept that calls on businesses to take a leadership role in reducing the health and environmental impacts of consumer products. For example, producers should try to:

- design products to be upgraded instead of discarded;
- incorporate energy-saving features;
- use recycled materials in the product or its packaging, if feasible;
- avoid excess packaging;
- use renewable energy and recycled water in the manufacturing process;
- upgrade machinery and vehicles to energy-saving models; and
- minimize the discharge of pollutants into the environment.

Manufacturers and retailers can encourage recycling by providing free pickup of used goods, such as old appliances. They can sponsor education programs to identify the efforts being made to preserve natural resources.

Levent Konuk/Shutterstock.com

Many businesses today manufacture products using recycled materials and energy-efficient machinery.

Some businesses are taking back products that are no longer useable and offering free recycling to customers. Others are refurbishing used products for resale or donation. By planning for disposal during product design, producers can also minimize disposal problems.

Careers in Science, Technology, Engineering & Mathematics

What Does an Environmental Scientist Do?

Environmental scientists work to protect the environment by identifying problems and finding solutions that minimize hazards to the health of the environment and the population. They determine what is in the air, water, and soil to make sure that the environment is safe. These professionals also give advice on how to clean the environment. **Environmental scientists** typically:

- determine data collection methods for research projects;

- collect environmental data for scientific analysis;

- analyze samples, surveys, and other information to identify and assess threats to the environment;

- develop plans to prevent, control, or fix environmental problems;

- develop plans to restore polluted or contaminated land or water;

- provide information and guidance to government officials, businesses, and the general public on environmental hazards and health risks; and

- prepare technical reports and presentations that explain their research and findings.

What Is It Like to Work as an Environmental Scientist?

Most **environmental scientists** work 40 hours per week. The work environment is typically an office or laboratory. They may also spend time in the field gathering data and monitoring environmental conditions. **Environmental scientists** also travel to meet with clients.

What Education and Skills Are Needed to Be an Environmental Scientist?

- bachelor degree in environmental science or another natural science, such as biology, chemistry, earth science, or physics

- master degree may be needed for advancement

- analytical skills

- interpersonal skills

- problem-solving skills

- communication and computer skills

Checkpoint 17.2

1. What are some steps you can take in your home and community to improve and protect the world?
2. What is a home energy audit?
3. What are two ways you can reduce paper trash?
4. What are some programs communities sponsor to help protect the environment?
5. What are the issues on which the Environmental Protection Agency focuses?

Build Your Vocabulary

As you progress through this course, develop a personal glossary of personal finance terms and add it to your portfolio. This will help you build your vocabulary and prepare you for a career. Write a definition for each of the following terms and add it to your personal finance glossary.

biodegradable   recycle

home energy audit   composting

Chapter Summary

Section 17.1 Environment

- There are many natural resources that modern society relies on to produce the products and services needed to maintain good health and a high standard of living. Most natural resources are of limited supply. Scientists predict a future in which shortages of basic natural resources, such as water, food, and fuel, will affect a growing number of people.

- Scientists who study ecology have found that life on earth exists in a delicate balance. Current environmental issues include climate change, water and air pollution, depletion of natural resources, and land use. All of these issues can disrupt the balance needed to preserve the environment.

Section 17.2 Addressing Environmental Challenges

- There are many steps you can take in your home and community to improve and protect your world. Making small changes in your shopping habits, reducing your water and energy use at home, reducing waste, and conserving fuel all make an impact on sustaining the environment.

- At the local level, citizen action is often the driving force that protects a community's environment. Many communities sponsor a variety of programs to protect and enhance the environment. Some examples include recycling, carpooling, and clean-up programs.

- An important function of government is to ensure a safe and healthy environment for its citizens. Governments can use regulation, legislation, taxation, energy development programs, and water conservation programs to help achieve this goal.

- Businesses share responsibility for the environmental impact of the production, use, and disposal of their products. Companies can take a leadership role in reducing the health and environmental impacts of consumer products. They can also encourage recycling of used goods and proper disposal of hazardous products.

Check Your Personal Finance IQ

Now that you have finished the chapter, see what you learned about personal finance by taking the chapter posttest. If you do not have a smartphone, visit the G-W Learning companion website.

G-W Learning mobile site: www.m.g-wlearning.com

G-W Learning companion website: www.g-wlearning.com

Review Your Knowledge

1. What are three examples of renewable energy sources?

2. What are some examples of household hazardous wastes?

3. What are some factors that contribute to climate change?

4. What are some examples of valuable natural resources that are limited in supply?

5. What are the two main forms of energy used in the United States?

6. What are two sources of renewable energy that are used for green power?

7. What are three ways that you can conserve water in the kitchen?

8. What are three consumer groups that are good sources of information about protecting the environment?

9. Under a 1975 law, the Department of Energy (DOE) was required to set efficiency standards for major home appliances and several commercial products. What was the goal of these standards?

10. What are three things companies that produce consumer products can do to reduce the health and environmental impacts of consumer products?

Apply Your Knowledge

11. What are some of the problems that concern environmentalists today? What environmental problems concern you the most?

12. Investigate to find out where water shortages have been a serious problem in the United States. Find out how affected communities coped with the problem.

13. Why is it important for consumers to be informed about threats to the environment?

14. How can consumer spending habits and decisions serve as an environmental protection tool?

15. What are some environmental problems that exist in your community? How might they be solved?

16. What are some things you personally can do to address environmental issues?

17. How many active landfills are in operation in your area and what is the time estimated for each to reach full capacity? (Your local city government should be able to provide this information.)

18. In your opinion, what are the most important factors that contribute to pollution in your state?

19. By the year 2040, the world population is expected to exceed 9 billion people. Do you think the resources of the world can adequately sustain a population that large?

20. What can countries do to address the problem of overpopulation?

Teamwork

Work with other students in research teams to investigate one of the following sources or types of energy: nuclear, natural gas, coal, solar, geothermal, petroleum, wind, water, or underwater technology. Prepare a report on its use, cost, safety, effectiveness, availability, and impact on the environment.

G-W Learning Mobile Site

Visit the G-W Learning mobile site to complete the chapter pretest and posttest and to practice vocabulary using e-flash cards. If you do not have a smartphone, visit the G-W Learning companion website to access these features.

G-W Learning mobile site: www.m.g-wlearning.com

G-W Learning companion website: www.g-wlearning.com

College and Career Readiness

Common Core

CTE Career Ready Practices. A successful employee demonstrates creativity and innovation. Whether you see problems as challenges or opportunities, they often require creative thinking to solve them. Many new inventions come about from trying to solve a problem. Describe a situation in your life or in history where a problem led to the creation of a new way of doing things or a new invention.

Speaking. Using the Internet, research information on ergonomic solutions. What are some products available to entrepreneurs who need to create an ergonomic work environment? Make a presentation on your findings.

Listening. Informative listening is the process of listening to gain specific information from the speaker. Interview a person who works in the human resources department of a company. Ask that person to explain employee attendance policies for his or her company. Make notes as the policies are described. Evaluate the speaker's point of view and reasoning. Did you listen closely enough to write accurate facts?

Web Connect

Visit the website of the Environmental Protection Agency, the Department of Energy, or another government agency. Do a search for articles about urban sprawl versus smart growth. Summarize your findings. Make an effort to present a balanced view covering both sides of the issue. Cite authorities, events, dates, figures, pros, and cons.

College and Career Readiness

College and Career Readiness Portfolio

An important part of any portfolio is a list of references. A reference is a person who knows your skills, talents, or personal traits and is willing to recommend you. References can be someone for whom you worked or with whom you provided community service. Someone you know from your personal life, such a youth group leader, can also be a reference. However, you should not list relatives as references. When applying for a position, consider which references can best recommend you for the position for which you are applying. Always get permission from the person before using his or her name as a reference.

1. Ask several people with whom you have worked or volunteered if they are willing to serve as a reference for you. If so, ask for their contact information.
2. Create a list with the names and contact information for your references. Save the document file in an appropriate subfolder for your e-portfolio.
3. Place a printed copy in the container for your print portfolio.

Community Service Project

Many competitive events for Career and Technical Student Organizations (CTSOs) offer events that include a community service project. This project is usually carried out by the entire CTSO chapter and will take several months to complete. There will be two parts of the event, written and oral. The chapter will designate several members to represent the team at the competitive event.

To prepare for a community service project, complete the following activities.

1. Read the guidelines provided by your organization.
2. Contact the association immediately at the end of the state conference to prepare for next year's event.
3. As a team, select a theme for your chapter's community service project.
4. Decide which roles are needed for the team. There may be one person who is the captain, one person who is the secretary, and any other roles that will be necessary to create the plan. Ask your instructor for guidance in assigning roles to team members.
5. Identify your target audience, which may include business, school, and community groups.
6. Brainstorm with members of your chapter. List the benefits and opportunities of supporting a community service project.
7. This project will probably span the school year. During regular chapter meetings, create a draft of the report based on directions from the organization. Write and refine drafts until the final report is finished.

Unit 5
Economic Systems

Andresr/Shutterstock.com

The economic decisions of consumers impact the overall economy. Smart consumers avoid the pitfalls that a market economy can create.

Chapters

Personal Finance

Why It Matters

It is important to understand the basics of economics and its impact on your personal finance. Economic systems are based on choices—choices of what to produce, how to produce it, and how to distribute what we produce. These choices are necessary because wants and needs are unlimited and the resources to meet them are limited. This creates scarcity and requires us to decide which needs or wants to satisfy. In our market economy, buyers and sellers (consumers and producers) make free economic choices that determine what we will produce, how we will use productive resources, and who will receive the benefits of our productivity. The economic choices you make connect you to millions of other consumers in the United States and around the world.

Chapter 18
Economic Principles

Economics is the study of how individuals and societies use limited resources to satisfy unlimited needs and wants. We live in an economic world. Money is involved every time you buy a snack, rent a movie, ride a bus, turn on a light, send a text message, or see a doctor. Economic wheels turn to keep schools open, maintain streets and parks, and provide police and fire protection. Your home receives electricity, your television receives broadcasts, and your favorite stores are stocked with items you want to buy. Every day you use and depend on items generated by the US economy.

Focus on Finance

Why Study Economics

As the saying goes, knowledge is power. Studying this unit about economics will help you have a better understanding about the economy of our nation. Economic literacy gives you power to make decisions about how world events influence you. It helps you decide as a consumer if you should buy a house, invest in stocks, or save money. Economic literacy influences the career you choose, your role as a worker, and the part you play as a contributing citizen. When you understand the importance of economics in your day-to-day life, you make wiser personal choices for you and your family. By studying economics, you become an informed citizen and help shape democracy.

College and Career Readiness

Reading Prep. Before reading this chapter, go to the end of the chapter and read the summary. The chapter summary highlights important information that was presented in the chapter. Did this help you prepare to understand the content?

Check Your Personal Finance IQ

Before you begin the chapter, see what you already know about personal finance by taking the chapter pretest. If you do not have a smartphone, visit the G-W Learning companion website.

G-W Learning mobile site: www.m.g-wlearning.com

G-W Learning companion website: www.g-wlearning.com

Sections

Section 18.1 What Is Economics?

Section 18.2 How the US Economy Works

What Is Economics?

Objectives

After studying this section, you will be able to:

- Compare different types of economic systems.
- Explain the challenge of scarcity.

Terms

goods	marketplace
services	command economy
economic system	mixed economy
traditional economy	scarcity
market economy	nonhuman resource
free enterprise system	human resource
consumer	trade-off
producer	opportunity cost

Economic Systems

In earliest times, families were relatively self-sufficient. The family was the basic economic unit. It provided its members with food, shelter, protection, clothing, and other needs. Needs are items a person must have to survive. Needs differ from wants, which are items a person would like to have but that are not essential to life.

As families formed communities and moved away from an agricultural base, life became more complex. No longer were families self-sufficient. They became consumers who looked beyond the family to meet many of their needs. They began to trade with one another. Artisans and tradesmen became experts in their work.

As individuals and communities provided specialized labor, a wider variety of goods and services became available. **Goods** are physical items, such as food and clothing, while **services** refer to work performed. Examples of services include work done by a carpenter, plumber, or accountant. The interdependence of providers and users of goods and services marked the beginning of an economic system. An **economic system** is the structure in which limited resources are turned into goods and services to address unlimited needs and wants.

Every nation has an economic system. Economists have defined four basic types: traditional, market, command, and mixed economies.

Traditional

A **traditional economy** is a system in which economic decisions are based on a society's values, culture, and customs. Today, this type of economy mostly exists in developing countries or nations governed by strong cultural, religious, or tribal leadership.

In these areas, change comes slowly. People tend to stick with what they know and do as they have always done. For example, if you lived in a traditional economy and your parents raised sheep, chances are that you would, too. You would likely grow your own food and make your own clothing. You might barter or exchange goods and services rather than using money as a means of exchange. You would probably not be motivated to accept new ideas or try new ways of doing things.

In recent years, some traditional economies have begun to develop a new approach to economics. The people have come to recognize the advantages of technology and other advances in the modern world. There is a desire both to keep the old and to accept some of what is new.

Market

A **market economy** is a system in which privately owned businesses operate and compete for profits with limited government regulation or interference. It is also called a **free enterprise system** or *capitalism.*

In a market economy, consumers are important, and businesses react to their demands. A **consumer** is a buyer and user of goods and services. A **producer** is an individual or business that provides the supply of goods and services to meet consumer demands. Consumer choices create market demand, which largely determines which goods and services businesses will produce and sell. A market economy offers many opportunities for businesses to grow and profit by meeting consumer demands. It also offers hardworking individuals with education and training opportunities to develop their talents and succeed in fields of their choice.

In economic terms, the **marketplace,** or *market,* is not a physical place, such as a mall or a grocery store. It is an arena in which consumers and

Case Study

Living in a Market Economy

Anita and Juan are in their twenties and plan to marry in six months. They decide to buy their first home in the city and move to the suburbs once they have school-age children. They see two new one-bedroom apartments in their price range, but they prefer a higher-priced loft apartment. The cost of the loft is a little over their spending budget, but the high ceilings, wood floors, and interesting floor plan tempt them. The unit also has a new kitchen and laundry equipment. Their real estate agent says the loft should have an excellent resale value when they decide to sell and move in a few years.

Case Review

1. How are housing costs determined in a market economy? Why are they likely to be higher than in a command economy?

2. What would happen to housing costs in a market economy when the supply is severely limited? How would prices change when there are more sellers than buyers?

3. How would you describe the supply and demand for housing in your area? Would you rather be a buyer or a seller?

The word *market* is
derived from the Latin
word *mercaris*, which
means to trade.

producers meet to exchange goods, services, and money. The term *market* may refer to all goods and services in an economy or to a limited number of goods in a selected segment. For example, there is a market for children's clothes, for luxury cars, and for electronics. There also is a global market that encompasses trade among all the nations of the world.

Command

A **command economy** is a system in which a central authority, usually the government, controls economic activities. A central authority decides how to allocate resources. It decides who will produce what. It determines what and how much to produce and sets the prices of goods and services.

In this type of system, the needs and wants of consumers are not generally a driving force in the decision-making process. Consumers do not have broad freedom of choice. They often cannot decide for themselves how to earn and spend income. A command economy frequently exists in socialist and communist forms of government.

Mixed

Most economies are mixed. A **mixed economy** is a combination of the market and the command systems. For example, a mixed economy may function through a marketplace, although the government or central authority regulates the prices and supply of goods and services. The government may regulate certain industries, such as utilities and airlines, in a market system.

Although the US economy is technically a mixed economy, in this textbook and elsewhere it is often called a market of free enterprise economy. Compared with other mixed economies, the United States has minimal government involvement. The government's limited role in the US economy is varied and important. That role will be covered in detail in the next chapter. Currently,

Economics in Action

Marginalism

Marginalism is the added value versus the additional cost of one more unit or item. For example, suppose you buy two pairs of jeans at $65 and consider buying a third pair. Will the added pair bring you as much satisfaction as the first two? As you buy more jeans, the price per unit stays the same, but the "marginal," or extra, value of one more pair decreases.

You can also approach economic choices through a cost-benefit analysis, which is similar to marginalism. The cost-benefit principle states that you should take an action or make a purchase only if the benefit is at least as great as the cost. Using the jeans example, suppose you see a casual jacket that complements the first two pairs of jeans. With the jacket and those jeans, you could coordinate several outfits. A third pair of jeans, on the other hand, would not benefit your wardrobe to the same degree as the jacket.

These principles apply to economic decisions of individual consumers, businesses, and governments.

the role of government in the US economy has become a key political issue. Some people think that the government does too much, while others think that the government needs to do more.

Challenge of Scarcity

All economic systems attempt to resolve the problem of unlimited needs and wants and limited resources. Here the term *resources* refers to any input used to generate other goods or services. Resources that are scarce are in limited supply. The challenge of stretching resources to cover needs and wants is called **scarcity**. Individuals, families, companies, and nations are all limited in the resources available to meet needs and wants. Deciding how to deal with scarcity is the basis for the study of economics.

Over your lifetime, your needs and wants will never end. There are many reasons for this. The most obvious reason is that you outgrow your current needs and wants and develop new ones. For example, as your feet grow bigger, you need larger shoes. Your needs and wants change as you grow physically, mentally, and emotionally. Different things become important to you.

Also, fulfilling one want often creates others. For example, if you buy a smartphone, you will want apps for it. When your phone becomes outdated, you will want a new model.

Scarcity forces people, businesses, and governments to make choices in the use of resources and the needs to be met. There are two basic types of resources that are considered:

- A **nonhuman resource** is an external resource, such as money, time, equipment, or a possession.
- A **human resource** is a quality or characteristic that a person has.

Human resources include qualities that make workers more productive, such as good health, skills, knowledge, and education. Entrepreneurship is

Economists
Economists study how society distributes resources, such as land, labor, raw materials, and machinery, to produce goods and services. They may conduct research, collect and analyze data, monitor economic trends, or develop forecasts.

REDAV/Shutterstock.com

An employee's human resources include his or her skills, abilities, and knowledge.

a type of human resource, too. It is a set of personal qualities that motivates individuals to create, operate, and assume the risk of starting businesses.

Consumers have unlimited needs and wants for different goods and services. These needs and wants include food, clothes, housing, medical care, cars, and spending money. Since resources are limited while wants are unlimited, it is necessary to choose which wants to satisfy.

For example, suppose you must choose between seeing a movie and going bowling because you do not have time for both. You may need to choose between a new pair of gym shoes and a pair of boots if you do not have money for both. Families may have to choose between buying a new car and taking a family vacation or between buying a home and starting a business. Economic choices are endless.

Scarcity applies to governments in the same way. The needs of citizens far exceed the resources of governments. That is why it is necessary to make choices. Local governments may need to choose between raising taxes and cutting services. The federal government makes the same types of choices.

Trade-Offs and Opportunity Cost

The choices you make involve trade-offs and opportunity costs. A **trade-off** is the choice you give up when you make one choice over another. For example, there is a trade-off when you spend $50 to buy a jacket. The trade-off is the other ways you could have used the $50.

Making a choice results in a trade-off, and a trade-off results in an opportunity cost. **Opportunity cost** is the value of the option you gave up. If you turn down an after-school job because you have to be at soccer practice, there is an opportunity cost. The opportunity cost of playing soccer is the after-school job and the money you could have earned. The opportunity cost of working instead of playing soccer would be the pleasure and advantages you get from playing a team sport you love.

When you make a choice, you trade off, or give up, the other choices you could have made. The trade-off, or what you gave up, is the opportunity cost of the choice you made. When you choose one of two options, the one you did not choose is the opportunity cost of your choice.

Opportunity cost can be measured in terms of dollars, time, enjoyment, or something else of value. The opportunity cost of a decision often varies from one person to the next. It depends on what is valued by the person who makes the decision.

For example, if spending time with your friends is of primary importance to you, then missing time with friends may be the opportunity cost of going to soccer practice or taking an after-school job. If getting good grades is a priority, then losing time to study may be the opportunity cost of other choices.

Opportunity costs apply to economic choices of families, businesses, and governments as well as individuals. Weighing opportunity costs is a valuable decision-making tool.

Scarcity and Economic Systems

All societies are faced with the problem of scarcity and must make choices. The problem of scarcity applies to individuals, families, businesses, and organizations. Governments also make economic choices that affect everyone.

At the local level, governments make many choices in allocating limited resources. For example, a local government may need to choose between using funds to build a public swimming pool or to repave the streets.

The federal government makes the same types of choices. For example, the government may have to decide between drilling for oil or developing new energy sources or between defense spending and infrastructure improvements.

Major political and economic decisions center on how governments will divide limited resources among unlimited needs. These needs may include crime control, health care, environmental protection, education, national defense, and aid to the poor and homeless.

The scarcity of resources leads to three problems for all societies:

- What and how much to produce
- How to allocate resources in producing goods and services
- How to divide the goods and services produced

The way a society solves these problems defines its economic system. In a traditional economic system, a nation's religious or tribal leaders are likely to make these decisions. In a command economy, a central planning authority decides. In the US free enterprise system, market forces determine the answer to these questions.

Checkpoint 18.1

1. What is the difference between a *need* and a *want?*
2. What types of countries typically have a traditional economy?
3. What is another term for *market economy?*
4. What are some examples of nonhuman resources?
5. How can opportunity cost be measured?

Build Your Vocabulary

As you progress through this course, develop a personal glossary of personal finance terms and add it to your portfolio. This will help you build your vocabulary and prepare you for a career. Write a definition for each of the following terms and add it to your personal finance glossary.

goods	marketplace
services	command economy
economic system	mixed economy
traditional economy	scarcity
market economy	nonhuman resource
free enterprise system	human resource
consumer	trade-off
producer	opportunity cost

Section 18.2
How the US Economy Works

Objectives

After studying this section, you will be able to:

- Describe the factors of production.
- Discuss the qualities of a market economy.

Terms

factor of production	capital good
land	innovation
natural resource	profit
labor	supply
productivity	demand
capital	

Factors of Production

A circular flow of goods, services, and money takes place within the economy. See the model shown in Figure 18-1. The blue outer circle shows the flow of consumer goods and services from producers and sellers to

Entrepreneurs

Entrepreneurs are people who organize, operate, and assume the risk for a business venture or enterprise. Successful entrepreneurs have business management skills, marketing knowledge, and an understanding of the demand for the product or service they provide.

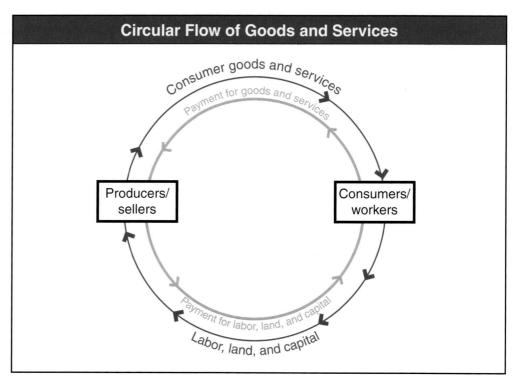

Goodheart-Willcox Publisher

Figure 18-1 This chart shows the circular flow of goods, services, and money between producers and sellers and consumers and workers.

consumers and workers. It also shows the flow of the economic resources from consumers and workers to producers and sellers. An economic resource (land, labor, capital, or entrepreneurship) is known as a **factor of production**.

The orange circle shows the flow of payments for goods and services from consumers to producers. It also shows the flow of payments for resources from producers to workers and suppliers. This model is a snapshot of how consumers and producers interact in the economy. However, it does not show the whole picture. For example, producers and sellers also are consumers. Businesses buy the goods and services that other businesses produce. In the next chapter, you will see how government fits into this picture.

Land

Land is all of the natural resources of a nation. A **natural resource** is a raw material, such as soil, water, minerals, plants, animals, and climate. All goods are made from natural resources. All services use natural resources in some form. However, natural resources are scarce.

Labor

Labor is the work performed by people who turn resources into products. Human resources were discussed earlier in this chapter. **Productivity** is a measure of the amount of work a person can do in a specific amount of time. A nation can make up for a lack of natural resources if its people are very productive.

Capital

Capital is the manufactured products that are used to make other products. A **capital good** is a manufactured product used to make a final product.

Entrepreneurship

Inventors, innovators, and entrepreneurs have always played an important role in the US economy. They are the engines that drive progress and prosperity. Out of approximately 220 of the greatest inventions of all time, 152 originated in the United States.

The inventor creates something totally new—a product, a process, or an idea. The new invention may have the capacity to change the overall economic and social landscape, as did the automobile, the lightbulb, and central heating. More recent inventions include television, the Internet, and the smartphone. Other inventions, such as crayons, can openers, and toasters, have a more limited impact.

The innovator brings inventions to life and practical use. Innovators make the most of an invention's capacity to bring change. Innovators also find new ways to use and improve existing products and processes to create new jobs, value, and growth.

The entrepreneur creates a way to produce and market a product or process, puts the necessary time and effort into its development, and accepts the financial and other risks involved in selling the idea. This hard work requires serious ongoing commitment. The rewards include personal satisfaction, independence, and profits.

Capital is another business term with different meanings. It is often used as the short form of financial capital, which is money that is used to buy capital goods. As a result, capital can be used to refer to capital goods or money.

Together, inventions, innovations, and entrepreneurship lead to new or improved products and services, higher productivity, more jobs, and higher wages overall. These three things are keys to job creation, growth, and ongoing prosperity.

The economist Joseph Schumpeter called this economic process creative destruction. According to Schumpeter, every new invention and innovation carries the seeds of destruction for existing products and processes. Consider the demise of the horse and buggy in the wake of the automobile, the diminishing business of the candle maker in face of the lightbulb, and the decline in typewriter sales following the introduction of personal computers. More recent examples include the impact that off shoring jobs has on local workers and the challenge to newspapers in a world of 24-hour televised news programs.

Consumers need to acknowledge and absorb the losses as well as the benefits of new enterprises and to consider the jobs lost as well as the jobs created. Growth and prosperity depend on reinventing our economy and moving forward, but it sometimes comes at a cost.

Market Qualities

You can gain a better understanding of how the US economy works by studying the basic qualities of a market economy. Three unique qualities that characterize a market economy are private ownership, economic freedom, and market forces. The dynamic combination of these three qualities explains many aspects of the inner workings of the US economy.

Private Ownership

Productive resources include the human and nonhuman resources used to produce goods and services. In the US economic system, citizens and businesses own these resources and decide how to use them. Businesses invest in the equipment, labor, and land needed to produce goods and services. They exercise the right to own private property. Individuals and businesses can buy and sell property; they can use it or give it away. On a personal level, you can own a home, a car, a business, and a vast selection of personal possessions.

Economic Freedom

In the United States and other market economies, consumers are free to make choices. This is good news for you. Free choice opens the doors of opportunity in many areas. Both individuals and businesses have the right to decide freely how they will earn, spend, save, invest, and produce. You choose:

- What you will buy
- Where you will buy it
- How much you are willing to pay
- Whether you will use cash or credit
- Whether you will spend or save

Minerva Studio/Shutterstock.com

In the United States, consumers are free to make choices about how they earn and spend money.

Businesses respond to consumer choices by producing and selling the goods and services consumers want. In our economy, the combined choices of individual consumers make the greatest economic impact. Your decision to buy a new cell phone will not greatly impact the manufacturer's profits. However, if thousands of consumers buy it, the company will make money.

You are also free to choose how to earn your money. There is a vast menu of job possibilities in a free market economy. Your future income will depend on the career choices you make and the abilities and skills you develop. If you are willing to work hard and get the training and education required, you are likely to succeed in a market economy. This is not always true in a command economy where a central authority controls much of the opportunity.

A free market economy is also ideal for starting your own business. The path of the entrepreneur is not an easy path, but it is open to anyone with a sound idea and the willingness to take risks and work hard. Take a look at the stories of those who founded well-known corporations, such as Microsoft, Apple, and Walmart. Almost all of them started with an idea that greatly appealed to consumers.

Market Forces

Our market economy is controlled by market forces. Individuals are free to make economic decisions, but the market forces influence those decisions. There are three market forces: competition, the profit motive, and supply and demand.

Business Management & Administration

Business Development Managers
Business development managers plan strategies to improve a company's performance and competitive position. They analyze, interpret, and evaluate various types of data in order to make sound business decisions.

Competition

Economic competition occurs when two or more sellers offer similar goods and services for sale in the marketplace. Each seller tries to do a better job than the other in order to attract more customers, make more sales, and earn more profits. Businesses compete with each other in many ways. They compete in the areas of price, quality, features, service, and new products.

In a market economy, innovation is the engine that sparks growth and prosperity. **Innovation** is the process of creating something, such as new or improved products and new ways to do things and solve problems.

Research and development (R&D) is the key to realizing the potential of innovation. It is an investment in the future. In simple terms, the innovator comes up with a new idea, explores its practicality, and turns it into a new product or service. Businesses, universities, and government agencies all participate in research and development, both independently and in cooperation with each other.

Historically, the United States has invested more money in research and development than any other country. This is one reason America is among the most prosperous nations. The same is true of businesses. Those that invest the most in research and development tend to be the most competitive and successful.

Technological advances are a major force in the creation of new products, services, and businesses. Technology is the application of scientific knowledge to practical uses and product development. Wi-Fi, smartphones, and hybrid automobiles are examples of recent technological advances.

The companies providing the best products and services at the lowest prices generally achieve the highest sales and profits. Ideally, this results in higher quality at lower prices for consumers. Competition encourages competence and efficiency in the production and sale of goods and services.

Electronic products are a good example. Consider the development of smartphones that started out as simple cell phones. Today, you can use the multipurpose smartphone to make and take your calls, surf the Internet, text, take photos and videos, and store and play music. In addition, smartphones can run countless apps that allow you to play games, access the news and sports scores, enjoy social networking, manage your finances, find addresses and directions, keep a calendar with reminders of important dates, and much more. You get more for your money with each new development. Most of this innovation is driven by competition and the profit motive.

There is also competition in the job market. The highest incomes go to the most educated, trained, and skilled workers who produce the goods and services in greatest demand. This demand increases the competition among workers. Workers try to update their skills and education in order to qualify for better jobs and be able to earn higher incomes and better benefits. This situation, in turn, improves a company's ability to compete.

Profit Motive

The promise of earning money inspires the worker, shop owner, manufacturer, and investor to engage in economic activity. For businesses and investors, **profit** is the total amount of money earned after expenses are subtracted from income. The profit motive drives businesses to produce goods and services to meet consumer demand.

For individuals, profit comes in the form of income. Individuals sell their productive resources, such as labor, ideas, land, and capital. In return, they receive income or a return on their investments. This is what brings people into the workforce and motivates investors to put their money to work.

If there were no opportunities to earn profits, the US economy would falter. Individuals would be less motivated to work. Investors would not invest in businesses and provide the money needed to turn resources into goods and services. Businesses would not grow or try to increase sales. All businesses, from a corner grocery to a worldwide corporation, depend on profits. The *profit motive,* or the desire for profit, drives both individuals and businesses to produce.

Supply and Demand

The key principles of private ownership, free economic choices, the profit motive, and competition come together to create a dynamic, ever-changing economy. Individuals, families, and businesses are free to act in their own best economic interests in the marketplace. By doing this, they make the economy work better for everyone.

Remember the economic challenges common to all societies? In short, the challenges are: what and how much to produce, how, and for whom. The US economic system addresses these questions largely by letting the forces of supply and demand operate in competitive markets. **Supply** is the amount of a product or service producers are willing to provide. **Demand** is the quantity of a product or service consumers are willing to buy.

Supply and demand are closely connected to price. For example, suppose you own a gym shoe company. When you price shoes at $80 a pair, you sell 1,000 pairs. At $40 each, you sell 3,000 pairs. When the quantities and prices are plotted on a graph and connected, they form a line called the *demand curve.* Price and demand move in opposite directions, so the curve has a negative slope. This illustrates the law of demand: the higher the price of a good or service, the less consumers will demand.

As a producer, you want to sell your goods for the highest possible price. If you think you can get $80 for each pair of sneakers, you would want to produce more. If you think you can only get $20 a pair, you would decide to produce less.

Go Green

A variety of electronic equipment, such as computers, cell phones, and other tools, are necessary to enable business to run efficiently. Care must be taken to keep equipment clean and maintained on a regular basis. Avoid chemical cleaners when removing the smudge marks from an LCD or TV screen or a computer monitor. Chemical cleaners may ruin some equipment finishes, and some are bad for the environment. Look for environmentally friendly cleaners that will not harm equipment to protect your investment as well as the environment.

When the prices and quantities are plotted on a graph and connected, they form a line called *the supply curve.* Price and supply tend to move in the same direction, so the curve has a positive slope. This illustrates the law of supply: the higher the price of a good or service, the more producers will supply.

The laws of supply and demand work together. When demand and supply are relatively balanced, the market is said to be in *equilibrium.* As shown in Figure 18-2, equilibrium is the approximate point at which the supply and demand curves intersect. It is the price at which the quantity supplied equals the quantity demanded. At this point, the market is operating at maximum efficiency.

Equilibrium is more an idea than a reality. Markets are usually not in equilibrium. Changes in supply or demand trigger price adjustments. When a price for a product is set too high, products stack up on store shelves. When a price is set too low, there are shortages.

What conditions might cause prices to increase? Prices rise when the demand for an item is greater than the supply or when demand rises and supply remains the same. For instance, airline ticket prices are highest during peak travel times. Seasonal foods become more expensive when the season ends because they become less plentiful. Food prices also rise when crops are lost to severe weather.

Ethics

Ethics in communication is very important in both business and personal life. Distorting information for personal gain is an unethical practice whether in advertising, politics, or personal relationships. Ethical communications are truthful, accurate, and balanced. If information is an opinion, it should be labeled as such. When presenting material, it is important to credit sources of information. It would be unethical to take credit for ideas that belong to someone else.

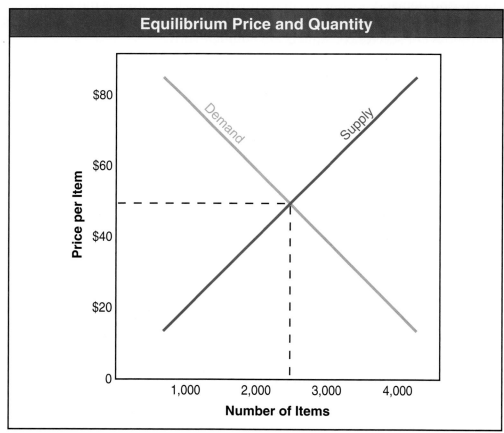

Goodheart-Willcox Publisher

Figure 18-2 The demand curve shows how much people will buy (*x*-axis) at different prices (*y*-axis). The supply curve shows how many products will be produced (*x*-axis) at different prices (*y*-axis). Equilibrium, $50, is the point at which the demand and supply curves intersect.

What conditions might cause prices to decrease? Prices fall when the supply for an item is greater than the demand or when supply rises and demand remains the same. For instance, at the end of winter, the demand for coats and gloves drops. Stores drop prices and hold end-of-season clearance sales.

To a large extent, demand in the marketplace determines *what* and *how much* is produced. Demand is expressed by the spending choices of consumers, businesses, and governments. These choices, to a large degree, determine what and how much producers will bring to the marketplace. In many cases, consumer demand leads to new and improved products.

Businesses generally own and control productive resources. They determine the right mix of productive resources and their use when they make products and deliver services to meet consumer demands. They decide how to produce goods and services.

The forces of supply and demand in the job market largely determine how to divide the goods and services produced. Those who can offer the skills, knowledge, materials, or capital needed for production receive income or profits. In job markets, those who have the qualifications to perform the work that is in demand generally earn higher incomes and can buy more of the goods and services they need. This helps determine how production is divided.

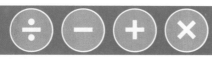

You Do the Math

Opportunity cost is the value of the option you gave up. To calculate opportunity cost, use the following equation:

cost of choice − cost of alternative = opportunity cost

Complete the Following Problems

1. Justin will graduate from high school in one month. He already has an offer for a full-time job that would pay $25,000 a year. He is also considering going to college for the next four years. Tuition is $8,000 a year. Room and board is $10,000 annually. If he works, he will not be able to make more than $3,000 a year doing part-time and summer work.

   A. What is the opportunity cost of attending college?

   B. What is the cost of tuition and room and board for college for four years, assuming the costs stay the same for four years?

2. Suppose that after graduating from college, Justin will make $50,000 a year for at least the next ten years. How many years would it take for college-graduate Justin to earn as much as he could have earned in four years if he had taken the job right out of high school?.

Careers in Human Services

What Do Personal Financial Advisors Do?

Personal financial advisors give financial advice to help clients plan for short- and long-term goals, such as saving for college and retirement. They recommend savings and investments choices to match their clients' goals. **Personal financial advisors** typically:

- meet with clients to discuss their financial goals and money needs;
- explain the types of financial services they offer;
- answer questions about savings and investment options and potential risks;
- recommend investment options to clients;
- help clients plan for specific circumstances, such as education expenses or retirement;
- monitor clients' accounts and determine if changes are needed to improve account performance or accommodate life changes, such as having children or loss of a job; and
- research investment opportunities.

What Is It Like to Work as a Personal Financial Advisor?

Many **personal financial advisors** work at brokerage firms, banks, or insurance companies. Many are also self-employed. They typically work full time and may meet with clients in the evenings or on weekends. Some work only with individuals, while others may have businesses as part of their client base. The work of a **personal financial advisor** is fast-paced and requires the advisor to stay current on savings and investments options, tax laws, and insurance products.

What Education and Skills Are Needed to Be a Personal Financial Advisor?

- bachelor degree in accounting, finance, or closely related area
- master degree and certification for advancement
- excellent communication and listening skills
- customer service skills
- decision-making skills
- attention to detail
- initiative
- math and computer skills

Checkpoint 18.2

1. Describe the flow of goods, services, and money that takes place within the economy.
2. Explain the roles of the inventor, the innovator, and the entrepreneur.
3. What are the three qualities that characterize a market economy?
4. In the US economic system, who owns the resources and decides how to use them?
5. What conditions cause prices to increase?

Build Your Vocabulary

As you progress through this course, develop a personal glossary of personal finance terms and add it to your portfolio. This will help you build your vocabulary and prepare you for a career. Write a definition for each of the following terms and add it to your personal finance glossary.

factor of production	capital good
land	innovation
natural resource	profit
labor	supply
productivity	demand
capital	

Chapter Summary

Section 18.1 What Is Economics?

- Every nation has an economic system. Economists have defined four basic types: traditional, market, command, and mixed economies. A market economy is also called a free enterprise system or capitalism.

- All economic systems attempt to resolve the problem of unlimited needs and wants and limited resources. The challenge of stretching resources to cover needs and wants is called scarcity. Scarcity forces people, businesses, and governments to make choices in the use of resources and the needs to be met.

Section 18.2 How the US Economy Works

- Land, labor, capital, and entrepreneurship are economic resources that make up a country's factors of production. Land is all the natural resources of a nation. Labor is the work performed by people who turn resources into products. Capital is the manufactured products that are used to make other products.

- Three unique qualities that characterize a market economy are private ownership, economic freedom, and market forces. A market economy is controlled by three market forces: competition, the profit motive, and supply and demand.

Check Your Personal Finance IQ

Now that you have finished the chapter, see what you learned about personal finance by taking the chapter posttest. If you do not have a smartphone, visit the G-W Learning companion website.

G-W Learning mobile site: www.m.g-wlearning.com

G-W Learning companion website: www.g-wlearning.com

Review Your Knowledge

1. What are the four types of economic systems?
2. Why is the economic system of the United States a mixed economy?
3. Describe the concept of scarcity and how it applies to individuals, families, and government.
4. Why are human needs and wants unlimited?
5. What is the difference between human resources and nonhuman resources?
6. What three challenges caused by scarcity must all societies face?
7. What are the basic qualities of a market economy?
8. Why is innovation important in encouraging competition?
9. What drives businesses to produce goods and services to meet consumer demand?
10. How do the laws of supply and demand relate to the prices of goods and services in the marketplace?

Apply Your Knowledge

11. What can you gain by learning more about the US economic system?
12. Suppose you started a service business, such as babysitting or dog walking. Describe how you would assess the demand for your service.
13. Demonstrate the concept of scarcity in your own life. Make a list of items you want and need over the next five years of your life. What resources will you use to get what you want and need? Will you be able to satisfy all your wants?
14. How do you and your family decide which needs and wants to satisfy? What trade-offs have you made in the marketplace? What were the opportunity costs of your trade-offs?
15. Create a list of pros and cons for each of the four types of economies: traditional, market, command, and mixed. Next, discuss with classmates the type of economy you think works the best, and why. Can your group agree on one? Why or why not?
16. Look around your classroom and select any item you see. Brainstorm to think of all the resources that were necessary to make the item. Create a list of at least five different resources.
17. Conduct an Internet search on famous inventors. Identify one of his or her inventions. What did he or she invent? What problem did the invention solve? Was it successful? Why or why not? Summarize your findings in a one- to two-page report.
18. Identify a successful business owner in your community. Prepare five interview questions about the goods or services the business provides and how the principles of supply and demand affect the business. Conduct an interview with the business owner and summarize your findings in a one-page report. Share your experience with the class.
19. Read a newspaper, magazine, or online article about prices rising or falling. What conditions are causing the change in price? Has supply or demand changed? Has the availability of resources changed?
20. Interpret the following quote: "One person's wage increase is another person's price increase."

Teamwork

Working as a team, create a bulletin board of newspaper and magazine articles and advertisements illustrating different economic concepts in action. Label each advertisement with the concept that is applied. What did you learn from this exercise?

G-W Learning Mobile Site

Visit the G-W Learning mobile site to complete the chapter pretest and posttest and to practice vocabulary using e-flash cards. If you do not have a smartphone, visit the G-W Learning companion website to access these features.

G-W Learning mobile site: www.m.g-wlearning.com

G-W Learning companion website: www.g-wlearning.com

College and Career Readiness

Common Core

CTE Career Ready Practices. There will be instances in which you will need to use critical thinking skills to solve a problem. One way to approach a problem is to create a pros and cons chart. Create a list of three needs that you currently have. Place all of the good or positive things about the needs on the pro side of the chart and all the negative things on the con side. Circle the items on your list that you consider the most important. Did the list help you come to a decision? Why or why not?

Speaking. Select three of your classmates to participate in a discussion panel. Acting as the team leader, name each person to a specific task such as time-keeper, recorder, etc. Discuss the topic of trade-offs and opportunity costs. Keep the panel on task and promote democratic discussion.

Listening. Active listeners know when to comment and when to remain silent. Practice your listening skills while your instructor presents this chapter. Participate when appropriate and build on his or her ideas.

Web Connect

Use the Internet to research the economic system of each of the following countries: China, Cuba, Brazil, and Congo. Identify the economic system for each one. Write a report documenting your findings. Footnote your sources and create a bibliography.

College and Career Readiness

College and Career Readiness Portfolio

Employers and colleges review candidates for various positions. They are interested in people who impress them as being professional or serious about a position. Being involved in academic clubs or professional organizations will help you make a good impression. You can also learn a lot that will help you with your studies or your career. While you are in school, you may belong to clubs. National Honor Society and Future Business Leaders of America are two examples. When you are employed, you may belong to professional organizations related to your career area. The American Nurses Association is one example. Update your résumé and online information to reflect your membership in clubs and organizations as well as relevant work experience and extracurricular activities. Make sure information about you on the Internet does not detract from your professional image. Review information you have posted on social networking websites, blogs, wikis, or other websites. Remove any information that does not give a favorable impression of you.

1. Identify clubs or organizations you can join to help you build a professional image. Give the name and a brief description of each one.
2. Save the file in your e-portfolio. Place a copy in the container for your print portfolio.

Written Events

Many competitive events for career and technical student organizations (CTSOs) require students to write a paper and submit it either before the competition or when the student arrives at the event. Written events can be lengthy and take a lot of time to prepare, so it is important to start early.

To prepare for a written event, complete the following activities.

1. Read the guidelines provided by the organization. The topic to be researched will be specified in detail. Also, all final format guidelines will be given, including how to organize and submit the paper. Make certain you ask questions about any points you do not understand.
2. Do your research early. Research may take days or weeks, and you do not want to rush the process.
3. Set a deadline for yourself so that you write at a comfortable pace.
4. After you write the first draft, ask an instructor to review it for you and give feedback.
5. Once you have the final version, go through the checklist for the event to make sure you have covered all of the details. Your score will be penalized if you do not follow instructions.
6. To practice, visit your organization's website and select a written event in which you might be interested. Research the topic and then complete an outline. Create a checklist of guidelines that you must follow for this event. After you have completed these steps, decide if this is the event or topic that interests you. If you are still interested, move forward and start the writing process.

Chapter 19
Government and the Economy

In our economic system, the most fundamental role of government is to provide the legal and institutional environment and the economic policies that permit and encourage productive economic activity. The system is based on the rule of law and leads to political and economic stability. This is what gives businesses and individual citizens the confidence to enter the marketplace as producers, workers, and consumers.

Government controls the money supply and levies taxes to pay for government operations and public services. These monetary and fiscal policies keep our economy stable and prosperous. Government enacts legislation to promote open and fair competition and to protect consumer interests. Laws and regulations cover everything from the purity of your food and water to the air you breathe and the money you borrow.

Focus on Finance

National Debt

In 2012 the national debt reached $16.3 trillion. The national debt is the total amount the government owes. It amounts to $61,000 per capita. In recent years, government spending exceeded its revenues each year by over $1 trillion. This deficit is added to the national debt, which means that the debt is growing by over a trillion dollars annually.

The annual interest on all this debt comes to approximately $224 billion, which is about the same as spending for education, the environment, and international affairs combined. Interest on the debt is expected to grow faster than any other item in the federal budget in coming years. This is money we cannot spend on other needs.

The debt has become both an economic and political issue, and possible solutions to the debt problem have been hotly debated. The one thing all sides agree on is that current policies regarding spending and revenues are not sustainable.

College and Career Readiness

Reading Prep. The summary at the end of the chapter highlights the most important concepts. Read the summary first. Then, make sure you understand those concepts as you read the chapter.

Check Your Personal Finance IQ

Before you begin the chapter, see what you already know about personal finance by taking the chapter pretest. If you do not have a smartphone, visit the G-W Learning companion website.

G-W Learning mobile site: www.m.g-wlearning.com

G-W Learning companion website: www.g-wlearning.com

Sections

eurobanks/Shutterstock.com

Section 19.1
Economics

Objectives

After studying this section, you will be able to:
- Describe the relationship between the US government and the economy.
- Discuss the economic conditions that are monitored by the government.

Terms

business cycle

recession

depression

inflation

stagflation

deflation

labor force

unemployment rate

underemployment

US Economic System

The US economic system is called a *market* or a *free enterprise system*. Compared with many other nations, the US government plays a small role in the economy. However, the economy could not function without certain types of government participation.

For example, the government provides the legal and institutional environment that permits and encourages economic activity. The government protects individual liberties and private property rights and enforces contractual agreements. It provides the political stability and the rule of law that are necessary for economic interaction. This is what enables individuals and businesses to carry out productive economic activities.

Government plays the following specific roles in the operation of our economy.
- It sets economic policies in an effort to create stability and prosperity.
- It makes tax and spending decisions in response to economic conditions.
- It controls the money supply.
- It regulates business and economic activity to ensure fair business practices and to protect the public's well-being and safety.

Economic Conditions Monitored by the Government

The US economy fluctuates between periods of economic growth and slowdown. This is true of economies in other industrialized nations as well. A **business cycle** is fluctuations between periods of economic growth and slowdown, as shown in Figure 19-1. Some economists prefer the term *business fluctuations* because there are not predictable patterns to the ups and downs. The business cycle has four parts.

- *Expansion* is a period when business activity is growing.
- *Peak* is the height of expansion and lasts until growth begins to slow.
- *Contraction* is a period of slow or no growth.
- *Trough* occurs when a contraction stops.

Each part can last months or even years. For example, the longest economic expansion in modern US history occurred during the 1990s and lasted ten years. However, the average length of an expansion is about three years. Economists use specific indicators to measure economic conditions and predict highs and lows. These indicators include gross domestic product (GDP), interest rates, business spending, unemployment figures, inflation, and consumer confidence. GDP is discussed later in this chapter. The following sections describe the most serious problems of a troubled economy.

Recession and Depression

When the business cycle starts a downward trend, people fear a **recession**, which is an extended period of slow or no economic growth. Technically, a recession exists if negative growth lasts two quarters or more. A recession is marked by:

- high unemployment;
- declining retail sales;
- lowered average personal incomes;
- decreases in consumer spending; and
- reduced spending by businesses on equipment and expansion.

Overall economic activity declines in a recession. Many workers lose their jobs and businesses fail. It may also be difficult to obtain a mortgage for a home or to start a new business. When a recession goes on for several years, which is rare, the economy is said to be in a **depression**.

During the Great Depression of the 1930s, one out of four workers was unemployed. Pay cuts were common among those who had jobs. People lost

Occupational Health and Safety Specialists
Occupational health and safety specialists inspect workplaces and recommend ways to reduce and eliminate disease or injury. They look for biological, chemical, physical, and radiological hazards and identify ways to increase workers' safety. Specialists are employed by federal, state, and local government agencies.

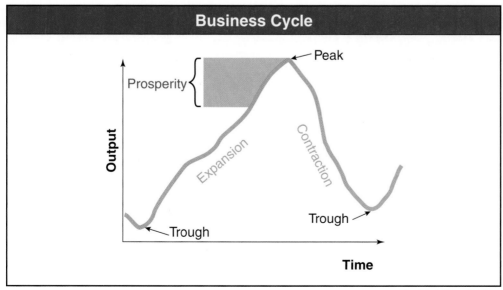

Goodheart-Willcox Publisher

Figure 19-1 One business cycle consists of the time from one trough to the next.

their savings and investments. Hunger and homelessness were common. Families migrated across the country looking for work. The depression lasted for almost ten years.

More recently, between 2007 and 2009, the economy went into what is now being called the Great Recession. Again, many people lost their jobs and homes, businesses failed, and the value of savings and investments fell dramatically. Unemployment exceeded 10 percent among unskilled and uneducated workers. In 2009, a fragile recovery began with slight improvements in GDP and employment figures. Economists estimate that the impact of the recession could last for years. Some of the consequences that may lie ahead are discussed in the following paragraphs.

The business year is divided into four, three-month quarters.

Inflation

Inflation is an overall increase in the price of goods and services. It threatens the nation's prosperity because it decreases the value of a dollar. Due to inflation, today's dollars buy less than dollars from past years. For example, you would need $15 in 2012 to buy what would have cost $10 in 1995. The CPI Inflation Calculator at the website of the US Department of Labor's Bureau of Labor Statistics can be used to calculate the cost of inflation.

According to government data, the US inflation rate is fairly low compared with the rates of many other countries. For example, in 2012, the estimated rate of inflation in the United States was 2.9 percent. In India, it was estimated at 8.8 percent. In Russia, it was about 3.7 percent, and in China, it was 3.6 percent. Inflation is especially hard on individuals and families who live on fixed incomes. Income stays the same over the years, while costs climb. There are several types of inflation.

Demand-Pull Inflation

Demand-pull inflation occurs during recovery and peak periods of the business cycle. When the economy is growing, consumers are more likely to be employed and spending money. Spending increases at a faster rate than

You Do the Math

This chapter uses graphs to present statistical information. A graph can be used to depict the unemployment rate over time. A line graph shows fluctuations in the business cycle over time.

Complete the Following Problems

For each of the following, state which type of chart would best express the information.

1. Show fluctuations in the rate of inflation over the past 25 years
2. Show the proportion of new US citizens who came from each of the world's continents
3. Show total taxes collected by the federal government during the past ten years

d13/Shutterstock.com

Inflation affects the price of most goods and services.

supply. Put another way, there are too many dollars chasing too few goods. According to the laws of supply and demand, as demand goes up, so do prices.

Cost-Push Inflation

Cost-push inflation is triggered by an increase in the price of a widely used product. For example, when the price of oil rises, consumers pay more for fuel to power their cars and heat their homes. Many other goods and services, from food and flowers to building materials and airfares, increase in price as well. This increase happens because many businesses require fuel to operate and bring goods to market. Petroleum is also a necessary ingredient in many other products.

Stagflation

Stagflation is a period of slow growth (economic stagnation) and high inflation. The best-known episode of stagflation took place during the 1970s. Oil producers raised oil prices, which triggered inflation because the costs of many goods and services rose. This occurred at a time of slow growth and high unemployment. Some economists predicted another period of stagflation following 2012 for both the United States and the world.

Deflation

Deflation is a period of declining prices. When prices continue to fall, consumers and businesses tend to defer spending while they wait for still lower prices. Eventually demand falls off, causing business failures, unemployment, and lower incomes. Extended deflationary periods can lead to an economic depression. The Federal Reserve uses monetary policy to avoid sudden and severe ups and downs in the price levels of goods and services.

Unemployment

A nation's prosperity and stability depend on full use of its productive resources, including the labor force. This is one of the goals government seeks to achieve through its economic policies. The **labor force** is composed of people, age 16 and over, who are employed or looking for and able to work.

The **unemployment rate** is the percentage of the labor force that is out of work and seeking employment. The unemployment rate in the United States is reported by the Bureau of Labor Statistics. These figures are closely tied to business fluctuations. The highest unemployment rates occur during periods of contraction.

Historically, from 1948 until 2012, the employment rate in this country averaged 5.8 percent. When the Great Recession began in 2007, unemployment was at 5 percent. In October of 2009, it peaked at 10 percent as shown in Figure 19-2.

Unemployment hurts workers and their families. When family breadwinners are unemployed, the entire family suffers. Some families must move because they lose their homes or cannot afford to make rent or mortgage payments. Some people go into debt and lose health benefits that are usually provided through an employer. Unemployment is also associated with health problems, such as stress-related illnesses, depression, and substance abuse. There are several types of unemployment that economists consider.

Frictional Unemployment

Frictional unemployment is short-term unemployment that affects people who are between jobs. These are people who have moved or changed jobs or careers. They can often find employment by matching their qualifications to available jobs. Some workers will be temporarily unemployed even in a strong and growing economy.

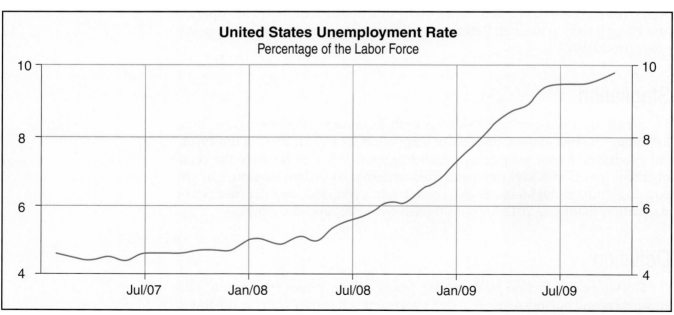

Source: United States Bureau of Labor Statistics

Figure 19-2 The US Department of Labor keeps track of the civilian unemployment rate.

Structural Unemployment

Structural unemployment tends to be long-term, difficult to correct, and the most damaging to both workers and the economy. It refers to unemployment among workers who drop out of the labor force or do not enter. There may be a mismatch between their skills and available jobs. Examples of structural unemployment include jobs lost because of technological advances, failure of a major employer in an area, and outsourcing of jobs to cheaper labor markets.

Cyclical Unemployment

Cyclical unemployment normally is tied to the business cycle. It occurs when the economy slows or is in a recession. Demand falls and workers are laid off. There are more job seekers than available jobs. When the economy moves into the recovery phase, workers are rehired.

Seasonal Unemployment

Seasonal unemployment is related to jobs that depend on seasonal activities. These jobs include those for the extra workers hired for the holidays, for vacation seasons, and for crop harvesting. Seasonal jobs end when the short-term demand for workers ceases.

Underemployment

In addition to the unemployed, a percentage of the labor force will be underemployed. **Underemployment** is a condition in which workers are employed only part time or are overqualified for their jobs. They are skilled workers who hold jobs requiring few skills. Some of these workers are underemployed by choice, but most workers cannot find work at their skill or educational level.

Continuing prosperity and stability require the workforce and other productive resources to be employed at full capacity. This is one of the goals government seeks to achieve through its economic policies.

Max Topchii/Shutterstock.com

Many ski resorts hire extra employees for the winter season. These workers are sometimes affected by seasonal unemployment after the winter months.

Checkpoint 19.1

1. What are the roles government plays in the functioning of the US economy?
2. Name the four parts of the business cycle.
3. Recession is marked by what factors?
4. What are two types of inflation?
5. What typically happens during a period of deflation?

Build Your Vocabulary

As you progress through this course, develop a personal glossary of personal finance terms and add it to your portfolio. This will help you build your vocabulary and prepare you for a career. Write a definition for each of the following terms and add it to your personal finance glossary.

business cycle   deflation
recession   labor force
depression   unemployment rate
inflation   underemployment
stagflation

Section 19.2
Economic Policies

Objectives

After studying this section, you will be able to:

- Discuss the gross domestic product and the consumer price index.
- Describe how the government uses monetary policies to combat inflation and recession.
- Differentiate between monetary and fiscal policy.
- Identify the laws and government agencies that protect consumer interests.

Terms

gross domestic product (GDP)

consumer price index (CPI)

labor union

monetary policy

Federal Reserve System

discount rate

fiscal policy

tax

subsidy

deficit spending

surplus

national debt

perfect competition

monopoly

oligopoly

collusion

Economic Indicators

The economy is incredibly complex and difficult to understand and predict. Government policies attempt to provide price stability, growth, full employment, and ongoing prosperity. The tools the government uses to influence the economy include monetary and fiscal policies. Existing economic conditions dictate the policies the government follows.

In making policy decisions, the government looks to economic indicators. An economic indicator is a piece of significant economic data that economists use to evaluate the overall health of the economy.

The GDP and the consumer price index (CPI) are two key indicators that influence monetary and fiscal policies. Other important indicators include the consumer confidence index (CCI), the retail sales report, and employment figures.

Gross Domestic Product

The economy is described in terms of many indicators. The best measure of economic growth is the gross domestic product. The **gross domestic product (GDP)** is a measure of the value of all goods and services produced by a nation during a specified period of time, usually one year. The GDP includes the following measures.

The underemployment rate is also referred to as *U6* and is considered the broadest measure of unemployment.

The change in GDP from one quarter to the next is measured in chained dollars. Chained dollars are based on the average cost of goods and services in successive pairs of years. The second year in a pair of years becomes the first year in the next pair, so the amounts are chained.

- *Personal consumption expenditures.* This is a measure of consumer spending.

- *Gross private domestic investment.* This is a measure of the money businesses invest in buildings, equipment, technology, innovation, and inventory.

- *Net exports of goods and services.* This is the value of the goods and services exported minus the value of goods and services imported from other countries.

- *Government spending.* This is a measure of government consumption expenditures and gross investment.

The US Department of Commerce's Bureau of Economic Analysis (BEA) calculates the GDP each quarter. The growth or decline in production is measured by the change in the real GDP from one quarter to the next. Although the GDP is calculated quarterly, it is expressed as an annual rate.

The US GDP dropped by 0.3 percent in 2008, and by 3.5 percent in 2009, as shown in Figure 19-3. These were the first declines in 16 years. They were

History of Finance

Adam Smith and John Maynard Keynes

Two economists instrumental in shaping modern economics were Adam Smith (1723–1790) and John Maynard Keynes (1883–1946). The ideas of Smith and Keynes continue to foster debate about the role of government in the economy today.

Adam Smith lived at the dawn of the industrial revolution. Previously, most people lived in rural areas and produced most of what they needed themselves. The industrial revolution brought people to cities to work in factories. Factory workers became part of an assembly line, each specializing in a small task that contributed to a finished product.

In his book *The Wealth of Nations*, Smith hailed specialization, or division of labor, that created greater economic efficiency, mass production, and markets for goods. He argued that a free market economic system was superior to other systems because it harnessed a powerful force that motivated people: self-interest. In a free market economy, people have the freedom to do what is best for themselves and wind up doing what is best for the economy. For example, in order to maximize profits, producers avoid wasting resources. To increase earnings, workers learn new skills. This give and take between people acting in their own self-interest is the "invisible hand" that runs the economy. Smith opposed government interference in the economy.

John Maynard Keynes witnessed WWI and the Great Depression. He and others saw the depression as a failure of Smith's invisible hand theory. The economy was damaged, and only government intervention saved it. New government programs created jobs and stimulated the economy. Spending on WWII created new demand that finally lifted the United States out of the depression. In his book, *The General Theory of Employment, Interest, and Money*, Keynes argued that economic stability and prosperity depends on government playing a role in the economy.

evidence of the severe economic problems the United States faced during the recession.

A falling GDP indicates a weakening economy. A rising GDP indicates economic growth or the beginning of a recovery from recession. An unexpected spurt in GDP may indicate that the economy is overheating and inflation could result.

Gross Domestic Product		
(billions of dollars)		
Seasonally adjusted at annual rates		
Year	Quarter	GDP
2007	1	13,611.50
	2	13,997.20
	3	14,158.20
	4	14,291.30
2008	1	14,328.40
	2	14,471.80
	3	14,395.10
	4	14,081.70
2009	1	13,893.70
	2	13,854.10
	3	13,952.20
	4	14,133.60
2010	1	13,270.30
	2	14,413.50
	3	14,576.00
	4	14,735.90
2011	1	14,814.90
	2	15,003.60
	3	15,163.20
	4	15,321.00
2012	1	15,478.30
	2	15,606.10

United States Bureau of Labor Statistics

Figure 19-3 During the Great Recession, the US GDP dropped.

Consumer Price Index

The **consumer price index (CPI)** charts the ups and downs in the prices of consumer goods and services. It is a measure of the average change in prices over time for selected goods and services. It sometimes is called the *cost of living index.* The CPI measures annual price changes for a bundle of goods and services that average consumers purchase against the prices for the same goods and services in a base period of a previous year.

The CPI is used to measure cost of living changes and to adjust wages for workers who are covered by collective bargaining agreements. These agreements are contracts between employers and labor unions. A **labor union** is a group of workers who unite to negotiate with employers concerning issues, such as pay, health care, and working conditions. The CPI is also used to determine the cost of living increases applied to Social Security and pension benefits.

The CPI charts price changes by collecting data from over 50,000 households and 23,000 establishments in 87 areas across the country. The CPI does not include changes in real estate prices, income tax and other taxes, or Social Security taxes paid by individuals and businesses. These expenses represent substantial price increases for consumers.

Monetary Policy

Monetary policy is the actions the Federal Reserve Board takes to manage the supply of money and credit in the economy. The Federal Reserve Board, also called the Fed, is part of the **Federal Reserve System.** The Federal Reserve System is a system that regulates the nation's money supply and the banking system. Created by Congress in 1913, this system is comprised of the Board of Governors, 12 Federal Reserve Banks, and the Federal Open Market Committee. The Fed looks at economic indicators and an analysis of economic conditions to determine what actions to take. It uses the following three tools to manage the supply of money and credit: reserve requirements, the discount rate, and open market operations.

Reserve Requirements

The level of bank reserves mandated by the Fed is the cash reserves that banks and other financial institutions must set aside rather than lend to customers. It is expressed as a percent of their deposits. For example, suppose the reserve requirement is 10 percent. A bank that has $10 million in deposits from its customers can only lend $9 million. The other $1 million must stay on deposit. High reserve requirements reduce the amount of money available for lending. As a result, the supply of money and credit falls. Low reserve requirements have the opposite results.

Discount Rate

The **discount rate** is the interest rate Federal Reserve Banks charge commercial banks for credit when they borrow. This affects the rates that banks charge consumers and businesses. A high discount rate discourages bank borrowing and reduces lending activities. This lowers the amount of money in circulation. Low discount rates have the opposite effect. One of the first steps the Fed takes to address an economic slowdown is to lower the discount rate. This makes credit available at a lower cost and encourages businesses to expand and consumers to buy more goods and services. During the Great Recession of 2008, the Fed lowered the discount rate to less than one percent. In periods of inflation, the Fed is likely to increase the discount rate.

Open Market Operations

Open market operations refer to the Fed's buying or selling of treasury securities in the marketplace. Treasury securities are debt obligations of the US Department of the Treasury. They include treasury bonds, notes, and bills. When the Fed buys these securities, it increases the money supply and available credit. When the Fed sells government securities, the money supply shrinks because the dollars paid for these securities are no longer in circulation.

Easy versus Tight Money

When the Fed follows an easy monetary policy, money and credit are readily available. Interest rates are relatively low. Under these conditions, consumers and businesses tend to spend. They buy or build more homes when interest rates for home mortgages are lower. Companies borrow more money for expanding their businesses. Entrepreneurs borrow money to start new businesses. Farmers borrow to buy machinery and land to produce more crops. All these activities stimulate the economy and create jobs. However, if too much money is pumped into the economy through Federal Reserve policies, inflation may result.

In times of inflation, the Fed turns to tight monetary policy. It increases reserve requirements, raises the discount rate, and sells government securities. These actions reduce the money supply and discourage the use of credit. As economic activity slows, price increases tend to level off or fall.

It may sound simple for the Fed to speed up or slow down the economy, but maintaining a balance between supply and demand is no easy task. All the parts in the puzzle are constantly changing. When facing stagflation, the Fed's job becomes even more challenging. If it tightens the money supply, which is the sure cure for inflation, it risks further slowing the already depressed economy. In addition, it can take months for monetary policies to bring about

Government & Public Administration

Labor Economists
Labor economists study changes in the supply and demand for labor. They analyze reasons for unemployment, identify factors that influence the labor market, and collect data on wages. Labor economists usually work for the government. Visit the Bureau of Labor Statistics website (www.bls.gov) to learn more about the Labor Department's statistical data.

Go Green

If you use a lot of paper, look for environmentally friendly products. Paper manufacturers are always looking for new ways to produce paper products from renewable sources. Currently, some paper is made from by-products of sugar cane instead of wood. Sugar cane biodegrades faster than wood, is less expensive, and is cleaner to use in the production process. Many office supply companies now carry sugar cane paper with more new products to come.

the desired changes. Finding the right balance and the right timing is critical and complicated. Government policymakers must be extremely careful in wielding their power.

Sometimes the government enacts policies that make a bad situation worse. For example, during part of the 1930s, the government followed a tight monetary policy. Some economists say this policy may have led to a deepening of economic troubles that became the Great Depression. The Depression did not end until the government pumped millions of dollars into the economy through a vast jobs program. The entry of the United States into World War II boosted demand for military weapons, uniforms, machinery, and many other goods and services that created jobs and economic growth.

Overall, government fiscal and monetary policies are intended to moderate the ups and downs in the business cycle. The government's goal is to create longer periods of prosperity and full employment with less severe downturns and upswings in the economy. The government's attempts to control recession and inflation are outlined in Figure 19-4.

During the Great Recession beginning in 2007, the Fed took steps to stimulate the economy by increasing the money supply. It lowered interest rates and reserve requirements imposed on banks. In addition, the Fed bought financial assets from banks and other institutions. These Fed purchases increased the supply of money available for lending, spending, and investment. Many economists believe that the prompt action by the Fed early in the recession prevented a complete economic collapse. There is an

Fiscal and Monetary Policies			
Economic Conditions	**Likely Fiscal Policy**	**Likely Monetary Policy**	**Expected Results**
Inflation A period of rising prices	• Increase tax rates, leaving consumers and business less money to spend • Reduce government spending to cut the amount of cash flowing into the system	• Raise reserve requirements so less money and less credit are available • Increase the discount rate, making credit more expensive • Sell government securities, drawing money out of circulation	• Decreased credit availability • Less money in circulation • Decreased spending • Decreased demand • Decreased production • Slowing economy
Recession A period of economic slowdown and unemployment	• Lower taxes, giving consumers and businesses more money to spend • Increase government spending to pump more money into the economy	• Lower reserve requirements, permitting banks to lend more money • Lower the discount rate, making credit more affordable • Buy government securities, pumping money into the economy	• Increased availability of money and credit • Increased spending • Increased demand • Increased production • Business expansion and job creation

United States Bureau of Economic Analysis (Revised December 31, 2012)

Figure 19-4 The government uses fiscal and monetary policies to alter economic conditions.

ongoing debate on expansionary policies versus austerity measures in the face of recession and a record-breaking national debt. This is one of the most pressing economic problems facing the nation. The pros and cons will play out over time. To be informed, you will need to study both sides of the issue.

Fiscal Policy

Fiscal policy is the federal government's taxing and spending decisions. Government often uses fiscal policy to stimulate the economy in periods of recession and high unemployment. When government increases spending, it puts more money in circulation and stimulates greater economic activity, which creates more jobs. Fiscal policy can also slow economic activity in periods of inflation or rising prices. Tax increases take money out of the economy and tend to dampen an overheated economy. Congress controls taxing and spending decisions.

Taxing and Spending

As mentioned earlier, a recession is a period of slowing economic activity. Overall economic activity declines. To stimulate demand for goods and services during a recession, the government acts to increase the amount of money in circulation. With more money available, economic activity tends to expand. The government may increase spending to stimulate the economy. It may also lower taxes to leave more money for consumers and businesses to spend, which also increases demand. Ideally, economic and business activities expand to meet the increased demand.

Inflation occurs when demand is greater than supply. Increased demand drives up the prices of limited supplies. To combat inflation, the government may increase taxes and reduce its own spending. This takes money out of circulation, reduces demand, and slows economic activity. Such action should help control inflation and bring prices down.

Government taxing and spending decisions make a significant impact on the overall economy. These decisions determine the amount of taxes individuals and businesses will pay. The decisions also determine the services that the government will provide in return.

The circular flow diagram of the economy in Figure 19-5 is similar to one presented in the previous chapter. However, this diagram incorporates the government's role. The inner circles, in black, show how government participates in the flow of goods, services, and money. Producers and sellers provide goods and services to the government and receive payment in return. Consumers and workers provide labor and capital for the government and receive payment in return. The government provides services for which citizens and businesses pay taxes. A tax is a fee imposed by a government on income, products, or activities and paid by citizens and businesses.

Tax revenues pay for government operations. These operations include expenses connected with Congress, the court system, presidential offices, law enforcement, and a host of federal agencies and commissions. Taxes also pay for public goods and services that private citizens and businesses cannot or do not produce. At the federal level, these goods and services include national defense, social welfare programs, highways, transit systems, environmental protection, and certain areas of research and development.

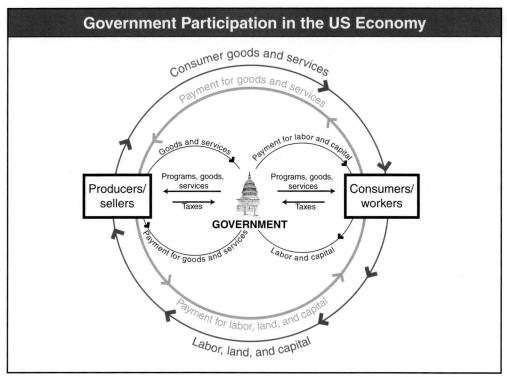

Goodheart-Willcox Publisher

Figure 19-5 A circular flow of goods, services, and money takes place within the economy. This chart shows how government participates.

At the local and state levels, tax revenues pay for government operations and for public goods and services closer to home. These goods and services include schools, libraries, hospitals, roads, airports, parks, and fire and police protection. Citizens and businesses "buy" these goods and services from government with tax dollars.

Government spending of tax revenues creates demand for goods and services. For example, the government pays for public schools with tax dollars. Private contractors build the schools with materials produced by private industries. This spending feeds money into the system, creates demand for goods and services, sparks business activity, and creates jobs.

During periods of inflation, government spending has a negative impact on the economy. It increases demand in the marketplace. When the combined demands of the government and consumers are greater than the economy's capacity to produce, prices go up. This is why reductions in government spending help fight inflation by reducing demand.

Redistribution of Income

When the government chooses to tax those who have more money to provide for those who have less, it redistributes income. One way to achieve this goal is through a *progressive tax.* With a progressive tax, those people with higher incomes pay a higher rate of tax than those people with lower incomes. The federal income tax system is progressive.

The government also redistributes income through transfer payments. Transfer payments include income and benefits that the government provides for individuals and households in the form of social programs. The three most familiar programs are Social Security, unemployment compensation, and Temporary Assistance to Needy Families (TANF). These program benefits are paid largely by taxing those who do not receive them.

A **subsidy** is a form of transfer payment that gives financial assistance to a business or entity, such as those in education, agriculture, the arts, or health care. It may come in the form of a direct payment, a tax benefit, or some other advantage. The government pays billions of dollars in subsidies each year.

The principal goal of subsidies is to benefit the public in some way. For example, government may subsidize small farmers so they can compete with corporate-owned farms. A subsidy paid to milk producers guarantees them a reasonable profit and ensures a supply of milk for consumers. Many farmers who grow subsidized crops, including corn, wheat, cotton, soybeans, and rice, also get money from the government. The flow of money in these cases is from taxpayers to those receiving the payments or benefits.

To date, the federal government supports over 2,000 programs involving some form of subsidy. The cost is in the billions. To learn more about the impact of subsidies on the federal budget and the overall economy, visit the Subsidy Scope website.

Deficit Spending and the National Debt

Often, the cost of government programs and services is greater than the tax revenues it collects. Just as consumers borrow or use credit to pay their bills, the government borrows money to cover its expenses. The money is raised by the sale of treasury and savings bonds to individuals, companies, and foreign countries.

Deficit spending is the amount the federal government spends each year beyond the amount it receives in revenues. When the government receives more than it spends, it is called a **surplus.**

Over the years, deficit spending and government borrowing have created a huge national debt. Each year's deficit increases this debt. The **national debt** is the total amount of money the government owes at a given time. Like consumers, the government must pay interest to borrow money.

The money paid in interest on the national debt leaves less to spend for health care, education, environmental protection, defense, and other needs. When government borrows excessively, there is less credit available for business expansion, home mortgages, and other business and consumer needs. Dollars spent by the government are dollars that are not available to the private sector where growth generally is created.

You and other taxpayers must pay for the debt. As government spending and debt increase, revenues and taxes must also increase. High levels of government spending and national debt threaten future economic growth and represent a huge burden on future generations.

This situation is another area of current debate related to the Great Recession. Some propose to slash government spending in the midst of the recession, which could dampen or reverse a fragile recovery. Others agree on the need to cut government spending, but they believe that the recovery should be on firm footing before huge reductions in government spending are made. Further debate surrounds the items to cut or eliminate in the federal budget. To be informed, you will need to study the pros and cons presented on both sides.

Government Regulations

Almost every phase of business and economic activity falls under some form of government regulation. For instance, the simple hamburger sold across the nation is subject to thousands of local, state, and federal regulations. Rules cover everything: fat content of the meat, ingredients in the ketchup, advertising slogans, hiring practices, wages, restaurant inspections, disposal of trash, and so on.

The earliest regulations were drafted mainly to promote fair competition and to ensure public well-being and safety. The regulations focused on preventing practices that interfered with fair competition. They were also aimed at protecting consumers from unfair and possibly harmful practices in the marketplace.

Fair Competition

Fair competition is one of the hallmarks of a market economy. It works best when there are many sellers offering similar products. Competition between producers results in more innovation, better products and services, and lower prices for consumers. **Perfect competition** is a condition in which no single seller can significantly influence the market price of a product or service. It exists as a goal but is never fully achieved.

A monopoly is the opposite of perfect competition. A **monopoly** is a situation in which there is a single seller or producer of a given product or service. Since it has no competition, a monopoly business can charge high prices, and it has little incentive to improve productivity or products and services.

Elected Representatives— State or Federal

Representatives are elected officials who serve as legislators at the state or federal level. They serve a leadership role in government by making decisions, analyzing government regulations and policies, and enacting new laws and regulations.

Blend Images/Shutterstock.com

When competition exists in the market, consumers have a wider selection of goods and services from which to choose.

The oligopoly is another threat to perfect competition. An **oligopoly** is a situation in which a few large companies dominate an industry. Oligopolies today include the automobile industry and the airline industry. Wireless providers are another example. AT&T, Verizon, T-mobile, Sprint, and Nextel control 89 percent of the market.

Laws known as antitrust laws were passed to promote competition and fair trade and to prevent trade restraints in the marketplace. The best-known antitrust laws are as follows.

- The *Sherman Antitrust Act of 1890* prohibits monopolies.
- The *Clayton Antitrust Act of 1914* prohibits price fixing and other unfair trade practices.
- The *Federal Trade Commission Act of 1914* created the Federal Trade Commission. This commission was given the power to investigate unfair or deceptive trade practices and to enforce compliance with lawful practices.

Although monopolies are illegal, exceptions have been made for some industries. For example, cable television companies were allowed to monopolize cable service in particular areas. It was impractical to have two or more companies rigging wires and cables throughout a community. In addition, when a drug company develops a new product, it becomes the sole provider of the drug for a period of time. During this period of no competition, the company earns high profits. In this way, it is reimbursed for the costly process of bringing a new drug to market.

Oligopoly is legal, but the companies in an oligopoly are not allowed to make secret agreements among themselves. **Collusion** is making a secret agreement among companies to shut out smaller competitors and to engage in price fixing. *Price fixing* occurs when two or more businesses in an industry agree to sell at a set price and eliminate price competition.

Public Well-Being and Safety

In 1906, Congress passed laws regulating the labeling of food and drugs. It also passed laws to ensure that meat was inspected before it could be sold. In 1913, the Federal Reserve System was established to oversee banking activities.

The Great Depression of the 1930s brought widespread unemployment and business failures. In response, Congress passed new laws that increased the government's power to intervene in the economy. New legislation provided for unemployment benefits, retirement income, and insured bank deposits. It also regulated the sale of securities and gave workers the right to form unions.

Since 1906, government involvement in the economy and public life has taken on a life of its own. Today, we have more than 100 federal regulatory departments. Each department includes many regulatory agencies within it. The same types of regulation exist in every state, county, and municipality. Almost every aspect of public life falls under some form of government regulation. Laws that ensure public well-being and safety cover a number of key areas, including:

- equal opportunity;
- fair labor practices;
- workplace safety;

- environmental protection;
- pure foods, drugs, and cosmetics;
- product safety;
- truth in advertising and labeling;
- truth in lending and saving; and
- homeland security.

Costs of Regulation

Government regulations have a major impact on the economy. For example, they cover every phase of the auto industry, from the manufacturer to your local service garage. The government regulates working conditions, employee benefits, car warranties, auto financing, servicing, registration and licensing, insurance, and advertising. Important and necessary as they are, federally mandated safety features, pollution controls, and fuel economy requirements add thousands of dollars to the price of a new car.

In the United States, federal laws are passed by Congress and signed into law by the president. Some regulations may be necessary to protect consumers and to ensure fair business practices. However, as the number of regulations and regulatory agencies increases, so do the costs to government, to businesses, and ultimately to consumers.

The scope of regulations and the paperwork they require increases the cost of complying with the laws enacted. Historically, government regulations were directed at a specific product or industry. Today, laws, such as the *Occupational Safety and Health Act (OSHA)*, the *Consumer Product Safety Act (CPSA)* and the *Environmental Protection Act (EPA)*, apply to almost every existing business and product. In addition, regulations require far more recordkeeping and paperwork than in the past.

It is costly for businesses to comply with government regulations. In 2010, small firms with 20 or fewer employees paid as much as $10,000 per employee each year to comply with federal regulations. For larger businesses with 500 or more employees, compliance costs were close to $8,000 per employee. These costs make it difficult for businesses to compete in world markets and increase the prices they must charge for their goods and services.

Government Agencies Serving Consumers

Government agencies assist consumers by establishing and enforcing laws and regulations at the local, state, and federal levels. They protect consumers from unsafe products and unethical business practices. These agencies represent consumer interests in many areas.

At the local and state levels, government agencies provide information, protection, and many other services. They regulate food standards and sanitation practices, credit and insurance transactions, and business and trade practices. They also govern the licensing and certification of groups, such as medical professionals, hospitals, nursing homes, funeral homes, lawyers, and others who serve the public.

Several key federal government agencies with a brief description of their primary functions are discussed in the following paragraph. All these agencies have websites that fully describe their functions and services.

The *Department of Agriculture (USDA)* provides various programs and services related to the food supply, natural resources, economics, and international trade. In the interests of consumers, the USDA researches the nutrient content of food and ways to improve the quality and safety of food, crops, and livestock. It also provides food assistance to needy consumers and nutrition education to the public.

The *Department of Energy (DOE)* works toward a reliable, affordable, and clean energy supply for the nation. To achieve that goal, current programs focus on energy, environmental, and nuclear challenges. DOE priorities include the development of alternative fuel sources and better fuel economy.

The *Department of Labor (DOL)* promotes the welfare of wage earners and retirees, improved working conditions, and better job opportunities. This department enforces labor laws that include minimum wage, child labor, anti-discrimination, maximum working hours, and safety and health regulations. It also administers the Bureau of Labor Statistics and the Occupational Safety and Health Administration.

Case Study

Government Regulations

Jake worked for many years in a bakery. Eventually, he opened his own business. He baked high-quality breads and rolls. The business was successful and demand soared.

Jake wants to enlarge his plant, buy improved equipment, and hire more help to increase production. However, the expansion will make his business subject to more government regulations, including:

- mandatory safety equipment and materials
- employee health and retirement benefits
- new content and nutritional labeling
- packaging specifications
- more inspections by the City Health Department
- additional and more detailed recordkeeping connected with these regulations

Jake will have to raise prices to cover the costs of the additional regulations. If the demand for bread falls, the cost of meeting the regulations may become too high. He might be forced to close his business. If Jake decides not to expand, the jobs he would have created and the increased productivity will not benefit the economy.

Case Review

1. Regulations ensure Jake uses wholesome ingredients and is fair and honest with employees and customers. How much and what type of regulation do you think is necessary to achieve these goals?

2. Some people argue for more regulations, stronger consumer protection, and broader government powers. What do you think? What evidence can you find to support or oppose this position?

3. Critics of government regulations claim the cost is too high. They argue money spent to comply with regulations reduces the amount available for capital improvements. The cost is ultimately passed on to consumers in the form of higher prices. What do you think? What evidence can you find to support or oppose your view?

The *Department of Health and Human Services (HHS)* serves the needs of citizens from birth to old age through a variety of programs and assistance. It administers financial aid programs, promotes public health, and works to control drug and alcohol abuse. HHS supervises and coordinates the work of many offices, including the Centers for Medicare and Medicaid

Careers in Finance

What Does an Economist Do?

Economists study, analyze, and interpret economic issues, including markets, jobs, taxes, interest rates, and government economic policies. Macroeconomists study the economy as a whole, while microeconomists study the economic decisions of individuals and businesses. **Economists** typically:

- collect data to predict market trends;
- advise legislators and businesses;
- recommend solutions to economic problems;
- compare current and historic economic conditions to make predictions;
- explain economic concepts and events in publications;
- research the impact of globalization on worldwide economic issues.

What Is It Like to Work as an Economist?

Approximately half of the nation's **economists** work for federal, state, or local governments. Others work for corporations or in research fields. Some **economists** teach at the college or graduate levels. Still others work as journalists or commentators, interpreting economic events for the public. An **economist** is likely to work regular hours in an office setting independently or as part of a team.

Economists typically work with statistics, charts, mathematical models, and surveys to collate and interpret economic data. They may be asked to make oral or written presentations of their findings and to attend economic conferences and meetings.

What Education and Skills Are Needed to Be an Economist?

- bachelor degree with coursework in economics, calculus, and statistics for entry-level jobs
- master degree or doctorate degree in economics
- experience in finance and other related fields
- analytical and critical thinking skills
- advanced computer and math skills
- active interest in economics and related fields

Services, the Office of Public Health and Science, the National Institutes of Health, the Centers for Disease Control and Prevention, and the Food and Drug Administration. The first priority of HHS is to protect the health of all Americans and to provide essential human services.

The *Food and Drug Administration (FDA)* protects the public against impure and unsafe foods, drugs, cosmetics, and other hazards. It operates national centers for drug evaluation and research, food safety and applied nutrition, and veterinary medicine. The FDA aims to promote public health and food and drug safety.

The *Social Security Administration (SSA)* promotes economic security by managing the federal government's retirement, survivors, and disability insurance, as well as the supplemental security income programs.

The *Department of Housing and Urban Development (HUD)* supervises programs related to housing needs, fair housing opportunities, and community development. It administers mortgage insurance to promote home ownership, rental assistance for low- and moderate-income families, housing safety standards, urban renewal programs, and federal real estate laws.

Checkpoint 19.2

1. What data on price changes is not included in the CPI?
2. How do reserve requirements affect the supply of money and credit?
3. What advantage does a monopoly have in the market?
4. What is the purpose of antitrust laws?
5. In general, how do government agencies assist consumers?

Build Your Vocabulary

As you progress through this course, develop a personal glossary of personal finance terms and add it to your portfolio. This will help you build your vocabulary and prepare you for a career. Write a definition for each of the following terms and add it to your personal finance glossary.

gross domestic product (GDP)

consumer price index (CPI)	deficit spending
labor union	surplus
monetary policy	national debt
Federal Reserve System	perfect competition
discount rate	monopoly
fiscal policy	oligopoly
tax	collusion
subsidy	

Chapter Summary

Section 19.1 Economics

- The US government provides the legal and institutional environment that permits and encourages economic activity. The government protects individual liberties and private property rights and enforces contractual agreements. It provides the political stability and the rule of law that are necessary for economic interaction.

- Economists use specific indicators to measure economic conditions and predict highs and lows. These indicators include gross domestic product (GDP), interest rates, business spending, unemployment figures, inflation, and consumer confidence.

Section 19.2 Economic Policies

- The gross domestic product (GDP) is a measure of the value of all goods and services produced by a nation during a specified period of time, usually one year. A falling GDP indicates a weakening economy, and a rising GDP indicates economic growth. The consumer price index (CPI) charts the ups and downs in the prices of consumer goods and services.

- The Federal Reserve Board looks at economic indicators and an analysis of economic conditions to determine what actions to take. It uses three tools to manage the supply of money and credit: reserve requirements, the discount rate, and open market operations.

- Monetary policy refers to actions the Federal Reserve Board takes to manage the supply of money and credit in the economy. The Fed sets reserve requirements, establishes a discount rate, and performs open market operations. These actions speed up and slow down the economy depending how they are carried out.

- Fiscal policy refers to the federal government's taxing and spending decisions. The government often uses fiscal policy to stimulate the economy in periods of recession and to slow economic activity in periods of inflation.

- Almost every phase of business and economic activity falls under some form of government regulation. Antitrust laws were passed to promote competition and fair trade and to prevent trade restraints in the marketplace. Government agencies assist consumers by establishing and enforcing laws and regulations at the local, state, and federal levels.

Check Your Personal Finance IQ

Now that you have finished the chapter, see what you learned about personal finance by taking the chapter posttest. If you do not have a smartphone, visit the G-W Learning companion website.

G-W Learning mobile site: www.m.g-wlearning.com

G-W Learning companion website: www.g-wlearning.com

Review Your Knowledge

1. What is government's fundamental role in a free market economy?
2. What signifies that a recession has begun?
3. How does inflation affect the nation's prosperity?
4. What causes stagflation?
5. Name and describe four types of unemployment.
6. What are some consequences of rising unemployment and underemployment for families?
7. What is monetary policy and how can it be used to stimulate or slow down the economy?
8. What is fiscal policy and how can it be used to stimulate or slow down the economy?
9. How can having a high national debt hurt the economy?
10. What are three government departments or agencies that serve and protect consumers? What is the focus of each one?

Apply Your Knowledge

11. How can too much government interference in the economy have a negative impact? What is too much? What is necessary?
12. In your state, what is the sales tax rate? How does the government use the money generated from sales tax?
13. How has your community chosen to use public funds or taxes to meet public needs and wants for services, such as education, police protection, street repairs, parks, and recreation?
14. Read a newspaper, magazine, or online article about unemployment. What kind of unemployment does the article describe: frictional, structural, cyclical, seasonal, or underemployment? What economic conditions have led to the unemployment?
15. How do laws that prohibit monopolies protect the consumer's right to choose?
16. What public goods or services do you and your family routinely use? How would life be different without them?
17. What are the costs of regulation for governments and for businesses? In what ways do consumers pay these costs?
18. What has been your experience with consumer protection agencies and laws?
19. Research one of the three antitrust laws mentioned in this chapter. What circumstances led to this law being created? Why is this law historically significant?
20. Conduct an Internet search for one of the government agencies listed in this chapter. Research how this agency is funded and how it uses its funding. Write a one-page report on your findings.

Teamwork

The Fed took action several times to stimulate the economy during the economic crisis that began in the winter of 2007. Describe what the Fed did and the pros and cons of its actions. Working with your team, research the press coverage of the crisis. Share your findings with your class.

G-W Learning Mobile Site

Visit the G-W Learning mobile site to complete the chapter pretest and posttest and to practice vocabulary using e-flash cards. If you do not have a smartphone, visit the G-W Learning companion website to access these features.

G-W Learning mobile site: www.m.g-wlearning.com

G-W Learning companion website: www.g-wlearning.com

Common Core

College and Career Readiness

CTE Career Ready Practices. To become career ready, it will be important to learn how to communicate clearly and effectively by using reason. Create an outline that includes information that workers need to know about unemployment in the workplace. Consider your audience as you prepare the information. Using the outline, make a presentation to your class.

Reading. Read a magazine, newspaper, or online article to find the current US unemployment rate, GDP, CPI, and Federal Reserve discount rates. Determine the central ideas and conclusions of the article. Provide a summary of the material that contains all the most important details.

Writing. Research current trends in the stock market in the United States and worldwide. How does stock market performance affect insurance company profits? Write a report that answers this question and describes the trends as well as the outlook for future stock market performance.

Web Connect

The CPI Inflation Calculator at the website of the US Department of Labor's Bureau of Labor Statistics calculates the cost of inflation. Visit the Bureau of Labor Statistics' website to find the CPI Inflation Calculator. Use the calculator to find out what one dollar is worth today compared to the year you were born.

College and Career Readiness

College and Career Readiness Portfolio

You have collected various items for your portfolio in earlier activities. Now you will organize the materials in your print portfolio. Your instructor may have examples of portfolios that you can review for ideas. You can also search the Internet for articles about how to organize a print portfolio. You should provide a table of contents for the items. This will allow the person reviewing the portfolio to find items easily. Keep separate the sections of the portfolio that are for your use only, such as your contacts database and sample interview answers. You should continue to add and remove documents as you complete assignments or gain new skills. Update the table of contents when you make changes to the portfolio.

1. Review the documents you have collected. Select the ones you want to include in your career portfolio. Make copies of certificates, diplomas, and other important documents. Keep the originals in a safe place.

2. Create the table of contents. You may also want to create a title page for each section.

3. Place the items in a binder, notebook, or other container.

Careers

Many competitive events for Career and Technical Student Organizations (CTSOs) competitions offer events that include various careers. This competitive event may include an objective test that covers multiple topics. Participants are usually allowed one hour to complete the event.

To prepare for the careers objective portion of an event, complete the following activities.

1. Read the careers features in each chapter of the text. As you read about each career, note an important fact or two that you would like to remember.

2. Do an Internet search for *careers*. Make notes on important facts about each.

Chapter 20
Consumers in the Economy

In a free market economy, consumer behavior influences and is influenced by economic conditions. On a personal level, economic choices are a determining factor in one's standard of living. Collective consumer behavior makes an impact on overall economic conditions and prosperity, or the lack of it. While a market economy offers economic freedom and many other advantages to consumers, it also presents problems and challenges. For example, the vast selection of goods and services available in the marketplace can make choosing difficult. In some cases, consumers create their own problems in the marketplace. When consumers fail to plan their spending or fail to seek necessary information on goods and services before buying, they can make costly mistakes. Impulse purchases can lead to overspending and other consequences. Be aware and alert to avoid common consumer mistakes and to get value for the money you spend.

Focus on Finance

Fear as an Economic Problem

Since it is often described with data and charts, the economic system appears to function according to logic, science, and cold, hard facts. However, human emotions play a huge role in the economy. The best example of this is the ups and downs of the stock market. It can be highly volatile, fluctuating with consumer confidence and anxiety. The feelings and behaviors of consumers can cause economic upturns and downturns. When consumers are optimistic about the economy, they spend more money, which boosts the economy. When they are feeling anxious or pessimistic, they curtail their spending, which depresses the economy.

The US economic system is built on faith and trust. For example, millions of people put their money into banks because they trust that it will be safe there. The banks make money by taking in deposits and lending to businesses and other consumers. If anything should happen to frighten large numbers of depositors, they can demand their money and a bank failure can result.

College and Career Readiness

Reading Prep. Skim the Review Your Knowledge questions at the end of the chapter first. Use them to help you focus on the most important concepts as you read the chapter.

Check Your Personal Finance IQ

Before you begin the chapter, see what you already know about personal finance by taking the chapter pretest. If you do not have a smartphone, visit the G-W Learning companion website.

G-W Learning mobile site: www.m.g-wlearning.com

G-W Learning companion website: www.g-wlearning.com

Sections

Section 20.1 Consumer Behaviors

Section 20.2 Economic Challenges

Section 20.1
Consumer Behaviors

Objectives

After studying this section, you will be able to:

- Identify how economic activities determine your financial well-being and the state of the overall economy.
- Discover which factors affect a nation's standard of living.

Terms

prosperity

investment

asset

standard of living

GDP per capita

labor productivity

Economic Activities of Consumers

You live in a market economy. Your economic activities, such as spending, saving, and voting, all make a difference. A market economy, with its freedom of choice, offers many advantages. However, living in a market economy also can present problems and challenges. Making wise choices and managing money carefully are important skills for consumers in the marketplace.

The collective economic activities of consumers play a vital role in a market economy. Consumers earn, spend, borrow, and save. They invest their dollars. They share financial risks through insurance. They pay taxes and vote for the candidates who support policies and programs that will affect the economy. The way consumers perform these activities determines how well they live and how well the economic system works.

Earning a Living

A market economy permits you to choose the work you wish to do. You can also decide on the level of education and training you want to attain. These choices largely determine your job opportunities and earning power.

The ability to find work depends on job skills, experience, and education. It also depends on your career choice and the demand for workers in your chosen field. Qualified people who want to work in high-demand fields are likely to find employment and earn a comfortable income.

Once hired, job performance helps determine how far and how fast a worker will advance. Hard work and the ability to work well with others are important qualities in almost every field. In today's fast-changing world, and particularly in response to the recent recession, it is especially important to continually update job-related skills.

Spending

A market economy permits you to make your own spending choices. The way you make these choices determines what your money will buy. Getting the most satisfaction for the dollars you spend requires careful choices in the marketplace.

Your spending decisions help create a demand for the goods and services you buy. You contribute to the profit and success of the businesses from which you buy. Your individual spending may not be major in creating a demand for specific products or in supporting one business over another. However, as a group, you and other consumers determine the success or failure of specific goods, services, and businesses.

Consumer confidence is a key factor in determining the state of the economy. It is an assessment of the optimism or pessimism of consumers regarding current economic conditions. When consumers believe the economy is strong or improving, they tend to be optimistic and to spend more. This creates a sense of prosperity. **Prosperity** is a time period of growth and financial well-being. These periods of prosperity are marked by high employment, job security, and overall stability.

When consumers are doubtful about the economic future, they spend and borrow less. This lowers the demand for goods and services. Business slows down because sales decline. Jobs are harder to find. Workers are laid off. These conditions can lead to a recession, or a period of economic slowdown. As discussed in Chapter 19, a recession is marked by rising unemployment, falling demand, slowed production, and declining economic activity.

Saving

People think of savings as money that is put aside for the future. However, anything that improves a person's financial position is considered savings. This includes the cash value of a life insurance policy, home improvements, and the purchase of durable goods. Goods that have lasting value, such as furniture, appliances, and cars, are called *durable goods*. Savings such as these increase your financial well-being as long as you do not spend beyond your ability to pay.

In a market economy, the money you and other consumers transfer to financial institutions is pumped back into the economic system, as shown in Figure 20-1. It is loaned to businesses and other consumers to pay for business growth, building construction, and home purchases. Savings used this way

Economics in Action

Consumer Confidence

Consumer confidence is a key indicator of the state of the economy. It is based on a survey that asks people in 5,000 US households how they view their financial well-being, spending power, job opportunities, and confidence in the future. Researchers at the nonprofit Conference Board process their answers and reduce them to a number.

The Consumer Confidence Index is a value between 0 and 100. By following the index from month to month, researchers gauge whether consumers are more or less optimistic. A high number indicates optimistic public opinion. To see the current Consumer Confidence Index values, check the Conference Board website.

Flow of Money

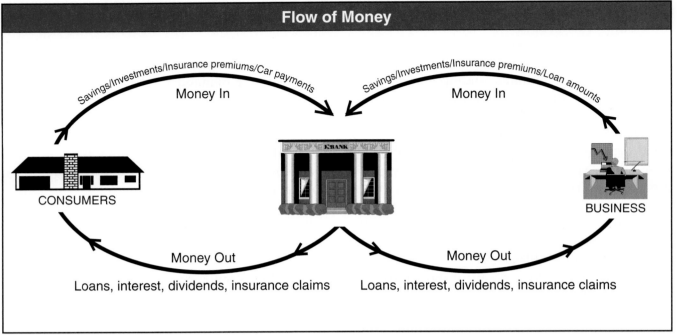

Goodheart-Willcox Publisher

Figure 20-1 This diagram shows the flow of money into and out of financial institutions—banks, credit unions, and insurance companies.

help generate more jobs, greater productivity, and a growing economy. Therefore, the health of the economy is closely related to the savings rate, or the amount of money people save.

Borrowing

Each time you use a credit card or charge account or take out a cash loan, you are borrowing. These are forms of *consumer credit*. Credit is a tool that lets you buy now and pay later. There are good reasons to borrow. Borrowing is sometimes the only way consumers can pay for major purchases, such as a house, car, or college education. Saving enough money to pay for these large expenditures all at once is difficult. Credit can also help you pay for unexpected expenses, such as a large medical bill.

In most cases, you pay a fee for using credit. Credit is costly in another way, too. When you use credit, you spend future income. This means part of your future earnings must be used to pay what you owe. The use of credit reduces future income. People who do not monitor and control their borrowing can get into serious financial trouble. Chapter 6 discusses both the sound and risky uses of credit.

Consumer borrowing has two important effects on the economy. It increases the amount of money in circulation, and it increases the current demand for consumer goods and services. For example, when you borrow, you have more money to spend. As you and other consumers use borrowed money, you increase consumer demand in the marketplace.

When the economy is in a recession, the use of credit to buy goods and services increases demand and stimulates productivity. This is why the Federal Reserve System may lower interest rates to encourage the use of credit during a recession. Lower interest rates help stimulate growth.

Consumer borrowing can have a negative impact on the economy during periods of inflation because it increases the current supply of money. When the supply of money grows faster than the supply of goods and services, it increases demand. This causes prices to rise, and inflation is the result.

Another reason for the cautious use of credit is its long-term effect. Unfortunately, the overuse of credit carries the seeds of an eventual economic downturn because the credit used today must be repaid with tomorrow's dollars. That means tomorrow's dollars will be paying today's debts rather than supporting future demand. Using credit increases immediate demand, but it decreases future demand. Excessive consumer debt threatens economic prosperity.

Buying Insurance

Insurance is a risk-management tool. It offers protection against certain financial losses. When you buy insurance, you and other buyers pay a fee called a premium to own an insurance policy. The policy outlines the specific terms, the risks covered, and the amounts the insurance company will pay for specific claims.

You can share financial risks related to life, health, and property. For example, suppose you and 5,000 others buy health insurance. If you must go to the hospital for an illness, the insurance premiums of those who do not need to be hospitalized will help pay your expenses. Insurance companies invest the premiums paid by policyholders. The premiums and the investment earnings are used to pay the claims of policyholders who suffer financial losses. The number of people who suffer losses at any given time is much smaller than the number of policyholders in the insurance pool.

Insurance strengthens the overall economic stability of the nation. It spreads financial risk and stabilizes income for citizens who face serious financial losses or loss of income. Social or government insurance programs include Social Security, Medicare, Medicaid, unemployment insurance, and workers' compensation. These programs provide income, health care, and other services to citizens who are retired, ill, disabled, or unemployed.

In addition, insurance companies invest billions of dollars of insurance premiums in business enterprises each year. This investment contributes significantly to the strength of the economy. Personal insurance needs are covered in detail in Chapter 8.

Go Green

As more transactions are handled with debit and credit cards, less cash is needed. This affects how much money is printed. The number of dollar bills rolling off the presses has been declining in recent years. Production of $5 bills has dropped to its lowest level in 30 years. No $10 bills were printed in 2011. With less paper currency printed, the US Treasury saves paper, ink, and energy. The trend toward more electronic transactions and less paper money can be good for both consumers and the environment.

Investing for the Future

When you have saved enough money to provide for emergencies and some goals, you will want to think about investing your money. An **investment** is an asset you buy that can increase your wealth over time, but it also carries the risk of loss. An **asset** is an item of value you own, such as cash, stocks, bonds, real estate, and personal possessions. Consumers invest money to improve their financial position and increase their future economic security. The purpose of investing is to make more money than you invest. Investments include financial instruments, such as stocks and bonds, business ownership, valuable items, and real estate.

Investments usually give consumers a greater return on their money than savings. However, the risk of loss is greater for investments than for savings accounts. The desire for profit motivates people to invest. Investors hope to sell their investments eventually at a higher price than they paid for them. However, there is the chance that they will lose part or all of their investment. That is why it is important to do careful research before you invest.

Consumer investments pay for a large share of business growth and activity. Businesses use the money consumers invest to purchase new plants and equipment. Investments also help pay for the research and development of new technology and the marketing of new products and services. Economic development and growth are directly related to the investments and savings of individuals as described in the following example.

If an airline company wants to expand its service, it can issue new stock for sale to the public. When investors buy the stock, the company gets the money it needs to buy new planes. Companies building the planes create jobs. Operating the planes creates more jobs, better service for consumers, and a profit for the airline.

If the company continues to make a good profit, the price of its stock usually rises. This encourages more investors to buy stock in the company with the hope of making a profit. Investors make money on the investment, and workers receive more job opportunities. The company makes money on the new planes, and consumers benefit from more flights and better service. Investment dollars start this type of chain reaction in businesses of all types, as shown in Figure 20-2. The benefits of investment ripple through the economy.

Paying Taxes

In the previous chapter, you learned that government provides many of the goods and services that citizens want and need. These goods and services include the military, the judicial system, schools, parks, government operations, and much more. Tax revenues pay for the many government departments and agencies and for the programs and the services they provide. Local, state, and federal governments provide a wide variety of services for citizens. The types of taxes governments levy to pay for their services and programs include the following.

- *Income tax.* Income tax is a tax individuals and corporations must pay on their earnings. The federal government, most states, and some city governments levy income tax.

- *Sales tax.* Consumers pay sales tax on the price of goods and services they buy.

Ethics

Consumers have a responsibility to use technology in an ethical manner. Using software downloaded from the Internet without a license is unethical and illegal. It is important to obtain licenses for any technology product that is used.

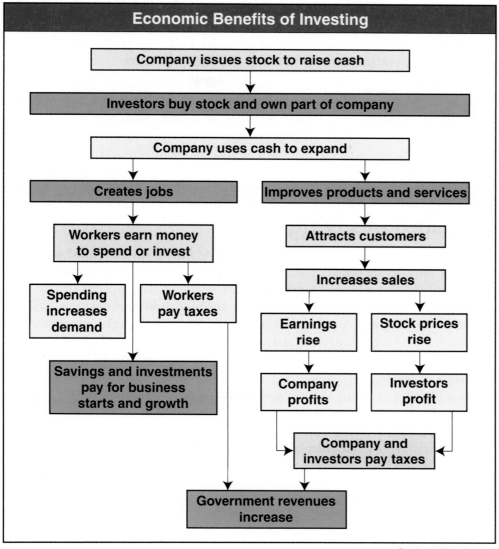

Economic Benefits of Investing

Company issues stock to raise cash

Investors buy stock and own part of company

Company uses cash to expand

Creates jobs → Improves products and services

Workers earn money to spend or invest → Attracts customers

Spending increases demand

Workers pay taxes

Increases sales

Earnings rise → Stock prices rise

Savings and investments pay for business starts and growth

Company profits → Investors profit

Company and investors pay taxes

Government revenues increase

Goodheart-Willcox Publisher

Figure 20-2 This diagram shows how consumers and business work together through consumer investments to keep the economy going.

Market Researchers
Market researchers help companies understand what types of products people want and at what price. They gather data on competing products, successful methods of marketing and distribution, and future sales potential. Their evaluations help companies decide whether to expand product lines or develop new ones.

- *Property tax*. Owners must pay property tax on the assessed value of their property.
- *Estate tax*. Estate tax is a tax heirs must pay on the value of an estate that is greater than the exemption the law allows.

In the United States, voters indirectly decide what they want to "buy" from government. They decide the level of taxes they will pay for their purchases. For example, citizens vote for more taxes every time they vote for a new school, more police protection, or a new highway. They vote for higher taxes every time they vote for a candidate who advocates new government programs without reductions in government spending.

As you learned in the last chapter, government economic policies play an important role in the overall economy. The government's spending of tax dollars stimulates the economy. It creates demands for goods and services that are usually met by private businesses. Excessive government spending can harm the economy. It can drive prices up and cause inflation. It also can contribute to the national debt.

When the government spends more than it receives in tax revenues, it must borrow money. This borrowing is called *deficit spending*. Year after year of deficit spending increases the national debt. US citizens ultimately pay for government spending and the national debt through taxes.

Government has the power to increase taxes in order to pay for its spending. When government increases taxes, it tends to depress the economy because it reduces the amount of money available for business activity. During a recession, the government may cut taxes to help stimulate the economy. Taxes and government spending are discussed in more detail in Chapter 19.

Standard of Living

As you advance on the job, your income and your personal standard of living should increase. **Standard of living** is the degree to which one has the ability to obtain the goods and services one needs and wants. If your income rises faster than prices, more goods and services will be available to you, and your standard of living will rise. For most people, that translates into a higher quality of life and overall level of well-being. Your earning power and job performance are directly related to your standard of living.

Besides determining your personal wealth, your earning activities contribute to the nation's wealth. The *national standard of living* is the level of prosperity in the country. It is measured by income levels and the ability of citizens to acquire necessary goods and services. These goods and services include housing, food, health care, education, transportation, and communications. As a nation, the United States has one of the highest standards of living in the world.

Customer Support Specialist

Customer support specialists are employed by companies to serve as a direct point of contact for customers. They interact with customers and are responsible for ensuring that customers receive appropriate, courteous service and help with questions and concerns.

GDP Per Capita

There are different ways to measure a nation's standard of living. Many economists use GDP per capita. As you will recall, *gross domestic product (GDP)* is a measure of the market value of all final goods and services created in an economy during a given time period. *Per capita* simply means per person. **GDP per capita** is the market value of final goods and services produced per person. It is the national GDP divided by the number of people in the country. GDP is usually adjusted for inflation and stated in dollars.

When GDP per capita is high or rising, incomes are rising and more goods and services are available to each citizen. This rising GDP per capita indicates that people are consuming more and their standard of living is rising. On the other hand, when GDP per capita is falling, it indicates falling incomes. Fewer goods and services are being produced. A lower GDP signals a lower standard of living.

There are some problems with using GDP per capita to measure standard of living. It assumes that everyone gets an equal share, although that is false in reality. Also, GDP as a measure of output does not account for unpaid work, such as housework, childcare, and volunteer work. However, despite these omissions, GDP per capita is the most common way to measure living standard.

Ant Clausen/Shutterstock.com

High labor productivity is one indicator of a strong economy.

Labor Productivity

Economists also use labor productivity as an indicator of a nation's economic health or prosperity. **Labor productivity** is the value of the goods and services a worker creates in a given time. High labor productivity indicates a healthy economy. To raise labor productivity, businesses and governments need to invest in productive resources, such as technology, infrastructure, factories, and the education and training of workers. Top-performing workers use efficient tools and technology to increase their own earnings. In turn, their high productivity also boosts the nation's wealth.

Your earning activities, plus those of all others in the job market, make a huge impact on the economy. At the same time, the state of the economy affects your earning potential. Economic conditions influence the number of jobs that are available, the type of work in demand, and salary levels. Demand in job markets is ever-changing.

Checkpoint 20.1

1. How does consumer spending affect the overall economy?
2. How does the use of consumer credit influence current consumer demand?
3. Why does overuse of credit eventually lead to an economic downturn?
4. What role do consumer investments play in the overall economy?
5. How does a person's income affect his or her personal standard of living?

Build Your Vocabulary

As you progress through this course, develop a personal glossary of personal finance terms and add it to your portfolio. This will help you build your vocabulary and prepare you for a career. Write a definition for each of the following terms and add it to your personal finance glossary.

prosperity   standard of living

investment   GDP per capita

asset   labor productivity

Objectives

After studying this section, you will be able to:

- Give examples of consumer economic challenges that can arise from free market characteristics.
- Outline consumer economic problems that result from consumer mistakes.

Terms

high-pressure selling

deceptive advertising

conflict of interest

impulse buying

overspending

Economic Challenges for Consumers in a Market Economy

A market economy offers you, the consumer, both the privilege and the challenge of making free economic choices. You are free to choose how to earn a living and what to do with your money. You can choose to pay cash or use credit. You can decide to spend or save. Free choice offers you the opportunity to decide for yourself how to get the most satisfaction from your money.

Free choice does not guarantee satisfaction. Certain characteristics of a market economy can complicate choices. Some of these characteristics are discussed in the following paragraphs.

Confusing Variety of Products

Businesses compete with one another in a market economy. As a result, the same or similar goods and services are sold by a wide variety of outlets. Choosing a reliable seller and finding the best product for the best price is a challenge. It is necessary to learn something about the sellers as well as the products and services you buy.

A market system also supports the development of countless new products and ideas. The system rewards producers who give consumers what they want. As a result, the variety of goods and services found in the marketplace is extensive. Consider all the fabrics, styles, and colors of clothing you can buy. Think about the many sizes, models, and features of cars. Count the specialties in medical care and the number of choices in home furnishings. Think of the many forms of consumer credit, types of insurance, and ways to save and invest money. Even the many flavors, types, and brands of ice cream can make choosing difficult.

You Do the Math

Place value is a basic element of a number system. A digit's position, or place, in a number determines the value of the digit. Each place represents ten times the place to its right. This is a *base ten system*. The number shown below is seven trillion, eight hundred sixty-three billion, one hundred fifty-nine million, two hundred thirty-seven thousand, five hundred eighty-four and one thousand eight hundred seventy-five ten thousandths.

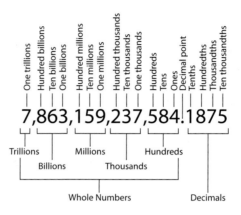

Complete the Following Problems

A country's standard of living, or level of prosperity, is measured by GDP per capita. Using the figures for GDP and population, calculate the GDP per capita for each of the following countries. Round to the nearest dollar.

1. India: GDP = $1.209 trillion; population = 1.17 billion
2. Guatemala: GDP = $67 billion; population = 14 million
3. France: GDP = $2.499 trillion; population = 64.3 million

The choices open to consumers make it possible to meet almost every need. However, these many options also make it a challenge to choose intelligently. Careful comparison shopping, particularly for costly purchases, is one way to reduce the confusion and make satisfying choices.

Questionable Selling Methods

In a system where the survival of a business depends largely on attracting consumer dollars, selling plays an important role. Businesses want to sell as much as possible at the highest price they can get. With this goal in mind, most companies advertise and market their goods and services aggressively.

While most businesses are honest and fair, some may use questionable selling methods to increase their sales and profits. Techniques such as less-than-truthful advertising, contests, and free offers are examples of high-pressure selling and can encourage you to buy for the wrong reasons. **High-pressure selling** is attempting to convince a buyer to make a quick decision. Too often, factual information is not part of a sales pitch. You need to focus on what is important to you before making purchases.

Keep in mind that deliberately misleading advertising and other dishonest business practices are illegal. **Deceptive advertising** is information that purposely misleads a consumer through dishonest claims. If you question the ethics of a store or selling method, contact the local Better Business Bureau, the chamber of commerce, or the nearest office of the Federal Trade Commission. Through these agencies, you can report practices that may be illegal or unethical.

Conflict of Interest

To a certain extent, buyers and sellers want different things, creating a conflict of interest. A **conflict of interest** is a situation in which a buyer and a seller have competing interests. Suppose you are in the business of selling cell phones. You want to sell as many phones at the highest price you can get. You want to be able to pay your business expenses and make a good profit.

When you are buying a cell phone, you want the phone that best fits your needs at the lowest possible price. You want to have money left over to spend on other items. In other words, sellers want the highest price possible, while consumers want the best quality at the lowest price.

The free-market system helps resolve the conflict of interest between sellers and buyers. Both profits earned by the seller and prices paid by the buyer are tied to the forces of supply and demand. Everyone depends on these forces to achieve the proper balance between profits and prices. The system strives to create a supply of goods and services to meet demand at prices that will keep the producer in business and the buyer able to buy.

Public Information Coordinators

Public information coordinators serve as advocates for businesses, associations, and other organizations. They build and maintain positive relationships with the public by working closely with print or broadcast media. They also handle other tasks, such as organizing special events and mediating conflicts.

Monkey Business Images/Shutterstock.com

Illegal business practices can be reported to the Better Business Bureau, chamber of commerce, or Federal Trade Commission

Careers in Law, Public Safety, Corrections, & Security

What Does a Customs Inspector Do?

A **customs inspector** enforces the laws governing imports and exports. **Customs inspectors** examine luggage, cargo, vehicles, and people entering and leaving the country. Customs inspection is a part of the Department of Homeland Security. **Customs inspectors** typically:

- check individuals and property crossing US borders;
- enforce trade regulations working with federal, state, and local law enforcement;
- identify illegal substances, potential threats, and individuals banned from entering the United States;
- interact with law enforcement agencies, such as the Drug Enforcement Administration and the FBI;
- communicate with freight, logistics, and transportation companies; and
- verify documentation of citizens, tourists, and shipments.

What Is It Like to Work as a Customs Inspector?

Most **customs inspectors** work in international ports where people and goods enter and leave the country. They work with K-9 units as well as other law enforcement personnel and agencies. **Customs inspectors** wear a uniform and often carry a firearm. Depending on their assignments, some inspectors may be trained dog handlers. Others may be proficient in a foreign language.

The work may be stressful because it can involve dealing with people who are intent on bringing dangerous or prohibited materials across the border. The job also involves the possibility of encountering and apprehending criminals.

What Education and Skills Are Needed to be a Customs Inspector?

- high school diploma, preferably with additional schooling
- US citizenship with proof of residency
- military or law enforcement experience
- security clearance
- foreign language proficiency a plus
- communication and computer skills

Consumer Mistakes Leading to Problems

For a variety of reasons, consumers sometimes make poor choices when presented with the many options offered by a market economy. These choices can lead to economic problems. Some common consumer mistakes are discussed in the following paragraphs.

Lack of Planning

Some of the worst consumer economic problems are caused by lack of planning. When consumers fail to plan ahead, they lack direction for their spending. They do not set goals for the use of income or build savings for future needs. Lack of planning also makes it difficult to control the use of credit.

Consumers who do not plan ahead often have trouble paying routine monthly bills. They may have difficulty buying groceries to make nutritious meals at reasonable prices. Finding clothes that fit into your wardrobe requires planning. Buying a car that meets your needs for transportation and fits into your budget requires planning. You also need to plan ahead to have money available for occasional expenses, such as birthday gifts, insurance payments, vacations, and taxes.

Poor planners often find it difficult to save enough for big expenses, such as a car, a home, an education, or retirement. They often make purchases that do not meet their needs and wants. Careful planning is the only way you can take charge of your financial well-being. It allows you to match the highs and lows of expenses with the highs and lows of income over a lifetime.

Case Study

Consumer Mistakes

Lamont has a pay-as-you-go cell phone. He figures the 1,000 minutes he purchased will last a month. However, he uses the minutes in three weeks and does not have the money to buy more.

Sarah's friends are taking a trip together during spring break. She intends to go, too, but spends her savings on a new jacket. Now she does not have enough money for the trip.

Ken gets a job and opens a savings account at a bank. He plans to deposit his paycheck, and eventually, he plans to buy a car with his savings. However, he cashes his paycheck instead. A few days after payday, he has no money left to deposit.

Case Review

1. How does poor planning affect each person in the case?
2. What would you have done differently in each situation?
3. What did Ken do right? How did his good intentions go wrong?

Failure to Use Information

The failure to investigate thoroughly and to ask questions concerning a future purchase can lead to disappointment and even big mistakes. For instance, Mariko signs up for an $800 online course in communications. She does not finish the course because the assignments take more time and hard work than she expected. It also is difficult to get help from the school because she gets a different instructor every time she has a question. She drops the course and loses her $800.

These types of situations are avoidable when consumers seek and use available information. Reliable facts can be found for almost every product and service you want to buy. When reliable information is not available for a given product or service, you would be wise to make another choice. Sources of information abound, and the Internet can be used to retrieve consumer information in seconds. Salespeople and other consumers who have used specific products and services can be helpful, too.

The fastest and easiest way to get information is to ask questions. Make it your rule to ask first and buy later. Getting the facts first is especially important where health, safety, or large amounts of money are involved. Making uninformed choices can be costly, disappointing, and even dangerous.

Impulse Buying and Overspending

Even informed consumers sometimes indulge in impulsive or thoughtless spending. Others habitually overspend, which can lead to debts that are difficult to repay.

If you are like most consumers, you sometimes buy things without thinking about your needs and goals or the consequences of spending. This is called **impulse buying**. When done regularly, this type of spending can consume a sizable amount of money. Thoughtful spending will leave more dollars for the needs and wants that are truly important to you.

Overspending is spending more money than you can afford to spend. Overspending happens most frequently using credit cards. When you use cash, you cannot spend more than you have with you. You think more carefully before making a purchase. A budget or spending plan can help you control spending and stay within your means.

Poor Communication

Most businesses want to know the likes, dislikes, wants, needs, and problems of their customers. Failure to speak up, ask questions, and complain when necessary can be costly. An open line of communication can lead to greater satisfaction with products, services, and sellers.

Consider this example. Charlene calls to request servicing for her furnace. She is told that a repairperson could come on Monday afternoon. Since Charlene works during the week, she takes Monday afternoon off to let the repairperson into her house. She is docked $80 from her paycheck. Later she learns that the repair could have been done on Saturday or in the evening. If Charlene had requested a different day or time, she would not have lost pay. Using better communication would have saved her money.

Checkpoint 20.2

1. How does a market economy lead to a variety of products and sellers?
2. What are two questionable selling methods?
3. Explain the conflict of interest between consumers and sellers in a market economy.
4. Name four common mistakes consumers make in a market economy.
5. What tools can help you control spending?

Build Your Vocabulary

As you progress through this course, develop a personal glossary of personal finance terms and add it to your portfolio. This will help you build your vocabulary and prepare you for a career. Write a definition for each of the following terms and add it to your personal finance glossary.

high-pressure selling   impulse buying

deceptive advertising   overspending

conflict of interest

Chapter Summary

Section 20.1 Consumer Behaviors

- Consumers earn, spend, save, invest, pay taxes, and vote for the candidates who support policies and programs that will affect the economy. The way consumers perform these activities determines how well they live and how well the economic system works.

- GDP per capita and labor productivity are two indicators of a nation's standard of living. A rising GDP per capita indicates that people are consuming more and their standard of living is rising. High labor productivity indicates a healthy economy.

Section 20.2 Economic Challenges

- Certain characteristics of a market economy can complicate choices consumers are free to make. Consumers must choose from a confusing selection of goods and services. They must also deal with questionable selling methods and conflicts of interest with sellers.

- Consumers sometimes make poor choices when presented with the many options offered by a market economy. Consumers can create problems for themselves by failing to plan their spending, failing to use available information, and engaging in impulse buying and overspending.

Check Your Personal Finance IQ

Now that you have finished the chapter, see what you learned about personal finance by taking the chapter posttest.
If you do not have a smartphone, visit the G-W Learning companion website.

G-W Learning mobile site: www.m.g-wlearning.com

G-W Learning companion website: www.g-wlearning.com

Review Your Knowledge

1. How do consumer attitudes about the economy affect spending?
2. What can be considered savings?
3. How does the use of credit affect immediate consumer demand?
4. Explain how investments stimulate the economy.
5. What type of tax is paid on real estate owned by individuals and corporations?
6. What does the GDP per capita indicate about a country's standard of living?
7. How can consumers complain about questionable selling methods?
8. Explain the consequences of consumers failing to plan ahead.

9. When reliable information on a product or service is unavailable, what should a consumer do?

10. What is the difference between impulse buying and overspending?

Apply Your Knowledge

11. Explain how savings, investments, and insurance premiums serve as the source of credit for consumers and businesses. Illustrate your explanation with a chart or drawing showing the flow of money.

12. What industries suffer most when consumer spending is down? For example, what happens to the housing and construction industry? What related industries are likely to suffer? What industries seem to suffer the least during a recession?

13. Look in your local newspaper for an article about taxes. What services does your community "buy" from the local government with tax money?

14. What choices or goals can you make now that will improve your standard of living later in life?

15. Conduct an Internet search for *GDP per capita by country.* How does the United States rank in comparison to other countries? Did you expect the United States to rank higher or lower? What conclusions can you draw from this research?

16. What consumer problems do you consider most serious? What do you think can be done about them? What consumer problems have you experienced? How might you have avoided them?

17. Find an advertisement in a newspaper or magazine for a product that you or your family uses. Does the product work in the way that it is advertised, or is the advertising misleading? Explain how your experience with the product compares or contrasts with the advertising claims.

18. Have you or someone you know experienced the consequences of impulse buying or overspending? What problems arose? How could they have been avoided?

19. Pretend that you are making a large purchase, such as buying a car or a television. Use the Internet to locate reliable sources of consumer information that relates to your purchase. Create a short presentation that summarizes your research and how it affected your purchasing decisions. Share your findings with the class.

20. Describe a time when you experienced the consequences of poor communication as a consumer. How could the experience have been improved with better communication?

Teamwork

Working with your team, research a period of economic prosperity in the United States. What events led to this period? What events caused an eventual downturn? Report your findings to the class.

G-W Learning Mobile Site

Visit the G-W Learning mobile site to complete the chapter pretest and posttest and to practice vocabulary using e-flash cards. If you do not have a smartphone, visit the G-W Learning companion website to access these features.

G-W Learning mobile site: www.m.g-wlearning.com

G-W Learning companion website: www.g-wlearning.com

Common Core

College and Career Readiness

CTE Career Ready Practices. Contributing citizens pay their fair share of taxes to support the government. Select two tax laws that generate funds for government services. Describe how the revenue generated from these taxes help contribute to the betterment of the community.

Speaking. Create a presentation about current trends in the stock market using your choice of digital media. Include information that describes these trends as well as the outlook for future stock market performance. Use examples that will enhance understanding and to add interest to your presentation. Present your findings to the class.

Listening. As your classmates make their presentations on the current trends in the stock market, evaluate each presenter. Review the presenter's point of view and use of digital media. Was the presentation effective?

Web Connect

Use the Internet to find the most current GDP and total population for each of the following countries:

- Ethiopia
- China
- United States

College and Career Readiness

College and Career Readiness Portfolio

You created items for your e-portfolio in earlier activities. Now you will decide how to present your e-portfolio. The items should already be organized in folders. Review the files you have collected. Select the ones you want to include and remove others. Keep separate the files with information for your use only, such as answers to interview questions. Decide how you want to present the materials. For example, you can create an electronic presentation with slides for each section. The slides could have links to documents, videos, graphics, or sound files. Websites are another option for presenting the information. You might have a main page with links to various sections. Each section's page can have links to documents, videos, graphics, or sound files. The method you choose should allow the viewer to navigate and find items easily. The files can be placed on a CD or a website.

1. Create the slide show, website, or other vehicle for presenting your e-portfolio.

2. View the completed e-portfolio to check the appearance.

Preparing for the Event

Regardless of the competitive events in which you choose to participate for a Career and Technical Student Organization (CTSO), you will need to be well organized and prepared. Of course, you will have studied the content exhaustively before the event. However, you also have to prepare by making sure you have the tools you need for the event and travel arrangements are made. Buttoning down all the details well in advance of an event will decrease stress and leave you free to concentrate on the event itself.

To prepare for a competition, complete the following activities.

1. Pack appropriate clothing, which includes shoes and proper undergarments.

2. Prepare all technological resources that you might need to take to the competition. Double-check to make sure that any presentation material that is saved electronically is done so on media that is compatible with the machines that will be available to you at the event.

3. If the event calls for visuals, make sure you have them prepared in advance, packed, and ready to take with you.

4. Bring registration materials, including a valid form of identification.

5. Bring study materials, including the flash cards and other materials you have used to study for the event. If note cards are acceptable when making a presentation, make sure your notes are complete and easy to read. Have a back-up set in case of an emergency.

6. At least two weeks before you go to the competition, create a checklist of what you need for the event. Include every detail down to a pencil or pen. Then use this checklist before you go into the presentation so that you do not forget anything.

Chapter 21
Global Economy

Economic globalization is the increasing economic connections among governments, businesses, and citizens of the world. Goods and services, money, labor, technology, and ideas all move rapidly across national borders. International trade plays an essential role in every nation's economic system. It influences supply and demand, prices, competition, consumer choice, and government policies. It affects job opportunities and living standards.

In recent decades, globalization has intensified. You will need to keep up with this new global environment. Understanding it will help you to hold your own in the job market and in the marketplace.

Focus on Finance

Antiglobalization Movement

Some people and groups do not view international trade agreements or groups positively. The label *antiglobalization* describes individuals and groups who oppose globalization. These groups include labor, environmental, and human rights groups all over the world.

Many of these groups say they are not against globalization. Rather, they object to a type of globalization driven by the needs of wealthy countries and multinational corporations. They charge that trade agreements and global economic institutions put profits above the well-being and livelihood of people. For example, NAFTA critics say that it hurts small farmers, especially in Mexico. Lowered trade barriers opened the Mexican market to US agribusiness. Unable to compete with cheap imports, many Mexican farmers lost their livelihoods and became migrant workers.

The basic goal of many groups in the antiglobalization movement is to promote social justice and human rights. They especially work for the elimination of inequities between the poor and the rich around the world.

College and Career Readiness

Reading Prep. Read the chapter title and write a paragraph describing what you know about the topic. After reading the chapter, summarize what you have learned.

Check Your Personal Finance IQ

Before you begin the chapter, see what you already know about personal finance by taking the chapter pretest. If you do not have a smartphone, visit the G-W Learning companion website.

G-W Learning mobile site: www.m.g-wlearning.com

G-W Learning companion website: www.g-wlearning.com

Sections

Section 21.1 Economic Globalization

Section 21.2 International Monetary System

Section 21.1
Economic Globalization

Objectives

After studying this chapter, you will be able to:

- Describe the flow of goods and services in the global economic system.
- Explain the flow of labor among countries.
- Analyze the effect of multinational corporations on the global economy.

Terms

economic globalization

international trade

imports

exports

specialization

comparative advantage

economies of scale

migrants

multinational corporation

outsourcing

offshore outsourcing

insourcing

cartel

Flow of Goods and Services

After silencing an alarm clock manufactured in China, an American consumer gets dressed in jeans produced in Thailand and a T-shirt made at a factory in Israel. Breakfast is cereal sprinkled with California raisins made from grapes picked by migrant farm workers. Before leaving, the consumer brushes his teeth with toothpaste made in a Nigerian factory by employees of an American corporation. Once outside, he gets into a vehicle made in the United States by a Japanese automaker. He drives to work at a multinational corporation with offices in 30 countries.

Like this fictitious consumer, you live in a world that is becoming increasingly globalized. *Globalization* refers to the process of becoming worldwide in scope. **Economic globalization** is the flow of goods, services, labor, money, innovative ideas, and technology across borders. It is changing the way people communicate, shop, and conduct business.

International trade is one of the major forces behind globalization. **International trade** is the buying and selling of goods and services across national borders and among the people of different nations. It has been going on for thousands of years. Many of the earliest travelers were traders looking for natural resources, new products, and new markets for their goods. They created trade routes that crisscrossed continents and oceans.

Most trade today occurs between individuals and businesses in different nations. The government in each nation regulates and sets the parameters for international trade.

International trade is discussed in terms of imports and exports. **Imports** are the goods and services that come into a country from other countries. The *importer* is the business or consumer who buys goods and services that come from other nations. **Exports** are the goods and services grown or made in a particular country and then sold in world markets. The *exporter* is the party who sells goods or services in foreign countries.

What Is Traded

For many people, the subject of trade conjures images of giant containers being loaded and unloaded from ships at US ports. This is the trade in products or goods. As you will recall from Chapter 18, goods are physical items, such as food, furniture, toys, computers, car parts, and all other items on store shelves. World imports and exports also include intermediate goods, such as lumber and oil, that are used to produce other goods.

Trade in services accounts for a sizeable piece of imports and exports. These services are provided by businesses, including banking, transportation, insurance, law, telecommunications, and entertainment companies. This sector is rapidly increasing as the world seeks more professional services in research, consulting, and information processing.

Finally, money flows between nations. International capital flows refer to the purchase or sale of financial or real assets across national borders. Money flows into a country when foreigners invest in its assets. Money flows out of a country when its citizens, businesses, or governments invest in foreign assets. You will read more about this later in the chapter.

Why Trades Occur

Two parties trade with each other because each expects to benefit from the transaction. One party receives a product or service and the other receives a payment. You probably make dozens of trades a day. For example, you might go to a bakery, give the clerk some money, and receive a blueberry muffin in return.

Steve Rosset/Shutterstock.com

Imports are goods and services that come into a country from other countries.

Buying what you need is easier and more efficient than trying to make all the items yourself. The same is true for countries. No country can produce all the goods and services that its people and businesses want. However, it can provide a range of products and services. Then it can trade these for whatever it cannot produce. This is called specialization. **Specialization** is a method of production in which a particular range of products and services is produced. A country can then trade for whatever it cannot produce. The types of goods and services that countries specialize in depend on the factors discussed in the following paragraphs.

Climate, Geography, and Natural Resources

Climate, geography, and access to natural resources vary from one country to another. In part, these factors determine what a particular country can and cannot produce.

For example, the tropical climate of Costa Rica makes it an ideal place to grow bananas. Thailand, China, and Indonesia produce most of the world's rubber. Bolivia has the largest stores of lithium that is used in batteries. The vast natural gas fields of Russia supply that country with more natural gas than it needs. Likewise, Saudi Arabia has vast reserves of oil. The climate and geography in parts of the United States make it well suited to grow much of the world's corn, wheat, and soybean crops. Each country exports what it produces in excess of its needs.

Climate, geography, and natural resources also can limit what a country is able to produce. A tropical climate or a desert cannot produce the variety of foods that its people require. Even the United States, a country with varied climate and geography, cannot grow enough coffee and cocoa to meet consumer demand. Nations tend to import those goods and services they cannot produce in sufficient quantities to meet demand.

Available Human Resources

The quality of the labor force in a particular country determines what it can and cannot produce. For example, what is the literacy rate? Does a large share of the population have computer skills? How many colleges, universities, and specialized training programs are available?

Industries that require a highly skilled workforce would not take root in a country where most workers are uneducated and unskilled. In these

Ethics

Unethical individuals might set up a website, accept electronic payments, and then disappear without shipping products to the buyer. Before purchasing anything online, consumers should verify the seller. The Better Business Bureau evaluates sellers and informs consumers about sellers' trustworthiness.

Go Green

As a consumer, it will be necessary to find phone numbers and other contact information for business and personal use. Instead of using a print directory, consider using an online resource. Notify the company that sends print directories that the business no longer needs a print copy. However, if a print directory is needed, recycle it when the new copy is available. By recycling these directories, thousands of tons of paper each year and space in the landfills can be saved.

countries, most jobs would be low paying, such as those in the garment-making industry and in factories that require low-skilled workers.

Other labor force factors include pay scales and cost of living. Shoes and clothing are examples of labor-intensive products that often are made in countries where labor is plentiful and pay scales are relatively low. The workers generally earn less than US workers who do the same jobs. For example, a worker in a third-world factory may make only $5 a day for a 14-hour workday.

Some companies move their manufacturing operations overseas to take advantage of lower labor costs along with more favorable tax laws and regulations. Their products are then imported into the United States for sale.

Consumer Preferences

Some products are imported because they are specialties of particular countries or regions. These products can be made just as efficiently in the importing country. However, the foreign-made products offer style and performance qualities that consumers prefer. This has been the case in high-fashion clothing from European designers, high-performance automobiles from Japan and Germany, and a variety of electronic products, primarily from Asia.

Comparative Advantage

If a nation could produce all the goods and services its citizens and businesses need, there are still advantages to trade with other nations. An economic concept called comparative advantage explains why. **Comparative advantage** is the benefit to the party that has the lower opportunity cost in pursuing a given course of action. The opportunity cost of a specific choice is the value of the alternative choices not made.

Consular Officers
Consular officers receive and review applications for nonimmigrant visas. They also provide a range of services to American citizens overseas.

The following example explains how this works. Suppose a doctor and a nurse staff a small medical office. The doctor sees 20 patients a day. Each appointment is billed at $100. The nurse is paid $250 per day to run the office.

The doctor is more efficient than the nurse at both treating patients and running the office. Can the doctor save money by firing the nurse and doing both jobs? Looking at opportunity costs provides an answer. Without a nurse, the doctor has less time to see patients. He would have to cut his patient load by five patients per day. The doctor's fees, which total $2,000 at 20 patients, would be reduced by $500 if he sees only 15 patients. For the doctor, the opportunity cost of managing the office is $500. However, the nurse is paid half that amount. It makes financial sense for the doctor to treat more patients and hire a nurse to manage the office.

When individuals, businesses, or nations specialize in the activities for which their opportunity costs are lowest, everyone benefits. Countries tend to export what they produce most efficiently. They import the goods and services produced more efficiently in other countries. When nations trade with each other, consumers gain more choices and lower prices.

One of the reasons for comparative advantage is an economic concept called economies of scale. **Economies of scale** is the concept that the cost of producing one unit of something declines as the number of units produced rises. The costs of production are spread over more units. If a business can sell more of a product by expanding into overseas markets, it can take advantage of economies of scale.

US Trade

The United States is a dominant power in global economic markets. It is the world's largest importer and a major market for more than 60 countries. Millions of people across the globe depend on the United States for their livelihoods. When the US economy falters and consumers decrease spending, workers at home and around the world lose their jobs.

The United States is the world's third largest exporter of manufactured goods. China is one of our major trading partners. According to the US Census Bureau, the United States imported about $399 billion worth of goods from China in 2011 while exporting $104 billion. This has created a $295 billion trade imbalance with China. You will read more about that in the following pages.

The United States imports more products than it exports, as shown in Figure 21-1. However, it exports more services than it imports, as shown in Figure 21-2. The United States has a trade surplus in services and a trade deficit in goods. Top US trading partners for both imports and exports are listed in Figure 21-3.

US Commerce		
Category	**Imports**	**Exports**
Industrial Supplies	Crude oil	Organic chemicals
Consumer Goods	Automobiles, clothing, medicines, furniture, and toys	Automobiles and medicines
Capital Goods	Computers, telecommunications equipment, motor vehicle parts, office machines, and electric power machinery	Transistors, aircraft, motor vehicle parts, computers, and telecommunications equipment
Agricultural Products	Cocoa, coffee, and rubber	Soybeans, fruit, and corn

Goodheart-Willcox Publisher

Figure 21-1 The United States has a trade deficit for goods, meaning it imports more than it exports.

US Service Exports
Financial services—investing services, insurance services
Information services—computer consulting, data processing
Other services—architectural design, construction, engineering, legal services, advertising, marketing, accounting, management, technical training, travel, tourism, entertainment, transportation services

Goodheart-Willcox Publisher

Figure 21-2 These are just a few examples of US service exports.

Top US Trade Partners	
Exports	**Imports**
Canada	Canada
Mexico	China
China	Mexico
Japan	Japan
Germany	Germany
United Kingdom	United Kingdom
Netherlands	Saudi Arabia
Korea	Venezuela
Brazil	Korea
Belgium	France

Source: Foreign Trade Division, United States Census Bureau
Goodheart-Willcox Publisher

Figure 21-3 These are the top nations the United States trades with in the world market.

A high percentage of what is consumed in the United States is produced in the United States. However, products and services that cannot be provided in sufficient quantity or quality at the desired price are imported. Imports represent dollars flowing out of the country.

Flow of Labor

In addition to increasing the movement of goods and services between countries, globalization increases the flow of labor. People who move from one place or country to another are **migrants.** Today, almost three in every 100 people in the world are migrants. Some are refugees or asylum-seekers that flee their birth country because of persecution. Many are members of a minority ethnic or religious group who are denied basic rights by their government. Millions of others cross borders to escape war, economic crisis, and natural disasters. Some leave to escape rampant crime and corruption.

However, many people are economic migrants seeking better opportunities to work and earn a living wage. The gap between wealth and poverty in countries is a major cause of migration, both legal and illegal. For example, a person can earn on average nine times more working in the United States than working in Mexico.

History of Finance

The Silk Road

One of the most famous trade routes was called the Silk Road, created around 100 BC. It was a network of roads that connected Europe, North Africa, and Asia. Caravans of traders exchanged gold, glass, perfumes, and other Western goods for the East's silk, ceramics, spices, and iron. People, plants, animals, ideas, knowledge, and culture also flowed back and forth.

The developed countries, such as the United States, are beacons for people seeking economic opportunities. More than 40 million people, or 13 percent of the US population, were born in another country. Most recent migrants came from Latin America, Asia, and the Caribbean.

As US businesses open offices and factories in foreign countries, a growing number of Americans are becoming economic migrants. However, their numbers are much smaller than the number of migrants coming into the United States.

Impact of Multinational Corporations

Multinational corporations are also referred to as *multinationals*.

Much of globalization is driven by the growth of multinational corporations. A **multinational corporation** is a business that operates in more than one country. Some multinational corporations are so large that their assets are greater than the GDPs of entire countries. These large companies have greatly increased the amount of global trade.

Multinational corporations often are created when several companies in different countries are combined. An example of a multinational corporation is Johnson & Johnson, which was incorporated in 1886. With corporate headquarters in New Jersey, it is comprised of 250 subsidiary companies in 57 countries. A *subsidiary* is a business that is controlled by another business. Johnson & Johnson employs more than 117,000 people.

US multinationals employ millions of people in their subsidiaries across the globe. Also, millions of Americans work for US-based subsidiaries of multinational corporations headquartered elsewhere. For example, Japanese automaker Toyota employs thousands of American workers. Multinationals have altered world trade in important ways that are discussed in the following sections.

One Product, Many Origins

A product label that reads "Made in the USA" or "Made in China" only tells part of the story. Many of the world's largest companies operate across the borders of several countries. Today, the parts and labor that go into the production of almost any product come from many different countries. The idea of country of origin for manufactured goods has lost its meaning in a globalized world.

Electronic products, for example, require components from suppliers all over the world. US companies buy these components chiefly from India, Philippines, Russia, China, Canada, Taiwan, and Ireland. An estimated 90 percent of iPhone parts are made in other countries. The phones are assembled largely in China. Even so, Apple is credited with creating well over 300,000 jobs in the United States while outsourcing thousands of jobs to other countries as well.

Outsourcing is moving sections of a business to other companies or to subsidiaries in other locations in the United States. **Offshore outsourcing** is moving sections of a business to another country. Today, labor is cheaper in many other nations, and foreign manufacturers often offer the flexibility and industrial skills companies seek. Workers put in long hours with few benefits to meet production deadlines.

Case Study: The World Economy

Profit Squeeze

Walter owns a small business in Illinois. In recent years the cost of running his business has increased across the board. The cost of doing business threatens to reduce profits to the point that it is not worth Walter's time, effort, and investment to keep his business going.

Walter has two options. He can either increase his prices, or he can decrease his production costs. Nothing about Walter's business requires him to be located in Illinois. Cost savings is the chief advantage of moving all or part of a business to a country with low-cost labor and a favorable tax structure. In addition, there would be far less government interference and oversight.

Unfortunately, if Walter decides to do this, his 70 employees will be left jobless. Relocating them would not be practical.

Case Review

1. Do you think Walter is justified in moving his business to another country? What other alternatives might he have?

2. If Walter decides to move the business, what do you think he should do about the employees he must let go? Does he have a responsibility to them?

3. What do you think could be done in the United States to encourage businesses to stay in the country? How does the economy suffer when businesses leave?

When a US company moves a piece of its operations to another country, it creates jobs in that country. Often those jobs offer workers in the host country better opportunities than were previously available.

While outsourcing offers companies substantial cost savings and greater productivity, it also results in job losses for workers at home. These displaced workers must upgrade their skills and seek retraining to find new jobs. This is one painful reality of globalization.

Insourcing is a process in which foreign companies open subsidiaries in the United States and create jobs here. Some American companies also are insourcing when they return operations from other countries to the United States. Today, US subsidiaries of foreign companies account for over five million jobs in America. Foreign-owned companies insource millions of good paying jobs each year. For example, BMW recently completed a billion dollar expansion in North Carolina, and Toyota is building new plants in Mississippi and Texas. These companies provide good, high paying jobs to American workers. Nestle USA, T-Mobile USA, Sony Corporation of America, and Volvo Group North America are among the companies that insource jobs to the United States.

Flow of Capital Investment

The growth in multinational corporations has increased the flows of capital and investments around the world. *Capital* is money used to generate income or to invest in a business or asset. Many economists believe that this flow, rather than the flow of goods and services, is the most powerful force driving globalization today.

Money flows from one country to another when a parent company builds a factory overseas or lends money to a foreign subsidiary for expansion. A large share of global trade today is the movement of raw materials, goods, services, and product parts from one subsidiary of a multinational to another.

Another type of international investment occurs when investors buy or sell the stocks and bonds of foreign companies. Investors include individuals, businesses, and groups of people who pool their money in pension and mutual funds. These funds are then used for international investments.

Cartels

A **cartel** is a group of countries or firms that controls the production and pricing of a product or service. It has the same economic effect as a monopoly. An example of a cartel is the Organization of Petroleum Exporting Countries, or OPEC. OPEC nations collude to set prices for oil by controlling the supply. Their decisions largely determine market prices and, ultimately, the amount you pay for fuel to run your car and heat your home.

Chapter 19 covered several forms of market control. Monopoly occurs when one firm controls the entire market for a particular product or service. An oligopoly exists when only a few large companies control an industry and set prices. However, companies making agreements among themselves to engage in price fixing is illegal.

Many multinational corporations have achieved worldwide dominance in their industries. For example, some large agribusiness companies control the world market for seeds and other agricultural products. The enormous wealth and power of some corporations can give them significant influence over governments and global trade policies.

Checkpoint 21.1

1. What is the difference between economic globalization and international trade?
2. Why do people trade?
3. Does the United States have a trade surplus in goods or services? Does it have a trade deficit?
4. Explain the influence of capital in globalization.
5. Does a cartel function more like a monopoly or oligopoly?

Build Your Vocabulary

As you progress through this course, develop a personal glossary of personal finance terms and add it to your portfolio. This will help you build your vocabulary and prepare you for a career. Write a definition for each of the following terms and add it to your personal finance glossary.

economic globalization

international trade

imports

exports

specialization

comparative advantage

economies of scale

migrants

multinational corporation

outsourcing

offshore outsourcing

insourcing

cartel

Objectives

After studying this chapter, you will be able to:

- Describe the relationship between currency strength and the balance of trade.
- Explain the government's role in global trade.
- List several trade organizations and their purposes.
- Describe what you can do to develop the skills needed to succeed in a global economy.

Terms

exchange rate

balance of payments

trade deficit

trade surplus

free trade

trade barrier

European Union (EU)

North American Free Trade
   Agreement (NAFTA)

General Agreement on Tariffs and
   Trade (GATT)

World Trade Organization (WTO)

International Monetary Fund (IMF)

Foreign Exchange Market

When people in the same country buy and sell goods to one another, they use the same currency. In the United States, that currency is the dollar. However, when buyers and sellers are in countries that use different currencies, they must first figure the value of one currency in relation to the other. This involves the *foreign exchange market,* or *foreign currency market.*

The currencies of different countries are bought and sold on the foreign currency exchange market. A currency, like a product, has a price. The **exchange rate** is the value of one currency compared to another. The exchange rate tells you how much you must pay in US dollars to buy a unit of foreign currency.

Exchange rates are constantly changing. Buyers and sellers in the foreign exchange market generally set currency values. The currencies of countries that are politically and economically stable are more desirable to investors. The more desirable a currency is, the greater the demand for it.

The value of a nation's currency also can be affected by changes in its interest rates. The higher an interest rate, the greater is the return on an investment. Higher interest rates draw foreign investors, and this increases the demand for a currency.

The foreign exchange market affects your life every day. It determines how much you pay for the goods and services you rely on. However, most people only learn of the foreign exchange market when they travel to another country.

For example, if you go to Canada, you may need to exchange American dollars for Canadian dollars. The exchange rate is the rate at which one currency can be converted to another. For example, if the exchange rate is $1.10 Canadian for each US dollar, a traveler should get $110 Canadian for each $100 USD, minus fees. Figure 21-4 shows international currencies.

You can exchange money at banks, airports, and currency exchanges. Airports usually charge the highest fees. A number of online currency conversion calculators are available.

Businesses must also use the foreign exchange market when conducting business in other countries. For example, suppose a business located in China wants to buy road-building equipment from a US company in Peoria, Illinois. The equipment costs $500,000. To make the purchase, the Chinese firm needs to convert its currency, the Yuan Renminbi (CNY), into US dollars (USD). How much Chinese currency do they need to convert?

Suppose that the foreign exchange rate on the day of purchase is:

1 USD (US dollar) = 6.21 CNY (Chinese Yuan Renminbi)

500,000 USD = 3,105,000 CNY (They may need a little extra to cover fees.)

When US businesses buy Chinese products, they may be able to trade in dollars rather than converting to the Yuan Renminbi. This is because many countries, including China, accept the USD because of its stability relative to other currencies. The USD is the *international reserve currency.* However, converting to Chinese currency may be less costly.

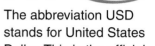

The abbreviation USD stands for United States Dollar. This is the official currency code for US money and is most often used in international business.

International Currencies	
Country	**Currency**
United States	Dollar
European Union	Euro
United Kingdom	Pound
Australia	Australian dollar
Canada	Canadian dollar
Mexico	Peso
Japan	Yen
South Korea	Won
China	Renminbi
Brazil	Real
Saudi Arabia	Saudi riyal
Venezuela	Bolivar fuerte
India	Rupee
South Africa	Rand

Goodheart-Willcox Publisher

Figure 21-4 International Currencies

Foreign currency can be exchanged for US dollars at banks, airports, and currency exchanges.

Trade and Exchange Rates

The value of a nation's currency, including the US dollar, goes up and down with the demand for it in other countries or in world markets. At times, the value of US dollars is high, or strong; at other times it is weaker.

When the dollar is strong, goods and services imported into the United States cost less. This raises demand for imports. When the value of the dollar is high compared with the currency you are buying, you get more for your money. Your dollars go further when you travel in that country. Foreign buyers must pay more for exports from the United States when the dollar is strong, so they buy less. When the dollar is strong, foreign investors must pay more for US companies, real estate, and stock; so they tend to invest less.

When the dollar is weak, goods and services imported into the United States cost more. This reduces demand for imports. Traveling in other countries costs more because dollars buy less. Foreign buyers pay less for exports from the United States when the dollar is weak, so they buy more of our exports. Foreign citizens, businesses, and governments get more for their money when they invest in the United States. They tend to invest more. A weak dollar also attracts more tourists to the United States.

Exchange rates change daily. They are published regularly and can be found in travel sections as well as the financial pages of most major newspapers and online.

US Trade Deficit

To understand international trade, you need to know the meaning of balance of trade. This is the difference between total imports and total exports of goods and services. These numbers are recorded in the **balance of payments.** This is an account of the total flow of goods, services, and money coming into and going out of the country. When a country buys, or imports, more products than it sells, a **trade deficit** develops. The country has an *unfavorable balance of trade.* If it sells, or exports, more than it buys, the country has a **trade surplus.** The country then has a *favorable balance of trade.*

The United States has run a substantial trade deficit since 1976. It imports more goods and services than it exports, as shown in Figure 21-5. Currently, the United States runs the largest deficit among worldwide trading nations, and China runs the largest surplus.

The deficit makes it possible for China and other nations to accumulate more US dollars. With accumulated dollars, these nations can buy more US goods, services, and assets, such as real estate, securities, and businesses.

The United States actually needs more foreign investors to buy treasury bills, corporate securities, and real estate to help pay off the growing national debt. Most economists think that, in the long run, this is not a healthy situation. They think that trade deficits and budget deficits coupled with the growing national debt weaken the US economy and its leadership position in the world.

Government's Role in Global Trade

Governments regulate trade. Government trade policies are often described as free trade or *protectionism.* **Free trade** is a policy of limited government trade restrictions. Individuals and businesses are relatively

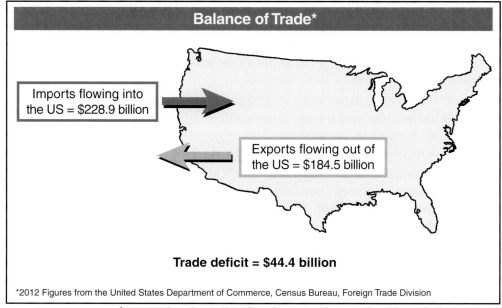

Balance of Trade*

Imports flowing into the US = $228.9 billion

Exports flowing out of the US = $184.5 billion

Trade deficit = $44.4 billion

*2012 Figures from the United States Department of Commerce, Census Bureau, Foreign Trade Division

Source: 2012 figures from the United States Department of Commerce, Census Bureau, Foreign Trade Division

Goodheart-Willcox Publisher

Figure 21-5 The United States has run a substantial trade deficit since 1976. Each year its imports are greater than its exports.

free to buy and sell goods and services from people and businesses in other countries. Governments generally favor free trade that opens markets for the goods and services they export. Imports may be restricted. Trade restrictions are often called protectionism. They are designed to protect businesses at home from foreign competition.

Why Nations Favor Free Trade

Theoretically, trade among nations benefits all the trading nations. Therefore, everyone benefits when tariffs and other impediments to trade are kept to a minimum. Some of the arguments for free trade have been discussed earlier in this chapter. In summary, free trade is beneficial for the following reasons.

- Free trade stimulates growth and raises productivity and living standards in the countries that open their economies to world markets.
- Free trade allows countries to specialize in those goods and services they produce most efficiently and trade for those that they produce less efficiently. This is the comparative advantage argument.
- Free trade produces a greater variety of goods and services at lower prices as a result of worldwide competition and innovation. Consumers enjoy a greater selection of goods and services at lower prices.
- Free trade generates more innovation and product improvements as a result of competition and the international exchange of ideas and technologies.
- Free trade creates new investment opportunities stemming from capital flows across international borders.
- Free trade promotes cooperation and peaceful relations among nations who become trading partners. When a country needs and wants goods and services produced in other nations, there is a strong incentive to maintain working relationships.

Customs Inspectors

Customs inspectors enforce laws governing imports and exports. They inspect cargo, baggage, and articles worn or carried by people, vessels, vehicles, trains, and aircraft entering or leaving the United States.

Why Nations Favor Restricted Trade

Nations, including the United States, restrict trade for various reasons, including the following.

- *To protect domestic industries.* Governments often seek to protect home-based industries from foreign competition.
- *To protect the jobs of workers.* Labor, capital, and materials often cost less in other countries when compared with the United States. This means foreign companies can offer their goods at lower prices. If these goods are allowed into the US marketplace, US companies making similar goods could not compete. This could drive them out of business and lead to job losses.
- *To reduce dependence.* Countries may want to avoid dependence on single sources of necessary items. For example, the United States depends on OPEC sources of oil. These oil-producing countries can cut the supply of oil or raise prices, causing serious economic problems in the United States.
- *To control distribution.* Countries may want to control the distribution of products or technologies that threaten national security. For example,

You Do the Math

It may be necessary to convert currency when doing business with another country. To determine the exchange, you can use one of the many currency converters found on the Internet.

Complete the Following Problems

You want to buy two books published only in the U.K. The cost of the books is £17.98. The current exchange rate is $1.00 = £0.60797.

1. What is the cost of the books in US dollars? (Round up to the nearest cent.)
2. Shipping from the U.K. is £9.97. What is the total cost of your purchase including shipping in US dollars?
3. What is the current exchange rate for the pound? How much will this book cost in US dollars using the current exchange rate?

---

the United States restricts the export of technological know-how and materials that could be used to build weapons that might be used against the country.

- *To address unfair trade practices.* For example, importers may engage in dumping. This refers to the sale of imported products at lower prices than those charged in the domestic market for similar products. Once the imported products dominate the market and drive the domestic producers out of business, the importer raises the price. To combat dumping, governments may tax these imports to raise their prices so domestic companies can compete.

Critics of free trade have other arguments. In the United States, they claim that free trade increases the US trade deficit in world markets as the United States continues to import more than it exports. Others say free trade benefits larger companies and developed nations at the expense of smaller businesses and emerging nations. Many people think that free trade also threatens cultural identity and individuality as large multinational corporations replace small local businesses. They seem to create a "worldwide sameness" as they become a dominant presence around the globe. In many countries, there is a fear that imports bring foreign values and cultural identities with them at the expense of local traditions, values, and culture.

How Governments Restrict Trade

Governments can limit opportunities for foreign companies to sell their products or services on an equal footing with domestic companies. This is called *protectionism,* and it refers to government policies that restrict trade. Protectionist policies can backfire as other countries retaliate by imposing their own trade barriers.

Trade Barriers

Government policies can discourage imports through trade barriers. A **trade barrier** is any action taken to control or limit imports. There are several types of trade barriers.

- A *tariff* is a tax on imports that makes them more expensive to consumers. It is intended to make domestic products more cost competitive with imports.

- An *import quota* is a limitation on the number or quantity of imports allowed into the country.

- A *nontariff barrier* is a type of regulation, such as environmental quality regulations or safety requirements.

- An *embargo* is a law used by a government to prohibit trade with a particular country for political reasons.

Subsidies

Subsidies, which were discussed in Chapter 19, are another form of protectionism. A subsidy is a payment, tax break, or other incentive paid by a government to a local business or industry. Subsidies allow businesses to offer their goods for sale at lower prices. This lower price enables the goods to compete successfully with foreign products. Subsidies are often attacked for creating an unfair advantage for the business receiving the incentive.

For example, suppose an electronics company in another country receives subsidies from its government. The company ships its products to the United States. Since the company receives subsidies, it can charge less for its products than a US company making similar products. The US company cannot afford to meet the low selling price. Eventually, the majority of customers buy the cheaper import, and the US company goes out of business.

Currency Manipulation

Currency manipulation refers to action taken, usually by a government or central bank, to increase or decrease the value of currency. The forces of supply and demand in the currency exchange markets determine the value of the US dollar. This is true of most other currencies as well. When a nation sets the value of its currency without regard for the market, it is said to be manipulating its currency.

If a nation artificially lowers the value of its currency, it can gain competitive trade advantages. The International Monetary Fund (IMF) prohibits currency manipulation for the purpose of gaining unfair trade advantages.

When a nation's currency is weak, its exports become cheaper in world markets. Its imports, however, become more expensive. As a result, the country tends to increase its exports and decrease its imports. This creates a trade surplus. A weak currency also invites more foreign investment into the country. This often translates into new factories, new jobs, and more products for export.

For trading partners, the consequences include trade deficits and unfair competition in domestic markets. For example, in recent years China has kept its currency artificially low. This allowed China to sell its products in the United States at lower prices than similar products manufactured in this country. In some industries, this unfair advantage could drive firms out of business. American workers could lose their jobs. In addition, the United States' trade deficit with China continues to grow, and China's trade surplus with the United States increases. Low-priced imports from China are a short-term advantage for US consumers; however, these low-priced imports may create an unhealthy long-term situation for the US economy.

Trade Organizations and Agreements

The United States has existing trade agreements and partnerships with a number of other individual nations and regions of the world. These agreements are called free trade agreements (FTA). The goal of these agreements is to create economic benefits and opportunities for all participating nations as a result of free trade and investment across their borders. Figure 21-6 lists some of the many trade organizations in the world today.

The **European Union (EU)** is the largest trade sector in the world, surpassing any individual country. As of 2012, the EU had the largest GDP and it was the largest importer and exporter of goods and services. Twenty-seven nations belong to the EU. Seventeen of these countries share a common currency called the euro. The main trading partners of the EU include the United States, China, Switzerland, and Russia.

Trade Organizations		
Abbreviation	**Organization**	**Country Members**
ASEAN	Association of South East Asian Nations	Brunei Darussalam, Burma (Myanmar), Cambodia, Indonesia, Laos, Malaysia, Philippines, Singapore, Thailand, and Vietnam
CAFTA-DR	Central America-Dominican Republic	Costa Rica, Dominican Republic, El Salvador, Guatemala, Honduras, and Nicaragua
EU-27	European Union-27	Austria, Belgium, Bulgaria, Cyprus, Czech Republic, Denmark, Estonia, Finland, France, Germany, Greece, Hungary, Ireland, Italy, Latvia, Lithuania, Luxembourg, Malta, Netherlands, Poland, Portugal, Romania, Slovakia, Slovenia, Spain, Sweden, and United Kingdom
NAFTA	North American Free Trade Agreement	United States, Canada, and Mexico
OPEC	Organization of the Petroleum Exporting Countries	Algeria, Angola, Ecuador, Indonesia, Iran, Iraq, Kuwait, Libya, Nigeria, Qatar, Saudi Arabia, United Arab Emirates, and Venezuela
SADC	South African Development Community	Angola, Botswana, Democratic Republic of Congo, Lesotho, Malawi, Mauritius, Mozambique, Namibia, Seychelles, South Africa, Swaziland, Tanzania, Zambia, and Zimbabwe

Goodheart-Willcox Publisher

Figure 21-6 These are some of the many trade organizations around the world.

North American Free Trade Agreement (NAFTA) is an agreement between the United States, Canada, and Mexico that lowered trade barriers and opened markets among the three countries. Canada and Mexico are top trading partners of the United States, and trade has increased dramatically among the three nations.

World Trade Organization (WTO)

Interpreters
Interpreters translate or interpret written or oral communication into another language. They need to be sensitive to the cultures associated with the languages they translate.

Most governments believe that fair and open trade among nations benefits all. Governments, even friendly allies, constantly negotiate trade terms with one another. Disputes often involve access to markets. Trade disputes arise over certain policies and practices that create unfair competition, in the view of at least one country.

Issues of protectionism and unfair trade are controversial and complicated. They often involve more than economic considerations. Trade restrictions, or trade sanctions, are political weapons that can be used against the economies and governments of other countries.

The **General Agreement on Tariffs and Trade (GATT)** was formed after World War II by the Allied nations to aid post-war recovery. This agreement is a set of international agreements that promote free and fair trade among nations. GATT agreements attempted to reduce the use of tariffs, quotas, and other trade restrictions.

In 1995, the **World Trade Organization (WTO)** was created to expand the work of the GATT. The WTO is an international organization that mediates trade disputes among 155 member nations and establishes trade practices that are acceptable and fair to all nations. WTO agreements are signed by practically every trading nation in the world. Besides trade in goods, the WTO is also involved in the regulation of trade in services, inventions, and intellectual property.

Other Important Global Organizations

Many of the world's nations have come together in other organizations and forums to achieve mutual goals. These goals include the establishment of world peace; elimination of hunger, poverty, and disease; and sustainable growth and development. Many of the groups, which often work together, directly or indirectly influence trade and global economics.

World Bank

The World Bank has a membership of 187 countries. Its primary mission is to fund specific projects that promote economic development, reduce poverty, and raise living standards. To this end, the World Bank provides financial and technical assistance to developing countries. Financial assistance consists of grants and low- or no-interest loans. For more information, check out its website at www.wto.org.

International Monetary Fund (IMF)

The **International Monetary Fund (IMF)** is an organization with the mission to oversee the international monetary system. It works to stabilize exchange rates and eliminate trade barriers. Its 188 member countries are advised on how to better manage their economies. The IMF also helps member nations head off and resolve economic crises.

Like the World Bank, the IMF provides loans and technical assistance to countries. However, unlike the World Bank, these monies are not intended to fund specific projects. They are meant to help stabilize the overall economy of the country and promote growth. The IMF Center is located in Washington D.C.

G20

The Group of Twenty Finance Ministers and Central Bank Governors (G20) is a forum for 19 countries plus the European Union. Besides the United States, the G20 countries are Great Britain, Japan, Italy, France, Russia, Canada, Germany, Australia, Argentina, Brazil, China, India, Indonesia, Mexico, Saudi Arabia, South Africa, South Korea, and Turkey. The heads of state of G20 countries meet annually to discuss issues ranging from health and the environment to trade and terrorism. The leadership role rotates among the member countries.

United Nations (UN)

The United Nations (UN), headquartered in New York City, is an international organization of 193 member countries. When it was created after World War II, its primary purpose was to maintain peace and security in the world. The UN is known as the entity that provides humanitarian assistance in areas ravaged by war and natural disasters. It is a forum where member countries can condemn political aggression and human rights violations. Its programs promote better living standards for people around the world. For more information about the UN, go to www.un.org.

Organization for Economic Co-operation and Development (OECD)

The Organization for Economic Co-operation and Development (OCED) was established in 1961 to promote policies that improve the economic and social well-being of people around the world. It addresses critical global issues and helps governments deal with the economic, social, and governance concerns of globalized economies. It has 34 member nations.

Globalization and You

Globalization presents advantages and disadvantages, hopes and fears, pros and cons. It dramatically affects economic conditions and trade in every nation. Both consumers and producers operate in world markets. This is why it is important to understand the role of globalization in your economic life.

You are already buying goods and services from other countries. As a worker, the goods or service your company produces will likely be sold in other countries. You may work for a multinational corporation at some point in your life. Your managers and coworkers may be born in other countries. You will be competing for jobs with workers around the world.

You can prepare for a global market by continuing your education, learning a foreign language, and following current world events.

As a Worker

Globalization affects you as a worker because it influences demand for both goods and services. This, in turn, influences job creation and opportunities. Increased exports mean growth, and growth means jobs.

When a US company gains access to foreign markets and competes successfully in the sale of its products and services, the company will grow and expand. It will need more workers. There will be more jobs. This also is true when foreign companies open plants or offices in the United States. This creates new jobs in the United States.

As a worker, you may be unfavorably affected if you work in areas that are subject to foreign competition. Foreign competition may also lead to a loss of jobs for US workers in certain sectors. When US companies must compete with popular imports, as happened with the auto market in recent years, US workers may lose their jobs. In some industries, there may also be layoffs and shifts in employment as a result of offshore outsourcing.

Jobs commonly outsourced are those in the manufacturing industries. However, service and professional jobs, especially those in information technology, are also being outsourced. For example, when you call a computer company's service department, the person who answers is often a half a world away. Accountants living in another country may prepare your tax returns. X-rays and other test results can be read and interpreted by medical professionals in distant locations.

What You Can Do

You need to prepare for employment in a global market and for the changing cultural and political landscape that lies ahead of you. Some suggestions are listed below.

- *Continue your education.* Completing high school and getting postsecondary education and training are more important than ever. With offshore outsourcing and the Internet, competition for jobs is global. Jobs for the uneducated and unskilled are moving to places where workers are paid a small percentage of a US worker's salary. The more education and professional and technical skills you have, the more opportunities and job security you will gain.

- *Consider science- and math-related occupations.* The United States currently imports workers to fill many jobs that require science and math backgrounds. There is a great need for workers who have solid foundations in these subject areas.

- *Improve your skills and knowledge.* After you enter the work world, keep the door to education open. Stay informed about trends in your field. Take advantage of retraining and educational opportunities on and off the job. Go back to school to learn new skills.

- *Learn a foreign language.* Fluency in almost any foreign language is a key asset in the work world. Becoming proficient in Chinese (Mandarin) and other Asian languages, Russian, or Arabic will open doors to job opportunities around the world.

- *Learn about world affairs.* Regularly read newspapers, magazines, and websites that report extensively on international affairs and foreign policy issues. Seek out books about areas of the world that interest you. Tune in to radio and television programs broadcast from other countries. Find out about international organizations and their function in the world economy.

- *Travel or live abroad.* Enroll in a student exchange program. Spend a summer working, studying, or doing volunteer work abroad. Visit relatives and friends who live in other countries. Learn about other cultures while having the adventure of your life. As the world grows more interconnected, global issues will become more important to everyone.

In the future, the citizens of every nation will become, in a sense, citizens of the world. Common interests will include policies governing the use and sharing of resources, environmental concerns, and controlling terrorism. Other issues include broad access to necessary medicines and health care services, alleviating poverty, and educating citizens for life in a global society.

As the world grows smaller, the United States will have to decide whether it will become more involved with other nations in a variety of areas. Nations will need to cooperate with one another in addressing issues such as the environment, poverty, terrorism, AIDS, and disaster recovery. Peacekeeping in areas of conflict will continue to call for international cooperation.

The future is likely to hold both more cooperation and more competition in global markets. There will need to be international agreements on the use of world resources. You will also likely see a continued increase in the exchange of ideas and developments in the fields of science and technology.

Careers in Government and Public Administration

What Does the President of the United States do?

The **US president** is the highest position in the US government. The position is given to the winner of a national presidential election, held every four years. The **US president** typically:

- is the head of state and the head of government;
- serves as commander-in-chief to the US armed forces;
- leads the executive branch of the US government;
- influences Congress when laws are being made; and
- inspires Americans as a role model and leader.

What Is It Like to Work as the President of the United States?

The **US president** often works in an office environment, but travels around the globe to meet with other world leaders. The job of **US president** comes with much responsibility and many challenges. **US presidents** also have a high level of notoriety and respect.

US presidents earn relatively low pay, when compared to chief executive officers at many private companies. **US presidents** have extremely long workdays in a very stressful work environment.

What Education and Skills Are Needed to Be a President of the United States?

- strong background in politics or law, but a degree is not required
- experience working in government at the local, state, or national level
- comfortable with public speaking
- must be a natural-born citizen of the United States
- must be a permanent resident of the United States for 14 years
- must be 35 years of age or older

Checkpoint 21.2

1. How does a strong US dollar affect US exports?
2. What are some reasons nations restrict trade?
3. Explain the purpose of a tariff.
4. What is currency manipulation?
5. What is the World Bank's mission, and how is it achieved?

Build Your Vocabulary

As you progress through this course, develop a personal glossary of personal finance terms and add it to your portfolio. This will help you build your vocabulary and prepare you for a career. Write a definition for each of the following terms and add it to your personal finance glossary.

exchange rate

balance of payments

trade deficit

trade surplus

free trade

trade barrier

European Union (EU)

North American Free Trade Agreement (NAFTA)

General Agreement on Tariffs and Trade (GATT)

World Trade Organization (WTO)

International Monetary Fund (IMF)

Chapter Summary

Section 21.1 Economic Globalization

- Economic globalization is the flow of goods, services, labor, money, innovative ideas, and technology across borders. International trade is one of the major forces behind globalization. World imports and exports include both goods and services.

- Globalization increases the flow of labor among countries. Many people are economic migrants seeking better opportunities to work and earn a living. The developed countries, such as the United States, are beacons for people seeking economic opportunities.

- Multinational corporations have greatly increased the amount of global trade. Multinationals employ millions of people. They greatly affect the origins of parts and labor for products, the flow of capital around the world, and the pricing and availability of products.

Section 21.2 International Monetary System

- A nation's currency strength can affect its balance of trade. Foreign buyers must pay more for exports from a country when its currency is strong, so they buy less. Foreign buyers pay less for exports when the currency is weak, so they buy more exports.

- Governments regulate trade. Government trade policies are often described as free trade or protectionism. Theoretically, trade among nations benefits all the trading nations. However, some nations restrict trade for various reasons.

- The United States has existing trade agreements and partnerships with a number of individual nations and regions of the world. The goal of these agreements is to create economic benefits and opportunities for all participating nations as a result of free trade and investment across their borders.

- You need to prepare for employment in a global market and for changes in the cultural and political landscape. Continuing your education, learning a foreign language, learning about world affairs, and traveling abroad are examples of things you can do to develop the skills needed to succeed in a global economy.

Check Your Personal Finance IQ

Now that you have finished the chapter, see what you learned about personal finance by taking the chapter posttest. If you do not have a smartphone, visit the G-W Learning companion website.

G-W Learning mobile site: www.m.g-wlearning.com

G-W Learning companion website: www.g-wlearning.com

Review Your Knowledge

1. What is economic globalization?
2. What is the purpose of specialization regarding trade between nations?
3. How does comparative advantage affect trade with other nations?
4. What are migrants and what role do they play in globalization?
5. What is the role of multinational corporations in globalization?
6. What is the difference between outsourcing and offshore outsourcing?
7. Explain the nature of exchange rates.
8. Explain the difference between a trade deficit and a trade surplus.
9. What are three advantages of free trade?
10. What forms can protectionism take?

Apply Your Knowledge

11. List three ways international trade affects you.
12. Describe how you think the world would be different with minimal or no globalization.
13. Describe the climate, geography, and natural resources of your state. What is your state known for producing? How do these three factors make your state ideal for production of these goods or services?
14. Using the Internet, research one of the specialized industries you identified in question 13. Can you identify any countries that trade with the United States for this product or service? What does that country specialize in?
15. Conduct an interview with someone who moved to the United States from another country. Be sure to ask why he or she decided to move to the United States and what the similarities and differences are between the United States and his or her country of origin. Record your answers and share the interview with the class.
16. If you were to lose your job to offshore outsourcing, what steps would you take to find a new job and recover financially? What do you think your employer and the government could and should do to assist you?
17. Use the Internet to compare the exchange rate of the US dollar with the currencies of at least five other countries. Create a table comparing your results. Be prepared to present your results to the class.
18. Read a newspaper, magazine, or online article about the value of the US dollar in international markets. Does the article describe the US dollar as being weak or strong? What economic factors have led to whether it is weak or strong?
19. Research one of the trade organizations mentioned in this chapter. Write a two- to three- page report that explores why the organization was formed, its history, and the trade-related issues that it handles.
20. Outline what young people can do today to prepare for working in a global economy and to protect themselves against future job dislocations. What can you do personally?

658

Teamwork

Working with a teammate, discuss international trade. One person should be for open markets and the other person against open markets. Create a chart with your opinions and discuss some of the problems and disputes that have arisen among nations over trade policies.

G-W Learning Mobile Site

Visit the G-W Learning mobile site to complete the chapter pretest and posttest and to practice vocabulary using e-flash cards. If you do not have a smartphone, visit the G-W Learning companion website to access these features.

G-W Learning mobile site: www.m.g-wlearning.com

G-W Learning companion website: www.g-wlearning.com

Common Core

College and Career Readiness

CTE Career Ready Practices. Whether you see problems as challenges or opportunities, they often require creative thinking to solve them. Many new innovations come about from trying to solve a problem. Describe a situation in which a challenge could keep a business from going global. How could a business turn that challenge into a positive situation and enter the global market?

Reading. Go to the Social Security website and use the search function to search for *glossary*. In the search results, locate the glossary and open it. Read each term and determine its meaning from the definition.

Writing. Research the issue of reforming Social Security. Write a one-page paper describing what you believe to be the best option. Draw evidence from your research to support your position.

Web Connect

Research current exchange rates for various currencies against the US dollar. Include the British pound, Japanese yen, Indian rupee, Canadian dollar, Mexican peso, Chinese yuan, and the euro. Create a chart that shows your findings.

College and Career Readiness

College and Career Readiness Portfolio

You have probably used the Internet as a resource while creating your portfolio. The Internet also provides ways to help you present and store materials for an e-portfolio. Perhaps you created web pages to present your e-portfolio. You could create a personal website to host the files. However, another option is using a website that specializes in e-portfolios. Some sites charge a fee to help you develop and host your e-portfolio. However, free sites are also available. Free sites may be sponsored by a school or some other organization. Some sites offer a basic account for free and charge for an account with more services. These sites typically have tutorials, templates, and forms that make placing your materials in an attractive e-portfolio easy. Be sure you read and understand the user agreement for any site on which you place your materials.

1. Search the Internet using the term *free e-portfolio*. Review sites to learn what portfolio tools and resources are offered for free by at least two websites.
2. Write a short summary for each site that includes the website name, the address, the sponsoring organization, and the tools or resources offered on the site.

Day of the Event

You have practiced all year for this Career and Technical Student Organization (CTSO) competition, and now you are ready. Whether it is for an objective test, written test, report, or presentation, you have done your homework and are ready to shine.

To prepare for the day of the event, complete the following activities.

1. Be sure to get plenty of sleep the night before the event so that you are rested and ready to go.
2. Use your event checklist before you go into the presentation so that you do not forget any of your materials that are needed for the event.
3. Find the room where the competition will take place and arrive early. If you are late and the door is closed, you will be disqualified.
4. If you are making a presentation before a panel of judges, practice what you are going to say when you are called on. State your name, your school, and any other information that has been requested. Be confident, smile, and make eye contact with the judges.
5. When the event is finished, thank the judges for their time.

Math Skills Handbook

Table of Contents

Getting Started

Math skills are needed in everyday life. You will need to be able to estimate your purchases at a grocery store, calculate sales tax, or divide a recipe in half. This section is designed to help develop your math proficiency for better understanding of the concepts presented in the textbook. Using the information presented in the Math Skills Handbook will help you understand basic math concepts and their application to the real world.

Using a Calculator

There are many different types of calculators. Some are simple and only perform basic math operations. Become familiar with the keys and operating instructions of your calculator so calculations can be made quickly and correctly.

Shown below is a scientific calculator that comes standard with the Windows 8 operating system. To display this version, select the **View** pull-down menu and click **Scientific** in the menu.

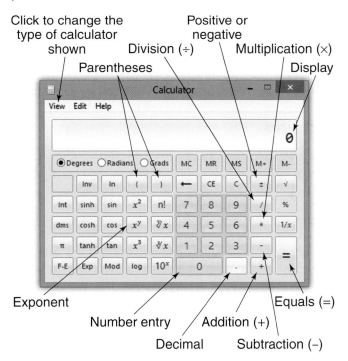

Click to change the type of calculator shown

Parentheses

Positive or negative

Division (÷)

Multiplication (×)

Display

Exponent

Number entry

Decimal

Addition (+)

Subtraction (−)

Equals (=)

Solving Word Problems

Word problems are exercises in which the problem is set up in text, rather than presented in mathematical notation. Many word problems tell a story. You must identify the elements of the math problem and solve it.

There are many strategies for solving word problems. Some common strategies include making a list or table; working backward; guessing, checking, and revising; and substituting simpler numbers to solve the problem.

Strategy	How to Apply
List or table	Identify information in the problem and organize it into a table to identify patterns.
Work backward	When an end result is provided, work backward from that to find the requested information.
Guess, check, revise	Start with a reasonable guess at the answer, check to see if it is correct, and revise the guess as needed until the solution is found.
Substitute simpler information	Use different numbers to simplify the problem and solve it, then solve the problem using the provided numbers.

Number Sense

Number sense is an ability to use and understand numbers to make judgments and solve problems. Someone with good number sense also understands when his or her computations are reasonable in the context of a problem.

Example
Suppose you want to add three basketball scores: 35, 21, and 18.
- First, add 30 + 20 + 10 = 60.
- Then, add 5 + 1 + 8 = 14.
- Finally, combine these two sums to find the answer: 60 + 14 = 74.

Example
Suppose your brother is 72 inches tall and you want to convert this measurement from inches to feet. Suppose you use a calculator to divide 72 by 12 (number of inches in a foot) and the answer is displayed as 864. You recognize immediately that your brother cannot be 864 feet tall and realize you must have miscalculated. In this case, you incorrectly entered a multiplication operation instead of a division operation. The correct answer is 6.

Numbers and Quantity

Numbers are more than just items in a series. Each number has a distinct value relative to all other numbers. They are used to perform mathematical operations from the simplest addition to finding square roots. There are whole numbers, fractions, decimals, exponents, and square roots.

Whole Numbers

A whole number, or integer, is any positive number or zero that has no fractional part. It can be a single digit from 0 to 9, or may contain multiple digits, such as 38.

Place Value

A digit's position in a number determines its *place value.* The digit, or numeral, in the place farthest to the right before the decimal point is in the *ones position.* The next digit to the left is in the *tens position,* followed by next digit in the *hundreds position.* As you continue to move left, the place values increase to thousands, ten thousands, and so forth.

Example

Suppose you win the lottery and receive a check for $23,152,679. Your total prize would be *twenty-three million, one hundred fifty-two thousand, six hundred seventy-nine dollars.*

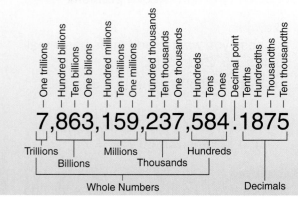

Addition

Addition is the process of combining two or more numbers. The result is called the *sum.*

Example

A plumber installs six faucets on his first job and three faucets on his second job. How many faucets does he install in total?

$$6 + 3 = 9$$

Subtraction

Subtraction is the process of finding the *difference* between two numbers.

Example

A plumber installs six faucets on her first job and three faucets on her second job. How many more faucets did she install on the first job than the second? Subtract 3 from 6 to find the answer.

$$6 - 3 = 3$$

Multiplication

Multiplication is a method of adding a number to itself a given number of times. The multiplied numbers are called *factors,* and the result is called the *product.*

Example

Suppose you are installing computers and need to purchase four adaptors. If the adaptors are $6 each, what is the total cost of the adaptors? The answer can be found by adding $6 four times:

$$\$6 + \$6 + \$6 + \$6 = \$24$$

However, the same answer is found more quickly by multiplying $6 times 4.

$$\$6 \times 4 = \$24$$

Division

Division is the process of determining how many times one number, called the *divisor,* goes into another number, called the *dividend.* The result is called the *quotient.*

Example

Suppose you are installing computers and buy a box of adaptors for $24. There are four adaptors in the box. What is the cost of each adaptor? The answer is found by dividing $24 by 4:

$$\$24 \div 4 = \$6$$

Decimals

A decimal is a kind of fraction with a denominator that is either ten, one hundred, one thousand, or some power of ten. Every decimal has three parts: a whole number (sometimes zero), followed by a decimal point, and one or more whole numbers.

Place Value

The numbers to the right of the decimal point indicate the amount of the fraction. The first place to the right of a decimal point is the tenths place. The second place to the right of the decimal point is the hundredths place. As you continue to the right, the place values move to the thousandths place, the ten thousandths place, and so on.

Example
A machinist is required to produce an airplane part to a very precise measurement of 36.876 inches. This measurement is *thirty-six and eight-hundred seventy six thousandths* inches.

36.876

Addition

To add decimals, place each number in a vertical list and align the decimal points. Then add the numbers in each column starting with the column on the right and working to the left. The decimal point in the answer drops down into the same location.

Example
A landscaper spreads 4.3 pounds of fertilizer in the front yard of a house and 1.2 pounds in the backyard. How many pounds of fertilizer did the landscaper spread in total?

$$\begin{array}{r} 4.3 \\ + \ 1.2 \\ \hline 5.5 \end{array}$$

Subtraction

To subtract decimals, place each number in a vertical list and align the decimal points. Then subtract the numbers in each column, starting with the column on the right and working to the left. The decimal point in the answer drops down into the same location.

Example
A landscaper spreads 4.3 pounds of fertilizer in the front yard of a house and 1.2 pounds in the backyard. How many more pounds were spread in the front yard than in the backyard?

$$\begin{array}{r} 4.3 \\ - \ 1.2 \\ \hline 3.1 \end{array}$$

Multiplication

To multiply decimals, place the numbers in a vertical list. Then multiply each digit of the top number by the right-hand bottom number. Multiply each digit of the top number by the bottom number in the tens position. Place the result on a second line and add a zero to the end of the number. Add the total number of decimal places in both numbers you are multiplying. This will be the number of decimal places in your answer.

Example
An artist orders 13 brushes priced at $3.20 each. What is the total cost of the order? The answer can be found by multiplying $3.20 by 13.

$$\begin{array}{r} \$3.20 \\ \times \ \ \ \ 13 \\ \hline 960 \\ + \ 3200 \\ \hline 41.60 \end{array}$$

Division

To divide decimals, the dividend is placed under the division symbol, the divisor is placed to the left of the division symbol, and the quotient is placed above the division symbol. Start from the *left* of the dividend and determine how many times the divisor goes into the first number. Continue this until the quotient is found. Add the dollar sign to the final answer.

$$3\overline{)9.60} = 3.20$$

9↓	Product of 3 × 3
06	Bring down the 6
6↓	Product of 2 × 3
0	No remainder

Example
An artist buys a package of three brushes for $9.60. What is the cost of each brush? The quotient is found by dividing $9.60 by 3.

$$3\overline{)9.60} = 3.20$$

−9↓
06↓
00

Rounding

When a number is rounded, some of the digits are changed, removed, or changed to zero so the number is easier to work with. Rounding is often used when precise calculations or measurements are not needed. For example, if you are calculating millions of dollars, it might not be important to know the amount down to the dollar or cent. Instead, you might *round* the amount to the nearest ten thousand or even hundred thousand dollars. Also, when working with decimals, the final answer might have several more decimal places than needed.

To round a number, follow these steps. First, underline the digit in the place to which you are rounding. Second, if the digit to the *right* of this place is 5 or greater, add 1 to the underlined digit. If the digit to the right is less than 5, do not change the underlined digit. Third, change all the digits to right of the underlined digit to zero. In the case of decimals, the digits to the right of the underlined digit are removed.

Example

A company's utility expense last year was $32,678.53. The owner of the company is preparing a budget for next year and wants to round this amount to the nearest 1,000.

Step 1: Underline the digit in the 1,000 place.

$$\$32{,}678$$

Step 2: The digit to the right of 2 is greater than 5, so add 1.

$$2 + 1 = 3$$

Step 3: Change the digits to the right of the underlined digit to zero.

$$\$33{,}000$$

Fractions

A fraction is a part of a whole. It is made up by a numerator that is divided by a denominator.

$$\frac{numerator}{denominator}$$

The *numerator* specifies the number of these equal parts that are in the fraction. The *denominator* shows how many equal parts make up the whole.

Proper

In a *proper fraction,* the numerator is less than the denominator.

Example

A lumber yard worker cuts a sheet of plywood into four equal pieces and sells three of them to a carpenter. The carpenter now has 3/4 of the original sheet. The lumber yard has 1/4 of the sheet remaining.

Improper

An *improper fraction* is a fraction where the numerator is equal to or greater than the denominator.

Example

A chef uses a chili recipe which calls for 1/2 cup of chili sauce. However, the chef makes an extra-large batch that will serve three times as many people and uses three of the 1/2 cup measures. The improper fraction in this example is 3/2 cups of chili sauce.

Mixed

A mixed number contains a whole number and a fraction. It is another way of writing an improper fraction.

Example

A chef uses a chili recipe that calls for 1/2 cup of chili sauce. However, the chef makes an extra-large batch that will serve three times as many people and uses three of the 1/2 cup measures. The improper fraction in this example is 3/2 cups of chili sauce. This can be converted to a mixed number by dividing the numerator by the denominator:

The remainder is 1, which is 1 over 2. So, the mixed number is 1 1/2 cups.

$$2\overline{)3} \\ \underline{-2} \\ 1$$

Reducing

Fractions are reduced to make them easier to work with. Reducing a fraction means writing it with smaller numbers, in *lowest terms.* Reducing a fraction does not change its value.

To find the lowest terms, determine the largest number that *evenly* divides both the numerator and denominator so there is no remainder. Then use this number to divide both the numerator and denominator.

Example
The owner of hair salon asks ten customers if they were satisfied with the service they recently received. Eight customers said they were satisfied, so the fraction of satisfied customers is 8/10. The largest number that evenly divides both the numerator and denominator is 2. The fraction is reduced to its lowest terms as follows.

$$\frac{8}{10} = \frac{8 \div 2}{10 \div 2} = \frac{4}{5}$$

Addition

To add fractions, the numerators are combined and the denominator stays the same. However, fractions can only be added when they have a *common denominator.* The *least common denominator* is the smallest number to which each denominator can be converted.

Example
A snack food company makes a bag of trail mix by combining 3/8 pound of nuts with 1/8 pound of dried fruit. What is the total weight of each bag? The fractions have common denominators, so the total weight is determined by adding the fractions.

$$\frac{3}{8} + \frac{1}{8} = \frac{4}{8}$$

This answer can be reduced from 4/8 to 1/2.

Example
Suppose the company combines 1/4 pound of nuts with 1/8 cup of dried fruit. To add these fractions, the denominators must be made equal. In this case, the least common denominator is 8 because

$4 \times 2 = 8$. Convert 1/4 to its equivalent of 2/8 by multiplying both numerator and denominator by 2. Then the fractions can be added as follows.

$$\frac{2}{8} + \frac{1}{8} = \frac{3}{8}$$

This answer cannot be reduced because 3 and 8 have no common factors.

Subtraction

To subtract fractions, the second numerator is subtracted from the first numerator. The denominators stay the same. However, fractions can only be subtracted when they have a *common denominator.*

Example
A snack food company makes a bag of trail mix by combining 3/8 pound of nuts with 1/8 pound of dried fruit. How much more do the nuts weigh than the dried fruit? The fractions have common denominators, so the difference can be determined by subtracting the fractions.

$$\frac{3}{8} - \frac{1}{8} = \frac{2}{8}$$

This answer can be reduced from 2/8 to 1/4.

Example
Suppose the company combines 1/4 pound of nuts with 1/8 cup of dried fruit. How much more do the nuts weigh than the dried fruit? To subtract these fractions, the denominators must be made equal. The least common denominator is 8, so convert 1/4 to its equivalent of 2/8. Then the fractions can be subtracted as follows.

$$\frac{2}{8} - \frac{1}{8} = \frac{1}{8}$$

This answer cannot be reduced.

Multiplication

Common denominators are not necessary to multiply fractions. Multiply all of the numerators and multiply all of the denominators. Reduce the resulting fraction as needed.

Example

A lab technician makes a saline solution by mixing 3/4 cup of salt with one gallon of water. How much salt should the technician mix if only 1/2 gallon of water is used? Multiply 3/4 by 1/2:

$$\frac{3}{4} \times \frac{1}{2} = \frac{3}{8}$$

Division

To divide one fraction by a second fraction, multiply the first fraction by the reciprocal of the second fraction. The *reciprocal* of a fraction is created by switching the numerator and denominator.

Example

A cabinet maker has 3/4 gallon of wood stain. Each cabinet requires 1/8 gallon of stain to finish. How many cabinets can be finished? To find the answer, divide 3/4 by 1/8, which means multiplying 3/4 by the reciprocal of 1/8.

$$\frac{3}{4} \div \frac{1}{8} = \frac{3}{4} \times \frac{8}{1} = \frac{24}{4} = 6$$

Negative Numbers

Negative numbers are those less than zero. They are written with a minus sign in front of the number.

Example

The number −34,687,295 is read as *negative thirty-four million, six hundred eighty-seven thousand, two hundred ninety-five.*

Addition

Adding a negative number is the same as subtracting a positive number.

Example

A football player gains nine yards on his first running play (+9) and loses four yards (−4) on his second play. The two plays combined result in a five yard gain.

$$9 + (-4) = 9 - 4 = 5$$

Suppose this player loses five yards on his first running play (−5) and loses four yards (−4) on his second play. The two plays combined result in a nine yard loss.

$$-5 + (-4) = -5 - 4 = -9$$

Subtraction

Subtracting a negative number is the same as adding a positive number.

Example

Suppose you receive a $100 traffic ticket. This will result in a −$100 change to your cash balance. However, you explain the circumstance to a traffic court judge, and she reduces the fine by $60. The effect is to subtract −$60 from −$100 change to your cash balance. The final result is a −$40 change.

$$-\$100 - (-\$60) = -\$100 + \$60 = -\$40$$

Multiplication

Multiplication of an odd number of negative numbers results in a *negative* product. Multiplication of an even number of negative numbers results in a *positive* product.

Example

If you lose two pounds per week, this will result in a −2 pound weekly change in your weight. After five weeks, there will be a −10 pound change to your weight.

$$5 \times (-2) = -10$$

Suppose you have been losing two pounds per week. Five weeks ago (−5) your weight was 10 pounds higher.

$$(-5) \times (-2) = 10$$

Division

Division of an odd number of negative numbers results in a *negative* quotient. Division of an even number of negative numbers results in a *positive* quotient.

Example

Suppose you lost 10 pounds, which is a −10 pound change in your weight. How many pounds on average did you lose each week if it took five weeks to lose the weight? Divide −10 by 5 to find the answer.

$$-10 \div 5 = -2$$

Suppose you lost 10 pounds. How many weeks did this take if you lost two pounds each week? Divide −10 by −2 to find the answer.

$$-10 \div -2 = 5$$

Percentages

A percentage (%) means a part of 100. It is the same as a fraction or decimal.

Representing Percentages as Decimals

To change a percentage to a decimal, move the decimal point two places to the left. For example, 1% is the same as 1/100 or 0.01; 10% is the same as 10/100 or 0.10; and 100% is the same as 100/100 or 1.0.

Example
A high school cafeteria estimates that 30% of the students prefer sesame seeds on hamburger buns. To convert this percentage to a decimal, move the decimal point two places to the left.

$$30\% = 0.30$$

Representing Fractions as Percentages

To change a fraction to a percentage, first convert the fraction to a decimal by dividing the numerator by the denominator. Then convert the decimal to a percentage by moving the decimal point two places to the right.

Example
A high school cafeteria conducts a survey and finds that three of every ten students prefer sesame seeds on hamburger buns. To change this fraction to a percentage, divide 3 by 10, and move the decimal two places to the right.

$$3 \div 10 = 0.30 = 30\%$$

Calculating a Percentage

To calculate the percentage of a number, change the percentage to a decimal and multiply by the number.

Example
A car dealer sold ten cars last week, of which 70% were sold to women. How many cars did women buy? Change 70% to a decimal by dividing 70 by 100, which equals 0.70. Then multiply by the total number (10).

$$0.70 \times 10 = 7$$

To determine what percentage one number is of another, divide the first number by the second. Then convert the quotient into a percentage by moving the decimal point two places to the right.

Example
A car dealer sold 10 cars last week, of which seven were sold to women. What percentage of the cars were purchased by women? Divide 7 by 10 and then convert to a percentage.

$$7 \div 10 = 0.70$$
$$0.70 = 70\%$$

Ratio

A ratio compares two numbers through division. Ratios are often expressed as a fraction, but can also be written with a colon (:) or the word *to*.

Example
A drugstore's cost for a bottle of vitamins is $2.00, which it sells for $3.00. The ratio of the selling price to the cost can be expressed as follows.

$$\frac{\$3.00}{\$2.00} = \frac{3}{2}$$

$$\$3.00\!:\!\$2.00 = 3\!:\!2$$

$$\$3.00 \text{ to } \$2.00 = 3 \text{ to } 2$$

Measurement

The official system of measurement in the United States for length, volume, and weight is the US Customary system of measurement. The metric system of measurement is used by most other countries.

US Customary Measurement

The following are the most commonly used units of length in the US Customary system of measurement.

- 1 inch
- 1 foot = 12 inches
- 1 yard = 3 feet
- 1 mile = 5,280 feet

Example

An interior designer measurers the length and width of a room when ordering new floor tiles. The length is measured at 12 feet 4 inches (12′ 4″). The width is measured at 8 feet 7 inches (8′ 7″).

Example

Taxi cab fares are usually determined by measuring distance in miles. A recent cab rate in Chicago was $3.25 for the first 1/9 mile or less, and $0.20 for each additional 1/9 mile.

Metric Conversion

The metric system of measurement is convenient to use because units can be converted by multiplying or dividing by multiples of 10. The following are the commonly used units of length in the metric system of measurement.

- 1 millimeter
- 1 centimeter = 10 millimeters
- 1 meter = 100 centimeters
- 1 kilometer = 1,000 meters

The following are conversions from the US Customary system to the metric system.

- 1 inch = 25.4 millimeters = 2.54 centimeters
- 1 foot = 30.48 centimeters = 0.3048 meters
- 1 yard = 0.9144 meters
- 1 mile = 1.6093 kilometers

Example

A salesperson from the United States is traveling abroad and needs to drive 100 kilometers to meet a customer. How many miles is this trip? Divide 100 kilometers by 1.6093 and round to the hundredth place.

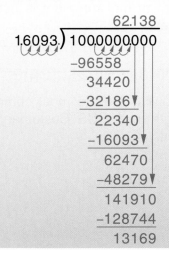

Estimating

Estimating is finding an *approximate* answer and often involves using rounded numbers. It is often quicker to add rounded numbers, for example, than it is to add the precise numbers.

Example

Estimate the total miles a delivery truck will travel along the following three segments of a route.

- Detroit to Chicago: 278 miles
- Chicago to St. Louis: 297 miles
- St. Louis to Wichita: 436 miles

The mileage can be estimated by rounding each segment to the nearest 100 miles.

- Detroit to Chicago: 300 miles
- Chicago to St. Louis: 300 miles
- St. Louis to Wichita: 400 miles

Add the rounded segments to estimate the total miles.

$$300 + 300 + 400 = 1{,}000 \text{ miles}$$

Accuracy and Precision

Accuracy and precision mean slightly different things. *Accuracy* is the closeness of a measured value to its actual or true value. *Precision* is how close measured values are to each other.

Example

A machine is designed to fill jars with 16 ounces of peanut butter. The machine is considered accurate if the actual amount of peanut butter in a jar is within 0.05 ounces of the target, which is a range of 15.95 to 16.05 ounces. A machine operator tests a jar and measures the weight to be 16.01 ounces. The machine is accurate.

Suppose a machine operator tests 10 jars of peanut butter and finds the weight of each jar to be 15.4 ounces. The machine is considered precise because it fills every jar with exactly the same amount. However, it is not accurate because the amount differs too much from the target.

Algebra

An *equation* is a mathematical statement that has an equal sign (=). An *algebraic* equation is an equation that includes at least one variable. A *variable* is an unknown quantity.

Solving Equations with Variables

Solving an algebraic equation means finding the value of the variable that will make the equation a true statement. To solve a simple equation, perform inverse operations on both sides and isolate the variable.

Example
A computer consultant has sales of $1,000. After deducting $600 in expenses, her profit equals $400. This is expressed with the following equation.

$$\text{sales} - \text{expenses} = \text{profit}$$
$$\$1,000 - \$600 = \$400$$

Example
A computer consultant has expenses of $600 and $400 in profit. What are her sales? An equation can be written in which sales are the unknown quantity, or variable.

$$\text{sales} - \text{expenses} = \text{profit}$$
$$\text{sales} - \$600 = \$400$$

Example
To find the value for sales, perform inverse operations on both sides and isolate the variable.

$$
\begin{array}{rrr}
\text{sales} & - \ \$600 & = \quad \$400 \\
& + \ \$600 & + \quad 600 \\
\hline
\text{sales} & & = \quad \$1,000
\end{array}
$$

Order of Operations

The order of operations is a set of rules stating which operations in an equation are performed first. The order of operations is often stated using the acronym *PEMDAS*. PEMDAS stands for parentheses, exponents, multiplication and division, and addition and subtraction. This means anything inside parentheses is computed first. Exponents are computed next. Then, any multiplication and division operations are computed. Finally, any addition and subtraction operations are computed to find the final answer to the problem. The equation is solved from left to right by applying PEMDAS.

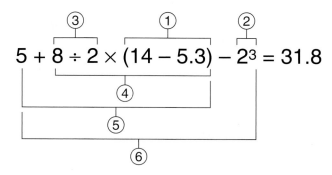

$$5 + 8 \div 2 \times (14 - 5.3) - 2^3 = 31.8$$

Recursive Formulas

A *recursive formula* is used to determine the next term of a sequence, using one or more of the preceding terms. The terms of a sequence are often expressed with a variable and subscript. For example, a sequence might be written as a_1, a_2, a_3, a_4, a_5, and so on. The subscript is essentially the place in line for each term. A recursive formula has two parts. The first is a starting point or seed value (a_1). The second is an equation for another number in the sequence (a_n). The second part of the formula is a function of the prior term (a_{n-1}).

Example
Suppose you buy a car for $10,000. Assume the car declines in value 10% each year. In the second year, the car will be worth 90% of $10,000, which is $9,000. The following year it will be worth 90% of $9,000, which is $8,100. What will the car be worth in the fifth year? Use the following recursive equation to find the answer.

$$a_n = a_{n-1} \times 0.90$$
$$\text{where } a_1 = \$10,000$$
$$a_n = \text{value of car in the } n^{th} \text{ year}$$

Year	Value of Car
n = 1	$a_1 = \$10,000$
n = 2	$a_2 = a_{2-1} \times 0.90 = a_1 \times 0.90 = \$10,000 \times 0.90 = \$9,000$
n = 3	$a_3 = a_{3-1} \times 0.90 = a_2 \times 0.90 = \$9,000 \times 0.90 = \$8,100$
n = 4	$a_4 = a_{4-1} \times 0.90 = a_3 \times 0.90 = \$8,100 \times 0.90 = \$7,290$
n = 5	$a_5 = a_{5-1} \times 0.90 = a_4 \times 0.90 = \$7,290 \times 0.90 = \$6,561$

Geometry

Geometry is a field of mathematics that deals with shapes, such as circles and polygons. A *polygon* is any shape whose sides are straight. Every polygon has three or more sides.

Parallelograms

A *parallelogram* is a four-sided figure with two pairs of parallel sides. A *rectangle* is a type of parallelogram with four right angles. A *square* is a special type of parallelogram with four right angles (90 degrees) and four equal sides.

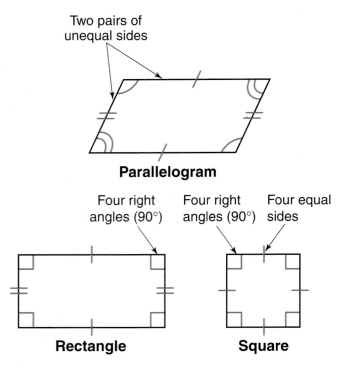

Parallelogram

Rectangle   **Square**

Example

Real-life examples of squares include ceramic floor and wall tiles, and each side of a die. Real-life examples of a rectangle include a football field, pool table, and most doors.

Triangles

A three-sided polygon is called a *triangle*. The following are four types of triangles, which are classified according to their sides and angles.

- *Equilateral:* Three equal sides and three equal angles.
- *Isosceles:* Two equal sides and two equal angles.

- *Scalene:* Three unequal sides and three unequal angles.
- *Right:* One right angle; may be isosceles or scalene.

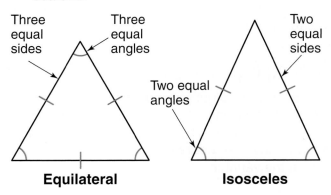

Equilateral   **Isosceles**

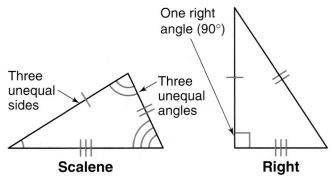

Scalene   **Right**

Example

Real-life examples of equilateral triangles are the sides of a classical Egyptian pyramid.

Circles and Half Circles

A *circle* is a figure in which every point is the same distance from the center. The distance from the center to a point on the circle is called the *radius*. The distance across the circle through the center is the *diameter*. A half circle is formed by dividing a whole circle along the diameter.

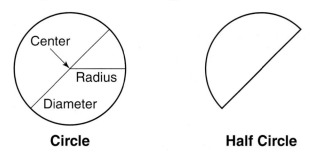

Circle   **Half Circle**

Example

Real life examples of circles include wheels of all sizes.

Perimeter

A *perimeter* is a measure of length around a figure. Add the length of each side to measure the perimeter of any figure whose sides are all line segments, such as a parallelogram or triangle. The perimeter of a circle is called the *circumference*. To measure the perimeter, multiply the diameter by pi (π). Pi is approximately equal to 3.14. The following formulas can be used to calculate the perimeters of various figures.

Figure	Perimeter
parallelogram	2 × width + 2 × length
square	4 × side
rectangle	2 × width + 2 × length
triangle	side + side + side
circle	π × diameter

Example

A professional basketball court is a rectangle 94 feet long and 50 feet wide. The perimeter of the court is calculated as follows.

2 × 94 feet + 2 × 50 feet = 288 feet

Example

A tractor tire has a 43 inch diameter. The circumference of the tire is calculated as follows.

43 inches × 3.14 = 135 inches

Area

Area is a measure of the amount of surface within the perimeter of a flat figure. Area is measured in square units, such as square inches, square feet, or square miles. The areas of the following figures are calculated using the corresponding formulas.

Figure	Area
parallelogram	base × height
square	side × side
rectangle	length × width
triangle	1/2 × base × height
circle	π × radius² = π × radius × radius

Example

An interior designer needs to order decorative tiles to fill the following spaces. Measure the area of each space in square feet.

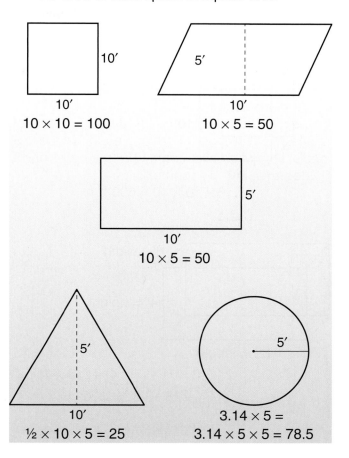

Surface Area

Surface area is the total area of the surface of a figure occupying three-dimensional space, such as a cube or prism. A *cube* is a solid figure that has six identical squares faces. A *prism* has bases or ends which have the same size and shape and are parallel to each other, and each of whose sides is a parallelogram. The following are the formulas to find the surface area of a cube and a prism.

Object	Surface Area
cube	6 × side × side
prism	2 × [(length × width) + (width × height) + (length × height)]

Example

A manufacturer of cardboard boxes wants to determine how much cardboard is needed to make the following size boxes. Calculate the surface area of each in square inches.

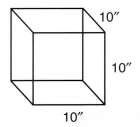

$$10 \times 10 \times 10 = 1000$$

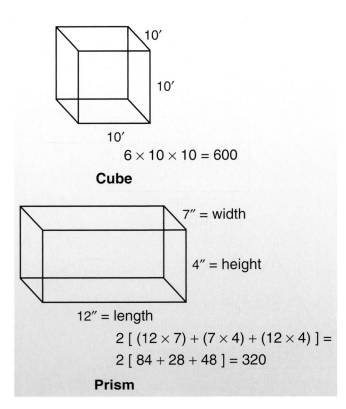

$$6 \times 10 \times 10 = 600$$

Cube

$$2\,[\,(12 \times 7) + (7 \times 4) + (12 \times 4)\,] =$$
$$2\,[\,84 + 28 + 48\,] = 320$$

Prism

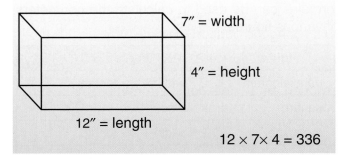

$$12 \times 7 \times 4 = 336$$

Example

Find the volume of grain that will fill the following cylindrical silo. Measure the volume in cubic feet.

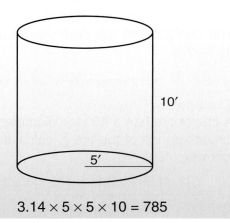

$$3.14 \times 5 \times 5 \times 10 = 785$$

Volume

Volume is the three-dimensional space occupied by a figure and is measured in cubic units, such as cubic inches or cubic feet. The volumes of the following figures are calculated using the corresponding formulas.

Solid Figure	Volume
cube	side³ = side × side × side
prism	length × width × height
cylinder	$\pi \times$ radius² × height = $\pi \times$ radius × radius × height
sphere	4/3 × $\pi \times$ radius³ = 4/3 × $\pi \times$ radius × radius × radius

Example

Find the volume of packing material needed to fill the following boxes. Measure the volume of each in cubic inches.

Example

A manufacturer of pool toys wants to stuff soft material into a ball with a 3 inch radius. Find the cubic inches of material that will fit into the ball.

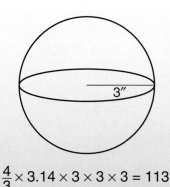

$$\frac{4}{3} \times 3.14 \times 3 \times 3 \times 3 = 113$$

Data Analysis and Statistics

Graphs are used to illustrate data in a picture-like format. It is often easier to understand data when they are shown in a graphical form instead of a numerical form in a table. Common types of graphs are bar graphs, line graphs, and circle graphs.

A *bar graph* organizes information along a vertical axis and horizontal axis. The vertical axis runs up and down one side; the horizontal axis runs along the bottom.

A *line graph* also organizes information on vertical and horizontal axes; however, data are graphed as a continuous line rather than a set of bars. Line graphs are often used to show trends over a period of time.

A *circle graph* looks like a divided circle and shows how a whole object is cut up into parts. Circle graphs are also called *pie charts* and are often used to illustrate percentages.

Example

A business shows the following balances in its cash account for the months of March through July. These data are illustrated below in bar and line graphs.

Month	Account Balance	Month	Account Balance
March	$400	June	$800
April	$600	July	$900
May	$500		

Example

A business lists the percentage of its expenses in the following categories. These data are displayed in the following circle graph.

Expenses	Percentage
Cost of goods	25
Salaries	25
Rent	21
Utilities	17
Advertising	12

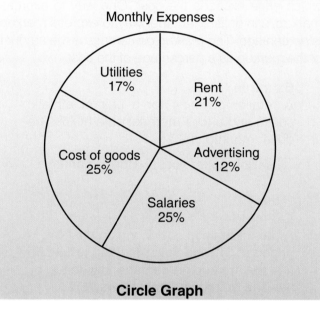

Monthly Expenses

Circle Graph

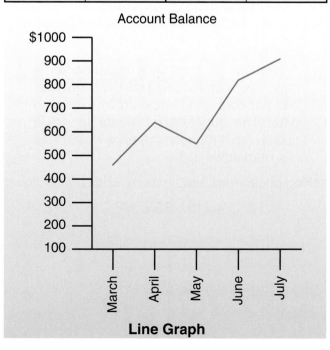

Account Balance

Line Graph

Math Models for Business and Retail

Math skills used in business and retail are the same math skills required in everyday life. The ability to add, subtract, multiply, and divide different types of numbers is very important. However, this type of math is often focused on prices, taxes, profits, and losses.

Markup

Markup is a retailing term for the amount by which price exceeds the cost. One way to express markup is in dollars. Another way to express markup is percentage. The *markup percentage* is the amount of the markup as a percentage of the cost.

Example

A retailer pays $4 for a pair of athletic socks and prices them for sale at $7. The dollar markup is $3.

selling price – cost = dollar markup

$$\$7 - \$4 = \$3$$

Example

A pair of athletic socks, which cost $4, is priced at $7. The dollar markup is $3 . To find the markup percentage, divide $3 by $4. The markup percentage is 75%.

markup dollars ÷ cost = markup percentage

$$\$3 \div \$4 = 0.75 = 75\%$$

Percentage Markup to Determine Selling Price

The selling price of an item can be determined if you know the markup percentage and the cost. First, convert the markup percentage to a decimal. Next multiply the cost by the decimal. Then, add the markup dollars to the cost to determine the selling price. Another way to find the selling price is to convert the markup percentage to a decimal and add 1.0. Then multiply this amount by the cost.

Example

A pair of athletic socks costs $4, which the retailer marks up by 75%. Find the selling price.

1. Convert the markup percentage to a decimal.

$$75\% = 0.75$$

2. Multiply the cost by the markup.

cost × markup = dollar markup

$$\$4 \times 0.75 = \$3$$

3. Add the $3 markup to the $4 cost to find the selling price. The selling price is $7.

$$\$4 + \$3 = \$7$$

Example

A pair of athletic socks costs $4, which the retailer marks up by 75%. Find the selling price.

1. Convert the 75% markup percentage to 0.75 and add 1.0.

$$0.75 + 1.0 = 1.75.$$

2. Multiply 1.75 by the $4 cost to find the selling price.

$$\$4 \times 1.75 = \$7$$

Markdown

A *markdown* is the amount by which the selling price of an item is reduced. Sometimes a markdown is also called a *discount.* To find the amount of a markdown, subtract the new or discounted price from the original price. A markdown can also be expressed as a percentage of the original price. Sometimes this is called a *percentage discount.*

Example

A package of meat at a supermarket is originally priced at $10. However, the meat has not sold and is nearing its expiration date. The supermarket wants to sell it quickly, so it reduces the price to $6. This is a markdown of $4.

selling price – discounted price = dollar markdown

$$\$10 - \$6 = \$4$$

Example

A package of meat at a supermarket is originally priced at $10. However, the meat has not sold and is nearing its expiration date. The supermarket wants to sell it quickly, so it marks down the price by $4. The markdown percentage is determined by dividing the $4 markdown by the original $10 price.

markdown ÷ selling price = markdown percentage

$$\$4 \div \$10 = 40\%$$

Gross Profit

Gross profit is a company's net sales minus the cost of goods sold. *Gross margin* is often expressed as a percentage of revenue.

Example

A wristband manufacturer generated net sales of $100,000 last year. The cost of goods sold for the wristbands was $30,000. The net sales of $100,000 minus the $30,000 cost of goods sold leaves a gross profit $70,000.

net sales − cost of goods sold = gross profit

$$\$100,000 - \$30,000 = \$70,000$$

Example

The gross profit of $70,000 divided by the net sales of $100,000 is 0.70, or 70%.

gross profit ÷ net sales = gross margin percentage

$$\$70,000 \div \$100,000 = 0.70 = 70\%$$

Net Income or Loss

Net income or loss is a company's revenue after total expenses are deducted from gross profit. Total expenses include marketing, administration, interest, and taxes. A company earns a *net income* when gross profit exceeds expenses. A *net loss* is incurred when expenses exceed gross profit.

Example

A wristband manufacturer had a gross profit of $70,000. In addition, expenses for marketing, administration, interest, and taxes were $50,000. Net profit is calculated by subtracting the total expenses of $50,000 from the gross profit of $70,000. The net profit was $20,000.

gross profit on sales − total expenses = net income or loss

$$\$70,000 - \$50,000 = \$20,000$$

Break-Even Point

A *break-even point* is the number of units a company must sell to cover its costs and expenses and earn a zero profit. Use the following formula to find a company's break-even point.

total costs ÷ selling price = break-even point

Sales Tax

Sales tax is a tax collected on the selling price of a good or service. The sales tax rate is usually expressed as a percentage of the selling price. Sales tax is calculated by multiplying the sale price by the tax rate.

Example

Suppose you buy a T-shirt for $10.00. How much is the sales tax if the tax rate is 5%? Convert 5% to a decimal (.05) and multiply it by the sale price.

sale price × sales tax rate percentage = sales tax

$$\$10 \times 0.05 = \$0.50$$

Return on Investment

Return on investment (ROI) is a calculation of a company's net profit as a percentage of the owner's investment. One way to determine ROI is to divide net profit by the owner's investment.

Example

Suppose you start a dry-cleaning business with a $100,000 investment, and you earn a $20,000 net profit during the first year. Divide $20,000 by $100,000, which equals a 20% return on your investment.

net income ÷ owner's investment = return on investment (ROI)

$$\$20,000 \div \$100,000 = 0.20 = 20\%$$

Glossary

529 plan. Savings plan for education operated by a state or educational institution. (15)

A

ability. Physical or mental skill developed through learning, training, and practice. (15)

acceleration clause. Statement in a contract that allows the creditor to require full and immediate payment of the entire balance if a payment is missed or the terms of the contract are not followed. (6)

adjustable rate mortgage (ARM). Mortgage with an interest rate that can be adjusted up or down periodically. (13)

advertising. Any paid public announcement promoting the sale of a product or service. (9)

amortization. Process of paying back a loan in equal monthly installments. (13)

annual percentage rate (APR). Annual cost of credit a lender charges. (6)

annual percentage yield (APY). Rate of yearly earnings from an account, including compound interest. (5)

annuity. Contract with an insurance company that provides regular income for a set period of time. (7)

apartment. Living unit that is often among similar units. (12)

appraisal. Written estimate of the value of real estate. (13)

apprenticeship. Combination of on-the-job training, work experience, and classroom instruction. (15)

aptitude. Natural physical or mental talent. (15)

asset. Item of value that is owned, such as cash, securities, real estate, and personal possessions. (2)

ATM card. Card issued by a bank that allows the holder to check account balances, withdraw and deposit cash, and transfer money from one account to another using an automated teller machine. (4)

B

bait and switch. Strategy that involves advertising one item and then substituting another item. (10)

balance of payments. Account of the total flow of goods, services, and money coming into and going out of the country. (21)

bank statement. Record of checks, ATM transactions, deposits, and charges to an account that is provided by the bank. (4)

bankruptcy. Legal state in which the courts excuse a debtor from repaying some or all debt. (6)

bear market. Extended period of uncertainty and pessimism when stock prices fall. (7)

beneficiary. Person or organization named by a policyholder to receive the death benefit of an insurance policy after the policyholder's death. (8)

bill of sale. Legal document that spells out important features of the sale and transfers rights from the seller to the buyer. (14)

binding arbitration. Method of settling disagreements through an objective third party. (10)

biodegradable. Ability to be broken down naturally by microorganisms into harmless elements. (17)

biofuel. Fuel composed of or produced from biological raw material. (17)

bodily injury liability. Insurance coverage that protects a person who is responsible for an auto accident that results in the injury or death of other parties. (8)

body composition. Proportions of muscle, bone, fat, and other tissues that make up body weight. (11)

bond. Certificate of debt issued by a corporation or government. (7)

bonus. Money added to an employee's base pay. (3)

brick and mortar. Business that operates out of a physical location. (9)

brokerage firm. Place where a variety of investment products can be purchased as well as savings accounts can be opened. (5)

budget. Plan for the use of money over time based on goals, expenses, and expected income. (2)

bull market. Extended period of consumer confidence and optimism when stock prices rise. (7)

business cycle. Fluctuations between periods of economic growth and slowdown. (19)

business plan. Formal document that states the goals of a business and includes a detailed strategy of how goals will be achieved and how the business will be grown. (16)

buying incentive. Special offer by sellers designed to help sell goods and services. (9)

C

capital. Manufactured products that are used to make other products. (18)

capital gain. Income that results from selling an asset for more than the purchase price. (7)

capital good. Manufactured product used to make a final product. (18)

capital loss. Loss of money that occurs when the selling price of an investment is less than the purchase price. (7)

career cluster. Grouping of general occupational and career areas. (15)

career ladder. Outline of jobs in a given career field that are available at different levels of education, training, and experience. (15)

career plan. Outline of steps or actions that can be taken to reach a career goal. (15)

cartel. Group of countries or firms that controls the production and pricing of a product or service. (21)

cash advance. Loan against the available credit on an account. (6)

cash flow statement. Summary of the amount of money received and the amount paid for goods and services during a specific time period. (2)

cashier's check. Special type of check that the bank guarantees to pay. (4)

caveat emptor. Term that means let the buyer beware. (10)

certificate of deposit. Savings account that requires a deposit of a fixed amount of money for a fixed period of time. (5)

certified check. Personal check that a bank certifies is genuine and that there is enough money in the account to cover the check. (4)

certified used car. Previously owned vehicle that has received a thorough mechanical and appearance inspection along with necessary repairs and replacements. (14)

chain letters. US letters or e-mails that promise a big return for a small investment. (10)

Chapter 13 bankruptcy. Bankruptcy that permits debtors with regular incomes to pay all or a portion of their debts under the protection and supervision of the court. (7)

Chapter 7 bankruptcy. Bankruptcy that eliminates most types of debt and stays on a credit report for 10 years. (7)

charter. License that authorizes a bank to operate. (4)

check. Written order for the bank to pay a specific amount to the person to whom the check is written. (4)

check register. Record of account deposits, withdrawals, checks, fees, and interest. (4)

class action lawsuit. A legal court action brought by a group of individuals who have been similarly wronged. (10)

climate change. Shifts in measurements of climate—such as temperature, precipitation, or wind—that last decades or longer. (17)

closed-end credit. Loan for a specific amount that must be repaid with finance charges by a specified date. (6)

closing cost. Fee or settlement charge that must be paid before the sale of a home is final. (13)

codicil. Document that explains, changes, or deletes provisions in a will. (7)

coinsurance. Percentage of the service costs that patients pay. (8)

collateral. Property that a borrower promises to give up in case of default of a loan. (6)

collection agency. Business that specializes in debt collection. (6)

college access. Building awareness about college opportunities, providing guidance regarding college admissions, and identifying ways to pay for college. (15)

collusion. Making a secret agreement among companies to shut out smaller competitors and to engage in price fixing. (19)

command economy. System in which a central authority, usually the government, controls economic activities. (18)

commercial bank. Business owned by investors, and its primary functions are to receive, transfer, and lend money to individuals, businesses, and governments. (4)

commission. Income paid as a percentage of sales made by a salesperson. (3)

common stock. Stock that has voting rights and receives dividends declared by the company. (7)

community bank. Type of commercial bank that is locally owned and operated. (4)

community college. Two-year postsecondary school offering both academic and occupational courses. (15)

commuter service. Type of mass transit that runs mainly during business hours and caters to commuters. (14)

comparative advantage. Benefit to the party that has the lower opportunity cost in pursuing a given course of action. (21)

comparison shopping. Process of gathering information about products, services, and prices to find the best buy among similar products and services. (9)

compensation. Payment and benefits received for work performed. (3)

composting. Natural process that transforms materials, such as food waste, leaves, and grass clippings, into useful soil-like particles. (17)

compound interest. Amount calculated using the principal (money deposited) plus the interest it earns. The interest previously earned is included in the total before new interest earnings are computed. (5)

condominium. Form of multifamily housing in which a person typically owns the unit he or she occupies. (12)

conflict of interest. Situation in which a buyer and a seller have competing interests. (20)

conservation. Protection and management of the environment and valuable natural resources. (17)

consumer. Buyer and user of goods and services. (18)

consumer advocate. Group or an individual who promotes consumer rights. (10)

consumer cooperative. Nonretail association owned and operated by a group of members for their own benefit rather than for profit. (9)

consumer price index (CPI). Measure of the average change in prices over time for selected consumer goods and services. (19)

contingency clause. Part of a contract that calls for certain requirements to be met before the contract is binding. (13)

continuing education. Pursued after formal education and training is completed. (15)

contract. Legally binding agreement between a borrower and a creditor. (6)

cooperative. Form of home ownership in which a person buys shares in a corporation that owns the apartment building. (12)

copayment. Flat fee the patient must pay for medical services. (8)

copyright. Exclusive right to copy, license, sell, or distribute material. (16)

corporation. Business that is a separate legal entity that is owned by investors called stockholders or shareholders. (16)

cosigner. Responsible person who signs the loan with the person to whom the loan is granted and promises to repay the loan if the borrower fails to pay. (6)

cost-benefit analysis. Method of weighing the costs against the benefits of an action, a purchase, or a financial decision. (1)

coupon. Printed or electronic offer giving a discount for products or services bought before a certain date. (9)

cover message. Letter or e-mail that is sent with a résumé. (16)

credit. Medium of exchange that allows individuals to buy goods or services now and pay for them later. (6)

credit card. Plastic card that allows the holder to make credit purchases up to an authorized amount. (6)

credit counseling service. Organization that provides debt and financial management advice and services to people with debt problems at little or no cost. (7)

credit fraud. Fraudulent use of someone else's credit information. (6)

credit report. Record of a person's credit history and financial behavior. (6)

credit score. Numerical measure of a person's creditworthiness at a particular point in time. (6)

credit union. Nonprofit financial cooperative owned by and operated for the benefit of its members. (4)

creditworthy. Having the assets, income, and tendency to repay debt. (6)

culture. Beliefs, behaviors, and other characteristics common among members of a group or society. (1)

cyberbullying. Using the Internet to harass or threaten an individual. (16)

D

debit card. Card that allows a person to make purchases by swiping the card through a point-of-sale terminal that is usually located at the merchant's checkout counter. (4)

deceptive advertising. Information that purposely misleads a consumer through dishonest claims. (20)

deductible. Amount that is paid toward medical expenses before the insurance company begins to pay. (8)

deficit spending. Amount the federal government spends each year beyond the amount it receives in revenues. (19)

deflation. Period of declining prices. (19)

demand. Quantity of a product or service consumers are willing to buy. (18)

demographics. Statistical characteristics of a population. (1)

dependent. Individual who relies on someone else for financial support, such as a child, a spouse, or an elderly parent. (8)

depreciation. Decrease in the value of property as a result of use and age. (8, 14)

depression. Recession that lasts for several years. (19)

dietary supplement. Product that is intended to enhance a person's diet. (11)

disability. Limitation that affects a person's ability to function in major life activities. (3)

discount rate. Interest rate Federal Reserve Banks charge commercial banks for credit when they borrow. (19)

discretionary expense. Amount spent for an item that a person could do without. (2)

diversification. Spreading risk by putting money in a variety of investments. (7)

dividend. Portion of a corporation's earnings paid to stockholders. (7)

dollar-cost averaging. Strategy of investing a fixed dollar amount at regular intervals. (7)

down payment. Portion of the purchase price paid before a loan is issued. (14)

E

earnest money. Deposit made when a purchase agreement is signed to show that an offer is serious. (13)

easy-access credit. Short-term loan at a high interest rate that is granted regardless of the borrower's credit history. (6)

ecology. Study of the relationship between living things and their environment. (17)

e-commerce. Buying and selling goods and services online. (9)

economic conditions. State of the economy at a given time. (1)

economic globalization. Flow of goods, services, labor, money, innovative ideas, and technology across borders. (21)

economic system. Structure in which limited resources are turned into goods and services to address unlimited needs and wants. (18)

economies of scale. Concept that the cost of producing one unit of something declines as the number of units produced rises. (21)

education. General process of acquiring knowledge and skills. (15)

electronic funds transfer (EFT). Movement of money electronically from one financial institution to another. (4)

emergency fund. Amount of money that can be easily accessed in case of unexpected expenses. (5)

employee benefit. Form of noncash compensation received in addition to a wage or salary. (3)

endorsement. In banking terms, signature on the back of a check that transfers ownership of the check (4). In insuranse terms, an attachment to existing insurance coverage, such as a family policy, to protect expensive items taken to college. (8)

endowment insurance. Type of insurance that pays the face value of the policy to beneficiaries if the insured dies before the endowment period ends, or pays the face amount to the insured if he or she lives beyond the endowment period. (10)

ENERGY STAR program. Voluntary partnership of the US Department of Energy and the Environmental Protection Agency, product manufacturers, local utilities, and retailers to encourage the purchase of the most energy-efficient consumer electronics and appliances. (9)

EnergyGuide label. Label that shows the estimated annual cost of operating an appliance and other information. (9)

entitlement. Government payment or benefit promised by law to eligible citizens. (3)

entrepreneur. Person who owns and operates a business. (16)

environmentalist. Person who is concerned with the quality of the environment and how to maintain it. (17)

equilibrium. Point at which the demand and supply curves intersect. (9)

equity. Difference between the market value of property and the amount owed on the property. (12)

ergonomics. Science of adapting the workstation to fit the needs of the worker and lessen the chance of injury. (16)

escrow account. Account for holding money in trust for others. (13)

estate. Assets and liabilities a person leaves when he or she dies. (7)

ethics. Moral principles or beliefs that direct a person's behavior. (1)

European Union (EU). Largest trade sector in the world and is composed of 27 countries. (21)

eviction. Legal process of removing a tenant who is not paying rent from a rental property if the tenant does not leave voluntarily. (12)

exchange rate. Value of one currency compared to another. (21)

exclusion. Medical service that is not covered in an insurance plan. (8)

exclusive buyer agent. Real estate agent who works for the buyer and not the seller. (13)

executor. Person appointed to carry out the terms outlined in a will. (7)

exemption. Amount that a taxpayer can claim for each person who is dependent on that person's income. (3)

expense. Cost of goods and services one buys. (2)

exports. Goods and services grown or made in a particular country and then sold in world markets. (21)

extended warranty. Warranty that covers servicing and repairs that may be required after the initial warranty expires. (9)

F

factor of production. Economic resource, such as labor, land, capital, or entrepreneurship. (18)

falling hazards. Sources of potential injuries from slipping or falling. (16)

family financial crisis. Major problem that changes the future of the family and its lifestyle. (2)

family life cycle. Stages a family passes through over its lifetime. (2)

Federal Reserve System. System that regulates the nation's money supply and the banking system. (19)

fee-for-service plan. Health insurance plan that pays for covered medical services after treatment is provided. (8)

finance charge. Total amount paid by a borrower to a lender for the use of credit. (6)

fiscal policy. Federal government's taxing and spending decisions. (19)

fixed expense. Amount that must be paid each budget period. (2)

fixed rate mortgage. Mortgage with a guaranteed fixed or unchanging interest rate for the life of the loan. (13)

focus group. Group of consumers that evaluates products before they go on the market. (9)

foreclosure. Forced sale of property. (6)

Form I-9. Form used to verify an employee's identity and that he or she is authorized to work in the United States. (16)

Form W-2. Form that shows earnings and the amounts of income, Social Security, and Medicare taxes withheld from income during the year. (3)

fossil fuel. Organic substance, such as coal, petroleum, and natural gas, derived from the decomposed remains of animals and plants that lived in prehistoric times. (17)

franchise. Agreement that permits the franchisee to market and sell goods and services in a given area that are provided by the franchiser. (16)

free enterprise system. System in which privately owned businesses operate and compete for profits with limited government regulation or interference; also called a market economy. (18)

free trade. Policy of limited government trade restrictions. (21)

freeware. Software that is fully functional and can be used forever without purchasing it. (16)

FTC Used-Car Rule. Law that requires dealers to fully disclose to buyers what is and is not covered under a used vehicle's warranty. (14)

G

game of chance. Situation in which the participant must wager something to win. (9)

garnishment. Legal procedure requiring a portion of the debtor's pay to be set aside by the person's employer to pay creditors. (6)

GDP per capita. Market value of final goods and services produced per person. (20)

General Agreement on Trade and Tariffs (GATT). Set of international agreements that was formed after World War II by the Allied nations to aid post-war recovery; currently they promote free and fair trade among nations. (21)

generic drug. Drug that is sold by its common name, chemical composition, or class; and it usually costs considerably less than a similar brand-name drug. (11)

global warming. Steady rise in average temperatures near the earth's surface. (17)

globalization. Worldwide spread and integration of production, markets, communications, and technology. (1)

goal. Objective that an individual wants to attain. (1)

goods. Physical items, such as food and clothing. (18)

grace period. Time between the billing date and the start of interest charges. (6)

graduated payment mortgage. Mortgage that allows the buyer to pay low monthly payments at first and higher payments in the future. (13)

gross domestic product (GDP). Measure of the value of all goods and services produced by a nation during a specified period of time. (19)

gross pay. Worker's earnings before payroll deductions. (3)

H

hazardous waste. Substances—liquids, solids, and gases—that are dangerous or potentially harmful to health or the environment. (17)

health savings account (HSA). Tax-advantaged savings account available to people enrolled in qualified high deductible health plans. (8)

high-pressure selling. Attempting to convince a buyer to make a quick decision. (20)

high-yield savings account. Account that pays a higher interest rate than passbook and statement savings accounts. (5)

home energy audit. Assessment of how much energy a home uses and ways to reduce consumption. (17)

home equity loan. Type of loan in which the borrower uses the equity in his or her home as collateral for the loan. (13)

human resource. Quality or characteristic that a person has. (18)

hypoallergenic. Substance or product does not contain ingredients likely to cause allergic reactions. (11)

I

identify theft. Form of credit fraud that involves stealing someone's personal information and using the information to commit theft or fraud. (6)

implied fitness. Unwritten promise that a product is fit for any performance or purpose promised by the seller. (9)

implied merchantability. Unwritten guarantee that a product is what it called and does what its name implies. (9)

imports. Goods and services that come into a country from other countries. (21)

impulse buying. Buying things without thinking about needs, goals, or the consequences of spending. (20)

income. Form of money received, such as an allowance, paycheck, or gift. (2)

inflation. Overall increase in the price of goods and services. (19)

infomercial. Paid television program designed to sell a service, product, or idea. (9)

innovation. Process of creating something, such as new or improved products and new ways to do things and solve problems. (18)

inpatient. Person whose care requires a stay in a hospital. (8)

insourcing. Process in which foreign companies open subsidiaries in the United States and create jobs here. (21)

insurance. Form of risk management that pools the premiums of a large group of people to cover the expenses of the smaller number within the group who suffer losses. (8)

interest. Activity that is enjoyed, a subject that is liked, an idea that is fascinating, a sport that is played, or a hobby that is enjoyed. (15)

interest-bearing savings account. Type of demand deposit account that pays interest and allows for regular deposits and withdrawals. (5)

International Monetary Fund (IMF). Organization with the mission to oversee the international monetary system; it also works to stabilize exchange rates and eliminate trade barriers. (21)

international trade. Buying and selling of goods and services across national borders and among the people of different nations. (21)

internship. Short-term position with a sponsoring organization that gives the intern an opportunity to gain on-the-job experience in a certain field of study or occupation. (15)

interview. Employer's opportunity to meet with an applicant and discuss the job and qualifications for the job. (16)

investing. Purchasing a financial product or valuable item with the goal of increasing wealth over time in spite of possible loss. (7)

investment. Asset bought that can increase wealth over time, but it also carries the risk of loss. (20)

investment portfolio. Collection of securities and other assets a person owns. (7)

itemized deduction. Allowed expense that can be deducted from adjusted gross income. (3)

L

labeling law. Government regulation that requires certain information be placed on labels for certain products. (10)

labor. Work performed by people who turn resources into products. (18)

labor force. People, age 16 and over, who are employed or are looking for and able to work. (19)

labor productivity. Value of the goods and services a worker creates in a given time. (20)

labor union. Group of workers who unite to negotiate with employers over issues such as pay, health care, and working conditions. (19)

land. All the natural resources of a nation. (18)

landfill. Permanent waste disposal site for most solid, nonhazardous waste. (17)

landominium. Type of residential property in which the homeowner owns both the home and the land on which the home is built. (12)

lawsuit. Civil action brought by a person (a plaintiff) against another party (the defendant). (10)

lease. Contract that specifies the conditions, terms, and rent for the use of an asset. (12)

legal document. Paper that can be filed with a court officer or used to uphold an agreement in a court of law, such as a marriage certificate, auto loan, mortgage, or credit card agreement. (2)

lemon. Vehicle that has serious mechanical problems that the manufacturer has been unable to fix after a reasonable number of attempts. (14)

lemon law. Law that requires a seller or manufacturer of a defective vehicle either to replace or repair it or to refund the buyer's money. (14)

lessee. Person who rents property. (12)

lessor. Person who owns and rents property to the lessee. (12)

liability. Current or future financial obligation. (2)

license. Legal permission to use a software program. (16)

lien. Legal claim on a borrower's property by a creditor who is owed money. (6)

lifting hazard. Source of potential injury from improperly lifting or carrying items. (16)

limited liability company (LLC). Business that is organized as a proprietorship, but the liabilities (debts) are limited to the assets of the business. (16)

limited warranty. Guarantee for service, repairs, and replacements only under certain conditions. (9)

line of credit. Preapproved amount that an individual can borrow. (6)

loan shark. Someone who lends money at excessive rates of interest. (6)

loss leader. Item priced at or below cost to attract buyers in the expectation that they will purchase other merchandise as well. (9)

lottery. Activity in which prizes are awarded to participants by chance in exchange for some form of payment. (10)

M

managed care plan. Type of health-care plan in which the insurance company contracts with specific doctors, hospitals, and other health-care providers to deliver medical services and preventive care to members at reduced cost. (8)

management. Process of organizing and using resources to achieve predetermined objectives. (1)

manufactured home. Single-family house built in a factory and shipped to the home site where it is erected. (12)

marginal benefit. Change in total benefit of using one additional unit. (1)

marginal cost. Change in total cost of using one more unit. (1)

market economy. System in which privately owned businesses operate and compete for profits with limited government regulation or interference; also called a free enterprise system. (18)

marketplace. Arena in which consumers and producers meet to exchange goods, services, and money. (9, 18)

mass transit. Public transportation where a large number of people can travel at the same time. (14)

material-storage hazards. Sources of potential injury that come from the improper storage of files, books, or office equipment. (16)

Medicaid. Government program that pays certain health-care costs for eligible, low-income individuals and families. (3)

Medicare. Federal program that pays for certain health-care expenses for older citizens and others with disabilities. (3)

migrants. People who move from one place or country to another. (21)

minimum wage. Lowest hourly wage that employers can pay most workers by law. (3)

mixed economy. Combination of the market and the command systems. (18)

monetary policy. Actions the Federal Reserve Board takes to manage the supply of money and credit in the economy. (19)

money management software. Computer program used to organize daily finances and keep track of income, spending, saving, debts, investments, and other financial data. (2)

money market account. Type of savings account that requires a higher minimum balance than regular savings accounts, but it offers a higher interest rate. (5)

money market fund. Type of mutual fund that deals only in high interest short-term investments, such as U. S. Treasury securities, certificates of deposit, and commercial paper. (7)

money order. Payment order for a specific amount of money payable to a specific payee. (4)

monopoly. Situation in which there is a single seller or producer of a given product or service. (19)

moped. Low-powered motorized two-wheeler with an engine capacity less than 50cc. (14)

mortgage. Type of secured loan used for buying property. (13)

motor scooter. Two-wheeled motor vehicle with an engine capacity of 50cc to 250cc. (14)

multinational corporation. Business that operates in more than one country. (21)

mutual fund. Investment created by pooling the money of many people and investing in a collection of several securities. (7)

mutual savings bank. Financial institution that is owned by its depositors. (4)

N

national debt. Total amount of money the government owes at a given time. (19)

natural resource. Raw material, such as soil, water, minerals, plants, animals, and climate. (18)

need. Item a person must have to survive. (1)

net asset value (NAV). Net asset value is a mutual fund's assets minus its liabilities. (7)

net pay. Gross pay (plus bonuses, if any) minus payroll deductions. (3)

net worth statement. Written record of an individual's current financial situation. (2)

netiquette. Accepted social and professional guidelines for communicating using the Internet. (16)

no-fault auto insurance. Type of insurance plan that eliminates the faultfinding process in settling claims by having each policyholder make a claim to his or her own insurance company after an accident. (8)

nonhuman resource. External resource, such as money, time, equipment, or a possession. (18)

nonrenewable energy. Power source that can be used up or cannot be used again. (17)

North American Free Trade Agreement (NAFTA). Agreement between the United States, Canada, and Mexico that lowered trade barriers and opened markets among the three countries. (21)

nutrients. Chemical substances found in foods that furnish energy, build and maintain body tissues, and regulate body processes. (9)

O

obsolete. Something that is no longer useful because a newer version exists. (9)

Occupational Safety and Health Administration (OSHA). Federal agency that enforces safety and health regulations in the workplace. (16)

occupational training. Education that prepares an individual for a specific type of work. (15)

offshore outsourcing. Moving sections of a business to another country. (21)

oligopoly. Situation in which a few large companies dominate an industry. (19)

online–only bank. Financial institution that conducts customer transactions via the Internet. (5)

open-end credit. Agreement that allows the borrower to use a specific amount of money for an indefinite period of time. (6)

opportunity cost. Value of the option that was given up for another option. (18)

option. Feature available for a particular car. (14)

organic food. Food produced without synthetic fertilizers, pesticides, growth stimulants, or genetic engineering. (9)

outsourcing. Moving sections of a business to other companies or subsidiaries. (21)

overdraft. Check written for more money than the balance of an account. (4)

overspending. Spending more money than can be afforded to spend. (20)

over-the-counter drug. Nonprescription medication available on supermarket and drugstore shelves. (11)

P

partnership. Business that has two or more owners. (16)

pawnshop. Business that gives customers high-interest loans with personal property, such as jewelry, held as collateral. (6)

payday loan. Short-term, high-interest loan that usually must be repaid on the borrower's next payday. (6)

payroll deduction. Subtraction from gross pay. (3)

perfect competition. Condition in which no single seller can significantly influence the market price of a product or service. (19)

philanthropy. Act of giving money, goods, or services to meet the needs of others and to promote good causes. (2)

phishing. Crime commited online that involves the use of fraudulent e-mails and copies of legitimate websites to trick people into providing personal, financial, and other data. (6, 16)

physical fitness. State in which all body systems function efficiently. (11)

piecework. Wage based on a rate per unit of work completed. (3)

point. Amount that is charged by lenders at closing, and it equals one percent of the mortgage. (13)

policyholder. Person who has purchased insurance. (8)

Ponzi scheme. Investment operation in which money from new investors is used to pay earlier investors. (10)

postdated check. Check written with a future date. (4)

preexisting condition. Illness or an injury a person has before signing up for health-care insurance. (8)

preferred stock. Type of stock that pays regular dividends at a set rate. (7)

premium. Amount of money regularly paid to an insurance company for a policy. (8)

prescription drug. Medication that can only be obtained with a physician's orders. (11)

primary care physician. Physician who is trained to diagnose and treat a variety of illnesses in all phases of medicine and oversees general treatment for most patients. (11)

principal. Amount of money borrowed on a loan. (6)

priority. Value or goal that is given more importance than other values and goals. (1)

private mortgage insurance (PMI). Insurance policy that protects the lender from loss if the borrower defaults on the loan and the home goes into foreclosure. (13)

probate. Legal process of winding up the affairs of an estate, paying final expenses, and distributing the balance of money and property to beneficiaries. (7)

producer. Individual or business that provides goods and services to meet consumer demands. (18)

product placement. Means of showing a brand name product or its trademark in movies and television programs. (9)

productivity. Measure of the amount of work a person can do in a specific amount of time. (18)

profit. Total amount of money earned after expenses are subtracted from income. (18)

property damage liability. Insurance coverage that protects an individual who is responsible for an auto accident in which the property of others is damaged. (8)

property survey. Map of the property drawn by a surveyor to show size, boundaries, and characteristics of a property. (13)

prospectus. Legal document that gives a detailed description of a security. (7)

prosperity. Time period of growth and financial well-being. (20)

proxy. Stockholder's written authorization to have someone else cast a vote on his or her behalf. (7)

purchase agreement. A contract between a homebuyer and a seller that includes a description of the real estate, its location, the purchase price, the possession date, and any other condition and terms of the sale. (13)

pure risk. Risk with a possibility of loss but no possibility of gain. (8)

pyramid scheme. Fraudulent investment plan. (10)

R

real estate broker. Person licensed to arrange for the purchase and sale of real estate for a fee or commission. (13)

rebate. Cash back offer for purchasing an item. (9)

recession. Extended period of slow or no economic growth. (19)

record keeping. Process of setting up an organized system for financial and legal documents. (2)

recycle. Reprocess resources so they can be used again. (17)

reference. Person who is qualified and willing to speak on a person's behalf. (16)

regular charge account. Account that lets an individual charge goods and services in exchange for a promise to pay in full within 25 days of the billing date. (6)

renewable energy. Power source that is continually available or can be replenished. (17)

rental agreement. Written agreement that permits the tenant to move out at any time as long as the required notice is given. (12)

rent-to-own. Arrangement in which a consumer pays rent for the use of a product and eventually owns it. (6)

repossession. Taking of collateral when a borrower fails to repay a loan. (6)

Reserve Officers' Training Corps (ROTC). College program for training commissioned officers for the United States armed forces. (15)

résumé. Summary of an individual's educational background, work history, and relevant interests. (16)

retail stores. Business that sell directly to consumers from their place of business. (9)

review. Critical report or comments about an item. (10)

revolving credit account. Type of credit agreement that offers a choice of paying in full each month or spreading payments over a period of time. (6)

risk. Measure of the likelihood that something will be lost. (8)

risk management. Process of measuring risk and finding ways to minimize or manage loss. (8)

Roth IRA. Individual retirement account in which individuals contribute after-tax income and qualified withdrawals are not taxed. (7)

Rule of 72. Equation that estimates how long it will take to double an investment with a fixed interest rate. (5)

S

saving. Setting money aside for future use. (5)

savings account. Account designed for accumulating money for future use. (5)

savings and loan association. Financial institution that provides many of the services offered by commercial banks. (4)

scarcity. Challenge of stretching resources to cover needs and wants. (18)

secured loan. Loan that requires collateral. (6)

securities exchange. Secondary market where securities are bought and sold through stockbrokers. (7)

security deposit. Amount a renter pays to help protect the property owner against financial losses in case the renter damages the property or fails to pay rent. (12)

services. Work performed. (18)

share account. Savings account at a credit union. (5)

shareware. Software that can be installed and used on a trial basis. User should purchase if they decide to keep using it. (16)

simple interest. Interest earned only on the principal, which is the amount of money originally deposited. (5)

single-family house. Detached house, usually with a front and back yard, a driveway, and often an attached carport or garage. (12)

skill contests. Opportunity to win prizes by demonstrating skill instead of chance. (10)

small claims court. Part of the court system that offers a simple, prompt, and inexpensive way to settle minor differences involving small amounts of money. (10)

SMART goal. Something to achieve stated in terms that are specific, measurable, achievable, realistic, and time based. (5)

social responsibility. General sense of concern for the needs of others in the community, country, and world. (16)

Social Security. Federal program that provides income when earnings are reduced or stopped because of retirement, serious illness or injury, or death. (3)

software piracy. Illegal copying or downloading of software, including scanning or downloading images or music. (16)

software viruses. Computer programs that cause harm to computer systems. (16)

sole proprietorship. Business that has a single owner. (16)

specialist. Physician who has had further education and training in a specific branch of medicine. (11)

specialization. Method of production in which a particular range of products and services is produced. (21)

speculative risk. Risk that may result in either financial gain or financial loss. (8)

stages in the family life cycle. Typical patterns of social and financial behavior families follow at different periods in the life cycle. (2)

stagflation. Period of slow economic growth and high inflation. (19)

standard deduction. Fixed amount that can be deducted from adjusted gross income. (3)

standard of living. Degree to which one has the ability to obtain the goods and services one needs and wants. (20)

stock. A share in ownership of a corporation. (7)

stock trade. Purchase or sale of shares of a stock. (7)

stockbroker. Agent who buys and sells securities for clients. (7)

store credit cards. Credit cards primarily issued by major department store chains that permit the user to charge purchases only with the merchant issuing the card. (6)

subprime mortgage. Mortgage made by lenders who charge higher than prime rates to borrowers who have poor or no credit ratings. (13)

subsidy. Form of transfer payment that gives financial assistance to a business or entity, such as those in education, agriculture, the arts, or health care. (19)

supply. Amount of a product or service producers are willing to provide. (18)

surplus. When the government receives more than it spends. (19)

sustainable. To be kept in existence, as in resources that can be used without depletion or permanent damage. (17)

sweepstakes. Promotional offer that gives participants the chance to win items of value or prizes. (10)

systematic decision-making. Process of choosing a course of action after evaluating available information and weighing the costs and benefits of alternative actions and their consequences. (1)

T

tax. Fee imposed by a government on income, products, or activities and paid by citizens and businesses. (19)

tax credit. Amount that can be deducted from the taxes a taxpayer owes. (3)

tax deduction. Amount that is subtracted from adjusted gross income, which further reduces taxable income. (3)

tax deferred. Taxes on the principal and/ or earnings are delayed until the funds are withdrawn. (5)

tax exempt. Free of certain taxes. (5)

t-commerce. Sale of merchandise on television through shopping networks or TV commercials. (9)

technology. Application of science and research to human life and environments. (1)

telemarketing. Sale of merchandise by phone. (9)

term life insurance. Type of insurance that provides protection only for a specific period of time or until a specified age. (8)

testing and rating service. Group or organization that tests products and rates them according to certain criteria. (10)

tip. Money paid for service beyond what is required. (3)

title. Legal document that proves ownership of property. (13)

title insurance. Type of insurance that protects the buyer if problems with the title arise after the purchase. (13)

title loan. Short-term loan made using a borrower's car as collateral. (6)

townhouse. Home that is attached to adjacent houses. (12)

trade barrier. Action taken to control or limit imports. (21)

trade deficit. When a country buys, or imports, more products than it sells. (21)

trade-off. Choice given up when one choice is selected over another. (18)

trade surplus. When a country sells, or exports, more than it buys. (21)

traditional economy. System in which economic decisions are based on a society's values, culture, and customs. (18)

traditional IRA. Individual retirement account that allows individuals to contribute pretax income to investments that grow tax deferred. (7)

training. Instruction on a specific skill or task needed for a job. (15)

travel and entertainment cards. Credit cards that are typically used for business and usually require the user to pay the entire balance each month. (6)

traveler's check. Special form of check that functions as cash. (4)

trust. Arrangement through which a person transfers assets to a trustee, who then oversees and manages the assets on behalf of beneficiaries. (7)

trustee. Person or institution named to manage an estate on behalf of the beneficiaries. (7)

U

umbrella policy. Insurance policy that covers loss amounts that are higher than those covered by primary policies. (8)

underemployment. Underemployment is a condition in which workers are employed only part time or are overqualified for their jobs. (19)

unemployment rate. Percentage of the labor force that is out of work and seeking employment. (19)

unit price. Cost per unit, weight, or measure. (9)

unsecured loan. Loan made on the strength of a signature alone. (6)

V

value. Personal belief about what is important and desirable. (1)

value system. Overall structure of values and goals that guides behavior and provides a sense of direction. (1)

variable expense. Cost that changes both in the amount and time it must be paid. (2)

variations in the family life cycle. Patterns that differ from the typical family life cycle. (2)

vehicle identification number (VIN). Unique number assigned by the automobile industry and used to identify an individual auto. (14)

W

walk-in clinic. Health-care facility that provides certain routine medical attention. (11)

want. Nonessential thing a person would like to have. (1)

warranty. Guarantee that a product will meet certain performance and quality standards. (9)

wealth. Abundance of money and other assets. (2)

whole life insurance. Type of insurance that provides basic lifetime protection so long as premiums are paid. (8)

will. Legal document stating a person's wishes for his or her estate after death. (7)

work order. Document that describes the work that will be performed. (9)

World Trade Organization (WTO). International organization that mediates trade disputes among 155 member nations and establishes trade practices that are acceptable and fair to all nations. (21)

written roommate agreement. Document that includes the rules related to living arrangements and expenses and is signed by all roommates. (2)

Index

E